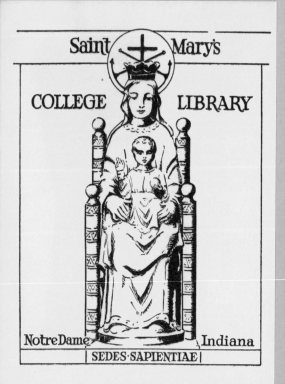

OTHER PUBLICATIONS OF *Paul Weiss*

BOOKS

Reality
Nature and Man
Man's Freedom
Modes of Being
Our Public Life
The World of Art
Nine Basic Arts
History: Written and Lived
Religion and Art
The God We Seek
The Making of Men
Sport: A Philosophic Inquiry
Philosophy in Process, Vol. 1: 1955–1960
Philosophy in Process, Vol. 2: 1960–1964
Philosophy in Process, Vol. 3: 1964
Philosophy in Process, Vol. 4: 1964–1965

With Others

American Philosophy Today and Tomorrow
Science, Philosophy, and Religion
Moral Principles in Action
American Philosophers at Work
Dimensions of Mind
History and Philosophy
Law and Philosophy
Human Values and Economic Policy
Right and Wrong: A Philosophical Dialogue Between Father and Son,
  etc.

EDITOR, with *Charles Hartshorne*

Collected Papers of Charles Sanders Peirce (SIX VOLUMES)

PHILOSOPHY

By PAUL WEISS

IN PROCESS

VOLUME 5

September 3, 1965 – August 27, 1968

Southern Illinois University Press
Carbondale and Edwardsville

Feffer & Simons, Inc.
London and Amsterdam

PREFACE

THE FOURTH VOLUME of this work, like its predecessors, has been well received. Paul G. Kuntz and Robert Neville, in particular, have subjected it to thorough and perceptive examinations, bringing into focus issues that I, among others, did not realize were so crucial and central.

Unfortunately, most of the philosophical journals have taken no notice of the existence of any of the volumes. This is regrettable for a number of reasons, not the least of which is that they contain a number of independent investigations of topics at the forefront of current discussion. This is true especially of the present volume which looks at the nature of rules, language, logic, action, mind, perception, being, and phenomena from a not too familiar perspective. The detailed index and page headings should make it comparatively easy to locate these and other matters of primary concern.

Many of the questions here dealt with, however, will not have much interest for most contemporaries. Though the methods pursued and the answers provided are often new, still they are not, I think, alien to the spirit which has dominated philosophy over the course of history and is still operative today. How significant the work is, in whole or part, is of course for others to decide.

December 1970
Washington, D. C.   P. W.

PHILOSOPHY IN PROCESS

1965

Actualities can be understood to be members of complexes governed by Actuality and by the encapsulated modes of Being, God, Ideality, and Existence. The actualities benefit from them. Thus, God and actualities make one complex. The actualities obtain from God a qualitative tonality, a solidarity, accredited achievements of the complex, distinctive roles with respect to other actualities in God, and relations to actualities as in the other complexes.

There has been a partial recognition of this affecting of actualities in my discussions over the last few years. The accretion by actualities of the qualitative tonality which is God has been acknowledged in references to the qualifications of God which make the actualities into sacred objects. The distinctive role that an actuality has with respect to other actualities in God has been acknowledged in the references to the affiliations of the actualities due to God. The solidarity of actualities due to God has been acknowledged in the references to the community of believers and to the nature of the dedicated community. The relations to actualities in other complexes have been acknowledged in the reference to the burdens transferred from one mode of Being to another. And the achievements of the complex as distributively accreditable to the different actualities has been acknowledged in the consideration of service as the outcome of men's participation in the divine. It was not seen, though, that all of these were to be understood as so many different affects which God as an encompassed mode of Being produces in the actualities He encompasses. And it was not seen that there did not have to be a reference to such human or consciously acknowledged situations as a dedicated community or a participation in the divine. The various affects are to be found in all actualities.

We have a similar affecting of actualities by Ideality and Existence. All five ways of being affected should be distinguished and given distinctive names. And then another kind of complex should be recognized in which Actuality is the governing encompassing Being, and this too should have five distinctive affects on the actualities. As a consequence, the actualities should be qualified in four distinctive ways, have four distinctive solidarities, have accredited to them four distinctive kinds of complex achievement, have four distinctive types of roles, and have four distinctive types of relation to one another as in the other complexes.

In all cases, there should be a recognition of the affect of actualities in the Beings which govern them, due to the fact that the actualities make up a quantitative totality, function as individuals, have some freedom from one another, have their individual activities sum to a total, and are all related to one another in a way which abstracts from the distinctiveness of the different modes of Being. The actualities, as involved with those modes of Being, specialize a more neutral way of being related to one another. This aspect of the complexes has been somewhat neglected by me; I have paid insufficient attention to what actualities do to the different Beings, though there are hints here and there, pointing up the fact that the actualities make a difference to those Beings.

It would not be too much of an exaggeration to say that in *Reality* I dealt primarily with the actualities in relation to one another, but that in the *Modes of Being* I dealt with them as affected by the modes of Being, and that the final story involves the uniting of these two. In the first chapter of the *Modes of Being,* there is consideration of the fact that the actualities affect the Beings, but this is dealt with as a kind of action, whereas the present discussion is emphasizing a kind of inevitable transference of meanings and achievements from the actualities to the Beings.

It could be well argued that the actualities form complexes only with the encapsulated modes of Being, and that as in Actuality they do not have any other role but that of being neutrally related one to the other. But such a suggestion, which seems eminently reasonable, is also up against the consideration that Actuality does seem to endow all actualities with an equal status as realities, and this could be said to be a way of giving them something of a qualitative tone, a solidarity, etc. I think the two suggestions can be reconciled by seeing the encapsulated modes to have comparable though distinctive affects in actualities, but that Actuality (though it too has five kinds of affects characterizable in the same generic way) does not affect those actualities in ways which are really comparable to the affects of the encapsulated modes of Being. If this answer be accepted, similar things must be said about the pluralities to be found in each mode of Being.

All these different affects are ontological. When we bring into account human interests and insights, we bring ourselves into separate domains, activities, and disciplines. Thus, though every entity is *sacred* (because of the qualitative modification which the total qualitative nature of God has on its members), only some are *sacramental*, i.e., conspicuously sacred. These sacramental objects can be known only from the position of one who is interplaying with other beings in a special way—who, for example, has a special kind of solidarity with them, special relations to them, etc. Outside of that situation, no one could know what was there known to be sacramental; but consideration of the omnipresence of God would allow one to know that everything was sacred.

Something of the sacred character is carried over into the actuality when it functions as a rationally classified entity (because of Ideality) and a concordant entity (because of Existence); conversely, the sacred must be understood to have its rational and concordant aspects.

September 4

The reality of complexes, from the perspective of a theoretically known world of submicroscopic particles, is evidenced by the discrepancy that exists between the acknowledged distribution and functioning of those particles and their conceivable, independent, and random action. The reality of the theoretical world of submicroscopic particles, from the perspective of actual limited complexes, is evidenced by their members' capacity to escape that membership and become members of other complexes. More generally: confronted with entities of a certain kind, we infer that they are in fact governed by some complex when we note that their behavior is not independent and their distribution not random; we infer that they are part of one totality when, starting with them as members of particular wholes, we learn of their freedom to dissolve that membership and become members of other wholes.

Given men in a religious community, we infer that there is a divine governance of them, by noting that they are united and that they function in ways which are not as independent or as random as they could be. The difference is a matter of degree, testifying to the fact that we are comparing the men, not as in complexes and as parts of a single total whole, but as in different complexes. Given the religious community, we infer that men are not wholly constituted by their life there and that they are in fact distinctive individuals, when we see that they can escape the community and be parts and members of other complexes. Similar things must be said with respect to actualities in relation to Ideality and Existence.

To say that we infer that there is a divine governance by noting that men are more intimately related than otherwise is to use a variant on the teleological argument. It is to say that there is something characteristic of men that requires a reference to a governing power; for reasons given in the *Modes,* this is only a premiss for an argument. But it is a premiss which is in the spirit of the teleological argument, since it sees some feature additional to what the scheme of things has natively.

In the ordinary teleological argument it is usually supposed that the world cannot have an order of its own, and that apart from a divine governance the entities would function in a purely chance way. This argument supposes that the theoretically known world is identical with the conceivable world of independent, randomized items. (It is to be noted that I am now using "random" in the more traditional sense, and in contrast with the way I used it some time back, when I spoke of the particles being "randomized" by the complexes in which they were.) Once we void that supposition, we are forced to look for the divine dominance, not when we find any order beyond that which mere chance combinations of random entities provides, but when we find the particles and their complexes to have less freedom and a distribution which is not accountable for by the theoretically known world, or by any limited complex or complexes of those particles.

What is death? The question is asked from the position of living organisms, and refers then to the members of it as standing away from its control. Death is the state where the members acquire a degree of freedom as great as those of any members in other complexes.

What is life? The question is asked from the position of particles which are not alive. It refers to them as subject to a control which makes their distribution and action different from what they are in other kinds of complexes.

What is the cosmic meaning of death? It is the state where the members acquire a degree of freedom as members of a single totality of particles. What is the cosmic meaning of life? It is the particles as subject to controls making their distribution and actions different from what they are in the single totality of particles.

From a cosmological point of view, the problem of life does not differ in principle from the problem of any existence in any governing complex—a stone, a mountain, a sea, even a drop of water, or a piece of salt or chalk. It is a distinctive problem only from the position of other complexes, referring to some complex which imposes a degree of solidarity on its members greater than those complexes do.

From a cosmological point of view, the problem of death is only a variation on the problem of the dissolution of any complex. It is a distinctive problem only from the position of a living being for which the degree of freedom which is exercised by its members is maximum.

Life and death, from a cosmological point of view, are but special cases of the control and freedom characteristic of all complexes in relation to their members, and which are, strictly speaking, inexplicable from that point of view. But then, a piece of salt will be just as mysterious as a living being, the corroding of a mountain is just as mysterious as the death of a mouse.

September 5

In a thoughtful and in many places ingenious and subtle article in the current *Review of Metaphysics,* Richard Rorty argues for the thesis that it makes sense to speak about the behavior of brain cells or fibers in place of sensations. Faced with the case where a man reports that he has a sensation of pain but there is nothing observable in the brain corresponding to that occurrence, Rorty suggests we override him, and say he doesn't know what a pain is. This is a fascist conclusion, and I think violates the very intent of a scientific enterprise, which Rorty would like to follow. I call it fascist because it says that if there be an individual who does not conform to the consensus we are to ignore or dismiss him.

Suppose that the man were to say, "All right, I am not using the word 'pain' in the way others think it should be used. But it still is true that I am undergoing a feeling which is disagreeable and is alike in its disagreeableness to other feelings which you allow me to call 'pain.' " Rorty cannot handle that case I think. But someone who wanted to support the thesis which Rorty offers ought to go on to say that he thinks that if one were to extend the range of observations to include, say, movements of the heart or toe, vibrations of certain nerves, etc., he would find the answering observational occurrence.

The finding of a recalcitrant item is but an occasion for looking for what is to answer to it, what is to substitute for it, in an area wider than that which one had acknowledged before. No one would be willing to override a responsible person who, in the absence of any observable alteration in his bodily movements, nevertheless reported his experience of an unusual sensation. Should such an occurrence take place, and should it be true that, no matter how wide one spreads one's net there is nothing to be discerned, the conclusion must be that this occurrence belongs in a distinct complex, and that the nature of it is evidence of the distinctive, unique character of that complex and those features which it gives to the item there.

Sensations can be said to be occurrences in the mind; brain cells can be said to be in the body, which is a different kind of complex. Let us suppose, however, that sensations are in fact the very kind of entities which are brain cells, but as existing in a distinct kind of complex from them. We would then have to change the thesis of Rorty to one which claimed that the members of some complex also have another role in some other more readily observable or controllable or publicly evident complex. This would not preclude the continued existence of the items in a complex by virtue of which they have the character of sensations.

A sensation which had no answering role in another complex such as the body would be theoretically understandable in terms of material elements so far as account was taken of the sensation as that which was only in the feeling complex of a conscious man at such and such a moment. From the theoretical point of view, there would be no reference to the man, but only to the position and functioning of the element as distinctive and as contrasting with other elements which are to be found in other complexes, and perhaps in this one too, where the element is now located. Though the element as a sensation was privately acknowledged and could not be publicly observed, it nevertheless could be understood to be in the same theoretically known world as the elements which were publicly acknowledged.

The thesis that sensations can be dealt with materialistically is not a thesis which substitutes observables for unobservables, or more observability for less, but one that offers a theoretical account of the sensation in terms which are appropriate to material occurrences. The sensation is viewed as a theoretical particle, but with a distinctive position and activity which it obtains from the complex in which it is. That complex is not known from the position of the theoretical world; but then too, neither is the complex of brain or body known from that position.

September 18

A possible preface to a possible second edition of the *Modes of Being*:

This book claimed to tell us about four ultimate realities in themselves, in relation to one another, and in relation to substantial space-time objects such as ourselves and the things with which we interplay. It says a good deal, and I think correctly, about the relation of those realities to one another. Some rather plausible things are said too, about three of the realities in themselves, with hardly a word directed at the mode of Being, Actuality. Considerable confusion is exhibited in the references of the Beings to space-time objects. Little more than hints are given as to the relation of Actuality to those objects; and instead of speaking of the three other modes of Being in relation to those objects, it deals with the relation of delimited forms of those modes of Being in relation to them.

As was made evident in *Philosophy in Process,* the present work thus gives us an account of the encapsulated (by Actuality) forms of three modes of Being in relation to particular actualities, and makes evident how those delimited forms are related one to the other. Read as an account of the interplay of three limited forms of ultimate realities in relationship to one another and to substantial objects, i.e., actualities, it is on the whole I think sound and illuminating. But it does presuppose an understanding of all four modes of Being as apart from actualities, and in relation to one another. This I think can be extracted from the discussions in *Philosophy in Process.*

(The above is a draft and should be rewritten. But the point is the one that ought to be made.)

September 19

One of the disservices which religious apologists performed for mankind is due to their insistence that religion offers the only alternative to a life of licentiousness, folly, and irrationality. When men discard religion, they then have the apologists' sanction that there is nothing else to be done than to do as one likes. Had it been seen that there is an ethics which needs no divine sanction, that there is a politics which has its own rationale, its own laws and definitions of rights and duties, that there is a world of art with its own demands and values, that there is a common history in which all are caught and which all can help direct toward the achievement of a world civilization, and that there are group loyalties which are awakened and sustained in work and sport, one would have been able to show that those who discard religion are far from having discarded all standards, demands, prescriptions, obligations, and values.

A stab at a subjectivistic history of philosophy: Thales fell into a well, and came out saying everything is water. Anaximander was rather vague in his views, and concluded that the real was the indefinite. Protagoras had a rather large following, and therefore thought that everything was number. Heraclitus was a passionate poet and said that reality was fire. Parmenides thought he was immortal and said that non-being altogether was not. Zeno was a devoted disciple, and argued that there was no motion.

September 20

We are at the beginning of metaphysics when we ask after the being that confronted actualities have. They are not the Being which they have, as their coming to be and passing away reveals. We achieve a minimum metaphysics when we affirm that there is Being; we explain the actualities with which we began, by acknowledging that they are by virtue of this Being. We need not affirm that they were generated out of that Being, created by it, or even sustained by it. The domain which they constitute can well be as co-eternal as the Being; that domain could be constituted by some actuality or other, always. A minimal metaphysics will not, however, be able to account for the presence of those actualities or the domain they occupy.

We complicate our minimal metaphysics with the acknowledgment that actualities are subject to forces not of their own making, and distinct from Actuality, the Being which they momentarily, fragmentarily, and diversely possess. Thus, the recognition that they are contemporaries through time, that they are all facing a common future, and that they are affiliated in ways which are not dependent on their proximity or likeness, leads to the acknowledgment of Existence, Ideality, and God. But we have as yet no warrant for the supposition that these are Beings in the sense in which Actuality is. They can well be realities within Actuality, operating in some independence of it.

To get to a full metaphysics, one must move from the acknowledgment of Actuality to the acknowledgment of three other modes of Being. This can be done in a number of ways. 1] The Being which is Actuality can be shown not to fully be unless it is over against other Beings which are as eternal and basic as it is. There must be at least two Beings if there is one. That there are four Beings could be shown by making evident that the relation between two Beings is as substantial as the Beings, and that this relation must have a counterweight in the form of another equally substantial Being. 2] The Actuality can be seen to function with respect to actualities in ways which cannot be accounted for by remaining with either one of them or even with both. The reality of Actuality over against actualities, which could not be accounted for in the minimal metaphysics, can, though, be explained as the result of the operation of God, the Being, on Actuality. The similarity of the actualities to Actuality is to be accounted for by the operation of Ideality, the Being, on Actuality. The extension of Actuality over all the actualities is to be accounted for by the operation of Existence, the Being, on Actuality.   3] Myth, intuition, and mysticism are correlative with speculative knowledge, reaching to Ideality, Existence, and God, respectively.   4] Actuality is qualified in a number of ways, and thereby offers evidence of the reality of other Beings, which can then be proved. Actuality is said to be intelligible, effective, and unitary, because we approach it from the position of Ideality, Existence, and God, respectively.

All four of these ways seem to lead most readily to God, rather than to the other two modes of Being. Actuality is then seen to be only because it is over against God; to be over against actualities only because affected by God; to be apprehended in a way which is correlative with a mystical vision of God; and to be unitary because it is approached from the perspective of God. Having arrived at God in one or more of these ways, one can then look for characterizations of the two of them (Actuality and God) together (which will yield Ideality), or for relations between them (which will yield Existence). Having reached Ideality, one could then try to show how it is related to Actuality and God via Existence; having reached Existence, one could try to show that it relates Ideality to Actuality and God only because Ideality is acting as a counterweight.

September 21

A man seeks to complete himself by mastering what is not himself, thereby freeing himself from external conditions. The mastery is most complete if the others are completely subordinated to himself, to become nothing more than constituents or parts of him. This he does when he eats; but since he can eat but little, he must engage in other kinds of activity—restructuring, controlling, classifying, and knowing. Knowing is superior to all the others in that it has an unlimited range. But it fails to get the others in their being. Metaphysics is the attempt to get to that being through knowing. All other forms of knowing deal with actualities in terms of parts, principles, or categories pertinent to them, or with some Being or subdivision of it, as having pertinence to man's nature or particular needs. In metaphysics the primary concern is to grasp Being in its Being, or as I have tried to make evident, in ultimate Beings. This means that we there reach the limit of knowing, since what is left over are the careers of the Beings in relation to one another, and to actualities and other delimited entities that there may be. Without metaphysical knowledge, what would be left over is not only those careers, but the intelligible natures of the Beings which have the careers.

Because of the action of Ideality, Actuality has a nature similar to that of actualities. This conclusion is, of course, one of the main tenets of the microcosmic-macrocosmic school, and of the Whiteheadians. But it does not follow that if Actuality has the same nature as actualities it interacts with them, or that its career is to be understood in terms similar to those that are pertinent to actualities. What in fact does interact with actualities are delimited forms of Beings which are unlike those actualities.

The similarity of nature in Actuality and actualities means that we can understand the former by means of concepts which are pertinent to the latter. It is of course true that Being is not of the same order as entity, or actualities. They both are, but in different ways. This is only to say that they have different careers, different ways of functioning. The similar natures that they have are displayed in different contexts with different results.

Metaphysical speculation has two stages, one of which is reached easily, the other of which is reached only with difficulty. The first involves a conceiving of Being, the other involves an encounter with Being, a seeing it function in the shape of four interlocked modes. Being is nothing other than myself or any other actuality freed from an involvement with other actualities, and thus as denuded of the features it thereby accretes. The encounter requires a facing of the transcendent reality which lies beyond all actualities; this requires a retreat way within oneself and a discovery of a resting place for one's initial wonder.

But might one not urge that actualities are because of the Existence that is in each? What need then is there to refer to Actuality? Is it not that existents could conceivably be of different grades of reality? The past, for example, exists because something like existence has been imposed on its facts. But this illustration does not really show that present things, things which now all have the same kind of existence within them, may have different grades of reality. May we not say though, that were it not for Actuality, that a larger entity, or one which lasted longer would, because it had more Existence in it, be superior to others? I think so. It is because of this that we must have recourse to Actuality as the

Being which makes all actualities equally real. Actuality has no magnitude in and of itself; no entity therefore can be said to be more real than another because it has more of Actuality within it.

But now it becomes clear that I ought not to say that actualities have a Being (Actuality) which they themselves are not. The actualities are because they have Existence in them; and they are oriented toward Actuality which is over against them, and which equates them as equally real by the fact that it is over against them all in the same way and to the same extent. This morning's observation (it is now after lunch, and I have taken up this argument after working on the draft for the book on democratic values—which was soon abandoned [May 15, 1966]) about the two stages of metaphysics must now be revised. We should say something like: actualities come and go, but despite their diverse magnitudes and durations, they are all equally real, when they exist, because they are all equally related to Actuality.

Our stages are now: 1] the recognition that all actualities exist through the presence of a portion of Existence in them;   2] the recognition that all equally are wondrous, regardless of how much Existence they have in them;   3] the recognition that their equality of being is due to a power other than Existence;   4] the confrontation of a Being which can equalize the reality of whatever is oriented in or toward it.

More comprehensively: we might find it wondrous for all actualities to be equally real, equally intelligible, equally present, equally unitary or private, and look for the distinctive ultimate Beings which make these equalities possible. Metaphysics on this view would not be the study of Being qua Being, or even Beings qua Beings, until it had passed the stage of studying how actualities are equalized in these four ways. Because of the fact that Actuality is the only ultimate in the role of an ultimate equalizer (the others having their roles only as within the confines of Actuality), equality of reality is in a different ontological position from equality of intelligibility, presence, and unity (or privacy). It is as equal in intelligibility, presence, and unity that actualities are equally real, for Actuality abstracts from the differentiations which the confined Ideal, Existence, and God, make to the different intelligibilities, present extensions, and unities.

The first metaphysical question would then seem to be, in what sense are the diverse entities about us alike? The scientist says they are alike in their constituents, apparently assuming that the diversity is due to the mere grouping of those constituents. But we can go on to ask what the various groupings have in common. Would it not be enough to answer that they have extension, intelligible form, and self-centeredness in common? What need then would there be to refer to Actuality? We made such a reference before because we considered different extensional distances, different degrees of complexity, different values. But now we have generalized beyond these differences.

Why not say that the actualities have in common the generic features of what they diversely exhibit? Because these are evidently abstractions, whereas what is being sought is something concrete, basic, a commonality which equalizes, not by abstracting from differences, but by overriding their claims to ultimacy. We seek then to know what *makes* the actualities equal, not how they can be conceived to be equal. The equality which we seek to explain is due to a power, a constraint, a re-evaluation, not to a generalization.

The past does not have an extension, nor do its items have a self-centeredness, and the actualities in their full concreteness as unique beings seem not to be intelligible, taken in and of themselves. Yet there is a sense in which the past is as real as the present, since it excludes and is excluded by it; and each actuality in its full concreteness is precisely what is on a footing with every other. Past, de-existentialized items do not, to be sure, have that full concreteness, but they are all equally real as past items; as excluding and excluded by present items, they have, through the agency of God, a kind of concreteness which allows them to be as real (though not active) as present items. But here I am far from sure, and certainly far from clear.

September 22

The basic question is not, why is there something rather than nothing. Such a question supposes that the being of what is, is somehow alien to it, that it might not have been. It is true, of course, that the things in this world come to be and pass away, but it does not follow that none might have been. If there always is some actuality or other, and this because there must be a plurality within and over against Actuality, there never is a time when it is possible to have nothing.

The philosophic quest begins with the attempt to say something about all actualities in their severalty, as distinct items. Atomists look to ultimate particles as grouped in various ways; Aristotelians analyze the actualities into matter and form, or essence and existence; Thomists see them all sharing in a divine, or divinely produced existence. In these various cases, there is no explanation provided for the individuality itself, for the actualities as distinct one from the other. Groupings and combinations can be duplicated, and a single existence stemming from God would seem to destroy any individual differences.

Instead I think we should look outside the actualities for factors which are pertinent to them all, but which, precisely because the actualities are not identical with those factors, the actualities can face in individual ways. We can see that the actualities are all *conditioned by, self-bounded from, oriented toward,* and *condensations of* some commonality distinct from them. (These four answer to the perspectives of Ideality, Existence, Actuality, and God. The first two, though, seem discoverable without reference to any modes of Being. We see them in the latter two guises I think only after we have come to know something of Actuality and God, perhaps on the basis of what we had already come to know of Ideality and Existence. In any case this seems to be the way I came to know them.)

Actualities are conditioned by the future possibilities they are to realize; by whatever enables them to be present; by whatever allows them to be over against their past; and by whatever equalizes them in these different situations. We have here conditioning by the Ideal, Existence, and God, and a final, overall conditioning by Actuality to make them all equally real.

Actualities are self-bounded from one another, from an absolute Other, from the common Being which they diversely face, and from the merely possible and merely past. We have here self-bounding in Existence, with respect to God, with respect to Actuality, and with respect to the Ideal. The final, overall self-bounding seems to be with respect to Actuality.

Actualities are oriented toward the possibilities they are now tensed to realize, toward what lies alongside them in a common Existence, toward God in terms of which they are evaluated, and toward Actuality, as that Being with respect to which they all are equal. Here again Actuality offers the final, overall factor. This third case is the inverse of the first, for where the first begins with conditions, the third begins with conditioned actualities and looks toward that which could condition them.

Actualities, finally, are localizations of Existence, instantiations of Ideality, complexes of repetitions of a divine identity, and equalized by Actuality. These are all condensations of modes of Being, with Actuality once again having a kind of priority.

We have actualities pointing to Actuality in four ways—as that which conditions them, that from which they stand apart, that toward which they are oriented, and that which they mirror in limited ways.

In all these cases, we start with the position of some Being, even though we speak and think as though we were attending only to the actualities. Respect for the actualities in their severalty makes the second approach the more congenial. It defines our most basic question to be: how is it that actualities though final, private, and individual are in the same sense? And our answer here is that they all are over against the same ultimate Being, Actuality. We can then go on to say that they had been equalized by being conditioned by Actuality, that they are final as equals by being oriented toward Actuality, and that their equal beings can be understood as condensations or imitations, duplications or reflections of the kind of Being which Actuality is, though there must be no implication here that they are somehow derivate from it.

This account would seem to lead to a distinctive method for metaphysics. One must begin by generalizing what one knows of actualities in the effort to escape from the special conditionings of one's time, place, experience, and society. But one must continue to acknowledge the actualities in their severalty. And this requires one to look beyond the actualities to what it is that they all have closed themselves off from, in order to be the distinctive actualities that they are, to the same degree and in the same way. But can we know that there is something from which they have closed themselves off unless we know it is there conditioning them? But this would require us to know something more than actualities to begin with.

Either we find all the actualities closed off in such a way that they show that there is something from which they are closed off, or we find them oriented toward something which we arrive at by some transcendence, or we begin with that something conditioning the actualities or providing them with a paradigm. Because the Christian tradition takes the last of these alternatives, it is forced in order to account for the reality of the world and particularly of men, to speak of a fall from the state where men and God are not altogether separable.

Perhaps the movement is a complex one? Does it not begin with the acknowledgment of actualities as oriented toward a common future, move from this to a conditioning by Existence, from there go to an instantiation of God, and end with a closing off of actualities from Actuality? We find ourselves subject to the future and controlled by Existence. And when we investigate the way we function, it is necessary to acknowledge God which we as privacies and unities, and in terms of our analysis as identities, can be said to instance. It is the interrelating of these which is the work of Actuality; this is known to be its work because Ideality, Existence, and God have a reality (over against themselves as Beings) of their own and in relation to actualities. Were there no Actuality beyond them, they would be finalities involved with what was not real, in any sense in which they were. And that Actuality would absorb them, have them merely as a function of itself, were they not directed at the actualities. And those actualities would not be data for them, were they not over against them and Actuality as well.

Oriented toward Ideality, conditioned by Existence, instantiating God, actualities are irreducible realities holding themselves over against Actuality all in the same way and same extent. That Actuality is known to be real because of the way it interrelates the orienting Ideality, the conditioning Existence, and the paradigmatic God.

September 23

When we are discontented with the confusion, errors, inconsistencies, and imprecisions of common sense we 1] *generalize.* Common sense has already generalized, and we may accept some of its results, as we do when we use its ordinary language. We thus may speak of things, of men, of tools. But to escape the limits of our own society, our generalizations should go further. And thus we get to actualities (i.e., substances) living and nonliving. Phenomenologists who pride themselves on staying with the concrete generalize as surely as others do. They speak of men and things, anxiety, shame, and so on, and not about this or that single occurrence. We can also generalize to properties and get extension, quality, number, etc.

Having generalized, we proceed to 2] *classify.* As the above cases illustrate, we can accept some of the commonsense classifications; but once again it is better to go beyond the limited and unsystematic classifications, to attend to those that are primary and those that are derivative, those that are active and those that are passive. The usual classifications can be taken to be involved with various subdivisions of these.

From classification we proceed to 3] *describe.* Here attention is paid to the distinctive features of the members of the different classes. Classification must make use of some description, but having used it, it makes possible further descriptions, particularly when two or more classes are contrasted.

After description we can 4] *divide.* We now break up the entities with which we began, in order to isolate those parts which make up a single theoretically known world out of the particles of all entities. This is the move that atomism makes, but it wrongly supposes that the initial entities have been annihilated. Division is an intellectual act, and leaves untouched the whole which is divided.

From division we move on to 5] *evidence*. Evidencing has a number of forms. A] There is the evidence from factoring. Here entities are analyzed into factors which have a being apart from their union in those entities. This is what Aristotle did when he distinguished form and matter and found form in its purity to be one with God, and the matter to be a single cosmic reality. Factoring makes one aware of actualities as so many condensations of ultimate realities.

B] There is the evidence of integrity, of the way in which actualities maintain themselves over against one another and whatever else there be. They maintain themselves as distinct extended beings, as actualized possibilities, as privacies, and as finalities, thereby leading us to take them as self-bounded from ultimate realities having the guise of a cosmic extension, a realm of possibilities, an ultimate privacy, and a final version of themselves, i.e., Actuality.

C] We find them to be limited in magnitude, in what they can do, in relation to their past, and in that each is coordinated as a reality with all other actualities. Their limitations give us evidence that there is something which is beyond them and which keeps them not as persistent or as strong as they otherwise might be.

D] Actualities reach into the future, accumulate their past, reach out into their environment, and are together in one universe. These functionings offer evidence of their orientation toward other realities.

These evidences do not reach to the Beings which they evidence. They direct us toward them. To get to those Beings, we must engage in new acts of apprehension. We 6] *speculate*, attempting to acknowledge more than actualities. The conditioning that we feel, particularly by the Ideal in the guise of prescriptions and by Existence in the guise of force, leads to the consideration of these Beings. But we do not yet have them in the form of ultimate modes of Being. This we achieve only after we find that they must be supplemented by God, and that all three of them are themselves conditioned and offer evidence of purer forms of themselves by their limitations and by their functionings. They have roles relative to actualities, but must first be in order that they can have such roles.

To account for the relativization of the Beings, we look for a power other than themselves, and this is Actuality. To look for them in a purer form we 7] employ *dialectic* and *proof*. These enable us to reach them as coordinate with Actuality.

The speculative move (6) could have taken account of the fact that the actualities are contemporary, grouped, affiliated, and real in the same sense even while individual, and that these point to powers which operate on them. This approach takes account of a plurality of actualities, whereas the other takes account of them singly. I suppose the second is preferable. Since the fourth characterization leads to Actuality as a mode of Being, we here have already a beginning for a dialectical discovery of the other modes.

Summarily: We find our generalized actualities to be so conditioned that they are grouped, contemporary, affiliated, and equally real, and therefore move on to consider three Beings encapsulated in a fourth. The three encapsulated Beings also have a status of their own, a status which makes it possible for the fourth Being (Actuality) to be a Being in a sense other than that of the other three as now functioning with respect to actualities.

Making actualities coordinately real does not evidently involve a relativization of Actuality; they can be said in fact to make themselves coordinately real through their common self-bounding from Actuality. They will not, strictly speaking, be conditioned by Actuality, and their orientation toward it will be only the inverse of their bounding themselves from it. But they can all be taken to be condensations of Actuality, provided we can legitimately say that Actuality is a factor in them in something like the way in which Ideality, Existence and God, in their delimited encapsulated guises, are factors in them.

October 2

There are three kinds of judgments, 1] *judgments what,* 2] *judgments that,* and 3] *judgments at once what and that.* A "judgment what" unites units horizontally. It is this judgment which alone is emphasized by analysts, language philosophers, and idealists. There is no reference here made to anything beyond those elements. Truth will, for this type of judgment, relate either to the customary usages to which the judged is put, or to the way in which the elements are related to one another. For Hegel, the relation can be said to be one in which the predicate absorbs the subject, and itself gives way to another absorbing predicate until we reach the absolute end.

A "judgment that" is characteristic of realism. It refers something in the mind or language to a reality beyond. This is the kind of judgment which Bradley is occupied with in the first chapter of his *Logic.* It also concerns *Principia Mathematica*; there, a ϕ is attributed to an a which is an individual. But in the *Principia Mathematica*, we seem to have no discriminable individuals; *a* seems to have no features which would enable one to distinguish it from a *b*. Consequently, the ascription of the ϕ to it must be in error, for a naked *a*, an *a* which has no features, would then be wrongly characterized as having the character ϕ. If we instead held that it did have that character, we would make our judgment tautological, since we would be ascribing to a ϕ'd *a*, the character ϕ.

"Judgments what" cannot claim to be true of anything; "judgments that" have nothing intelligible of which they can say something significantly true. Both are abstractions from a basic act of judgment where we A] analyze components of what is given;   B] relate these in a "judgment what";   C] unify them to make something which we claim to be true of that object; and   D] refer this judgment to the object (and thus have the "judgment what" as a component in a "judgment that").

In this last form of judgment, the copula has three roles. It unites the elements of the "judgment what"; it orients the "judgment what" in the individual asserting it; and it refers that judgment to the object.

There are four different meanings of "proper name" that can be distinguished, though only three are viable. There is the logical proper name, the name which merely denotes. This is the *a* in ϕa. Such a logically proper name has never been found, nor does there seem to be an entity answering to it. But there is the *grammatical* proper name which functions as a subject in the "judgment what"; the *denotative* proper name which is the entire "judgment that"; and the *summational* proper name which is the designation of the location where one derived the elements of the "judgment what," and to which one refers the "judgment that." "Socrates is mortal" uses "Socrates" as a grammatical subject, as a designating term for that which is named "Socrates" and is mortal, and as the name of the unit being which we had judged in this double way.

If the "judgment what" be defined as a hypothetical, we can go on to say that it will have a categorical use in that it will be the unit which is "predicated" in the "judgment that." The nature of the entity to which one refers in the "judgment that" determines the kind of consequence which is rightly linked with the antecedent of the hypothesis. This means that we make "judgments what," not by combining any entities, but by combining those which reality underwrites.

It is true to say that "If I were rich, I would not spend my money wildly," since I am a man of such and such habits and interests, and my being rich would not affect these. It is false to say that "If you were I, you would be taller than I," for you in becoming I must be sustained by me, and I have a certain height. But what of "If I were you, I would be taller than I am?" Evidently the subject here is you and this requires me to change into a being of a different height.

October 6

Each actuality is fully a being. It is distinct from a mode of Being in that it is oriented toward Actuality as that which makes all actualities, no matter when, or where, or how large, to be equally real. The contingency of the actualities is due to the fact that they are existent, by means of the possession of a portion of Existence within them. The portion within them is not altogether separable from Existence outside, which goes its own way as an encapsulated mode of Being.

There is Existence in Actuality and other modes of Being, but this is Existence as a qualifier, as that which is effective on them. Actuality does not contain (though it does encapsulate) other modes of Being as an integral part of itself in the way actualities contain the encapsulated modes of Being. Each mode of Being offers a position in terms of which the rest can be characterized and understood, and which dictate various functions to them.

If an actuality exists contingently, must it not also be contingently intelligible and be a unity contingently? After all, it is related to the Ideal and God in somewhat the way in which it is related to Existence. Existence has no prior or subsequent role to these others; yet it does seem as if an actuality can acquire and lose Existence while remaining intelligible, and continuing to have some kind of unity. Does it have an intelligibility as an actuality here and now; does it have a unity as an actuality here and now? Is not the intelligibility of the actuality, which seems to be untouched by the coming and going of Existence, the intelligibility of the possibility of the actuality? Is not the unity of the actuality, which seems to remain despite the movement of Existence, the unity of the meaning "actuality"? Yes. The point perhaps can be more readily seen if we think of the contingency of the existence of an actuality to be only the contingency of being contemporary with other actualities. We can then also see that those actualities are contingently grouped with one another, and contingently affiliated with one another.

This last suggestion makes the contingency of the actualities an outcome of the diverse exercise of powers on the part of the various encapsulated modes of Being. Instead of emphasizing the coming to be and passing away of an actuality or a number of them, it emphasizes the alterable ways in which they are together. An actuality then is contingent because it has such and such connections with other actualities for an undetermined period, dictated by the action of powers independent of the actualities.

We can say of an actuality that it, as grouped with others and as affiliated with still others in intimate ways, is also contemporary with others, not necessarily identical with any of the previous actualities. Still, when and so far as it is contemporary with certain actualities, it is also affiliated and grouped with them. Similarly, we can say that while contemporary with certain actualities, it may be grouped and affiliated with different ones, but that when in fact it is either grouped or affiliated, it is also contemporary with the items with which it is grouped or affiliated.

We have an independence in the operation of the different encapsulated modes of Being on the actualities, but we also have them all operative on the same actualities, once we take some one particular way of having actualities together as basic. We could have taken as basic the way in which actualities are related to actualities in the past, but this would not give us the situation where the actualities were grouped or affiliated as they are in the present. Still, if this be our base line, we can see how those very actualities in the past could be grouped and affiliated in a way they are not grouped or affiliated as merely present. Just so, we can think of actualities in the future as being grouped or affiliated, and then can see how they can be existentially related. However, we now abandon the idea of contemporaneity as the characteristic result of Existence, unless we suppose that the very fact of our considering the past and future make an "intellectualized" version of contemporaneity out of the considered items.

It would be better, I think, to hold to the idea of contemporaneity as involving only copresent substantial actualities. But then it would seem as if there were a priority to the idea of Existence, for actualities seem to be grouped and to have affiliations even when not present. And if it be said, as I did just a few minutes ago, that they are grouped and affiliated as substantial present actualities in a way they are not grouped or affiliated as past or future, it seems that Existence is once again given a priority over the others, as that which defines the presentness and contingency of the actualities.

October 7

When and as an actuality incorporates a portion of Existence, to become contemporarily together with other actualities, it is also grouped and affiliated with them in distinctive ways. Because the contemporaneity, grouping, and affiliation are under the control of Beings within Actuality, it is contingent in three ways.

In the next moment there will either be the same or different actualities. In the former case, the grouping and the affiliations may nevertheless have shifted. In the latter case, the new actualities may merely replace items in given groups and affiliations. It is only because we are dealing with present items that Existence is treated as the initial way of dealing with actualities; but when it is so taken, the grouping and affiliations are still independent, and the outcome of them may be a loss of existence on the part of some of the grouped or affiliated actualities.

October 8

A "judgment what" relates terms to make a syntactical judgment; a "judgment that" relates the result of a "judgment what" to an object. The "judgment what" is at the same time oriented in the judger; he claims that this, which is oriented in him and unified by him, is true of the object. The object, which he is claiming is a unity of the elements of the "judgment what," has consequences which parallel the conclusions that are entailed by the "judgment what."

A negative judgment can be understood in one of two ways. We can make use of a negative particle by infecting a positive one with a negation to give us a generic positive term. We take, say, some such term as "green," and infect it with a negation to get "non-green." This includes everything other than green, either within some limited domain or over the entire scheme of things. Or we can insist on positive particles only, and then infect the "is" with a negation to make it a relation of otherness. In the one case, we can continue to use the hypothetical form, where the antecedent or subject is thought to be the premiss or antecedent for the conclusion which follows from it, according to the rationale of the object to which the hypothetical is categorically referred. It allows us to say that both "If I were King of England, I would have a small standing army," and "If I were King of England, I would prove a failure, i.e., be unsuccessful" explicate me in terms of some disposition or potentiality which I have.

The second method requires one to consider two kinds of hypotheticals: one where antecedent and consequence are joined by an implication, and the other where the terms are related by a relation of otherness. The former I think is preferable, particularly if the negative particle is interpreted as having a restricted range, perhaps even of being a summary expression for a set of disjuncts, all of the same degree of particularity and of the same kind as the positive particle which the negative excludes, and which reciprocally excludes that negative.

Bradley, in his great *Logic*, tends to use only a "judgment that." When he deals with the negative judgment, he therefore speaks of it as involving a suggestion which is rejected by the object. Both affirmative and negative judgments can be excluded by an object; but both can be also true of an object. Bradley is actually speaking of an erroneous judgment.

An erroneous judgment is excluded by the object. But if every hypothetical has a categorical base, then this judgment must have a lodgement elsewhere. Is it not in the mind of the judger? Does he not, in making the false judgment, provide us with evidence of the kind of mind he has? Is he not one who is offering us the evidence in terms of which we can make a judgment about him? I think the answer to all these is "yes."

In error we have a "judgment what" which is oriented in us, but which we are not claiming is a judgment about us. The psychiatrist or the biographer takes the evidence and uses it to make a judgment *that* we are men of such and such a nature. One can therefore say that psychiatry is the metaphysics of error, the discovery of the truth value of false judgments about the world.

October 9

We know Beings in a way in which we do not know actualities. We cannot then say that our knowledge of Beings is the result of a generalization of what we know of actualities, for a generalization is a knowledge of the same type as that from which the generalization was made. Yet it is the case that actualities are affected by, qualified by, and in a sense constituted by Beings, or derivatives of them. Ought we not say that we can get evidences for Beings, and even get the material for generalizations from actualities, provided that we approach those actualities with an attitude, or with concepts, or from a position which is different from that we employ when we normally perceive, judge commonsensically, report, describe, or experience through our organs? But this would seem to make our apprehension of actualities bifocal—which does not seem to be the case. Better then would be the view that we can make a deliberate, distinctive approach to actualities so as to obtain categories in terms of which we can then understand Beings.

In our normal judgments of perception and common sense we deal with an actuality as intelligible, extended, unified, and perhaps also as a reality on a footing with other actualities. But we can also attend only to one side of it, say the intelligible; we then analyze the actuality and isolate a factor in it. It is this isolated factor to obtain which required no special unfamiliar power on our part, which we then, in a distinctive act, use as our agency for contemplating, judging, and eventually encountering the Being of Ideality. Intelligibility left free arises to meet that which is intelligible in itself, because the intelligibility becomes the carrier of a hope. The isolated intelligibility is carried to intelligibility as such through the agency of a hope, a hope which at last finds its appropriate object.

We can now say that though Beings are known in ways which are other than the way in which actualities are known, the actualities can provide agencies and evidence for such knowledge of Beings. But it also seems to be the case that we can get to a knowledge of Beings without attending to actualities, as Eastern thinkers have often maintained. In the given case of intelligibility and the (encapsulated) Ideal, we should then say that we can dispense with the acknowledgment or use of the intelligibility of the actuality and move directly, with a dislocated hope, to confront the Ideal. This is possible if we not only can detach ourselves from the world of actualities, but in such detachment can begin to make use of a hope appropriate to such a detached state.

If it be the case that both approaches to Beings arrive at the same point, it would no longer be necessary to say that when we start with actualities, we move from a grasp of them as totalities, objectives, and objects, and then point beyond the last to a relative transcendent of them, to a Being as involved with actualities (and not as it is in itself) and that is all. We will now be able to say that we can get to the transcendent in itself even when we start with actualities, though it would still be true that we can get to only a relativized transcendent Being then.

Can we also say that if we start with Beings, we not only can arrive at actualities as relatively transcendent to those Beings (and thus not yet confronted, not yet arrived at in or by themselves), but can also make use of some aspect of those Beings to provide us with the concepts appropriate to actualities in themselves? If so, we would be able to say that both actualities and Beings can be directly confronted in two ways; in one of these we start with the other type of reality. In both cases, we would use the same kind of referential act to get to the reality, to confront it as it is outside a relativizing situation. It seems evident that we can make this double approach to Beings; can we also make it with respect to actualities?

The category that would be appropriate to actualities is one in which the various modes of Being are together. It is the togetherness of them, treated as that which needs a concreteness and can find it only in a plurality, which must provide the category in terms of which we can directly face actualities from the base of Beings. But we here face a serious difficulty. The category does not now seem to include Actuality, or if it does include it, includes it in a different form. Either Actuality also has a self-encapsulated form, which seems redundant as well as mysterious, or Actuality functions as the power which requires the abstract togetherness of its encapsulated Beings to find a plurality of concrete embodiments in actualities. The second alternative requires Actuality to function as a kind of fourth pole of the category (taking the place of an "I"), and as a reference of the rest of the category to actualities. It would be behind and in front of the rest of the category treated as a three-ply togetherness, and thus as expressive of the nature of actualities. But I do not yet see how the pluralization takes place, nor how Actuality in fact functions. Would the category used in ordinary knowledge be derived from a grasp of this pluralizing togetherness?

October 10

If mathematics is a discovery of the necessities linking possibilities, it is occupied with the Ideal. The Ideal then is the realm of the intelligible. But I have said again and again that Actuality is the proper object of knowledge. If both contentions are to be upheld, we must conclude that the proper object of knowledge is not that which is intrinsically intelligible, but rather that which is the object of wonder.

But I have also said that the Ideal is identical with the Good when oriented toward man. The Ideal would seem then not to contain only possibilities which are intelligible, but normative possibilities as well. Are these also intelligible? If not, the Ideal cannot be identified with the intelligible. If so, then we must say that either mathematics is an intellectual way of facing our obligations, so that the non-normative is a kind of normative, or that the normative is the mathematical made into the norm for human action. On the first alternative, mathematics is ethics pursued by another means; on the second alternative, ethics is mathematics having an obligatory role. The first seems more promising, since it subjects the mathematical activity to normative conditions, whereas the second alternative would require us to say that the Good and other obligating possibilities have only a mathematical nature in themselves. The second alternative will of course appeal to Pythagoreans and others who look to mathematical science for a clue to the nature of ethics. Northrop would be a contemporary instance.

In any case, the kind of knowledge we get of the Ideal will be different from that which we get of Actuality. And starting with Actuality, we will have to understand how it is possible to have a direct knowledge that there is a plurality of actualities. Is it not that from the standpoint of Actuality, the other modes of Being are together, but do not make a single unity, that an approach to them from Actuality is inseparable from an attempt to have them unified, and that this attempt, precisely because it endeavors to make the conjunction concrete, pulverizes into an indeterminate number of equalized unifications of the three modes of Being? The category in terms of which we know actualities would then be the three Beings as equalized by Actuality, while the category in terms of which we know Actuality would be the wondrous nature of an actuality, detached from the complex nature of the actuality and allowed to terminate in its appropriate object.

October 11

The discussion of the last few days failed to make a distinction among a number of different questions. It did not distinguish the question of the direct knowledge of Actuality from the base of actualities, and conversely, from   A] knowledge of an encapsulated mode of Being from the base of an actuality, and conversely;   B] knowledge of a Being from the base of an encapsulated mode of Being, and conversely;   C] knowledge of an encapsulated mode of Being from some limited part of it, and conversely;   D] knowledge of a Being from some limited part of it, and conversely.

We can get a direct knowledge of Actuality by using the idea of an actuality as our concept and have this find its appropriate object by having it sustained by an attitude of wonder. We can get a direct knowledge of actualities by using the idea of Actuality as that which is to make concrete the togetherness of the encapsulated modes of Being, thereby forcing one to multiply the cases in which they are together. Do we in the first case start with the actuality, with an aspect of it which is wondrous, or with the reality of the togetherness of three factors—intelligibility, extension, and unitary value? I think it must be the wondrous reality of the actuality, the fact that it is a distinct Being, final and independent, in abstraction from its three factors, that offers the referent to Actuality, just as our referent to actualities is not Actuality, as affected by other modes of Being, but as independent of them.

Following that lead, we ought to say that when we wish to confront the other modes of Being as having roles within Actuality, we isolate an aspect of actualities and refer this, via distinctive ways of referring, to an appropriate terminus. There, hope, fear, or awe will be sustained without qualification. The aspect as isolated from all others is indistinguishable from a delimited portion of the terminus. Questions A and C turn out then to be the same.

We are left with the questions whether we can know other Beings, besides Actuality, from the base of an encapsulated form of them, or from the base of some limited part of them. But we do not seem to have any limited part of Beings which are coordinate with Actuality. The factors inside an actuality need not be similar in nature to these Beings. All we can do is to confront the encapsulated forms of these Beings, through the use of a delimited portion of them which has been abstracted from actualities, and then use the result as itself providing a base in terms of which we can have a direct knowledge of the Beings themselves.

From an actuality we can abstract its extension and use this as a concept of Existence (as inside Actuality) at which we arrive through an act of fear or the awareness of our weakness before overwhelming power. Having arrived at such an encapsulated Existence, we can use the result as itself referring to Existence as a Being. This reference is through a distinctive act of intuition, the counterpart of mythological absorption, mysticism, and speculative knowledge.

From the base of Beings other than Actuality, we can arrive only at their own subdivisions, or at themselves as having roles inside Actuality. We cannot, from those Beings, get to actualities or know that there are any. And when we get to their roles, we can know that there are actualities only as points or regions subject to those roles, and thereby made contemporary, grouped, or affiliated. The constitution of those actualities as having all three encapsulated Beings as factors is not known from the position of the Beings in their encapsulated roles.

If we can get to the Being of Ideality, Existence, and God via the limited forms of them inside Actuality, we can, as actualities, make contact with those Beings. We would not then make contact with them as directly as we do Actuality (since we would have first had to arrive at the limited forms of them), but we would nevertheless encounter them. The encounter would be inseparable from the reference to them. These references would then be quite distinct from that characteristic of our approach to Actuality.

We get to Actuality via inference, and must sustain this by an encounter. We get to the other modes of Being via their limited forms, but in such a way that we then and there encounter them. Wonder is different from hope, fear, and awe in that it arrives at its terminus only when made into an inferential act, whose terminus is then experienced by us as reducing us to the level of all other actualities.

If this is true, it must also be the case that the four modes of Being all make contact with actualities. Actuality does this by working through the togetherness of the confined forms of the other modes of Being; the other modes of Being do this by working through their individual confined forms. Actuality as a consequence makes contact with the actualities as substantial realities, while the other modes of Being make contact with them as instantiating them (in the guise of confined forms), and as nothing more.

October 13

When men are obligated by the Good, they instantiate that Good in the guise of a sense of duty. They also embody it in the form of a realization of a possibility, and are subject to it as that which allies them with others in distinctive groups. They instantiate Existence in their attitude of self-maintenance, embody it in their extensionality, and are subject to it as contemporaries. They instantiate God in their attitude of being His other, embody Him in their harmonious self-identity, and are subject to Him as beings who are affiliated with one another in various ways and in various degrees. All these are ontological cases; they are to be supplemented by accounts of men as involved with these limited forms of Being, in ethics and politics, art and history, and private and public religion.

October 15

Modern logicians speak of negation as a function or operator. This view has trouble with double negation. If the operation negation is like other operators, such as implication or disjunction, it leaves that on which it is operating untouched. The negation would then occur as if it were outside the bracket enclosing what is to be negated. The proper way to write "not p" on this view would be "$-(p)$" or "fp." But then the application of another negation would give us not an operator on a proposition, but on the negation sign, which is a different use than the previous operator exercised. Alternatively "ffp," which involves imposing a function on fp will return us to p, only if the "f's" operate in different ways.

If, on the other hand, we would like to have the negation act in the same way in both cases, we will find that we cannot return to the p at all. A negation which makes a difference to the item negated can be expressed not as a function, but as a qualifier. Not p is now to be written as $(-p)$, which is equivalent to a new term, q. If we negate this new term in the same way we negated the old, we get $(-q)$ or alternatively $(-(-p))$, i.e., r. This is not identical with p.

October 16

It is possible to treat negation as a dyadic function on a par with disjunction, conjunction and implication, by starting with two propositions, a "p" and a "non-p," or with what Frege called the true and the false, and take negation to be the function by which one replaces one of these by the other. Double negation on such a view will bring one back to the original proposition. But of course we do not then account for "non-p" on the base of "p," but take both of them to be equally given.

Modern logicians not only are not altogether clear about negation, they seem to be unclear about the laws of thought as well. It is true that one can have a system in which those laws are merely alongside others, but the question still remains as to whether or not those laws are used to make the system. And it is true that we can have systems where one or the other of these laws is not stated; but the question still remains as to whether or not they are operative, even where not stated.

The law of identity would seem to be characteristic of God; God is the self-identical. It is a law which would break down only if there were nothing distinguishable, if whatever we referred to was then and there pulverized, or flowed indistinguishably into something else. The law of inference would seem to be characteristic of Existence, for Existence is the domain of action. It is a law which would break down only if there were nothing relevant to anything else, precluding a move from one to the other. The law of excluded middle would seem to be characteristic of Actuality in relation to actualities; whatever is actual is either Actuality or an actuality. The law breaks down wherever there is generality. As Peirce observed, man is neither male nor female. The nominalist is evidently one for whom this law cannot be violated. The law of contradiction, finally, would seem to be characteristic of Ideality, for the law defines all that which is within Ideality to be logically possible. The law breaks down wherever there is vagueness, a merging of items. In Whitehead's account of the coming to be of an actual occasion, we have a merging of past and future in a single atomic moment; inside that moment the time is vague.

When a possibility is written as "*x*-or-*x̄*" we make it appear as though what was being denied is the law of excluded middle, since the items are not then disjoined. But if the above is right, the possibility should be given a generic characterization, such as "entity," or in a particular context, "color" or "sea-fight." Instead of saying with Aristotle that the sea fight tomorrow is "either won-or-lost," and that we cannot now say of that fight "it is won or it is lost," we should say that the sea fight now is only decidable and that it will be decided tomorrow.

All the laws together break down if there be nothing distinguishable, relevant, particular, or determinate, if all we have is at once flowing, unrelated, general, and vague. The validity of the laws depends on the fact that in thought and reality there are self-maintaining items, which have bearing on others, are specific, and oppose others.

October 21

Actuality both transcends and is immanent in actualities. It transcends them as a distinct reality which defines the actualities to be all equally real. This is a relative transcendence, since it is one having reference to actualities, even though it is from a position outside them, by a reality which is independent of them. An absolute transcendence by Actuality is had only so far as Actuality is related to the other modes of Being. As immanent, Actuality is the togetherness of the actualities, enabling them to constitute a single cosmos, where they are subject to the control of Existence, etc., and thereby become contemporaries, etc.

As immanent, Actuality is without any controlling power; yet it does not provide an empty togetherness, similar to that characteristic of the comma uniting the items in an aggregate. It has more the character of a whole, where the togetherness of the items has a nature and career. This means that the actualities, despite their punctuate, distinct beings, their privacies, and their status as beings-in-themselves, form no aggregate of items, but are "internally" related as members of one cosmos.

It would seem that I now am quite close to the idealistic position. But I am not more so than I was when I acknowledged that the comma itself was a one with respect to aggregated items. The present view is maintaining only that the nature of the togetherness of actualities, though immanent in them, is not constituted by those actualities, whereas the nature of the one of an aggregate is so constituted, even though it continues to have a being which is not reducible to the aggregate.

We have four basic kinds of "ones" in connection with actualities: a one whose nature is constituted by the many in which it is immanent; a one whose nature is not constituted by the many in which it is immanent; a one whose being and nature is a one for the many actualities; and a one whose being and nature is over against the many actualities as in the first of the three other foregoing manys. In the first we have the actualities in an aggregate; in the second we have them in a cosmos; in the third we have them equally real; in the fourth we have them aggregated but over against Actuality.

October 22

There are three squares of opposition: *1]* Aristotle's, where all the propositions have existential import;   *2]* a "Platonic" where none of the propositions has existential import; and   *3]* Modern logic's, where the particular propositions are taken from the first, and the universal propositions are taken from the second.

1]   Aristotle (but apparently not all Aristotelians) took his universal propositions to refer to real beings; it was therefore possible for the particular propositions to be viewed as subsumed under them.

2]   The Platonic square of opposition denies that "some" means existents. It takes "some" instead to refer to a part of what has been marked out by the "all." Here too, subsumption of particular under universal is possible.

3]   In the two foregoing, all the traditional relations of the square are preserved. For the modern logician only the relation of contradiction is maintained. For them, "some" means existent, but "all" may refer to what does not in fact exist. Consequently, of the nonexistent, both "some are" and "some are not" are false, and their contradictories "none are" and "all are" are true. But if we can say of x's both that "All of them are y" and that "None of them are y," we in fact say that x is vague, since it allows for the presence of both y and non-y. No definite conclusions can be drawn from a universal regarding that which does not exist.

But is it not true that "All centaurs have the torso of a man," and false that "No centaurs have the torso of a man"? Is it not true that in a vacuum (which does not exist) bodies fall at the same rate, and false that they fall at different rates?

October 24

If we have a One *for* a Many, we must also have the Many united by a distinctive One. A One for a Many thus presupposes a Many in which a One is immanent. The One for a Many also must be grounded in a One which is over against the Many (in which a One is immanent), for it cannot be a One "for" without being something by itself, having a Many facing it to which it will apply in the guise of a One for that Many.

Given a Many with a One immanent in it, we need make no reference to a One for that Many, unless we can show that there is something happening to that Many which cannot be accounted for except by making reference to a force, power or domain which is operating on that Many. One can, of course, define the Many as having integral to it whatever powers we find that it is subject to. The entities in the Many as not involved in those powers will then be defined as abstractions, and any powers beyond those now acknowledged to be integral to the Many will be defined as nonexistent, or will be treated as arbitrary or irrational factors.

A monist is one for whom a Many has nothing other than an immanent One. He can isolate the items in the Many only by abstracting them, and thereby making them be nonreal. His Many is bound together in a single internal relation which allows for no additional power, and from which nothing can be distinguished without falsification. Wittgenstein is a linguistic monist with respect to his various languages, for these are means by which men are bound together in a single public world, precluding their being able to have private languages and perhaps privacies. For Leibniz, on the other hand, we have only monads, which are not even together except from the position of God. Once he acknowledges that the monads are merely together in a Many in which each is completely external to all the others, he has to account for the fact that they keep pace in time, have common objectives, are affiliated in various ways, and are all equally real. These facts are taken by Leibniz to be the result of a divine decision. God, for him, is the One for the Many monads, and is the source of features in that Many which cannot be derived from a consideration of the members of it as merely together as self-contained monads.

We gain nothing by taking as the real only isolate, atomic entities, for we will have to have them together, and thus as connected by an immanent One. To account for such facts as contemporaneity, etc., we will be led to look outside our atoms to a single universal power able to affect the mere togetherness, so that the items act in some consonance with one another.

Nor do we gain anything by attributing to the Many in and of itself an intrinsic contemporaneity, an intrinsic self-defined objective, an intrinsic set of valencies, and an intrinsic equality in reality, for we would then not be able to deal with the items severally, except as falsifications or distortions. We cannot therefore take the Many to have its One entirely immanent in it.

Nor do we gain anything by trying to combine these two positions— which is what in essence Sartre does. He takes the world to have a One immanent in the Many, but man to be an independent being standing over against whatever else there be. Consequently, when he finds himself or any man in that Many, he thinks the situation inexplicable, absurd. It is his view (and apparently Heidegger's as well) that men are thrown into that world, made to belong to a Many even though they are in themselves atomic units, independent of a position in that Many.

If Wittgenstein can distinguish a plurality of languages, he is evidently able to have a Many in which the languages are units. Is not that Many subject to influences which cannot be accounted for by attending to the several languages or their mere togetherness? Do not the languages develop in some accord with one another? Do they not express the same civilization? If so, then we must acknowledge a One outside those languages. We must take the languages to be so many separated worlds, quasi privacies which the One will bring together. But if we can do this with languages, we should be able to do this for the words in the different languages, and for the men who make use of the words and the languages. The words and the men will be private just so far as they are not governed by a One; i.e., just so far as there is a One for them, and they consequently have some kind of independence with respect to one another.

Monism and monadology are extremes which try to deny one another. But the first has no one who can deny, and the second has no one to whom to deny. To be able to deny is to escape the unified totality, to stand over against it as an independent unit. To have someone to whom one can deny is to belong in the same world with him, to constitute a Many with him, united by an immanent One in the shape of a denying.

To avoid these extremes, we must affirm that there are beings which have some independence of one another, and which together constitute a single Many in which a One is immanent as a kind of aggregational togetherness. We never get a situation where we have only a One or only a Many. We always have a Many in which items are loosely together, and which nevertheless function in more intimate ways, pointing up the need to acknowledge a One for them, and then beyond this a One in itself which *can be* a One for them.

Thinkers differ as to just how loose or tight the items in a Many are held together, and therefore how much of what is true of them is to be accounted for by referring to a One (or a number of Ones) outside them all. The more they tend to monism, the less acknowledgement beyond must they make; but they do this at the price of denying the independent being and action of the items in the Many. The more they tend to monadology, or atomism, the more independence they allow; but they do this at the price of having to treat common features of the items in the Many as the effect of some outside One. The Humean tries to reject a number of commonalities that most thinkers find to characterize the Many of experience; but sooner or later he has to introduce a mind which endows the Many with the common features that he denied it to have intrinsically.

We cannot avoid having to acknowledge a Many of actualities and a mode of Being which functions as a One for them. We can avoid acknowledging more than one mode of Being only if we can treat all the other features of the Many as intrinsic to it, or if we can reject them as illusory or surd. But since the features do not appear to be any more intrinsic or illusory or surd than the feature which leads us to acknowledge one mode of Being, we cannot avoid a reference to other modes of Being as well.

Let us suppose that we want to affirm only that all the actualities are together in a single time, whether we take this to be psychological, local, or cosmic. We could suppose (with Aristotle) that the very togetherness of the actualities has a contemporaneity intrinsic to it. If so, we will have to look to a One to account for their groupings or common goals. If this be thought to lead to a One outside the merely temporalized Many, we can then go back and ask whether the same reasoning does not require us to acknowledge that the common time is also an effect of some external One. Or alternatively, we can see the Many as having its grouping intrinsic to it, and then will have to account for time by looking to a One outside that Many; we can then return to the original Many and ask if the grouping is not as alien to the items in the Many as the common time is.

The basic argument of the *Modes of Being*, particularly as interpreted in this *Philosophy in Process*, is that there are four features of the Many actualities which require a reference to Ones for that Many. A more monistic system would allow one to acknowledge less than four; a more monadic one would, of course, force us to acknowledge more than four. Atomism is extravagant, monism is timid metaphysics. Yet it is the atomists who often speak of themselves as anti- or non-metaphysical, and the monists who call themselves metaphysicians. Both suppose that the metaphysician acknowledges a One in itself. This he does, but not without also acknowledging a One for the Many—and this neither of them has.

October 25

A machine yields a sequence of items. They could conceivably be in the form of words. But those words do not form a sentence, even if they begin with a capital letter and end with a period. A sentence makes a claim to be true for every one. If that claim is wrong, someone is to be criticized for misleading the rest, for being careless, for being a blunderer, or for deceiving us. We could charge the machine with being inefficient or in poor condition, but we cannot charge it with making an error.

In order to claim that what the machine presents us with is a sentence, we must take it together with a man who made it or programmed it. It is the two of them together who make the sentence. In relation to the machine, the man can be said to be a One for its many words. Taking the machine alone to be visible or present or available and known by empirical means, we can say that the man is the mind of the machine.

It is possible to give a machine a series of sentences which make claims, and ask the machine to order them in some way. The machine would not then be writing a book or telling a story. It would merely put the sentences in an order. But a message requires that the sentences be related in accord with some rationale. If it is a scientific message, they are related as having a rational connection; if it is a mathematical message, they are related by deductive processes primarily; if it is a story, they are related by aesthetic principles governing contrasts, tensions, climaxes, taking account of the weights of the words and their overtones.

We can allow any kind of associations to take place, but to acknowledge something to be a message of some kind we must take it to have a primary set of connections. Such connections presuppose that with each sentence there is a readiness of a certain kind to relate it to the others. The message, if spoken or gestured or exhibited in the shape of a song, for example, must have its component parts accompanied by gestures, tendencies to act, and some area of communication, respectively. The units must be parts of a language which is shared by others. If someone wants me to take the sequence of sentences as making a message, he must provide me with a context in which each sentence functions as a unit in an interplay with other men. If the message is written down, it must be part of a language which others can use; this means that it must have a structure, have the units in it interconnected in such a way that something is clarified from a plurality of positions.

A novel tells us what man is by showing us the plausible outcomes of certain suppositions made regarding men; a prose work tells us what the real is by showing us how different truths about it hang together. But it takes something outside the given totality of units to allow the totality to be a single story or message. The "mind" of the novel is the individual author in a social setting. It is he who tells us to read the sentences with various inflections, to note the different nuances, to stress this or that episode. If there were no author, we would be the creators of the novel, using the material given to us, in what seems to be a novelistic form, to make a novel in fact. In the usual case, both where we are given sequences of words and sequences of sentences by a machine, we take it for granted that there is an author for them.

Suppose there were a million monkeys hitting the typewriter keys, and what they produced were libels, forged checks, plagiarisms and the like, and that they then sent them off to newspapers, etc. Whom would we hold responsible? Is it not the man who sat those monkeys down at those machines and allowed them so to function? He might say to us that he did not intend to have them produce what they did. We would then have to treat him somewhat the way we treat those who find that they have an irresistible impulse to shoot or kill. We would have to say of him that though he did not forge a conscious intent, and though he had no control over his agents at that moment, he had set himself in the situation where the undesirable consequences were produced by what he had made possible. It is because we do not like what the monkeys produced that we look for the man who was responsible for setting them to work.

If what the monkeys produced was only gibberish, we would be content to allow that the result was the work of the monkeys and nothing more. But if something makes sense to us as a message, we have the alternative of looking for the "mind" or "One" behind the plurality of items, which makes the message have a single unity, or of supposing that we had ourselves created the message out of sheer data, as we sometimes do when we read tea leaves, clouds, etc. In the absence of accompanying gestures, without knowing what language it fits in, and thus without knowing how to relate the sentences one to the other (e.g., making some take a subordinate role, others to be corollaries and the like), we cannot say whether we are faced with mere data or with a message. We assume the second as the more likely, and eventually take it to be the work of whoever communicated the message, organized and printed it in a book, or who set the machines or machinelike animals to work in the way they did.

We do not take a complexity of sentences to be a single work unless it instances a style which is to be found elsewhere as well. The novel is taken to be the work of an artist only if there is something else he does which exhibits that same style, that same way of bringing parts together to make something excellent or distinctive. If we have only one novel, or only one message, we must put it in the setting of the life of the individual. In the absence of such an individual, we must place it in the history of literature or science, where it will be related to other works of the same or different genre, as dated in a certain century, and as characterizing a certain society. The novelist is the "mind" of his novel; that mind is a One for his novel as a member of a Many, made up of his products.

In all these cases, the mind belongs to something outside the evident producer of the content achieved. As so belonging, the mind has a dignity that such a producer cannot provide it. We look to the (individual) man who made the machine, the (social) man who programs the machine, and the (creative) man who relates one work of a machine to another to get us from words to sentences, from sentences to a message, and from a message to a unified work of art or science, inside a life or a history of art or science.

It is possible to treat the program as already introduced into the machine as the "mind" or immanent One of the machine. But that One presupposes a One *for* the machine, a One which does the programming and which has the right and obligation to make claims on behalf of the units turned out by the program. The program will be the representative of the mind, working in the machine, somewhat as my habits are the representatives of my intentions.

It is possible to have a message be part of the very uses of units, by treating them as parts of a language. This will bring us to the level of animal intelligence, for the animal uses its noises and gestures in a social and public interplay. We will then nevertheless presuppose a One for the socially immanent "mind" so far as we are offering an ordered account of something. And it is possible to have a unified work as representing the limit of our achievement. We would then be on the level of an animal which had built its nest or had given birth. But to understand the unitary event as meaningful in a life, and not merely as that which gives meaning to the rest of the life, one would have to take account of the life as a unitary pattern of which the unified work was but one instance.

The mind of a man is a potentiality for instances of unifications of data, all connected by a single life-style. No particular unification or set of unifications can be said to exhaust that mind; the mind of a man not only links unifications already produced, but points to others which are to be produced. Should a man die, we refer to what he has projected forward to give sense to what has already been produced as not exhausting what he was. A man's mind is that by virtue of which we say that what he has done is not all he could have done. He is immortal in the sense that what he has accomplished is part of a larger whole of which the remainder is a possibility.

The mind does more than give a meaning to individual acts of the body; it does more than relate those acts to one another to produce significant actions. It makes the body into a source of a plurality of central unifications, of perspectives and conditions all related in a single life style which reaches beyond those unifications to the possibility of still others.

The death of a man requires us to look to the accomplishment of others as ways of realizing the prospect which he made possible. They make that prospect become part of a civilized whole, linking him with the other producers of that civilization.

There is much in the foregoing which is in consonance with Wittgenstein. He clearly says in the *Blue Book* that there is a consciousness accompanying thoughts; it is evident then that he is not denying privacy. But skipping over the case of the machine and its production of words in a sequence, he occupies himself primarily with sentences (though he usually speaks of words), and tries to show that they are part of a social language of some sort. He does not go on to deal with the question of the way in which the language or a single work produced in it is related to other works. His illustrations are rarely from art, and when they are they are trivial. He also fails to see how the immanent structure or rule (which for him defines what is significant) presupposes and is in fact often a surrogate for a transcendent One that is responsible and is held accountable for the consequences which are the outcome of the use of that rule. But he is alert to the fact that sequences are different from ordered patterns, and that if there is to be any message, sentences belong in languages where individuals interplay with one another in multiple ways.

A mind is never exhausted in any set of bodily acts. To have a mind is to be detached from what is about, in the sense of having or being a single One for it, to be expressed in the shape of smaller Ones for what is confronted, and to be manifested in the shape of immanent Ones which allow what is presented to be accepted by another as a sentence, a message, or a unified work. The mind is no substance over against the body; it is the body as related to other bodies, the world about, the world to be, and (since those relations are determined in part by what the body underwent in the past and how it is related to what happened in the past) the world that had been. It is a One which is tensed to connect the body as it is now to whatever else there be, has been, and can be.

Up to now I have been speaking as though what was, was only the empirically observable; but the mind can relate what the body does to what lies outside the regions of the body. This it does when it reflects, speculates, or engages in dialectic. It then relates the body not to something yet to come, to what now is, or what had been in the world of the body, but to what lies on another plane. The detachment which the individual requires in order to be able to make what the body does be a One for what is encompassed or faced, can be carried out to the point where the individual is detached with respect to all that occurs in this space-time world, but in such a way as to recognize that it is a world. And then he can go a step further and detach himself from that world by turning toward other realities, with respect to which the entire space-time world and its members are subordinated. The Wittgensteinians never consider this case; as a consequence, when they want to deal with God they find themselves unable to speak of Him in any other sense than that of an entity somehow alongside or involved in this world.

An historically minded thinker will want to reduce the One for the Many of the historical world to an immanent One, expressing the way in which men and various works were related to one another. For him there is no other meaning to God than what He means to men over time. This is essentially the Hegelian view. Whatever justification an Hegelian can provide for this reduction will justify the Wittgensteinian, for he in effect has reduced the Hegelian history to a language. But he in turn can be reduced on the same basis to an existentialism with its individualistic claims to be and to know. And the existentialist in turn can be reduced to a pure behaviorist with his sequence of occurrences. In each reduction we lose a kind of unity which we in fact must acknowledge if we are to do justice to the nuances and complexity of what we are and know.

Each of the reductionists has an argument by which he rebuts the reduction of his own view, and justifies reducing the One for him to a One in his Many. The rebuttal appeals to facts of meaning, import, or totality; the justification proceeds by an appeal to experience or encounters. The Wittgensteinian does not allow that God, for example, is only a God in history; he wants to reduce that God to a language about God. He says that if we are to communicate or know anything about God, we must speak of Him, and this requires a use of a language. But we not only speak of God; we also organize our society, tradition, mythology, and historic life in the light of Him. But we also go further; we evaluate the historic life, note that as a whole it is transient and defective, and see it in terms of a God outside it.

We can be said to embody the One for the historic world in the same way that we embody any other One; we then become prophetic, religious representatives of God who, by relating ourselves to the historic world in a certain way, constitute, together with that world, another kind of universe where both are at once part of it and apart from it. Such representatives inevitably make a reference to God as still over against them. We can never get to the point where we have only an immanent One for the Many of this world. Even when we act as representatives of a transcendent One, and as such representatives help constitute a new immanent One, we will have either to acknowledge a transcendent One beyond us, or to suppose that we have passed an arbitrary judgment on all else, because we do not in fact represent any One beyond both us and the world of history.

The religious man justifies his appeal to God (and then in the guise of something like a mind) by his claim that the totality of things has a value or import which requires a measure and judge outside it. Deny that measure and you make history the last resort; but then on the same grounds, you can deny the ultimacy of history, etc., etc., until you come down to a sequence of words or sounds—atoms of the world of experience —and have these alone as final. Then sentences, messages, books, history, and religion (to use these as the names of the series we have been examining) will all have to be accounted for as products of ourselves. It makes no difference whether we call them errors, distortions, illusions, or mistakes; the fact is that we will have to make a reference to a mind of man which has the power to produce these. We will then be back where we started from, placing all structure, intelligibility, and organization in our minds, rather than in the world.

By allowing a One over against the entire historic world, we give the world a freedom from that One. And we can then take that historic world to be a One for individuals and their works, and so on. If instead we insist on having the final One be immanent in the world, we lose the freedom of that world; and if we take the opposite tack and insist that there is no immanent One (unless perhaps it is that of an aggregate of atoms), we lose the ingredient meaning of the world, and then make our minds a One for it.

Language has a career which is not said in the language, though we can now get a language (having a career) in which the first career is stated. The assessment of a career is not in the career, though we can get a career for the assessment. And of course a sentence belongs in a context or language which is not said in the sentence, though we can make a sentence about the language. And, finally, a word belongs in a sentence which is not mentioned in the word, though once again we can find a word which names that sentence. If we place the word outside the sentence as on a higher level, we can also place the assessment of a career on a higher level than the career, and the career on a higher level than the language, and the language on a higher level than the sentence. But putting something on a higher level is making it a One *for*, which will only lead to the acknowledgment of a One *of*.

October 27

It has often been remarked that attempts to grasp final realities always leave us with a residuum which is still outside our reach. God has been called an "absconding Being"; Existence has been said to be that which we refer to or which is given, but which itself is not known; ideas and ideals have been said to enable us to know things but are themselves a base, part of an "I think" itself either not knowable, or without content or meaning; and Actuality (under some name or other) has been treated as a condition for the reality of actualities, but not graspable, since all we can grasp are actualities and not what they presuppose.

There are two ways of meeting this contention, one of which is more appropriate to Existence and God, and the other of which is more appropriate to Ideality and Actuality. The Existence which is thought always to be a content over against us, forever receding before our attempt to encompass it, can be adjusted to. The individual then, instead of taking himself to be over against Existence, makes himself be continuous with it, a part epitomizing the whole. He does not encompass the whole, but he no longer has it escaping him as something at which he wants to arrive but which forever flees before him. Instead he is on a level with it, embodying its texture. Similarly, when he becomes involved with God, he constitutes a situation with Him, and thereupon achieves the status of being a part of the same universe with God. God does not thereupon lose His status as a Being over against him and other realities, but He no longer is something at which he is trying to arrive, but rather something with which he constitutes a single whole in worship, or prayer, or submission. He is affected by God, possesses Him as that which enables him to be a part of that situation.

In both of these cases, we recognize ourselves to be limited realities only so far as we see ourselves as part of a larger whole; the remainder of the whole is continuous with ourselves, while retaining a Being of its own. We are flooded by the rest of the situation constituted by Existence or God, and thereby experience them. This outlook has been stated in theology under the doctrine of a prevenient or necessarily antecedent grace, without which acts of faith are not possible.

The second way of avoiding the endless pursuit of forever receding realities is to recognize the power of concepts to flood Ideality and the power of actualities to flood Actuality. Here the concepts point not merely to objects beyond them, but to the domain of which those concepts are a part. We know the concept of concepts, the Ideal of which the various possibilities are specifications, by treating these possibilities as possibilities, i.e., by speaking of the concepts as concepts. When we so speak, we are not applying "concept" to the concepts in the same way that the concepts are applied to objects; instead we are grouping the concepts, coordinating them, and in that act acknowledging the concept of them to be their domain. Similarly, when we acknowledge ourselves to be one among actualities, we then and there acknowledge Actuality as that in terms of which we are one among those actualities.

I haven't got this problem altogether straight, and I seem to be only on the edge of something that could be called an answer.

November 5

Every series of occurrences has a One immanent in it. And, at least so far as men of intent, will, desire are concerned, every series in which they manifest themselves has a One for that unified Many. That One may be the same or different in nature from the One in the Many. We cannot decide this question until the series has gone on for a while. In each discipline, and in connection with each kind of objects, the series has a different stretch. We are ready to infer that a man is a murderer if he kills on two different occasions. We would not be ready to infer that we have made a wrong selection of insured clients because on a given day or even for a week or a month they seem to be among those most prone to accidents or death; but after two months we may be willing to say that there is a selective process operating, either with respect to the clients we chose, or the manner in which we chose them.

Every series exhibits a style so far as the One which is immanent in it is identical with the One for it. The supposition that we have gone far enough to determine what is the One for a unified many, is identical with the supposition that we have discerned the style of that many. Should we discover that, at the time the style has been recognized to be present, the individual has had a different intent in mind from what he in fact has exhibited, we dismiss that intent as a mere wish or hope, and maintain that his real intent, his character, or his nature was such that what he in fact did was what he "intended."

Wittgenstein was right to remark that we cannot tell from a short run whether a man is following a certain rule; but he did not go on to remark that we can and do tell that he is following such a rule (which is a One for the series) after a certain period. Should the man thereupon do something not in accord with such a rule, we would then say that he had changed his rule, and not that the rule had not been followed up until then.

He who acts courageously over a period is courageous; should he thereupon act cowardly we must say that he changed his nature. Until the time came when we could call him courageous—a matter determined by experience, convention, convenience, and the like—it is ambiguous whether or not he is so. He can be said not yet to have a well-defined habit, but instead to have a habit which could become a habit of being courageous or something else. The One for the Many, up to a point, is a One which is ambiguous as to just what kind of One it is—like or unlike the One that is now immanent in the series.

Not all rules are produced by habitually acting out something; we can be given directions, recipes, etc., and prepare to follow them out. We have the problem of speaking of habits only when we know only a series of acts; but we could begin by knowing the rule, and setting ourselves to act in consonance with it. If we know the rule and find ourselves acting in consonance with it, we cannot yet be said to have the rule immanent in what we did. We can say this only when we have arrived at some later point in the series, where we define the series as long enough to sustain a style. But we are following the rule before we come to the point, even though another cannot say that we are.

We can be said to be rule- or law-abiding only when we have carried out a series to the point where there is a style; but we can follow a rule, and can work in consonance with a law before we arrive at the place where we are rule- or law-abiding.

All our reasoning follows contingent rules; no one reasons by following logical rules. The contingent rules tell us how to operate on something so as to get something else. They are as numerous as there are relational expressions, since any relational expression can be treated as telling us how to pass from one term to the other. We ought not to ask then whether our reasoning is valid, but only if it is plausible, whether the rule we use is efficient, effective, reasonable, or helpful for getting some desired end. Nevertheless, it is possible to add the rule to the premiss to make, as Peirce saw, a single premiss from which the conclusion followed necessarily, i.e., in consonance with a logical rule or law.

We get the premiss by colligating data. Colligation, or the formulation of contingent rules, however, is an act of abduction. To say that we have arrived at the point where we can legitimately obtain a rule, a One for a unified series, is to say that the items are sufficiently numerous to make worthwhile a unification of them in terms of an explanatory or justifying principle, exemplified in the series as its style.

In *The World of Art*, science was treated as a theoretical subject whose space, time, dynamics, and objects were abstractions. In this work, I have in places supposed the theoretical world of science to be real. But the correct answer now seems to me to be somewhere in between these two. We ought to affirm that there are submicroscopic entities; we discovered they were real after we had theoretically decided that there were such.

The evidence for the existence of positrons seems strong. They were discovered by men who dealt with these particles as though they constituted a world of their own, uninfluenced by bodies on another level; but it would seem to be more correct to say that though the entities are real, the relations they bear to one another are not, as a matter of fact, what the theories state. The positrons are in fact bunched together inside various macroscopic bodies, where they behave in ways which do not exactly conform to the theoretical laws.

The real sun is over against other actualities and as such encompasses a limited number of ultimate particles in a distinctive way. The nature of that way is suggested by the sun as perceived. We *perceive* how the theoretically structured ultimate particles are capable of being bunched; we *conceive* how the perceptual sun might result from the intersection of sets of ultimate particles as theoretically related. The real sun is somewhat like the commonsense sun in that it is both open to a perceptual and conceptual approach, e.g., by a sailor with his calendar of risings and settings. But it is distinct from such a commonsense sun in that its conceptualizable side is known through theoretical astronomy, and its perceptual side is freed from the conventions and mythologies which characterize the commonsense outlook. It might be called an existential sun, if this is freed from a limited reference to human beings and their concerns, and is allowed to stand over against such human beings as a genuine actuality on a footing with them.

November 6

A premiss can be obtained by abduction, the process by which one converts a plurality of items into a single unity. Colligating premisses to make a single premiss involves abduction. There is abduction also involved in moving from a judgment or proposition which is true, because it answers to some matter of fact, to a premiss—where the proposition possesses a truth value as something which is to be transferred from that premiss to the conclusion, or is to be transformed in the course of the movement to the conclusion.

Abduction is an inference. Since the move from a proposition as true of something beyond itself to a premiss which is true for the purpose of inferring is abductive, we either will presuppose an endless series of abductions before we can have an inference, or there are inferences which do not depend on prior abductions. At some point we must just accept something, take it as our beginning. We could start by merely constructing a premiss without regard for whether or not there is a reality answering to what it asserts. Or we could start with a judgment or proposition and abduct to a premiss. Or we could start with given data and abduct to the judgment or proposition. Or we could start with a situation and abduct to the data to be used for making a judgment, and so on.

We come to formulate rules in two ways. We can abduct them from a set of items, and we can formulate them apart from any set of items. When we try to determine the nature of a disposition, habit, character, etc., we follow the first procedure; when we give commands, orders, directions, etc., we follow the second.

We can say that every situation embodies a rule. This tells us that the items in the situation make a whole, that they have a relevance wih respect to one another. If we have only two items, we can say that there is a rule operating between them. But we also can see these two items as part of a larger whole, governed by another principle of relevance and thus by another rule. Such an overarching rule may govern every item, and thus be a rule for all the subordinate rules, or it may skip some of the items as mere blocks or incidents and not relevant to what the rule demands, and thereby reveal itself to be a rule like the encompassed ones but covering a longer stretch.

Let a man begin counting by twos. After he has counted, 2, 4, 6, let

him count by threes, 9, 12, 15, 18, and then after that, let him count by
fives, 20, 25, 30, 35, 40. I think we should say that he now exhibits three
rules, a counting by 2's, by 3's, and by 5's. But we could also say that he
followed the rule of counting according to a more complicated system,
say by taking a number first ten places away, then another thirteen places
away, and then another fifteen places away, to give the sequence 2, 12, 25,
40. The skipped items would be irrelevant to this sequence, intrusions to
be accounted for in some other way. We can also acknowledge a rule for
the various countings, which in the present case would be a counting by
2's followed by a counting by 3's, and this by one by 5's. Such a rule is a
rule of rules, a One for the various rules which in fact are Ones in the
sequences. It is the rule of rules which is expressed as a style, and which
is to serve as the link amongst all the different embodied rules in what
one does. Behaviorism attends only to embodied rules; it can therefore
know of a style only after it has defined a whole as complete, and recognized that there are parts of that whole which embody their own rules.

A woman says that she is writing a long letter to her daughter. She
has written a paragraph, but is now putting on her coat to go shopping;
when she returns, she will clean up, and prepare for the children to come
home for lunch, etc. We can say of her that her letter writing is an action
which stretches over her daily chores; we could also say that being engaged in chores is one type of act, with its own characteristic relevancies,
time, and events, and that writing is another type of act with its own
relevancies, time, and events. We could also say that she engages in her
chores and writes her letter as a dilatory person, or as one who does not
like to write, or as who does not love her daughter, etc. In the last cases,
she has a rule for rules. Consequently, her chores or writing cannot exhaust her intent, disposition, character, habit, meaning, style, or purpose.
Only the exemplification of the rule for rules can do this.

We will sometimes be able to say what kind of a dilatory person the
woman is by seeing exactly what kinds of rules she has embodied in the
various unitary activities in which she engages; we always will be able to
know what kind of dilatory person she is by seeing the way in which these
activities are related to one another in fact. But apart from such actual
manifestation of the dilatoriness in the relation between these various
activities as embodying rules, she remains partly unexpressed. We can, if
we wish, deny that as unexpressed she is yet definite enough to be characterized in one way or another, but this will not permit us to deny that she
is offering a One or rule for the various rules, and may in fact be determining just what the governed rules are.

If we deny that the rule for the relating of various rules has any definiteness until it is embodied, we come close to Croce's view that intentions and the like have no natures except as expressed. We also will deny that there is anything like character, intention, or purpose until it has been manifested. But if we have a rule for relating rules, we have not manifested it until we have already had at least one rule carried out. I think we ought to say therefore, that though a rule for rules, a character or disposition governing a life or a career, is not altogether definite until it has become immanent in the entire set in which the various rules operate, it has some definiteness before that time. It is already realized in whatever set of items we have already acknowledged as governed by it, which precludes it from being a disposition of quite a different sort, e.g., one which excludes such a realization of a rule.

Before there is any realization in the shape of some rule, what kind of status has a rule of rules? This would seem to be analogous to the question as to what kind of status a habit, command, order, etc., has before or apart from being acted out. They seem to be projects, ways of referring to the future, and thereby isolating the possibilities that are realizable. If so, they are principles of selection amongst possibilities, or alternatively, ways of specifying certain possibilities. One can know something of what they are like only so far as one knows the nature of the activities in which they are.

In turn, the rules we exhibit and the rules governing the relation of rules to one another (and which may in fact dictate even the kinds of rules to be related) are to be understood to be specializations of a natural or ontological project. Because a man speaks no French there can be no rule for counting in French for him; there is surely no rule for connecting his various countings in French. If he knows French, he can face the possibilities of making various kinds of counts in French, but we do not know whether those possibilities will be realized until we see him realize them. He is able to realize them because his nature as one who knows French already made counting in French be within the area of his projection of that nature.

November 7

I once said (*Reality*) that the ontological argument argues that if p is possible, it is necessary. Hartshorne's statement is alternative to this; he holds that God either is necessarily or is not necessarily, which is to say that He cannot be contingent.

Does it follow that if God is possible, He necessarily is? When we speak of God as possible, we refer to Him as involved in our world of space-time objects. The necessity which we take to follow in the onto-logical argument is then the necessity for Him in that world. God is that Being who in our space-time-dynamic world is not only not contingent, but also not intrinsically necessary. But then in our world He is, as Findlay remarked, impossible, for our world is a world where there are only contingent beings.

If we want to prove the existence of God, we must move from con-tingent beings to a Being in-itself, and thus make use of the cosmological argument. What we get to will have a status which is to be defined in new ways. If we wish to use the modal terms, possible, impossible, neces-sary, etc., we must then use them in a new sense. Now it is conceivable that a Being may vanish when and as all contingent beings pass away; it could fade out of reality, as Kant suggested. But then it would be like a contingent being, something which need not be always, even though it is also true that it never was not, always was, and that it had neither be-ginning nor end, even that it was necessarily. To prove the existence of God, we must then not only show that it is impossible for Him to be inside the contingent world (unless it be in effect, role, act, etc.), but that if He can be beyond that world, He necessarily is there in the sense of never attaining the position of not-being.

To such an argument, it will be answered of course that the passing away of God will involve Him in time and thus make Him part of this world, which is contrary to the hypothesis. But to this, one can answer that He would not necessarily pass away over the course of a time, but like a Humean impression would just pop into Being and pop out of it, be vivid and then fade away utterly. And if it be argued that the actuali-ties would have no Being in which they then could be said to share, one can counter with the observation that the Being which is God need not be taken to be except while actualities are.

The situation does not change when we acknowledge not one but four modes of Being, or when we refer to the Being of Ideality, etc., rather than to the Being which is God. And this means that we cannot prove the reality of Being or Beings by merely making use of a modal logic.

To avoid confusing the necessary with the everlasting, it would be better to take the necessary to be the constitutive, that which would be identical with the immanent One throughout all actualities. To say of something that it is not contingent, in the sense of not being able to be among those actualities, is to say that it is either nonconstitutive or constitutive of them. If there must be a constitutive entity in order that they be *all* the actualities, and thus have a One immanent in their Many, we arrive not at God or any other Being, but only at the domain of actualities. This result is somewhat in accord with Anselm's ontological argument, which is concerned with proving the existence, not of a transcendent God, but of one who is involved with the world. But we would then need to take further steps to prove the existence of a God who transcends the world, and show how He is related to Himself as immanent in the world. If we could do this, we would prove the reality not of God, but of Actuality as related to another necessary reality, the constitutive domain of actualities. We would in effect have had to acknowledge that there were two necessities, neither of which was God—the constitutive domain of actualities, and Actuality, over against which the domain had reality.

If we acknowledge only a constitutive One, we have something like a pantheism. That constitutive One though, is not God. If we acknowledge in addition a transcendent One of which the constitutive is an expression, we have something like a "panentheism," though again we have no right to call that One "God." If we acknowledge the transcendent One to be that which is over against the domain of the actualities as constituted by an immanent One, we most clearly acknowledge Actuality and a domain of actualities, operating in independence of one another (despite the fact that the Actuality could be said to define all the actualities to be equally real). This function though, could be accredited to an immanent One; then we would leave to Actuality only the role of encompassing the other modes in relation to the domain of actualities or to the actualities severally.

November 8

Let it be supposed that there are four Ones immanent in the totality of actualities, and that all of them change in nature in the course of time and in consonance with changes in the functioning of the actualities. Let it be also supposed that one of these Ones exercises the power of equating all the actualities as realities, when and as that One in fact unfolds itself as the One of those actualities. We can then go on and treat all the other Ones as prescriptive for the totality of actualities as already equated by the initial One.

The initial One, which equated all the actualities, would be somewhat like Actuality as I have been viewing this over the last few years, except that it would not encompass any modes of Being within itself, nor would it have the status of a mode of Being over against the actualities. It would be the Being of the actualities as immanent in and thereby constituting the totality of them. Instead of having three modes of Being encompassed by Actuality and thereby operative on the actualities, we would now have them operative on the actualities as already governed by Actuality. Such a view would bring us back quite close to that presented in the *Modes of Being*, where Actuality was more or less ignored, and attention was directed instead to the other three modes of Being and their interplay with acutalities, and eventually with one another.

If this alternative position be adopted, we would no longer have to distinguish between the Beings, their subdivisions, and their roles. They would be Beings which functioned in relation to actualities, not Beings in which the actualities shared. That sharing would be only with respect to the Actuality, which was immanent in and constitutive of the totality of actualities. We could, of course, continue to speak of the other three modes as having a Being over against the actualities when the modes in fact were involved with one another, and as standing over against one another when the modes were involved with actualities. There would be no role which Actuality played with respect to them, and so we would not have subdivisions which were equal in reality to one another or to the whole in which they were. Nor would we have to speak of these other modes of Being as enabling the Actuality to stand away from the actualities, as extending over them, or as having a nature similar to theirs (which is what I over these last years have been saying is what God, Existence, and Ideality do for Actuality). Instead we would find that the totality of actualities would be subdivided by these other modes into various affiliated sets, contemporaries, and groups, in contrast with the actualities as mere units in the whole which was produced by Actuality.

Each of these other modes of Being could be said to have subdivisions which it produced as a totality in the very way in which Actuality produces a whole for actualities. With respect to those subdivisions, there would be prescriptions imposed by Existence and Ideality. The question that remains is whether Actuality would be able to function with respect to the subdivisions of other modes of Being in somewhat the same way that the other modes of Being function with respect to actualities. If we say this, we will move back again to the position which I have been outlining these last years. But if we do not say this, we deny, apparently arbitrarily, to one of the Beings the power to prescribe to the subdivisions of others in a way analogous to that in which they prescribe to its subdivisions.

Does Actuality equalize the reality of the items (or perhaps better, the particularities) in the other modes of Being? If so, the items would have to be thought to be unequal apart from its action. Yet if each of the other modes of Being is constitutive of the totality of its particularities, it would seem that each should be able then and there to equalize them as realities. Must we not then say instead, that what Actuality does is to equalize the reality of the particularities with the One which immanently constitutes them? If so, we would have to conclude that it is Actuality which endows God's roles with a, reality equal to that enjoyed by Himself as a Being.

I think I have now come to a position which is a union of the position taken in the *Modes of Being* and that developed in this work over the last years. As in the *Modes*, I am not now dealing with Actuality as over against actualities, but instead am taking the ultimate truth to be the interplay of three interplaying modes of Being with actualities. But when I turn to consider these modes of Being in relationship to one another's particularities, I see them to be functioning somewhat the way I have been remarking on in the previous volumes of this work. The late insight that the Being of actualities is Actuality is preserved, together with the early insight that the other three modes of Being have a direct affect on the actualities. We will have to add however, that though Actuality acts on the particularities of other modes of Being, it does not act on the other modes of Being to enable them to be or function in a certain way with respect to their particularities.

The modes of Being, as is said in *Modes of Being*, must be seen to act on one another as Beings, and on one another's particularities, but not on one another as concerned with their respective particularities. As involved with one another, they would constitute a fourfold reality which was abstract because it was separated from the various particularities.

Since the various modes of Being are here thought to have a constitutive role with respect to actualities (though Actuality is given priority over the others), they will not so far have any particularities of their own. Either they will function as constitutive Ones just so far as they are not ultimate but are subdivisions of such ultimates, or they will achieve the stage of having subdivisions only when they are prescriptive for actualities as constituted by an immanent Actuality. The first of these alternatives says that they are Beings which have a constitutive *role* with respect to actualities; the second says that they as mere Beings are constitutive of actualities, and that only so far as they are prescriptive do they have something of which they themselves can be primarily constitutive in the way in which Actuality is of actualities. The first seems to be the more cautious view; it forces us to find arguments for supposing that there are Beings which are outside the domain of actualities. In the absence of such proof, we must be content with saying that the Beings have a relative transcendence just so far as they are viewed as prescriptive for what is constituted by Actuality. This transcendence does not mean that they have distinctive subdivisions and particularities which they themselves constitute in the way in which Actuality constitutes the domain of actualities. We could recognize subdivisions and particularities in them as so many specialized and limited stresses imposed by actualities so far as they are concerned with those transcending Beings.

On this view, what we have are four constituting Beings, three of which also prescribe and therefore transcend the constituted domain of actualities, and which are in turn focused on by actualities and thereby specialized in the guise of a number of roles and subdivisions. In connection with God, this would mean that we have Him as immanent in the world of actualities and also over against that domain as a mere Being which can have and in fact does have an immanent role with respect to them as already constituted by Actuality, and that when those actualities refer to Him they demarcate various subdivisions and roles as relevant to those actualities.

The domain of actualities as constituted by Actuality is a world of distinctive individuals, self-enclosed. But as such they are made to form groups, etc., and face possibilities, etc. It is possible to view them as also constituted by two more modes, and having the third over against them. Let that third be Ideality. Then we would have to say that a domain of actualities has God and Existence immanent in it, so that they are at once individuals, affiliated, and contemporaries (or in one time-space-dynamic totality where they are related in ways which may not match the affiliations), and as such have over against them the Ideal as focused on in the shape of various possibilities. We never get to the stage where we have only constitutive Ones; though each mode can have the role of a constitutive One, for any three (of which one is always Actuality) there will be a fourth which is prescriptive to and specified by actualities as a plurality of relevant subdivisions or roles.

The more I insist on my individuality, the more I define myself to be part of the domain constituted by Actuality and thus as having over against myself the other modes which then prescribe to me while I specialize them in the shape of subdivisions and roles. I, the private being, face God, the affiliating Being, who judges and who has a reality as a single One which can be immanent, and is so just so far as I am affiliated by Him. Such a view leaves open the question whether God has a reality apart from my being an individual in the domain of actualities, or whether He too constitutes a totality of actualities, and stands over against the domain constituted by Actuality only because an actuality retreats from the affiliation. In the latter case, we would have to say that God (as a transcendent Being) exists only so far as I am (or any actuality is) or present myself (or presents itself) to be an individual in the domain of actualities constituted by Actuality.

Analogously, we must say that the space-time-dynamic Existence of cosmological physics has a being of its own only so far as it is set over against distinctive actualities—or what is the same thing, so far as distinctive individuals are ignored. And since those individuals can have Ideality and God immanent in their totality, cosmological Existence can be said to be when we ignore individuals, their grouping, and their affiliations. We move from such a theoretically known Existence to it as germane to actualities by taking it to have regions where there is some kind of bunching to occur with respect to the spatio-temporal-dynamic units, i.e., with respect to the ultimate particles of science—which are, I think, to be identified with the ultimate units of extension (or Existence as a Being which makes actualities contemporary, and which they specify).

Similarly, we will get the Platonic heaven of forms only so far as we hold it over against a world of actualities which has God and Existence immanent in it. That heaven ignores affiliations and the spatio-temporal-dynamic. Actualities can be said to specify that heaven of forms as so many relevant limited possibilities or ideals for the actualities.

November 9

Actualities related by an immanent One, are to be explained as being governed by a (different) One. As such, the actualities have over against them some Being which, together with the actualities as governed by the (different) One, can be viewed as constituting the initial situation.

Every plurality has an immanent One. This plurality can be understood and explained as the product of the union of itself (as governed by a different One) with still another One which is not immanent. Since the totality of individual actualities has Actuality immanent in it, it can be understood to be the product of:

a transcendent God and an immanent Ideal which is a One of the
    actualities

a transcendent God and an immanent Existence which is a One of the
   actualities

a transcendent Ideal and an immanent God who is a One of the actualities

a transcendent Ideal and an immanent Existence which is a One of
   the actualities

a transcendent Existence and an immanent Ideal which is a One of
   the actualities

a transcendent Existence and an immanent God who is a One of the
   actualities.

Most men today would not use God as an explanation, particularly for
what is occurring in the world of actualities. Consequently, the only cases
they would consider to be viable are:

a transcendent Ideal and an immanent Existence which is a One of
   the actualities

a transcendent Existence and an immanent Ideal which is a One of
   the actualities.

Of these, they prefer the first, since they take actualities to be in space-
time and thus to make a cosmos where Existence is immanent. But all of
the cases are equally satisfactory. The East would use the second as better
than the first, and of course theologically oriented thinkers would accept
some one or more of the other cases.

The view most congenial to the West today accepts the reality of a
plurality of distinct individual actualities and attempts to account for
them as a totality. The totality is taken to be the product of the (same or
different) actualities as natural beings which are somehow united with an
Ideal. This way of putting the matter is quite close to Northrop's, though
he sees the West as trying to insist on the transcendent Ideal and the East
as stressing the immanent Existence. And I am not sure whether he would
hold that the combination of these would give us the totality of individual
actualities as constituting a domain of its own, and thus as having an immanent Actuality as its One.

November 10

We cannot explain the totality of actualities by reference only to
the actualities taken severally and to a unitary Actuality. If there be a
plurality of actualities, they are together in some way already, so that the

explanation of actualities as constituting a domain in which Actuality is immanent will require us to refer to actualities as already unified by Existence, the Ideal, or God, and having over against that totality one or the other of the two remaining modes. We would have to explain the totality of actualities in which Actuality is immanent by speaking of the actualities as united by Existence, for example, and confronting the Ideal or God. Our explanation of the totality would then consist in affirming that an existent totality of actualities is conjoined with the Ideal or God to produce the Actualized totality of actualities. Actuality would not then be shown to be a product of the existent actualities and some transcendent mode of Being; but the totality in which it was immanent will have been explained in this way.

We seem though to have a choice of a number of explanations in every case; the Actualized totality of actualities can, on the above account, be explained with reference to   A] the actualities as having Existence immanent in their totality and as being conjoined with either God or Ideality as transcendent of that totality;   B] the actualities as having Ideality as immanent in their totality and being conjoined with God or Existence as transcendent of that totality;   C] the actualities as having God as immanent in their totality and being conjoined with either Ideality or Existence. Any given totality then is to be explained in any one of six ways.

A sociologist is concerned with groups of men; his observations should be directed to the way in which those groups interplay with one another, how they grow, decay, etc. If he wishes to explain the grouping, he must have recourse to men as standing outside the groups. These are not the men studied in psychology, where we read into them in the form of drives or capacities the traits they manifest in the groups. Instead we must make reference to men as constituting a mankind (i.e., where Actuality is immanent in their totality), as existing in nature (i.e., where Existence is immanent in their totality) or as affiliated in various ways, e.g., sexually, as old and young, by congeniality, by color, etc., which can be said to have God immanent in the totality of actualities. Sociologists would undoubtedly choose the second, where the men are taken to be units in nature. But then they must envisage a common humanity, a common goal, or a common judge or control as the other factor which will, together with the men in nature, explain the fact that they are in the groups which the sociologist studies.

The men in nature and the common humanity, etc., are, from the standpoint of sociology, theoretical constructs. That the totalities have a reality of their own is something to be known through observation in other disciplines; the knowledge that the transcendents have a reality of their own is, of course, to be known only speculatively, or through analogous transcendent acts having such transcendents as their proper terminus. The combination of the two is also something to be known philosophically. It involves an alteration in the factors which are combined until they appear as the single totality of actualities as governed by Ideality.

November 11

The world of every day is popularly viewed as having been created by God. Most theologians would agree, but only if one removed the patina which convention, secular tradition, etc., has imposed on this view. It is the latter world in any case which the scientist is trying to understand. If he is a cosmological physicist, he wants to understand it by attending to ultimate real particles in rational, mathematically intelligible combinations. This means that he must use two principles: one which assures that the particles are distinct and real, and the other of which determines their grouping. These principles are but formalizations of Actuality and Ideality. And they must be taken to operate on the particles as interrelated in a cosmic space and time—i.e., in Existence. The explanation the physicist provides is in effect an explanation for a world in which what is explained is interrelated through affiliation, i.e., in a divine-like way. This is what is acknowledged and then explained by referring to the principles and the existent particles.

When the philosopher faces the problem of reconciling the object of perception with the object known to science, he in effect is trying to explain a world of macroscopic actualities over against one another, i.e., as governed by an immanent Actuality. He accepts the result which is the outcome of the use of the two principles and the existent particles (a result which is not identical with what was to be explained, since it gives only the rationale of this and not it in its concreteness or in its operation), and uses the percepts as principles of affiliation, i.e., as surrogates for the divine. The percepts tell us how to relate the grouped real particles to one another so as to constitute a world in which there are groups of these particles over against one another. What is being explained is evidently then a world of substances. But the substances have to be acknowledged first if the percepts and the scientific objects are to be treated as explanatory of them.

Substances as over against one must be lived with and through; they can be explained only by taking account of factors which are not identifiable with them. One of the factors may be an abstraction from them (the percepts) and the other may be treated as an idealization from them (the scientific object), though there is no need to proceed in this way. It is possible to provide good explanations by turning one's back on the object to be explained and constructing new schemes, or by attending to other Beings from which principles may be obtained.

If we take the world to be sacramental or created, our explanation of it will be "safe and stupid," to use Plato's expression, if we treat it as some amalgamation of God and stuff. A scientific account offers a better explanation of such a world since it is clearer, bolder, grounds predictions, and allows for the derivation of laws. But no such explanation recovers the explained; the explained has its own characteristic qualia and career which the explanation dissects and then tries to reinstate in a formal way. It tells us that the explained is the unity of the principles and the given material, but it does not show this unity nor see it function. It is therefore inclined to slight a consideration of the principles which must be acknowledged if there is to be an adequate explanation, and to content itself with the acknowledgment of what it is on which the principles must operate.

Cosmologists are occupied primarily with telling us the nature of the universe of existent particles not yet affirmed to be fully real as individual entities, nor to be grouped as we usually find them in the macroscopic bodies. Materialists are their philosophical counterparts, for materialists tend to dismiss percepts and to accept only the scientific objects on which the percepts are to operate as principles of affiliation. They are reductionists. They would not cease being such if they were content to make use of percepts or other principles in order to give a rational account of substances, for the combination of principles with data is achieved formally only. Failing this their account denies the distinctive reality of what is thereby being explained.

He who allows his synthesis of explanatory factors to replace the reality he is trying to explain is a reductionist. Rationalists are all reductionists, for they take the formal outcome to be the real, and dismiss what they experience (and of which that formal outcome was an abstract reconstruction) as unreal. Aristotle at times comes close to this kind of reductionism with his theory of form and matter; that is perhaps one of the reasons why he treated qualities as "accidents" to be put aside in any scientific study. His view is in consonance with the view of most scientists today; like him, they take the real to be identical with either one of the factors—or when they are most adequate, with all the factors as formally united—dismissing what is left over as "accident," illusion, something subjective.

Appearances must never be allowed to disappear; the discovery of their causes or of factors in terms of which they can be explained and which can be united to give a rational counterpart for those appearances, must not therefore be allowed to replace the appearances. Explanations do not make the explained vanish; they tell us about it and may even give us a formal counterpart of it. A rationalist in maintaining that only what is formal is real, is at a loss to account for evidence, common sense, experience, etc., except as mysterious confusions and illusions.

November 12

I have in the past held that *modus ponens* involves a risk, since it involves moving from a rule where the premiss and consequence are internally related and going to the position where they are detached, and in fact where the conclusion replaces the premiss. But this would hold only if the premiss could be said to be identical with the antecedent of the rule. If this supposition be avoided, we can make another and I think better interpretation of the *modus ponens* and thus of the nature of reasoning.

We first have a rule, which could be obtained by summarizing past experiences, but which could also be freely constructed by a mathematician or theorist, or just arbitrarily. This rule is produced in these various cases by abducting from a set of items, and coming up with a new synthesis of them. In any case, the rule is a given structure, divided off from the process of inference by a line which is always in operation, separating off the rule from any process.

In order to reason or do anything in consonance with a rule, we must make the rule internal to ourselves. The first step that must be taken is to get a starting point in the world and from there project an outcome. The starting point is not identical with the antecedent given in the rule; it occurs in another world and need not have any more in common with the other than say "count by twos" has with numbers, or "salute when you see a superior officer" has to do with the living soldier, actual saluting, or a real officer. All we want from the accepted position is that it be accepted as that which is symbolized by the antecedent. What is projected from there is the possibility of the terminus. The projection is the intentionalizing of the rule, the accepting of it as part of one's tendency, or disposition, or purpose; it tells us what the rule means in us, and not merely what it is as a bare rule, not yet effective, not in fact used.

Reasoning is the process by which we convert a prospective terminus into a real terminus. The process produces a structure in the course of its progress. That structure is related to the initial rule in the same way that the antecedent of the process is related to the antecedent of the rule, and in the same way that the final outcome is related to the consequence expressed in the rule. There is no necessary identity, no necessary similarity; all we need have is the same kind of distance, the same kind of relation, which connects our initial starting point in the inferential act to the beginning of the rule, to hold for the rest of the factors in the inference, i.e., for the "therefore" and for the terminal conclusion.

We can now state the *modus ponens* as:

$$
\begin{array}{cc}
1] & \underline{p \;\; R \;\; q} \\
2] & p \quad\;\; q \\
3] & \qquad\quad \therefore \\
4] & q \\
\end{array}
$$

1 expresses the rule. This rule in reasoning tells us that we can go from a proposition p, having property value x, to proposition q, having property value y. If we specialize this general rule of inference to deal only with the same property values, we obtain rule $1'$: p as having property value x (e.g., truth) is related by R (a relation expressing substitutability or replacement) to a q having the same kind of property value. If instead we specialize the general rule to deal only with the same propositions we specialize it as $1''$: p as having property value x (e.g., necessity) is related by R to itself as having a different property value (e.g., truth).

2 internalizes *1*; it turns it into an intention, a purpose. P might have been acquired by attending to some proposition true of a matter of fact, or it might have been freshly entertained; in either case it is distinct from the p above the line, and is to be understood as facing a prospective q, a q which is as yet undetermined comparatively to that p.

The "therefore" (*3*) expresses the process by which one converts the possible q into an actual q, the q on line *4*. It is this process which can be said to produce a structure R', which has the same relation to the R of the first line that the p and the q of the second line have to the p and the q of the first line.

On this account there is no genuine reasoning unless there is at least an intention with respect to a prospective conclusion. But if this is the case, no behavioral account of reasoning will ever be adequate, for behaviorism has no way of acknowledging an intention which has not yet been carried out. All it can do is to acknowledge that we first have a p

and then have a *q*, and that these are perhaps in a relation which has been described in some publicly knowable rule or set of directions. But it is one thing to act *in accord with* such rule or directions, and another to act *in terms of* it. Reasoning, because it is an act by which one moves in terms of a rule, requires us to internalize it in the shape of a project which we will then proceed to carry out by converting the projected outcome into an actual outcome.

November 13

The different components in the *modus ponens* are relevant to one another; but they are also independent.

The rule (which has its counterpart in connection with other activities in commands, instructions, tickets, programs, formal structures) may be perfectly respectable and yet never be internalized or followed. And if it is followed, it may be with interruptions and side moves of which it does not speak. The working out of a problem according to a rule may involve all sorts of false starts, errors, repetitions, and scaffolding. One may have a good ticket for a ride, but actually stop off along the route for a short side trip, in order to picnic, etc.

The internalization of a rule (by the adoption of a position with a project of getting to the end) may be achieved without attending to the rule at all. One may give oneself a purpose which had not been formalized or known in any rulelike way. And having the purpose does not mean it is going to be expressed, or if expressed that it will be fulfilled in the most efficient way.

The process of drawing a conclusion may not follow any purpose and may not be in accord with any explicit rule. And where it follows a rule and carries out a purpose, it may take a roundabout way. The girl takes all day to write in her diary; the fact that she goes to school, speaks on the telephone, etc., does not mean that the writing in her diary was not an all-day job. One could of course break down her day into a number of parts —going to school, speaking on the telephone, interspersed with jottings in her diary, etc. And this we perhaps will be inclined to do, so long as we do not know that she had a single purpose in mind, to write in her diary, throughout all these different tasks—or at least that she was governed by a tendency, habit, or disposition to write in her diary, which took precedence over all other shorter ranged tendencies in that it gave meaning and order to them in relation to one another. The strict empiricist who wishes to exorcise all references to purposes, etc., except so far as they have been exhibited, cannot make sense of such common expressions as "the woman took all day to write her letter," "the villain behaved with great consideration for a time," "the war lasted a year (though there were times when there was no fighting)."

The carrying out of the activity necessarily involves the production of a structure, an ingredient form which can be said to be the residuum left after the activity is over and which can be known by the historian. But that structure need not have anything in common with the structure of the given rule or of the intention. But it should, if the reasoning is to be genuine reasoning and thus be in terms of a rule and an intent, have its main pivots related to those of the rule in the same way that the beginning and ending of the process are related to the antecedent and consequent of the rule.

At the end of the inference, we arrive at a conclusion which has inherited a property value from the antecedent. But we do not want to have it remain in this guise, for it then makes at least an implicit reference to that antecedent. We must convert the property value which it has inherited into one which is directed at the world. What we then do is to reverse the movement by which we obtain a premiss from a true proposition that speaks of a matter of fact. The premiss used in our inference, if grounded in a truth of a matter of fact, had to take the truth (which was referring to the fact) and make it into a characterization of the proposition, i.e., turn it into a "truth-value." It is this "truth-value" which in the ordinary inference is inherited by the conclusion, and which must now be converted into a truth of a fact answering to that conclusion. If we do not make this conversion, we merely arrive at the conclusion and fail to conclude with it.

November 17

God is immanent in three ways. He is immanent in each dedicated community, when the members of it bind themselves together with their accepted past to constitute a religious people; He is immanent when a limited number of men achieve an intimacy of relationship (Buber's I and Thou); and He is immanent in the entire cosmos as providing the members of it with a union which is inexplicable in terms of an Ideal grouping or an existential conjunction in space and time. However, if God were only immanent, He would be multiplied by the various religions with their opposing claims; He would be too limited and episodic if He were present only in human encounters of a special sort; and He would be too impersonal if He were merely cosmically immanent, hardly different from the whole of nature, or mere togetherness, or the One of the Many actualities.

We have a warrant for calling the above immanents "God" because and so far as we can and do point beyond to Him in an act of worship, in an act of individual faith, and in a reference to a cosmic power to bind. The last can be known only through cognition; the others in religious acts. But no one of them provides a guarantee that there is really something to which one is pointing. This relative transcendence must be supplemented by a radical, absolute transcendence.

There are two absolute transcendencies: mysticism and speculative thought, the one religious, the other secular; the one immediate, the other discursive; the one beyond articulation, the other articulate. Each arrives at the Being of God as that on which the terminus of worship, faith, and acknowledged role depends. But he who arrives at God's Being never rests there; he moves on toward the object of worship, faith and role, but now as that which is an expression of God's Being.

The three dimensions of God—immanence, relative transcendence, and absolute transcendence—do not put a distance between actualities and God. Absolute transcendence arrives at the very Being which is immanent, but recognizes it to have another status. God the Being is God as immanent, but understood to be in Himself. Just as we do not depart to another world when we refer to a man as a substance while acknowledging him to be visibly present, so we do not depart to another world when we acknowledge God the Being. But this does not mean that one must then suppose that there is nothing more to God than an actual or potential togethering of actualities. God in His Being must be understood to be over against the actualities, but not to be remote in space, and indeed not remote in any sense but that of contrast. Viewed as prescriptive, He is that Being who is exercising a role with respect to actualities. He is then in the state of a relative transcendence of those actualities, but one which is achieved from the base of His own Being.

A consideration of the way in which we are all involved with the future suggests that we may have to go still another step in our understanding of God. As was observed in *Reality*, all beings are subject to a mellontological causation, i.e., they are all to be understood as inseparable from the incipient future. What will be can be, and will be only because it can be. No being is simply in the present; all are related beyond themselves to relevant possibilities which their actions and sometimes just their presence enable them to realize at a subsequent moment. We have teleology only where the possibility is determinative of how the realization is to take place.

The acknowledgment of purpose, intention, meaning, etc., does not introduce a new factor, but only a new way in which old factors operate. Mechanism has trouble with teleology primarily because it tries to deal with the world as though it were atomistic in time; to account for any stretch of relevant occurrences it can come up with nothing better than habit or achieved sequences; it never knows nor can say that there is an end which is being sought, often confusing the conditioning which the end provides with the causes which make one attend to that end. In a mere teleological situation, the operation of the end may be not known; such a situation could be said to be dominated by a tendency, a disposition, an appetite, or an inclination. When consciousness intervenes, we speak of intentions, desires, goals, and the like.

A possibility can dictate to us without necessarily affecting us and our acts. This is the case sometimes when we face the prescriptive possibilities of ethics. We are then obligated by the possibilities, but may act in disregard of them or even in opposition to them. The possibilities can be said to define the kind of beings we are—obligated ones—but themselves not to be more than mellontological termini. It is this role which Actuality, God, and Existence can also assume with respect to a world in which they are immanent. All could be said to be inseparable from the being of actualities, but also to be distinct from and outside them. All could be said to define the kind of beings those actualities are.

A full man, a man who is most fully, realizes his promise: he is one whose actions are governed by all four modes of Being. At one and the same time he acts in such a way as to be distinctive, to realize an ideal end, to be existentially adjusted, and to be in spiritual accord with other actualities. Since he is together with other actualities, and thus is one of a Many whose immanent One is provided by one of the modes of Being, in three of the cases his action may serve to enable some other modes of Being to be immanent. Thus if he is an actuality related to other actualities by Actuality, his action may succeed in making the Ideal not only be realized in the shape of some possibility (or of itself as the Good), but as the immanent One of other actualities. But now I am beginning to lose the thread.

November 20

From an involvement in the world of actualities, we can be led to attend to God, or to engage in some religious activity, in a number of ways.

1] We may find something astonishing in the shape of a statement or an act, which we think requires God for its explanation. Revelations, prophets, miracles, and the like are the names for such astonishing occurrences, or vehicles of them.

2] We may find ourselves so dissatisfied, disillusioned, frustrated by what we are, find, and do in the world, that we detach ourselves from it and turn elsewhere. This is the view held by the Buddhist and the Hindu; it is also the position taken in my account of how and why we turn to God.

3] We may find ourselves in despair because we have not been able to see anything in the world which answers to our condition, and therefore look for something else which could satisfy this primordial need. Here we are viewing both the religious and secular concerns as something like specializations of a primary appetite, with the religious answering to it better or more completely, perhaps even adequately. However, if there be some satisfaction given in the secular world, it would seem as if the religious would have to be taken as correlate with it, a specialization and not a completely adequate way of providing satisfaction to our primal need. This seems to be John E. Smith's position.

4] We may find ourselves in despair and take the secular world to be a perversion of a primal need. Such a view requires that there first be a concern for God. This is perhaps what is at the root of Tillich's discussions.

5] We may find ourselves compelled, invited, lured, somehow pulled away from our present situation in the world and made to attend elsewhere—some men, it is said are called, or have been benefited by grace and the like.

There is no inconsistency in saying that all of these may occur. But each one would have to be justified by an account of man, his involvement in the world, and the nature and position of God in relation to man. The first takes God to act in the world; the second takes us to be oriented in a number of directions toward different Beings; the third takes the distinctive involvements, such as the second recognizes, to specialize a more basic ontological drive; the fourth is essentially from the position of religion and is to be matched by other positions taking other outlooks as basic; the fifth recognizes man to be subject to compulsions which are traceable to God, compulsions which need not affect what he is in the world, but which in fact turn him away from it.

Does the awareness of the supranatural in terror or fear add another case? It can be said to do so: 6] Here we are forced to turn away from the world not by something that lures us but by something in the world which forces us to do so. But unlike the astonishing, considered in the first case, where we confront a signal object, we here are forced to turn away from all objects and to open ourselves up to something else. We are close to the second case, except that here the turning away from the world is compulsive, whereas there it seems to be voluntary or at least semivoluntary.

November 21

Abduction, the logic of getting new ideas, forming hypotheses, getting explanations, moving to rules, etc., can be put in a *modus ponens* form:

1] "If you are given z, and if aRz, bSz, cTz, etc., then select that antecedent from which we can get z most readily and make possible the derivation of other desirable conclusions in equally ready ways."

$$2] \quad z. \ aRz, \ bSz, \ cTz \rightarrow a$$
$$3] \quad z. \ aRz, \ bSz, \ cTz$$
$$4] \qquad\qquad\qquad \therefore$$
$$5] \quad a$$

The difference between an abduction and other forms of inference then lies simply in the fact that we make use of a distinctive rule in abduction, which tells us how to find the antecedent for a rule that we will want to use.

November 22

An abduction may start with fact, proposition, rule—anything in fact. And it may arrive at a premiss, a rule, an hypothesis—at anything which will serve to ground the initially accepted item. If the abduction moves to an explanation, it will end with something having the structure of a rule. If it arrives at an explanation for some observable occurrence, or some law, it takes its start with something having the structure of a rule. Consequently, in this case, we have something like the following situation:

If you are given z (with the structure lMn, where l is the antecedent, n the consequence, and M the relation between them), and if aRz, bSz cTz, etc. (where R, S, T, express not relations of deduction, but relations of grounding or justification), then select that antecedent from which we can readily explain or justify the z as well as other similar kinds of occurrences. The selected antecedent will itself have the structure of a rule, $\phi O \psi$.

Having accepted the rule: 'If you are given z, and aRz, bSz, cTz, etc., select a or b or c, etc.', we can engage in *modus ponens,* by affirming the given, and then moving on to obtain the isolated a (or b or c). We will then, having started with z, i.e., lMn, end with $\phi O \psi$. These are related as premiss to conclusion. Though we have come to the antecedent of z, along a *modus ponens,* that antecedent need not function as a premiss from which we move to the initial z as a conclusion; it may function merely as a rule guiding us.

If abduction can be expressed in a *modus ponens* form, are we not involved in an infinite regress? To get a premiss from a true proposition about a matter of fact, to forge a rule out of data, are steps we had to take in order to forge *modus ponens*; but these are abductive processes. Is not the answer: we can engage in an inference in order to begin a particular kind of inferring; but we can also start with something given and then infer? Which of these alternatives applies to judgment? Bradley thinks that a judgment is not inferential, because there is no development or unfolding of what is accepted to begin with. But there need never be an unfolding in an inference, even of the most satisfactory kind; a premiss is merely a beginning of an act which is to end in an acceptable outcome, and that outcome may not have anything in common with the beginning. A judgment is inferential as Peirce saw; it involves an abduction (and thus a *modus ponens* inference, if I am right) from given data.

November 23

If God's cosmic immanence be thought of as a *de facto* set of affiliations which actualities have to one another, we can then go on and take an institutional religion to provide the means by which men can come together in dedicated communities from time to time in order to intensify the *de facto* immanence. Having intensified it, usually through ceremonial and ritual and the identification of the community with some event in the past, the members of the dedicated community could then be thought to make it their concern to try to intensify and modify the *de facto* affiliations which still characterize those outside the dedicated community.

On this account no reference is made to God as a transcendent Being, except perhaps as a device to enable the dedicated community to hold on to its past, or for its members to so act together that they become more effectively and even differently affiliated than they were in their *de facto* affiliation, as members of a single cosmos. We come here very close to the new "atheistic" theologians, except that they do not seem to see the difference between a cosmic and religiously determined affiliation.

To recover something like the classical view, and to be in closer consonance with what I wrote in *The God We Seek*, one would have to show that there was an actual insistence on our intensifying our affiliations, and that such intensification could not be produced by us merely by coming together and carrying out some rituals. If we could not do this, we would have to give up prayer and worship, and deny the doctrines of grace, judgment, divine punishment, incarnation, and creation, for all these presuppose a Being who is outside the immanent situation. On the present account God is nothing but the name for the totality of affiliations which can be intensified and altered when men deal with one another or perhaps engage in some ceremonial.

In the *Modes of Being*, an attempt was made to prove the reality of God by attending to facts which could not otherwise be accounted for; but what is wanted now is some experience of pressure, some subjection to a power, or some necessity to make a transcendent reference for which we can be assured there is a terminus. The last is what is used by the religious man who, with a mystic, can both point beyond immanences and enjoy a transcendent Being. But it would be desirable to have an experiential justification, which was open to all others. Is this not possible? If not, we have only the choice of accepting or rejecting the reports of the religious man of faith and the religious mystic. And it could be well argued that it makes sense to reject those reports, since otherwise we divide men into two different kinds, the religious and the nonreligious, with different powers and relations to the real.

There have been theologians who have spoken as though faith and mysticism are not possible without the intervention of God, and that these are the only ways in which we can apprehend Him. But they must then be charged with making the above division into the religious and nonreligious—and this is something which the rest of us need not accept. The best defense of religious activity and insight is provided by showing that others have the desirable results in only minimal ways. This is best done perhaps by showing that a love directed at fellowman never succeeds as well as one which has first or also been directed at God, who is experienced as completing, forcing, or redirecting one. I haven't got this situation right yet, for I am now once again asking for something only a religious man can provide within his own context—unless it be possible for him to provide empirical evidence for his transformation by God, which seems most unlikely.

I think this may provide some focus: the religious man loves his enemy; this is presumably what no one can do unless God helps him. But this means that it is wrong to urge people to love their enemy; instead one must urge them to love God who will enable them to love those they otherwise could not.

November 24

It might be of interest to see what a more or less typical day is like, and what I envisage as I sit down to work. I have just finished a rewriting of the book on education, and await the Christmas vacation for a clear period in which I can type out the whole, and then give it to a typist for a clean copy. My typing is too careless to serve for a manuscript copy for the publisher. And I have just sent off to the press my corrected copy of the manuscript for part of volume 2 of *Philosophy in Process*, answering questions put by the publisher's reader—on the copy that is to go to the printer.

I am now completing the reading of the typist's copy of my manuscript for around February 1965, which will more likely than not be part of volume 4 of this work. I have been working over that typist's copy for an hour or so a day for the last week; I should finish with this section of her work this week.

In addition to correspondence to answer, I have on my desk a manuscript of a student, sent in by Rudd Fleming of Maryland, a copy of a plan to begin graduate teaching at University of Delaware, on which William Reese wants me to comment, a copy of the *Architectural Record* in which King Lui Wu wants me to read about the excellent Manuscript Building that he put up a while back, and books in process of being read —*The Two Worlds of American Art,* by Barry Ulanov; *A Practical Manual of Screen Playwriting,* by Lewis Herman; *Quarterly Review of Literature; The Political Vocation,* edited by Paul Tillett, and miscellaneous offprints which have been sent to me. I will not turn to the reading of these until late afternoon; the rest of the time will be spent in thinking and writing, and working over manuscripts.

It might be of interest, too, to have me state how I think it is that the ideas expressed in this work come about. They originate usually as a consequence of my trying to formulate to myself some idea or view I had previously expressed, but which I must present to a class, or to a lecture audience. But quite often as a consequence of the questions raised or as a consequence of some lecture heard, or even more frequently because of something read, I find myself faced with a view or position or distinction that I had not considered. I then ask myself if and how my own views could be made to fit into this new one. (This procedure is the reverse of Robert Hartman's, who tries to see how well his own spacious view accommodates the view he has heard others express. His method gives strength to his own position; mine allows me to criticize and modify what I once had held.) I often find that I must alter my previously stated position or the one I have just heard, in some minor degree, but then find that there are questions left over that the new view cannot accommodate, I thereupon try to introduce into the new situation distinctions, considerations, facts, etc., which make me hold a much more expansive view than that which I had before, or had heard expressed by another.

Today, for example, the "new" theologians are putting a great emphasis on the immanence of God, and are denying that there is any meaning to His transcendence or to any personal dealings which He might have with men. This sounds to me as though theirs was a reiteration of the position of God as cosmically immanent, or at least immanent in mankind. How does this view fit in with the acknowledgment of historic religions, dedicated communities, detachment from the world, faith, and the problem of whether or not the immanence of God in the world can be understood without reference to Him as a Being who can become so immanent? Giving as much weight as I can to the new proposals of these young theologians, I find I am left over with some such question as that with which I ended yesterday: what would be the evidence that a religious man can provide to show that his behavior with respect to other men was determined by God? My answer to this was that there was an act, such as forgiveness, or loving one's enemies, which one could not perform by oneself but only as a consequence of an antecedent or accompanying involvement with God, in which God enriches or strengthens men.

Having arrived at this position, I try to criticize it. I present myself with the question, granted that men are so enriched when they worship or pray, or participate in a religious community—something which not everyone would grant but which could be said to be definitory of a genuine religious experience, rare though it be—might it not be that the mere fact that they speak of God or make a reference to such a Being, strengthens them, whether or not a God exists? Could we ever determine whether this is the case? Must we not sooner or later take an intellectual approach to God to determine whether or not there is a Being with such a power? Must we not sooner or later move beyond faith to mysticism to determine whether or not there is a Being who can become involved with men? I think that the answer must be in the affirmative in both cases.

November 26

One can avoid the acknowledgment of Existence as a mode of Being by accounting for the contemporaneity of actualities by a doctrine of divine preestablished harmony, and for the experience of distance and resistance as being the product of the individual's constructions, native ideas, and categories. But it is to be noted that we then acknowledge God as a mode of Being and give Him a task we do not know in fact that He assumes, and that we ascribe to ourselves the production of extension and insistencies (or resistances) which in effect deny that there is a real space with real objects that we confront. Since it is the task of philosophy to hold on to experience as given and not take this to be a kind of fiction until we are forced to do so by the fact of error or incoherence in our views, this alternative to acknowledging Existence cannot be accepted.

We can get rid of the view that Ideality is a mode of Being by supposing that both the future and the universal grouping of all actualities as actualities are unreal or merely imagined, and that the experience of being obligated, prescribed to, is the product of our own projection and a submission to what we have projected. But the first supposition will not allow us to acknowledge possibilities and the involvement of entities in the incipient future, nor will it allow us to say why all that occurs in limited regions of Existence are actualities in the same sense, all equally intelligible. And the view that the experience of obligation can be taken to be the product of a self-imposed prescription will have us somehow create that to which we feel forced to submit. Since the Ideal applies to all that is, we would on this alternative view have to suppose that we can conceive of an unreality or imaginary entity which we cannot make vanish, and that we can project a cosmic obligating entity to which we find ourselves subject, even when we do not want to. But now we introduce powers into our supposed imaginings and projects for which we do not have any evidence; in effect we will give to something finite and recondite the cosmic power that Ideality is said to have on any view which takes it to have a reality of its own.

We can avoid the acknowledgment of God as a mode of Being by taking Him (as the other of us) to be something created by our language or beliefs, and by taking the experience of Him, as empowering us to love our enemies, i.e., make radically new affiliations of an eminently desirable sort but which otherwise seem impossible, to be the experience of a delusion on our part (perhaps even caused by our coming together in a religious community). But we will then endow our language or belief with the force of deluding us into thinking that we are genuinely absolute others, and by taking a delusion to be so powerful that it works unknowingly to empower some of us to do an eminently desirable good. The delusion seems now to be something divine-like, with a career of its own; and the creation of an "other" in language or belief would seem to be inseparable from the understanding of ourselves as unique, but on the present alternative only delusively so. But we have no knowledge of such a delusion nor any understanding of how it might work.

Finally, we could get rid of Actuality as a mode of Being on the supposition that the other three modes are merely together, and that our experience of Actuality as that which makes all its parts equally actual is verbal or illusory. But not only must Actuality be recognized to be immanent in the totality of actualities, but it is the task of the other modes of Being, in their nonexperiential guise, to enable Actuality to stand away from those actualities (the task of God), to be similar in nature to those actualities (the task of Ideality), and to extend over them while transcending them (the task of Existence). And it is the task of Actuality to adjust these modes of Being in their experiential guise (so that what one Being does has bearing on the others) and to equalize actualities despite their difference in size, power, and value. Actuality in its experiential form makes possible the distinction between "x is y" and "it is the case that x is y," where the latter refers to a world that is completed. We avoid the acknowledgment of Actuality only by accepting some immanent kind of harmonization amongst the other three modes in their experiential guise, and a separation and involvement of actualities with Actuality, for which no reason is to be given; by the very fact that they are they will have to be said to be equally actual and contingent, depending on nothing for the being which they contingently possess.

These different answers to the possible rejection of the modes of Being in their ontological and experiential forms are uneven. It is desirable to sort out the various arguments I have urged over the years regarding the reasons and functionings of the various Beings in order to make a strong case for the undesirability of these other alternatives. The best defense for the modes will be the demonstration that the other alternatives but attribute to unknown powers special tasks, and that it makes us deny the validity or finality of what we experience merely because of some theory we have, and not because of any evidence we can produce. But enough has been said I think to show that the opposition to the acceptance of some mode of Being must take place both on an ontological and an experiential level. After one has argued, for example, that the increase in power and satisfaction felt by a religious man when and after he is involved with God could be explained by holding that man's delusions have the ability to empower and enrich him, one must go on to show that the status of being an absolute other, of being independent of Actuality, of having a unity, of having a real past to which one can refer, of facing exterior prescriptions and realizable relevant possibilities, and being over against the unity of Existence, all can be better explained in other ways, than by referring to God.

November 27

It is hard to avoid acknowledging Existence as a mode of Being. It is not only the topic of the cosmological physicists, accounting for space, time, and causation, but it is also experienced in the shape of compulsions, seems to be illuminated by art, is necessary to the understanding of history, and explains the fact that actualities continue to be contemporary over the course of time, even though some are at rest and others in motion, some are sluggish and others swift in change and motion. To account for all these things by reference to a divine act, etc., is not only not to avoid the acknowledgment of a mode of Being, but is to attribute to God powers which but repeat in another form the facts which are acknowledged by one who accepts the reality of Existence.

The reasons for accepting Ideality as a mode of Being seem to be almost as persuasive as those which persuade one with respect to Existence. There is, to be sure, a lack of support by the scientists, but this is counterbalanced by the support of logicians, mathematicians, and ethicists. The commonality of ends for a multiplicity of actualities, the presupposition of a possible future for any occurrences in time, the fact that every and all the items in this world can be criticized as defective, limited, incomplete, and that purposes, duties, and the like can be accounted for as acceptations of an objective prescription, all support the view that Ideality is a basic mode of Being. We cannot get rid of it without denying that there are prescriptions (and therefore holding that by some agreement, conscious or unconscious, the laws of logic and the obligations imposed by ethics could be changed) and will still be unable to explain how what will be can be without there being a "can be," i.e., a possibility presupposed, which will either be identical with, a part of, or a subdivision of the Ideal.

We have harder going when we deal with Actuality. Why might this not be said to be a function of all the actualities, or identical with the juncture of the Ideal and Existence? Why should not the Ideal and Existence equalize all the actualities? Why not consider the contingency of actualities to stand in contrast with the eternity of the Ideal and Existence? Why must the having of Being by actualities require that Actuality be the Being on which they have a momentary hold?

And we seem to have an equally hard time holding on to the view that God is an ultimate mode of Being. Why suppose that any actuality ever achieves the status of being an absolute other, requiring a transcendent other over against it? And why may not its other be the union of the Ideal and Existence? If an actuality achieves the state of being absolutely private, over against whatever there be, it will contrast with the transcendent Beings, Ideality and Existence; if it achieves such a state only to some degree, it will be more or less involved with other actualities at the same time that it is more or less involved with the Ideal and Existence.

Why may not the enrichment and empowering of individuals who believe in God be the result of a delusion? After all, the idea that God enables one to love his neighbor is a view peculiar to only a few religions, and does not seem to have much to do with Islam, Buddhism, or Hinduism, and perhaps even Judaism. Also, some people who believe seem to be weakened, confused, and even turned on a path of destruction and hate by their religion and its God. Those who see these to be the result of a delusion on the part of man usually take only tendencies toward evil to be the outcome of the power of a delusion; but if a delusion can have this much power, why cannot it have just as much power in other men or at other times, to enable men to do good?

If we deny the reality of Actuality, we will of course deny that actualities have a distinctive Being in which they participate, or we will have to view actualities as combinations of instantiations of the Ideal and Existence. This view is not altogether incompatible with an Aristotelian outlook, with its doctrine of essence and existence, though Aristotelians would be inclined to deny that there is an Ideal realm—despite Aristotle's admission of one in the *De Anima*, where he discusses the active reason. If we take this view, we need not suppose that actualities are instantiations of the Ideal and Existence; these instantiations can be thought of as abstractions from the actualities.

If we deny the reality of God, we dismiss the beliefs of a multitude as mistaken. We could still make sense of religion, and even provide some meaning for the term "God." Religion would be the experience of alienation and reconciliation with the Ideal and Existence, as unified and as transcendent of their immanently sustained roles as the togetherness of actualities. So far as there was an alienation, the unity could be called "God"; so far as there was a reconciliation, it could be called "Actuality." Or, taking God to be the principle of affiliation, the power by virtue of which certain actualities have an openness to some and a closedness to others (apparently no less worthy and apparently at times in no way different in Being, performance and nature from the others), God would be identifiable with the *de facto* affiliation for one who took the secular world to be "God's footstool" or who started with the omnipresence of God, and with the affiliations which were brought about by those who accepted some creed or participated in some religious ceremony or community. God in the latter sense would be the power for good which men acquired in certain kinds of relations with one another.

Bonhoeffer was inclined to take the secular world to be entirely devoid of God, and to stand over against a transcendent God. His view is much more orthodox than his followers suppose. Some of these at least want to take the world itself to be permeated by God, and therefore find no need to make a reference to God as transcendent. Their position, strictly speaking, is the opposite of Bonhoeffer's. The view I am now suggesting gets somewhere between these two views. With Bonhoeffer, it is allowing for the reality of God as capable of making more of a difference than is now evident in even the most devout, but it does not suppose that He has a Being of His own; with the "new theologians" who follow Bonhoeffer, it is allowing for the reality of God in the world, particularly when men do good, but it allows one to stand over against Him in some degree, though He will then not be a person but a union of the Ideal and Existence.

The suggestion allows for two modes of Being having an immanent and a transcendent status. It takes Actuality and God to be understood as the immanence of those Beings together, the one emphasizing what is common to all the actualities, the other emphasizing how they are related to one another by affiliation. It also allows one to understand God to be over against the actualities (just so far as they are private beings, without going so far as to suppose those privacies to be absolute) and to be the union of the two transcendent Beings. And it allows one to understand Actuality as that unity of those transcendents which the unity of the actualities instantiates.

The present suggestion does not avoid metaphysics or transcendentals; but since it demands of us the acknowledgment of no more than two modes of Being, it would seem so far to be superior to the position offered in *Modes of Being*. That book would then be right to have neglected Actuality, particularly in the main body of the work, but it would still be in error because it insisted on the reality of God.

November 28

If we suppose that God is the togetherness of Ideality and Existence, we do not escape a reference to Him as transcendent, since as the Other of all else (to which I as the representative of all else can be the correlative Other), He will not be immanent. The Ideal and Existence have a transcendent status as well as an immanent one, and God as the togetherness of those modes of Being is therefore also transcendent. God as the togetherness of these modes of Being when they are immanent has the status of an affiliator. This last supposition leaves no room for Actuality, unless it be what Existence and the Ideal have in common; it also endows the immanent togetherness with some kind of power, which a genuine togetherness does not have.

On this view God as transcendent will have neither nature nor power, and all references to Him as ennobling, empowering, enriching, and judging men will have to be rejected. We are now quite close to Buddhism. With it we can speak of men emptying themselves to confront the eternal emptiness, which does not impose any demands on them. If the Buddha goes back into the world, he does so voluntarily, out of pity, not because this is a power and a duty which he acquires from an involvement with God.

We seem then to have two basic approaches to God, the one characteristic of the West, and the other of the East. The former takes God to be a Being who not only acts on actualities and the immanent totality they form, but who stands over against the actualities as a kind of inwardness, enabling men to do things they otherwise could not. The latter takes God not to be a Being and not to act, and to be delusively referred to as a judge, a power, an affiliator, and the like. How are we to choose between these?

One way of making the choice is to ask which does more justice to the facts, which clarifies more, the view that men, as detached from the world and facing God, are more like Being or more like non-being? Those who hold the latter can with Hume say that they never come upon anything in the investigation of the self but particular impressions; or with Kant they can say that the "I" is merely the accompaniment of all perception, without power, or meaning, or personality of its own. But something possesses the impressions, something is the locus of the perceptions, something persists over time and perhaps forever. Moreover, it is the actuality as other than God which is an other for the world. If an actuality were a mere togetherness, how could it be an other *for* anything? Must not an "other for" have a being and a nature of its own?

We take the position of the West, in the Hebraic, Christian, or Muslim form, then, on the ground that the self has a reality and a power which requires that its other also have a reality and a power, and cannot therefore be a mere togetherness of other modes of Being. Consequently, we have some ground for rejecting the otherwise unsupported and apparently irrefutable view that we delude ourselves when we suppose that God can or does empower men to forgive those who hurt them, to love those who hate them, to walk in His ways doing justice to all, and so on. It may, of course, be true that God is a Being who *could* empower men, but does not do so in fact. But now the denial that God empowers one is not a matter which may or may not be possible, but one which may or may not take place. Since we cannot find ourselves deluding ourselves to engage in these difficult but desirable works, it would be simpler to explain our feeling that we are so empowered as being the result of the action of one who has already been recognized to have that power. And one should do so even if, like me, one has never had an experience of such empowering, except in the sense of making rapprochements with individuals without having anything or much in common with them.

What is wrong with the new theologians and the Buddhists, we must conclude, is their idea of the private nature of man, from which it follows that they are mistaken regarding the kind of reality that God has as transcendent, and therefore also in their supposition that an enrichment or power achieved in a religious setting is the outcome of a delusion.

November 29

A dedicated community through its ritual, ceremonial, prayers, and recitals should have a plurality of effects. It should bind the men together with one another, with the past members of the religion, and with great religious figures and events. And it should empower them so that they will, on leaving that community, make intimate contact with some other individuals, and also will belong more firmly to one mankind than before. These effects should not be aimed at, and may not even be mentioned; they come about because of a worship. Nor should the effects be detached from their causes and treated as though they were themselves of the essence of religion, as the followers of Buber are inclined to hold with respect to intimate contact of individual with individual, and the new theologians are inclined to hold with respect to mankind.

We can know that these effects are the result of the working of God, rather than of the working of a community which takes God to be both present in it and transcendent of it and all else, because there is another effect of worship, besides that just indicated. Worship makes the individual aware of himself as the other of God; the richer he is, the more evident it is that God is a Being who has the power to make those who worship Him to have more intimate contacts with some men, and to be more firmly part of mankind than they otherwise would be. The more one can see oneself involved with other actualities in other than these ways, the more surely one can see that, though as a private being one is then an other *of* and *for* them, one will be other *than* God, a being over against Him. Reciprocally, the more God is involved with other Beings, the more surely will He be other *than* actualities, and other than any actuality that represents all else.

We remain within the area of experience and religion so far as we stop with men as individuals who are involved with God by being others *for* and *of* Him. We must turn to speculation to know what His nature is, and what kind of involvement He has with other modes of Being; and we must turn to mysticism to experience Him as an other *of* us, who penetrates us, and we Him.

The return to the secular world with a desire and a power to become more firmly part of mankind, and thus to be affiliated with others in a way one had not been before soon loses its strength, requiring one to renew the involvement with God in a dedicated community. A dedicated community is at once a place for binding men to one another in that community and in that religion, and an occasion for a renewal or for an increase in strength and confidence.

December 1

From a biological point of view, a man can be said to be the totality of organs, one or more of which functions as a One for the others, in such a way that what it does is done on behalf of those others. The heart beats for the hand, mouth, kidneys, and liver, and the hand and mouth function for the heart, kidneys, and liver, etc. We here dispense with any idea of a single unitary organism except in the sense of an immanent unity of all the organs. The position is similar to what we can take with respect to the nature of a group, family, society, or state. Here men act representatively for the rest; a family, for example, is a father working for the mother and child, the mother taking care of the child and father in the home, and the child uniting the two through its needs and responses. But there is a difference between a family and a man. The family has a career in time and interplays with other families and the like, but all the work is done by the individuals. We could, of course, say that all the work done by an individual is done by the various organs together. He eats with his mouth, circulates his blood with his lungs and heart, etc.; whatever he does is done via some particular organ or organs. So far the situations are parallel. But a man can criticize himself as a totality, can discipline himself as a totality, is self-identical despite changes in the totality, and is able to detach himself from his body and what it is connected with, to attend to the Ideal, God, Existence and Actuality—nonbiological acts. The state is not a final reality in the sense in which a man can be said to be one, because it has no single act in which it can engage over against and as conditioning every representative member of it; it is not able to engage in acts which have no human agents.

If chemicals can act representatively for one another, we can explain the cell in terms of them; if electrons, etc., can act representatively for other electrons, etc., we can explain chemistry in terms of them. The representatives will then be unifiers, operants, solidifiers, polarizers, and not merely entities in a context; they will not so far explain how the totality can act on similar totalities.

A diplomat functions as a representative of the totality of representative men and those they represent; but he is no more or less a man than those whom he represents collectively. Just so, we could envisage chemicals functioning representatively to constitute with others the totality we call a cell, and acknowledge some of those chemicals to function on behalf of the totality in relation to other totalities. Should we do this, we would have "reduced" biology to chemistry, though not without endowing the chemicals with "polarizing" functions with respect to others, to enable them to constitute a single totality with them, and with "polarizing" functions for the totality in relation to other totalities. Is this a true "reduction"?

It is conceivable that we could "reduce" all the sciences eventually to physics in a similar way. This does not mean that we will have reduced man, for as was observed above, and was initially remarked in *Nature and Man,* man has powers, even nonmental ones, which allow him to act with respect to other men and the modes of Being.

December 2

If we wish to have all the sciences reduced to physics, we must suppose that some of the particles of physics not only polarize others to constitute chemical units, but that some of the particles (not necessarily identical with those which were the "chemical polarizers") so acted on one another that some chemical sets of them were polarized with respect to one another, and that some of the particles (not necessarily identical with any of the previous polarizers) so acted on one another that some sets of sets of chemical entities were polarized with respect to one another, to constitute complex biological entities. We would have to say that a walk was not correctly described as a movement with the legs in order to arrive at some destination; nor as a mere movement of legs; nor as a mere movement due to tendons and muscles; nor as a displacement of a living body; nor as a displacement of a group of organs or cells; nor as a displacement of chemicals; but only as a displacement of physical particles which formed larger and larger groups because some of the particles were able to polarize groups of particles on behalf of the groups in which those polarizing particles were a part. The walk itself would be characterized as the product of some physical particle acting with respect to some distant place in such a way that the physical particles said to be in, or at, or to constitute the living body, engage in various motions which we combine and refer to as the use of tendons and muscles, etc.

The analogy here would be a state. Just as the citizens of a modern state live in families and help constitute towns, counties, and the entire single state, so the physical particles could be said to be parts of different groups. And just as some of the citizens can represent the others in the towns, counties, and the entire single state, so some of the particles can represent the others in molecules, cells, organs, and the entire body. And just as some of the citizens can represent the entire state in its commerce with other states, so some of the particles can represent the entire set of particles making up the body, when that body is involved with other bodies.

This kind of reductionism does not deny that there are complex bodies, walks, etc., but it does deny that they are ultimately real. It thinks it can explain them in terms of ultimate particles; but then it must endow these particles with polarizing or representative functions of a special sort. There is some willingness on the part of physicists to allow for such functions just so as far as these allow for an understanding of chemical and biological units.

Reductionists have tended to deny the reality of complex organisms or their functioning, understanding some such activity as a walk for example as nothing more than a sequence of steps, and these as nothing more than a sequence of motions. But a walk would seem to be no less real than a biological division of cells, or a combination of chemicals. If we acknowledge the occurrence of such divisions and combinations, even when denying that they are ultimately real, and try to account for them by ascribing representative functions to particles, must we not offer a similar explanation for a walk? And if we can deny that there is a walk, and treat it instead as a sequence of physical motions (thereby avoiding speaking of the representative function of particles with respect to distant positions), should we not deny that there are organisms, cells, chemicals, for the same reason? If we follow the last lead, we will have a simple reductionism; here physical particles will have representative functions only with respect to other physical particles so as to constitute complex physical entities; every other, more complex being will then be treated as a mere aggregate of the complex physical entities, and their activities.

On either reductionistic scheme we would still be unable to handle prescriptions, other-worldly enterprises, privacies, individuality, self-discipline, self-sacrifice, self-denial, self-criticism, self-identity, artistic appreciation, knowledge, will, and mathematical and logical necessities.

December 3

A genuine religious experience would seem to involve two movements, one somewhat like that emphasized in the East, and the other somewhat like that emphasized in the West. To begin with, there must be an involvement with what is an other of oneself; this is possible only so far as one manages to be detached from all that is not God—which according to the Buddhists would be all that is determinate, distinguishable, and characterizable. One need not go all the way with the Buddhist; it is enough to remark that as a self, having put aside all concern with one's body, the existent cosmos, ethical ideals, and even the Being which is common to all actualities, one finds oneself distinct from and yet interplaying with what has an inwardness equal to one's own. It is in that interplay that one becomes empowered to engage in acts beyond those normally pursued. One is confident that this empowerment is not due to an illusion or delusion, precisely because one finds oneself over against that with which one is interplaying. The empowerment is due to the presence of something which is the other of oneself.

It is conceivable that what is the other of oneself may be the togetherness of all or some of the other realities, though it is hard to see how one can get an inwardness for such a togetherness. We would then not be empowered by a delusion which we had forged for ourselves, but we would not yet have any assurance that that with which we interplayed had any being of its own, or even a being which could be in interplay with us. Only by shifting our attitude and attending to whatever else there be do we know that there is a Being over against us, a Being which is other than us, in the direction where we interplayed when we were detached from all else. We then are able to act in the world as responsible for all else, as representative of all else. We are then over against God and thus His correlate who faces Him as a self which interplays with everything else.

He who shifts from a detachment from all else with an involvement in God as other than himself to an involvement with all else as other than God, loves his neighbor, forgives his enemies, does justice, etc., not merely by interplaying with some other actualities, but as one who is responsible for them, who represents them all. Someone else might love his neighbor to the same degree, but he will not do so religiously, if he only interplays with that neighbor, makes a closer contact with him. In a religiously governed interplay, one loves his neighbors because one has been involved with what are others of oneself as detached, and who, as representing all the non-divine, has returned to deal with them. It is the recognition that one's other (which was encountered when one detached oneself from what was non-divine) is an other of what is responsibly (or alternatively, representatively) involved with what is non-divine.

The "therefore" in an inference is a process which may involve selection, props, and many steps. It must, to be reckoned a part of reasoning, be at once valid and deliberate, the one by virtue of a conformity to the demands of a rule, and the other by virtue of a conformity to an intention to arrive at the conclusion in a rational, controlled way. If we have only a valid move, we have an outcome that is not unsatisfactory, but we cannot ourselves be said to have produced it. We have merely arrived at it.

But if we make a deliberate move only, we have an outcome which we intended to arrive at (i.e., which we faced as a possibility, and thus as somewhat indeterminate) but which may itself not be validly reached.

December 4

The process of abductively arriving at an explanation of something can be given the simplified form:

$$1. \quad zPa$$
$$2. \quad z \rightarrow a$$
$$\overline{}$$
$$3. \quad z$$
$$4. \quad \therefore$$
$$5. \qquad a$$

This differs from the ordinary form of *modus ponens* solely in the fact that P represents a movement to an explanation of some kind—causal, theoretical, something more general, etc. If we read it in accordance with the usual way of reading a rule governing an inference, we would say "if z then a"; our "therefore" would then express the fact that we had started with the z in the light of the rule (line *1*), and the intention to obtain a (or some general form of it) as expressed on line *2*.

The problem of abduction is then not the obtaining of a as an explanation, but the obtaining of it as the consequence of the hypothetical, "if z then. . . ." But might this not be achieved in many ways? We could produce it in accordance with some method, say that of finding a mathematical expression for z, an historic antecedent for it, its most proximate cause, or a set of propositions from which z could be deduced, etc. Is this different from the process of finding a material consequence for some supposition, such that the consequence is acknowledged as the terminus of some route, not necessarily an implicational one? Thus we can say, "If the rate for insuring men under thirty is x, then the rate for men over sixty is $2x$." We can here take "doubling the rate" to be expressed by the "then" or we could have it produce the consequence "rate for men over sixty is $2x$." Just so we can say that "If we are given z, then the best explanation for it is a," and suppose either that the "then" is a way of stating the method by which we relate the z to the a, or that it is a way of connecting the z to an a which had been obtained by some accepted method. The more orthodox view I suppose is to hold that the "then" relates us to a consequence which has some logical relevance to the antecedent, as deducible from it perhaps, or as implied by it in accordance with logical rules. Accepting that position, we should say then that the abductive rule in *modus ponens* should read:

If *z*, then *a* (obtained by some operation which may or may not start with *z*).

If this be the procedure, the issue of abduction comes down to the operation by which *a*, as a consequence logically implied by the *z*, is obtained. But can we say that *z* logically implies *a*? It is not a consequence of it in the way in which in the ordinary *modus ponens* form, *p* implies *q*. The latter can be obtained in accordance with truth table rules, etc.

We do say, "If you want to be rich then you must save, work hard, be shrewd, etc." What does the "then" here express? Something like "then, in accordance with past experience and the nature of the world of business, etc."? The "then" is evidently a shorthand expression to be followed by some statement of the method or rule by which the consequence is thought to be pertinent to the premiss.

In the ordinary case of *modus ponens,* we would say (on the last interpretation) that "if *p*, then *q*" is to be understood as saying "if *p*, then (attending only to cases where the consequence is implied by the premiss in accordance with truth tables or intensional meanings) *q*." It would appear, consequently, that the only difference between one kind of premiss and another is given in the bracket following the "then." But now instead of showing that abduction falls under the regular deductive form, we seem to reverse the situation, and have even the deductive form involve an operation in accord with a method, to give us the consequence of an hypothesis or rule.

December 5

Only he is religious who not only loves his neighbor, forgives his enemies, etc., but does so as one who has been "called," "sent" to do so. And one can know that he has been "called" only if he is able to attain the state of being other than God. And this he can do if, having involved himself with God in a religious community, he can take himself to represent all else (including all that goes on in the religious community) and thus to be a kind of epitomization of all else, facing God, the other of this. He who receives the call receives it insofar as he is naked, alone, yet responsible, representative of, standing for the other realities over against God. The empowering, the being sent, occurs in some involvement with God, inside or outside the dedicated community, but the fact that it is a divine empowering is knowable only so far as one knows that one is absolutely other than God.

Only he is genuinely religious, religious in his being and not for some psychological or personal reason, who as private is involved with God. And he can be private only so far as he is able to detach himself from all else. He will then be over against the rest of reality, be other than it, as one who represents God, who faces all else as that which is not God—which is what the Hindus see and stress.

December 6

I detach myself from all else in order to be involved with God. I am then defined by Him to be His representative, to be one who should act in His name. When I look toward that from which I detached myself, I then act on His behalf, seeing all else as my responsibility to deal with in His terms. Should I eventually interplay with what lies beyond, I can be said to be a religious man only so far as I continue to view that with which I interplay from a divine perspective. It makes no difference to the religious experience if the involvement with God is constituted by the act of detaching from the rest of things, for all that is wanted at this stage is that all else be seen to be the other of myself as representing something divine. If I made myself into such a representative, it is still true that the world is seen to be not alongside but the correlative other of God.

I face God as my absolute other if I stand before Him as the representative of all else. When I interplay with Him in worship, etc., I can be said to do this authentically, to be following the spirit and not merely the letter, if I do so on behalf of all else, so that what is achieved by me is then in keeping for the rest. When I turn to all else as that which with me stands over against God, I define it to be divine-like.

For the religious experience, there is nothing known about God but that He is my absolute Other in terms of which I deal with all else. It is conceivable that I gave myself the position of dealing with all else in the guise of His Other, or that He so constituted me. In the first case, I must be said to be the other of an X, which is then given religious import by the fact that I ascribe to that X the status of being the Other of myself who is acting on (what I say are) His terms. In the second case, I directly act on all else in terms which He provides by virtue of His being my absolute Other. Religion cannot decide between these cases, and does not care to, so far as action on the world is concerned, since all it wants is that divinely sanctioned acts be done. But there would be no genuine exercise of the spirit unless God were really my absolute Other, and unless I represent all else when I stand over against Him. If I give myself the role of being His Other, I ascribe to Him a power which makes Him a God for me and all else, without granting that He is a God in and of Himself.

When I am detached from the world, I am involved with God; I represent Him when I stand over against that world. When I stand over against God, I am involved with the world; I represent the world when I face Him as the absolute Other. A man who acts in the world is religious only so far as in involving himself with the world, he continues to represent God; a man who interplays with God has a religious experience of Him only so far as, involving himself with God, he continues to represent all else.

What is said here of God should have counterparts in observations regarding the Ideal, Existence, and Actuality. We must for example detach ourselves from all else to become involved exclusively with the Ideal; we then represent that Ideal, are carriers of its imperatives. And we must continue to represent it when we involve ourselves with the world from which we had detached ourselves. Also, we represent the world when we face it as an absolute Other of all else, and we must continue to represent the world when we are involved with the Ideal in obligation and duty.

These formulae point up the fact that religious and ethical men, when they behave as other men do, are nevertheless sustained by an attitude these others do not have; they take themselves to be acting in the name of something else, to be sent by what they had been involved with (though the sending is defined by what stands over against). And they can be said to be involved with these transcendentals only so far as they stand for all else, a position they can acquire only by first interplaying with all else.

The religious man who loves his neighbor differs from another who does so, not in any overt act, but as a representative of a God with whom he interplayed in an act of faith or worship. But if there is no difference in the practice why have a difference in attitude? Is it not that the religious man claims to have an experience of being empowered, and has a reason justifying this claim? He experiences a capacity to act as a divine representative when he becomes involved in his religious worship, and then sees that he must act on all in those terms. This is not possible except so far as there is a God with whom he is not involved but who is the Other of all, and thus an Other of himself as acting as His representative.

When the Buddhist turns away from the world to attend to what else there be, he faces a mere indeterminate from which he cannot distinguish himself. But were he to turn back to the world so as to act on it in terms of his enlightenment, he would in that act define the blank (to which he had tried to attend but with which in fact he interplayed) as a power to which he was giving the status of a concerned God, just so far as he acted on those others in the name of, for the sake of, or as a representative of that transcendent blank. He, with all else, would be an Other of a distinctive kind, making that blank have a distinctive nature, as a correlative.

In the religious situation, the religious man is empowered to be a representative of what is absolutely Other than himself as together with all else. It makes no difference to him if the empowering is due to the situation, to himself, or to the Other, just so long as it is the case that as he acts he is representative in fact of that Other. Similarly, in the secular situation, a man is empowered to be a representative of what he is detached from when he becomes involved with God; he does not care if the situation, or himself, or the detached world empowers him, just so long as, as one who represents all else, he is involved with God.

Just as the religious man represents God as the absolute Other, the ethical man represents the Ideal, the artist represents Existence, and the inquirer represents Actuality. All achieve some power or status when they interplay with limited forms of these modes, and find that this change can be explained by acknowledging that they represent not only that with which they are involved, but absolute forms of these. The ethical man is obligated by interplaying with the Ideal in some limited guise, and acts in the light of this obligation as the other of the Ideal in its Being. Such an otherness on his part means of course that he must represent the Ideal, not only for actualities, but for God and the other modes of Being as well.

Religion offers a reason for what one does: the change in nature acquired in the religious setting is carried out as what ought to be done by a representative of God, the absolute Other. But this that ought to be done, why should it not be taken to be what is required by the Ideal as the absolute Other? Because what is to be done is in part some benefit to the Ideal itself. We justify our wanting to realize it by saying this too is demanded of the representative of God, the absolute Other, just as we can justify our religious involvement by saying that this is in part something required by one who acts as the representative of the Ideal as the absolute Other of himself and of that with which he is involved. Or, to move to neutral territory, where the ethical requirement might be that we should enhance that on which we work, the religious requirement might be that we should respect even that which we use to achieve the enhancement. In ethics we make good the loss of the material in the larger good that ensues; in religion we affirm the value of that which has been lost or is used, as having its own final dignity.

Ethics begins with the religious acknowledgment that everything has value; religion begins with the ethical acknowledgment that value is to be preserved and enhanced. A religious love of enemy is appreciative of him as a human being; the ethical love of enemy is appreciative of what he can become. Better: The ethical man loves his neighbor because that is better than hating him, but the religious man does it because there is something lovable in him which can be discerned from the position of God.

The ethical man will try to improve the situation with his love, appreciating whatever he discerns to be of positive value there; the religious man will begin with the acceptance of something of positive value there (even though he does not discern it) and will work to make it better. If the ethical man cannot see any good in the man, his love will end at a lower level, or will require a degree of effort which is not true of the religious. From the side of truth, the ethical man will affirm that another should be loved by him though he does not see that this is the case; the religious man will affirm that he must be lovable intrinsically though he knows this only by taking the position of God.

Religion says all things have worth; ethics that they are to be improved; art that they are to be worked over so that some new value can find residence; inquiry or truth that each item is as basic as any others. From the standpoint of the last, we should say that a man is to be loved because of something in him, because he can thereby be improved, and because the outcome will be something elegant or admirable. From the standpoint of ethics, we should say that the man is to be loved because we thereby improve our relation (of intimacy) to him, improve him in making him a superior being, and improve the possible position he has in relation to us and whatever else we know. From the standpoint of art, we should say that he is to be loved because we thereby change him into one more pleasing to behold in relation to us, in himself, and as something to be known. From the standpoint of religion, we should say that he is to be loved because we see him as having worth as ethical, worth as transformed through our act, and worth as the object of knowledge. (I am now not altogether clear about these distinctions.)

A capsule statement bringing in all four approaches might clarify the issue more: If we ask religious and ethical men to love their neighbors, we can also ask the artist and the inquirer to do so. But where the religious man acknowledges something intrinsic, and the ethical man points to a good result to ensue, the artist would assert that the love itself is desirable and productive of something desirable, whereas the inquirer would say that the love is an agency for letting us know what in fact is the case.

December 7

The religious man, the ethical man, the artist, and the inquirer can all "love their neighbors" or "forgive their enemies" or "love their enemies" etc., but they all will do it in different ways, with virtues and defects not characteristic of the others. This view I think brings together all the threads of argument and suggestion I laid down these last days.

Let us use "love" as epitomizing what is to be done. The religious man attends to something latent in another, which he deals with as the representative of the absolute Other, God. He does not have in mind the improvement of the other; he does not spend time mastering the art of love; and he does not use the outcome as a means of enabling him to understand the other better. As a consequence, he may remain with the latent feature too long, may not bring about a better situation or as good a one as possible, may behave awkwardly, and may not know the other any better than before.

The ethical man has in view an objective to be realized via the love. He does not know exactly what the other is now like, he has not mastered the art of love, and he does not use the outcome as a means for enabling him to understand the other better. As a consequence, he may begin at the wrong place, may not act altogether properly, may not know the other any better than before, and will perhaps take longer and do less than he ought.

The artist is occupied with the creative act of love. He does not know what the other is like, does not have in view some desirable objective to be obtained through the love, and does not come to know the other any better because of the love.

If the religious man really means to love the other, he must recognize that he not only must love what is latent in that other, but must see that men approach that other in different, supplementary ways. All of them must cooperate if justice is to be done to the other. To insist on one's own approach is to make an idol of one's own way of dealing with him.

When then a minister goes on a protest march, he must not be supposing that he is doing what the others are doing, unless he denies his own vocation. He must take himself to be supplementing them, cooperating with them in the acknowledgment of a situation which is regrettable, but concentrating on the seeing the latent virtue, which can be known only from the perspective of God. When and as he so concentrates, he may incidentally try to become less awkward, attend to the good that should be achieved, and use his love as a means for learning what is the case, but these must never be his primary considerations.

If there are to be worker-priests, they should, while sharing in the lives of the workers, always see them as men who are not primarily to be helped, dealt with appropriately, or understood, but primarily as unique individuals whom he, as a representative of an absolute God, acknowledges to have a core that is precious, but which no one else can discern, and which even he (the worker-priest) cannot know is there except as one who has been empowered to acknowledge it.

"Love" is the religious man's term; more justice is done to the other approaches if we recognize that their terms are "duty" or "concern," "creativity" or "beauty," and "inquiry" or "knowledge." Can we now go on and say that there are different inquiries, e.g., which concern different types of men? Does the religious man inquire because and in the light of the fact that God created him or enlightened him? Does the ethical man inquire because it is a way of bringing about greater good? Does the artist inquire because it is a form of creativity? They do not do these things; but they can and ought. If so, we must say something like this: all men must love, do their duty, create, and inquire, but they will do these in different ways and with different results. The ethical man's love, as we saw before, is not like the love of the religious man; but his creativity also is not like the artist's, nor are his inquiries like the intellectual's.

There evidently are four kinds of cooperation: cooperation in love, in ethical action, in creativity, and in discovery. Each one of these will be the special concern of one type of man. The religious man will want to have a cooperation in love, though this will require him to recognize that the others will engage in this love in a way that is distinct from his. At the same time he will be willing to cooperate with others in their type of approach, always recognizing that this is subordinate to, and even subject to, his characteristic love. He will see himself in these other cooperative enterprises as giving them the incidental fruit of his more basic approach of love.

If the religious man goes on a hunger strike on behalf of flagrant injustice, it is out of a love which he hopes will be supplemented by others; in the course of that love he will incidentally act ethically and supplement the ethical acts of others, incidentally be creative and supplement the creativity of others, and incidentally come to learn more about the situation and supplement the inquiries of others. He must avoid two confusions, one with respect to the nature of his love (which is distinct from what supplements it), the other with respect to the nature of the supplements he is to offer to others (for these are to be by-products of his love, subordinate to and not intended to be alongside it).

From the perspective of the religious man, the supplements others provide are taken to be of lesser worth; but they are not so in fact. They are so from the position of the religious man (who takes his love to be primary), and from the position of the others (who take the love they engage in to be incidental or to be specializations of some more basic way of behaving). It is only from an outside position that we can say that the religious man is supplemented by and supplements coordinately in the four approaches. And what is true of him is true of the others.

The religious man loves coordinately with three other kinds of men. He sees the love they offer to be more important than the other things they do, but he also treats their offering as less important than his own. They see the supplements which he offers them to be more important than the love which he characteristically expresses, but to be less important than what they themselves characteristically provide.

The outside position from which we can say that they must supplement one another as coordinate, even while viewing one another as not doing all they ought, is one which we can obtain by abstracting from them as acts, and allowing them then to constitute a single mesh of systematically interrelated positions. To engage in an act is to disengage one of these positions and to define the disengagements from the other positions in terms of this.

The different types of men have one primary and two incidental forms of action. The religious man, for example, is primarily involved in attending to the hidden lovability, while incidentally loving and acting in the ways characteristic of the ethical, etc., men. He looks as if he were one of those other men so far as we overlook his characteristic primary activity, or treat his incidental activities as though they were primary either for himself or for others.

December 9

Poems after the Chinese:

The years rush by as driving rain
Over the frozen minutes;
Brother struggles with brother
Bruising time and eternity.

A philosopher's poem:
Truth is very near
Reach and it is yours.
Where has everything gone?

Think not of the morrow
Think not of the past
Why do you borrow?
It's better to fast.

To know is to love
To love is to know
One comes from above
The other looks below.

December 14

In the last few days I have written two one-act plays, grounding them in my understanding of one or more of the types of men I had distinguished last week—the religious, the ethical, the creative, and the cognizing. In the one I wrote first, "Chocolate and Vanilla," I tried to make evident that a merely religious man did not really know how to do justice to the other dimensions and that he does not (without some awareness of those other dimensions) know how to do full justice to the religious dimension either. The point is not made explicit but is nevertheless, I think, evident. In the second play, "Tintorobi," I tried to show the limitations of the merely ethical and creative approaches, but I think the distinctions between them are not conspicuous. I would not judge one play to be superior to the other on any other basis than their dramatic value, and of this I cannot be sure until I see them on the boards.

December 18

If the contingency of actualities be stressed, we seem driven to hold that they are oriented in Actuality, within which the other modes of Being are also to be found in a reduced form. But if instead we stress the plurality and independence of the actualities from one another, all four modes of Being can be treated as on a level, each offering a distinctive ground or way in which the actualities are interrelated. The actualities as in a space-time-dynamism are also affiliated, grouped, and defined to be equally real. The modes of Being as so functioning are here and now, not remote, obscure, recondite; they provide actual interrelationships for the actualities, and that is all. But the modes of Being are not exhausted in any *de facto* interrelationship. They must therefore have a reality outside the particular relationships that hold at any given time. They are relatively transcendent to the immanent relationship of all the actualities. But they cannot have this transcendent status without also being absolutely transcendent, for otherwise they would not be, and therefore would not be able to become immanent.

The difference between the modes of Being A] as immanent in the world of actualities, B] as relatively transcendent of them but as capable of being immanent, in different degrees at different times, and C] as absolutely transcendent as realities which can exercise this power, is a matter of status, not of remotion, or distance, or obscurity. The modes of Being are no more than different cosmic ways in which actualities are together, grounded in distinctive natures or realities. It is the very reality which is now exhibited as the contemporaneous interconnection of actualities, for example, which is able to keep them contemporaneous, and which has a distinctive nature in and of itself. The metaphysical question of the relation of the four Beings in themselves to one another is the old question of the One and the Many, and is I think dealt with rather satisfactorily (with the qualifications expressed in this present work) in chapter 10 of the *Modes of Being*.

In addition to the relative and absolute transcendence of the various modes of Being, we can also distinguish a "completive" transcendence. Here we start with the immanence of the modes of Being in a situation comprising a limited number of actualities, and refer to the modes of Being as immanent in *all* the actualities. As so immanent in all the actualities, the modes of Being are completively transcendent to themselves as immanent in only some of the actualities.

Could one take this last kind of transcendence to be sufficient to account for the prescriptive and compulsive power of the modes of Being? If this were possible, one might be able to avoid a reference to their relative and absolute transcendence by treating these as alternative expressions for the completive transcendence. If we could say that the ethical obligation which we have is nothing other than the demand of the rest of the grouping of actualities on us to become part of it, we perhaps could dispense with any reference to an Ideal Being making any demands on us—and so on for the other modes of Being. We would then be able to return to a position somewhat close to *Reality*. There would be no genuine modes of Being, but only various ways in which limited numbers of actualities were related and in such a way as to refer to the need to be together with all the rest as interrelated in a somewhat similar way. The brute force of what I have called "Existence" would be nothing other than the force of contemporaneity characteristic of other actualities than ourselves and those with which we have a vital interplay. We would have no need to suppose that there ever is a single Existence, etc., except in a most attenuated sense in which the compulsion felt by this contemporary group here would relate the group to all other contemporary actualities. One could even go with modern relativity theory and hold that the contemporaneity holding amongst other actualities was different in its meaning or value from that holding in our limited frame, while adding that we do feel a compulsion to be together with those other entities as in other frames.

I have now opened up what seems to be a genuine alternative to the position taken in the *Modes of Being*, with or without the modifications suggested in this work. It is not yet evident to me just how all the issues raised before, all the solutions offered, all the facts dealt with are to be handled on this alternative view, but for the moment I am aware of no insuperable obstacle.

December 19

Granted that actualities are united with one another in four ways —as equally real individuals, as grouped in various ways, as contemporary, and as affiliated, we have to account for the fact that each actuality and sometimes a number of them are subject to the demand that the present way of being united be altered. Can this fact not be accounted for by understanding by Actuality the demand on each actuality that it take itself to be together with others, equally individual and self-enclosed;

by understanding by Ideality the demand for a harmony of subordinate groupings; by understanding by Existence the compulsion exerted on a limited number of actualities; and by understanding by God the lure which makes one or more actualities seek to be affiliated with the rest?

If we follow this suggestion, we are faced with two further subordinate alternatives. We can suppose that actualities are only in one context and that the above distinctive roles are but ways of dealing with the actualities as belonging to that context; or we can suppose that there are four distinct contexts, but that they function with respect to actualities in somewhat like the above distinctive ways. We must take the second of these alternatives, for actualities as contemporary are not identical with themselves as affiliated, etc.

We should speak of the immanence of the four modes of Being as relating the many actualities *de facto* in such and such ways. And we should speak of their transcendence so far as the actualities as individuals are not fully integral to the context of them all, so far as their groupings are not in harmony, so far as they form pockets of interplaying items and are about to slip into the past, and so far as they have only minimal affiliations with some actualities; they then reveal the presence of demands on them. We have here only a relative transcendence, for we here make reference to Beings or contexts (or parts of them operating on other parts) only in relation to the actualities, and make no reference to the Beings in themselves. There is of course a relation to be found amongst the various contexts, but this is provided by the actualities in those contexts; each actuality is a connection between the contexts.

We have now arrived at a neo-naturalism where something like the position of *Reality* is achieved, but with some account taken of a demanded equalization, an obligating ideal harmony, a compulsive power of Existence, and a luring force of affiliation. To test this view we must see if it can do justice to the independence and togetherness of actualities; to the prescriptiveness of logic and ethics and the reality of possibilities; to the ongoing of the world, space and time, and the brutal nature of Existence; to religion and mysticism.

One problem which faced the older naturalisms has now been overcome. There was no way in which they could refer to something which was over against the actualities; they could only dislocate abstractions from those actualities or project something from them; but these do not permit a turning back on the actualities with a demand to be realized by the actualities. But on the present view, actualities in one or more contexts can be held over against themselves as able to enter into other contexts—and conversely, as not yet understood in some context, they can be understood to be in three other contexts.

The present approach, as the last sentence illustrates, converts what had been an ontological problem in the *Modes* into an epistemological issue. It is not, however, a purely epistemological matter, for a context has its own integrity, and imposes demands on actualities as surely as they impose demands on it. Though neither actualities nor context on the present view has a full reality in and of itself, both make a contribution to the single fourfold whole of actualities in a context. The actualities taken severally are all seen to have vectors toward one another; their context taken as a whole is seen to need to be for all the actualities in the maximal way that is now enjoyed by some. We have here no private individuals struggling to get into a public world any more than we have an Absolute trying to be realized; we have a plurality of real actualities in a single all-encompassed fourfold Context, but with only some actualities connected in harmony and with greater intensity than that enjoyed by others, and with the contexts therefore broken up into limited subcontexts.

December 20

Neo-naturalism is a view which, without departing from the acceptance of a universe whose only members are actualities, does take account of the fact that there is a prescriptive logic, a necessitarian mathematics, an obligating ethics, a compulsive existence, real space, time, causation, religion, theology, and even mysticism. It treats metaphysical speculation as providing scaffolding, allowing one to see what is achieved if one exercises maximum sympathy; and it finally denies the reality of the entities acknowledged in such speculation by dealing with them as simply contextual dimensions of the world of actualities. This is a position alternative to that of the *Modes*; it can be maintained only so far as one can avoid the affirmation that there are powers in the contexts which depend for their being on powers beyond those contexts.

A context is existential, so far as the location and activities of individual actualities in it are limited and directed by the rest of actualities. It is divine-like so far as any affiliations are approached from the perspective of the most intensely experienced or occurring affiliations. It is ideal in nature just so far as there is a context for all the actualities in harmony. And a context can be like what has been termed Actuality, and thus can be said to be the Being of the actualities, so far as it is a context for all the actualities as distinct individuals, over against one another.

The mystic is concerned with the achievement of a maximal affiliation with any and everything, without distinction. The mathematician is concerned with the ideal context from the position of the existential context, and thus sees the ideal context as divided into a plurality of ideal centers or possibilities. Logic provides those rules which we must follow if we are to avoid converting the distinct into the indistinct or vague, and the particular or determinate into the general or indeterminate. Religious men feel the attraction of the maximal affiliation and have a desire to give it a cosmic application.

Ethical men respond to various demands. They are alert to the meaning of obligation, attending primarily to the ideal context as not only the source of one of the demands but as that which itself must be realized. Men also meet a demand to act to increase the range of intensive affiliation, to maintain themselves as individuals over against other actualities, and to adjust themselves to other actualities. But in connection with the demands of the Ideal, they act on the others in terms of the nature of ideal context itself, as that which is to be the context for them all as making a single harmonious totality.

I seem now to have "naturalized" the metaphysics of the *Modes of Being* without losing the range which that work enabled one to master. This naturalization is the result of an act of sympathy by which full weight is given to logical and ethical prescriptions, religion, art, history, space, time, causation, mysticism, speculative and dialectical thinking, individuality, the reality of actualities and the reality of their togetherness in contexts which have distinctive natures of their own, but no reality contrasting with the reality of the actualities.

In all these cases, the contexts are *de facto* Ones *of* the Many actualities. As such they are no less real than the actualities in them. The proof of the presence of a One of the actualities is given in chapter 10 of the *Modes* to the effect that there cannot be a single Many without a One of them which enables them to be together as a Many. It is the awareness of the different ways in which actualities are *de facto* together that makes us distinguish the various contexts from one another.

None of the contexts is maximally realized. All need a better realization. Two of them, the Actuality-like and the Ideal-like (representable by the comma and the implication sign) demand the realization directly; the other two, the divine-like and the existential (representable by the dot and the therefore) make no such direct demand, but are represented by the most intense affiliation and by the rest of the universe, respectively.

We end then with the paradox that on this view God is understood to be powerless, making no demands at all, while the cosmos of space-time-causation has no unity, being essentially one in which the mass of all the rest acts on each. There will still be a transcendence of God and Existence in the sense that each is a One *for,* just so far as there is no cosmic maximal affiliation, and no complete unification of the actualities as extended and in space, time, and becoming. But we will have lost all transcendents in themselves, Ones over against the Many, or over against the Many as distinct from Ones *of* and *for* that Many.

The *de facto* contexts exhibit neo-naturalism as a "pantheism" where this term is freed from theological connotations; the contexts as not maximally realized exhibit neo-naturalism as a "panentheism" where once again the term is freed from theological connotations. But though in both guises the contexts are real, the only genuine plurality of beings that we have is that of actualities. The actualities here are beings together in four distinctive ways. These ways have distinctive reality just to the degree that some actualities are together in ways others are not.

December 21

From the neo-naturalistic standpoint, a religious man (in detaching himself from actualities as constituting the secular world in an existentialistic context) will not achieve a privacy over against those actualities; instead he will be in another context with them. Nor will he be able to engage in an act of prayer or faith, if this be viewed as a private involvement with some ultimate Being. His detachment from an involvement with the actualities in all but a divine-like context makes him one who has a sympathetic attitude toward the reality of all the other actualities. It is that sympathetic attitude which is intensified in the dedicated community, and which the religious man wants to have maximally intensified, and then with respect to every actuality. Such intensification is a process of strengthening the affiliations, an acceptance of all as finalities.

The religious man does not turn from an involvement with other actualities in the affiliating divine-like context; he continues to remain there, trying to intensify and extend the affiliations he has already achieved. He can of course turn from that context to some other. But if he is to continue to be a religious man, he will turn to some other context (say, that which is ideal-like) as a representative of the actualities with which he had been affiliated, just as he can enter into the affiliating context as a representative of the actualities with which he was involved in other ways.

The religious man is the other of all the rest of the actualities in the affiliating context only as if A] he is representative of all those actualities as in the other contexts, and B] he seeks to be maximally affiliated with all the actualities. As a representative, he is a nonreligious other; as seeking maximal affiliation, he is a religious other. As the first, he is not yet detached; as the second, he is detached from actualities in the other contexts but is already attached to them in less than maximal degree in the affiliating context. He is not yet a genuine other.

Privacy will characterize an actual man only so far as he is in the context of equalization, the Actuality-like context, for here he stands as a punctuate entity on a footing with all the others, and together with them as a mere unit being.

Is too much lost in this neo-naturalistic view of religion? We no longer have a God, an absolute Other, perfect detachment, private faith, sacral objects (except as agencies promoting one's desire or aptitude to become better affiliated). And no explanation is provided as to how a maximal affiliation operates on what is now not maximally affiliated. But none of these seem to be difficulties in principle, and merely express divergencies from views which acknowledge God to be a Being with which man can interplay and over against which he can be an other.

December 22

A philosophy should combine two rather opposed tendencies. It must be generous, expansive, sympathetic, catholic; but also cautious, critical, sceptical, analytic. If it is not the former, it will neglect or dismiss areas of interest to multitudes, tend to reduce disciplines to some favored one, and allow itself to be caught within the prevailing outlook as to just what is respectable and allowable. If it is not the latter, it will be romantic, perhaps incoherent, disorganized or confused; it will not be sharp or clear on difficult and borderline matters.

If we begin with the former, we will move toward ontology; if we spice the former with the latter, we will move toward the production of a system of ontology. If instead we begin with the latter, we will produce a context-theory, allowing only actualities to be real and then only as together; if we spice the context approach with generosity, we will make it fourfold.

A fourfold context-theory allows one to acknowledge punctuate individuals merely alongside one another, as the personalists and the Jains would be inclined to hold; it allows one to acknowledge a merging of all the individuals into a single affiliated whole, as the Buddhists hold; it allows one to acknowledge a subjecting of all individuals to a single set of standards, as the Confucists hold; and it allows one to acknowledge a togetherness of all individuals in a single space and time, as the Aristotelians hold. But it does not allow us to have a private individual who is religious, or ethical, or artistic, i.e., occupied with something which is pertinent to him, but which may perhaps not be pertinent to others unless they too achieve a privacy which is turned away from all contexts.

A systematic ontology allows for the acknowledgment of a plurality of Beings with which the individual in his privacy can be concerned. It does not give sufficient weight to the fact that actualities are together with one another, since it allows that the Beings could be detached from all involvement with actualities and be involved instead with one another. But such an ontology does some justice to the position of the Jews, Christians, Muslims, and Hindus, for all of these acknowledge the reality of individuals as sealed off from one another but as open to God; it does some justice to Kantianism, with its awareness that ethics has to do with self-legislation and men as ends; it does some justice to the intent of art, with its attempt to use individual creative powers to penetrate to the very being of Existence; and it does some justice to man's awareness of the precariousness of both individual and collective life.

If we opt for a context-theory, we minimize what can happen privately; if we opt for a systematic ontology, we minimize our status as beings alongside others. If we want to have them both together, must we combine them or have them alternatively? But if we combine them, we end with a blur. What the one denies, the other affirms: the one acknowledges Beings with which the private individual can interplay; the other acknowledges only contexts where the actualities are together in various ways. But we can move from the acceptance of either to a recognition of its limitations, then to a view where those limitations are overcome, and then (aware that this view also has limitations) back to the initial position where the view's limitations are themselves overcome. But this solution is not satisfactory. Not only does it avoid the question as to whether either one of these views is tenable, but it does not reveal how we can think of both of them.

A better solution acknowledges the ontological and the contextual views at the same time and in sequence. This can be achieved by having the subordinated criticism and sympathy expanded so as to be continuous with themselves as occupying a primary position. Thus the criticism which the ontology embodies can be made continuous with criticism characteristic of the context view, and the generosity of the context view can be seen to be continuous with the generosity of the ontology. When holding the context view, one will be aware that one is not and cannot be completely generous, and when holding the ontology view, one will be aware that one is not and cannot be completely critical. From either position, one can now try to find an equilibrium point where the two dispositions are balanced, so that neither will be subordinated to the other. This point will be one where we have less than the generosity of the ontology and less than the criticism of the contextualist; or alternatively, where we will have more than the generosity of the contextualist and more than the criticism of the ontology.

The equilibrium point can be described in a number of ways. It can be said to be the point where either position can be accepted, but only as allowing for the other as also legitimate. It can be taken as the point where the two dispositions are in equipoise, each limiting the other. Neither disposition would be exercised, for such an exercise would require that it subordinate the other. Instead, each would define a problem, the one insisting on the reality of a functioning privacy and the other insisting on the reality of contexts. Alternatively, we could adopt one of the approaches while actually living through the other. As members of a context, we would have an ontology; as private beings involved with Beings, we would have a contextual theory.

I am uneasy about these answers, for none of them tells us what is the case. But for the moment I do not know what else to say.

The last few hours, I have been typing a revised version of the education book, *The Making of Men*. But all the while I have been keeping the present problem in the back of my mind. A hopeful lead would seem to be that of taking each of the answers to make use of the virtue which is now coordinate with its own, and A] applying this to itself, B] applying it to the other, C] taking that other to use the virtue to make its alternative possible, and D] taking itself to make possible the exercise of the virtue by the other. Thus one who acknowledges the context-theory will A] take a generous approach to itself so as to make provision for all the dimensions of experience, B] acknowledge ontology as an allowable enterprise, C] see ontology as using generosity to make possible a fourfold Context, and D] see itself as making possible the generous development of an ontology with its various Beings. And one who develops a systematic ontology will 1] view it critically, 2] acknowledge the significance of an enterprise whose primary method is criticism or a rejection of ontology,   3] see the context as making possible, through a critical approach, the enterprise of ontology, and   4] see itself as that which makes possible a strong critical context.

The whole weight and value of an ontology is to make for the best contextual living, and the whole weight and value of a context is to enable one to have a private life involved with Beings. This is *4* above. We get *3* when each is appreciative of what the other does for it. We get *2* when each sees the legitimacy of the other. And we get *1* when each looks at itself exteriorly in the spirit exhibited by the other.

December 23

In theory and in fact, each view, the ontological and the contextual, sees the other as   A] that which it makes possible,   B] that which makes it possible,   C] as that which is coordinate with itself, and   D] as that which has a subordinate form of the virtue that is characteristic of itself. The context position   A] enables one to function as a private being;   B] is produced by a private being;   C] needs the Beings of ontology to oppose it in order that it might have a final being; and   D] needs to be expanded so as to be complete. A privately acknowledged ontology   A] makes it possible to have a unified complex context;   B] is produced through the use of a public language;   C] needs a plurality of particulars in order to be explicated; and   D] needs to be contracted in order to be precise.

In effect, this says that the Hegelian solution of oppositionality offered in the *Phenomenology of Mind* is only half a solution and needs a systematic ontology as a counterpart with which it can become united. In Hegel's language, there must always be substance as well as subject.

But is this solution I am offering not one biased toward the generous facet of philosophy? A contractive approach would refuse to combine the ontological and the contextual. But then it would be faced with two views, the ontological and the contextual, neither of which would acknowledge the existence of the other, and each of which would take the claim of the other to be unintelligible, to be dismissed as errors of language, as illusions, or as myths. The expansive solution I am offering knows that the contractive answer will involve two limited schemes, each with its own inexplicables, the outcome of the refusal of each view to acknowledge that the other is making legitimate claims. It sees ontology to be in no favored position so long as it does not yield to an expansive solution of the problem of how to deal with the claims of both the ontology and the context.

The expansive solution knows that each part, if taken as final, will not realize that there is another position alongside it. In compensation, it allows for the presence within itself of both answers, each taking itself to be final; it allows therefore for the contractive answer to occur within its confines. To the objection that this is but to reassert the expansive answer, and to refuse to have the contractive alongside it, one can reply that the contractive answer breaks up into two answers (one of which supports expansiveness), of which it is aware only one at a time, that both of these answers have inexplicables within them, and that neither is able to account for itself.

We end then with an ontology and a context as requiring one another, each being pursued with the same combination of generosity and criticism, but differing in that they begin at different points. The expansive solution gives a greater role to both criticism and generosity than either the context or the ontology by itself allows, since it not only sees that each attitude has a place inside the position sustained by the other attitude, but that it can be extended to cover the other position without in any way subordinating it. It sees that criticism can be made to stretch over the entire speculative enterprise as a way of refining it, and that generosity can be made to stretch over the entire contextual field as a way of enabling it to be.

December 24

From the standpoint of an expanded systematic account, both the ontological and the contextual standpoints fail to do full justice to their own characteristic virtues, and in the end defeat themselves. The ontological is not sufficiently generous, since it fails to acknowledge the contextual standpoint as one where the generosity can also be displayed; the contextual is not sufficiently appreciative of criticism, for it does not acknowledge that it can be displayed in the ontology. The ontology defeats itself in that there is a dimension of reality which it is unable to acknowledge, though its thesis is that it will acknowledge all that is real. The contextual standpoint defeats itself, because its refusal to acknowledge the ontology makes the ontology stand over against the contextual standpoint in the same dogmatic, limited, and self-centered way that the contextual view itself exhibits.

The ontology is incomplete but does not know it; the contextual standpoint is only one of two nongenerous standpoints but does not know it. The one is not generous enough, since it finds no room for the ontological; the other is too generous, since it allows for two nongenerous positions. The one is too critical, since it does not allow a place for the contextual, the other is not critical enough, since it does not eliminate an alternative to itself, and indeed by its narrowness makes room for it.

December 25

A religious man who gives himself to the work of improving the lot of fellowman makes the mistake A] of forgetting that the proper way to enter that context is from a position of an involvement with the Ideal, and B] of neglecting the demands of his own appropriate context, where he is to be acceptive of all others as belonging to one world, worthy of respect as such. If he is content to be in his own context, he will not be all that he should be, for he will then not be functioning as a representative of God, with whom he had been involved in an act of faith. Consequently he will sympathize, but will not actually forge a bond of love or other deep affiliation with other men and beings. He ought to enter a divine-like context only as one who had been involved with God and now represents Him for all the others. Such a man should have represented all the others when he faced God. He should also be aware that it is equally appropriate to deal with other modes of Being and in terms of them to enter into appropriate contexts with other men. And what is true of him is true of the ethical, the artistic, and the cognizing man.

An ethical man should come into the context of doing good works from the position of one who is obligated to realize the Ideal, and who is able to be obligated because he came to the Ideal from a context in which good was to be done to others. If he detaches that context from the ontological involvement with the Ideal, he will act properly, but not as one who is doing what he ought. He ought also to recognize that there are other contexts where other attitudes are to be assumed, and that there are other kinds of Beings with which a man could be involved.

In general, there can be A] an overconcentration on one mode of Being, B] a confrontation of a mode of Being without any connection with a context, C] a confrontation of a mode of Being from the wrong context, D] an entrance into the wrong context from the position of some mode of Being, E] a living in a context without reference to a connection with some mode of Being, F] an overconcentration on one's own context, i.e., without reference to any other context. While in one context, one must be aware of other contexts, of one's inseparability from an appropriate mode of Being, of the reality of other modes of Being, and of the fact that one's involvement with one mode of Being is conditioned by a distinctive context.

1966

The position, from which one can see the equal right of ontology and contextualism, might be charged with adopting the magnanimity which made ontology possible. But to this one can counter that the ontology is so generous that it denies itself when it asserts that one should attend to the ontology and the context severally. But now one might be faced with the objection that one is then too critical. To this it can be replied that the criticism stops soon enough to allow for the presence of critical view's own denial.

After one has completed an ontology, one might still be confronted with the objection that all its results can be expressed in a language. But to this one must answer, *1]* that there are many ways of dealing with languages, from those which take it to be a set of actual sounds, to those which take it to be a merely formal ideal structure, or a set of terms with differing colorings, or a set of unit acts; and *2]* no matter which one of these be selected, the language of ontology will be a peculiar one, unlike all the other languages, for its terms, though having beings and meanings given in the language, will also be and have meanings which cannot be understood without reference to Beings outside the language.

Whatever actual entities there be are substances which are in contrast with Actuality, and have an import with respect to one another which is dictated by the fact that each can represent all the others. If we were to find a counterpart for these substances in a language, we would forge a language of transcendental terms in which each encompasses all the others.

Actualities are in a Context with four dimensions, or contexts. In each of these dimensions, the representative actualities are related in different ways—as separate items, as implicated with one another or classified, as coordinated with one another, and as affiliated.

What is true of Actuality with its fourfold Context for the actualities which are over against it (but whose status as contingents with the power to represent all others cannot be understood without referring to Actuality) is true of the other modes of Being. Ideality, for example, has over against it a plurality of possibilities in a fourfold Context. Those possibilities, though they have meanings and beings in relation to one another, also are and behave in ways which cannot be understood without reference to the Ideal. They are delimitations of the Ideal, instantiations of it, and at the same time are capable of classifying that on which they are applied.

It is not only true that one can find a way of re-expressing in a context what is discovered in ontology (though always at the price of having a new form of context-behavior which is different from that of other languages—since it will use transcendentals, meanings, cosmically localized acts or terms of address whose weights and grammar are distinctive) but one can find a place in ontology for whatever context one confronts. A plurality of actualities cannot be understood without reference to the *being* of a Context in which those actualities have a distinctive relation to one another, expressive of the fact that they need one another.

Each of the four modes of Being faces distinctive kinds of entities in a fourfold Context; and each mode of Being offers a context for three other types of entity. We have God and a fourfold Context of spiritual unities, and a divine context for actualities, possibilities and localizations in Existence. A religious man, when detached, becomes part of the fourfold Context of spiritual unities; he can then return to this world and live in the fourfold Context for actualities. But he will function as a religious man in that Context only so far as he stays in the divine dimension, where he will, as a man, be (like a prophet) guided by what he understands of the divine, and will in fact have not his individual self as he had before, but a self which is sustained by and stands over against God.

We escape a reference to an oddly behaving language either by taking that language together with a Being which it is to express, or by attending only to items so far as they have their being and meaning determined by a Context. Similarly we escape a reference to oddly behaving particular beings—beings which truly are and come to be and pass away —either by taking those beings together with the context in which they occur, or by attending to them only in their severalty, as distinct items. If we take the second of both of these alternatives, we give up reductionism to content ourselves with a limited contextualism and a limited ontology.

January 14

The possibilities which an entity will realize are not only those that specify the Ideal. As in a fourfold Context, the entity has to face a prospect which will be vitalized in the shape of the same or other relations with other entities. When and as it is realizing the possibility of being of a certain nature, it is also realizing the possibility of being in a certain position, the possibility of being together with the others as equally real, and the possibility of having a certain dignity as a unitary being. These possibilities can all be said to be generic forms of the very relation which now connects the entity with others. Each entity then would be correctly described as not only being in a fourfold Context, but as standing outside it in the shape of a vectoral being, facing a generic form of that fourfold Context, which it then proceeds to realize by uniting itself more firmly with each of the four facets of the Context.

The generic form of the relations which connect entities can be carried by concrete objects. The perceptual object sustains the generic relationship, somewhat in the way in which the police can be said to sustain the laws that are to be carried out by the people. The relationship in its cosmic reach is similarly sustained by the modes of Being. The speculative mind knows those Beings, submits to them, and allows them to guide its understanding of the actual embodiments of the relationship. These are not blind embodiments; but if they were, the actions would still be teleological, since they would be actions governed by the generic, the not-yet-realized. They are embodiments engaged in with the effort to accommodate the relationship, and under the pressure of Beings which insist upon themselves, even on those which are not conscious of them.

January 18

I have been trying for some time now to see if I could not develop a neo-naturalism which would do full justice to the reality of prescriptions, commands, ideals, possibilities, sacred objects, and the like, but I do not think I have had much success.

The most hopeful direction seems to be that suggested in *Reality:* the various realities which are in fact contemporary can be dealt with as futures for one another. When an entity *a* is ready to act it faces other entities, *b*, *c*, etc., to which it will respond as actualizable in another concrete situation where *a* (or some modified version of it) is once again alongside *b*, *c*, etc. (or modified versions of them). The *b*, *c*, etc., as termini of a response of a readied *a* and which are to be made concrete through *a*'s activity, can be said to be the product of a generic form of the relation connecting *a* with the others, which have the roles of mere carriers of that generic form. A readied *a* therefore faces, not the entities that are in fact alongside (for these are alongside not the readied *a* but the *a* as here and now in a concrete relation with them). A readied *a* is an *a* which is disconnected from the concrete situation, and faces others as also disconnected.

This account applies to every entity whatsoever; all have to be treated as readied to act with respect to combinations of generic relations which are carried by dislocated contemporaries of the entity. In the case of the higher living beings, there can be a conscious focusing on the carrier, on the generic form which the carrier sustains, or on a combination of the two. If there is a focusing on the carrier, we have perception; if on the generic form, we have reflective knowledge of the transcendent; if on the combination of the two, we have a delimited version of the object of reflection, with which we can deal through action.

Action with respect to the entity, which is faced as a unity of present, dislocated object, and generic relation, involves the production of a concrete relation connecting the acting being with the others, no longer in the guise of carriers and thus no longer as dislocated. The relation converts the acting into a mere term for the relation. The response to what is faced is thus a production of a new set of contemporary entities. The generic relation, as specified by the carrier, is realized in the guise of a concrete relation having a specialized form of both the responding entity and that to which it responds.

This account deals with action from the position of one entity; but, of course, the other entities with which that entity is concretely related are responsive to it, so that what is realized is either a common generic form sustained and perhaps transformed by different entities in different ways, or the outcome of the realization of a plurality of different prospects. When and as the generic form is realized in the guise of a particular concrete relation, its termini are realized as concrete terms by the responding entity in interplay with that to which it responds. If entities *a* and *b* are at a distance in space, then from the position of *a*, entity *b* is transformed into a carrier of the generic "distance." When *a* responds to the carrier as together with the generic distance, the generic terms which are termini for the generic relation become realized as an *a* at such and such a particular distance from an equally specialized *b*.

When *a* and *b*, or different parts of these, confront a common prospect, they face it as that which is carried by an amalgam of *a* and *b* transformed into carriers. Where *a* is a complex being, it faces *b* as carrying the generic relation between the parts of the complex being; as a carrier *b* is then nothing other than the parts transposed and united. The food that the animal faces is, let us say, its mouth and legs united as carriers for the generic relation connecting them. But now, *b*, as a distinctive entity, is lost.

Ought we not say instead then, that *a* and *b* face *c*, which though it has a position alongside them, functions as the carrier of the relation between them, treated generically? This would mean that there would be no universal relation which one faced; the most cosmic relation would be one which was carried by one entity and was the common prospect of all the rest. But it does seem as if it were possible to have a prospect for all entities whatsoever.

If we acknowledge that both *a* and *b* can have positions similar to *c*, we can say that the concrete situation of *a*, *b*, *c* is faced with an amalgamation of all three as carriers for the generic relation uniting them in fact. Each of them can focus on a subdivision of the amalgamated three and on some limited version of the generic relation which this subdivision carries. But what does the amalgamation of *a*, *b*, *c* look like; what kind of being has it; how does a man come to know the whole generic relation which the amalgamation is supposed to sustain?

Let us consider only one entity *a*, as in a given state at a given moment. We can then say that just so far as *a* is able to retreat from the actual state so as to be able to act, it then and there attaches itself to a generalized form of the given state as carried by *a* as having another meaning. In other words, it can be said that *a* as in a given state is analyzed into   1] *a* as ready,   2] the given state as generalized,   3] *a* as having another meaning than what it is as in that stage or as ready,   4] the factor 2 supported by 3,   5] 1 as inseparable from 4. Action on the part of *a* as ready will be the specialization of 2. To be ready to act with respect to a generalized version of one's state is to be oriented toward oneself as having another meaning. If *a*, to begin with, is an intelligible or an existent entity, it will have its generalized state supported by itself as a sacred object or as an individual, or (where intelligible) as an existent, or (where existent) as intelligible.

January 19

An actuality can be said to have three dimensions: it is in a given state at a given time; it is a unity of an intelligible, an individual and an existent fragment; and it is potential. The actuality is all three of these at once; at one and the same time it is fact, being, and power. These three dimensions are not separable from one another; yet we can distinguish them, and they do stand apart just so far as we consider the actuality as that which is incipiently future.

When the actuality withdraws preparatory to acting, it sets its potentialities over against itself as in the other dimensions. Those other dimensions then constitute a situation with it. But since the potentialities have been withdrawn, and are thereby transformed into a tendency to act, the fact and the being of the actuality are also transformed. Instead of the fact in its concreteness, we then get the fact made indeterminately intelligible, vaguely individual, unanalyzably unified and fluidly existential—in short, indefinite. And instead of the being of the actuality continuing to be integral to the fact and potentialities, it is made into a carrier of the indefinite fact, and the target of the tendency to act.

No individual exists by itself; when and as there is an effort to realize the indefinite fact of itself, there is an effort to act with respect to the indefinite fact of other entities in interrelation, as carried by the beings of those other entities.

If we think of actualities as having various degrees of intimacy with one another—what I have been calling a relation of affiliation—we can say that in the course of its act to realize the unanalyzable unity of the state of other actualities, the individual is ready to act to realize the unanalyzable unity of its own state.

On this account there would be no being which was God. We would have only individual and collective states where the actualities were sacred and affiliated respectively. Indeterminate versions of these are carried by the actualities as the counterweights of the potentialities for realizing the indeterminate versions. God would be the indeterminate state which was carried by actualities and which was to be realized through the exercise of the tendency to act. He would be inseparable from other forms of indefinite states, and would be realized in definite states when and as the other forms were. We could concentrate on one form or the other, but whether we do or not, they are all realized at the same time.

The indefinite state seems then to have three distinct roles. In a part of it, it is oriented toward the separate actuality, as that which it is to make into its own state; it is the indefinite which is carried by all of the other actualities and which the separate actuality is also endeavoring to realize, by moving beyond the part which is germane to it as a state that might possibly be achieved; and it is the indefinite which relates the separate state to the state which is pertinent to all the other actualities as facing the separated actuality.

The perceiving individual brings to realization a state of himself when and as he acts toward something at a distance as that which is sustained by actualities devoid of potentialities and abstracted from their states, serving only as counterweights to the acting entity. If adumbration allows for a penetration to the potentialities of the perceived, it can occur only so far as perception involves some kind of realization of the indefinite state which the actuality confronts, for such realization yields an actual state inseparable from beings with potentialities. Perception as a confrontation arrives at an indefinite state sustained by a sheer being, and moves on, via judgment, to allow us to attend to a definite state as integral to the being and its potentialities.

We do not as a rule notice the indefinite states which in fact we are acting to realize; instead, we attend to delimited forms of these which appear for the acting being as the features of their carriers. The hungry animal confronts its prey, as that which could be chased or eaten. The being chased or eaten is a specialized version of the indefinite form of the state which the prey is in; it then becomes the target of the hungry animal's readiness to act. For the hungry animal, the prey's look or smell or move is a feature of the prey, but in fact it is the indefinite form of the prey's state, specialized by the prey which also acts as a carrier of that specialization.

In this attempt to give a naturalistic account of the transcendent aspect of the various contexts in which actualities are, there is much unclarity. But what seems clear so far is that the so-called transcendent beings are here indefinites which are being realized in the guise of relational states. What is acting (which could be all of the actualities severally) in the guise of actualities acquires distinctive states qualifying those actualities. The actualities are thereby related to one another in realized forms of the indefinites which are germane to all the actualities. God, for example, would be the actual state of affiliation which actualities have at a given time, and also the indefinite form of that state which is sustained by the actualities and can be realized through the actions of those actualities. To face other actualities not as affiliated, but as mere beings which together sustain an indefinite form of the affiliation (but qualified by them so as to have some observable guise), would on this account be identical with the acknowledgment of a transcendent God. There would, though, be no being to that God as an entity over against the indefinite state or the beings which sustain and specialize that indefinite state.

January 20

The current discussion brings me to the outcome that an actuality can be said to respond to an indefinite version of the features of that which it confronts. We respond to the "red" of an object which in fact has only one of a number of shades of red. This sounds like a mild, empirical observation, but reference to previous analyses and to the distinctions that I have made in my draft of the Presidential Address to be delivered at the December meeting of the Eastern Division of the American Philosophical Association in Philadelphia shows how rich it is, and how many problems it involves.

Each of the indefinite features can be considered as an overspecialized version of a more cosmic general nature, which is to be understood as having the essential features of what I have in the past been calling "modes of Being." This means that there are at least four distinct kinds of features with which an actuality must be said to be occupied. The position is now rather close to that presented in the first chapter of *Modes of Being*, where it was not affirmed that there were Beings with which actualities interplayed. However, it goes beyond that chapter in that it affirms that the features are sustained by the actualities as they are then and there in concrete interrelationship.

The expression "responding to an indefinite version of a feature of an actuality or set of them" is biased toward observable aspects. There should then be a counterbalancing expression to the effect that a fact is the product of the interaction of a responsive being and the indefinite feature. Here we are biased toward non-observables. In both cases, however, there is a dependence on the kind of considerations dealt with by the other. The observable is the factual, and the response and the indefiniteness are taken to be aspects of it. But they are aspects which function independently of it. If we tried to deal with them as dimensions of the factual, we would find that they behaved in ways which did not conform to the way in which the definite, here and now, factual did; they are interlocked in a tensional relation. On the other hand, the non-observable, potentially acting actuality, and its correlative prospect in the form of an indefinite feature, cannot be made intelligible except so far as one is here and now with other actualities constituting a factual world. If we tried to deal with the factual as though it were nothing more than an empty conjunction of these observables, we would find that it had a reality of its own, defying the use of the categories appropriate to the unobservables.

The factual is explained by the potential and indefinite which it presupposes; these can be treated as factual aspects only so far as their behavior is aberrational. The non-observable is oriented in the factual which it presupposes, and which can be treated as really factual only by using categories that are alien to the non-observable.

Is it possible to combine both accounts into one? Only in the sense that we enter into the domain of the factual or the non-observable and allow for aberrational cases. But we cannot enter into both domains at the same time. All we can do is to enter into one while making reference to the other as a possibility. But do we not then favor the account which stresses factuality (though in the shape of a particular outlook, even one favoring non-observables) while making a reference to another condition to which we could respond? No; because we have so far not entered into that particular outlook, so that it could be more correctly said that we favor the account which stresses unobservables, for we are confronting two possible avenues, neither of which has been chosen. But even this bias is qualified, for we entertain the two possible avenues only so far as we here and now have adopted some position which favors some fact or some unobservable.

Here and now, we either speak of responding to the indefinite feature, or of having potentialities with respect to a prospect. At the same time, we face the possibility of systematically dealing with the components from the perspective of fact or of unobservables. Each way of speaking presupposes what it cannot account for and which, if expressed in terms appropriate to the presupposed, would yield odd expressions or odd realities.

But has an account of facts and non-observables left any room for "speaking" or for a language? I think so, and in a double way. A language could be identified with the facts or with the non-observables, i.e., either one or the other might be said to have neither being nor meaning except as a unit or expression in language, or at least to have its meaning exhausted in the language. But we can also view the language as the counterpart of that with which we were concerned. The factual can then be said to presuppose language as a field in which response and indefinite features were termini; the non-observable can be said to presuppose language as a fact whose presence is to be explained as the result of a conjunction of potentialities and prospects. The second account of language allows us to deal with it as the presupposed. But then it becomes evident that it will in turn presuppose either the factual or the non-observable, and will, if it tries to accommodate these, have to acknowledge occurrences outside its control or expressions which have a different grammar from those items with which the language previously dealt.

We remain wholly with the factual if we refuse to explain how we are able to respond or how the indefinite can have a nature of its own, exerting power or influencing activity. And we remain wholly with the non-observable if we refuse to explain how there can be sheer facts having an obstinacy and a rationale of their own.

God can be said to be relatively transcendent just so far as He is the cosmic indefinite form of actual affiliations. We have no need to refer to Him as absolutely transcendent, unless we find that He has a nature and a career apart from any reference to Him. He is relatively transcendent as explained from the basis of actual affiliations; but if He is to be able to be relatively transcendent, He must be something more. We have a potentiality to respond to Him only so far as He has a Being which can, but so far is not, in relation to us. God as our absolute Other, God as making it possible for a man to be one who can respond to Him, God as that power which makes men and other beings behave in ways which cannot be otherwise explained—commitment, loving one's enemies, desire to respond—is God the absolutely transcendent, about whom we can, however, speak here and now, though not in the ways we speak about particular things.

There are two kinds of occurrences which require us to look to the transcendent for explanation: A] disconnections from the world of fact, such as the I, faith, obligation, prescriptions, otherness; and B] aberrational patterns such as exhibited by transcendent terms, terms of address, worship, agreement, commitment, etc. And there are two kinds of occurrence which testify to the reality of facts: the interrelation of items with some intimacy, even those which refer to potentialities and possibilities; and the factuality of all references, knowledge, and reports of the transcendent.

None of these shows that there is an absolute transcendent or that fact is ultimate. To get to the former, the relative transcendent must be treated as somehow one with fact, as understandable from a similar perspective, but as nevertheless allowing for some disconnections and aberrational patterns; to get to the latter, the relative transcendent must be treated as somehow one with the absolutely transcendent, as understandable from a similar perspective, but as nevertheless not able to accommodate or account for certain connections or for its own acknowledgment here and now.

The more anxious we are to avoid reference to an absolute transcendence, the more surely we must hold the relative transcendence away from the world of factuality. If instead we insist on treating it as though it were fact made indefinite, the more we will have to disconnect the I (so as to understand that whole of fact), and the more surely will terms such as God, Ideality, Existence, Actuality, Being, and their cognates have an aberrational grammar (e.g., as involving necessities or nonempirical influences and relations) to be learned only by looking toward absolute transcendents as guides to be imitated rather than cognized. To deny significance to such disconnections and aberrational patterns is to confess that one does not see how to accommodate them—which is a correct conclusion for one who refuses to allow anything which a given perspective cannot handle. But this, of course, is a gambit which can be carried out on the other side; he who accepts both the absolute and relative transcendent over against fact has no way of accounting for the factuality of his act, nor for the way in which he and his doctrines are connected with other men and doctrines. And if we dismiss these factualities as unrealities, we but repeat in another place the highhandedness of those who try to remain solely with facts and treat the relative transcendent as of a piece with it, finding no room for the meaning or grammar of disconnected items and transcendent terms.

Better: It is the disconnection of items in an immanent or factual scheme that requires a reference to what transcends this. The transcendent is relative if we start with empirical material; it is absolute if we start with a combination of the relative transcendent and the empirical. The erratic pattern in the immanent domain is due to the attempt of that domain to encompass the transcendent. Conversely, it is the connection of transcendents with one another over empirically grounded distances that requires a reference to the factual, either from the position of a relative or an absolute transcendence. The facticity of the acknowledgment of the transcendent is due to the attempt of the transcendent to encompass the reality of the immanent domain, which resists this encompassment even to the degree of orienting the confrontation of the transcendent within it.

We have then a world of interconnected factuality with an inevitable number of disconnected items, and a world of final realities with an inevitable interrelation of them in another real domain. The realm of metaphysical realities is no more distant than the being of any disconnected item, for this is inseparable from a counterweight in the shape of that to which it can respond. The realm of sheer fact is no more distant than the interrelation of others with ourselves, who are private beings thinking on the nature of the realm of sheer fact.

The traditional teleological argument faces up to the aberrational functioning of order or purpose in a supposed chance world; the traditional cosmological argument faces up to the factuality of a cosmic meaning. Neither refers to the disconnection of the individual (or anything else) from the whole. Peirce suggests something like such a disconnection in his discussion of Musement. I suppose it is behind the ontological argument of Augustine and Anselm, and behind the view of Descartes, when he speaks of the self whose idea of God is connected with the Being of God. In essence the argument is: I stand away from the rest of the world, and must so stand away in order to understand it as a whole; therefore God (I would say, together with other finalities) exists. I am able to be with God, therefore God and I are now others of one another, existing *in* and *by* ourselves.

January 21

To move to ontology from the base of empirical fact, we must A] generalize the definite until it becomes the generic form for all definites of that type; B] cosmologize it, i.e., acknowledge it to encompass all actualities whatsoever; C] acknowledge its integrity as that which is now, and can be over against oneself as a distinct being.

The third step is the most important and involves a recovery of one's privacy in detachment from the rest of the world of actualities, and the acknowledgment of some kind of insistence—compulsion, necessity, equalization, and assessment, answering to Existence, Ideality, Actuality, and God respectively. The acknowledgment of the third kind of insistence points up the fact that every actuality whatsoever must be seen to have a status outside of its context, just as surely as the individual's ego does. The difference between an inanimate entity and a speculative man is not a difference in status, but in the kind of activity they engage in as detached, the former then having no recognizable activity, the other having one involving understanding, submission, acceptance, identification, etc. (Conversely, a confrontation of Beings is imbedded in a plurality of contexts, and thus is subject to conditions which particularize and perhaps distort.)

Every actuality is eccentric in that it has a being of its own, and as such has a transcendental import, just as surely as the ego does. And if the term "ego" is a transcendental, we must also say that the name of any actuality, so far as it designates it as a distinct entity, is a form of transcendental address, requiring the entity's relations and interplay with other distinct entities to be dealt with in the light of the way in which it is related to what lies outside their common context.

We have then two kinds of transcendentals: those which refer to the actualities as distinct (and therefore relate to those actualities as involved with the indefinites beyond them), and those which refer to those indefinites themselves. "An actuality," "substance," "ego," "individual," are transcendentals of the first type, whereas "Existence," "God," "Being," are transcendentals of the second type.

The easiest way for most men to move to metaphysics, I suppose, would be by a consideration of space or time. The acknowledgment of these as cosmic and yet not exhausted by any set of actual occurrences would leave us with them as mere functions of the things that are related, abstractions derived from actual limited spaces and times, unless one could show that they were correlative to our separated selves (which is what Kant in a sense does when he contrasts them with the categorial forms of judgment) and that they had a distinctive integrity, say in the form of a distinctive rhythm or geometry (which Aristotle would not allow, since for him, time is the number of whatever motion there be, and there is no space, but only a place whose "geometry" is determined by whatever there be in it). Because the Aristotelian cannot grant the time and space a genuine being or a status as dimensions of some genuine Being, he cannot get to ontology by this route; his way is via the acknowledgment of substances, i.e., of actualities as distinct which need a reference to Actuality (which Aristotle calls God, who in the guise of the unmoved mover is a substance somewhat like actualities) as that which equates them as equally real.

January 24

"Individual" has at least five distinct meanings. It may refer to the distinctive intelligible nature, involving ego, character, emotion, and experience; it may refer to a distinctly located entity in space, time, or process of causation; it may refer to a center of rights and dignities, a being infinitely precious and induplicable; it may refer to an active, substantial being which is together with other similar beings, or their derivatives; and it may refer to that which is finally real. The last two are difficult to keep apart, since they refer to the individual as together with others and thus as subject to Actuality as immanent, and to the individual as over against all others, but as oriented with respect to Actuality as transcendent.

When we say of an actuality that it is real, we are not then viewing it as something on a footing with us. Instead, we are ascribing to it an indefinite, uniquely flavored, all-encompassing feature which we recognize so far as we are detached from the world where we are together with the actuality. Our action with respect to it, turns it and us into entities which are together in a way somewhat similar to that which prevailed before.

January 25

Faced with possibilities, the individual actuality makes itself a member of a class with others; faced with existents, it makes itself be in an extended relation with others; faced with sacred objects, it makes itself be in an affiliated relation with others; and faced with realities, it makes itself be in situations with others where it retains its distinctiveness but is encompassed in some kind of whole. In the discussion about individuals yesterday, I referred to the actuality as facing various prospects and to it also as making itself into a unit in a situation. Evidently three cases were there omitted: the individual as in a class, as at a distance, and as affiliated.

When the actuality faces others as realities, it is a detached entity. It acts to realize the prospect of itself as real when it moves toward the realization of the reality of others in a situation with itself. For a reflective man, the reality which is oriented in particular actualities has a nature of its own; when he attends to this, he sees that all of the actualities, while being made into parts of limited situations, are also parts of one single situation in which all actualities are. The acknowledgment of that cosmic generic reality allows one to see that all of the actualities are in a single Actual situation, the cosmic generic reality being in fact Actuality as it transcends all situations.

The self-identical individual is directed toward others as sacred, real, etc.; it could also be identified with reality, etc. It is directed so far as it is occupied with particular actualities; it is identified so far as it has managed to achieve the position of a speculative mind. At every moment, the individual realizes itself as somehow together with other actualities, as the outcome of its action directed to the realization of the real which is carried by some or all of the actualities that there are.

January 26

If the various contexts or ways of being together of the actualities be described in terms of the dot, comma, horseshoe, and therefore, the current discussion shows that these are the result of a determination of indeterminates carried by the actualities which some given one is responding to. These forms of togetherness are distinct from those which connect the indeterminates (or speaking more ontologically, the modes of Being).

Might it not be the case that the different modes of Being carry an indeterminate form of "Being as such," and that this is realized through the actual interplay of the various modes of Being? One need not suppose that the "Being as such" has an independent reality, for there is no evidence that it exerts a force, a compulsion on the Beings, though this seems to be the case with respect to the indeterminates which transcend those that the actualities sustain. The connections amongst the modes are barren, without sensuous features, extension, binding power, incapable of constituting situations, whereas those amongst actualities have such features.

January 30

Lulled by Plato and Aristotle, I have too often assumed that the Ideal which we strove to realize was, when related to man, identifiable with the Good. But again and again, I recognized that the Ideal was to be identified with the domain of the possible or rational, and that the Good was a transcendental.

It is necessary to distinguish the prospect which an actuality faces from the kind of outcome it achieves. It faces a fourfold prospect enabling it to be rational, positioned, to have dignity, and to be an actuality. All of these are realized at the same time in the shape of limited structures or meanings, places, rights, and self-centeredness. The conjoint realization of them in harmony is the achievement of the Good; this is correlative with a fourfold achievement of Existence, unity, and reality.

Reality, Good, Existence, and unity are results which were not aimed at, except in the sense that the actuality strives to be in equilibrium with respect to the prospect it is occupied with realizing. Each of these transcendentals points to an ultimate mode of Being. The Beings as relevant to actualities are faced as prospects and are realized as structures, places, etc.; as in themselves the Beings are referred to through the combination of these realizations.

It is no longer necessary then to speak of the Ideal having to be kept exterior, or being guaranteed realization by God. If God is necessary to guarantee anything, it would be the achievement of unity on the part of an actuality which is faced with the fourfold prospect of being rationalizable, placeable, with dignity, and possessed of individuality. The evidence of God would be provided, not by the fact that the Ideal was made exterior or relevant as the Good which actualities are to realize (which is what I contended in the *Modes* and subsequently), but by the fact that the actuality was unified. This now seems like the indirect proof of the *Modes of Being*, where universals ingredient in actualities provided evidence for the action of God, but not for His nature. If we wanted to find the analogue of 4.18 and/or 4.19 of the *Modes of Being*, we would have to deal either with the Good as a transcendent, one of whose components was a realization of a divine-like prospect, or with the Ideal to which that Good referred.

An actuality as a unity is one with itself as the absolute Other of God (the absolute Other). To deal with subordinate possibilities, in a parallel way, we would have to say that there is a kind of unity which possibilities have and which enables them to be absolute Others of God as well.

The arguments for God in the *Modes of Being* suffer from various defects. A] They start from actualities and not from Actuality. B] They deal with Ideality, not by itself and as there bearing testimony to a divine action producing a result which is like God, but with it as related to actualities. C] If they are to be allowed to deal with actualities as providing testimony, they should consider possibilities and portions of Existence as doing this as well—or conversely, if Existence be treated as a mode of Being which, by virtue of its opposition to its own essence, needs God and thereby in fact testifies to Him, we should deal with Actuality and Ideality as somehow having acquired some feature from Him.

Some time ago I suggested that God enabled Actuality to stand away from actualities, and enabled Ideality to stand away from its possibilities. In any case, the kind of evidence that these modes of Being would offer for the reality of God is different from the kind of evidence that actualities provide, either by virtue of their dignity or sacrality, or by virtue of the unity they have through the harmonization of the sacrality with intelligibility, location, and individuality.

Positively stated: actualities face a fourfold prospect, which is an indeterminate version of the fourfold Context in which they in fact are. In realizing that prospect in the shape of a fourfold factual state, they incidently realize transcendentals which refer to absolute versions of the components of the fourfold prospect. Each of the components of the fourfold prospect is faced in independence of the others; otherwise there would be no problem of harmonization of them with a more or less successful exhibition of the transcendentals, unity, etc.

Actualities then not only feel the force of the modes of Being when and as they face the fourfold prospect, but in their realization of the prospect produce transcendentals which refer to that which controlled them.

January 31

Are the transcendentals realized independently of one another? They should, since they are related to distinct Beings. Each Being sustains the fourfold Context in a distinctive way, and when the Context is realized in the guise of the actual states of affairs in which the actualities are, the actualities realize the Beings in the guise of transcendentals that refer to those Beings.

Do the transcendentals realize some kind of possibility? They must, for whatever will be can be, and what can be is a possibility. It is, of course, not a possibility in Ideality, for that would make Ideality and the other modes of Being subdivisions of Ideality. It is a relative transcendent inseparable from the prospect which the actualities face as indeterminates sustained by one another or by the totality of actualities.

The four modes of Being are realized in the guise of transcendentals. Is the togetherness of the transcendentals a possibility in some sense? It must be, if what will be must first be that which can be. It is the possibility "Being" which is inseparable from the Beings as involved with the prospects which the actualities face. This "Being" is more indeterminate than any of the Beings, and seems to have no power at all. The relatively transcendent Beings exhibit power, but neither the fourfold prospect nor the "Being" inseparable from the meaning of the relatively transcendent Beings exhibits power. The power which the relatively transcendent Beings exhibit is one which is derived from the modes of Being themselves, as absolutely transcendent.

The actuality, on withdrawing from a given state, faces the fourfold prospect. In order to be able to face that prospect, it should be in a position to confront the relatively transcendent Beings. These involve some kind of compulsion on any attempt to realize the fourfold prospect. The actuality has a being in and of itself only so far as it stands over against the mere "Being" which is inseparable from the relatively transcendent Beings. That mere "Being" is realized as the singularity of the combination of the four transcendents which refer to the Beings from which mere "Being" is inseparable.

On this account we can say that an actuality is an absolute Other, not of God, but of "Being" as such. It will be the other of God only so far as God represents all actualities and the other modes of Being, or so far as the actuality represents everything else. Apart from such representation by God or self of all else, an actuality will be concerned with a divine prospect of affiliation, a relatively transcendent "possibility" of a sacralizing power, or an absolutely transcendent Being which is a specific locus of an indeterminate "Being" that in fact has no other reality than that of being the common indeterminateness of all the specific loci of it.

"Being" as such, which is realized in the guise of the conjoint presence of four transcendentals in an actuality, is a "can be," something like that of the fourfold prospect. Apart from the four modes of Being it has no reality, being only the product of a generalization or neutralization of different realities. It is, but only so far as it is inseparable from the Modes of Being, which give the relative transcendentals, lying beyond the fourfold prospect, their power.

Only the four modes of Being (and their independently functioning subdivisions) are finally real. The fourfold prospect is a generalization of the state in which actualities are at a given moment, and is at once carried by actualities and empowered by the relatively transcendent Beings. The relatively transcendent Beings are relativized versions of the modes of Being and exist only as such empowered versions. "Being" is a prospect constituted by the four modes of Being together, and is realized as the singular union of the transcendentals which refer to those modes of Being.

Just as we need not conceive of a possibility "the pair x and y" on a footing with the possibility "x" and the possibility "y," but yet must acknowledge it to be possible, as that which is in fact realized when we realize both the possibility "x" and the possibility "y," so we must conceive "Being" to be a possibility which is not a possibility in the sense that the modes of Being are possibilities for realization in the guise of transcendentals. "Being" is a constituted and sustained possibility, having no other being or power than that which it obtains from the more basic modes of Being.

February 2

Over the past months, I have had in the back of my mind the idea of writing a philosophy book for youngsters. It is in the attempt to formulate my views in such a way as to communicate with them that has led me again and again to epitomize my entire outlook, particularly as having an empirical or naturalistic base.

The individual faces the world about him as A] that which he would like to understand but which, on understanding, he finds to be subject to the restrictive demands of logic, mathematics, proof, etc.; B] that with respect to which he wants to act, but under the restrictions imposed by some force; C] that with respect to which he takes an attitude of sympathy or appreciation, but subject to various commands or considerations respecting the dignity of others; and D] that with respect to which he wants to be on a footing as an individual, but under conditions which define him to be real together with them. The attempt to discover the source of the demands, force, commands, and conditions is the attempt to move away from that which one confronts to what makes it possible. Such a movement alights on what is to be faced as answering to one's value, existence, unity or reality, all making up a final singularity.

Might it be possible to introduce a child to such a scheme by attending to the fact that what it confronts is an arena of action? What is a wheel? Something to roll. What is a shoe? Something to put on or take off, to tie, to kick with, etc. But then we should ask: "Don't you kick a balloon in a different way than you do a basketball?" "What is this which is different in them?" "Is it not force, compulsion, power, in one degree here and another there?" "Is it not the world in which we are trying to fit (and which we are accustomed to call by such names as 'nature' or 'Existence')?" "What is this Existence by itself, apart from the way it is expressed as force here and there?" "Is it not space-time-causation?" "And is it not known by our looking beyond the particular things to something they all have in common, but as being there even if there are no particular things?" "When I see myself as an existent entity do I not point to that Existence?" "And do I not, as that existent entity, encompass an intelligible, real, significant extension?"

Some such development, put in concrete terms, with clear illustrations, would be the substance of what I would try to convey. But for the moment, I still feel far from being able to make the first step, in part because this epitomization is not altogether in sure focus, and in part because the vocabulary for references to mere Existence, space, extension, etc., is too abstract.

February 9

I sent off my *The Making of Men* about a week ago and haven't had an idea since. I have no notion about what I want to study or write about. Last night while listening to Nathan Millstein playing Beethoven's only violin concerto—which I did not particularly like, though most of the audience apparently did—I returned to an idea with which I had been toying on and off. I decided then to try to give a philosophic account of sports.

One of the main tasks in a philosophic account of sports is that of classifying them. An obvious set of divisions is by skill, speed, endurance, and contests. Skill relates to some capacity to manipulate, and defines a sport by itself when treated as involving a single individual and requiring little exertion—e.g., fly casting, gymnastics, bowling, canoeing, and shooting. Speed involves acting within a well-defined spatial limit and attempting to decrease the time spent in traversing it. Endurance pits the stamina of the individual against time; it endeavors to determine the capacity of the individual to continue until some goal is reached or until he arrives at some temporal end, beyond that at which men normally stop. Contests involve the interplay of men individually or in groups with one another. They may of course involve speed, skill, and endurance, separately or together. But they also bring in an element of cooperation, even when there are only two individuals involved, for the sport cannot continue except so far as each is allowed his role and perhaps sustained in it.

Another mode of classification would attend to the aspects of the individuals that are involved. We have sports, such as chess and checkers, poker and bridge, which make use of mental faculties—mind, imagination, shrewdness, memory, daring—unaccompanied by any but elementary and minor bodily functioning. We have others which involve the entire body—wrestling and swimming; the legs—walking, running, jumping, skating, skiing; the arms—shot put, hammer throw, weight lifting. But there are many muscles which one sport will ignore and another utilize; a complete roster of possible sports would take care of all the muscles. Sports such as football, baseball, basketball, soccer, and bull fighting, involve the entire individual, though putting a primary emphasis on only some of the individual's powers. But other sports, even those which seem to involve only the legs or the shrewdness of the individual, cannot be treated as though they had absolutely no bearing on other parts of the individual.

These two kinds of classification—according to the facet of man that is being tested, or according to the power that he is using—should be related. Thus one might speak of a sport involving a skillful use of the arms—lassoing; a speedy use of the arms—boxing; an enduring use of the arms—weight lifting; and a contest involving the arms—tug of war, fencing. But there is much overlap here; the principles of classification are not altogether satisfactory.

It would not be amiss to list the major sports given in an encyclopedia of sports: angling; archery; automobile racing; backgammon; badminton; ballooning; baseball; basketball; bicycle racing; billiards; birling; boating—canoe, ice, motor, yacht; bobsledding; bowling—duck pins, lawn, ten pins; boxing; bullfighting; canoeing; checkers; chess; cockfighting; codeball; cornhusking; cricket; croquet; cycling—bicycle, motor; darts; dicing; diving; dog racing; dominoes; fencing; fieldball; figure skating; firearms—pistol, revolver, rifle, skeet, trapshooting; fishing; flycasting; football; fox hunting; gliding; golf; gymnastics; handball; hockey—field, ice; horse racing, harness horse racing; horseshoe pitching; hunting; hurling; jai alai; jujitsu; lacrosse; logrolling; battle royals* (starred items were listed under Miscellaneous Sports); bull riding*; chinning*; club swimming*; diving*; duck calling*; El Gato*; faceslapping contests*; fish fights*; frontentis*; horseback riding*; horse jumping*; lotto*; mountain climbing*; purring*; rope skipping*; roulette*; rowing*; running—backwards, cross country, in sack, three-legged*; soap box derby*; spelunking*; throwing*; walking on hands*; water skiing*; woodchopping*; woodsawing*; wrestling—belt, fingerhooking*; paddle tennis; pigeon racing; ping pong; platform tennis; playing cards; polo—horse, roller, water; quoit pitching; racing—airplane, bicycle, etc., dog sled, etc.; racquets; rodeo; roping; roque; rowing; rugby; sculling; shuffleboard; skiing—downhill, jumping, slalom; soaring; soccer; softball; squash—racquets, tennis; swimming; tennis—court, lawn, paddle, racquets, table; track and field; trapping; trotting; volleyball; walking; weight lifting; yachting.

There is some overlap here, and there are places where distinctions should have been made—e.g., track and field covers a number of different sports. But the list can serve as an initial test for our initial classifications.

February 10

Another classification of sports: spectator sports, such as greyhound racing and cock fighting where there may or may not be previous preparations and training, and where men do not participate; direct participative sports, e.g., wrestling, boxing; combination sports, where men are conjoined with one another or with some animal to constitute a single functioning unit, e.g., in a tug-of-war or polo team; complex sports with the individuals having distinctive roles, e.g., in baseball, football, rugby; agency sports where men use devices of various kinds in order to produce a result, e.g., rifle shooting and automobile racing.

This new classification, like those of yesterday, is not grounded on any clearly understood principles.

February 11

The participant in a sport exercises his will in an habituated way, achieved through training and discipline, as an agency of control, or as a means of committing himself. The first enables him to acquire a style and achieve smoothness in performance; the second determines his accuracy and precision; and the third enables him to endure and to stretch himself to the breaking point. He must combine these uses of the will with a practical judgment which tells him when and where to act, modify, advance, or retreat. The spectator, in contrast, identifies himself with the participant; he is primarily emotional and finds that he is purged in the process of the participation.

The spectator of a sport is distinct from a spectator in a drama, despite the fact that sports are sometimes exciting, and that in both places the emotions are purged. The purgation of the drama-spectator is prearranged; there are definite positions where he is to be excited and satisfied; also he is to identify himself with each of the characters and not merely with one of them. In the sports, the climaxes and the purgations come as the sport develops; they are sudden. The identification of the spectator is with one side as opposed to another—and the sides could be defined by animals, or even by nature in relation to an animal or to man.

The practical judgment shown by the participant in the sport is somewhat analogous to that exercised by men in law, business, and everyday affairs, except that in the case of sports the judgment must as a rule be made quickly in climactic situations, which appear unexpectedly. He is therefore closer to a soldier or officer in the midst of battle, even in such a quiet game as chess.

The use of the will to commit oneself entrains the virtue of fortitude; the judgment that is required is essentially what the medieval called "prudence," a union of mind and body in a practical situation. The two together define the participant as a dedicated man who understands where the main joints are, and is ready to act with respect to them as a trained individual who has his body under control.

February 12

The athlete and the craftsman are quite similar. Both have to be trained and disciplined until they have good habits and a style; both must exercise control so that accuracy and efficiency are secured; both are committed to bringing about something excellent. The craftsman, however, does not as a rule face crises. But one may well conceive of him doing so; one can imagine, for example, a maker of a bow stretching himself to the ultimate limit in order to make it bend as it had not been bent before with such and such a wood. If craftsmen can face crises which are like those that some athletes face, the difference between them will be at most one of degree unless some other consideration can come into play.

The craftsman has an objective in view; he makes something excellent for a purpose. Though he may himself be involved in the process and may even be caught up emotionally (though this does not often happen), he nevertheless attends to the object made as serving a purpose beyond itself. The athlete instead is a craftsman of play, or better perhaps, a maker who is a self-maker. The craftsman may make himself to some degree, but this is incidental; his attention is focused on the work and the end it is to serve, whereas the athlete is one of the items that is being made.

An athlete might think of himself as one who is entertaining the crowd or who is working for a boss, or for honors, etc., but if his activity is tailored for such ends, we speak of him as an entertainer rather than as a sportsman. A sportsman can, of course, have moments where he entertains, but his activity as a whole will not be directed toward the entertainment, but toward the situation in which he is tested and transformed, either alone, or together with a transformation of something or someone else.

February 19

I mean what I say; that is, I am trying to tell the truth; what I am saying, I am claiming to be true.

I do not mean what I say; i.e., what I say is less than what I intend to convey and in fact do convey. Every judgment, of which the saying is an expression, has a twofold unity which is not said. It is united on the side of the subject as that which he asserts or claims, and on the side of the object as the adumbrated counterpart of his unity.

I say what I mean; i.e., what I mean, the particular, the experiential, the existential, the sensuous, etc., is now expressed in the form of a judgment or a saying. What I mean is not changed into a saying, but the saying is the saying of what I mean.

I do not say what I mean; I mean the particular, the singular, and this I am unable to express in terms of universals, etc.—the point that Hegel makes. This which I mean though is something that I can say, though when I say it there is always left over something meant but not said, and something said but not meant.

A family is "natural," as that which perfects man. This is the view Aristotle takes. But he does not make evident in a way that is plausible today why it is that a man allows himself or why he wants to be more or less permanently attached to a woman—or why a woman wants to be this with respect to a man. On his account, the woman is always subject to the man and he needs her for "psychological reasons," while she needs him to rule her. It would be better I think to say that each finds the other somewhat strange, that they are able to look at one another with sympathy and yet critically, because there is an area where they do not compete, since they are oriented toward different things (public affairs over against the family, the impersonal world of interchange over against the home, etc.), and that each permits the other to be unbuttoned without danger of being destroyed. These of course are ideal cases, and individual men and women do in fact sometimes not provide these benefits. But what I am suggesting is that there is some awareness of these benefits dimly before them, though they may never focus on them because prevented by the driving demands of sex, the need for companionship, the effort to imitate one's parents, by social custom, law, and the need to be supported. But these are not basic conditions for the establishment of a permanent relationship; sex, for example, can often be satisfied better outside the familial situation; companionship is perhaps better provided by those of one's own sex; the imitation of one's parents can be in other roles than in the parental; social custom and law have themselves to be explained as perfecting men, and the reason why they should support a permanent relation between man and woman would have to be explained.

Why are children wanted? Is it because one wants to see if one could do a better job than one's parents had? This is Robert Thom's suggestion to me. There may be some element of truth in this, but I think that the primary reason is a more forward-looking one. The child allows us to see what innocence is; it allows us to watch it unfold without its being aware that it is observed. But these reasons seem to depend on more calculation and reflection than is characteristic of most men. Is it not that there is some feeling of loneliness or incompletion that the man and woman find in one another, some incompatibility of rhythm and temper for which the child is the answer? Malinowski would oppose such a view; according to his account of the Trobriand Islanders, they do not relate the having of children and sex; they think the children come as it were by good fortune. But the question is still open whether or not they want the children, and why. It is compatible with the present hypothesis to say that the Trobriand Islanders want children for the same reason that the rest of the world does, but that they think that this is to be achieved apart from sexual involvements.

February 20

In *The World of Art*, I say that "Play is self-contained activity without serious or definite purpose productive of . . . pleasure . . . an expressive use of energy . . . exhibiting a spontaneity . . . detached from any interest in what lies beyond." I then go on to say that a child or a puppy plays, but that an adult does not. What I did there, evidently, was to choose one of many meanings which the term "play" has, in the attempt to separate out the nature of games and sports (the one taken to be play subject to rules, the other to be games in a social context) and to isolate the factor of spontaneity in a *work* of art.

When we turn to games and sports, the meaning of "play" seems to be different from what it is in connection with the arts. "To play a game" or to "play at a sport" involves a subordination of the spontaneity of play to the rules and the context. The artist has a genuine moment of free play in his working, whereas those involved in games and sports do not. We ought to distinguish "free play," "playing in" a game, and "sharing in" a sport.

It seems correct to say that a game is play subject—or more sharply, subjected—to rules. But sports seem to be more than games in a social context. There should be a reference to some commitment, to the necessity for training, to the exercise of skill, to the fact that the individual is put to the test, and that he at once makes something and himself. This, it must be confessed, is a comparatively new meaning, and one which exists alongside another, almost synonymous with "play." The word "sport" itself is a derivative from "disport" and carries a strong overtone of "frolic," "make merry." The present meaning seems closer to what had once been inseparable from "game," where the stress is on competition and winning. Over the course of centuries, we have in effect come to treat a game as less serious than a sport, and to view "free play" as without any serious import at all.

Sports are exhibited in the form of games. Here "game" means some particular instance in which the pattern or nature of the sport is presented. "Sport" then has a generic meaning, specified in a plurality of games. It is like habits, training, intent, purpose, which are generic features made manifest in the guise of specific acts. If we accept this, we must say that the game makes manifest a commitment, allows one to put to the test the excellence of one's training and skill, and offers an occasion for making oneself while producing something graceful or otherwise desirable.

On this last interpretation, the game would be an instantiation of a sport which was participated in through the instantiation of the responsiveness to the pattern of the sport. These instantiations would encompass play, but would always keep it subordinate.

February 21

I mean what I say has two senses;   1] what I intended to express I did express;   2] what I convey I intend to convey. The first refers to the truth that I must speak in universals, and that I accept this fact. The second refers to the truth that what I confront is a unity, and that though I express myself in terms which are universals, they do make a unity by virtue of my unifying judgment, which refers to the adumbrated unity before me.

I say what I mean also has two senses;   1] my expression does justice to what I understand;   2] my expression does justice to the reality I am judging. The first refers to the fact that I understand in terms of universals, and that the expression answers to this. The second refers to the fact that my expression is a unity which answers to the unity that I adumbrate when I judge.

Hegel and the linguistic analysts all seem to take only the first of these senses. But if we expand their views to include the second as well, do we not return to some form of language philosophy or other variant of an objective idealism and its coherence or consistency theory of truth? No, because we cannot acknowledge the language as encompassing a plurality of words without going outside it to the unity which judges and the unity which is judged, or which is adumbrated in the judgment.

We play in a game, engage in a contest, and participate in a sport. Playing the game involves some spontaneity, but since the game is a sport-event it makes one subject to the rules which define the sport. By playing in the game, we participate in the sport. It is possible, of course, to play in a game without participating in a sport—e.g., a game made up on the spot. A sport has records, traditions, rules; a game may not. A contest is a test; it is occupied with victory, the demonstration of superiority. This is also done in games, both those which are and those which are not parts of sports; but the primary object of the game is not winning.

Contests are not college activities, if the latter are to be defined as having character building and the production of a gracefully achieved outcome as their aim, unless the contest is used solely as a measure of progress, skill, readiness, and the like.

February 22

The gambler sees games and parts of games as contests. He commits himself to some outcome by putting up something valuable. In some cases, he is able to exhibit memory, understanding of human nature, shrewdness, and even skill. In all he must depend in part on luck and good fortune—the latter being luck which is thought to be providential, having some concern for the gambler, and testifying to his being distinguished from others. When he is so distinguished, he feels himself to be in possession of some signal quality which (though he may not be able to isolate it) he thinks provides the reason why he is the object of good fortune.

A run of good luck is soon taken to be a sign of good fortune, and thus to provide the gambler with an assurance of his signal worth. If this be correct, it is perhaps right to conclude that the gambler is a man who is unsure of himself and seeks the assurance which good fortune provides. Some of the evidence for this conclusion can be obtained from the gambler's attitude towards money, or whatever else that is valuable that he uses to express his commitment. Though he lives a life gravitating around money, though he depends on his gambling to provide him with his necessities and luxuries, and though he needs money with which to gamble further, he rarely holds on to his money. He lets it go in part because it came so easily, and in part because he thinks of himself as a man of good fortune who can get more money in the very way in which he had obtained this.

There are men who gamble but who are not gamblers. These are in a sense investors who try to judge or guess some outcome in the attempt to improve their financial situation. They have less interest than the gambler in style of play, and are usually without preparation or understanding of the nature of the game. Both, though, are interested primarily in outcomes; they are not participants except in card games and games of chance; but even here, though they may find excitement in the course of the play, the focus is on the outcome of the contest where it is decided whether or not they have won or lost, and how much.

Since there is perhaps no game in which some factor of luck does not enter, it is inevitable that one engaged in a game will share something of the spirit of the gambler, and take a run of luck to mark him as someone favored. The player, though, exerts himself and makes himself while trying to produce a good game. Even in a card game, there is a difference between an expert amateur and a gambler. The latter, because concerned primarily with the nature of the outcome, may cheat, take undue advantage, or take himself to be at the moment an object of ill fortune; the former, who may play no better or worse than the other, will be more self-critical and try to determine what he is doing that is wrong.

The gambler has a confidence which the non-gambler does not, since the latter is willing always to take some of the blame on himself. A gambler, of course, can notice errors that he has made, and a non-gambler can hope for a run of luck, but the gambler sees the errors as slips, and the non-gambler sees the run of luck as supportive and adventitious, and not something to be looked for or even hoped for.

We speak of those who take risks in order to obtain some gain as "taking a gamble." If the risk is not reasonable, we have something close to gambling as a form of investment; if the risk is reasonable, and grounded on a knowledge or experience which shows a good likelihood that the reward will be forthcoming, we have something close to professional gambling, where the "risk" lies only in the uncontrolled and un-predictable acts of fortune. He who is taking a gamble looks to fortune to provide propitious circumstances which are to so structure the con-tingent world that the risk will be shown to have been worth taking.

February 23

It is often said that sports provide a nonviolent expression of hostility. Such a view does not take account of the fact that sports also often involve cooperation, loyalty, and sacrifice, that they provide a test, give one a pleasure in winning, and allow for the expression of relief, joy, justice, courage, and judgment. It would be better I think to view sports as an effort to determine human limits, to find out who one is by being pitted against well-defined situations. This of course applies pri-marily to the participant in the sport. The spectator, however, can be thought to be embraced by this view when consideration is given to his initial identification with the athlete or side. He then does not, of course, come to know his own limits; but he comes to know the limits which other men face, and can know this in a crisis situation—which is what is missed by those who know about sports only through the reading of newspaper reports or record books.

One can treat sports in a way that is somewhat analogous to the arts, by viewing them as aimed at the embodiment of the ideal in the shape of character, where this is understood to be an habituation of mind and body in harmony, for the mastery of what can be humanly mastered. The will is then fixed at certain ends in the service of memory, judgment, skill, speed, endurance, severally and together in various combinations.

Juggling is a skill; it becomes a sport and thus is expressed in games or gymnastics only when it has a tradition, records, rules, and there is not only a commitment to do well, but some awareness of a benefit to the in-dividual.

It is evident that I am still in the dark regarding the fundamental questions of sports—classification, motivation, structuralization, the kind of function they have, and their relation to other enterprises. All these need much more clarification and explanation.

February 26

A game can be viewed as an event in history which involves prior training or knowledge, has been separated from antecedents and consequents, is subject to rules, and is aimed at improving men through a graceful or superior performance. Similarly, we can say that technology is a form of action which has been dominated by knowledge, involves planning regarding the future, controls a limited portion of existence, and separates off a humanized realm; that leadership is a form of politics which involves superior knowledge, an ideal objective, a human realm, and men in their individuality; and that public worship is a dedicated community governed by ritual, has an idealized creed, is separated from the surroundings, and makes a man attend individually to God. In all these cases, we have a public domain occupied in terms which character-ize private experiences.

In some games men test themselves. They see how much they can en-dure, how strong they are, how precise they can be, and how rapidly they can respond. They see how long they can survive under certain condi-tions, how much they can lift, how accurate their eye and hand, say in casting, and how quickly they can coordinate, say in skeet shooting. In other games men define an area (hammer throwing) or see how far they can reach (archery, shooting with pistols, shot put). They can be said to be occupied here primarily with exhibitions of strength, accuracy, or speed, or combinations of these. Men can also be involved in the trav-ersal of a space with strength, accuracy, or speed in endurance walks, div-ing, and racing. And they can also be involved in team sports so as to make possible feats of endurance—climbs; accuracy—baseball and foot-ball and soccer; and speed—relay races.

It is possible also to divide sports or games into those where men function singly, make use of some agency, such as a ball, racket, ski, skate, or bow and arrow, or manipulate something, such as an airplane, horse, or sled.

Are cockfighting and greyhound racing sports? They are called "sports," but they are distinguished from the foregoing by being essen-tially "spectator sports," with men doing nothing beyond training and refereeing. They offer not games but contests. If they are considered sports, they are to be placed in a special category of "spectator sports" and dealt with in terms of their effect on the spectator.

Are juggling, acrobatics, and gymnastics sports? They do involve men, they do allow for the making of men in an excellently made situa-tion, and they do allow for some kind of testing. The fact that they em-phasize skill rather than strength or speed no more disqualifies them than it does fly casting, rifle or pistol shooting, and similar activities which emphasize accuracy rather than the other achievements.

Cornhusking, woodchopping, logrolling are primarily time-oriented sports, since their primary object is to see how much can be accomplished within a given time. Deep-sea fishing would seem to be concerned with endurance as well as skill. These stand over against the space-oriented sports, such as the shot put or hammer throw.

Craps, roulette, etc., are games. Though records are kept of great successes, and though there are some who claim to have systems or to be experts in these games, they are essentially games of chance with perhaps some element of shrewdness having a role. Their emphasis is on the winning, the gambling, the fortunate outcome; there is nothing delicate in the performance, and apparently no virtue or dignity achieved by the players except the manifestation of fortitude in failure and modesty in success.

February 28

To be part of a game is to be engaged in the making of an event. It is therefore to be like a figure in history, except that the former acts more like an artist or craftsman than like a representative of the human realm. Spectators identify themselves with gamesmen—a term which covers athletes, card players, jockeys, and sportsmen engaged in fishing, hunting, etc. They are then able to see a segment of something like history with a directness otherwise not available to them. Ordinary men may help bring about some historic event, but usually in some minor role without an awareness of the nature of the crises, the direction of the movement, the reasons for its occurrence, or the structure of the events. But when they share in a game, they see the structure of something which is quite close to an historic event.

Each game is a single event, cut off from all else. There is to be sure a history of sports, and the gamesmen in different events are part of it. But there is little or no accumulation from one event to another, though there are traditions in style and lessons passed on. The history of a sport is largely a history of successive advances made on some record. It is possible, of course, to have a history of sport where there is a gradual development or sequence of significant events recorded, and we do have something like this in connection with bullfighting, baseball, and football. But then we have a history of a segment of mankind, something analogous to a history of art or technology, and not history in the broadest sense, which involves all mankind, or representatives of all mankind, or segments of these, in the guise of peoples, nations, or states.

The history of a state is distinct in type from that of the history of a sport or technology, even where each event is controlled and well structured, not because it involves larger numbers of participants, but because the events contribute to the history and not, as in the case of the history of the sport or technology, made without concern for what is to be thereafter. In politics, one is immersed in the present, and has a present situation to resolve, but this is always governed by the historic "ought to be" which is accepted in intent as an outcome that is not only to be realized in some guise in the present event, but in subsequent ones as well.

What is true of the gamesman is true of the technologist, the leader, and the public worshipper. Each brings into a public setting something of the spirit which governs a private performance. The technologist involves himself in activities that are governed by knowledge, plans, and rules, but in such a way as to humanize them. Those who merely use the results grasp the nature of what it means to subdue nature, to be in control of the environment. The leader involves himself in political and social affairs in accordance with felt ethical or moral principles. Those who follow him use his orders, directions, and achievements to become part of a human realm which is then and there being constituted. The worshipper makes himself part of a dedicated community by bringing in his private faith, to produce a sacred object. Those who watch him, or accept him, or (if he be a priest) imitate him, share in the benefits of the sacred object, without themselves becoming sacred.

The gamesman and the artist, particularly the performing artist, become indistinguishable when they relax and change their objectives to become entertainers. But they give up different things then; the one gives up the effort to make himself under the conditions of the game, while the other gives up the effort to make something beautiful, with an incidental making of himself.

The game controls, but this does not mean that one must merely keep to the rules. When the referee is thought to rule incorrectly, it is a practice in tennis for the player who has been thought to be improperly benefited to throw the next point away. This is not in the rules, but it is part of the game. And in games of skill, the rules are but the guide lines for activities in which there can be considerable inventiveness, spontaneity, and freedom.

March 1

To produce a humanized episode, the gamesman makes a series of events. In the limiting case, a single event will constitute the entire episode. In order to make an event, he must be prepared. The preparation will involve A] training; B] knowledge of the rules (which could be conveyed in the shape of a training); C] an attitude of wanting to be involved; D] bodily readiness; E] adjustment to equipment; F] adjustment to apparatus; G] having material available (balls, bats, rifles, bullets, etc.); H] taking a position in space; I] taking a position in relation to things (targets, starting line, logs, etc.); J] taking a position in relation to another man or other men on one's team; K] taking a position in relation to another man or other men who oppose one.

Not all of these preparations will be found in every game or event; the more complex the game though, the more all these preparations will be required. The possible indispensable ones would seem to be A] training —though there are exceptions here, for example, when a new game is invented and tried out then and there, or when men begin a game making use of nothing more than their native powers; B] knowledge of the rules, provided this not be taken to require explicit formulation or communication of the rules; C] attitude of wanting to be involved, though it does seem that occasionally a man might be indifferent, lax, indolent, refusing to "play the game" and yet be said to be part of a game; D] bodily readiness, which could be brought under the former heading—were it absent, we would have to say that a man was caught up in a game and did not play it. Not all games involve equipment or apparatus, but H] there has to be some position taken, if only to sit at a card table, or to stand on the floor in order to do push ups or knee bends. Only some games require positions in relation to things or to men.

Only B, knowledge of the rules, seem to be indispensable; the others can be defined to be indispensable only if one demands a conformity to conditions beyond knowing what the rules of the game are, where "knowledge of the rules" means also a willingness to produce the event in terms of the rules. B could be more sharply stated as a readiness to make a humanized event in accordance with definite rules. And the least addition that one should be content with in order to define a game is C, an attitude of wanting to be involved. Combining B and C would give us as the minimal preparation a genuine desire to make a humanized event in accordance with definite rules. If the gamesman has had no training, the desire must be expressed in tension; but if trained, it is possible for him to be relaxed at the start.

The making of the humanized event involves 1] expenditure of effort, 2] judgment in estimating what the situation is, 3] judgment in estimating what the incipient situation will be, 4] control of one's acts,

5] control of the equipment, 6] control of the apparatus, 7] use of the equipment, 8] use of the apparatus, 9] control of material, 10] use of material. Apart from the desire, the various preparations should be determined by the various factors involved in the making of the event. To the above, there should also be added 11] the intent to attain some result, though this could also be viewed as nothing more than the persistence of the desire throughout the act, except that where before the desire was directed toward the participation of the individual, it is now directed toward the achievement of a certain outcome. (The two can be combined if we speak of the desire as having two components, one of which leads into the game, and the other of which leads to the close of the game.) It would seem then that the indispensable element in the game is the exercise of a genuine desire to make a humanized event in accordance with rules.

How does this help constitute a character? How can one know that there is a genuine desire present? Why need there be anything more than a desire to merely share in the game, without making any particular effort? I think there need not be more than such a mild desire except on the part of those who are athletes, men dedicated to the project of making humanized events or episodes. The other two questions require more thought.

March 2

The athlete is the producer of concrete "therefore's."

We sympathize, identify ourselves with the athlete but not with the gambler. The gambler is an individual alone in the cosmos.

The desire to enter into a game is an intention directed at a goal to be arrived at in consonance with rules.

The desire which governs participation governs the production of "therefore's."

Sports are tragic (in something like the classical sense applied to drama) because they involve a basic challenge to be met seriously. Entertainment is comic in something like the classical sense, for it seeks to please.

The Negro comic, Dick Gregory, said that they don't care in the South how close you get, so long as you don't get too big, whereas in the North they don't care how big you get, so long as you don't get too close. A philosophic rendition of this would be: In the South you must remain inferior, but in the North you must remain an instance of a category.

Gregory's is more vivid and has direct bearing on men; mine allows for an extension and application in other places. But now I need a different kind of illustration than that which Gregory provided. Thus: in the South they don't care how equal you get, so long as you show that you are subservient, whereas in the North they don't care how unsubservient you are, as long as you show that you think you're not yet equal. This lacks the wit and bits of Gregory's remark, but then I am not a comic.

We move from being men with intent to men who are inferring or making something, not by departing from the one and moving into the other, but by remaining men of intent while selecting some one of the positions in which we in fact are, or which we can occupy as the position which is to be followed by the playing of the game. If I intend to run a race, I am ready to run it when I accept some position as the start. I always am at some position among other positions. What I do is select one of those positions as distinctive. There is then no being merely a man of intent and then becoming a man of action, but only of adopting this or that position as the position from which the action is to begin.

But may not one have an intent which calls for a distinctive act to be produced rather than for the selection of some position among actual positions or positions related to the one that is now occupied? I think not, for the moment of time in which one engages in some act is a moment which is selected, and not something into which one moves from the position of intent.

The question of the expression of the will pivots on the issue of how one selects a position. Do we use the origin point of the intent, the idea that from a beginning x we are to reach terminus y, as a variable, and then in the world of positions take one of them to be its value? It seems so. The taking of it to be a value always has some arbitrariness to it, even when the value can be seen to have a general aspect describable in terms of the variable, for a mere variable is surely distinct from itself as involved with a specific value. What we select may be conspicuous, arbitrarily assigned, or marked out in some way, but it becomes the beginning of a process of exhibiting the desire or intent through the acceptance of it as instancing the variable.

An intent should be understood to have a beginning point which faces in two directions; it faces toward a possible terminus which is wanted, and toward the world of actual positions from which one position will be accepted as appropriate. Without the latter, the intention becomes only a wish. After a period in which the intent, despite its reference toward actual positions, is not carried out, we must say that it becomes just a wish. The first kind of wish is pure and hopeful, the second is residual and defeated. A paralyzed man who "intends" to raise his arm in fact has the second kind of wish; a healthy man who "intends" to keep his arm by his side indefinitely, but is not alert to the difference between one position and another, and thus who in effect ignores all actual positions from which to begin this situation, makes a wish in the first sense.

A man can be said to have an effective intent if and so far as he looks at the position he is in, and others with which it is connected, in terms of the variable that defines the beginning of that intent. At the very least he must face his present position as "not the starting point," and treat all subsequent occupied positions in the same way, until he defines one as "the starting point." Should he designate this from afar, he will tacitly take all the others not to be proper starting points.

We have then 1] a wish, 2] an intent which will be expressed, 3] an intent that is always being expressed until the exhibition of it is in fact begun by moving away from an accepted starting point. The expression usually will initially involve a rejection of the position in which one is and the turning to some other.

A man intends to run, we say, because he is moving toward the starting line. He does not need another intent in order to start running. If he is at the starting line under accepted conditions for starting, he will start. But may he not change his mind at the last moment and refuse to run? Yes, but that means only that he changed his intent. He intended to run all the time that he was moving toward the starting point (defined in terms of place, time, and act); but before he got there, he changed his intent. Once he has come to a starting point, he cannot but run. He may of course quit the race before it is through, or even after he took a step or two, having changed his intent.

What if he refuses to budge when the gun goes off, even though he had not previously resolved not to move? Must we not say that he intended to start, but only wished to run? I am not sure, but this can perhaps be treated as a case of nonrecognition, and thus in effect as a rejection of an acknowledged proper starting point.

March 3

Some of my earlier characterizations of preference, choice, and will need alteration. We can be said to exercise free choice when we forge an intention, for it is then that we choose means and end together. The freedom of preference will be exhibited in the rejection of actual positions which are being occupied. A freedom of will, will be exhibited in the acceptance of a position in advance of occupation. This means that we can have a free will with respect to a starting point as well as with respect to the terminus of an event, the starting point which is freely willed being then the terminus of an intent. It is evident now that one can combine a freedom of will with a freedom of preference by rejecting particular positions at the same time that one focuses on some desired position. The occupying of the desired position can, however, be said to be an expression of a preference in a positive mode.

March 5

I visited George Schrader in the hospital this morning where he was resting after he had been treated for some persistent but not serious pains. He was talking with David Carr who was writing his thesis with George. As an outcome of the conversation I had with them, it seems right to say that there is a basic potentiality in entities which is expressed in outward form and behavior. The difference between the inward and the outward of a thing would lie only in the relation which the inward has to a future, in contrast with that which the outward thing has to other things. This potentiality could be oriented toward those other things but only so far as they were dealt with as futures, rather than as correlatives.

When we come to man, we must go further and recognize different inward modalities of the spirit which articulate a basic life-style. This will be manifest in the same way that things' potentialities are and a body's are (where a body is a mere biological or chemical entity). The intentions of a man will be manifest in his selection of positions, etc. The most idle of fancies, the simplest wish, the mere toying with possibilities can then be said to be manifest in some distortion or modification of the life-style, intentions, plans and the like, either by over-rigidifying them, or by allowing them to be carried out more mechanically or carelessly, precisely because the individual is not altogether involved in them.

We can go still further and maintain that the occupation with God, Ideals, Existence, and Actuality—with, in fact, any transcendent reality —will be manifest in some modification of the life-style. But if there be such Beings, so that an occupation with them is not merely an interlude for entertaining mere fantasies, we should find that there is a coherent pattern that the occupation with Beings introduces into the life-style, enabling one to set this over against the pattern which characterizes an occupation with daily matters. A life-style, in other words, though manifested in and through the body, is not expressed as an aptitude to deal with daily things, but in an attitude toward them, which could be divided into subattitudes where they are taken seriously, and others where they are reevaluated. To account for that reevaluation, one would have to acknowledge the attachment of the individual to realities outside the daily world.

Might one not act out a role with which he is not involved? Yes. If we here refer to an actor, we must, though, take account of the drama and other actors, of a situation where he engages in a specific task. If instead we refer to one who is simulating, pretending and the like, we must say of him what we say of one who is merely wishing—his life-style is modified in that he is not fully occupied with it, but is overlaying it with this pretending behavior. We may allow ourselves to draw incorrect inferences from it as to what we are to expect him later to do, but we are not in error in taking him to be expressed in that behavior. We would be right to expect him to act later in some consonance with that behavior—for example, if he is a confidence man who is acting as though he were one's friend, we can expect small acts of kindness and generosity from him, without having to suppose that he will always act with our interests in mind.

He who pretends is different from an actor and from someone who is involved with other realities than those which dot the familiar world. But like the person involved with other realities, his activities may have a distinctive pattern; unlike his, the pretender's will be a pattern, not alongside, but inside that which characterizes his relation to the things about. He speaks the common language, as it were, but speaks of different things than he normally does, whereas the person involved with other realities speaks a different language about everyday things.

Does not a mad man also speak a different language about everyday things? Yes, but it offers itself as the same language. Suppose it did not? Then we would say that it is expressing something, the madman's mind, as something distinctive, but that he does not know this. He cannot prove that there is something answering to his language. But a philosopher, a theologian, an ethicist, and an artist have coherent languages; those languages look aberrant only so far as we abstract from the Beings toward which they are oriented. The madman's language is coherent too, but only for one who takes it to be the articulation of a peculiar mind.

To discover the basic life-style of a man, we must start with him as now in such and such a state in relation to such and such entities, and turn this into a hypothetical. If he is walking, we must say that "If he is walking, he will arrive at such and such a point at such and such a time." We must then alter the antecedent and consequent in such a way that the difference which the new antecedent has to the old will be exactly proportional to that which the new consequence has to the old. The two hypotheticals will then express the same potentiality or life-style, whose characterization will then be made in terms of variables which can take these different antecedents and consequences as values. The meaning of the life-style is expressed in the "then," in the fact that it is just this consequence which is connected with this antecedent, that consequence with that antecedent, etc. The life-style is thus a law in-gredient in the man, inseparable from an exhibition at every moment in some particular occurrence.

The life-style and its subordinate modalities are always expressed or exhibited in the "exterior" in the shape of contour, organ, expression, gesture and/or act; but it is never entirely expressed or exhibited in any or all of these. To suppose it is never expressed, or may at some time not be expressed, is in effect to turn the "inner" into a distinct substance living a life by itself; to suppose it is ever exhaustively expressed is to lose it in the "outer" and thus to deny that there are any but bodily po-tentialities; it is to allow potentialities for bodily act and no potentialities for thought, desire, etc., that can be expressed or exhibited bodily. If we move, we realize a bodily potentiality; if we act, we realize an "inner" potentiality, though we exhibit it in a movement. We distinguish the latter from the former the way we distinguish an amble from a walk, i.e., by attending to the determining end characteristic of the latter, an end which is outside the reach of the mere body.

There are those who would like to reject all potentiality, bodily or otherwise. But then they must be content with mere simples without careers, promise, or capacity to move or react. If, with Hume, they would like to make bundles of these, they must take account of the mind's capacity or potentiality to make those bundles. The only question then is how many and kinds of potentialities one acknowledges, and the way in which the most basic potentialities are sometimes overlaid with lim-ited modalities which exhibit different patterns in fact.

March 6

Reuben Abel and Andrew Reck in their otherwise favorable reviews think that my occupation with a fourfold scheme in *Philosophy in Process,* volume 1, is almost obsessive. I do not deny that it seems so; but in fact what I was doing was testing the notion, trying to see where it would break down, pushing it as far as I could. I was not defending it or even using it as a matrix; at most I used it to help me uncover facets and areas which I otherwise would have neglected. No one who had worked as hard as I had on the Peirce *Papers* could avoid being alert to the danger of being caught inside some methodological scheme or fundamental matrix. It certainly would give me a much simpler outlook to have acknowledged only one reality or dimension. And I have often constructed schemas which contained less and others which contained more than four independent items.

Yesterday's discussion, as I see it now, was too simpleminded in good part, because it did not take sufficient account of multiple dimensions, and perhaps even of the four modes of Being. It should have begun with the acknowledgment of the life-style or soul or root potentiality of a man as at least four-dimensional, and then gone on to note that the manifestation of that potentiality in and through the body will have a corresponding four-ply character. If a man kneels, it could be that he is acting only as an existent, as an individual, as one offering a sign of his loyalty to a political ruler, or as one who is worshipping. Any fantasy or wish would have to be understood as affecting one of these dimensions of expression. And the law of one's being would have to have a fourfold character too, though perhaps it might be possible to find a superlaw which will equate the four laws in the ways in which these equate instances of themselves.

March 7

We express what we are in and through our bodies, most obtrusively in actions which make for smooth commerce in daily affairs. But we sometimes find that there are occurrences which seem dislocated, lacking the efficacy or order of the acts which are in accord with the necessities of daily life. When this occurs, we can do a number of things. A] We can dismiss the occurrence as an aberration. But this is only to label it as something which is distinctive—which, of course, is what is also done when we speak of it as mad, nonsensical, foolish, etc. B] We can take it to be a performance, an act of some kind, and therefore to involve a distinctive setting and some intention, carrying out a program which is distinct from that of our own life-style. The entire performance will then be a single expression of that life-style, with the intention serving as the condition that unites all the subordinate acts. c] We can take it to express an unconscious, a self, or a soul whose nature and drives are distinct from those which are manifest in daily life, or to express a collective unconscious which was coming out through this or that individual channel. The act would then have to be said to be undesired, unexpected, not intended by the individual in any way in which the daily activities are intended. d] We can take it to be an imitation of some other act in that it is governed by no other basic intent than that of wanting to deceive or to duplicate another's acts. Here the act, though as closed off as that of an actor's, involves no effort to interplay with others, or to follow out what might be an explicit script, and does this in some chosen artifactual setting which emphasizes the detachedness of that which is being done. e] We can take it to be an expression of some dimension of the life-style which is coordinate with that which is being expressed in ordinary reasonable behavior.

If we take the last of these positions, we will treat the act as an item in a larger pattern in which the individual will be involved with others in new ways. His acts, on the hypotheses, are the very acts which are being dealt with from the position that they are imitations, aberrations, etc., but now as linked with others (which are also aberrant from the perspective of ordinary life) in a direct and distinctive way.

Let us suppose that a man kneels and says a prayer. The behavior could be treated as an aberration, as carrying out a role, as an imitation, as an expression of a psyche, or as a bodily expression of an attitude of awe taken toward God. (In addition to these, of course, it could be treated as a social phenomenon, an occurrence in history, etc.)

When we take praying and kneeling to be an aberration, we refuse to account for them; it is only when we treat them as an imitation, a performance, as the expression of the unconscious, or as a function of the society, that we try to provide a rational account. It is only when we ground them in some reference to a reality which is coordinate with that of Existence that we can take them to be reasonable, and see them therefore as part of an entire life-pattern in which they have a distinctive integrity.

The religious man who kneels and prays may be self-sacrificing the next week in what seems to be an aberrant way; it is reasonable to understand the sacrifice to be related to the kneeling and praying as another expression of the worship of God. (This of course is not the only possible correlative to the attitude underlying daily commonplace life.) If there never are such other acts, if all that follows is normal in a commonsensical sense, we will have to have recourse to other explanations. Recourse is had to transcendent realities in order to make reasonable what otherwise could be made only rational, i.e., which could be understood only in terms of some principle or law determining nonusual behavior.

Transcendent realities—which are manifest as immanent contexts possessed of a power and status of their own—have efficacy. They affect individuals. Consequently, it is not entirely accurate to say that prayer and kneeling express only an individual's attitude of awe or worship; they do express this, but they also express the conditioning of the individual in his privacy by the reality to which it is then related. As a consequence, we must say that the commonplace behavior of the individual does not merely express a dimension of his life-style or basic potentiality; it also expresses a space-time-dynamic conditioning by Existence—a point faintly seen in the Jungian interpretation of behavior in terms of a cosmic Unconscious.

What is expressed in and through the body is the private individual, but not an isolated one; it is the private individual as subject to conditioning by Beings and with which the individual more or less consciously interplays. Intentions must be understood from inside one or another of the conditions. The effect of wishing or hoping is to be shown in the way the expression of the individual, as conditioned in this way or that, is modified.

A man can kneel as conditioned by Existence (or nature, which is a subdivision of this), by God (even when he is not religious, but so far as he has some privacy and detachment), by the Ideal (as a consequence of an obligation or a political demand), or by Actuality (to express his equality with others). He can intend each one of these expressions; or he can merely wish to express himself in these ways at some given time and in a particular manner.

There are cultures in which, and there have been times when ethics (stoicism), religion (Buddhism), or individuals (Kant's kingdom of ends) were thought to be the normative forms, and the commonsensical or existential taken to be aberrational. But there is no more warrant for taking one of these to be normative than there is for taking the commonsensical. Each is normative with respect to relevant intentions and wishes, and not normative with respect to what is done in terms of a different conditioning. It is the case, though, that only the commonsensical or daily reasonable attitude is spelled out in the shape of particular acts by every man, whereas the other conditionings are sometimes not expressed in any other way than in the form of unplanned groupings, affiliations, and confrontations. One may wish to express oneself in some particular way when subject to such conditioning; e.g., one might wish to pray. The wish will be expressed then in the guise of a rigidification or looseness in the position occupied as a unit in the conditioning.

May not there be a rigidification or looseness in the position one occupies in the dominant type of expression, which is usually reasonable, commonsensical, practical, and familiar? To answer this in the affirmative is to say that a wish is expressed in all the expressions of the completely conditioned life-style. This is perhaps more correct than the view that a wish is expressed in only one dimension.

Is it possible to abandon all reference to self, transcendentals, and the like? Yes, if one is willing to accept a pattern (or language) which has an odd grammar whose rules one cannot state in advance—since they are in fact defined by the self and the transcendentals. When Ryle says that we can mindfully drive a car in the same sense that we can drive a car carelessly, and thus do not need to speak of a mind in addition to the body which is attending to the driving, he in effect is saying that the mindful driving is a kind of driving. He is also supposing it is different from careless or habitual driving, and thus exhibits a distinctive pattern. If one takes habitual driving as a norm, the careful or mindful driving becomes aberrant.

The view that Ryle holds—and Wittgenstein as well—is that there is a plurality of patterns with distinctive "grammars," no one of which is the norm. But almost at once they go back to common sense or science as providing a norm. The refusal to acknowledge anything but behavior is in effect the acceptance of a plurality of patterns, none of which has the right to be treated as a norm for the others. One moves to a metaphysics when one accepts a norm, even that of common sense. The acknowledgment of aberrations from some norm is one with the acknowledgement of other norms.

March 8

A metaphysical first principle: I and other entities are subject to common constraints. This tacitly acknowledges Actuality as that Being in terms of which actualities are equated as equally real. The principle refrains from speaking about all actualities, since it is by no means clear that the ultimate particles which science is trying to know are subject to the same kind of constraints as the macroscopic substances which we come to know in a partly conventionalized guise.

Were there no common constraints, the relations between entities is all we would have to acknowledge, and these could be viewed as functions of the entities themselves. The fact that the entities are subject to common constraints makes evident the presence of some other type of reality.

There seem to be four kinds of constraints—in addition to that which is expressed in the principle. There is the constraint to be in time with contemporaries, the constraint to be in a single intelligible class with other entities, the constraint to be affiliated in some way or other with other entities, and the constraint imposed by the presence and activity of whatever ultimate particles there be. The first three of these are studied in metaphysics, and the fourth is the topic of science. The last differs from the others in that it expresses the constraint differentially as varying from entity to entity, and then in a specifiable manner, since it is supposed to be a function of the ultimate particles' number, position, combination, and arrangement, expressible presumably in mathematical ways. (Though the constraint to affiliate may be felt in different degrees at different times, it is nevertheless cosmic in its functioning; the other constraints apply indifferently to all the entities.)

Radical monists would deny our principle, but then they would also have to deny themselves and their assertions—and this denial. Contextualitists would deny our principle, but then they would have to deny the reality of the constraints or take them to be inexplicables. The world of actualities is, according to this principle, the outcome of a juncture of actualities and the manifestation of other realities; the principle allows us to acknowledge the distinctive reality of actualities, their punctuate reality, at the same time that it allows us to acknowledge the theoretically known entities which are within them, and the threefold constraint which affects the relationship and activities that they exhibit together.

A phenomenologist is able to acknowledge actualities as in a constraining context, but since he does not turn away from these, he is unable to explain that which he confronts. Science and metaphysics alike seek explanations, but the explanations are of different kinds.

If we start with the first principle, we take an approach to realities distinct from those which start with awe, wonder, etc., unless these be directed at the occurrence of constraints. And if we say that the acknowl-

edgment of constraints in the sense desired is at least tacitly an acceptance of the verification thesis of the positivists, to the effect that whatever is asserted must have an empirical instantiation, it is necessary to
add that the source of the constraint—or the being which is able to exhibit that constraint—is itself not observed, but must be known through
reflection, dialectic, and speculation.

March 16

Using some of Aristotle's terminology, we can say that every
actuality is made up of a matter and form. The matter here though, will
be the theoreticably known particles of science, and the form will be the
individual unity of the actuality. They are necessary to one another, for
the particles are clustered by the unity, and the unity functions as it
does because of the particles. When a scientist speaks of a world of
those particles he makes a double abstraction—he takes them away
from their unities and he breaks up the clusters to make the items related
to one another without the mediation of their unities.

An actuality is a single being. An Aristotelian, and more particularly, a Thomist, would say that it was an existing essence. But it would
be more correct to say that it was a sacred, individual, existing essence.
Aristotle would go on to say that it was in a place and in time, but it
would be more correct to say that it was constrained to be together with
other actualities as a reality, as intelligible, as existing (spatially, temporally, and causally) and as affiliated, with the constraints being traceable to the very contexts in which the actualities were, but as having a
reality of their own.

I have sometimes spoken of man as essentially afraid, as one who
adventures, as one who trusts. It can also be said that he is one who is
challenged, and this in a double way. He is challenged by what intrudes,
by what insists on itself and which must be subjugated and used so that
it is in consonance with his integrity and needs. He is also challenged by
that which stands in the way of his expressions, his movements, and his
adventures, and which he must somehow overcome and use or avoid in
order to make himself manifest exterior to himself.

We can distinguish a number of challenges: there is the challenge
of his own body, with its lusts and appetities, its impulses and needs.
The body can be said to intrude upon his thoughts and desires, and it
can be said to be an obstacle to the full or pure expression of what he
has in mind. There is also the challenge of his sex, so that what another

sex can do is taken to be something which he must also be able to do, or take himself to be bound by his own sexual nature. The sex that he has also has an intrusive side, but it also, for the female athlete, has the shape of an obstacle, which she tries to overcome by trying to do what men do. There are also challenges offered by nature, society, and mankind.

The athlete seems to take account only of the challenges of body, sex, and nature, and then primarily as obstacles or conditions defining what he is to do in order to test himself maximally. The rebel sees society as a challenge, and the religious thinker, and perhaps the artist and the philosopher, sees mankind as a challenge. Mankind is also a challenge for the mystic and the Eastern religious thinker.

March 9

Sooner or later, almost everyone comes to the conclusion that God is not an entity in our space-time world, contingent, locatable, and palpable. This does not mean that men then abandon all views which locate His power, influence, effects, or primary residence in some place at some time; but they do see that He is not exhaustively definable as a being who is only at a particular location at a given time, interacting with other entities in accordance with the laws which govern their interaction with one another.

Do the Greek mythological gods conform to this insight? Do the totemists? Do those heresies which proclaim that Christ was wholly God, and did not have another locus or status? I think so. Though the Greek gods exhibit lusts and jealousies and many other weaknesses of men, and though they at times had the appearance of men, they dwelt in another universe, were immortal, and apparently did not occupy space in any sense in which they did when they appeared to and interplayed with men. The god of the totem is a god who may be located in the totem object, but he has a being not to be confined to the functioning or presence of the totem object. And even those who think of the Christ as an individual observable being, when they view him as a god, suppose that he is made of different stuff from men, and thus is one who in fact is not the palpable object that he seems to be.

The clearest rejection of the view that God is not a being among other beings in this space-time world is perhaps provided by the deified Roman emperors. Though the deification marked them off as distinctive kinds of beings, it in no way altered the fact that they were limited entities who, though deserving of worship, were not able to be in any other position or to engage in any other activities than those which were in principle within the scope of human beings.

Once it be admitted that God is not a being among the beings of the world, one must face the question whether or not He is like those beings in some respect. This question can be answered affirmatively in two ways. He can be said to be like the things as a reality, and like those things with respect to some power. Aristotle and Whitehead take the first of these positions and treat God as a reality to be subject (with modification) to the same categoreal scheme which pertains to other actualities. Orthodox Judaism and Christianity—the latter more surely than the former—would say that God is like man in some respect, as is evident from the acceptance of the view that man was made in His image. They take God to be a person, concerned with men or the world. Thomas Aquinas attempted to unite these two views, for he took God to be a substance and to be a person (more precisely, three persons in one substance).

Those who suppose that God is a substance, or some other kind of reality, and not a person are at most deists. Those who suppose that God is a person, but not a reality in any way comparable with any of the entities in this space-time world, are at most personalists. One can mute the deistic position (which usually holds that God did create the universe but no longer concerns Himself with it) so that it becomes one with the affirmation that God is a Being to be contrasted with the contingent beings which populate this universe. And one can note gradations in personalistic views which allow God to be occupied with men or the cosmos in various degrees. (No one apparently wants to hold that God is a person, somewhat the way we are persons, and yet has no involvement with the world or any part of it. To hold that He has no involvement with the world or any part of it is one with affirming that He is a Being—i.e., substance, reality, ground, or unity, to be known if at all through reflection. The person of God apparently is to be known only through revelation.) God the person could be the God of history, the God of a people, the God who judges eventually.

For many, God is thought to be a person who is intimately involved with everything one did, and then as a judging, conscious being. It is these who are shocked by great evils, for they cannot envisage a concerned and good personal God allowing these evils to occur. But they could face these evils and still take God to be such a concerned person if only they would suppose that He has purposes in mind beyond our capacity to judge. This is the line taken in the story of Job; it is also followed by Augustine.

If it be the case that even where God is thought to be effective in this or that place, and to have the status of a person, He also transcends it, one is faced with the question as to just how one is to speak of Him. If He is a substance, we can either make use of analogies or try to forge a new language where new kinds of terms in a new grammar are used. This latter is the metaphysical answer. If we view Him as a person, we must depend in part on revelation, encounters, and religious and mystical experiences to provide us with this reference. But if we speak of God as a reality only, we need do nothing more than try to find a language appropriate to Him as a Being who is unlike the entities in this cosmos.

If we deny the legitimacy of a metaphysical approach, we must have recourse either to a negative theology which, while acknowledging the reality of God, denies the legitimacy of any discourse about Him, or must, with the positivists, say that anything of which we cannot speak in the terms of empirical science or experience, has no reality whatsoever.

Whether or not one accepts the reality of God as a being or a person, and then as one who can be known through analogies, metaphysical discourse, or "negatively," one can acknowledge God in an experience, or affirm Him to be immanent in the world, not as a locatable entity, but as a power which binds or orders or permeates them. Those who, with the positivists, reject all reference to the transcendent may nevertheless, even without any religious reference, acknowledge Him to be an immanent power. It is this perhaps which the current "death of God" theologians are maintaining. They have neither an interest in nor a capacity to acknowledge God as transcendent; they also reject the idea that He is a person, and as a consequence, are left with the idea of Him as an immanent reality. But once God is acknowledged to be immanent in the universe and yet to be distinct from any kind of entity in it, I think it not too hard to move on to acknowledge Him to be transcendent as well, even if only in the guise of a reality which is to be known, not through experience, but through metaphysical speculation. If this is correct, then the only issue that really remains is between those who think that God must be a person and those who think that He need not be.

The "death of God" theologians are disillusioned about a God who is a concerned person, and are antagonistic toward any attempt to deal with transcendents. In the end then, they are left only with an "impersonal," though perhaps humanly pertinent, immanent reality into whose ground and presupposition they do not care to inquire. Such a failure to inquire reveals them to be preachers rather than theologians or philosophers.

April 10

A number of strong objections can be made to the demand that one obey, no matter what or whom. Obedience A] subjects one to the will of another; B] makes one dependent on the decisions of another; C] denies one's own freedom of decision and thus the right to learn through experience and adventure; D] defines one as inferior to another; E] opens one to the risk of doing what might not be good to do, and this without providing one with the opportunity to determine whether or not what is being asked is proper to do in fact, under the circumstances, or for oneself; F] gives another a position of independence which may be too great for any individual to bear, and which may never be deserved; G] reduces one to the role of a puppet and may encourage dependence, fear, laxness, and cowardice.

A demand for obedience can be defended by showing that the demand is rooted in a right which has an overriding value with respect to the self-expression or the freedom of the individual who is being asked to obey.

A¹] The right can be taken to be identical with the power to enforce the demand of obedience. Not to obey him who has the power is to suffer more than otherwise, or it is to fail to accept the truth that the possession of power is its own justification—or both of these considerations at once.

In *Modes of Being*, I argued for the right of might, but I abandoned this position when I came to write *Our Public Life*, for I could not see clearly that might by and of itself entailed a right, and a right proportionate to the might. But that leaves untouched the consideration that one could be said to rightfully obey him who had superior might, because in this way he avoided the loss of other values, such as freedom from suffering, life, freedom of movement.

B¹] The right might spring from one who has a position of authority. Here he is representative of some institution or tradition or group, and on behalf of it demands that the individual in his individuality give way to what has a superior status. This is the position which Hegel, and for the most part Hobbes, would take, since for them the nation or the state has a right which is greater than that possessed by an individual.

C¹] The right might flow from the superior knowledge or maturity or wisdom of the individual, who therefore when asking another to obey is actually acting on behalf of that other in the light of considerations beyond the knowledge or use of that other. This is the kind of right which the teacher, the coach, and the parent claim with respect to the student, the apprentice, and the child, respectively.

D[1]]   The right may spring from a consideration of what it is good for a man to be. Here one views freedom as dangerous, as unchannelled and disordering, and takes obedience to be a way in which one achieves an order. Obedience on this view would be good for everyone; it would be a kind of disciplining, but one whose rules and control were given from without. This view would maintain that a man cannot limit his own impulses or spontaneities sufficiently for maximum good, and that he needs to have another put a limit on these.

E[1]]   Closely related to this last case would be one where the individual is thought to be too self-centered for his own good, and should obey in order to free himself from this limited perspective. By virtue of his obedience, he would belong to something other and perhaps larger than himself.

Obedience can be thought of as something forced upon one, something achieved through threat and punishment, or something which is voluntary, perhaps by virtue of the recognition that some one of the above reasons for obedience has plausibility. Those who view obedience as something undesirable must be forced to obey; but even in those cases where it is desirable, it may be thought to be undesirable, and the obedience may have to be produced through pressure. It may also prove to be the case that even where obedience is thought to be desirable and is so in fact, that it will have to be produced through pressure, since the individual who might see the value of obedience might not be in sufficient control of himself to be able to make himself obey as he ought.

Both sides of the question have merit. The individual gives up something desirable in himself when and so far as he obeys; but he also gains something in obeying. The issue then comes down to a balancing of the gain and the loss. Depending on what the demand for obedience rests on, the nature of the individual who is asked to obey, and the kind of outcome which results from the obedience, both for the one who commands and for the one who obeys, we might in one case stress obedience and in another stress its rejection.

April 11

The mind is united with the body in a number of ways.   A]   It is united through a control, exhibited in what Aristotle would call the intellectual virtues, or more particularly, the virtue of prudence. This is manifested in the mastery of the body and the instruments which the body uses. B] It is united through the will, where this is understood to be a reference to something exterior both by the mind and the body, so that an emphasis by one of these will have the effect of directing the activity of the other. The will is manifest in determination and endurance. C] The emotions are inchoate ways of having mind and body together, and come to expression best when creatively employed in art. D] What Aristotle calls the moral virtues, such as courage and temperance, unite the body and mind through a submission of the body to the mind's control, and thus as the reciprocal of the first mode of union, through prudence or intellectual virtues. This is manifested in skill. E] The habituation of the body in such a way that the mind is without efficacy, and serves only to record what the body is doing. Here the manifestation is in the shape of efficiency, grace, and craftsmanship.

The athlete is, produces, and expresses all these forms of union. But his primary stress is on the conjunction of control with skill, and thus with the unification of mind and body through an imposition of the mind and a submission of the body. He is Plato's state writ small, and thus, in Aristotle's terms, the embodiment of justice and temperance, the virtues where each part does its proper task, and the body is willed to be and is willingly subordinate to the mind—once we free the virtue of temperance from the Aristotelian association of it with pleasure of some kind.

The athlete imposes his disciplined mind on his body, and disciplines his body so that it is controlled readily by the mind. This outcome he tests and promotes through his involvement in his sport, with the result that he becomes one whose mind and body are well-integrated. Does this allow him some freedom of mind, some time and capacity to pursue intellectual matters, having no bodily import? It is, of course, the intent of the colleges to insist that this is the case; they can make their point if it be true, as I think it is, that the control of the body by the mind and the submission of the body to the mind does not require the full use of the mind.

A woman is primarily her body, but a man uses his body. The athlete approximates the stage where the woman already is by nature. The woman does not have her mind entirely involved with the body, and when she engages in sport, it is this portion of the mind that she utilizes. She utilizes it somewhat the way in which the professional athlete does; she engages not in the formation and exhibition of character or virtue, but in a work.

There is little difference between a woman amateur and professional; both take their athletics to be work; but there is a great difference between a male amateur and professional, for the former is involved in character formation and expression, whereas the latter is engaged in an activity making use primarily of that union of the mind and body that arises from habituation. That habituation is sustained by a prior union similar to that of the amateur, differing from it in that there is no necessary prior use of the mind, but only an incidental and subsequent use of it in the light of what is bodily accomplished or demanded. Professional athletes, and often the leaders among the amateurs as well, have their minds control their bodies. They do this by allowing the bodily adventures to dictate the limits and directions in which the mind is to be used, and then employed to control.

April 12

If skill be taken to involve an understanding of what is to be done, a judgment in the application of rules, and a control of the body, we can say that the athlete combines skill with commitment (expressed through the will), involvement (making use of the emotions) and technique or power (expressed as the stabilized and habituated body). Endurance will be primarily the product of the commitment, and speed with strength will express power. We have then skill, endurance, and power, sustained by an emotional involvement, producing the character of an individual whose mind and body are in accord. That character is made and remade by being exercised in sports.

Bodily health is the body as united with a mind which is merely incidental or is controlled by the body. The counterpart of bodily health is intellectuality, where the life is devoted to intellectual pursuits with only an incidental concern for the body. It is possible to attend to these extremes at different times, and subsequently to try to unite them in commitments and involvements, where endurance and emotional expression have priority. This is perhaps what everyone after a period of youth must do—even the athlete. The body and the mind will then be allowed to function at their best in some independence of one another, and then later combined by focusing on a common objective, or by expressing one's emotions in a controlled way.

May 2

I have just received a copy of my birth certificate, which I need in order to be enrolled in Medicare. I have sometimes said that my father was a laborer. The birth certificate lists him as a coppersmith, and this he surely was. Indeed, toward the end of his life, he was a foreman in a boiler factory. It is misleading then to speak of him as a laborer, though he did tell me that he was engaged in manual labor in connection with the building of a bridge or some other structure at the fair in St. Louis (I think in 1892). The birth certificate says that he was 37 when I was born, that he was born in Hungary, and that we lived at 205 Avenue C, Manhattan. My mother was Emma Rothschild, 31, born in Germany, and it was recorded that there were two previous children still living. One of these died when I was quite young. I had another brother who died before I was born. I grew up as one of four boys. My older brother and my next younger brother are now both dead, leaving only myself and my youngest brother, Arthur.

My present certificate is dated October 18, 1905, and was apparently obtained in order to permit me to enter kindergarten. I do not know why the original was not consulted; it does not seem reasonable that there was no record made of my birth at the time.

German philosophers are deadly serious; they rarely say anything witty, and rarely tell a joke unless it be to point up some idea. If they have genius, they do great new things in philosophy; if they lack it, they are dull, and function either as disciples or as historians of ideas. English philosophers are not serious at all, but primarily witty, clever, and adroit. If they have genius, they say arresting things about rather minor matters; if they lack it, they occupy themselves with trivia, spoken about with some expertness. American philosophers are in between these two types, since they unite some wit or ease, with considerable seriousness. If they have genius, they write a vitalized and understandable philosophy; if they lack it, they become academic, talking only to one another, and imitating the Germans or the English.

We live in what Plato would call a world of the mixed. This is the world of common sense; it has a transcendent and an empirical component, neither neatly distinguished. It is fringed too, by a genuine transcendent and a genuine empirical reality. Philosophy should engage in a process where we move first to one of these fringes and then to the other, in the attempt to have them in their purity and thus to be in a position to unite them so as to get a better union than we were vouchsafed initially.

There seem to be a number of arts which occupy themselves with all three dimensions of Existence: communication, celebration, and cinema. All seem to be able to enter into any place, any time, and to involve a plurality of dynamic processes. All seem to have relaxed forms, where there is no endeavor to produce the excellent, and where the unity of the highest expressions of these arts is broken down into endeavors which may stress one or the other of the dimensions that the arts unite. Communication turns into socialization with its accompanying propaganda; celebration turns into sport with its accompanying professionalism; cinema turns into confrontation with its accompanying advertising.

Communication and celebration are to cinema what architecture and sculpture are to painting. The first possesses, the second occupies, and the third exhausts a dimension of Existence. And, as some recent works in art would seem to indicate, since it is possible to make works in which possession, occupation, and exhaustion of a dimension occur together—for example, in some of the painted free structures which mark off a region of space—it would seem that we should be able to forge a single art in which communication, and celebration were combined with the cinema. We of course can in a documentary communicate by means of the cinema, and we can use the cinema to serve as an agent in a celebration. What I am now referring to is a combination of the cinema with the other two, but I am unable to imagine the result. It will, however, not be an art including all the arts or all their virtues.

The cinema is distinctive in that it is able, through the agency of the camera and through editing, to take up the position of any and all of the actors, any and all of the objects, at any place or time, and to relate them dynamically to one another in multiple ways.

May 3

A language may be invented for a number of reasons.

1] It might be desirable to deal with some limited area in a highly specialized way. Words, rules, and special symbols are used in various trades, sports, and disciplines, such as mathematics and logic.

2] It might be desirable to speak about the languages one in fact uses. It is this which has led to the development of "metalanguages" by men such as Carnap, though they make the tacit assumption that the language spoken about is either ordinary commonsense language or the language of science. But evidently we can have metalanguages to speak about the language used by metaphysicians, religious thinkers, artists, and so on.

3] It might be thought that ordinary languages and even the languages of special disciplines are not precise enough, or widely ranged enough, or that they include contingent or extraneous elements, and that one would like to have a language which was occupied with what was unchanging or necessary. This is apparently what Gustav Bergmann is occupied with. He seems to suppose that he thereupon is able to speak of the real constituents of the world. But how can he know that, even if he has found the invariant factors in the language of every day, he has found a language appropriate to speaking of what is real, except by making the supposition that the only reality is what is invariant in the objects of ordinary language?

4] One can take as one's aim the forging of a language appropriate to what is real. But now one must attend to the real, and in the light of the nature, relationship, and rationale of the items that are real, try to construct a language appropriate to them. There are some, however, who deny the possibility of knowing anything at all except through the agency of a language, and thus who would deny that this last represents a real alternative. But were these people right, they could not know whether or not the objects to which they referred in their language were constituted or produced by that language, since they have no way of looking at those objects to check on their status as independent realities apart from the language. To this I suppose, an answer would be given to the effect that we can make those entities the objects of other languages. But if those other languages are appropriate to their objects, the entities as appearing in those other languages would be different from what they were as appearing in the given language. The most one can do is, I think, to try to find out what is invariant in all the languages, and to maintain that this alone refers to what is real. But here one supposes that the real is what is constant in or for all the languages, overlooking the kind of languages and their justification referred to under *1*.

We seem to be able to think without speaking—even to know what we are unable to express. We can feel discomfort without being able to describe exactly what it is we are feeling, or even without being able to name it. The infant cries out when in pain; it seems foolish to say that it has no knowledge of pain, though, to be sure, it has no publicly viable knowledge, no knowledge which it can communicate in articulated grammatical sentences.

A language, in the sense desired under *4* could be forged when and as one was confronting the real in intuition, speculation, imagination, self-consciousness, or as a consequence of a dialectic or systematic way of handling what one already knows. Such a language would not have antecedently defined words, rules, grammar, etc., but would partly produce these while confronting the entities, and trying to relate them and one's grasp of them to what one had already mastered.

May 4

In the performing arts, the spectators have a constitutive role; they alter the rhythm and define the location of the work. In communication, celebration, and the cinema, and in their related forms of socialization, sport, and confrontation, the spectator can change the tonality of the occurrence, but only because he is so far an intruder. In communication and socialization, an observer is irrelevant, and when there is one he may make the participants self-conscious. Celebration and sport, though these can be made into activities designed to interest or please spectators, in their pristine forms are occupied with producing something through individual and cooperative acts, without regard for those who may be watching. They allow for the watching, and that watching may make a difference to the spontaneity and freshness of the enterprise, but ideally, it can be abstracted from and the celebration and the sport carried out as though there were no spectators. Confrontation, and more sharply the cinema, though allowance is made for some outside spectator to see what has been produced, are completed in their entirety before they are made available to spectators. One can even say that advertising, graphic design, and similar activities, which fall under confrontation, are completed before there is an opportunity to have a spectator present, even one who is to be altered by the confrontation and can therefore be thought to be one for which these activities are "performed."

The performing arts serve to alter the spectator along lines of the performers' alterations. His emotions are to be spent in a controlled manner with the consequence that they are "purged." But in the three-faceted enterprises, because of the independence of these from the spectator, what happens to the spectator is something quite different from what happens to the participants. The participants are makers, working as all artists do, with a consequent purging of themselves through the controlled expression of their emotions. But the spectator is caught by surprise; he confronts not something which he can read at leisure, or something which has a preestablished structure to it, dictating what is to be encountered, but a "happening" where the unexpected is the source of the "purging." It is as if he were present in the very making of a work whose development was not yet under the control of the artist. A celebration may be well planned; there may be considerable strategy and preparation in advance of the playing of a game, but the actual production is something which must be lived through and with in order to be known, and then with respect to something which is unrehearsed and unexpected.

If these considerations are allowed to be of primary importance, it would be necessary to distinguish a dance which was a celebration from one which was a dynamic art. Folk dancing offers a celebration; the ballet or the modern dance offers a dynamic art. Similar distinctions should be made in connection with music and the theatre, for both of these can be products where spectators are not confronted but merely allowed to be present.

May 5

There are some who deny the existence of time, but they evidently mean that there is a nontemporal world which is more real or more ultimate than the temporal, or is a ground of it. If we do not grant reality to a temporal world, we will have to deny reality to our learning that it is unreal and to our movement to what we take to be real. And no matter how insistent we may be in declaring our commonsensical temporal world to be unreal, it is true that, compared with illusions, hallucinations, and errors, what we encounter in that world (and the purged versions of this) is real.

If we accept time as real, we are faced with a number of difficulties: 1] Time is extended; next week is more remote, at a greater distance in time from now than tomorrow is, and last year is more remote from us now than last week is. But there is something paradoxical about these assertions, for if time is that which flows, there is as yet no time from now to the future, and the time which connects us with the past has no genuine extension of a measurable sort comparable to that characteristic of the present moment, not to speak of the fact that there is no passage in the past either. The remoteness of the future is also questionable in the light of the fact that the idea of a possibly possible is dubious, and the remote future seems to be only a possible whose nature depends on a prior occurrence of what precedes it. We must say, I think, that the future has no distinguishable extensions within it, and that when we say that it is extended, we mean that there will be a sequence of extended presents in which distinctions in the future will be realized. We must also say that the past is made up of what had once been extended presents. And we must go on to say that the present is now extended, separating the past and the future.

2] Most thinkers hold that there is only one time, but then they diverge as to just what time this is. Some would take the time that is of interest to the physicist or astronomer to be basic; some would take the time of common sense to be so; while others would insist on the reality either of historic or religious time. It is more correct to say that there are many real times. This view agrees with all of the above affirmations, but rejects their denials of the rights of the other positions. This leaves it with the problem of reconciling the various times. This can be done by thinking of each time as involving certain items in relevantly defined stretches, with other items functioning as obstacles. If *a, b, c, d* are connected in a secular historic time, items *a, c,* may be connected in a religious time, with *b* having the role of making the unit *a, c,* take as long to pass as the portion *a, b, c* does in secular time.

3] There are longer and shorter presents. A battle is now, and so is the war, but the present of the battle is shorter than that of the war. The battle passes away before the war is over. But then the present war must have as part of its present the battle as past. This means that the present of the war stretches into the past, and then has as part of its present mere facts, for that is what the past war is. If now we envisage a single historic present for all of western civilization, we seem to have a single present whose end is still future and whose beginning must be set in the remote past.

The alternative to this odd view is that there is no extension to the present, or that there is only a minute extension at each moment and everything else is a construction out of or combination of such minute extensions. But the first of these alternatives would deny extension to time, truth to experience, reality to historic occurrences, and would reject the reality of the commonsense world, or what we can salvage from it by removing conventional and other accretions. The second alternative is favored by those who rest their cosmologies and ontologies on the acceptances of the current science.

No matter how small one makes an extension in the present, one will have to distinguish in it a before and after, and deny that the items are also earlier and later. Within that present, any distinguishable element would be related to the whole as a battle is to a present war. There is, however, a difference between the two cases; in the case of the smallest unit, there is no allowance for the actual occurrence of distinguishable elements, but in the case of the war, the battle does occur as a distinct event, in its own present.

One can understand an atomic present, i.e., the smallest possible present (whether this be thought to occur only in the physical world or in some other, in terms of which the physical could be thought to be an abstraction) as a profile which is filled out by intensification. Such an intensification it would seem, however, has degrees, and these are either in an order of before and after, or in an order of earlier and later. In the first case, we have the same problem over again, and in the second, we break down the atomic present into smaller presents, each occupied by one degree of intensification. Consequently, we must say that the present occurs without such a set of intensifications; each component of it must be as fully concrete in any mathematically defined subdivision of the atomic moment, or it must have being only so far as one takes account of the other components in that interval. The latter alternative is better for the atomic moment, for that moment makes no provision for the reality of any occurrence of smaller duration than itself, and thus precludes the presence of fully concrete components in it having such a smaller duration. But when we come to events which do occur and which are nevertheless part of some larger present, such as a battle in a war, we cannot deny that there is a concreteness to the enclosed item. But we can deny that as enclosed, it has that concreteness.

We should distinguish between a mere battle which has its own present, and that very same occurrence as inseparable from other battles and to be understood only in relation to them. Though the battle has passed away and been replaced by another occurrence in a real present, we are then driven to say that it must also be part of the present of the war, and as such to be only before that replacing battle, and indeed before even events that have not yet occurred in their own present and as parts of the war.

The last admission seems fatal; if something has not yet taken place and thus is not part of the war, it cannot be said that the war is present with all its items only in a relation of before and after, for the later battles will be at times later than earlier ones. It would seem that what we must say is that the war is occurring now in the shape of a present battle, and that this battle cannot be separated from future battles as after it, and from past battles which are before it. The future and past battles will be later and earlier than the present battle, taken as mere battles; but taken as parts of the war, they will be related to the present battle as in a present war. This seems to imply that the battle actually occurs and that the war is merely defined to be present. But then we can say the same thing about the various events which make up the sequence of the battle that we now say about the war: the events will then be linked by the battle which in fact does not occur. Following such a procedure, we will end with an atomic present, and a consequent denial of the equal reality of other kinds of presents.

The longer present must be said to be in a shorter present which is related to other shorter presents which had been and which will be. But then surely there will be a difference between the longer present which is in the last shorter present to occur in it, and that longer present as still needing the appearance of that last shorter present. A war which is in the middle of its development has a different content from one which is at the end. But then which one is present? And must not the latter be said to come later than the former?

Is it an escape from this difficulty to say that it is the last battle as a prospect which is in the present with the other battles, and that the war is in whatever battle happens to be taking place? On this view there is nothing peculiar in the presence of the war in the last battle; it is present in whatever battle there is, no one of these defining its present. We will then give up the idea that the war needs the appearance of the last battle, and instead say that it needs some battle or other, and has all of them together as before and after in relation to the prospective last battle. It remains to be seen whether this can be maintained after further reflection.

May 7

In different periods, different types of lives were viewed as complete. The complete life for the Greek was that of the wise man; for the Romans, the political man; for the Medieval, the religious man; for the Renaissance, the artist; for the "age of science," the scientifically oriented man; for the Romantic, the imaginative man; for the nineteenth century, the cultured man; for today, the technically oriented man. There were, of course, other stresses in those periods, but it does seem to be the case that these different types of life not only were looked upon as superior to others, and even as the limit of possible and desirable attainment by men, but that they were in fact pursued then as they were not at subsequent or previous periods.

Where today the philosopher, the religious man, and the artist would be viewed as "escapists," in previous ages they were thought to have a greatness and be fulfilling. Plato, Aristotle, and the sophists flourished at the time that wisdom (in part because of their teaching, to be sure) was taken to be the primary value for man; Michelangelo, da Vinci, and Raphael came at a time when art was not only appreciated, but when the artist himself or others saw the artist (or those who really appreciated art) as the complete man.

It does not seem that we ever return to the old ideals; there seems to be a new ideal life looked to and carried out in each epoch. It may be that the occurrence of such a new ideal defines the epoch; but even if this were the case, it does not seem that some later epoch is similar in nature to an earlier one. If this be true, we can expect a new epoch with a new ideal to succeed the present. What will that new ideal be?

Possible lives, not hitherto treated as ideally complete are: a life of action, an ethical life, an historical life, and a community life. But one might well argue that discoverers, conquerors, explorers, and adventurers of the sixteenth century, after the period of the Renaissance, lived a life of action, and were thought to be superior to all others, and seemed to live as though they were carrying out their actions to a degree and with a success not equalled before or after. And do not men like Alexander, Caesar, and Napoleon (who cannot be put in one epoch), though they think of themselves as political and military men, belong with the conquerors? The last illustration shows that there may be great individuals who live or are thought to live complete lives which are not duplicated or imitated during their time.

The only clear case seems to be that of the ethical man. He is a secular man occupied with promoting and preserving what is good. He would be the most perfect of men if he could engage in acts of heroic proportions in multiple situations, and in such a way that the virtues of other kinds of lives would be captured or replaced. Apparently it is such a man that some of the younger theologians have in mind when they ask the religious to turn away from a concern with the past, with tradition, and even with God, to attend to fellow man.

If I am right in my treatment of the necessary limitations of any one life, no one of these supposedly actual or possible complete lives is genuinely complete. Homer, Michelangelo, Shakespeare (to attend to different arts and to break down the idea that a complete life in some epoch is directed toward accomplishments only in some one area) did not have the wisdom of a Plato or Aristotle, the religious grasp of a St. Augustine, the cognitive mastery of a Newton, the imagination of a Blake or Yeats, the cultivation of an English squire, or the skills (or the knowledge of skills) of a research scientist in our technological laboratories. (These judgments, I think, do not penetrate very far; they depend in part on undefined and unfocused characterizations of greatness in different areas, and of the nature of different epochs. Nor have I made clear what I mean by a "complete" life, or justified the view that in their different epochs these different men were thought to be complete rather than outstanding men.)

The treatment of "causation" in *History: Written and Lived* is not entirely clear with respect to the question as to whether or not there is a genuine causation, a genuine production, a genuine making something come about in history. It speaks as though men in groups came together with nature at every moment to constitute an historic occurrence, and that they then separated off to continue acting apart from the historic situation which they constituted, only to come back again to constitute another historic occasion. But surely things happen in history. Must then there not be substantial realities in history, beings who are able to act?

Things happen in history; the implication that there are substantial realities in history must be pursued. But why should this cause trouble to anyone who holds, as I do, that the political state has a kind of substantiality, even though it is one which is produced through the interlocking of men and institutions? There is a human realm and it has its own integrity and causality carried out by men linked together under the governance of institutional structures. Just as men can and do remain in the human realm, even though and while they are subject to the laws of nature—which are relevant to all entities in space-time—so the human realm and nature can unite to constitute an historic occurrence. This utilizes the energies the realm and nature provide so as to yield a new unit of energy which can be transmitted to the next event in history. If one wanted to adhere to the view that no actual energy is carried from one historic event to another, one would then have to say that the human realm and nature continue to contribute their energy during the time that they are united so as to constitute a single complex historic energy, and that their contribution continues over more than the length of one historic occurrence.

May 8

The view that in some act or other we inevitably betray what we are, faces a number of problems. It must decide whether what is betrayed is the very center of a being, his unconscious, his character, or his intent, some combination of these, or all of them together. This question can be clarified by attending to another problem, that of properly characterizing the betraying factor. If this is treated as though it were an item alongside others, one would have the right to say that it should then be dealt with as those others are, and not as a sign of some inward reality. The betraying factor must be something aberrational, which cannot be explained in the way in which other occurrences, say purely physiological or biological ones, can be explained. Once this point is recognized, one can go on to distinguish betrayals in the context of deliberate acts, in the context of inadvertant acts, in the context of social acts, and in the context of uncontrolled, "freely" associated acts. The first would lead to the acknowledgment of unstated intentions or purposes, the second to an acknowledgment of dispositions, the third to the acknowledgment of moral character, and the fourth to the acknowledgment of an unconscious.

A third problem involves the recognition that the betrayal factor does not tell us the nature of that to which it refers us, as it is by itself. An intent, for example, is not exhausted in its being or meaning by the factor which betrays its presence; all we learn from the factor is that there must be an intent of such and such a nature to make intelligible its occurrence, but the intent itself may be more complex than this and have grounds, relations, and consequences which are not revealed by the betraying factor.

The third problem is not faced by those who think we have only a single kind of access to anything, since they suppose that we must begin with experience or the empirical and end by pointing to what is "inward." They deny the reality of the intent, etc., as anything more than that which is exhausted in the betrayal factor, or deny that this reality can be known. A more dialectical spirit would have led them to ask if it were not the case that one can in fact attend to the inward directly, and become aware that there are occurrences outside it (since one is confronted with realities which are not capable of being fitted into the categories appropriate to the inward). It is then not that we face some external reality, but rather that in the very heart of the (transcendent) inward we find contingent, transient occurrences which we cannot account for except by taking them to be distinct realities which are termini of what is outward and experienceable in a public world.

May 9

Yesterday's discussion at the end, where it tried to explain how we, when attending to transcendent realities, come to know that there are contingent occurrences as well, did not, I think, find the correct factor. Instead of saying that the realities are intruded upon, it seems more correct to say that we, in knowing those realities, know that we know them as distinct from us and our knowing. When we take ourselves as fixed, we then speak of those realities as absconding, as remote; when we take the realities to be fixed we take our finite act of knowing to be possessed by those realities; when we take both of them to be basic (as we ought, since they are distinct from one another) we see them as othering one another, and thus as realities in different senses.

To such an account, a number of difficulties can be raised. Is it not the case that we also find ourselves over against empirical entities? Yes, that is why we take them to be real. But don't we take them to be real in the same sense that we are? Yes. But we do not take the transcendents to be realities in the same sense? We do take them to be no more and no less real than ourselves. Must we not then explain why in the one case, we take the realities to be the same in kind and in the other, not to be the same in kind? Yes.

The knowledge that we have of other empirical entities requires a different use of the mind than does the knowledge that we have of transcendent realities. In the one, our minds become identical with the structure, the very context of the world in which we and the other entities are, but in the other, our minds become identical with the essence or meaning of the realities which we come to know. Because we share in the same context with the other empirical realities, we know them to be real in the same sense we are. (We do not know if they are equally real, real to the same degree, unless we take them and ourselves to be oriented in Actuality, or take the context which we share to be an expression or representative of that reality.) We do not share a context with the transcendent realities. We are related to them, to be sure, but as distinct, as oppositional. We try then to forge a context with them, through an interplay, possession, submission, inquiry, or other agencies which bridge the gap which spreads between actualities and the Actuality in which they are oriented.

If this is right, the usual way of speaking about our knowledge of ourselves is wrong. We usually speak as though we were knowing ourselves from a deeper, more inward position, but the present account requires us to say that the inward is known from an outward position, that we look into ourselves from a distance—just as we understand that there is an inward by identifying some external factor as a betraying one because we in fact look at it from an inward or transcendent position.

That something betrays an intent is known only from the position of one who already stands somewhere where intentions are forged. That there are real occurrences which are over against Actuality, despite the fact that they are transient and contingent and it is permanent and transcendent, is known only from a position which is caught in the context of the transient and contingent. This last contention comes rather close to what most opponents of discourse relating to transcendentals maintain. They hold that we are always caught in the realm of the finite and contingent, and therefore cannot have knowledge of such transcendents. What I am saying is that we do have a knowledge of them, and that we know them in a distinctive way.

In knowing transcendents, we know truly and in a distinctive way, but we find that, despite our identification with the very structure or essence of those transcendents, we cannot make ourselves one with them. We fail, not because we find their content escaping us, but because we cannot free ourselves from the grip of the world of empirical entities.

Must we also say that when we come to know betraying factors, and even when we come to know other actualities, we find ourselves oriented in Actuality in such a way that we cannot free ourselves from it entirely? But surely the betraying factors must be understood in a way different from that in which we know ordinary factors, and therefore other actualities, in their ordinary careers. Surely if we cannot escape the position of a finite contingent being, it would not seem possible for us to be inescapably oriented in Actuality, and conversely!

Only the betraying factors require us to be in the position of a transcendent. And the impossibility of escape holds only so far as we have an object of knowledge. It is only so far as we know a transcendent that we are forced to say that we are over against it in a contingent world; it is only so far as we know an empirically discerned betrayal factor that we are inescapably oriented in a transcendent.

What I have been calling a "betrayal factor" is an empirical occurrence which is not like ordinary empirical occurrences, and cannot be explained by the laws which govern them. To say this is to say something which involves no reference to an orientation of ourselves in a transcendent self or in a (transcendent) Actuality. We are oriented in these only so far as we identify an occurrence as one which betrays an intent. We could not say this unless we were already grounded in the area where intentions and similar kinds of occurrences take place. We do not then use the betrayal factor as a sign or report of an intention. Instead, we take the aberrational occurrence to be an occasion for us to take another position toward our data than we normally do; we then move out of the context where we come to know ordinary occurrences to take our stand in the transcendent. But when we want to know the transcendent, we root our knowledge and judgments in ourselves as caught in the context of contingent, finite beings.

We cannot avoid being transcendent when we know empirical realities; we cannot avoid being empirical when we know transcendents. But while we are empirical and transcendent we have transcendental and empirical knowledge respectively. Such a conclusion has many consequences, one of which is the fact that a religious detachment from the world is a detachment from categories, meanings, and concepts appropriate to the world, and not a detachment from a place in the world, and that a religious man's service in the name of God involves a return to those concepts without losing an orientation in God.

May 13

The empirical ego knows the transcendent; it is empirical ontologically while it functions transcendentally. The transcendent ego, in contrast, knows the empirical, for it is transcendent ontologically while it functions empirically. The being of the ego is in one domain when it is occupied with knowing something in another. The being provides the unstated framework within which the knowledge takes place. Radical empiricists must end where Wittgenstein did, with a frame of which he cannot speak; radical transcendentalists begin in a frame which they cannot explain—as is evident in the acknowledgment of "appearances" by monists.

This way of putting the matter exaggerates the separation of egos from one another. But we live in a mixed world; and only for short periods, and then in the course of a rhythmic movement which reverses the stress of a previous moment, are we able to concentrate on the ontological or the empirical realities.

It is when we see the ordinary acts of a man that we also see what betrays his intentions. The former and the latter are seen from an ontologically transcendent position. But the latter is also accepted as testimony; in that case, we identify ourselves with an empirical position, enabling us to acknowledge another's transcendent intentions.

We become metaphysicians when we accept or identify ourselves with the empirical as testifying to the transcendent; we become empiricists when we accept or identify ourselves with the transcendent as testifying to the empirical.

May 17

When we attend to transcendent realities, we find that every once in a while matters become somewhat obscure. There are elements that do not hang together, that seem out of place in a domain that is free of all contingency and external conditioning. We account for the obscurity by noting that we knowers are not identical with the transcendents, that we in fact are introducing the obscurity by virtue of the fact that we are behaving according to conditions which are set outside those transcendents. In a word, we are then aware that there are other kinds of reality. We get testimony to the nature of another reality when we order the obscurities and find a rationale in them. This ordered set of obscurities gives us the pattern, betrays the context in which other realities (actualities) are set.

Similarly, when we attend to empirical entities, we find ourselves facing patterns, sequences, and stretches of occurrences which have no intelligible order to them. We find that we can account for these by noting that we understand what we confront in terms which the confronted does not provide. The odd patterns are in fact reports of the reality of contexts other than the empirical. Therefore when we attend to them, we can know that there is a nonempirical world. But we will not know from that position what that world contains, except so far as we attend to the several items in the pattern and use these as testimony regarding the nature of the reality outside the empirical.

These observations bring together two lines of thought I have been following recently, without a sufficient awareness of their differences and relations. In one line, I looked for ways of knowing that there was more than one kind of reality or context; in the other, I looked for evidences as to the nature of those other realities or contexts. What is now evident is that we cannot be pure ontologists or empiricists, for the other realm makes manifest that it too is.

The obscurities or patterns are sources of evidence for the nature of another realm. Only because we know something about the empirical can we give a proper order to the obscurities; only because we know something about the transcendent can we know how to divide the pattern into distinct items, each answering to some fundamental nonempirical fact.

The shifty eye of the confidence man is out of keeping with the rest of his behavior; this tells us that there is another "intention" which his behavior expresses. But we would not know how to use the shifty eye as a referent to that intention had we not seen the eye as part of a distinctive pattern reflecting the presence of a realm of intentions. Conversely, a metaphysical system encompasses a systematically ordered set of obscurities or difficulties, which evidences the presence of another kind of reality than that with which it is primarily occupied through the use of transcendental terms. This fact would not have been known had one not first faced the obscurities singly, and then seen that each occurred because the metaphysician was caught also within another domain than that with which he was primarily occupied. His metaphysical world has breaks, gaps, pluralities which he cannot account for, except by seeing that they say to him that there is a world of particulars. That world he can come to know by attending to the gaps or failures of his system, for they report the nature of the context in which the particulars are caught.

The mind is evidenced by a sequence of bodily occurrences not explicable in the same way as are occurrences for which no mind was invoked. It is because men act in ways which cannot be explained by means of the laws governing the activities of things or even animals that we speak of the mind. But the nature of that mind we cannot know, except by attending to particular isolated occurrences which do not fit in with the pattern governing thing-like activity. Conversely, starting with a formal language, we can know what is ontological only by noting the places where constants and special axioms must be introduced; and we can come to know the nature of the world to which one is committed by systematically uniting those constants and axioms, for they then define the frame of that world.

If this is correct, then we must say that no one empirical act betrays an intent except so far as one had already established the reality of a realm of intentions by acknowledging some odd pattern of activity. Conversely, when the Wittgensteinians insist that the meaning of the expression "I am in pain" is to be determined by a host of accompanying grimaces and gestures and words, they are not only not remaining in the realm of behavior, but have as a matter of fact defined a pattern which is to be accredited to the "mind." No information is thereby obtained regarding what goes on in that mind. To get that information one must break up the pattern into distinct items, each of which is to serve as the name of some dimension of the mind. The expression "I am in pain" could be said to tell us what is going on in us privately just so far as the entire pattern of grimaces, etc., is recognized to be distinctive, not assimilable to other behavioral patterns, such as those governing our biological functionings, etc.

It would also be the case that though we could not know just what was in fact going on in the empirical world if we take our stand with transcendents, we can nevertheless know that there is such a world by noting the inexplicable gaps and obscurities in the transcendent world. And we can then go on, and through our rational organization of the gaps and obscurities, know the context in which the still unknown empirical occurrences take place.

We can agree then with some modern logicians who look to the constants and the quantifiers in formal expressions to tell them what it is to which they are "ontologically committed," but we must refuse to suppose that we then learn anything more than that there is an ontological domain—which is perhaps all they would be willing to say. We can, though, go on and interrelate the constants, say hierarchically, or as merely independent, etc., to get an understanding of the structure of the world to which we were ontologically committed. What we could not learn is just what happened in that world, unless we were to abandon our formal language and be part of the world to which we had found ourselves committed. But the supposition of some logicians (Gustav Bergmann I take it is one of them) is that the formal language itself will tell us what is the case.

The Kantian "metaphysical deduction" is the prototype of all efforts to try to know the nature of the empirical world by attending to certain formalities—forms of logical judgments, axioms, linguistic necessities, etc. If the preceding account is correct, Kant is warranted in moving from such a realm to something else, say categoreal features pertinent to the world, only so far as logic itself was flawed by gaps and obscurities whose interrelation made an intelligible pattern. Does not Kant tacitly admit this with his recognition of the role of space and time?

The Kantian "transcendental deduction" is an instance of an attempt to move to presuppositions from the position of what is given. On the preceding account, he would be warranted in moving in this way if what he encountered were patternings which were not "given," and then took account of the items in them as distinct occurrences. Is this not what Kant in fact does when he deals with the problem of causation, and eventually attempts to account not only for the causal nexus as not "given" but for the expression of freedom in that causal nexus? But then he should have provided two sets of arguments—one which showed that the causal nexus was not given and could not be given in the manifold offered to the pure forms of intuition (but was nevertheless observable), and that specific causal situations were to be known only by seeing them to be newly instituted and then from the side of the categories, and another which showed that the freedom of man was not given in the causal nexus (but was nevertheless observable), and that free acts could be known to be such only so far as they were severally related to a domain of freedom in man. I think he begins to see this second issue in the second *Critique*.

May 19

There are two kinds of aberrations. One is a pattern within which we seek to localize some occurrence, and the other is an occurrence which does not fit into the pattern where it apparently is. We have the first when a man is engaged in misinforming, misleading, or deceiving; we have the second when he is lying, and betraying that fact in some act.

It is because we know that there is such a thing as misleading, misdirecting, etc., that we are able to find a locus for the betraying act. That betraying act is used as the agency by which we lift the misleading pattern into the position of a "bad intent," as something which is privately grounded and in a way different from that of the other patterns. We could have localized the misleading pattern in a particular act of deception occurring here and now, but until we see that act as betraying some other dimension of the being, we will have to be content with recognizing the pattern of deception to be merely alongside other patterns which may have only physiological grounds. But we want the betraying pattern to stand out from all other patterns. This we can do, once we recognize that something cannot fit into the ordinary patterns and can serve in fact as the agency by means of which the aberrant pattern is treated as an instance of bad intent.

The betraying act occurs in the world of ordinary acts, but by virtue of our knowledge of it as part of an aberrational pattern, we see it to be the beginning of a bad intent. If we could not find any aberrational pattern in which it could be localized, we would refer it to the individual as a beginning of a bad intent which had not as yet any further expression. But we could make this move only if we had known that there was something like a deceptive pattern. We are able to lift the deceptive pattern to the position of a bad intent because of the looseness of the betraying act from the rest of the pattern.

What we can say of deception and self-betrayal can be said of error and illusion in perception. It is because we are caught in illusory situations that we are able to take an aberrant occurrence and term it an error—something which we have produced. Such an error allows us to take the illusory situation and treat it as distinct from all the others, and indeed as being sustained by an error in judgment. We need not do this of course; we can accept the illusory pattern as a mere happening. But then we should not call it illusory but merely one configuration alongside others.

When we turn to transcendent beings, we find that they are obscured. (I think it was wrong of me to say before that there were many obscurities.) In order to account for the obscurity, we treat it as a pattern or framework within which acts, expressions, and empirical occurrences can occur. If we take this man to be a liar, we can understand him as a mere self by taking the side of himself as liar to be an obscurity on his nature, to be separated from it by being made the pattern for a series of occurrences or statements by him, actual or projected. The psychoanalysts should find the obscurity in the individual and then use this to define the aberrational frame of his odd occurrences. When they name something a "complex" they in effect are doing just this.

If we find a man behaving in an odd way, we can say that he is being subject to odd influences alongside other influences. Should we find that we cannot locate those influences, we should look for signs of self-betrayal, which will serve to lift the pattern of odd behavior to the level of something produced freely.

We call a man free when we are able to make an otherwise aberrational empirical pattern into a case of intent, through the unification of it with a betraying item, i.e., one which does not as a singular event fit into the normal context. The item which does not fit becomes intelligible, and makes an aberrational pattern intelligible, by being united with it to constitute a case of intention.

May 20

If what was said yesterday is correct, one should expect an empiricist to create terms which betray the presence of transcendents in order to make an ontology into a language, and that an ontologist will create a genuine context in order to make empiricism intelligible and no longer obscure what is ontologically known.

Apart from such creations, there will be anomalous items and an obscurity. The former belong in new contexts or, as disconnected, refer one to the grounding of a new context. So far I have spoken as though a new context had to be one which reflected the presence of a transcendent. But this is to go too fast. We can find, say in the world of physics, certain occurrences which do not fit in that world, no matter how we might alter it. I think for example of living beings having their own time and space, and their own kind of environment. Such beings are aberrant from the position of a theoretical or observational physics. Why, confronted with these, do we try to deal with them as objects of a biological science, instead of—as some do, and as philosophers in the past have done—taking them to be the occasions for the acknowledgment of a soul or self? Why may we not, when confronted with aberrant behavior, always find a context in which to place it, and allow this context to be alongside all the others, open to the same kind of investigation, though perhaps as subject to different laws from those which pertain to the others? Why not be content with a sociology of fraud, lying, and expressions of pain?

May 21

I will call items which do not fit into some accepted context "eccentric particulars." When we are confronted with these, we try to place them in a context of their own. The new context is allowed to be alongside the old and to encompass different kinds of objects or acts. We are then left with the problem of how to relate these various contexts to one another. In the end, I think this will involve the acknowledgment of entities of which the previous items and the eccentric particulars are aspects.

Should we find our eccentric particulars to be orientation points in short-range contexts, to be somewhat similar to one another, and to be located at some limited region, we will attribute some transcendent power to them, and thereby define the entire context (embracing all the short-range ones) as an expression of that power. We take a number of eccentric particulars observable in a man to be so many different expressions of the mind, or of a disease, or of an inspiration. The mind, the disease, the inspiration would not then be known; they would be conceived unities which the eccentric particulars specify. If we refuse to do this, we will have to take the eccentric particulars as inexplicable occurrences belonging to short-range contexts which we do not know how to reconcile.

Did we not have an access to the mind, the disease, or the inspiration, or whatever transcendent unity we acknowledge as that which the eccentric particulars specify, we would have to term these "constructions," hypotheses, and the like.

When we turn our attention to the transcendents (which we can, by means of intuition, speculation, bracketing, and other ways of facing immediately that which is not experienced), we find that our apprehension of these is obscured. We can rid ourselves of the obscurity by turning it into a "regulative principle," a context. To make that context intelligible, we express it in terms of hypotheticals. The context is known as a set of intelligible laws when it is read as "if so and so, then thus and thus" or as a concatenation of variables. We will not know that there are any so and so's, or that there are values for the variables until we turn away from the transcendent and the regulative principle to face directly the actual entities which could serve as values for the variables.

It is possible for a man to be willing to affirm that there are minds and ultimate Beings, known through sympathy, intuition, speculation, etc., and yet balk at the idea that a disease can be known in this way. For him the disease might be merely a unity of symptoms. But if one thought of a disease as a malfunctioning of the entire individual, the disease could be recognized to be a reality; it would be the individual in a particular stance whose acknowledgment is to be achieved by attending to him as a person, i.e., one who is sensitive, conscious, with rights and duties living with others whose rights and duties are acknowledged, at least tacitly. Such a definition would deny that an idiot or an embryo was a person, for though it had rights and could be said to be sensitive and perhaps even be conscious, it would not recognize that others also had rights and duties. Be that as it may, the disease would be identical with the entire person who was specified in eccentric particulars in the shape of symptoms. (Defects in the embryo and idiot would then be called injuries, and not symptoms of a disease. Such a consequence can be avoided by taking the disease to characterize an organic being as a whole, which would allow a place for diseases shared by embryos, idiots, and normal men, and for diseases in animals. I think this desirable. Consequently, what was just said about the identification of disease with the particular stance of a person must be withdrawn, and the disease defined as the particular state of an organic being which exhibits a number of short-range contexts oriented in eccentric particulars, or symptoms.)

So far as eccentric particulars qualify or are imbedded in items in a normal context, we can account for their presence by referring to a reality in which the two kinds of entity are aspects, or we can refer the eccentric particulars to a power capable of intruding on the normal context. The first alternative would lead us to say that a man is a substance having a mental and a bodily aspect, the second would lead us to say that there is a mind which can express itself in the body, and that the mind and the body are separate powers or regions in which the substantial man is exhibited.

We can add to the second something of the first, and maintain that a man is a substance with diverse powers in which he fully expresses himself. This will allow us to say that a mind may intrude on the body, but that the intrusion is the work of the substantial man. We will not be able to make this answer in all cases; e.g., in connection with ultimate modes of Being, we must recognize certain occurrences to be the result of an intrusion of those Beings on our daily world, without having to suppose that there is a reality which subtends those Beings and the ordinary items. When we turn to the items as qualified by the Beings of course, we will have to see them as substantial, with both the qualification and the ordinary characters as aspects.

When we take account of the fact that there can be unexpressed intentions, or at the very least partially unexpressed intentions, and that the body has a rhythm and needs of its own, we know that we must give the mind and body some substantiality. But the present suggestion does not require us to suppose that this substantiality is anything more than the individual man in a particular role.

The mind and body on the first view are only roles; on the second, unmodified view, they are substances in their own right. The modified second view would hold that they are substances but not in their own right. The mind is not the body, the body is not the mind, but man is the mind and the body, and something more as well—a self or will pointing beyond both substantialized roles to an ideal objective for them both.

May 22

"If I were to see an ape with a book before him, turning the pages one after the other at about the pace a human being might, pausing here and there, putting his finger at a place and looking off, I would say of the ape *that* he had a mind."

"But he might be deceiving you; he might be making believe that he was reading."

"You are crediting him with a more subtle mind than I intended to acknowledge. To deceive is to have something in mind which one is trying not to allow another to know."

"He might be acting."

"That would mean he had an even subtler mind. To act is to assume a role for some fixed end which will guide the various moves and attitudes one assumes."

"He might have been trained to behave in the way you saw."

"He would then not have a mind of his own. He would be carrying out acts which express the fact that his trainer had a mind of his own."

"Then you don't know what the ape has in mind."

"Yes, that is true. But if I know that he is reading in fact, which is but to say if I know that he has a mind of his own manifesting itself in a context (to be contrasted with one produced merely biologically or even by training), I can know what he has in mind. I become clearer and clearer the more contexts of this sort I discover, and particularly if some of the elements in the initial context of reading, such as words, or the book, are used as eccentric particulars in other nonbiological or imposed contexts."

"But you don't then make contact with his mind."

"That's true. But I can, if I can sympathize with him."

"If I understand you correctly, you say that we must distinguish the question, Is it true *that* he has a mind, from the questions, What does he have in mind, and Can you directly know his mind."

"That is correct. And that means that we can answer the problem of the knowledge of other minds in three ways. We know that others have minds by viewing a number of eccentric particulars in limited aberrational contexts as instances or specifications of a mind, or as being mentally sustained. We know what others have in mind by attending to the nature of contexts which deviate from those which are the topics of biology, physiology, chemistry, and even social science, and which can be oriented in eccentric particulars that a being produces or manifests. And we know others' minds directly so far as we commune with them in sympathy and love, and perhaps also when we participate with them in some joint enterprise."

"A similar tripartite division should be possible in connection with the body."

"That is correct. I can attribute to the body and its various bodily contexts whatever I find obscuring the mind with which I sympathize, or whatever I find is distinct from the context of purposive, controlled, reasoned expressions I normally take to be a mental or intentional context. I can know what the bodily world is by attending to the various contexts which are oriented in merely biological or even social acts. And I can make direct contact with the body when I cooperate with it, struggle with it, and participate with it in various activiites."

"Can you tell whether primitive men of the past had minds?"

"I cannot, of course, make direct contact with their minds. But if their remains are accompanied by tools or works of art, I will be able to say that they had minds, and what they had in mind."

"You mean to say that you know what the message was that the cave dwellers were offering in their cave drawings and paintings?"

"If they were really drawing and painting, they were not communicating, but creating something which was to be accepted as a finality. I think that the cave dwellers made genuine works of art; what they had in mind then was to make something excellent. If they had left tools, I would say that what they had in mind was to alter something for some purpose."

"Might one say that we know that another has a mind, not through analogy, but through an acknowledgment of a unitary ground for certain contexts and their eccentric particulars, and that we know what he has in mind when we know the nature of those contexts?"

"Yes. And that means, I think, that when we ask whether or not we can know *that* another has a pain, what we are really asking is whether or not we can know *what* he has in mind. And to answer that, one must refer to a plurality of contexts, as Wittgenstein has so well insisted. But he was wrong in thinking that we cannot make direct contact with the pain of another; we surely do in sympathy. This does not mean that we too must be pained in the way another is, with the same grain and bite, but we can, as Whitehead insisted, feel with him and share in a feeling with him, each of us orienting it in ourselves in a distinctive way. Nor does it mean that we cannot know that another has a mind, a mind which can feel pain privately. To know what is privately felt, we must know what he has in mind; to know that he can be in pain is to know that he has a mind. When I privately acknowledge that I have a pain, I do not, as Wittgenstein thought, try to make use of a private language, spoken by no one but myself, and having application to entities which are accessible only to myself. Instead, I claim that I have a mind without providing evidence to another as to just what it is I have in mind." ("Mind," as I am using it here is, of course, shorthand for privacy, as embracing intention, will, hope, fear, purpose, a knowledge of the non-empirical etc.)

May 23

A work in the philosophy of education could be turned into one in the philosophy of psychotherapy by treating the stages in the growth of the student as stages in the achievement of a cure. If one were to make this conversion in connection with *The Making of Men*, my book on education, one would take psychotherapy to begin by building up the trust of the patient through sympathetic understanding, without much manipulation or guidance. He must be treated as an individual human being who is to find satisfaction in the therapy session in such a way that he moves on to the next stage, when there is to be a change also in the attitude of therapist to him. The therapy session will take him away from his ordinary environment for the period, and in that setting will try to help him recover his confidence in himself in the presence of others, and thus be one who has a basic trust first in the therapist and then in others who are also ill, and finally in other men.

May 30

The Making of Men is now at the publishers, awaiting editorial work before being sent on to be printed. President Brewster says that he would like to see it as soon as alumni reunion days are over.

Toward the end of that book, I try to show the nature of the full life. I say that it involves the dedicated pursuit of a type of life, while using the treasury of goods which others provide by their dedicated pursuit of other types of life. A comment by Marcia Guttentag has made me alert to the fact that this is too static a view. Answering my statement that politics offers one type of life, and art, for example, another equally precious, not to be sacrificed to politics (and even precluding a participation in marches, protests, and invasions into backward places), she remarked that one could be part of a steady stream of individuals who, while interested primarily in something besides politics, make themselves manifest in needed situations and areas. They would in that way give a kind of testimony to the cause.

If I carry over this perceptive judgment into the question of the full life, it leads to the observation that those who are primarily concerned with politics or business should provide testimony in the shape of money, concern, time, and other help to those who have given themselves to the life of art, knowledge, and religion. Each type would not merely give something to the common treasury, but would support what is best in the other types of life.

June 1

Women think that love always conquers. It does. It possesses the strong and overwhelms the weak.

Those who are defeated in life tend to take their stopping point to define the limit beyond which others should not go.

Why is it that men kill men, but lions do not kill lions, tigers do not kill tigers, etc.? Is it not because a man is always challenged to his depths by the very existence of other men? We are all failures in terms of the measure that every other provides; killing another is a way of removing that measure. But this can apply only to cases which are not directed at those markedly inferior, or conversely, which are carried out by those who think themselves not to be superior to all others.

June 9

It is possible to reconcile the various times which characterize different domains or types of activity by seeing them to offer different stretches at whose termini there would be entities common to all. A religious and secular time would, for example, both contain the occurrence of the birth of Jesus and his crucifixion. But the one would have a single event in which the birth and the death were terminal points, whereas the other would have single events in which say the birth was relevant to the first cry, or the opening of the eyes. In both histories, there would be birth as an initial terminus, but they would have different final termini as relevant to the initial one. In both histories, the death would occur, but what was relevant to the death in the one, say the birth of a man-God, would not be relevant to the other, which would take only the trial or perhaps the being crucified as the antecedent of the death. One stretch would contain the items of the other, as so many obstacles, slowing the time.

Why should there be a plurality of times? How are they possible? Is it not that each is imbedded in a Being? But then are there more than four types of time?

There are obviously more than four types of time. We can distinguish the times of the dance, music, and theatre; the times of secular and religious history; the times of biology, chemistry, and physics; the times of action and behavior; the times of private and public action, and so on. Whatever method be employed to determine just what times there are, each time would be sustained by something outside it. Each would be carried by a Being directly or indirectly, and could be qualified by it in some way.

As embedded in a mode of Being, there is a dimension of eternity, of non-passing. The future there, though not determinate, is a reality defining what precedes it to be part of one unity, by virtue of being subjected to it. As a consequence, both the present and the future will be part of one moment. This will be both preceded by an earlier present and past, and be together with the result in a relation of before and after; as preceded, it would be a mere possibility looked at from the perspective of the partly and the completely determinate; but as after, it would be a meaning sustained by a Being (or qualification of one) which also sustained and affected the items that were before it.

The past, similarly, would not merely be in a relation of earlier to a present and a future, but would also be before them in a single moment. It then would define the present and the future to be made determinate as continuations of itself. The war that is being now fought and is not yet over is "*this* war" because it is projected from the position of that past.

The present, similarly, must be said to have the incipient future as its project, and to have the relevant past as part of its meaning. The dynamism which is characteristic of the present does not exhaust the present—a point I have not before seen clearly. The present is present because there is a dynamism, but it is a present in a time, only because it is inseparable from both a future and a past, and this in a double way—as that which is encompassed by them, and as that which encompasses them.

The battle that is now raging is in the present. It is a battle in that war, governed in meaning, and therefore direction, pace, and thrust because it has issued from such and such a past. The past battles are no longer here, in the sense that they are not being fought, but they are here, in the sense that they make a difference to the way in which the fighting takes place. They are present in the fighting that is going on now, somewhat in the way in which past stadia are present in present substances—i.e., as dictating their uniqueness, self-maintenance, etc. (See *The God We Seek*.) The war that is not yet over defines the battle as part of a sequence of battles to come which are to terminate in the war. The battle has its own project, its own future terminus, but beyond this is another terminus which also affects the battles. We therefore have two "substantial" forms, the one in the future and the other in the past, which are effectively in the present in the guise of meanings that govern the course of the battle, at least in part.

The present has a project and a retroject which stretch before and after it, making it have an extension greater than that required for its ongoing. That ongoing is of course extensive, having within it a before-and-after, distinguishable, but not wholly determinate set of items. When the present passes away—and this it does with the passing of the ongoing—the project will be one which is still related to it. It is because the project which is now being actualized (and is thus a present) is the project of a present that is now past that we can say that the present has a retroject. The retroject of the present is a past for which this present was a project. The present has a past, in other words, only because there *is* a past for which that present once was only a project. The present must then be said to have a future only because there is a future for which that present once was only that which is to be retrojected.

The ongoing which is the battle cannot be broken up into shorter ongoings without our losing the battle. But the battle can be broken up into an ongoing, a project and a retroject, and that entire battle can be seen to be that which is retrojected by the war as not yet over, and to be a project for the battles that had been.

The ongoing which is part of the battle is part of a war only with respect to projects and retrojects having a longer stretch. The difference between the war and the battle then is that, despite having the same ongoing as constituting their being present, they have different futures and pasts inseparable from that ongoing.

The ongoing which is the battle is followed by another ongoing which is another battle in that war. The war thus has a number of ongoings taking place within the frame of its future and past. But this we can say only from the position of the battles. From the position of the war, there is only one ongoing environed by one future and past. If this were not the case, we would be able to speak of the war as though it were a sequence of battles in the order of earlier and later, and thus as though there never was a time when the war was taking place, but only battles. And then we could go on and speak of the different ongoings in the battles, thereby losing the battles for sequences of skirmishes. We could coninue this on and on, losing war, battles, skirmishes, etc., to end with punctuate events within which we would nevertheless have to distinguish an ongoing, a projected future, and a retrojected past, both sustained and governed by a real future and a real past.

A war has many battles, each of which (apart from the first and last) is a project or retroject (usually both) for others. The war does not have battles as a project or a retroject; its project has to do with victory or defeat, and its retroject with what brought the war about.

Better: Each occurrence has two projects and two retrojects. One pair concerns what is part of the occurrence itself, and the other pair concerns what is earlier or later than the occurrence. A battle has a project in its own future closure, and also a project in the shape of another battle to follow; it has a retroject in the shape of what is its own beginning, and a retroject in the shape of an antecedent battle. The battle to come and the battle which had been in their guise of projects and retrojects are now objectively sustained by the war; they are the present war envisaged from the position of an ongoing battle.

From the standpoint of the war, all the battles are on a footing; the present battle is, to be sure, ongoing, and tells us that the war is in the present; but the other battles had or will have this function too. As mere battles, they are all specifications of the war's own present stretch, one part of which is dynamic but continuous with and copresent with the nonstatic, projected, and retrojected parts of the war. The war, of course, also has a project and a retroject in the shape of what comes before and after the war.

If we consider the totality of all occurrences, we consider that for which there can be no further projects or retrojects. The totality is therefore not an occurrence, for this must have a project or a retroject other than that which expresses its own futurity and beginning. Let us call the totality, for convenience's sake, the whole of civilization. Civilization we must then say provides a sustaining for a single, final occurrence's project and retroject, but it has no project or retroject of its own. And though this single, final occurrence has within its confines smaller occurrences each with its own project and retroject, there is no hierarchy here. The civilization is not on another level than the smaller occurrences. It merely is, from their position, the locus of projects and retrojects which are outside the relevant beginning and ending of these occurrences.

June 10

An ongoing might be taken to be a single continuous process, but framed in a multiplicity of larger and larger projects and retrojects. The ongoing which is a present skirmish has an antecedent retroject and a subsequent project, all together making up a single present skirmish. The ongoing is also the ongoing of a battle (which comprises a number of skirmishes), environed by a project and a retroject extending beyond those of the skirmish. That very ongoing is the ongoing of a war, as environed by a project and a retroject extending beyond those of the battle. As a consequence, we can say that the skirmish, the battle, and the war are now going on, that all of them are in the present. All are more than ongoings, and all have their projects and retrojects sustained by actualities, combinations of these, by ultimate Beings, or by qualified forms of ultimate Beings.

A man has a project and a retroject which terminate in his death and birth. That project and retroject are sustainers of the projects and retrojects characteristic of his activities. When he combines with other men to constitute a society, he produces projects and retrojects which sustain the activities of that society. The war takes place within the field produced by the two armies.

An ongoing is continuous in the present; it is a single occurrence in which anything distinguished within it is in a relation of before and after, and not earlier and later. But a longer stretch allows for a longer ongoing as present than a shorter stretch does. The skirmish's ongoing is followed by another. But the two ongoings are indissolubly one as the dynamism of the battle. The ongoing of a battle is a single ongoing, to be followed by the ongoing of another battle. These ongoings are continuous, indistinguishable parts of a single ongoing which is the dynamic present of the war.

Conversely, the ongoing which is the war is subdivided into a plurality of ongoings which are battles, and this by virtue of the actualities that are involved in the battles. If we see the ongoing inside the entire temporal span of this universe, we will then have to say that its field (i.e., itself with its project and retroject) will be sustained by some ultimate Being, and that every subordinate ongoing is the product of the operation of some actuality's or actualities' projects and retrojects.

Whitehead supposed that there was a single ongoing, but that this self-divided to give punctuate events. But why should it so divide? And why suppose that we can have only a single cosmic ongoing, and a multiplicity of tiny subdivisions of this? We should acknowledge ongoings which have a shorter span than the entire cosmic present.

Any ongoing shorter than the cosmic present has a predecessor and/ or a successor in terms of which it is to be understood as later and/or earlier. But in the cosmic present, the two are continuous, present, framed within a final project and retroject—or a vector terminating in a possibility and another terminating in a settled fact. The possibility and settled fact have a reality apart from the vectors. The vectors terminate in them; they do not constitute them.

There are evidently then three sets of projects and retrojects for all but the final cosmic present. There are the project and retroject of the actuality or the event which are being traversed by the ongoing but which always extend beyond it; there are the project and retroject of the actuality or event which terminate in the future and past of the actuality or event, where another actuality or event will or did occur; and there are the project and retroject of some reality which sustain and qualify the other two. A battle has a beginning and an ending that define its present; it also has an antecedent in the form of some other occurrence, and will have a consequent in the form perhaps of another battle. The war is not a plurality of battles. It has a twofold field sustained by a third in the guise of armies.

The ongoing of a present is positioned sequentially throughout the vectoral field. The ongoing will be located at different parts of the extensive present in a relation of before and after and not earlier and later. I am alive in the present; my being alive as a baby occurs in the same present of myself as this individual human being. It is to be said to have occurred earlier than my present being alive only so far as we distinguish the event which is my being alive now from the event which is being alive then, and see each of these to have its own limited vectors.

Instead of treating an ongoing as at some position in the vectorial field, one can think of it as spread over all of it, but with maximum intensity at one point, or as achieving maximum intensity as it spreads from end to end. But none of these formulations seems to escape the paradox that the ongoing as here and now is later than itself as having been somewhere else or as having a different intensity before.

June 11

The battle raged first here and then there. On my walk, I first crossed this street and then that. The war took three years. How can such statements be reconciled with the view that battle, walk, and war are single events occurring in a present?

Is not the first equivalent to "There was a skirmish here and another there"? Is not the second equivalent to "During your walk, you crossed one street and then another, i.e., your steps took place in such and such areas"? Is not the third equivalent to "Before the war began and after it is over there are other kinds of occurrences; one kind is such that there are instances of it not only before and after the war, but while the war is going on"?

If these are equivalents (which they seem to be), we should speak of the events in terms of their own units when we are trying to say something about the way war developed, but should speak of the events in terms of other units when we are trying to communicate something about the events in neutral terms or at least in terms not defined by the events. We can say that the battle and the walk took place here or there, then or later, as we can with the war; and we can say of the war (as we can of the battle and the walk) that it embraced so many subordinate events—in this case, battles. The war is an eight-battle war; the walk is a long or tiring one with many stops; the battle involved many skirmishes.

We cannot say that the war is going on in the skirmish, any more than we can say that on our walk we lifted up one foot and then put it down, following this with the other, and so on. Skirmishes are ongoings which take place in a present battle and not in a war; lifting up a foot and putting it down is a sequence occurring within the span of a step and not in a walk. A sequence of skirmishes is a sequence of ongoings which occur within the span of the present battle; the battle's own ongoing is all those skirmishes as environed by one project or retroject, or both. The battle is taking place in each of the skirmishes; they are ongoings within the area of the battle's span. If we treat them as following one after the other, we treat them in terms of their own spans; they are then unit occurrences whose nature is to be understood to contain within it a sequence of smaller occurrences—and so on until we come to the smallest unit of action.

A smallest unit of action, defined perhaps by the smallest possible entity going at the fastest possible speed (see *Reality*) is not an ultimate particle to be added to others to build up a more complex unit and so on, until we arrive at a walk, a battle, or a war. A battle is indivisible from the perspective of the war; it is an ultimate ongoing unit just as much as the smallest unit of action is. The fact that the former can be understood to have other units within it is paralleled by the fact that the smallest unit of action can be mathematically subdivided, and the fact that the longest possible event has no antecedent or consequent, though the others do.

The war passes away in the passing of a battle, but nevertheless continues in the next battle. What passed away is the ongoing which is a battle. What has passed away is still present nevertheless and this in two ways. It is still present in that it is contained within the stretch which is the war—for this extends backward and forward to the ongoings that preceded and succeeded that battle. And it is still present in that it is an inseparable part of the war's ongoing. By being caught within the span of the war, it is kept in the present as a battle-of-the-war, and as part of the ongoing of that war.

When we say that a battle is over while the war is going on, we are referring to it not as an ongoing in a war, but as an ongoing which is followed by another ongoing in the guise of another battle, and which itself can be understood to embrace a number of skirmishes. We are also referring to it as a part of a war, but now as that which is resident in a (retrojected) area of the war. In the latter guise, it is nothing other than the factual filling of a part of the retrojected area.

The past battle then is A] a fact in the present war, B] a replaced ongoing, C] a part of the ongoing war. The first two are obvious; the third seems doubtful. How can an ongoing of the past battle have any being at all? It certainly is not taking place now. But is this objection not based on a misconception to the effect that the ongoing of the battle that is a part of the ongoing war is not the battle as having its own project and retroject, but as occurring inside the war's? The war that is now being fought in the guise of this battle is the very war that was fought in the guise of that past battle. The war's ongoing is either in both battles or it is in neither. If it is in neither, then the war is not fought in battles. If it is in both, then the war denies to the current battle the (exclusive) possession of the war's ongoing.

This is not yet in full focus.

Better: A battle defines an ongoing to be a skirmish, and thus to have a certain present stretch to it. The battle occurs in the skirmishes which follow one another in a sequence, the later ones replacing the earlier. To get the battle as a single ongoing we must have it in the context of a war; the war defines the war's unit ongoings to be battles. Such unit ongoings do not have within them a sequence of skirmishes; they are ongoings to be measured in external ways, i.e., by dividing them in accordance with the kinds of nonbelligerent events we take to follow or to precede the battles.

There is no half a battle which precedes a later half; there is only the single ongoing battle. But is not the dynamism of that single ongoing only in the present skirmish? If we say this, can we escape a regress into smaller and smaller units until we end with the infinitely small? If we can acknowledge any ongoing as extending over any single temporal span, we are in a position to acknowledge the battle as an ongoing unit in a war. It is because the war has vectors going backwards and forwards (but which are as present as the battle) that the stages of the battle continue to be ongoing in the war. As stages, of course, they succeed one another, but as merely distinguished facets of a single battle they are co-present in the vectors of the battle.

The issue is still not yet in full focus.

Two men die, one before the other, in different skirmishes. Let these skirmishes be identified as in the same battle. If we now take the position of a war, we can say only that they both died in the same battle, one before the other. There is no earlier and later in that battle to which they can be assigned. It is true, of course, that one man is dead while the other is still alive, but this is only to say that in the battle the death of the one comes *before* the death of the other. The first death in the battle cannot be isolated from the other death; they occur in the same battle, and thus in the same present moment, though they occupy different positions in it. The battle unites those deaths; its being consists in part in that unification.

June 12

The problem of the One and the Many has a dynamic as well as a static form. The latter seems to be the only one that has been considered in the past, in good part because the question—which has been bothering me these last days—of the nature of the present, has so rarely been faced.

The innings of a baseball game follow one after the other. If we attend to them alone we cannot explain why there were just these many innings. We need to encompass them within a single present game. We, who start with the innings, do not know the game; if we are to speak of the two together, we must say that the innings make a group, but what it is that makes them so we do not know. Conversely, the game takes time, even though it is in the present. We cannot know why it takes time unless we see the innings as themselves having a temporal stretch (which they have by virtue of the temporal sequence of the batters within them). But how can a present game take time to pass—how can the present include within it a time in which there is a genuine future, present, and past? Just as we cannot say, from the perspective of microscopic physics or cosmological physics, why atoms are bunched as they are, and just as we cannot explain, from the perspective of Aristotelian science, why bodies fall at the same rate, so we cannot say, from the perspective of the game, why it takes a certain amount of time nor, from the perspective of the innings, why these are clustered as they are in what we call one game.

If we speak of the game as taking time, or of the innings as clustered, we are viewing a single phenomenon from the position of the innings or of the game respectively. To take a neutral position we must see the game and the sequence of the batters together. And this we can do by facing them as over against ourselves as rule-dominated actualities, i.e., as beings whose plurality of parts or acts are governed by some general unitary principle. They then have the shape of a plurality of occurrences (each coordinate with our acts of attention), a game in process.

I, as a single game-minded man, engage in a plurality of acts of attention and observation. What I confront is a sequence of occurrences, the batters coming up one after the other. I hold them together by virtue of the rule I have in mind. I do not unite them to make a single bloc. They are in an actual process of being united into such a bloc, and I anticipate the result by virtue of my knowledge of the rule. They are producing the rule *in concreto* while I am facing them *in concreto*; I have the rule in mind while they are eliciting my different acts of attention.

The reality is that from which the present game and the sequence of batters are abstractions. The game is played only by virtue of a sequence of batters which cannot be known from the perspective of the game; the sequence of the batters occurs only in the game, which game is not known from the perspective of that sequence. But the actual game, as encompassing a temporal slab of a sequence of batters, is faced by me as a rule-dominated being, exhibiting a plurality of acts of attention directed at that sequence of batters.

This way of putting the matter tempts one to view the innings as schema in a Kantian sense, and thus as serving to unite the sequence of batters on the one side and to pluralize the unitary game on the other. But then the problem of the One and the Many is solved by saying that there is something, to wit the schematic innings which are both One and Many. The question remains: How is this possible? And in any case, the innings are such schemata only for the game with its sequence of batters.

The game itself is part of a schema for a sport and for innings; each batter is a schema for an inning on one side, and for a strike or a ball on the other. But what is wanted is not the understanding of some entity as having a double role—which it does—but the understanding of what it is as capable of having such a double role, and the nature of the unity of which we can say that it is a single extended present, embracing a plurality of presents in a sequence of earlier and later.

The emphasis on the rule distorts the reality of the played game toward the game as present; the emphasis on our attention distorts the reality of the played game toward the sequence of batters. We can reconcile the two distortions in the guise of a series of innings if we define ourselves as being at a game for so many hours. But if we take ourselves to be individuals with acts of attention answering to the sequence, we can understand the innings as productive of the rule of the game and as themselves being produced by the sequence of the batters. Taken in this way, the innings would be a schema produced by the batters, enabling one to pluralize the present game. If instead we take ourselves to be governed by the rule which defines a game, we can treat the innings as a schema to be quantified by the sequence of the batters.

Whether we take the innings to be neutral schemata or to be schemata for one side produced by the other, it is not the case that they are primary, or that they exhaust the reality of what is happening. The game is real as a single present; there really is a sequence of batters. And when I face the two, I do not face them as caught in innings; I face a sequence of batters in a game whose structure they are exhibiting. That structure is a concrete, specialized form of the rule of the game which I have in mind and which controls my observations of what is happening. But my observations are elicited by what I confront as a basic reality, the batters in their sequence. My observations and acts of attention, though controlled by the rule I have in mind, are in fact subject to what I face, the batters in their activities—and of course all the rest of the team.

It is possible to see my several acts of observation as a sequence which is productive of a pattern of attention or interest. We then reverse the way we have been looking at myself and the game. The game now will be a rule which governs the division of itself into innings, themselves not only encompassing a sequence of batters, but being constructed in the light of the way in which men pay attention.

These observations can be carried over to the question of reconciling Gestalt theory, with its insistence on patterns with their own dynamic closure conditions, and behaviorism, with its sequence of detached items. Since there is something over which the gestalt must stretch, and since the behaviors of individuals involve clusters of subordinate acts, each has something which it must take for granted. The one assumes a plurality of positions to occupy in an organic way; the other assumes the singularity of an act or situation in which it can insert its plurality. To reconcile them we must find a neutral position, which is the reality answering to myself as a single unitary being who has a number of punctuate acts or positions through which he goes. The objective situation is a pluralized gestalt—or better, a psychological unity with a physiological plurality within it—or alternatively, a physiological plurality organized by a purpose.

June 13

The Kantian schematism offers us time as a mediator between the a priori and the empirical, because it is (said to be) a universal on one side and a manifold on the other. The discussion of the last days is related to his conception to some degree.

In the discussions of the last days, I spoke of a ball game and innings, and of innings and the sequence of the batters. We could look at the innings as a kind of schematism relating the game to the sequence of batters. It would be better though, to see the innings as the production of interests on the part of a rule-dominated observer, confronting a sequence of batters, themselves sequentially productive of a rule. Carried over into the Kantian framework, this would be tantamount to saying that time could be considered to be the outcome of an individual with categories capable of living through an a priori, pure manifold, and of an empirical manifold of time which was productive of a governing rule. The two sides of time would be produced together. Time as a schematism would then be a joint product.

Kant wants to know how a round plate can be subsumed under the geometrically understood circle. According to the discussions of the last days, we must say that the round plate is gradually understood to have a describable form, and that the geometrical circle is gradually understood to be extendable in space. The schematism of the two is the extendable, geometrical circle as one with a rule for determining the relationship of the different "appearances" of the circle (as elliptical from this angle, etc.). Those appearances are interrelated episodes in a single "life" of the circle in experience. Kant sometimes speaks as though the schematism concerned only the first half of this account—that it is only a general rule of synthesis (of a plurality) under the governance of a rule. But were this all, how could we be sure that it answers to what is empirically the case?

June 14

The Kantian schematism is conceived in terms of the problem of subsuming an empirical concept under an a priori one. As such it is singularly successful, though more attention should have been paid by Kant to the empirical side of the time. That empirical side is a factual mode of linking groups of occurrences together. Time, on this view, is both made up of moments having stretches within which a plurality of occurrences take place, and a universal or general mode of breaking up the whole of time in accord with some a priori category. The success of the subsumption depends on the fact that the stretches of moments are in accord with the subdivisions of the whole of time.

If we separate off the formal concepts and their subdivisions from the empirical occurrences and their bundlings, we are faced with a number of alternatives:

1] The formal concepts and their subdivisions may both be formalities. A game on this view is to be divided into innings, though no such division in fact takes place, since no game is in fact played.

2] The formal concepts may have subdivisions which occur for reasons that the formal concepts cannot determine. Here the innings fit inside the formally defined game, but as their coming to be, passing away, and replacements make evident, the innings are defined by something beyond them.

3] The formal concepts and their externally determined subdivisions can be synthesized to constitute an actual game which takes as much time as is required for all the innings to occur.

4] The actual occurrences, say batters in a sequence, are bunched into actual innings. A game on this view is a sequence of innings, but why just this many is then in no way known. We merely stop the game as a matter of fact.

5] The actual occurrences are bunched into innings for a reason which transcends the fact. There is a game being played, but the nature of that game is not yet known. But it is known that the game does dictate the number of innings which belong together.

6] The batters in a sequence and the structure of an inning can be synthesized to constitute a set of batters in a sequence which passes away, to be replaced by another.

7] The formal concept can be a field or schema within which a plurality of unit occurrences take place. While I have the idea of a game as something to be played or which I intend to play, I go through a plurality of acts of attention.

8] The actual sequence of batters can be thought of as productive of an actual game. While the batters bunch themselves in various ways, they together constitute a single totality of batters playing one game.

9] The factors in 7 can be synthesized to constitute an enjoyed set of innings of the game. The innings are now synthetic products.

10] The factors in 8 can be synthesized to constitute an actual set of innings of the played game. The innings are now synthetic products.

11] The last two can be treated as over against one another. When and as I produce the idea of an inning which I live through in an enjoyment of acts of attention within the frame of a game, I face an actual set of innings produced by the union of actual batters in a sequence dominated by the plan or rule of the game.

The game has duration because the innings are replaced by others; the innings have duration because the batters are replaced by others. The batters are bunched in innings because they are playing a single game; the acts of attention are grouped in certain ways because they are carried out by a man who is attentive to the game.

The enjoyed game, as having endured, has innings which pass away because of the sequence of a set of subordinate items (acts of attention) within them. The actual game is able to be a single unit because the innings which the batters produce all belong together. Were it not for the acts of attention, the innings would be general subdivisions in the idea of the game. Were it not for the bunching together of these innings, we would not have a game, but only a sequence of innings in each of which there was a sequence of batters. The understood innings and the actual played innings are thus produced schemata, each a present within which there is a plurality, and all of which are related in the idea of a game and the actual game. The game keeps the innings together, but the plurality in the innings makes the innings pass. Conversely, the innings make the game pass, but the unity of the innings enables the sequence of batters and acts of attention to be together.

June 20

Women are attracted both to heroes and to cripples. The ideal object of their affections is obviously a crippled hero, an eagle with a broken wing. How can she find one? By marrying a hero.

It is the mother in her that makes the woman want to attend to the cripple; it is the daughter in her that makes her want to attend to the hero. The daughter role is better; she should reserve her mothering for her children. When she marries her hero, and discovers that he is also a cripple, she can protect her mothering by functioning as a daughter.

A man as father seeks to protect; as son, he likes sympathy. He can achieve both by protecting the woman who sympathizes, or by sympathizing with her whom he protects. As the first he is solicitous, as the second, he pities.

July 1

The Kantian acknowledges transcendental concepts. But he takes them not to have any objects of their own, but to concern themselves with ways of organizing what is known empirically. He takes this position because he supposes that empirical concepts are constitutive of what is known. But this position requires him to suppose that something is given for those empirical concepts (concepts which in fact have a non-empirical origin) and this cannot be known in any way.

There are two basic escapes from the Kantian position. One is to deny that there is a given for a concept in any other sense than that of a more inchoate or indeterminate form of the concept itself. The way is then open for the Hegelian answer, which takes both empirical and the transcendental concepts to be part of the same continuum with a supposedly given. This position, with minor changes in principle, is also taken by the Marxists and the pragmatists.

The second alternative is the "direct realistic." Carnap, who was originally a Kantian, particularly with respect to transcendental concepts (or what he called a metalanguage), gave up his Kantianism to accept the reality of submicroscopic physical entities. He then became a dogmatic metaphysician, differing from other metaphysicians only in what he was willing to accept as transcendentals having appropriate objects. (For Bergmann, a logically constructed metalanguage has appropriate objects, but there is no reason to restrict transcendentals to such a narrow range as a logically constructed metalanguage, or to suppose that no other transcendentals have appropriate objects.)

Metaphysics takes transcendentals seriously; it says that there are terms which are not reducible to empirical ones, but yet apply to any number, and perhaps all empirical entities. It does not say that those transcendentals apply to the use of empirical concepts, though they may, of course, do this when and as they make a direct reference to entities appropriate to themselves. Those appropriate entities might be factors in every empirical case, which is apparently what Aristotle took the transcendentals to be. But with Plato and Thomas Aquinas, with Descartes, Leibniz, and Spinoza, I think we ought to say that there are some transcendentals, such as "God," "self," "being," "good," and "existence," which have their own distinctive objects. Once this is acknowledged, we can avoid asking whether the referents can be verified in the way empirical referents are, for they evidently are not to be compared with what is empirical.

We should find ways in which we are able to have direct access to some transcendentals—deriving the others by inference, through speculative construction, and the use of dialectic (which demands that we complete what is now incomplete, by making reference to that which would make it no longer necessary to refer beyond). And then a Kantian can go on and maintain that the transcendentals constitute their objects in a way analogous to the way in which empirical concepts do. Such a Kantian will then have two "manifolds" to acknowledge, one of which is to be constituted by empirical, and the other by transcendental concepts. This alternative, of course, need not be taken; instead one can maintain that neither the transcendentals nor the empirical concepts are constitutive of what is known through their agency. But this which is not constituted by them is not something inchoate or unknowable, nor is it an indeterminate form of the concepts themselves. It is a plurality of realities in which the empirical concepts or the transcendentals are already embodied.

July 3

Men have the problem of fitting into different kinds of settings. They must 1] fit into a future governed by various conditions; 2] fit

into a present area which will constitute their viable environment;   3]
fit into a situation which has its own rationale;   4] fit into their own
bodies which have their own dynamics; and   5] fit into social situations
in which they make a contribution. These various fittings can have a
passive form, where the settings define what is being expressed or exhibited within them, or an active form, where the settings themselves are
modified. We have ten basic cases to consider:

1a]   We live in a world in which there are law-abiding occurrences;
within this there are social wholes, objects, and projects which have their
own structures. We play a game, we engage in work primarily intentionally, i.e., as involved with some ideal or objective to be realized. If
we play a game, there are rules that determine what must be done after
what. Despite the passivity of the individual who fits, he is not entirely
subject to the conditions; instead he allows himself to be governed only
in part, leaving the rest of himself uncommitted, out of gear. He then
lives only a partial life as one who is accepting some role, as a police-
man or a waiter might, keeping the rest of himself in abeyance.

1b]   An athlete or some other kind of purposive man not only fits
some condition, but adopts that condition, makes it his own. When he
does this, he may alter the condition so that it becomes the very structure of his activity, or he may merely accept it by altering and suppressing his other desires or interests. Whereas in the passive case he merely
allows part of himself not to become involved, in the active he deliberately brackets a part of himself in order to concentrate on being in accord with what the conditions demand.

2a]   We live not in our skins, but in space. We see beyond our bodies,
hear beyond our bodies, are occupied with objects which lie outside our
bodies, and sometimes outside our bodies' reach. We move from one
space to another, but find that the space has an extent and a contour that
we do not determine. We are enclosed within an area which has its own
geometry, determined in part by the other objects which occupy it. We
are spatial beings surrounded by other spatial beings which constitute
our environment, and we are oriented with respect to them, and define
our activities in terms of what these other spatial beings promise and
present. Our passivity makes this environment seem imperious, and sometimes threatening and overwhelming. We here do not keep a portion of
ourselves uninvolved, as in case 1a, but instead open it to assault and re-
conditioning by the environment in which we are.

2b]   We can treat the environment as a terrain, as a field in which we
are to act. Though it has its own geometry, it is one of which we are tak-

ing account in terms of our own desires and needs. We see it as an area to be traversed, to be used, to be exchanged, contracted, expanded, and modified in accordance with our demands.

3a] Within the spatial area, there are situations in which other items interact with us to constitute a single whole having its own rationale. This is the most conspicuous kind of setting into which we are asked to fit. When we fit into it passively, the others define in good part what we are and what we are to do. This is the circumstance in which the child and the stranger find themselves; it is in fact where most of us are most of the time. The situations in which we find ourselves are constituted by a plurality of items over which we have little control and about which we have little knowledge; they often have been in existence for some time and have their own momentum. When we seek to belong to something, a club, a situation, or want to share in some game or political enterprise we are often in this kind of case.

3b] Situations are sometimes reconstituted and redefined by some member of them. There is then an active fitting, a subjugation of the situation to oneself. When an athlete participates in a game, he of course is subject to rules; and when the game is performed by teams, he must yield to a situation that is in part defined by other men, on his team and on the other. But when he is called upon to perform in his particular niche on the team, he must function actively. Indeed were he and the others not to take such active roles, the situation would degenerate into an environment or spatial area. We have a game only because at least one member of the entire set of men constituting both teams is actively engaged in operating in the situation. But this does not go far enough. Mead, I think, is right in looking at each of the members of the team as functioning in the light of what the other members are, can do, and are doing. All of them can be said to be actively fitting into the particular situation, with only one or a few in a conspicuous role.

4a] Every human being has the problem of living in his body. That body has its own appetites and needs, its own impulses and energies. Over the course of time, we are all habituated in bodily ways. We usually drink when we are thirsty, and within limits, eat when we are hungry. Bodily needs dictate the time and place of many of our activities. Sometimes the bodily demands are imperious, and we are forced to abandon that in which we are interested in order to submit to the need to satisfy those demands. And, of course, we are assaulted from without through our sense organs, seeing and hearing much we would rather not see or hear.

4b]   The problem of the athlete is to identify himself with his body. When he does this, he does not submit to that body, for submission is a passive act, in which one merely allows the bodily conditions and acts to define what one is and does. Instead, the athlete accepts his body as the condition and the arena in which he will be. He brings into that body his own commitment, will, intention, and desire, but in such a way that they are there transformed and carried out effectively. He commands his body to do bodily things, but not on the basis of bodily impulses or conditions. He identifies himself (i.e., his spirit, or self, or mind, or intent) with the body, in the sense that he sets the body a task which the body can perform but which it may not of its own engage in, or engage in with that degree of commitment or energy.

5a, 5b]   One can question whether *5a* offers a distinct alternative to *3a*, even if we take it to involve other human beings, and *3a* to take account only of nonhuman ones, and particularly inanimate ones. In both cases, we have conditions set by others to which we try to conform, and which, when we do conform to them, become the structure of a whole of which we are a part. And what is true of *5a* in relation to *3a*, is also true of *5b* in relation to *3b*. Still, the work of sociologists and anthropologists is predicated on the isolation of *5a* and *5b*, as involving something distinctive about men. Though an individual man might invest a nonhuman situation with his own kind of meanings, there is no reciprocity here, except in the sense that those other entities have their own natures and mode of acting. In the case of men, they do to each other what each would be exclusively doing to the inanimate. Each imposes his meanings and values on the other men, both when they are passive and when they are active, to make the resulting situation one in which there is a conditioning by meanings and values as well as by natures, prospective acts, and presences.

July 4

A dedicated man accepts some condition as that to which he will be subject, passively or actively. A committed man is a dedicated one who has taken some ideal or result to define what he is to do. The limit of commitment is found in identification. Here one accepts some condition by endowing it with one's own vitality and even objective, so that what one has become identified with could be used in a dedication or commitment to something beyond itself.

An athlete is dedicated to the athletic life; he is committed to func-

tioning according to the rules in this or that game; he identifies himself
with his body so as to function as a purposed body in a game. If he goes
on to identify himself with the game, he becomes one who is playing a
role for the sake of winning the game. If he goes further and identifies
himself with the winning of the game, he uses the winning for some
further end, to which he may be dedicated or committed.

July 5

Some of our bodily responses to stimuli are learned; all are
qualified by our experience, training, punishment, and reward. Normally they are accompanied by idle thoughts, expectations, and intentions which are not altogether attuned to the way the body is ready to
respond. This situation can be met in at least three ways: we can accept
the body without qualification; we can make a selective acceptance of
the body; and we can take the body as a base in terms of which we occupy
ourselves with some end.

To accept the body without qualification is to keep no reserve, to
have no other desires or intentions. The body is then allowed to respond
as the stimuli demand. Whatever impulses surge to the fore are permitted unchecked. This is the answer taken by the self-indulgent man, the
sybarite, and the glutton. These are relaxed men who have withdrawn
any project which gears the body to acts and outcomes that it might not
of its own account produce.

The selective acceptance of the body is the special act of the athlete.
He does not accept his body entirely, but only his musculature, at the
same time that he suppresses or ignores his appetites, and resists various
responses to external stimuli. He is a man at once relaxed and determined, the relaxation being expressed in his identifications, and the determination in his refusal to identify himself with anything else.

The acceptance of the body as a base is the result of an acceptance of
some end as an end for the body. It is to will that something which is
relevant to the body be in fact that toward which the body should act.
Such a willing can come after the previous selection of aspects of the
body with which one has identified oneself. It can also follow on a complete identification, in which case some preferential order of response is
indicated.

Athletic preparation requires a selective identification. Athletic participation in a game requires the acceptance of the selectively identified
body as a base. Both depend on the capacity of the individual to have a

vectoral concern with something beyond the body, and on its ability to withdraw this or to allow it to function as a continuation of what the body is and tends to do. If a man takes the body as a base, but in such a way that what he projects is beyond the body's capacity, he is unrealistic, using bad judgment. Part of the art of training consists in so preparing the body that when we offer it the project of a game, we but continue in the future what it in fact has attained, allowing it to function as a body, but for ends it would not otherwise pursue.

July 6

A common theory of learning has the individual master the various steps of a process and then, when each step has been covered, allows the individual to engage in a single act. Apparently a similar, but in fact an actually diverse position, is offered by following the lead of the last days. Here learning is treated as involving a step-by-step identification with oneself, with this object, or as in this attitude, or position, or movement, so as to have a base in terms of which a project is defined. Though each step is like that treated in the common theory, the individual is now taken to be one who has accepted himself as at that step, as grounding an appropriate reference to something subsequent.

By identifying himself with something at a given step, the individual receives a satisfaction; he is completed then and there in a sense. This is not the case when the preparation is concerned with the mastery of parts of some desired complex activity. Moreover, in the ordinary case, after one has learned the totality of steps of a given act, one can do nothing more than exhibit that whole, whereas in the present case, the identification with the entire set of steps of a given act allows for the projection of another possible kind of act, thereby permitting one to utilize what one has learned, in a fresh and flexible way. Having mastered the various blows which should be part of a boxer's repertory, the boxer, on the suggested view, enters into the arena to bring about a result on the basis of what he has learned, and not merely, as the current theory would require, to exhibit what he had already mastered.

The present suggestion also allows for the approach to an identification from the perspective of a project. Most athletic training in fact proceeds in this way. Knowing what a game is like, one is able to train the individual in the various steps which make for a well-prepared participant in the game. Here the danger of falling into the traditional theory of learning is greatest; we tend to deal with the individual in training as though he has to master the various steps of the game piecemeal before he can enter the game—the game being already well-defined as requiring just these steps. But once again, it should be urged as an alternative that the steps into which the game should be broken are steps which allow for the identification of the individual with his body, some act, some object, and the like.

Can this or any other speculative theory be given empirical or experimental use? It can if we A] think of denials of some one or more of its components, B] formulate an alternative hypothesis in which those denials are a part, and C] set up experiments in which one can ascertain whether the one or the other hypothesis is confirmed. Thus we could ask if we get a better performance from men who identify themselves with their bodies at a given stage, than from those who merely allow themselves to be stimulated to respond. And we can tell if they have made such an identification by seeing if they have abandoned the usual conventional and unreflecting projects which overlay those of their bodies. And we can tell if they have abandoned those projects by seeing if they are not distracted from their present occupation with an identification, by something which would and does elicit a response by those who come into the experiment without any effort to give up any previous project, or expectation, or habitual way of looking at the world.

In such an application of the speculative to the experimental realm, we run the risk of making philosophy be occupied with the particular rather than with the general. The criticism of people like G. E. Morre, Carnap, and Wittgenstein about metaphysics supposes that metaphysics is in fact a philosophy of the particular. But this is not what it is.

A madman is a philosopher of the particular; he interprets the particular in terms that are not commonsensical or reasonable. But when a metaphysician says that time is unreal, or that a chair is a number, or an instantiated form, or a union of essence and existence, or of matter and form, or that it is an idea, etc., he is not saying that the chair as a particular is not a chair in the ordinary sense. What he is saying is that there is another context in which the chair and all other items should be placed so as to illuminate what is now and will remain obscure about their being, functioning, or presence.

A phenomenologist and an empiricist claim to be philosophers of the particular. Are they mad? No, because they do not believe what they say. They do not act in accordance with what they say they know to be empirically real. A genuine madman not only takes the particular to have a nature and a role distinct from that which common sense assigns to it and can understand, but believes and acts in terms of this understanding.

The phenomenologist and empiricist act as commonsense men, but talk like madmen. A speculative philosopher talks like a commonsense man about particulars, but like a madman about the principles which govern these and the kinds of contexts in which the commonsensical particulars fit and are illuminated.

July 7

The art of education consists in satisfying the student here and now, while luring him on to more advanced work. There are two types of cases. The one is best represented by the child, the other by the athlete.

A child, like everyone else, is tensed toward the future; it is expective, geared to what is about to be. But the expectation is vague, being only partly determined by what the child had gone through and what is still wanted. It is necessary to satisfy the child now by taking its present needs and impulses to define what it now requires, and then placing them in a context where the result will prove to be a base for an unfolding in another area. The child is to be satisfied now in such a way that it is ready to follow along a route that the teacher or society provides for it, a route which is a specification of its aboriginal expectancy, and reflects something of the nature of what the teacher wants the child to achieve.

The athlete is a man who has already specified his expectancies in many ways. He has filled them out with projects grounded in experience, qualified by convention, and expressing interests which transcend those of the body and sometimes those that can be satisfied empirically. The first task is to free the athlete from these specifications, and thus reduce him somewhat to the state where the child is.

What the child has by nature, the athlete must achieve by will; he must withdraw specifications acquired over the years in order to identify himself with his body or some objects here and now. His trainer then proceeds to deal with him as the teacher does with the child, placing the identified object in a context where it will unfold itself in such a way as to enable the athlete to arrive at a desired end. The identification is made at the price of withdrawing specifications, and the very meaning of the identification requires that another set of specifications, built on the identification, be provided either by oneself (which would require considerable trial and error) or by one's trainer.

It is sometimes said that a mother loves you as you are, because you are. If this be so, as I think it is, she can be said to make an identification with you then and there. But then she should place this in a context where you can continue to grow, so that you can be one who is to be loved because of what you have become. To sharpen the contrast between mother and father, or if one likes, to speak of these as ideal cases offering contrasting and supplementary positions, we should now say that the father loves you because and so far as you deserve to be loved by what you have shown yourself to be, and that this is oriented toward a future where you can be loved for what you are, as you are. Where the mother has a love which is ontologically grounded, in that it accepts the child as and because it is, the father's love is evaluationally determined and grounds a vector to the state where one is to be loved because he is, and as he is.

Both mother and father on this account allow for an identification with the child, the one ontologically, the other evaluationally. Both make this identification together with a specification of the expectancy they have for the child, as a being who is to arrive at the future, though the mother specifies the expectancy as one which will terminate in an evaluated being, where the father has it terminate in an ontological fact. The child as benefiting from both is at once accepted for what it is and for what it deserves, and is connected with the prospect of being more evidently what it is, and more deserving than it now can be.

When a man and a woman love, they identify themselves with one another. They then merge their diverse vectors to constitute a unique expectancy. It is this which defines them as a pair, and which is to be specified in the shape of particular projects reflecting the desire for, or the fact of a family.

July 8

We can relax in a situation indefinitely. But we might find an opportunity for identifying ourselves with it and then acting out a new role. This is what happened when Pope John XXIII was elected, when Truman took office, when Ben-Gurion became prime minister of Israel, and when de Gaulle became the ruler of France. These men were part of a system before they reached these levels; they there functioned as good members of the system, allowing their actions to be partly determined by what the system demanded. Such behavior, as a rule, is continued when men become leaders; the men then continue to function as they did before, but with an extra power of decision. Why the difference between these men and Pope John, etc.? Is it not that Pope John, etc., had accepted the system all along as something good, and not merely as something to which it was desirable to adhere? Is that not why, when they reach a position of power, they find it easy to identify themselves with the system? They humbly accepted the system and found a position in it, and when they arrive at a primary position in it, identify themselves with the system as a whole. Those who do not appreciate the system as that which is worthy of being identified with, or who do not recognize that someone has or could identify himself with it, will, when given a position of power, not identify themselves with it.

If we identify ourselves with only part of a situation, we leave over some possible activities; but if the situation is the only place where there can be roles, what is not used in the identification is repressed. There is also a kind of repression when the specification we impose on the system and values of society are blocked by the society, through the agency of threat or pain. Keeping the society's mode of expectancy (i.e., the kind of situation it provides) fixed, we are forced to change that with which we have identified ourselves. Keeping our identification with some specification fixed, we are forced to violate what was supposed to be our project.

That which is repressed has its own project, and this cannot be cancelled. According to Freud, the repression of some item but makes it come out unconsciously. This presupposes that we have identified ourselves with that which has been repressed. To repress is to identify oneself with something, but to deny its associated projected unfolding along certain lines because (according to Freud) we have accepted instead the project approved by society.

We can avoid repression if A] we do not identify ourselves with an impulse—but such a denial of identification is, according to Freud, impossible; B] we carry out the impulse—but society and parents forbid this; or C] we give up the project associated with the impulse—but this, according to the Freudian interpretation of dreams, is impossible. What we express is only part of ourselves, and then along projects which society endorses.

July 9

I jotted down these notes in shorthand yesterday evening:

Life is the self-maintenance of the individual. In death we become part of a single impersonal totality. While living we can represent that totality, and thus in life have within us the meaning of what defines our death. We will have thereby controlled death, not in the sense of making its advent impossible, but in the sense that the very meaning of our life is inseparable from the acceptance of that death.

The more we accept the world beyond as our own, the more we make the death we suffer our own achievement; we accept it as part of our meaning, instead of allowing it to be that which is externally imposed on us by a world alien to us. It means that we have another existence, but not as we live individually. Our individuality is the representing of the domain which makes us an imperfect part. Or we can identify ourselves with the impersonal domain and see our lives as an intensified and epito-mized form of this which we lose by ceasing to intensify and epitomize, and merely share in.

In his study of master and slave, Hegel takes the slave to avoid death by taking up the position of one who does the will of another. More gen-erally: to avoid death, put yourself at the service of a power that could destroy you, and in molding this power, turn it into yourself, make it bear the marks of your peculiar life. Then when you die, you but yield to your life in another form; you fall inside the very pattern of life that you have created. You are now a part of your own life in the shape of a transformed nature. It is the same as when you accept the punishment of the state as just, as your own punishment, as something which you as a citizen desire.

I conquer death by taking myself to be a unit in a brute nature which I, as alive, make into a support of myself as alive. Having accepted na-ture in idea as my own, which I possess when it makes me into a part, I find that I am a part of that which is no longer merely brute because its meaning has been "enlivened" by myself.

I avoid personal death by accepting the impersonal death by the world as a product of myself, and thus see the death as a product of the life and not as the terminus of it, as that which replaces life. To die is but to find a place in a context created by my life.

Guilt is a failure to live up to a desirable end, either because of a failure of self-acceptance to identify with some particular, or because of a failure of commitment to have a proper project toward that end. Meaninglessness is the failure to have an object with which to identify, or the failure to have a desirable end. Marcia Guttentag thinks that the former has given way to the latter, in the move from the nineteenth to the twentieth century—a judgment confirmed by many occurrences, from Sartrian existentialism and happenings, to pure experimentation in the arts. The position has strength if restricted to the movement from the state of being committed to the state of having no obligation, because lacking a desirable end. But we still have to go through the steps from self-acceptance to no acceptance of the self (or despair) which will, I think, inevitably lead to its opposite, unrestrained enthusiasm.

(After I wrote these lines, I went to the movies. When I came home, I jotted down the following.)

Our life is eccentric, to be explained by the fact that its very presence requires a reference to a reality outside the sphere of the interplay of actualities. To make it intelligible, we must see it as representative of death, of a realm of Being. It is Being brought inside another world. But then to die is but to be in another guise; it is on one side to be reduced to a normal particular, and on the other side to be understood in terms of the contours of ultimate Being. When life is made intelligible in the second way, there is a death which is nothing more than life made intelligible in new terms. Life becomes intelligible by becoming a report of Being. But to make it so is also to die. The intelligible nature of life is death, either because life remains a particular but is intelligible, or because it expresses what Being is.

(This morning I went on my walk; after reading the newspaper, and typing the foregoing, I returned to the reflections I went through in the course of that hour.)

One can think of life as a condensation of a biological domain, governed by its own laws of sporting, selection, and the like. Life would then be a momentary flicker exhibited now here and then there, as a kind of fulguration of the peculiar nature of that domain. This view, which has close affiliations with the Buddhist outlook on life, appeals to biologists because of its stress on the intelligible nature of the biological world, and because of its dismissal of the individual as a mere momentary condensation whose performance as an individual does not have a significance for biology. The position becomes unsatisfactory the more we attend to the individual, for the individual has a life having its own reality over against and distinct from that of the biological realm, even though it is never altogether sunderable from that realm.

A living being is part of a nonliving world, and is also inseparable from a biological one. Because of the former, it can be located, and its death can be described as the separation from the biological world of living beings (though of course it continues to be pertinent as organic matter). Because of the latter, it has a behavior which is eccentric from the perspective of the nonliving world. Life is a "mixture" as Plato observed, but not because it descends from some other realm, but because it is in fact a natural phenomenon which is to be made intelligible by being understood to be a way of referring and making articulate a biological world.

When an animal dies, it becomes a natural phenomenon as a mere particular, and as intelligible in itself becomes identical with the entire biological world. This new state means the extinction of the individual living animal, for it has no way of having the two sides together—which is what it did have when it was alive.

Man's consciousness immediately converts his species into one mankind. It also makes him one who, while alive, accepts mankind as the meaning of himself as eccentric in a world of otherwise normal, nonliving particulars. When on death, like an animal, he becomes one of those nonliving particulars, he also, like an animal, becomes, so far as eccentricities are concerned, identical with the entire realm for which those eccentricities were signs exhibited in the alien world of nonliving beings.

Having accepted mankind as himself, a man does not lose himself when he becomes one with mankind. But he does, of course, lose mankind as interplaying (in the guise of eccentric behavior) with the side of himself which is a normal nonliving particular (interplaying with other nonliving particulars). If in this life he could find some way in which the mankind, that he has accepted as the meaning or referent of himself as an eccentric particular, could be permanently united with the world of nonliving particulars (so that he in some way continues to be an eccentric particular even after he in fact dissolves the mixture of mankind and the nonliving), he will be able to continue to be a living being in the very sense in which he is able to continue to be identical with mankind after he dies.

Is this not merely to ask that a man accept the meaning of "mixture" as a juncture of units representing mankind, and units which behave normally in a nonhuman realm? Would it be enough for him to recognize the life of any man to be the life with which he can now identify himself, and thus which he can continue to live even after he in fact dies, i.e., after he dissolves his own particular bond? Is this not what men mean when they think of living afterwards in their children or in their race? One of course loses all distinctiveness of oneself when death ensues, but the affirmation that the mankind one has accepted as the meaning of one's own living meaning is to be thought of as combined with the intelligible nature of a nonliving unit, allows one to see another life as oneself in another part of the nonliving context.

What is here said about mankind, should be extended to cover other kinds of realms, such as those grounded in or identical with the various modes of Being, for man is not only a conscious being, but a reflective one who expresses not only mankind but more basic realities as well. By a roundabout route, do I now not come back to a rather commonplace idea, that a man avoids death by seeing his children as another version of himself? I think not. Firstly, it is not only one's children, but any living human being, and perhaps every human living being, which is being considered here, and secondly, the identification is shown to be not a simple acceptance of another's life, but a kind of reconstruction of it as the product of a single mankind and some impersonal particular which, though it results in a singular case—this living individual—is something which one has made his own.

My life is that of one who has identified himself with mankind and understood that mankind to be mixed with some nonliving particular. Another living being lives in his own way the life which is mine. He carries it out in a distinctive way without denying its general character as understood by me, or the fact that I understand it in a distinctive individual way.

July 10

From shorthand notes jotted down yesterday afternoon:

The generic union of a biological realm with a physical particular can be personalized by me. As so personalized, it can be seen to be my possession. As such a possession, it would be generic, to be personalized by another in a new way. That other now carries it, but does not change it any more than I do. Both he and I make a personal union of the realm and the physical particular—or more accurately, are ourselves such a union—but this is intelligible only as the generic which is possessed or oriented in one way rather than another. The actual personal union that I provide is a carrier or possessor of the generic union. So far as I possess or love another, the difference between us as carriers is lost.

If my love means that the other carrier is myself as well, for which I am responsible and in whose service I act, I am thereby preserved in the beloved. I possess not only what he possesses but that possessor as well.

Another formulation: The universal, "individuality," is instantiated by me and others; as known by me, it is made unique, but still allows another to instance it. I possess the universal in knowledge and recognize that others instance it, or I possess it in love and accept it as myself.

On my walk this morning, without thinking about the above formulations, I continued to think about the problem. As a result of these reflections, I would now put the matter differently. I can know the meaning of "individuality" by reflecting on the nature of the biological realm, the nature of a particular, and the kind of union that is possible to the two. Such a meaning is a universal, something general, but I can orient it in myself as a distinct, unique person. Then when I see that universal as being oriented in another, I see it as merely carried or quickened by that other without being altered. In the former case, I see that other as merely allowing the individualized universal another role so that the other becomes an occasion for me to be again. To be sure, that carrier is doing work I am not, and he has feelings and engages in activities which are not mine.

I can understand what a carrier is, and even what kind of feelings accompany such carrying. All that I fail to get is the living through of the individual feelings; this I cannot have without being him. That does not mean that I do not know what the feelings are like. Indeed I can duplicate them. After all, I can take the same attitude toward an individualized form of the generic "individuality" that another takes toward my individualization of it. I do this when I see myself as the inheritor of my ancestors. I then see myself (like them) to be a mere carrier of the individualized generic "individuality." My own feelings then seem irrelevant and distortive, preventing me from being what I want to be, a mere repetition of the individualized generic "individuality" which defines my ancestor as one who knew himself to be a union of a biological realm and a particualr. I can go further and actually try to live out the pattern which he provides. I then use my energies, and thus my distinctive individual nature, to fill out the generic individuality that he bequeathed to me.

I need not, of course, consider my ancestor in the guise of a generic individuality which he has cognized and oriented in himself, and which I then subsequently carry or vitalize. I can approach my ancestor via some story or myth which I would like to relive. This means that I can take the actual being which he was, and translate this into the form of a universal, oriented in him. This I think is the normal way in which I relive the past that I accept as my own.

The story I hear is a generalized version of the individuality of my ancestors, but one which continues to be personalized by reference to them. When I carry this, or vitalize it with myself, I do not distort what I inherit, but rather submerge myself in it. And I can understand another to do this with respect to myself.

I know another's "mind" so far as I have an individualized general knowledge of the nature of individuality and see that the other carries or vitalizes this, and nothing more. If I wish to know him as an individual, and thus as one who is able to provide an individualization for the general knowledge of individuality, I must know the difference he makes to that general knowledge. This I can know only so far as I can sense the difference between a report and an account, between an abstract piece of knowledge and a communication which I am expected to carry or vitalize. If I love another or sympathize with him, I know him via an account or communication, and not via a report or an abstract piece of knowledge.

I take the general items of knowledge, which I have in judgment or even in perception, as items to be carried or vitalized by me in the attempt to recover what they are as ingredient in others. My knowledge of the beloved's mind is achieved in an act of loving, in which I vitalize what I discern of the beloved, and thereby repeat the vitalization that he provided. But the beloved did not merely vitalize the universal "individuality" which I discern; he (a grammatical, not a personal referent!) made what I discern, personal, individual, and concrete. I give vitality to the universal "individuality" as that which had been concretely individualized by the other. How it had been individualized is expressed in the difference between the report and the account, in the difference between the request that I understand and what I vitalize of had been done to generic individuality by the other.

I love but few. Yet I can understand the "minds" of many, because I can sympathize, grasp the fact that there has been an individualization of the universal by them. That universalization I can not only carry, but in fact revitalize without distortion, by refusing to allow the intrusion of personal notes by me. I know the mind of another just so far, then, as I forego being a unique being, and serve only to carry or to vitalize the personally oriented universal I discern in and isolate from him. I have feelings and engage in various acts of my own, of course, but these reflect the effort I make in order to lose myself so as to be nothing more than a carrier or a vitalizer.

I reenact another's individualization of the generic universal—or since he does not begin with a generic universal and then subject it to an individualization (for this could not be possible unless he were an individual to begin with), I reenact what from the perspective of the generic universal is an individualized version of itself. This version the generic universal acquires when derived from another individual.

In coming to know another, I judge, or perceive, or acknowledge him to be a generic universal derived from, but still inseparable from, a concrete unique case whose particular nature I do not then know. That nature I can understand as an intensified form of a carrier, up to the maximum of complete absorption of the generic universal. In taking the universal to be that which I am to re-enact (i.e., as that which is subject to an intensification), I repeat what the other did, just so far as I minimize the intensification which I provide for the role of carrier.

The other is more than a carrier of the universal; he has it inseparable from an intensification which keeps it particular. When I face that universal as that which had been intensified by him, I allow myself to know it by suppressing my own intensification of it in favor of a vitalization or carrying of it, i.e., in favor of allowing that universal to remain unaltered except as that which had been uniquely intensified by the other. That other then continues to be in me, and lasts as long as I do.

When I present myself to others for a similar vitalization, I present myself to be immortalized by them. If they do not know me or do not want to repeat me in a vitalization of their own, I can nevertheless see them as carriers, and thus see myself as a personalized form of the generic individuality which is sustained by them.

We can be made to carry others, whether we know or desire it, or not; but we intensify those others only when we accept a universal as that which had been personalized by them and which we are to reenact in order to make evident again what that personalization was like. Our vitalization does not personalize the universal; all it does is to give body and energy to the fact that it had been personalized by another.

After I finished the above, I rewrote a chapter in the book on sports. Now it seems to me I can put some of the above in a clearer light: The origin of our knowledge of other minds lies in our reenactment of what is presented to us, not as a mere universal or as a record, but as a true story. This has the structure of a universal in that it is expressed in language; but it is organically constructed because derived from an actual situation.

Collingwood in his account of history had some such matter in mind. He thought of historic knowledge as a reenactment; he would be right if history were not a discipline, if it did not have records, and if it made no hypotheses or deductions, and sought only to "recollect" what had happened. Nor can he account for the fact that there had been a happening in the past, which cannot be recovered but only *re*-enacted, vitalized anew. An historical narration is an attempt to convert the historical record into a story; if it succeeds, we can then go on to carry the story or vitalize it by giving ourselves to living according to its rhythm, thereby experiencing something like the event which others have lived through, and which they leave behind in the form of a universal that has a personalized note, without being thereby made concrete or individual.

We take the story others provide to give us that which we might carry or vitalize. If I give myself to another, I am in effect asking him to carry my story or to vitalize it. At the very least, when I understand what it is to be a man, I interpret all others (who are particulars which unite with the biological and other realms) to be carriers, or at best vitalizations of my story. That story is expressed as the meaning of man oriented in, and thereby personalized by me, and yet free of me as here and now.

July 13

Women, through biological development, have an opportunity to become full persons more readily and sooner than men. When unconfused by male ideology, and not denied to be themselves, without reserve they can pursue careers, use their intelligence, and follow out their interests; their acceptance of themselves as women then, allows for a functioning with a minimum of failure, regret, or misstep.

The male must go out into the world to find himself. This is hard, and takes more time, considerable courage, and usually some luck. It is therefore no surprise that most men fail to be full men in the sense and to the degree that women succeed in being full women. The result is that women do not have an adequate choice of mates; too many marriages involve comparatively completed women and comparatively incompleted men, with the consequence that the women are forced into resignation, irritation, despair, or a concentration on their children, their homes, and their social work.

We say "time is money" and that we ought to "save time." The latter expression usually is interpreted to mean that we should not engage in wasteful action. But it is possible to take it to mean, perhaps unconsciously, that the time we have already lived through is to be preserved. There is some such notion behind the discussion of time in Norman O. Brown's *Life Against Death*—a suggestive, but also undisciplined and somewhat inchoate book which plays fast and loose with Freudian themes, but does face philosophic questions from this perspective and thus with some stimulating value for the reader. If there be some validity to this idea, then we save time when we remember, repeat, imitate, or live in terms of the past.

Given a well-defined project to which we are geared, we have considerable freedom in what we will do before we identify ourselves with some particular. The security provided by our union with the prospect allows us to play. Given a well-defined identification with something—our bodies, tools, acts—we have considerable liberty with respect to the specification we will impose on the aboriginal, indeterminate expectation. Our self-acceptance allows us to experiment as to just what we will bring about.

July 14

Ideally we ought to identify ourselves with something in such a way as to prepare for the carrying out of a project which will complete us. We fall short of that ideal in at least two ways: We may fail to identify ourselves with anything, and thus live an empty life; or we may fail to have a project, and thus live a meaningless life. We have empty but meaningful lives when we have projects without identifications; we have meaningless but satisfying lives when we have identified ourselves with something, but have no project which it is to serve.

The most common mistake men make is to identify themselves with something much beyond their power to make their own, with the consequence that they are forced to conform to it. This happens when they identify themselves with an institution, a nation, or even with some large work or sport or game. The identification cannot be carried out except so far as the very contours and behavior of the institution, etc., are accepted as defining what men are and what they are to do. But this means that they failed to get a project beyond themselves, and instead have made identification into a project. Though they can be said to have thereby made their lives have some meaning, they have not prevented it from being empty. But the fact that it is identification which they seek to achieve lulls them into believing that they have satisfying lives.

We make a somewhat similar mistake in education, when we give the child the task of identifying itself with some adult-size project. We fail then to satisfy the child, and allow it to have a meaningful life only in terms of the outside world which set this project for it. A child does not have a meaningful life in its own terms unless it faces a project rooted in something which satisfies then and there; that project should have its contours and activities vitalized and not merely submitted to.

When athletes are trained by being made to go through detached exercise after detached exercise, they are subject to a difficulty the opposite of which is faced by the child. They are given something with which they can identify themselves, but because it is detached, it is also something which does not lay the ground for a further project. There may be such a project in back of the mind of the trainer, but this is an exteriorly defined project for the athletes.

The athletes' exercises should all be satisfying then and there, and in such a way that a project is but the opportunity to use the exercise to arrive at some desirable goal. The identification may not be with what itself is desirable, but the identification is nevertheless satisfying because of what it opens up, and because it allows one to get definiteness for what one now is and is doing. The project, though terminating in something which should be desirable, may be faced as that which is onerous, unpleasant or dangerous; but it will nevertheless be a project which one ought to pursue because it allows one to become meaningful, to have something to which one can be committed.

July 15

A centaur, Jesus Christ, a workman, and an athlete have in common the union of otherwise disparate realities. The centaur is man and beast, Christ is God and man, the workman is man and tool, and the athlete is man and body. In all these cases, a superior being withdraws from its characteristic activity to identify itself with an inferior but insistent, brute reality. The identification involves a denial of some of the inferior's powers or tendencies, so that the result is something other than a combination of superior and inferior. The identification in the case of Christ, the workman, and the athlete is one which begins on a low level, the level of child, apprentice or trainee. (Is it legitimate to suppose that the centaur also had gradually to learn the ways of the horse?) The identification means that the inferior reality no longer is kept within its traditional pattern, nor yet allowed merely to respond to whatever stimuli might impinge on it. Without necessarily having any role for the inferior or for the combination, the identification by the superior makes the combination face a new future. That future is indeterminate with respect to the new combination, but it evidently has relevance to the nature of the inferior power and the kind of energies with which it is now endowed.

The superior power vitalizes the inferior, and thereby allows it to face a future which is better focused than one that the inferior would face by itself, or when merely overlaid with the intent of the superior. The superior power can also set an end for the combination which is to be arrived at by allowing the combination to develop in a trial and error way, so that a maximum identity and efficacy is achieved.

A superior manifests its superiority not only through its capacity to withdraw from its own project, or through its ability to identify itself with the inferior, but by its ability (once the identification has taken place) to assert itself by providing a frame or end toward which the identification, and the unfolding of it, can be directed. A Christ can give import to the life of man, and even to the life of a divinized man functioning here and now, by pointing up the nature of the superiorly defined world to which the life can be and should be subject. The athlete can attend to the problem of character building, or the attainment of excellence, when he has accepted himself as a splendidly functioning body, vitalized by himself as committed and focused. A workman can have some larger project before him, perhaps even the living up to the standards of the guild and/or participating in the work of mankind which allows him to evaluate what he is and has done as a union of man and tool. The centaur can be interpreted (in the absence of available characterizations of him as anything more than a man who has been dominated and merely carries out animal lusts) analogously to these others. He is more than an animal, having at least the desires of a man which are being expressed through the body of a beast. His desires, for example, make him direct himself toward women and not toward horses. When he allows himself to function as a humanly vitalized animal he must learn how to allow this to unfold in the course of time so that further satisfaction is achieved in his interplay with women and others, and must encompass this within a humanly evaluated totality that enriches and justifies the identification.

The acceptance of the inferior by the superior is but preliminary to the placing of the result within a context, defined by the superior, which lifts up the result into a new dimension. This outcome is to be duplicated by those who do not make the identification, but who accept it as desirable or who take it to be the exclusive product of one who was able to identify himself with the inferior. What Christ envisages as the future of himself as a God-man, can be adopted by others as their future, either because it has been opened up to them by Christ, or because they accept him. The spectator does something similar with respect to the athlete's final objective of being a full man in an excellent situation; the ordinary workman does this with respect to the master craftsman.

If we follow out this line, we ought to say that a centaur ultimately faces an end whose realization should ennoble him, and through him ennobles whatever there is that is bestial in man. The centaur humanizes the bestial side of himself, and places this in a setting where it acquires a new worth. All others should, by identifying themselves with him as one they would like to imitate or are willing to accept as model, be able to accept this setting as their own.

One can envisage an incarnation as involving the assumption of a mature body. Such incarnations characterize the Greek and the Hindu gods. But the incarnation of Christ (and of some of the Eastern religious leaders) is an incarnation first in the body of a baby. Is this not because the god in him must learn how to fit into the contours of the human, in somewhat the way in which an athlete must learn about his body and the workman about his tools?

In the foregoing there are three distinct ideas which are not sharply distinguished: 1] the unfolding of some base,   2] a projected outcome, 3] an evaluative set.

1]   The unfolding of a base is but the carrying out into action oneself as identified with some part of one's body or with some object, or event, or institution.

2]   The projected outcome is the anticipated result which is to be achieved at the end of an unfolding and which is defined in part by oneself as having identified oneself with something, and in part by oneself as standing away from such identification and giving a direction to what one is doing. The unfolding is an unfolding of means, with the projected outcome as a partly independently defined end.

3]   The evaluation is set by the individual or superior power apart from any control by the body and apart from anything with which the individual had identified himself. The evaluation is perhaps not possible until the identification has occurred; it is an evaluation of that identification and the way it unfolds. But it is an evaluation which has to do with the superior power as not involved with the inferior, and as such it is used to judge the superior power as so involved with the inferior. The involvement of superior with inferior makes possible the use of the superior to forge an evaluative scheme in terms of which the involvement of superior with inferior will be justified, as providing an agency by which the evaluation will be in fact realized.

July 18

One of the secrets for living a rich, strong, and affirmative life is to have a primary conceit. This is an eminently desirable prospect relating to one's abilities, virtues, achievements, status, or importance which, though it may not be in fact realistic, is nevertheless conceivably realizable by oneself. My personal primary conceit is to be a genuine philosopher, like Plato, Aristotle, and other great classical figures. I do not dwell on it, but it does enable me to avoid pursuing certain minor ends, to take defeats with respect to other aims with considerable equanimity, and to accept honors, rewards, and achievements, which fall below those that the primary conceit requires, without losing my stride or equilibrium.

I would guess that most leaders have a primary conceit, and that it is this which enables athletes to commit themselves to arduous tasks. It is also characteristic, I would think, of all fanatics.

It is tempting to say that the fanatics have a conceit which is not realizable in fact or at least by them, but it may well prove to be the case that others, not normally called fanatics, also have unrealizable conceits, though they seem to be realizable to them. It would be better, I think, to view the fanatic as one who acts in unreasonable ways, even though those ways may be appropriate for the realization of a primary conceit.

All leaders, athletes, all men whose life-style has an heroic cast, have a touch of the fanatic about them. If they did not, their conceit would have the shape of a mere wish or desire, since what they would be doing would not be appropriate to the realization of their conceit.

An individual with a primary conceit must act negatively and positively in terms of it. His negative activity will involve the denial that other pursuits are of primary importance; his positive activity will involve the acceptance of tasks and the devotion of self to enterprises and for periods which would not be characteristic of those who did not have that primary conceit.

Primary conceits drive out secondary ones from a position as criteria, evaluative principles, and controls. They are consistent with an involvement in multiple routine tasks, the pursuit of minor goals, the desire to achieve those goals, and a disappointment for not attaining those goals. But primary conceits are not consistent with a loss of confidence, equilibrium, self-knowledge, or devotion to long-ranged and even interminable enterprises.

Paranoia involves the acceptance of something like a primary conceit, bolstered with an unrealistic estimate of the paranoids themselves or of the place of their primary conceit in the scheme of things. They are inclined to suppose that their primary conceit is a conventional conceit like those accepted by most men, whereas it is instead a conceit which stands over against the conceits, beliefs, and aims of ordinary men.

He who has such a primary conceit deliberately contrasts it with the outlooks of others, and uses it to enable him to evaluate those outlooks, not as erroneous or unworthy, but as having a lesser import for himself. A primary conceit is thus essentially an evaluative principle governing one's behavior and one's attitude toward oneself, and then incidentally toward the behavior, aims, and achievements of others.

A primary conceit is accepted in such a way as to be constantly operative, even without being clearly apprehended as doing so. It is a principle of evaluation, and can be related to Freud's superego, when this is freed from its genetic grounding in the parental or societal demands, and is taken to be more than a merely moral principle defining one's guilt and responsibility. One can perhaps find the root of a proper primary conceit in the experiences of the child; attachment to it, though, could significantly be said to be the product of the attempt to free oneself from the superego as defined by society and parents, in order to have an independent principle of one's own. That is why it can be thought of as being on the verge of fantasy and wish, being saved from becoming these through the fact that it is not unreasonable to adhere to it, and because it has a preponderant pleasure tone.

Most men do not seem to have primary conceits. They settle for fantasies, or they spend their energies in trying to substitute one secondary conceit for another—or what is the same thing, in trying to vary the means which might help them arrive at a realization of a primary conceit. But since they are in fact involved with those means, they never have a primary conceit operating for them, unless it be as a lure or guide, or what they are striving to achieve.

One who has a genuine primary conceit does not strive to realize it by this or that means; he assumes an attitude to any and all that occurs as not of primary importance. This does not prevent him from seeing and using some things as effective means for approximating and perhaps arriving at the goal defined by his primary conceit. But he sees those means as replaceable by others, particularly when those means, through force of circumstances, are not available any longer.

One may not want to involve oneself in any means. One will then run the risk of having only a wish or a fantasy, and not a primary conceit. This risk can be minimized by making the primary conceit into a principle of evaluation of relative unimportance for whatever happens and as a principle of supportive evaluation for whatever one is.

A simple test as to whether or not one has a primary conceit is provided by an experience or even an imagination of a case where some virtue, nature, achievement, etc. (which has been accepted by oneself and others as one's own), is denied to hold. He who has a primary conceit will not be chagrined by this denial; he will not like it, but he will not be disturbed by the fact that some other virtue or perhaps a vice, some other achievement or perhaps some failure, is attributed to him. Nothing that has now been done or has not yet been done jeopardizes a primary conceit, unless it be such as to preclude its realization somehow, some time.

A primary conceit offers a rough translation of the meaning of God in human affairs. It offers a measure of worth for what one is and does. But then ought there not be also a primary resistance which expresses the nature of a brutality in existence which is of major significance, a primary ground resulting from an identification with some actual state or object, and a primary ideal objective which is reached through the unfolding of that primary ground? If so, we face the world, when we are at our best and in good focus, in terms of a plausible principle of evaluation that takes the sting out of the brutality and allows us to withdraw from the conventional world, thereby enabling us to identify ourselves with some primary ground that allows us to move toward a primary objective. The primary conceit continues to function, and therefore forces us to move on to the primary objective. Since it evaluates that objective too, the primary conceit does not allow one to remain there, but leads us to place the objective in a larger setting.

Most men do not have a primary conceit; instead they settle for wishes and hopes, while having only a rough idea of what is resistant, a loose grip on what might be a ground, and a blurred objective. They are not protected against the successes and failures which ensue on their slipshod use of what is available. They think only of tactics. When one tactic fails to bring them to a desired result, haunted by a sense of failure, they substitute some other; or if a tactic does bring them to a desired result, they puff themselves up with their shrewdness and good judgment, even though what they succeed in doing does not finally satisfy them.

July 19

A primary conceit does not affect one's usual practice, nor the relative evaluations one puts on the things ordinarily done. It assesses all things as not properly identifiable with oneself, and thus as never to be judged to be all-important, either as successes or failures. It does not make all things indifferent; if it did, it would allow an otherwise moral man to engage in shady practices. Still, so far as what one ordinarily did was dominated by what in fact is only a secondary conceit—pointing to some particular objective among the other objectives which men daily pursue —the possession of a primary conceit would allow one to become a little freer to engage in activities which convention or tradition or the usual associations with the secondary conceit do not allow.

A primary conceit also enables one to withdraw from projects (particularly in their usual form where they are blurred and not tenaciously pursued) in order to be able to identify oneself with some base in the shape of a present body, organ, act, or situation.

Religious men, so far as they have an apocalyptic vision, are inclined to emphasize a primary conceit's evaluative role. They emphasize its withdrawal influence when they give themselves to a religious life, since this requires them to abandon daily pursuits so that they can devote themselves to the carrying out of a religious vocation or a religious ritual.

Sometimes religious men say that if a man lost his primary conceit (say the conceit that he is surely saved), he would find that everything was allowable. Dostoevsky expressed such a view. But this is not a correct consequence. He who gives up a primary conceit, and he who does not have one, do not find that everything is possible. Instead, all is exactly what it had been before. He still lives a conventional life, pursuing socially approved goals in socially approved ways, more or less.

The view that everything is permitted if God (or a primary conceit having Him as a terminus) is not acknowledged to exist supposes that nothing has a value of its own, either intrinsically or because of its place in the ordinary social setting. But most people do not have a primary conceit, and yet continue to live lives in which very little is permitted, because they recognize that there are values to cherish, some of which are intrinsic and some of which are conventionally determined.

St. Augustine said, "Love God and do as you please." Many a man has urged that his religion points up one true value, allowing everything else to be considered to be valueless and therefore to be used as one likes. Such a man is a fanatic. His correlate, the man who thinks that if there be no primary conceit (or who thinks the only primary conceit is one which is religious, but which he rejects), everything is allowable, makes the same assumption that the fanatic does. For both of them, things have no values in themselves either intrinsically or socially, the one maintaining that they do get some value from God, and the other maintaining that they do not, for the simple reason that there is no God.

How is a primary conceit acquired? Why do some men have one, and others do not? How does it operate if it is not constantly before one's mind?

We cannot avoid having wishes and hopes; we have attractive models in the shape of ancestors and present heroes. The problem of the acquisition of a primary conceit is the problem of the conversion of these wishes and hopes into effective principles of evaluation. I suppose we endow the wish or hope at some time with the whole constellation of values which we take to be ourselves. But why do we do this? I suppose the answer is that we find that the values are not capable of being absorbed in a unity elsewhere. We find this out, perhaps, when we are frustrated or denied in some major effort and have the self-confidence to believe in ourselves, and to accept the values still, despite our present defeat. Those of us who do this are capable of an inward life, of a fantasy-existence, of imagination. But this answer, I think, does little more than repeat the question.

Granted that one has a primary conceit, it need not be before one's consciousness all the time. This does not prevent it from being used as a criterion or measure of value. Identified with our ego or self, it provides a frame or scale in terms of which we approach everything else, leading to the withdrawal of an interest in transient and minor goals, to allow for an identification with some base and its proper project.

July 20

It is possible to imagine oneself to be identical with someone in the past. He who lives in terms of this is a dreamer, someone lost in fantasy. It is possible too, to take someone in the past to be a model to be imitated, duplicated, or relived by oneself. He who lives in this way is a disoriented man, perhaps paranoid or schizophrenic. Ideally, one should take someone in the past to be the embodiment of a set of desirable values which are then made to function as providing a direction for what one is now and will be involved with, and for enabling one to withdraw from any particular project to concentrate on identifying oneself for the time being with something here and now, preliminary to an unfolding and a movement toward the end defined by the accepted desirable values. He who does this achieves a primary conceit. (Marcia Guttentag thinks that "primary" leads to the supposition that the conceit is primitive and unchanging; perhaps "basic" conceit would be a better expression for what is here intended.)

He who has a basic conceit adopts something from the past. It is this fact which makes the conceit have an antecedent plausibility. Since it is something which has been attained by others, it presumably can be attained again by oneself. It falls short of being a fantasy or something merely to repeat, because it is accompanied by a strong sense of what is going on in fact. Most men are aware of what is going on in fact, but have no basic conceit in terms of which it is evaluated, while those who have some principle of evaluation too often have no grasp of what is going on in fact, and merely submerge or cancel this in the light of the evaluation they have accepted.

The question of the acquisition of a basic conceit depends then on the double capacity to accept as desirable some quality which has been exemplified in the past in a normal course of activity. A basic conceit apparently is the product of the union of these two, with the desirable quality serving as a frame and a vector for what daily occurs.

Why do some men have only one of these capacities? Why do some exercise only one of them? Why do some men allow the results of these capacities to be alongside one another, while others, who have basic conceits, have one affect and condition and direct the others?

Do not these questions come down to the question as to why it is that some men allow what they admire in the past to provide an unshakeable criterion of excellence, and a fixed ground for themselves while they go about their daily rounds? Is it perhaps that they are disappointed in the kind of outcome they achieve in their daily rounds? Perhaps they do not then achieve the degree of success characteristic of their fellows, or the success does not provide them with much satisfaction?

Judging from my own experience and the reports of colleagues, it seems to be true of some academics that they went up that road because when they were young they discovered that they were not well adjusted to their contemporaries and found refuge in books or experiments which provided some satisfaction, and perhaps elicited praise and support from others. They are men who wanted to be successful in the daily world, but found it necessary to retreat in order to advance. Instead of merely retreating in themselves to be solitary, or retreating so as to project some longer-range project than that characteristic of their contemporaries, they retreated to an attractive figure in the past—some hero, adventurer, thinker, leader, or master whose exploits appealed to them—which they then took to be a carrier of what is desirable. They took themselves to be men who are to be for the future what those carriers are for them now. They therefore at once retreated into the past and projected its achieved virtues forward as what can be carried by themselves. They have a strong sense of both the future and the past, thus contrasting with others whose strongest sense is of the present, with hardly any grasp of the future, and only a tenuous hold on the past, particularly in the shape of exemplified excellence.

Denied satisfaction here and now, those who have a basic conceit find satisfaction in their acceptance of some past achievement, embodied in some concrete event or individual, and see themselves as grounding such an achievement for the future. They are modest and courageous at once, the modesty allowing them to accept the past achievement as a model for themselves, and the courage allowing them to see themselves as having a position for the future similar to that which their model has for themselves. They are in effect saying "I too can be a model."

July 22

Faced with defeat, one can persist in one's endeavors, trying by sheer determination and endurance to come out successfully at the end. One might also accept the situation and the position or roles in it which one has achieved or which have been bestowed. This is, I suppose, the normal answer, and is one which is tempting to those who have been brought up in what otherwise is a desirable atmosphere of trust (which seems to be an indispensable ground for growth in confidence and learning). A third answer is to retreat to fantasy, dreams, idle suppositions, wishes, and hopes. This would leave one in effect at the second position, but with the addition of an illusion that makes the result more tolerable. A basic conceit in effect offers a fourth alternative. It combines the second with something like the first answer, since it is one where the individual continues to struggle, though no longer inside the given situation, but in a larger setting where the given situation may provide a means for moving on, or where it is simply assessed as not being final.

The easiest supposition to make is that everyone takes each of the four answers at different times. No one gives up at once or struggles forever; no one altogether fails to settle for what is, and no one is wholly content with it; no one is without fantasy, and no one remains in it forever; no one is without a basic conceit, but no one has it operative always in all situations.

Why do some men sooner or later settle, though, for one of these or place it in a primary position? Why does even a young child assert itself, insist on itself, and thus refuse to accept the second position, but instead adopts either the first or the fourth?

The second and third positions accept the defeat, the one merely accepting the situation which defines where one is to be, the other allowing this to happen while one retreats to another plane. The third has an element of the defiance characteristic of the first and fourth positions. As a consequence, we can ask ourselves why it is that some individuals accept what is taking place and others defy it, either by indulging in fantasy, by continuing to insist on themselves, or by forging a basic conceit. We can include even the first of these alternatives, where the individuals accept what is taking place, under a kind of defiance, if it be remembered that no one is without some gleam of hope, some wish, or some expectation of deliverance or even luck. Consequently, our issue turns on the reason why one defies in one way rather than another.

We wish and hope when we cannot in fact master the situation now; when we indulge in fantasy, we admit the fact. We make a similar admission when we persist and when we accept a defeat. But when we wish and hope and fantasize, we do nothing about the situation now. The persistent individual acts to change it; a man with a basic conceit evaluates it.

The matter is now reduced to a case where some kind of defeat is acknowledged, and is met either with an answer which makes no difference to what is now happening, or an answer which makes a difference to its structure or its value. In one there is a letting go, and in the other there is a having oneself continue to be present in the situation in terms defined by oneself.

Talking with Richard Sewall this lunchtime about this question, what seemed to emerge is the view that those who achieve a basic conceit find in the face of some defeat that they get both pleasure and control by dealing at that time with some peripheral or irrelevant matter. They find that religion, or words, or argument, or knowledge, provides them with pleasure, as well as with an advantage over others who may have managed to deal better with the situation than they have.

Defeated or about to be defeated, then, some men (or better, some children) start off by finding a value—equal at least to what the success in that situation would seem to offer—in doing something else with some peripheral or irrelevant material, and then gradually build up a defense that revolves around the use of such material in a basic way. I suppose every child toys for a while for an answer to a possible defeat, but few have the good fortune to find something which allows for a pleasure and a mastery equal or superior in value to what the situation might have yielded.

The idea of a basic conceit combines the apparently antithetical ideas of an exaggeration of oneself or one's merits, and the introduction of a product of fancy, or wit, or imagination. It differs from pride (which plumes itself on actual achievements or possessions) and from arrogance (which makes a comparative judgment of oneself as superior to others). A conceit is more private, has an element of spontaneity or joyousness, and cannot be destroyed by anything that in fact occurs, as is evident from the careers of religious martyrs, saints, and leaders, from the careers of political leaders, and from the careers of great creative figures in the arts, sciences, and humanities.

July 24

There are at least two types of men who can be readily confused with those who have a basic conceit—gamblers and flexible worldly successes. Gamblers are not dismayed by defeats, and never take any particular success as final. They differ, however, from men who have a basic conceit in that they attribute their success to the cosmos, even when they suppose that it is a cosmos which answers to something distinctive in their own natures. A man with a basic conceit thinks that he can achieve some outstanding value, and this even in defiance of the world. The gambler never takes himself to defy the world, but to be in fact one who is unusually well adjusted to its basic intent or rhythm. Men who achieve a flexible success attain success in some socially eminent domain. They are leaders in business, industry, politics, the professions, in marriage, or in art. But they are never content to rest there; they supplement those successes with genuine interests in other areas, expressed either through escapes to other activities or in hobbies and adventures. That they do not have a basic conceit becomes manifest when they lose the position which they had achieved in the area of major success. They then become bewildered, disoriented, discouraged, or resigned. But one who has a basic conceit is not defeated even when he loses his position in some major worldly area of success.

If it be true that one acquires a basic conceit by fortunately coming upon some peripheral or irrelevant activity which gives power and pleasure in the face of a present defeat, and then using this to arrive at a position where some fundamental and unshakeable set of values is adopted as a reasonable objective for one to exhibit in one's own person and activities, the question arises why and how some men and not others arrive at that position?

The question could be answered if one supposed that men had a basic, indeterminate set of values initially, and that the chance discovery of what gives pleasure and power enables them to make this set of values determinate. Such a suggestion seems to carry the implication that all men have such an indeterminate set of values from the beginning, and that it vanishes after a time or is submerged when there is no fortunate discovery of something that gives pleasure and power in the face of defeat. I think much can be said for this alternative suggestion, since from the very start even the most passive and intimidated child seems in the face of circumstance to have some ego-insistence which can be reasonably supposed to sustain an attitude that refuses to accept what is here and now, or what is contingent or flawed.

If we take this supposition, we do not have to suppose that the basic conceit is built up out of the use of pleasurable and powerful replies to a situation where one is in fact defeated, but only that such replies merely offer ways for making determinate an aboriginal insistence on self. Ought one then not arrive at a determinate ego, which would lead to pride, arrogance, and self-importance, rather than to the acknowledgment of something bigger than oneself which one would like to live up to? I think so. To avoid this consequence, it is necessary to hold that the initial insistence is not personal, not an insistence on one's ego, but is rather an opening into something that is not viable in that situation. It is to open oneself to an area which can be filled out both with the determinate present content (yielding power and pleasure), and with images, beliefs, and memories relating to the past. The union of these images with the present content makes the ego "idealistic," filled with a hope that may prove to be illusory.

The illusory or fantasy element of a basic conceit now seems to be the product of two realisms—a realism which rests on the successful use of peripheral or irrelevant material in a defeating situation, and a realism which takes account of the fact that some time in the past a transcendent set of values had been realized by someone. The individual, as it were, says to himself, "I can continue to have the kind of success I now have through the use of this peripheral or irrelevant material, and it is not unreasonable for me to suppose that through its use I can be like some predecessor (who might be now living and who may be my father, teacher, model, hero, or guide), who has in fact managed to withstand all defeats and even successes."

The acknowledgment of a basic conceit throws some light on the phenomenon of upward mobility. Some cases of upward mobility exhibit the capacity of individuals, through energy and luck, to move from one social class to another. But some, particularly those of outstanding leaders (who so often come from a lower class) testify to an ability to reach positions in upper classes as a consequence of a drive and achievement in pursuit of aims that have nothing to do either with the class they are in or the class in which they fit later. They are men who are driven by a basic conceit, and who find that their attainment of what it outlines provides them with a worldly success and a position in some upper class that they then do not find of much importance. Those who move to an upper class position in this way are surely quite distinct from those who aim at such a position. It is one thing to try to make a good deal of money, and another thing to aim to be a great painter and find that an approximation to this goal in fact yields a good deal of money.

Is it necessary that there be a defeat before one accepts some irrelevant or peripheral item as a substitute, particularly when its use involves pleasure and power? I think not. One might run across that item by accident. The accident may take place in any setting, and as a consequence, one might suddenly find a satisfaction in the use of something which already frees one from the need to enter into a situation that might end in defeat. This seems to be what happens in the case of young musicians and poets. It seems also to be characteristic of athletes.

It would be odd to refer to athletes as men who have found alternative avenues to success from that which is daily offered, particularly when the latter is one where men are defeated. Usually the athlete, unlike the musician and poet, is well adjusted to the daily world; he usually has more than the usual allotment of dexterity, strength, and health. What seems to occur to him at an early age is the accidental discovery that such and such physical activities give him pleasure, power, and some social approval, and that he can continue to get these results without having to enter into ordinary situations. He therefore does not have the problem of finding an alternative in the face of a defeat, but rather that of maintaining, in cases where defeat might be possible to others and not necessarily to himself, an interest in athletic training, practice, and performance. His problem is to find some model that will give him the other half of his realistic dimension, which together with the particulars in which he now is interested (and with which I wrongly said some time ago he identifies himself for the moment) gives him an element of perhaps fantasied hope.

July 25

Men are driven by an urge to complete themselves. This urge is insistent, but indeterminate in content. Men tend to give it determination and application, the one by filling it with some attractive embodiment which allows it to function as a principle of value, and the other by having it provide a context for some particular which is now pleasurable and powerful. These two specifications, the determination and the application, are independent. Almost every one does something about both, but not in harmony. If there be a determination which has no bearing on what is now accepted as a pleasurable and powerful particular, we have myth, story, fancy, tradition, loyalty, and the like, without it having any effective import in one's life. If we have application to a powerful and pleasurable particular without determination, we have a vague sense of incompleteness, even while we are having satisfaction with something despite some possible failure in the ordinary course of events.

We want to reenact the determination, and we want to repeat the particular success. The reenactment makes us assume the status of a model for those to come, and the repetition enables us to continue to live in the world in a satisfactory or satisfying way. The union of the reenactment and the repetition is the work of the ego; it is an adventure which may end in failure, and so far as this possibility is open, the effort has its tinge of fantasy, of that which is merely hoped for and not that which is reasonable to expect will be attained.

When men settle for the position which they happen to achieve in some struggle with the world, they do not cancel their drive toward self-completion, but effectively frustrate it, since they not only rest for a while, but rest with that which does not in fact promote the self-completion. They are men who have a vague sense of being in an undesirable situation. This situation is overlooked by the pragmatists with their view that belief is or conduces a state of rest in thought and action, and that doubt leads one to reflect and to act so as to resolve what is otherwise indeterminate. No matter how firmly one believed, there would always be a drive beyond it; indeed, men act on their beliefs precisely because these provide a ground or stimulus for the carrying out of their drive for self-completion with some hope of success because it is grounded in what is accepted and stable. I suppose in the end Peirce and Dewey would agree with this view, but their formulation of the problem in terms of the bare dichotomy of belief and doubt (overlooking the overriding drive toward self-completion) forced them at times to speak as if doubt were the goad for activity, instead of being, as it is, one kind of tonality to a more primitive drive toward self-completion.

Sometimes one finds material for repetition before one has that which is to be reenacted, and sometimes it goes the other way. This is due to the fact that the one is a result of a hit and miss encounter with materials, and the other is the result of a hit and miss encounter with models, stories, traditions, etc. In very rigid cultures, where the activities of men are quite restricted, there will be a stress on what can be reenacted; in permissive cultures, where experimentation, particularly on the part of children, is permitted without much supervision, there will be a stress on what can be repeated with pleasure and power. The former stress penalizes the unusual members of a community, while the latter stress penalizes those who are well adjusted or unimaginative, and without a high degree of competence in what is finally acceptable.

There are primitive cultures where there is a good deal of permissiveness allowed to the children but little—and this seems to be characteristic of primitive cultures—to the adults. Were it not that the permissiveness relates to practices which are carried out by the adults in more disciplined ways, the cultures would be faced with the problem of eventually calling a halt to what is mastered in the permissive period. No culture can keep the permissive behavior inside well-defined boundaries without risking an intrusion of constraint into that behavior. The only thing it can do is to inculcate the reenactable state, and thereby reveal that what was permitted to be repeated at one time is no longer possible in terms of that reenactable state.

I would guess that the normal case is where a child experiments with this particular and that, at the same time that this or that past attractive model comes to the fore. The acceptance of the latter together with some appropriate form of the former is a creative move, and is successful just so far as the judgment is practically wise. The practical wisdom of the judgment is in part the result of the insight that the reenacted is relevant to the repeated, and is in part a product of the act of combining the two. We use a practical judgment to see what can be united, and we produce a practical judgment in the course of uniting what was proposed for union.

A strong enough grip on a past model will allow for experimentation after experimentation; a strong enough satisfaction and power obtained from a certain class of particulars will allow for a tentative acceptance of first this and then that model. The one results from well-told stories and good guidance, the other results from opportunities to make use of material that is peripheral or tangential to what brings success in this or that particular situation which is now being faced. (All this is evidently a variant on the Kantian schematism, although I did not have this idea in mind.)

July 26

There is a masculine and a feminine stress in love, with a corresponding masculine and feminine interpretation of death. Neither of these is the exclusive possession of males or females respectively, but it is more likely that they will be found in them than otherwise.

The male gives himself to an enriching experience. But there is a counter-note present in this, for he empties himself, loses focus on himself as distinctive, and becomes lost in a basic surge. This comes to the fore in the consideration of a masculine view of death.

Death is here the losing oneself within the totality of nature, the extinction of the individual by his becoming part of a larger and natural world. One can meet its challenge by bringing in the factor which was dominant in love. One then looks at the conversion into being part of nature as an occasion where one's own individuality has an opportunity to make its impress. He who does this will exhibit the same components as one who is in love, but the stresses will be reversed.

The female is possessed in love and thereby lifted up, made important, established as having a basic function. But here too there is a counter-note, in the form of a loss of identity, of being swallowed up, of being used, of being reduced to the status of being merely a woman. It is the latter that comes to the fore in the envisagement of death in a feminine sense.

Death is here the becoming abstract, the being given a role, the being made to serve. We can meet its challenge by bringing in the other factor, the note of being possessed as this individual. Death will then be seen to be a loss of individuality which is nevertheless seen to contribute to the enrichment of the possessor—which is to say, to mankind or civilization.

In anticipation of the male loss of self, there should be a stress on the fact that one has made an impression on nature; in anticipation of the female loss of concrete individuality, there should be a stress on the fact that one has enriched and sustained the process of being civilized.

Male loss of self is loss of identity, but it does not necessarily entail a loss of individuality, of being this distinctive being here and now. Female loss of concrete individuality does not necessarily entail a loss of self, of being a unique private being. The male loss of self is recompensed in part and imaginatively, by envisaging it to be accompanied by a forceful alteration in what remains in the world; the female loss of individuality is recompensed in part and imaginatively, by envisaging it to be accompanied by a permeating enlivening of what is abstract and formal.

These ways of dealing with death do not assuage the desire of most to understand themselves to be continued as selves and individuals. To have a self continue in the form of a diffuse impression on nature, and to have an individuality continue in the form of an enrichment of what is abstract or merely part of the formal whole of civilization, is to leave one's concern for personal immortality unsatisfied. The lover, though he exhausts himself, nevertheless continues to have a self, and the beloved, though she is possessed, nevertheless continues to be an individual. The dominance of the self and individuality in love is precisely what is wanted to be continued in death. To have it merely as a note qualifying an overwhelming loss of self and individuality will not satisfy one who would be immortal.

Suppose we speak of death as a love from which we do not recover, and thus as one where we continue the process of enriching and enlivening. What justification would we have for making this supposition? We can note ourselves in the process of dying, but we can also be aware that this process has a terminus in death, foreclosing the continuation of the process of dying, and presumably of enriching and enlivening. To make sense of our suggestion, we would have to hold that the self and the individuality are submerged in what remains after death, and there continue to maintain themselves, not necessarily consciously, but surely effectively. Men, though, seem to ask for consciousness, reflection, and energy permitting of some kind of creative and significant life after death. Ought they not then think of their selves and of their individuality as constantly fructifying that in which they are immersed or that which possesses them? Accepting this as a guide, we can say that men can be thought to be immortal in a partly satisfying sense if they are thought to continue as selves and individuals in an effective though not conscious way, enriching and concretionalizing what otherwise would be unfulfilled and abstract.

By speaking of immortality as allowing for the continuation of selves *and* individuals the masculine and feminine approaches are combined. Both should be said to enliven and enrich; it is as such that they continue to exist after death, making a difference to whatever may receive them and possess them.

August 25

I have just returned from Mexico where I have been for the last three weeks. This is the longest vacation I have ever had. In a sense it is also my second, the first having been taken during the Easter vacation when I went through Italy and France with Jonathan. They were vacations in the sense that I did not plan on doing any work on my books, though in the present case I did spend some time making a tape with Robert S. Hartman and another with Marcia Guttentag.

I think I like Mexico more than any other place I have ever visited. The spectacular sky, which one can see from a great bowl surrounded by mountains, changes in cloud formation and weather constantly; the geography is variegated and always arresting; the people, particularly in the provinces, are gentle and friendly; the crafts are local and always have something distinctive to them. The spirit of the place is one of quiet and calm, in a cosmic setting. I have been there some four or five times, and hope I will be there again as many more times in the future.

All men are born into families and grow up learning how to get along with fellowman in a society which is governed by rules and conventions. Can any one ever get into nature?

We fall according to the laws of cosmic gravitation; we guide our ships, or did, by the stars; we plant and harvest in accord with the rhythms of nature. But it is also true that we deal with gravitation, stars, and produce in terms which society provides. Our vocabulary, our tools, our seasons, and our clocks all dictate and define what it is that we are going to do with and get from nature, and when and how. As the existentialists insist, the nature that we know and with which we interplay is a humanized nature, a nature which is qualified by what we think, believe, hope for, decide, etc.

Yet we do escape from a merely humanized nature. There is such a subject as cosmology; there is such a subject as cosmological physics. We can deal with the stars, with biological growth and decay, with the forces of nature, its space and time, and with wild animals and natural forces in terms that are appropriate to them. If we did not succeed in transcending or cancelling out the humanizing intrusions which we impose on nature, and in terms of which we (as individuals) approach it initially, we would not have science, philosophy, and perhaps technology.

Everything we encounter has a brute side to it. We are forced to attend to it, to adjust ourselves to it, to yield to its insistence. Sometimes that brute side can be acknowledged as a note within a humanized context; but sometimes it is so overwhelming as to require us to attend to it in its own terms, and to see if we can find a rationale to it. It is only when we acknowledge a brute side to the humanized things we encounter but which cannot be explained as part of those humanized things, that we for the first time attend to the objects in nature as no longer, so far, subject to humanized values.

Before we get to the point of dealing with nature (and by extension, with Existence as such) apart from all human qualifications, we take account of it as something which is and can be qualified by human interests. From the position of having a nature which is humanized, we move first to the position where it is a nature on its own that is to be humanized, and then to the position where it is to be understood in terms appropriate to it as having a being apart from all human involvement.

Nature as humanized is excessively determined, and then by arbitrary and contingent rules. Nature as that which is to be humanized is at once brute and rational, but of a restricted size and containing only a limited number of objects. Nature as apart from all humanization, actual or possible, is Existence; it has an indefinite scope and contains all the entities that have a position in space and time.

When a man is sick, is he sick in a humanized nature, in a humanizable nature, or in Existence? He is of course sick in a community of men, but the sickness is biological and expresses the interaction of a human body with other bodies in nature, operating according to the laws of nature, no matter what interpretation men may impose on them. The sickness can be overlaid with humanized categories and may be treated as that which is to be so humanized; but in itself it is the result of the interplay of one human body with other bodies in nature. He is sick in Existence first, and may be made to be sick in a humanizable and in a humanized nature subsequently. (The "subsequently" need not take place after an interval of time; it expresses a dependence on the occurrence of an existentialized sickness).

August 26

There are at least three types of illness: somatic, psychosomatic, and psychological or mental. The somatic relates to one's body in interplay with other bodies, both occurring in nature. The illness, of course, is qualified by the society and the humanistic categories in terms of which men look out on nature. A psychosomatic illness involves other bodies as at once functioning as parts of nature and as qualified by our humanistic categories. That illness is qualified by other humanistic categories to make it an illness which is to be understood as requiring for its cure, (as is true of the previous case) something more than the removal of the somatic or psychosomatic causes. A psychological illness has to do with content which is entirely subject to humanistic qualifications; it too must be treated in terms that reveal the illness to be qualified in ways additional to those which affect the factors that enter into the illness itself.

An illness has causes which may be either natural or more or less humanistically defined. A cure of an illness is rarely produced by removing the "causes," by getting rid of the factors which brought it about in the first place, for the illness is almost immediately displaced into a new context where the ill person has a distinctive role from which he must be removed if there is to be a cure.

A person may be allergic to melons. Here we have a somatic situation; even if he likes to eat melons, he becomes ill due to the way in which the chemical composition of the melons affects the chemical composition of his body. But having become ill, he might take himself to be guilty, to be a burden, to be one who now can enjoy the attention and leisure which illness produces, etc. He cannot be cured by merely removing the melons, for he will have captured his illness within another frame, precluding one from eliminating it by merely removing the melons. He will nurse his illness, protract it, or perhaps suppress it or redefine it, and thus will not allow it to be treated as though it were solely a function of the items which caused it. In other words, though the illness is initially a function of the chemicals which the body and the melons involved, it is given a status of its own within a humanistic set of categories that preclude its denial by merely denying its components.

One can become ill from melons, not because they disagree with one's bodily constitution, but because one approaches them with a sense of guilt (perhaps because of some taboo, some superstition, some half-conscious or even unconscious association with regrettable incidents). The result will be an illness which is psychosomatic (so far as the melons have an untoward effect on the individual's body, if only as a weight or something which is to be digested) or is merely psychological (so far as one has made the melons, despite their possible satisfactory function in the body, into objects of repulsion).

These two cases, the psychosomatic and the purely psychological, are not always easily distinguished. A psychosomatic attitude toward melons will make them hard to digest; a purely psychological attitude toward melons can make them objects from which one might turn in disgust. However, if we can identify factors in the melons which can produce a purely somatic illness while we subject them to humanistic categories, we will have a psychosomatic illness. This would leave as instances of a purely psychological illness those disturbances with respect to objects which do not otherwise show them to have an adverse effect on the body.

A purely psychological illness can be achieved without there being any bodily assimilation or interplay with the disturbing object. The fact that the object may be made to interplay with the body is then found to be not a primary matter. The individual becomes ill on confronting or even on contemplating confronting, or using, or becoming involved with the disturbing factor; if we make him deal with it at length or more intimately he but intensifies the original illness. Yet one who is psychosomatically ill can be shown to have a constitution which does not operate compatibly with the factor, even apart from any knowledge had of its presence.

Is it possible to make a similar threefold distinction with respect to sacred objects, valuable objects, and objects treated as distinctive realities in their own right? Evidently these objects do not have a somatic import in the sense just dealt with, for this has to do only with their roles as part of nature or Existence. But these objects do have a being of their own, and as such must have some import for us as beings with which they can interplay. Granted that an object is sacred, for example, apart from any imposition of humanistic categories by us on it, there should then be proper and improper ways in which we might interplay with it. But can one become ill just by having an improper relation to a sacred object, even without knowing it and thus even without having subjected it to categories of our own? If there is to be a strict analogue between the cases that have been considered and this last (and of course of the valuable and the substantial), this question should be answerable in the affirmative. But for the moment I do not see how this is possible.

August 27

If illness of a somatic kind is the result of some maladjustment which our bodies make with the brute realities beyond it, there should be somewhat similar maladjustments to be found in connection with what is sacred (or divinely affiliated), valuable (or ideally grouped), and substantial (or actually equalized in reality). Each of these expresses an objective reality which we can humanize, or even approach in such a way as to ignore or to radically transform their distinctive features.

It has been customary to lump together something analogous to the somatic, psychosomatic, and the merely psychological approaches which we make to the sacred, valuable, and substantial as though they were all the products of a merely incorrect psychological attitude. This has been done because of a prejudice to the effect that the only genuinely root, nonpsychological maladjustment is a somatic one with respect to what is existentially brute.

If we distinguish something like a threefold form of maladjustment with respect to the sacred, etc., we should be able to say that there is a kind of ontological maladjustment possible with respect to them, of which the somatic is but a special case; that there is a kind of epistemic-ontological maladjustment possible with respect to them, of which the psychosomatic is but a special case; and that there is a kind of epistemic maladjustment possible with respect to them, of which the merely psychological is but a special case.

If this lead be followed, then what we have is a threefold distinction; the ontological, the epistemic-ontological, and the merely epistemic. Such expressions as "somatic" and "psychological" but point up the fact that this threefold distinction is being applied to what is merely brute, to that which is grounded in Existence.

What we now have are four kinds of ontological maladjustment, four kinds of epistemic-ontological maladjustments, and four kinds of mere epistemic maladjustments. In addition to the somatic form of ontological maladjustment, we have a spiritual one relating to the sacred, an estimative or evaluative one relating to the valuable, and a judgmental one relating to the question as to whether or not something was real (when it was only an illusion) or an illusion (when it was in fact real). These maladjustments should all be able to occur without consciousness, and have nothing to do with what one had in mind. They could be exhibited in actions, attitudes, ways of dealing with other entities.

One might not find oneself in any particular state of malaise if one were maladjusted with respect to the nonsomatic realities, but one would not be a whole man nevertheless. Just as it is possible for a man to be lax, tired, worn down without having any consciousness of inability or illness, and might even, due to excitement or some idea, conceive himself to be quite well, so it is possible for a man to think of himself as being in health and in good relation to the sacred, etc., perhaps because he does not take it to be sacred at all, and treats it as a mere brute reality, which has been overlaid by others with superstitious accretions.

He who is not properly adjusted to the sacred is alienated from others; he who is not properly adjusted to the valuable is cynical or sentimental; and he who is not properly related to the substantial is deluded, not in the sense that he sees what is not there, or does not see what is there, but in the sense that he misconstrues what he sees and takes illusion to be reality, and conversely.

Good adjustment to the realities about involves a grasp of them as sacred, etc. A good grasp of them as such can, of course, be overlaid with epistemic distortions to give us an epistemic-ontological illness; and of course the nature of the sacred can be obscured or even ignored by being made subject to purely epistemic categories.

August 31

It has been often observed that when a man is speaking of another, he frequently betrays himself. The criticisms and evaluations he makes of the other often reflect biases, prejudices, hidden desires, and aggressions on the part of the speaker. But is it not also true that when one man is speaking of another to a third, that he is also making an evaluation of that third? This seems to be especially true when a man is speaking to a woman about other women, to Jews about other Jews, to Negroes about other Negroes, particularly when the conversation involves a belittling of the others, with a seemingly presumptive praise of the man to whom one is speaking.

When criticizing another, particularly one who belongs to the same class as one's listener, and more surely when that class is thought to be disadvantaged, the speaker in effect is saying that he recognizes his listener to be in principle also disadvantaged but that the speaker is overlooking this, or that he discerns virtues which allow him to override these faults. He is ostensibly saying that the listener is outside of the class which is being criticized, at least so far as this particular fault is involved; often he is also implicitly saying that the speaker is superior to the listener, but that he is ready to ignore the distance between them, perhaps because of the listener's desirable virtues.

I think it is possible for a man to speak of another sincerely and in no way betray anything undesirable; it is also possible for a man to speak to a second of a third and in no way intend, implicitly or explicitly, to denigrate that second, particularly when he is engaged in denigrating the third. But it does seem true that both cases do occur.

If this be true, it should sometimes be the case that when men tell sex jokes to one another, when they speak of women in an impersonal or depersonalized way, when they speak contemptuously of their wives or their sweethearts, that they are also making a disevaluation of the other men. Here, of course, we have a case somewhat different from that first envisaged today, since it involves not a speaking to a woman about other women, but a speaking about other women to men. The talk may have the purpose and effect of promoting a solidarity amongst the men, but it can also have as its motive the viewing of other men as unable to understand the fine niceties of a relation of love or intimacy where the woman is treated with delicacy and understanding and with a genuine concern for and insight into her as a distinct individual.

So far as these observations have any merit, they point up the fact that an attitude, expression, or act which involves a conceived or incipient debasement of others often affects one's relationship to individuals who were not taken to be the topic of the discourse. A position which minimizes some individuals usually entails some minimization with respect to other individuals with whom one has come in contact, even when one speaks and acts as though one were making an exception of these latter individuals and were putting them on a level above the others, and perhaps even of oneself.

September 7

Psychiatrists and coaches have a somewhat common method. They try to combine firmness with kindness, direction with an encouragement to be free, sympathy with criticism. The coaches, however, have three advantages: their clients come to them confident rather than in despair; the objective to be attained is fairly clear; and there are well-defined tests to determine whether progress has been made.

The psychiatrist—or more generally, the therapist—could conceivably turn a despondent client into one who is confident that success will ensue, though perhaps the nature of the illness is such that this is a problem. If so, one might see the therapist as being first faced with the need to achieve the position of a coach, having to do with individuals who are confident that they will be cured. But this question is complicated by the fact that the other questions have not been resolved.

The coach wants his charges to achieve a degree of excellence, and perhaps to win in some contest. He knows whether or not they have achieved the excellence by making them face objective tests, often in competition with others. A therapist could conceivably say that he wants his patients to overcome a feeling of discomfort, perhaps accompanying a sense of failure or worthlessness, but it is possible that a man may have such a feeling because he fails to fit in with some undesirable situation or group. The coach does not face this question because he attends to a more objective criterion. He does not inquire into the question of the degree of comfort which his charges may feel, except so far as this may be of help in meeting the challenge which the contest may provide.

A therapist could argue that what he wants to do is to have men engage in socially acceptable tasks with some degree of publicly expressed satisfaction. But this would allow the therapist to prepare his clients to be part of undesirable societies, such as the Gestapo. His clients may then feel better than they had.

Coaches prepare their charges not only for contests, and not only for contests which are socially approved, but for contests which the vast body of mankind would approve, and in any case which are approved by those who belong to other political and social wholes. If the therapist would take the coach as his guide, he would seek to prepare his clients to do what would be approved by mankind. He would try to have his clients adopt the attitude of the therapist himself, which is to say to try to become sympathetic and critical, firm and kind with respect to the young, the dependent, and eventually with respect to everyone. Then he would try to have them engage in desirable activities, no matter how well or poorly they are placed. If a client be in Nazi Germany and forced to make a living, he would be helped to find those activities inside the scheme which would allow others to grow. He would try to teach neutral subjects, or acquire or spread knowledge of science, art, archaeology, medicine. Such knowledge might be misused and abused by those in power, but this would not affect the fact that the client had been improved.

Evidently many of those who go to therapists are in no position to learn how to be kind, etc. They are anxious or in despair. The first task is to get them to the stage where they are able to face the question as to what they should do that is positive. The therapist is then somewhat in the position of those who are involved with the rehabilitation of cripples, the injured, etc. Here the objective is to get men to arrive at the stage where they can become perfected.

We have then two stages of help: there is the help to get men to function in the normal ways in which the majority of men function, and there is the help to get them to function in ways which perfect themselves and others. Coaches get men who come for the second stage, whereas psychotherapists get them to come for the first stage. But is the first stage different in principle from the second? I think not. If a champion is taken as our model, all other athletes are defective in various ways; if a normal man is taken as our model, the physically and mentally ill are seen to be defective in various ways. The help needed by the latter demands that the guide proceed in the same way as the former —with sympathy and criticism, with vigor and gentleness.

September 8

I have been reading Hans Selye's Stress of Life. It makes plausible the view that the body not only makes specific responses to specific challenges, but that it makes specific responses to unspecific challenges, to the fact that it has been intruded upon, injured, challenged, forced to engage in activities in order to attain, if it can, the normal position which it had before this occurrence.

The view seems to depend on the supposition that a living body seeks to maintain itself, and that when confronted with some possible disturbance to this situation, it first takes alarm, then resists, and finally exhausts itself. Now, I have previously argued that no actuality is engaged in the activity of self-maintenance, and that this instead is a product of an effort to complete oneself. I objected to Spinoza's view that the body was occupied with the task of self-maintenance by remarking that there would then be no reason for any to intrude upon any other.

It might, however, be argued that self-maintenance is a preliminary state which must be achieved before there is a significant effort at self-completion. Self-maintenance could be said to be a consequence of self-completion, but one which must be attained before the self-completion could be treated as involving some intrusion or mastery of others. Conquest would then have to be understood to be the outcome of success, and not the outcome of some failure or defect. Or more accurately, there would always be a defect in the individual which he would try to overcome in his effort at self-completion, but this effort must result in the attainment of some stability, in some recovery of the position that had been occupied, before one went on to make use of that which had been confronted. Self-completion would then require that the intruder be utilized to get one to the stage where one could intrude successfully on others.

I am not sure how much of this is pertinent to the position Selye himself wants to develop. But it does lead to reflections on the nature of the individual as more than a mere body. One can start with the idea that an actuality seeks to maintain its own integrity, that it wants to be self-complete, and therefore tries to adjust itself to the kind of challenges which other entities provide. Those other entities can be said to be inseparable from or to represent the ultimate modes of Being, and it is as such that the individual body reacts to them so as to maintain its state as a normal self-contained individual.

The bodily case, which concerns Selye, can be understood to involve a challenge by dynamic entities to the existing individual who, as encapsulating a portion of Existence within himself, tries to adjust himself to any attempt to alter that Existence or the manner or degree in which it is possessed. We should on this basis be able to say that the individual may find his worth challenged by the presence of any sacral object, his freedom as a substantial reality challenged by the presence of any actuality, and his value challenged by the presence of any obligating entity. In these cases, we do not have an intrusion into the body of the actuality, but only a confrontation by that actuality of entities which evaluate it, and thereby in a sense challenge it as having not only a distinctive existence, but worth, freedom, and value (where worth or worthiness means a dignity in terms of some eternal judgment in contrast with value which is an embodied degree of excellence here and now).

The sacral, substantial, and valuable, no less than the dynamic, challenge the individual; in order for him to be in the same world alongside them, he must adjust himself to them by reassessing them through a change in his relations to them. Faced, for example, with some sacral object, or more sharply, with some conspicuous sacral object, the individual would have his worthiness challenged. The object would stand as a criticism of him, as a demand on him that he change himself so that he and it are coordinate. Would the individual then go on and try to complete itself by somehow subduing, mastering, or possessing this which he accepted as being alongside? If he did not, he would have to be thought of as an island, as that which seeks only to be with others and never to be with them as somehow under his control, so that no further assault will be possible and so that whatever values that other possesses will (without denying that other's independent reality and dignity) become part of the challenged individual. Individuals, whether treated as merely bodies or as something more as well, do not seek merely to be at rest; their rest is a position in terms of which they can act.

Illness can be defined as the need to adjust oneself so as to be only alongside that which assaults. But then health would be compatible with lassitude, idleness, inanition, and torpor. Homeostatis cannot be the aim of the organism; it can be only a state which one must reach in order to be able to function well. But functioning well involves the use and transformation of other entities.

Selye offers empirical evidence for the presence of the syndrome which results from a nonspecific attack on the organism. Are there analogous "syndromes" for encounters with sacral, etc., objects? Is there such a thing as a mere encounter with a dynamic object as over against the body and not as actually intruding on it? The answer to the second question seems to be that there is, for we do fear things which may hurt. The answer to the former question is more difficult. Are the feelings of guilt, humility, and insignificance unspecific responses to confrontations with valuable, sacral, and substantial objects? If so, ought not the challenge which is made by parts or representatives of Existence be something like the feeling of weakness or frustration?

Humility has a favorable connotation, at least in the literature. To express something analogous to weakness or frustration, we should speak of worthlessness. But then this must be distinguished from what has just been termed insignificance. Worthlessness answers to one's failure to live up to the demands imposed via sacral objects by God. Insignificance answers to one's failure to live up to the demands imposed via distinct actualities by Actuality. The one refers to the value one has in the eyes of eternity; the other refers to the status one has with respect to other actualities. The one is a judgment absolute and individual, the other a comparative judgment.

September 9

When a man responds to the presence of a sacral, valuable, or substantial object, he deals with it as answering to some state in which he then is, and as implicating the object's relevant mode of Being. If there is to be something similar in all four modes of Being, we are forced to conclude that when a man responds to some intrusive or threatening existent (i.e., some dynamic entity) through an alteration in some particular part of him, as well as through some form of stress, his response is expressive of some state of him as a single entity. He is not to be viewed as expressing the reaction of some part of his body, e.g., his joints and then in the form of an inflammation, but as being unprepared, as being too passive or active as a whole, and therefore about to express his reaction to the intruder in the form of an inflamed joint.

There are parts of the body which an individual in a given state can use to express the specificity of that state and its relevance to what is now threatening or intruding. Is there something analogous to be found in connection with the states of the individual answering to valuable, etc., objects? A man feels guilty when he does not face and deal with some object as valuable, and thus as at once deserving specific responses here and now and as representative of the nature of the Ideal. If there is to be an analogue to what happens when he faces a dynamic object, there should not only be some undesirable state in him, but also some particular part of him that is affected. Is this not the justification for our referring to his conscience? This suggestion places conscience on a footing with kidneys, liver, lungs, and heart, as a particular region in the individual which is directly affected by what now is not properly adjusted to. And it places character alongside conscience as a "part" which is affected when there is no appropriate relation to what is sacred, and self-evaluation alongside both of them, as a "part" which is affected when there is no appropriate relation to what is substantial.

We have then four types of part—physical parts of the body, conscience, character, and self-evaluation—each being affected by particular entities. The assertion seems odd, in part because the physical parts are palpable and readily distinguished one from the other. Ought we not then acknowledge other "parts" which, together with conscience, for example, help constitute the individual as one who can respond specifically to objects of value? Or ought we to treat conscience, etc., as on a footing with the entire organic body and look for subdivisions of it as capable of responding to particular values or valuable objects? Conscience, etc., on the second alternative would be equivalent to the individual as oriented toward the Ideal, just as the organic body is oriented toward Existence. Degrees and kinds of guilt would then be correlated with particular values or valuable objects with which we are not yet properly adjusted. This seems to be a plausible view.

We are still left with the fact that the various parts of the body are quantitatively determinable and clearly distinguishable one from the other in space, whereas the "parts" of conscience, character, or evaluation are at most degrees or tonalities, and not spatially distinguishable. What does this fact mean but that a body is extended and that Existence is spatio-temporal-dynamic, whereas the individual as involved with objects affected by other modes of Being is not extended in space? This reply seems correct, yet I cannot get over a feeling of uneasiness. I suggested that the different physical parts of the body were expressive of particular states, so as to remove the oddity of having Existence's objects alone be without an answering state in the individual. But now I am back with the fact that the body does have distinguishable parts which respond to these objects. If this be satisfactory, what need is there to refer to a state behind these parts, and which those parts express or convey?

If we could have nothing but states answering to the particular objects with which we were responding, we would have a complete symmetry amongst all four positions which an individual can take. But if there are particular quantitative parts in one case and only qualitative distinctions in the others, there would seem to be no warrant for adding to the former distinctive qualitative distinctions to match the qualitative distinctions in the latter.

September 12

Each mode of Being is inseparable from a plurality of entities. Each therefore can be approached quantitatively. Three of the modes of Being are also encapsulated inside Actuality and there have an effect on the various actualities, enabling one to see the contribution of those three modes of Being in a quantitative form. So far as we can view actualities, and particularly men, as answering on their unitary side to the various modes of Being, there should be quantitative ways of dealing with them. Each man, as a matter of fact, is transient and for a plurality of reasons, expressed by the dynamic, existent fact of other entities as located in space and time. Each is also dependent on other actualities for support; each is guilty with respect to the demands which the others make; and each lacks worthiness in terms of the acceptance that the others deserve. The dependence, guilt, and worthlessness, like the transience, are produced by any number of entities; those entities are inseparable from the various modes of Being, and as such are met by a single attitude on the part of the men. In other words, guilt, etc., is a single response elicited by any one of a number of actualities as having a value, etc., to which a given man is not adjusted properly.

The above not very clearly stated position is a generalization of Selye's view that the body of man is subject to challenges by other entities, and that the body not only reacts in specific ways to specific intrusions, but also in a nonspecific way, in the sense that the response can be elicited by any one of a number of agents and in any one of a number of ways. He also observes that there are particular occurrences in the body which express the fact of stress. Stress, though the response of the organism as a whole to the fact of threat and danger (as embodied by any one of a number of entities), has a specific, identifiable form, making a difference to the size and function, for example, of the adrenals. If there is to be a matching of the other modes of Being with what occurs in connection with Existence, we should hope to find particular "syndromes" in the individual answering to the fact that an "organic response" is being made to some intrusion by an intruder who is inseparable from some mode of Being to which the individual as a whole responds.

We should find, were the matching to hold throughout, that when a man is guilty, he not only fails to do justice to this or that particular claim, but that there is some specific combination of obligations which he then brings to the fore. The guilt should be expressed in him in terms of a distinctive readiness or reluctance to deal with value; similarly, his feeling of worthlessness or of dependence should be expressed in him in terms of a distinctive readiness or reluctance to deal with final evaluations or with entities as having a finality of their own. We would then have not only a relation to a mode of Being expressed as guilt, etc., but some particular change in the individual man expressive of this fact. Faced with a particular actuality, a man could then be said not only to respond to this in a specific way, but to respond to the Being by which that particular actuality is qualified, and to do this by means of some particular change in him.

Guilt, to take this as a paradigm, is the result of an improper treatment of some value claim made by some particular actuality. The same degree and kind of guilt can be provoked by different actualities, since the guilt reflects not the particular nature of the actualities, but the claim they make, and thus what they are as affected by the (encapsulated) Ideal. The guilt, though it is an "organic" response by the individual to the Ideal as represented by any one of a number of actualities, has its own specific form in the shape of a change in the attitude of the guilty being toward all else. This change is manifest in his ability to attend to value aspects of actualities as he had not before; he is now sensitive to them as having nonvaluational sides. To be guilty is thus to become aware that any and all actualities are more than instantiations of the Ideal. The guilt is due to the fact that the actualities have not been properly treated as such instantiations; it is due therefore to a failure to treat them properly as instantiations of the Ideal. This is equivalent to saying that guilt arises because valuable entities have been treated as nonvaluable. As a consequence, we must say that because we treat certain entities as nonvaluable, we become alert to the fact that all have a nonvaluable dimension.

None of the above is altogether clear to me, and for the moment I am not even sure that I am not at a dead end, following up a hopeless lead.

September 13

In *Reality*, I maintained that every being seeks to complete itself. The observation was made with respect to actualities in relation to one another. But it can be extended to apply to the modes of Being in relation to one another as well, and also to the modes of Being in relation to actualities, and to the actualities themselves. In all these cases, an entity insists on itself, while making an effort to subjugate the others, so as to make them conform to it.

The modes of Being do not merely subjugate the various actualities; they are felt by men to impose demands which, so far as they are not met, are felt by the men to express something unsatisfactory about those men. Men are guilty, without worth, without distinctness, and without individuality or dignity, because of the way in which they fail to be in a proper relation to the Ideal, God, Existence, and Actuality. This failure can be of one of two kinds. Either the actuality fails to meet the express demands of these modes of Being, or these modes of Being make unrealized claims on the actuality. The first of these can be treated as a consequence of the second, so that what we have is a series of claims made by the various modes of Being.

Should we not also say that each actuality makes a claim on other actualities, on the various modes of Being, and on the other actualities as affected by the modes of Being? If so, should we not also say that there is something like the feeling of guilt, etc., to be found in actualities, and particularly men, when and so far as they fail to do justice to the claims made on them by the other actualities and other types of particulars? We can be said to feel guilty because we fail to do justice to the claims of the Ideal; but do we not also have something like guilt, or something related to guilt when we fail to do justice to the value of objects as so many instances of the Ideal? Do we not have a sense of being unfair, indecent in such a case? It seems so. What we then have is not only a feeling of guilt because of the failure to meet the demands of the Ideal, but a feeling of having been unfair with respect to this or that valuable actuality, an unfairness that entrains a feeling of guilt with respect to the Ideal with which the valuable actuality is associated.

The feeling of unworthiness which arises because of a consciousness of one's inadequate relation to God accompanies one's perverse behavior with respect to what is sacred. The feeling of dependence which arises because of a consciousness of one's inadequate relation to Actuality accompanies one's incorrect estimate with respect to the equal reality of what is substantial. And the feeling of transcience which arises because of a consciousness of one's inadequate relation to Existence accompanies one's improper accommodation of other existent actualities.

The modes of Being have their own distinctive pluralities of particulars. Those particulars must be related to their respective modes of Being, and to what these encapsulate, in the way in which actualities are to their mode of Being and what it encapsulates. But just what these particulars are and what natures they have, the kinds of claims they make, etc., is hard to determine, because we have considerable difficulty in getting clear how a mode of Being functions with respect to its plurality, except in the case of Actuality.and its actualities.

When a Being encapsulates another, does it encapsulate the other's plurality? Does it encapsulate a version of the other? Does it encapsulate a version of the other? Does it encapsulate a version of the other Being together with all the plurality which the other Being faces? Or does a Being encapsulate the plurality or a version of the plurality associated with the other Beings? I think it most reasonable to suppose that what is encapsulated is the plurality which is associated with other modes of Being, with the consequence that actualities can be said to seek completion with respect to and be the target for various kinds of particulars as confined within the area of Actuality. But if this is so, in what sense does an actuality seek completion by trying to subjugate other modes of Being? By seeking to attain a proper relationship to Actuality, an actuality can perhaps be said to involve itself in an effort to adjust itself to the presence and action of other modes of Being, even though it has no direct relationship to them. (All this is not only somewhat obscure, but does not seem to have much bearing on the kinds of inadequacy felt by actualities, except so far as the clarification of fundamental issues makes evident what kinds of problems there are and how they must be dealt with in new ways.)

What I have been trying to get clear is how the various modes of Being and their different pluralities all need one another, and are suffered by one another to impose justifiable but unmet claims. Actualities, for example, must be said to need and claim to subjugate other actualities, Actuality, other modes of Being, and the pluralities associated with those other modes of Being. And what is true of actualities must be true of the entities in the other pluralities. And what is true of these must also be true of the modes of Being with respect to one another, and with respect to the items in their own and other pluralities.

September 14

When physicians tell a man to rest, what they mean is that he should relax for a period. Relaxation is the release of the various parts from a dominant unitary intent; it allows the various parts of the body to function with a minimal supervision. This is desirable just so far as there is an excessive stress due to the response of the organism to the pressures of some modes of Being as mediated by some particular.

Why is it not good to relax indefinitely? Is it not that A] the various parts of the body, if left without supervision, will sooner or later get in one another's way; B] that some parts, arms and legs, for example, need to be controlled in order to function at their best; C] that it is the persistent and insistent use of parts of the body that enables them to grow and to limit the process of decay; and D] that the organism as a whole has objectives of its own which should be pursued and in that pursuit govern the activity of the parts so that those parts function on behalf of those objectives?

A limited period of relaxation enables the parts to function more on their own than they had, and thus to prosper as distinctive entities; a longer period denies them the kind of guidance, direction, and control that is needed if they are to function maximally together. Evidently the organism as a unity is something like the conductor of an orchestra; without him the members of the orchestra would soon fall out of harmony. The analogy breaks down, however, when we think of a short period; the conductor's absence does not necessarily improve the playing, whereas the relaxation of the unitary guidance of the organism does permit an improvement in the functioning of the various parts.

The desirable state for the individual is one where he remains in control while providing for a maximization of the functioning of the parts. We have here a particular illustration of the question of the relation of the one and the many. If we envisage the mind or the organism as a whole as a one, and the parts of the body as a many, we have the further fact of the control by the one of the many to consider. There is also the unity of the one and the many. Does this mean that there are two or more basic ones?

The one of the organism is a one *for* many parts; so far as it governs those parts, it is a one *of* them. The parts, qua parts, to be sure, have a one *of* them apart from the organism, since any aggregate or collection of items has a one immanent in it. As having the power to govern the parts, the one *for* them cannot be a mere function of them, a mere being together of them even in a prescriptive guise—which is what is the case in connection with the modes of Being, beyond which there is no further being. When a being, functioning as a one, operates on a many which has some being of its own (and thus is governed by an immanent one of its own), it reorganizes the many parts, and thereby becomes filled out with those parts. The one that is the result of the domination of the organic unity over the parts of the body is nothing other than that organic unity as filled out by the parts which it immanently unites.

September 20

Sentiment discerns correctly; it is sentimentality that distorts.

Emphasis on a climax in art or sex defines what precedes as preliminary and what succeeds as anticlimatic. But every step should be satisfying and desirable, with the climax expressing only a major turning point.

Until a man is detached, he is unable to enter fully into anything.

A round of love makes a world.

It is one thing to be filled full and another to be fulfilled.

Different types of rules should be distinguished. There is the *general* rule which presents a mere structure: the knight in chess can move one space in one direction and two in another, or two in one direction and one in another. There is the *specific* rule which orients the structure in some actual position: the knight in this game can move from here to there. The "here" is any of the positions on the board and the "there" is any of the positions to which one can go by making use of the general rule. There is the *usable* rule, which is the specific rule oriented in some particular position: this knight in this position can move to this space or that. And finally, there is the *used* rule, which is the usable rule as it operates to bring one to this position or that.

When we use inference as a model, we tend to think of a rule as taking us from some beginning to a conclusion. We seem not to have to face any material conditions nor to be involved in any series of steps. There is only one movement, and this takes place in the mind. But when we come to the world of practice, we have a different situation. Here we must move from position to position, and do this under the conditions that prevail. We use a sequence of rules, all of which are selected under the influence of the end which we have in mind, making the progress to that end the result of a series of preferences, as defined in my *Man's Freedom* or in the *Modes of Being*.

The knight, let us say, is at Q4. The object of my move is to gain a further advantage. To do this, I must face all the pieces as providing a condition which I accept as the ground for a projection of my knight, as subject to a usable rule, so as to convert a possible advantage into an actual advantage.

When we think of rules as abstractly formulated, or when we view them as defining the path over which an inference is to move, rules are syntactical. When we think of rules as providing a connection between what we intend and what we will make out of what we confront, rules are semantical. But what we normally do in practical affairs is to move from an actual condition which we confront to a new situation by means of a rule which is selected under the pressure of some goal that we have accepted as that at which we would like to arrive.

A runner would like to run a four-minute mile. He decides that he will want to make a quick start and run ahead of all from the beginning. This is a usable rule. The use of the idea of running a four-minute mile dictates just how the rule is to be used. He will face the actual condition of the race in such a way as to try to exhibit his intent to have a quick start and to run ahead from the beginning. Every decision that he makes can be viewed as having the structure of a used rule which he makes concrete by starting at a given condition and attaining an alteration of it. The rule he uses is in fact then a plurality of subordinate rules, all of which are selected under the pressure of the end which characterizes the rule as a whole. The rule as a whole, oriented in a given condition and directed toward the goal, is used only by taking it to demand the use of a series of subordinate rules whose function is to take us from one condition to an altered form of it.

September 21

The reference to semantics yesterday overlooked what I once knew: if there is a problem of semantics, it cannot be solved, for such a problem supposes that there is a gap between two types of entity but that there is no third type of entity to bridge the gap. Any supposed bridge over the gap will consequently be found on one side or the other of the gap; it will never cross from one side to the other.

We can think of our ideas as alongside other entities of a similar general nature—sensations, sense data, etc.; we can think of them as having a physical nature and meaning alongside other physical entities, the so-called objects in the world; or we can think of them as having their own kind of nature and careers, but nevertheless related to external objects through the interlocking of the vectors of the ideas with the vectors of those objects, along the lines suggested in 2.12 of the *Modes*. In all these cases, we must acknowledge a complex situation which is to be transformed by the use of some component of it to bring about a new situation that can be anticipated only in a general way. We do not move from a state where we have nothing but ideas or words or private feelings into an external world, but instead have our ideas, words, feelings, etc., alongside objects, say in a relation of acceptance or conjunction, and then change our attitudes or the objects so as to produce another situation in which the ideas, etc., are alongside the objects in a relation of affirmation, identification, etc.

The Hegelian dialectic depends on the recognition that there are no real gaps between the various elements with which it deals. It is a difficult matter to decide just what makes his dialectic move—whether it is the completed Absolute luring the conjunction of the items on to become more solidified, or whether it is a self-moving fact produced by the mutual attempt of the components to adopt one another. In any case, the dialectic seems to be a special case of the kind of situation we find on every side. We are always in and observing situations in which items form some kind of unity that is to be transformed by altering the position or nature of one of the factors in it. One of those factors could be ourselves, or it could be something quite indifferent to us. The factor which is altered in position or nature embodies the usable rule; it gives the rule a use of a particular sort. As a consequence, what we have is the transformation of the original situation through the use of a rule as embodied in one of the factors.

A sequence of used rules is what is offered in an exhibition. In a game, we have instead some accepted objective, e.g., "checkmate," "more runs," "a four-minute mile," which serves to determine what usable rules are to be used in a particular action. Without the operation of that objective, the various usable rules have no necessary order among themselves; or they can be given a number of used forms amongst which we are not able to choose. The objective of checkmating makes the move of the knight to this place rather than any other the move to be made. It defines the use of the knight in accordance with the usable rule for knights.

A game is to be thought of, not as the locus of a rule or a number of rules, but rather as a set of rules governing different parts of the game, and different men, roles, and instruments which achieve an order amongst themselves only when those rules achieve a specific guise in the form of a use embodied in the alteration of some factor. The game of chess has rules for knights, bishops, etc., but tells us of no order in which they are to be played. If there were such an order prescribed, we would have the sequence of an exhibition. It is the objective of the game (which is a concrete form of a testing or a decision, that each side tries to translate into a "winning") which prescribes that this or that usable rule is to be used. The objective is reached by a creative process of relating used rule to used rule under the guidance of that objective.

To run a mile in four minutes—which is an objective within the reach of a good number of runners today—it is desirable to keep before one the prospect of a mile run at that rate. This prospect can have the form of a possible mile qualified by the character of being run in four minutes. It is such a qualified prospect which dictates to the runner whether or not he is to crouch or stand for the starting gun, whether he is then to remain slightly behind the leader or to take the lead, etc.

It is possible, of course, for a man to have no strategy, and to merely want to do his best, as the circumstances permit. Consequently he will, without reflection, crouch or stand, and will then respond to the other runners as the occasion seems to demand. He will in such a case make use of rules, for he will crouch, avoid interfering, wait for the gun, etc., as conditions for sharing in the sport. No attempt is then made to apply rules; all that is done is to act in consonance with the rules which the sport defines. But he will not usually be as effective as another who has a strategy, i.e., who has the objective operate in him so as to determine just what rules are to be used, and in what order.

We sometimes speak of applying a rule to a given case. Faced with a heterogeneous lot of balls, we can have the rule of picking out two reds and then a white one, two reds and then a white one, etc. But such a statement passes over the distinction between general, specific, usable, and used rules. We do not apply the general rule, pick out two reds and then a white; instead we accept the heterogeneous set of balls as the orientation point of a rule, thereby transforming the general rule into a usable rule. We could speak of this transformation as an application of the general rule, but it is in fact not yet applied. It is given a specific place in which it can operate. But it will not operate except so far as we engage in some act, such as picking out balls.

But what does it mean to say that the general rule is given a specific place in which it can operate? Is this not only a roundabout way of speaking of the application of the general rule? It would be better to attend to the fact that we encountered the heterogeneous set of balls and then went on to pick some out. We changed our attitude toward the set of balls. That attitude could have been changed under the guidance of the prospect of the general rule, but our movement in fact was a movement from one attitude to another with respect to the set of balls, and not a movement from a general rule to a specific use of it. The movement from one attitude to another (treated not as something private, but as a shift in the relationship which we in fact have with respect to the balls) is a shift from one "use" of the balls to another.

Does the shift in our attitude exhibit a rule? Are we using a rule when we encounter the set of balls? Unless there can be a completely isolated act, and thus unless the shift in our attitude conforms to no condition, it would have to be said to exhibit a rule. We must also be using a rule when we encounter the set of balls, for the encounter involves a distinctive use of the eyes and attention. The rules may not be known or ever formulated in a general form; they may be nothing more than structures, habits, or limits within which an occurrence takes place. Yet we can legitimately call them "rules," for they are indistinguishable from the patterns which in fact are instances of already acknowledged or formulated general rules.

September 25

The topics with which modern philosophers concern themselves are those initiated by the Greeks (with the possible exception of the philosophy of history) and reflect the basic interests of a leisured class. As a consequence, such fundamental concerns as are expressed in sport, business, sex, and the education of children have been neglected by the leading thinkers from the beginning of philosophic history.

Mankind, unreflectingly but insistently, exhibits a number of basic interests that have not been of primary concern to philosophers. Women seem to be primarily interested in the lives of idealized loved women and in the growth of children; men seem to be primarily interested in sports, sex, and worldly success. Is there a common character to these? I think there is.

In all these cases, we have an exhibition of a control for the sake of achieving a control or domination over other men or beings. The idealized loved woman is one who, through her body (understood to be naturally endowed but also controlled and cared for), is able to arouse and keep the interest of men, and thereby make her life glamorous and fulfilled. The growth of children is primarily a growth in the body which, when properly carried out, involves an incidental growth of the mind and a happy, fulfilled human being. In these two cases, the interest is directed at someone else, the one as a model, the other as the object of a task.

The interest in sports seems to be related to the mastery of the body in such a way as to make manifest what a man can do. There is, as is the case with the glamorous woman viewed by other women, an identification or acceptance by spectators of the athlete as a representative of mankind at its best. The interest in sex, which of course is not absent in women, is once again an interest in a body which is attractive, and also involves some concern for one's own body as that which is to function well. The interest in worldly success, however, does not involve a control of the body, except in the sense that the impulses are controlled so as to enable one to focus on the task of judging correctly, ruling others, exhibiting virtues of temperance and courage, and other powers needed in order to be comparatively powerful and secure.

There is a strong interest in crime on the part of men; this can be understood as an interest in the adventure characteristic of the athlete, but with a negative note—excellence and control directed in the wrong direction. There is a strong interest in religion, in the arts, and in inquiry, all of which involve something similar in the way of a control of the body, but for the sake, not of achieving a bodily dominated success, but one which ignores or minimizes the body's needs.

We seem here to have at least two kinds of control—a control of the body in order that the body perform excellently, and a control of the body in order that something else be done well. We can think of the woman in her concern for the child to be exhibiting something like the second of these, as do the businessman, the politician, the artist, the scientist, the religious man, and the philosopher.

In all these cases, a body is taken to be something within the ability of an individual to manipulate in such a way that something desirable is achieved, either in the form of a benefit for others, or as a rule in the form of some mastery by oneself of those who remain outside oneself. Mankind responds to individuals who have so disciplined themselves that, instead of allowing the body to follow its own impulses, they are able to dictate to it if and when it is to express impulses, and for what ends. Those who do this excellently awaken mankind's admiration.

Better perhaps: All men admire self-mastery, and some try to attain it. The self-mastery is made evident in the way in which one can use the body to make it function excellently in overcoming nature, one's own insistent responses, or other men. The immediate appeal that glamorous women make to women, and sports to men—these seem more basic and pervasive than a concern for the growth of children or the attainment of worldly success, and through not as demanding, seem more continuous than a vital sexual concern—is made by those whose self-mastery is essentially bodily, and involves the attainment of an ideal result.

Does it make much sense to view the interest in sex, the growth of children, nonworldly pursuits, and worldly success as derivative from a concern for a mastery of the body carried out best in glamorous women and athletes? A Freudian would surely insist on sex as more basic than these; Eastern thinkers would insist on the primacy of nonworldly pursuits; those who are economically or politically oriented would emphasize the factor of worldly success. But though sex is insistent, the achievements of sex do not awaken the admiration of men as much as sports do; at most, evidence of sexual prowess seem to awaken envy or awe. In any case, glamor and athletics are taken to provide evidence of sexual success, ability, or promise, particularly since in our society there is no opportunity to know about sexual prowess directly. Even in the case of the individual judging himself, it is questionable whether he would put sexual achievement as a more satisfactory sign of excellence or superiority than athletics, in part because the latter involves him in a competitive situation, and in part because it does involve a more severe kind of control and training—and an objective measure.

Men do want worldly success for themselves and do admire it in others, but I do not think that there is as much excitement or commitment for themselves, or as much admiration for others in this field as there is in athletics. But it would seem to be wrong to suppose that an interest in worldly success or an interest in nonworldly realities is derivative from the other. Men sometimes combine the two, and sometimes have them conflict. Of course a concentration on one will preclude giving full attention to the other.

October 3

If we judge from the interest and concern which men by and large manifest with respect to the activities of others, it seems to be true that there are not many types of major importance, and that these fall into two groups, one stressing something of value and the other something regrettable.

Women seem to be interested in glamorous women as having mastered themselves to become the object and source of love. They are also fascinated by the courtesan who seems to have the same power, but to use this for a less desirable end. They have a deep interest in the home and the proper relations of the different members to one another; incest seems to involve the perverse use of the same power.

Men seem to be primarily interested in worldly power; the hero, the tycoon, the millionaire are outstanding examples of those who have shown that they have such power. Those engaged in organized crime, mainly on the civil side, seem to use the same powers, but in a perverse way. Perhaps we should include here the despot and the traitor. Men also have a great interest in athletics; the brute seems to make use of the same powers, but for a perverse end. Another opposite to the athlete is perhaps a mentally ill man; he makes use of his body, but on behalf of a perverting psyche.

I don't think that the mass of mankind is interested to the same degree in the saint, the artist, or the scholar—in anyone who turns his thought away from the daily world. Nor is it as much interested in the negations of these—the villain who uses his abilities to injure and pervert, the mountebank or pornographer, and the magician or propagandist—though there is no question but that everyone seems to have some interest in them as unusual and perplexing individuals who may help or injure.

My focus for the moment is on the problem of sports. The question of just what it is that interests mankind is but a more inclusive form of the question as to why mankind is interested in athletics. It seems to be the case that mankind is interested in athletics as an area where one can see men in control of their bodies in such a way as to achieve an excellence otherwise not possible. One who has achieved such a mastery but makes use of his body for regrettable ends—say the powerful but brutal man operating in a somewhat lawless way—seems also to catch the imagination of mankind. The interest in the mentally ill is not perhaps as great, in part because apparently what basically interests one is the achieving of an unusual degree of power which could be used to show one's mastery of what challenges.

October 4

We are not the masters of ourselves for the most part, because we are immersed in a world which determines us. We react and respond to what confronts us, and as a consequence, what we do reflects what the world demands more than it does what we are or would like to have. To be sure, our reactions and responses are in terms of the nature, body, and interests that we have; but given these, the particular forms and times and ways in which they are manifested are determined from the outside.

To overcome this subjugation to outside forces, it is necessary to retreat from the world and thereby obtain a power by which one can approach the world in one's own terms. The retreat can stop at one of three stages. It can stop at our body, to make it something isolate, something which is to be redirected through a new determination and resolution. This stage interests those who have mastered the other stages, enabling them to make use of what they had obtained in order to conquer what lies beyond through the use of the body. It is a stage which can, however, also be stopped at without any consideration for the other stages. He who does that pauses for a while, takes a stand.

A further retreat is achieved by retreating not only from an immersion in the world, but from an immersion in the body. Then one treats the body as that which is to be accepted and used in terms of one's idea or will. It is to this stage that one must retreat if one is to train the body and to prepare it for a certain type of activity. All athletes must retreat to this stage; if they get only so far as the first, they may redirect the body, but will not have it working at its best, since the redirection will be for a body as it had been determined by the past involvement with the world.

A further retreat involves a turning from purpose or will, which has relevance to what the body might do, and attending to some transcendent reality. Here the retreat involves an orientation toward something which need not have any bodily import. But once such a reality has been acknowledged, it is possible to return to the second and first stages and use the awareness of that reality as a principle of assessment, dictating how one is to relate oneself to what else there be. In *The God We Seek*, it was seen that the religious man detaches himself from the world in this way. He so attaches himself to God that when he returns to the world, he does it in terms of the values and assessments which he, as a representative of that God, will inevitably impose on whatever he confronts.

An athlete ought not to be content merely to direct his body; he ought not to be content merely to prepare his body; he ought in addition to have oriented himself in Actuality, or in some delimited region of it, in order to be able to come back to the world as one who recognizes the equality of other men with himself. When he does this, he continues to approach all else as that which he is to master and in some sense conquer, but it will be a mastery and conquest of that which is recognized to have the equal right to try to master and conquer him.

To be part of a sport or game is to recognize that others are on a footing with oneself, at the same time that one is concerned with overcoming them. If there were no third stage of retreat, one would have no other alternative but to assert oneself over against others; there would be no need to recognize an overarching scheme in which the contestants were equal. The athlete need not go so far as to acknowledge Actuality as such, with a consequent acknowledgment of the equality of all actualities; it is sufficient for him to recognize and utilize Actuality only so far as it enables him to see himself as coordinate with the others who are competing with him.

A game is a specialization of Actuality in somewhat the same sense as some limited objective is a specialization of Ideality. Each participant should be a representative of the game in the sense that what it demands of the various contestants is accepted by each of them as a principle of assessment for himself and the others. He must approach the particular task not only from a particular position, but also from the perspective of a limited portion of Actuality which embraces that position and the position of others.

When I reflect and judge, I move to the first stage of retreat. I then face a world of entities, all of which are equal in the sense that they are exterior to me. I can then take some one of them, or all of them in turn, as representatives of all the others, in the sense of being foci or orientation points for them. Everything else can be understood in terms of this which I focus on, as a center, meaning, or position in terms of which they are to be understood, dealt with, or referred to. This which I take to be a representative of others can also be taken to be a representative of my own body. When I do this, I stand away from that body, for I, as having made this a representative of others, do not make it a representative of myself as making it a representative of them, but only of myself as one of the entities in the world with it. If I deal with x as a representative of all else, I leave out myself as so dealing with it.

In becoming the focus for my body as well as for other entities, there is a sense in which my body is in the orbit of another; it is then a body which has its meaning and value determined by that other. Only because I take that body of mine to be my body am I able to withdraw it from its external determinations, and therefore am able to oppose it. So far as I withdraw my body, the other has it only as a possible object to represent. My assertion of the body as mine is one with another's making my body function within its orbit.

Another can represent my body either as one entity alongside others, or as that which is possessed by me. If it does the latter, it faces my body as that which it can only partly represent. A portion of the meaning of that body is given to it by me, and is not determined by the position it has with respect to that which treats it as an object. If another represents my body as that which is not fully within its orbit, it is a being which acknowledges me to have a self. But such an acknowledgment is one with the having of a self of its own.

I may not know if another is treating my body as a mere body or as that which is possessed by me, but if it does treat it as possessed by me, it is a being with a self, for it acknowledges my body to be oriented away from that being. What has no self can represent my body only as an entity and never as that which is possessed by me.

Any object can be made by me to be representative of all else. If another allows my body to be a representative of all else, that other must have a self, for it is a self which determines whether one of the entities in the world is to be a representative of the others, or merely to be alongside them. Whatever can represent my body as that which belongs to me must have a self to which some other body can belong.

I may be wrong in thinking that x or y is a body for which there is a self. But if I am not wrong in thinking that my body belongs to me, and that something represents my body as that which belongs to me, I am not wrong in thinking that there is another self. I know my body belongs to me because I can retreat from it and repossess it; I know that something represents my body as that which belongs to me so far as it is treated as on a footing with that representative.

Whatever represents in the sense of offering a focus for all else, has all else as subject to its terms. But if it treats something else as an entity on a level with itself, it functions as a representative, not of that body, but of Actuality with respect to which it and that body are to be understood.

When I take something to be a representative of all else, I both subjugate it (for it is I who define it to be a representative), and ennoble it (for it then becomes a focal point for all else). If it has no genuine self, then my ennobling is but an ennobling within the framework of the subjugation; it is that which I ennoble and which is ennobled only so far as I so treat it. If it is truly ennobled, it functions on its own; my ennobling of it will then in effect be a freeing of it from the conditions which I impose in taking it to be a representative. Though I approach it from my perspective, I release it from that perspective in recognizing it to be that which has a perspective of its own. If it is a thing, it has a privacy and substantiality of its own, precluding me from subjugating it completely. But if it is a man with a self, it also has the power to assess me, as I assess it.

When I represent Actuality, I do not exhaust it; it remains what it is apart from me. I merely deal with others in terms of the values which it provides. When I see something as not only a representative, but as that which has a self (and thus which can be over against me) and also can acknowledge my body to belong to me, I see that thing to be oriented in Actuality. If that other is not a being with a genuine self, it will nevertheless be a being for which Actuality will function as a self.

The problem of other selves is a problem of particular selves. I do not know whether this which I face is a being with a self all its own. But I do know it as that which represents Actuality, either because I have made it do so as a substantial entity which is oriented in Actuality, or because it has retreated from the world and itself acknowledged Actuality. Only in the second case does it have a self of its own; but in the first case, it is a being which is possessed by a self. There are then only the alternatives: the body which I take to represent all else has a self which is its own, or represents Actuality in a limited way so that Actuality is made to function for it like a self.

If there were no other self and no Actuality, there would be nothing which could represent my body as belonging to me. But not to represent my body as belonging to me is to falsify it. If I am to do justice to the representative function of another, I must have that other be that which can treat my body as belonging to me, either because that other has a self of its own, or because it operates as that which is oriented in Actuality. To say "It is the case that my body belongs to me" is to say that there is another self, or Actuality in the role of self, for which my body belongs to me.

The things in the world are oriented in Actuality. I call them "things" because they are not seen to orient themselves in Actuality, to take themselves to represent it. But I allow them all to be bodies for a single "self" so far as I see them to be equally real with me, all oriented in Actuality with me. There always must be at least two selves, my own and Actuality, as represented by the various entities that I confront. There may be other selves as well, but this I will know only so far as I know that others are treating my body as my own, by the way in which they respect it, accord it rights, etc.

October 6

We can take up a number of positions with respect to the entities which we confront. *1*] We can confront them as entities forming a field for us. *2*] We can take some of them to be foci for the others (and perhaps also ourselves). *3*] We can take some of them to treat us as foci. *4*] We can take some of them to treat us as beings which use them as foci. *5*] We can see ourselves and others as members of some totality.

1] It takes considerable sophistication before we are able to see ourselves among all other entities in this world. When we do this, we fall under case 5. Initially and for the most part, we face a world of objects which define the horizon of our interests and activities, and which together as alongside one another constitute a field within which we can insert ourselves. We take this position by the very fact that we perceive. All beings by virtue of their position confront all others as part of a horizontal field.

2] Some of the objects which we confront become topics for attention, in terms of which we deal with the others, as somehow needed by or subordinate to, or functioning on behalf of the focused entity. We can subdivide this case into two: in one of these, we are not taking the entity as focal for ourselves, but only for some other entities; in the other, we also are focused on some particular entity. Eventually we may, in either case, take the focal entity to be one for every other, but it will then be an item of overwhelming importance. And we can eventually look at the world in such a way that each and every item in it can be treated as focal for some or all the others, in which case we will endow each and every item with a substantiality and ultimacy in terms of which the presence or actions of others are to be understood. This is a late achievement, the outcome perhaps only of considerable philosophic reflection. In all these instances we are self-conscious.

3] Some of the items behave toward us as demanding that they treat us as centers. They respond to our moves or preparations by a readiness to turn toward us and act in terms of our acts. In some cases we can have them behave toward us not only as foci but as beings who allowed or took them to be foci too. We then have selves.

4] To have a self is to have a mutuality in the acceptance of centers, with our accepting another as a center for us and others just so far as it accepts us as a center for itself and others. We then not only take things to have a reference to us in terms of which they are to act or have value, but take them to have a value at the same time. We in effect acknowledge a combination of 2 and 3, with the entities functioning both as substances with an ultimacy of their own, and as adjectives for us as the focal substantial entities. (When it is said that they "treat us as foci" it must not then be thought that there is a distinction between them as focused on us and some hidden power which makes them so act, except so far as we bring in case 2.)

5] We can acknowledge some general scheme under which we and others fall. When we do this, we see both of us as members of some situation in terms of which we are to be understood. In a sense, this is the position that is assumed when this rough fivefold classification is made, for it is a classification which is possible only so far as we have a perspective which includes ourselves and others. We are then reflective or speculative beings.

We can recognize that some entities are foci for ourselves and others, for we can see ourselves and others act in terms of them as centers. We move when they move, we retreat when they advance or retreat, we change our pace and ways in accordance with moves on their part. We can also see that some of them respond in similar ways to us. Our supposition that another has a self is a consequence of a double observation to the effect that we have one another as centers.

But surely there are mechanical devices which can be made to respond to changes in us, and which themselves function as centers for ourselves. Every object is substantial, and therefore can become a focus; and we can be determinative of what some of them do. Surely the responsiveness of a substance to changes in us does not show that the substance has a self coordinate with us. Yet the above discussion would seem to have this as a consequence.

A being with a self acknowledges other entities to be foci. If then I am to know that another is a self, I must know that it endows me or other entities with the capacity to function as centers for others, or that it acknowledges that they or I so act. It does have me as a part of its field; it does have me function as centered on it. But as a self, it must take me (or something else) to be a center too. Its activities as a center must be modified in the light of mine; its role must be a role in relation to mine.

That alone then has a self which takes me to have one too; I have a self only so far as I acknowledge that another has one too. We can know that we have selves only so far as we can see that our activities are not merely the activities of centers which also function as items centered about one another, but are modified activities, activities which are different with respect to one another as such centers.

If another changes his function as a center when we do, if his role as an item for other centers changes with changes in our own roles, then we rightly speak of it as having a self. Each of us will be a member of a situation which we constitute. We will have attained empirically what is transcendentally produced in the fifth case.

There is much that is not in focus in the above.

November 21

Most athletic contests end with one side victorious. Every athlete has tasted defeat, if not by coming out second to some other, then by falling short of his own standards or achievements. Defeat is an omnipresent prospect for all who engage in sport. But then why do athletes engage in it? Does the prospect of victory so overwhelm them that they are unaware of the prospect of defeat? Do the possible joys of success more than compensate for the possible or even actual pain of defeat? Do athletes forget their defeats quickly and dwell only on possible success? I suppose that there are athletes of whom it is true that they give little heed to the possibility of defeat. And then when it comes, it is hard to bear. But I should think that in most athletes the possibility of defeat is lively, and that it does not defeat them because it is but the counterpart of the sustaining possibility of victory.

Defeat as a prospect is inseparable from the prospect of victory. The athlete is tensed and somewhat disquieted; his confidence is tinctured with fear, and the hope of having good fortune on his side. He cannot expect victory if he does not see how hard it is to get, how precarious his opportunities are, and thus how imminent is the prospect of defeat.

The heightened expectation of victory, the great effort to get it, the awareness that its absence indicates a comparative limitation of oneself, makes defeat debilitating, humiliating, hard to bear. Yet something good comes out of it. A game is, after all, in between a drama and a common event. It has the artificiality, the conventionality, the detached separated nature of a drama, but it has the vital struggle, the actual effort to bring about some unpredictable result, which is characteristic of ordinary affairs. A defeat is in between the tragedies which are to be found in both.

The tragedy in a drama is self-enclosed; it portrays what it means for a vital value to be lost, but it itself does not exhibit such a loss of value. A tragedy in real life is open-ended; it involves a real loss of value, but in a setting filled with irrelevant details. The drama highlights the loss, but does not exhibit it; in real life we exhibit it, but rarely in a focused way. In the game, on the other hand, value is lost, as in daily life, but in a context where irrelevancies are excluded. But unlike real life, the loss of value is only a loss in terms of our estimation or expectation, not in fact; what happens is that one fails to measure up to some standard, and not that one has in fact reduced some value. And unlike a drama, the loss is actually worked through; there is no antecedent script which tells when and where and how and why the loss should occur. The game is like real life in that its problem is worked out in fact; it is like a drama in that it is cut off from the hurly-burly and the irrelevancies of daily existence and practical need.

November 22

Most actions involve two factors. There is an intention which reaches to the prospect to be attained and which serves to control, relate, and give a new import to the particular things which are done. And there are the particular things to be done—alterations, modifications, and changes instituted by the expenditure of energy. The two factors are capable of being held apart. One who had only the first would not act; one who had only the second would be engaged in a sequence of activities which had no intrinsic order or objective.

Learning by trial and error, or training through the mastery of particular acts, involves the holding of the second factor apart from the first. Getting the spirit of an enterprise, planning, and understanding what the ideal or standard may be, involves the holding of the first factor apart from the second. Mastery requires having both of them together.

It is possible to concentrate on some of the acts which are comprised within the intentional stretch of some other act. When this is done, we take the act to have an intentional aspect, and look to the subordinate parts of it as having to be produced in sequence under the aegis of that intentional aspect. Eventually though, we come down to unit acts which are not to be broken down into subordinate ones all related by virtue of an intentional end.

We come to rest on the individual's ability to clutch, turn, bend, glance, throw, lift, and the like. These are acts which have been learned in the course of the exercise of the body when growing. There are cases where they may have to be learned by going through a number of subordinate acts. We sometimes have to teach a very young child, or someone who has been injured, or who is seriously defective mentally, how to hold the laces of a shoe preliminary to tying a knot. We may have to help it to bring its fingers together, either by pressing them ourselves or by trying to induce the individual to imitate us. But in the usual case, we have as undivided acts such moves as gripping, opening the hands, stretching the legs, shifting the eyes, and the like, which are to be ordered with respect to similar unit acts in terms of some intentional result.

On the other side, we can have final acts which terminate in the very objective which had been intended in the inclusive act. The last battle may come at the end of the war; the last step we take comes at the end of the walk. And we can therefore have an intended act which is the very act that is carried out. We may intend to throw, and then in fact throw. We may intend to conclude to something, and in fact conclude to it. In these cases, it seems as if we have what Ryle thinks are occurrences which involve no process, no coming to be. But not only might one consider these to involve a passing through a sequence of obstacles or blocks, but the very fact that they might come at the end of a series of subordinate acts on the same level seems to indicate that the act which terminates the process is not equatable with the act defined by the intent.

In previous writings, I have spoken of acts as somehow realizing the prospect by filling it out, making it concrete, giving it specifications. But we would seem to have not only acts in which what we intend is controlling, and which can be thought of as being specified by the very acts which are controlled, but acts which are guided by an outcome, not necessarily intended but surely held on to by entities in the present, since they are inevitably oriented toward the future with its indeterminate prospects. In the case where there is some objective without any intent (consciously entertained or not), acts can be thought to realize and specify the vectoral structure which reaches from the present to that future objective. If this be granted, we have then two cases, one in which the acts are governed by and specify an intended end, and the other in which the acts specify the vectoral stretch between the present and the possibility with which that present is inevitably related. Simple acts such as clutching, turning, bending, etc., are cases of the second kind.

Whatever is done involves some sequence of alterations. We begin to refer to the realm of human activity when we take as our basic units the simple acts of clutching, etc., and have them governed by some intended end. The intended end, to begin with, may, however, not be an end for something we want to have done, except incidentally in order to have an act which is to be governed by some further intended end. We may want to clutch in order to keep a hold on something, which itself may be an act in a sequence of acts which we call "batting a ball." To teach a man to bat, we need not teach him how to bring his fingers together or to tighten his grip, but we may have to teach him how to have a good grip, where to place his hands on the bat, and how to swing. When we teach him how to have a good grip, we have to intend, and he has to intend to have a good grip. But once he has attained the stage where he has a good grip, we must get him to the position where he intends to swing properly, an intention which demands that the good grip be related in a definite order and way to the holding of the bat and the swinging of it.

November 23

The stoics were defiant men. They held themselves erect in the face of untoward circumstances and insisted on the dignity of man. But they were not defiant enough. When it came to the question of suicide they could say that when a chamber becomes too smoky, one should leave it. But there is first the question whether the chamber of life is ever too smoky, and then the question as to just where we ought to go when we leave it, and how. The alternative that the stoic envisages, suicide, seems to show that the stoic is not defiant enough.

A man ought to see himself as over against the whole of nature. Together with others, he forges a society which is a domain set over against nature, and possessing its own rules, rhythm, and being. And in that society, he should see himself as one who stands over against it as well. Just as he is a being in nature even when he is a member of a society, so he is a member of society even when he is a private being. He there defines what the world means and imports.

A man might commit suicide while in control of his faculties or while he is not. If he does the former, the question that faces him is whether any defeat in the world can equal the dignity that he has as a man. Those who consciously yield to the temptation to commit suicide place some limited end before themselves as though it were the only end possible, or the most inclusive end, or an irreplaceable or unduplicable end. Jilted, having lost status or a job, feeling lonesome, facing a period of stress or pain, they in effect yield to the forces of nature before they have been made to. They decide (which is a human privilege) to deny themselves the status of human beings who define what a man is in relation to what is outside him, and what intrudes upon him. But if a man does not have control of his faculties, his suicide is in effect the outcome of a natural force; he is in effect killed, even though the instrument for the killing is himself.

To such a view one might object that a man may face torture and pain of such intensity as to preclude him from being able to function as a man. Putting aside the question that the anticipation of such torture and pain is not equivalent with the actual suffering of it—and which may in fact prove to be less serious than had been anticipated—the envisaging of that situation is in effect an envisaging of a situation where one is no longer a man. What one does is then to anticipate a state where one is merely a creature of nature, a mere living being. But it is then questionable whether he can then be called a man.

It is possible, of course, to court death, and even to prepare to bring it about for the sake of some higher good. One might think of oneself as a representative of a nation or a people or a family, and willingly die in order to avoid betraying those who depend on one. But now suicide is in fact displaced by self-sacrifice, expressed in an act of self-destruction.

A man ought, when defeated by some particular occurrence on which he has set much store, to ask himself whether or not there are alternative courses which he can then live through. The death of a beloved cannot be compensated for; it is tragic, and one cannot do less than suffer through it. But that death is not the last act of the universe, and one should then set oneself to live, as once one had lived, without that beloved. What is true here, is true of one's fortune, job, status, achievements, promise, and the like. A man is a flexible being; to allow some particular outcome to determine the entire import of his life is to make that life too rigid, and thus in the end is to do injustice to what it is to be a man.

It is possible for one to suffer unremitting pain, which precludes his being able to do anything but look for anodynes. This is perhaps the smoky chamber of which the stoics spoke. But there is always a question here whether or not one is able to stand above and outside that pain. To be caught in the grip of it without hope of remission or conquest is to be but a living locus of what is undesirable. But to know this is already to be a man, defying even the pain.

Should it not be possible to do anything but to be conscious of pain, one is no longer a man in the sense of one who could be defiant. A suicide in that case would be an act deliberately brought about, and thus to require the intelligence of a man, but it would not be the act of one who was what he ought to be. But now I seem to be on the verge of a tautology, for I am saying that he who takes suicide to be an answer when he is in pain is no longer defiant as a man ought to be—but suicide is a confession of a refusal to remain defiant. The tautology is obviated by recognizing that when a man cannot be defiant, he is not truly a man. Suicide would be the act of one who was no longer defiant, but an act which nevertheless accepted the values and power of the world beyond in place of one's own. This means that we have to consider another state in addition to defiance and yielding. A nondefiant being may be determinative of a situation; a suicide is determinative just so far as he makes the decision to die, but his decision is also a decision to allow the course of the activity and the reason for the activity to be determined by something other than himself.

November 24

There are some features in common between the problem of moving from training to the accomplishment of a single act (in which the separate items that had been mastered in training are organically connected) and the problem of moving from some acknowledged assertion to an inference.

We are trained by mastering particular moves. Each of these can be said to have a "sessile" character, a feature which marks it as a distinct entity. A set of these moves is just a set of moves, and does not constitute a single act. To make a single act, it is necessary to turn the moves into constituents of the act. This is done by endowing them with a "projectile" character, one which can be transferred to the terminus. This projectile character may be the sessile character subject to an alteration, or it may be something entirely new. In either case, it is the product of the effect of the projected outcome on that which precedes it.

A move which we learn in training becomes the beginning of an act when it is related to a possible end. This is something like what happens when we take an assertion, p, and make it into a premiss for an intended conclusion, q. But in the case of the training, we also have intermediate stages to be mastered, whereas in the inference we are content with mastering the premiss only. But the intermediate steps can also be treated as agencies for transmitting the projectile character of the initial move. One move then would be taken to have a projectile character, and the other moves would constitute agencies for carrying that projectile to the end. The first step we take in a walk becomes the beginning of a walk through the fact that the other steps function as means for carrying the projectile nature of that initial move ("a walk to the store"), to the terminus of the walk. The terminus then is not merely the end of an activity, but the end of an activity with just that beginning. The terminus is an arrival at the store because it has projected into it the "walk to the store" from the beginning, and via the intermediate stages. And we can think of a significant inference as one in which the leading principle was in fact constituted of a number of distinct moves, but which nevertheless functioned to carry the projective "truth" of the premiss to the conclusion.

In both the inference and the learning, there is a replacement of a sessile feature by a projectile one. The replacement involves a projective excellence which is to be conveyed to the terminus.

In an inference, we are not content merely to transfer a projectile excellence (conventionally taken to be the "truth" of the proposition) to the terminus along the lines laid down by the rule. (In the rule, the initial excellence is projected but not transported to the possible terminus.) Instead, we try to hold that excellence apart from the act by which it is projected to the terminus; we want to hold it as a sessile feature of the conclusion so that we can assert the conclusion apart from the inference, in the very way in which we asserted the original proposition with its sessile character that we then replaced by a projective one. (The replacement could be the result of a conversion of the sessile character, or it could be the result of an endowment achieved by virtue of the relating of the initial proposition to the prospective conclusion.)

Do we want to hold the outcome of an act apart from the act, and for it then to have in a sessile guise the feature it inherited? It would seem not. Not only can we in training produce the terminus as a single separate move (when it possesses the sessile character without our having had to go through a process of projecting it from the beginning of the act), but we seem to be interested not in that terminus but in the act itself.

We can sometimes acknowledge a proposition with a sessile "truth" apart from an act of inference which projected a truth to that proposition from the base of some accepted premiss. But even in such a case, we might want to derive it by inference, for we might want it to be connected or justified by virtue of the premiss, even though we thereupon will affirm it apart from the premiss. We might want it to have a "sessilized" feature, a feature which was arrived at, even though it is now treated in independence of anything else. Even when we know independently that p is true and that q is true, we might want to derive q from p as a means for systematizing our knowledge. Just so, we can find it desirable to see the terminus of an act as something which brings a certain set of moves to a close.

We might want not merely to be at the store, but to arrive at it because we set out to get there. We might not merely want to hit the ball, but to hit it as the outcome of a proper lifting, gripping, and swinging of the bat. The ball cannot be hit unless we lift, grip, and swing the bat, but unless we deal with the swing as that which is to be arrived at from the position of a lift, as mediated by the grip and the swing, the hit will be something which merely happens after the lift, the grip, and the swing, even though it could not have occurred without them. They would be necessary conditions; but when we hit as part of an act, they are also sufficient conditions for the hit being a good hit.

But must we not say that for a poor hit, the lifting, gripping, and swinging are also necessary and sufficient conditions? And if we do, can we avoid treating the hit as a part of an organic act in which the lifting, gripping, and swinging are moves, which can be antecedently learned as discrete items, but which are components of a single act in which a hit is produced? And why should one speak of the hit as though it were the terminus, since it is but a consequence of our swinging and the place of the ball?

Let us take the swing to be the terminus of the act. It cannot occur without a prior gripping and lifting of the bat. But when one is trained to hit, one learns how to grip, how to lift, and even how to swing as separate items. The swing, though it requires a prior grip and lift, is then viewed not as having inherited anything from the grip or lift, but as a distinct type of move. It could, of course, be taught as a move where something of the grip and lift is transferred, but then what is being learned is the entire act of being at bat and not merely one of the moves presupposed by it.

We want to hold a conclusion apart from any act of inference which arrives at it by projecting some feature from the premiss. If we had known of the truth of the conclusion before we had engaged in an inference, we would hold it as something which was true in itself but pointed to in the course of some larger inquiry. Do we in a similar way want to hold the terminus of a physical act apart from the act? Yes, as that which had been arrived at, as that which terminates the act, as that which we had intended. We want its sessile feature to be a sessilized feature. In the same way, we want the sessile feature of truth which is possessed by a conclusion which we had finally concluded to, to be a sessilized feature in the sense of being acknowledged within the context of an inquiry, even though we then make no reference to any antecedent and allow it to stand as a single truth, in the same way in which the initial proposition was a single truth.

A conclusion of an inference differs from the antecedent proposition which we are going to use as a premiss, in that its sessile truth is seen to have been sessilized just as the initial proposition was treated as having a "projectable" truth, allowing it to be used in an inference. As having such a projectable truth, it is different from itself as a mere premiss with a possible and intended conclusion.

An initial proposition and a final conclusion have sessile truths, the one being projectable and the other being sessible, and thus as items for a possible inquiry or inference. When they function in an implication, the one has a projectable and the other has a sessible truth. When they function in an inference, the projectable, sessile, true premiss is replaced by a projected, sessile, but now sessile, true conclusion. The terminus of an act, we should similarly say, has a projected excellence which could be possessed by the terminus, and is now in fact possessed by it. And as now possessed, it allows the terminus to close the act and therefore permits us to enter into a new one.

A move which is like a terminus, but does not come about because something has been projected and conveyed to it, is merely one occurrence following on and followed by others. But as part of a single act, it terminates the act and thereby makes what had come before it relevant to it, and what comes after it part of another act. To arrive at a place is thus quite distinct from being there, or even to have come there; it involves a reference to what had been projected, and makes room for the beginning of another act.

November 25

In trial and error learning, and in learning a complicated act, two distinct steps must be taken. One must master a series of sessile moves, and one must then get these to be integrated into a single act. The moves themselves may have to be treated as acts, but we eventually come to the point where we have indivisible moves which we produce without reflection, achieve by simple imitation, or by being helped to put our hands here, our legs there, etc.

Let us concentrate on the sequence of gripping, lifting, waiting, and

swinging, which could be said to be the divisions that make sense in articulating what it is to swing at a ball with a bat. The pupil is first taught
how to grip the bat. He is told to hold his fingers thus and so, to bend his
body in this way, etc. He can then be taught to lift the bat. The two acts
are distinct; but he does not learn how to bat a ball or even how to lift
the bat properly until he has learned how to grip the bat in preparation
for lifting the bat.

The central problem of learning something complex after we have
mastered sessile moves is to turn the moves into mediators and conveyors
of what one has at the beginning. We start with the gripping, but when
we want to take this to be part of the single act of gripping-lifting, we define an antecedent move as a precondition. We take the gripping to be a
gripping in order to lift, and in that act acknowledge an antecedent interest in wanting to grip the bat properly.

What we have here is an analogue of a process of inference begun
with some antecedent; this antecedent is used as a source of a projectile
character only so far as we define a situation outside the inference as a
precedent one. We accept p as the antecedent of the inference only so far
as we at that time acknowledge p to be something we want to use. But in
the case of inference, this which we want to use, we would like to have
certified as desirable (say, because it is true) apart from our inference,
whereas in the case of training, we do not think we have to justify the
wanting to have a good grip. It is as if we said in inference that we want
to use p as our beginning, but do not then see if the p is in fact true. At
the risk of confusing our use of the term with what is a more common
usage, it could be said that our reasoning would then be "hypothetical,"
in that there is no assurance that what we take as our beginning has a
status of being true apart from that inference.

At the terminus of an inference, we end with something which we
wish to certify as having the sessile character of truth arrived at by a
projecting from our starting point. But the terminus q, should stand outside the inference in the same sense that p did. The p was outside the inference only as that which we would like to use as a premiss. We should
say then of q that it is what we would like to use as a conclusion—if the
analogue with training and learning holds.

These considerations point up the fact that what we have as an acknowledged entity before and after the inference need not be propositions
with truth values of a sessile nature, that become converted or are replaced with truth values which are projectable. All we need do is to have
an attitude: "wanting to use p properly as an antecedent of an inference."

At the end then, we should have "certified q." Similarly, an act ends with a lifting being done, and thus with our being ready to engage in another act from the position of a finished lifting, just as the inference ends with a "certified q" which allows us to use the q to begin another act, or to start another act having a new beginning, but one which we would not have started had we not come to have a "certified q."

Having mastered the act of gripping-lifting, we can go on to take "waiting" as the "leading principle" or conveyor of the excellence achieved, so as to arrive at the terminus of the waiting. We will grip-lift in order to wait properly, and will end with a proper wait which but makes us be in a position to swing. Having mastered the waiting, we are in a position to make a single act of gripping, lifting, and waiting, for which the approach should be "wanting to have these done (as one act) excellently," and which should be conveyed to a terminus by a "swing." The terminus will be the completion of the swing, as that which is an excellent finish, enabling us to then begin a new act, that of running to the base.

The second step of learning involves a thrusting backward from the sessile move to an external antecedent "wanting to do this excellently," and a pointing to an end, "having properly completed the act," which is the counterpart of that antecedent. Instead of starting, as is usually the case, in inference with an external antecedent which is sessilly true and concluding to an external consequence which is held to be sessilly true (though the truth had been achieved through a projection from the premiss), we remain in the act and try somehow to awaken an antecedent wanting, in order to make possible the use of the learned move as a transmitting agency. The antecedent wanting is a precondition for the consequent acceptance of the completed act and the allowance for the initiation of another act. It would seem, then, that a trainer cannot get the pupil to produce an act out of moves unless he can somehow induce him to achieve an attitude antecedent to his actually going through the moves as part of the single act.

Achieving the attitude and making the move part of the act are correlative enterprises; to do the one is to do the other, for the move becomes part of the act only so far as it is set over against an attitude with a sessile character (which may not have the same character as that which is in fact projected). The trainer must, while showing the pupil how to grip, for example, excite in him a desire to perform excellently. Or, having a pupil with such a desire, he must have him grip only as a way of moving to a proper swing.

November 28

There is a greater similarity between inference and the process of learning than I saw these last few days. When we have mastered a number of sessile moves—or to keep the problem to its simplest form, when we have mastered a sessile move—we have to move back to a position outside it, in order to make it function as a process. The movement back involves a consideration of two factors: one is an intention in which we envisage the entire process as beginning in such and such a way and ending in such and such a way; the second is the acceptance of such and such items as the appropriate items with which to begin.

We usually begin with some accepted item and an intention or rule before we infer. We go to training usually without such intentions and rules, and first learn to deal with the sessile move. We convert the sessile move into an act by having an intention which reaches the length of the move, and by having an acknowledgment of the factors which make a beginning possible. It is only because we make such an acknowledgment that we can end the act with the acknowledgment of something which we ought now to do.

The beginning which is external to an act is the reciprocal of the ending that is external to it. The one tells us that these materials are the proper materials; the other tells us that we are now ready to engage in another act. The process through which we go in effect is the transfer of the acceptability of the beginning to the acceptability of the ending, both of which are external to the process. That process is the sessile act converted into a dynamism by virtue of the acknowledgment both of an intention and of an antecedent beginning in the shape of an acceptable set of items to use in the process.

November 29

Peirce, in his account of inference, tended to confuse intention with rule. He thought one did not truly reason unless one did so in the light of a rule. But what he should have said is that one did not truly reason unless he did it intentionally, which is to say only if he took his beginning not merely to be related to the conclusion, but to point to it as that to which he is to conclude.

Peirce, also, by insisting on diagrams as essential to good reasoning, was in effect saying that inference was an act—which is I think correct—and that it is to be mastered by learning how to do a series of sessile moves—which is not necessarily true. Indeed, Peirce by his insistence on diagrams tended at times to forget that the act of inference was a single act in which the diagrammatic parts were but components, and not steps or stages. By forgetting the possibility of diagramming altogether, or by denying its relevance to the act of reasoning, some contemporaries make the opposite mistake and think that inference is not an act taking time to occur.

Training-learning and inference both need an intention, and both could use a rule in order to test the validity of the inference. In the case of training, the rule has the form of the coaches' ideals or models, a set of instructions, or the judgment of the coaches as viewed from the standpoint of the student. The rule or model is not necessary except so far as one wants something by which to determine whether the act is satisfactory.

The transition from training to learning involves the acknowledgment of two and perhaps three distinct factors which did not initially come into the training. The training involves the mastery of a set of sessile moves; the transition to learning involves the encompassing of these moves, as mere analytic components, within the single act. To make that transition, the student must A] intend to bring about the result, to finish the act in excellent form. The intention starts with the beginning of the act and points toward the end of it. B] The student must also acknowledge that what he confronts is satisfactory material to use, and (perhaps but not necessarily), C] he must acknowledge a rule or a model in terms of which he can know that his following out of the intent will be an act whose structure is ideal.

When we infer, the second of the above steps, B, is expressed in the acknowledgment of some truth. A true premiss (or a supposed true premiss, or in some cases even a false premiss or a doubtful one) is acknowledged to be satisfactory as a beginning for the inference. It possesses a sessile property which can provide us with a transferable property (the same or different in category as the sessile) when made part of an inference. The analogue in learning is the accepting of the material as satisfactory to constitute a satisfactory beginning of the act of reaching the desired end. That end, as arrived at, inherits the satisfactoriness of the beginning, by virtue of having been reached in the way it is. It is to be made to possess a sessile satisfactoriness so as to permit the next act to follow on it.

Having learned to put one's hands in this position and then to bend one's legs and tense one's muscles, etc., one is ready to engage in the act of gripping the bat. To grip the bat in a single act, it is necessary A] to want to grip a bat, and B] to accept this bat that is before one to be a satisfactory bat. Then either with or without a model, or even a habit well ingrained (which is a form of rule), one proceeds to grip the bat. The act comes to an end with the bat firmly in one's grip, able to be lifted to the shoulder quickly and well. The gripping firmly in this way is what is intended; it could be expressed in instructions, model, or rule; it is that state at which the next act is to begin. Gripping the bat firmly must then be something reached via the placing of the hands, etc., and be something which is accepted as satisfactory, having been so reached.

The consideration of learning makes more conspicuous the fact that we are not merely satisfied to come to an end of an act, but insist on having the terminus possess a sessile character apart from, though due to, the act. When we have "p therefore q" in an inference, we are not at an end merely by reaching the q, for the q then has only an inherited character, whereas we want it to have a sessile one. We must move from the q with an inherited character to a q as possessed of a sessile character. This q is the counterpart of the p which we acknowledged to be true to begin with.

We should not say, "p therefore q" as though this were the end of the entire process. Just as we had to take account of a p, before we brought it into relation to the "therefore," so we must take account of q as away from the "therefore." The "therefore" is ambiguous in that it sounds as though it were to be understood solely as involving a replacement of one item by another. This is the way I have been treating it in the past. But it should be understood to be an organic act, and thus to keep the p and the q together as surely as the rule and the intention do, but to warrant our holding the q apart as well, correlative to the p which we acknowledged before we began the inference.

The schema for both the learning and the inference should then be:

1. $p \ R \ q$ (rule or model)
2. $p \rightarrow q$ (intention)
3. $p.$ (acknowledged satisfactory unit for a beginning of an inference or act)
4. p therefore q (an organic act with a character transferred
         or   from p to q; the transfer is possible because
   better: from   of the way in which the intention combines
   p arrive at q: with the acknowledged unit for the beginning)
5. ———————   (acknowledged satisfactory term to use apart
         q from but because of the inference or act)

This line of thought has some bearing on the relation of the private and the public self. A man receives content from the external world either in the guise of what he observes or what another communicates to him. He translates this into content private to him which he relates to and replaces by further private content, to end with an expression which is externalized in the guise of content on a footing with that which he originally received. A living being, and particularly a man, returns to the world what is as at least as valuable as what he receives; in public intercourse, it is information and understanding similar to that which was presented to him.

All public content, all externally offered and returned material, has connections which are not constituted by the private being. One is tempted to say that it is content governed by a necessitarian rule of law and causality. But it is in fact a set of detached items, to be brought into an organic whole only by reading into the sequence some such expression as "possessed by or expressed by a reasonable man." Men usually return more than they receive because they are creative beings; we might define a man indeed as one who always returns more than he receives, and thus does not repeat but adds, if only by affirming what he took in.

There is something revelatory here about the nature of birth and death. We can see the life that we live as having been environed by a public giving of life to us, the receiving of natural conditions which we are then to carry out in ourselves. We can be said to be spending our lives in continuing to receive content from the world and society, but to add to this a giving out as well, a presentation to the external world of what we had produced in private. At the end of our career, we balance the initial one-way receiving that we had at the beginning with a one-way giving which is our death.

On death, we present ourselves to the external world in the sense in which we presented content all along, and in such a way as to balance what we had received, thereby making our death be on a footing with the conditions which we utilized in order to begin our lives. We will never have been born and will never in fact die, so far as we are beings who are conscious; our conscious life begins with the reception and conversion of the birth, and it ends with the presentation of ourselves, as no longer conscious, to the world out of which we initially issued.

The public acts which we receive and to which we contribute make up a set of detached items until we interpret them all as two sequences, one of which has us being given content and the other of which has us giving content. As being given content, our public acts are all the conditions which we normally say are prerequisite for our judgment or cognition; as content which we produce, our public acts are what we publicly are as men who have had a public birth and will have a public death, i.e., a birth which begins with social and natural conditions, and ends with our having a purely social or natural role.

November 30

A human birth is the outcome of the fulfilling of a series of conditions. It is a product of nature, society, and family—to mark out the more conspicuous factors. It is these which are converted into a human life. That human life repays the third of these in the act of a smile of recognition, the second of these in its normality, and the first of these in its acts of control and knowledge.

At every moment after birth, the human being takes natural, societal, and, for the most part in its early life, familial products, only to return in the form of acts, expressions, communications, and the like, something which is superior or at least equal in value to what it obtained, precisely because it has its roots in an individual consciousness. So far as an individual is conscious, decent, and healthy, he gives back to the family, society, and nature more than he obtained from them. Should he die at any moment, he has repaid what he owed. In a longer life, he has so much more of an opportunity to give back more than he received.

When life ceases, there is first (through will, plan, etc.) an externalization of consciousness (in the normal case) of what one is in the family; next there is a receding to the status of a dead man in that society, and finally, a receding to the status of a natural object. We give back to these three outside ourselves; the death which is here presented occurs after the act of our consciousness.

The last stage is the return of the physical body to nature. The nature with which we began—a nature which was something in itself but was functioning as that which makes a conscious life possible—is the nature to which we return in the guise of that which had been made possible by a conscious life. Though the corpse functions as a merely natural entity, it is returned by a man to nature, who so far makes nature a sacramental object—a graveyard or a crypt are examples.

Death is not something which we face, as those who define life in terms of consciousness lived through wholly from within are forced to affirm. We constantly externalize what we have received, and eventually come to the end of the process. That end is just a cessation of this type of act; it is followed by death, the actual conversion of the human into a mere factor in family, society and nature, as a way of returning into the conditions which made the consciousness possible.

The death which is correlate with the coming to be of a living human being is outside the consciousness of the individual, though of course he can imagine it and think about it. As conscious, he adopts the world on his own terms; and he returns to that world what he has himself conceived or consciously assessed. Strictly speaking, his birth and death have nothing to do with him as this conscious individual; they are the situations out of which he issued and to which he returns.

December 1

It is necessary to distinguish: A] start-finish,   B] antecedent-consequent,   C] base-prospect,   D] origin-terminus,   E] originating-terminating moves,   F] beginning and ending.

A]   The start and finish are isolated parts of an external setting; in the last resort, they are marked out parts of nature. One need not treat nature as a continuum with arbitrarily defined starts and finishes; it evidently has its own breaks, unit occurrences, and joints. Nor need we suppose that a start and finish are related by inexorable deterministic laws; there can be novelty and creativity between them. All we need acknowledge is that there may be many intermediary occurrences between them, whether produced causally or not. The start and finish are presupposed, but do not enter into acts of learning or inference. We acknowledge them merely by taking up a position, by encountering such and such materials.

B]   Antecedent-consequent constitute a rule or structure which can be used to guide activity, and which is to be used if one is to warrant the activity. Any factors in between the antecedent-consequent can be added to the former to constitute a larger antecedent, can be treated as constituting the actual material rule that is being used, or can be viewed as analyzable components which make the complex structure be articulatable. We now not only have a position, but see it in relation to another; we not only see a bat, but see it as something which we are to use.

C]   Base-prospect relates to an intention, where from some acknowledged entity we point to a possibility which is relevant to it and which is to be realized through our act. We can recognize a number of stages between the position we accept and the full realization of the prospect. We not only have a position here and another there, but intend to go from here, where we are, to there; we not only face a bat which can be gripped, but intend to grip it.

D]   Origin-terminus refers to the boundary of the act as outside the act. It relates to the start-finish but as relevant to what we are about to do. It could be said to be the product of the intent on the start-finish. In between the origin-terminus, there can be a number of auxiliaries in the form of props, diagrams, guides, and incidental aids. We now look at the position as the place from which a walk is to begin; we see the bat as that which we are to grip.

E]   We are not merely at an origin or a terminus, but move from the origin to the beginning, and move from the ending to the terminus; the moves in the one case are originating, and in the other, terminating. We take a first step and end with a last step. The first step as not yet completed is an originating one, and the last step as not yet completed is a terminating one. We reach for the bat and grip it. We accept this proposition as a worthwhile premiss, and present this proposition as a proper conclusion.

F]   Beginning-ending are the limits of an act, in between which we have a course or process that can be analyzed into subordinate but not truly abstractable components of the act. What we now do is to go through the process of gripping the bat, of making an inference, or of taking a walk.

The first three, A, B, C, belong together as providing the preconditions for an act. The second three, D, E, F, form a unity, When and as we move along F, from beginning to ending, we move from origin to the beginning, and (after the first move) finally from the ending to the terminus. We go through the act of gripping the bat as a single whole by interacting with the bat. We infer by attending to the premiss as that which has a truth of its own, to end with a conclusion as that which we want to have stand apart from us.

There is no such thing, then, as a mere act; the act as apart from an interaction with origin, auxiliaries, and terminus would be a mere intent, a thought, or a mere process of living. The "p therefore q" of the ordinary (and my own) account of inference is in fact to be seen as involving an interaction with origin, terminus, and auxiliaries while it moves on. The substitution of q for p is an act by which p is adopted, to be followed by the adoption of the auxiliaries, with an ending which is then offered as a terminus.

This does not mean that there is nothing private; a private act must, however, be conducted through an interplay of origins with beginnings, and of endings with termini, both of which can be privately entertained. This is in fact what usually happens in inference.

There is no simple passage from beginning to ending, but always an interplay with what is outside that course. Nor is there an abandonment of steps learned in training for the sake of going through an organic act; the organic act is the adoption of the steps learned in training, and the exteriorization of the process and ultimately of the ending, so that the process takes place in the body of the steps and the steps are qualified by the process.

The absorption of a dying (which is an ending) by a terminating (which is a yielding to nature) produces a terminus, death. The death can be imagined, but is not carried out as part of the process of life. At every moment in our interacting with what occurs after the origin, we are subject to this same process. Death is but the last of a series of outcomes of interactions of our living self with an external but available and relevant world.

Because there is an origin, auxiliaries, and a terminus, I am able to walk by having my legs come in contact with the ground. Because I am governed by an intent to walk, I am able to engage in an act of walking which, because it involves an interaction with origin, auxiliaries, and terminus, turns the latter into parts of a single organic and intended act. Man is the being who, via an intent which combines rule with start and finish, is able to interact with an origin and terminus, making the latter pair organic, while it makes the intended act into an actual occurrence. I articulate the organic act at the same time that I integrate the sessile moves into transient parts of a single actual occurrence.

Who am I? One who can make steps into a walk. Is that all? No, I can make paints into a painting, wood and metal into a gun, words into a claim. In what sense are these an advance? They carry my meaning, and sometimes a meaning of a world beyond them, into other contexts. They become me vicariously, giving my intent other embodiments by serving as causes and explanations of other origins-termini with which I do not then interplay. I am preserved in that with which I interplay; I outlast my life so far as I am preserved as well in that with which I do not interplay, but which is the product of that which I made in my interplay.

This is not yet a final answer. There are great achievements which have never been acknowledged and which have had no signal effect. It is also questionable whether any theory of outlasting a life which does not apply to all men can ever be satisfactory.

December 2

When I impose my intention on a series of steps, I turn them into constituents of a walk. I am then exteriorized, and so far become the walk, as embodied in those steps; and the steps, by that very act, are brought within the compass of my intentional nature, to be related to other objects of intention. But a walk is only one of the acts in which I engage. I can take it to be an object which I am going to vitalize through the introduction of a larger purpose, or by some principle of explanation, or by some way of intermediating it with other occurrences. I can continue this process until I am exteriorized in the world by making my intentions, knowledge, principles, emotions, intelligence, etc., all embodied in the occurrences there, at the same time that those occurrences are lifted up and made into elements within my total complex.

The existentialists seem to be interested in the second half of this process, and then only so far as it involves a kind of emotional vitalization of what is occurring (so far as they put a Kantian emphasis on their view) or as something which takes place from the very start without there first being some occurrence and an individual vitalization of it (a view which they tend toward, particularly since they are influenced by Hegel). But what they then do is to overlook the fact that we become the world as surely as the world becomes identical with ourselves by virtue of the impositions we make on the content it provides; they overlook as well the fact that the intellect, impersonal and objective, can be imposed, and is imposed on content as surely as are our individual and emotional sides.

What the existentialists have done is to anticipate the last stage of a long process. No man is simply identified with a walk or anything else which is merely produced through the objectification of an intent. An intentional object is vitalized by our intelligence, logic, science, ethics, and the arts; not until this has been done in such a way that the whole gamut of experience makes one single organized whole and we are in complete consonance with it (so that it is impossible to distinguish ourselves from the world), do we have the existentialistic result. We are then the very form of the world in which we live, and the world is the very content of our being. To have reached this stage is to be wise.

It is possible to reflect on the walk, and come to understand the nature of intention, purpose, and the conversion of mere physical sequential occurrences into components of single organic acts. Such reflection gives us the principles which we are to apply to the walk and other occurrences, thereby giving us a richer and wider-ranged way of having the particular occurrences of the world organically together.

There is a limit to this process. Though we can, of course, reflect on the nature of wisdom, we do not do this and ought not to do this when we are practicing wisdom. Thought about wisdom is thought about an ideal; when we are wise in the sense of making an integral unity with what lies outside us, we have neither time nor need for reflection. The existentialists are inclined to reverse this situation and to spend their time writing books about the desirability of being one with what lies beyond; they thereby show themselves to be not existentialists in fact, but to be aspiring to be so. And what they are aspiring to be is of a lower case than it need be.

A philosopher can take wisdom as his topic; it is a stage which he would like to attain. He does not mind affirming that he himself is not yet wise; his effort is to achieve wisdom by mastering those fundamental organizations of occurrences which allow him to be completely objectified and the world completely subjectified at one and the same time, and in one and the same situation. He and the world become harmoniously one when he is wise, but this is a result which comes about only after he has achieved a position where he can vitalize all that occurs in a single total scheme, a result which requires him to use not only his emotions and perceptions, but his intellect, and then in its most speculative and disciplined form. The existentialist achieves a degenerate form of wisdom only because he refuses to allow himself to be detached from the world sufficiently, so as to permit a broader and more basic way of dealing with all phenomena. Wisdom is an achievement, not a starting point.

Even if one views the outcome of wisdom as being due to the imposition of subjective or human factors on an external and neutral content, it does not follow that the content does not have in itself the very kind of structure which is imposed, and thereby makes a unity with man. And so far as we have exteriorized ourselves by making ourselves one with what is external to us, we exist when it does. Since we can make ourselves one with the entire cosmos by grasping the nature of its laws, its space and time, its dynamics, and its final beings, we are able to exist forever. We do not forever remain conscious of course, but the import of that consciousness, as exhibited in purposes, emotions, judgments, categories, and the like, is immortalized. The universe in a sense will objectify man, and in doing so will make the human remain forever. The existentialist, by reversing the stress and making content subject to man, in effect humanizes the universe and thereby makes it transient. This is another consequence of the existentialists' refusal to take an external world seriously.

The wiser we are, the more objectified we become, and the more humanized the entire scheme of things becomes. If we have the first without the second, we lose what is distinctive about man, individually and collectively, for we then become identical with the actual structure and process of the universe; if we have the second without the first, we lose what is distinctive about the universe, for it then becomes caught up in human concerns. But this means that man is immortal only so long as he subjugates the universe—or more generally, that man is objectified only so long as he remains in being and subjectifies the universe. Yet man can come and go and the universe continue. This surely is paradox.

Concentrating on the individual, we have reached the conclusion that he is immortal so far as he has made himself through his emotions, intellect, will, etc., in consonance with the scheme of things, but that this immortality is but the other side of a subjugation of the scheme of things to himself, who is but a transitory being. Does it make sense to overcome this paradox with the observation that we are objectively immortal only so far as we continue to maintain a meaning of immortality in the shape of the possession, in our own terms, of whatever there be? Our personal immortality would then mean that what sustains us forever is given meaning by us now, and that we are most truly immortal if we, in taking the universe on our own terms, understand ourselves to be that which is coextensive with that universe. But now, once again, I am losing the trail.

It seems equally true to say that when we perish, we obliterate a universe which makes us immortal, and that the universe by persisting immortalizes us who make it be a personal, transient reality. These stones which I arranged to form a series of positions cease to be positions when I perish, and yet those positions contain me and my meaning even when I am no longer; those stones have objectified me who have made them, for the moment, have the meaning of positions. Better: I am immortal as impersonalized, but the impersonalization is only at the forefront of and is inseparable from more and more personal and idiosyncratic ways of facing the universe; the universe is humanized, but the humanization is only at the forefront of and is inseparable from more and more objective, impersonal ways of existing. I am immortalized objectively, but I am here and now one who understands and feels that immortality; the universe is humanized subjectively, but it sustains that status as an objective reality.

December 6

In a purely mechanical world it is possible to have occurrences affected by others in such a way that they approach, turn from, and alter their movements in accord with the presence or actions of those others. A teleological situation involving these very items does not have the others affecting the occurrences directly. They affect some being which is the source of those occurrences. When an animal stalks another, that other, as an object of desire or intention, affects the animal which thereby acts in certain ways. Were we to look at this situation in a purely mechanical way, we would say that the various acts were a function of the (stalked) animal. The difference then is between the acknowledgment and the ignoring of an entity, which is the source of acts, as affected by another.

To convert a series of steps mastered in training into components in a single organic act is to move from the consideration of acts, as affected by the end to be attained, to that of an individual who is to be so affected, and thereby prompted to produce those acts. In this and other cases, it is possible to have a set of steps which come to no predesignated outcome, but which merely follow one on the other. When we take account of an individual who is occupied with that outcome, we do not have a more radical change in attitude than we had before. The mechanical situation in the one case had detached items all oriented toward some particular outcome; in the other case, it had those detached items without such an orientation. The change in the first case involved a reference to a being who was the source of the items; in the second case, it involved a reference to a being who was a source of the items and had some end in view.

When we turn to the problem of the passage from training step by step to performing a single organic act in which that training is utilized, we have no need to suppose that by introducing an intent, the steps which had been learned are somehow changed. The intention is the future as operative in us now in such a way as to make us include some occurrences and exclude others, and thereby define the steps as forming a single whole. Apart from the intention, the steps can be interspersed with other activities which, as occurring in a sequence with them, must be allowed to be on a footing with them; with the intention, those other occurrences are put aside as irrelevant or contributory to what the steps produce.

To concentrate on the various steps that are learned in training is in effect to have some kind of intention which allows one to attend to these steps alone. It is these steps that are to be learned and not some others. But though the steps are governed by some kind of intent, they are allowed to be members of a class instead of being possessed of an order governed by some prospective end. The shift to the act then is a shift in intent, from one where items form a class, even an ordinal class, to one where they are ordered by some prospective outcome. The intentional end which governs the ordinal class of steps learned in training affects the steps directly (or through the thought of the trainer); the intentional end which makes those steps be steps in a single act affects those acts via the individual as acting and not merely as thinking about the steps. One can ignore the steps in fact to concentrate on what might spoil the act, or what might make it a better act, all the while, of course, going through the steps in the process of carrying out the act.

The intention governing an acting individual is a vector which is affected by the prospective end; the intention guiding the training of an individual, by having him master particular steps, could have the act as its objective, but this act does not govern the training. It merely points to what will replace it.

December 7

"Grip the bat this way."

"Could it not be gripped this other way?"

"Not if you want to lift the bat."

"Oh, then there are two ways to grip a bat: just holding it tight, and holding it *in order that* . . ."

"That's true; but I can teach you to grip the bat in order to lift the bat, without having you pay any attention to the fact that you are going to lift it. I can teach you to grip it—as I began to do."

"What's the difference between teaching me to grip the bat in such a way that I will be able to lift it properly, and teaching me how to grip the bat in order to be able to lift it properly?"

"I must have the second in mind in order to teach you the first."

"But what is the difference in me?"

"You will have to keep in mind the fact that you are to lift it."

"What difference will that make?"

"You will follow one move by another, charge the whole with spontaneity perhaps, add other moves if this will improve the lifting, and exclude certain possible moves even though these had not been considered before."

From this dialogue, one can conclude that the trainer at least must have some end in view, even when he teaches only various steps or separate moves. He who learns step by step does not yet know how quickly the one is to follow on the other, nor does he have any reason to introduce any spontaneities, novelties, or nuances; he cannot know whether or not something else can or cannot be included in the act of gripping or in the transition from the gripping to the lifting, if this has not been already considered in the isolated step of lifting.

If someone were to count, 2, 4, 6, 8 . . . , we can never infer that he is counting according to a rule, or that he has an intention to count by twos (which is I suppose the same thing as to say that he is readied to count according to a rule which requires one to skip a number). It might be the case that he does not know any odd numbers, or that he is afraid to mention an odd number, or that he has an intellectual habit which prevents him from counting except by twos. We overlook this possibility when we tacitly suppose that he who counts by twos actually has the power to count by ones, to jump to fives, etc. When we ascribe to him an intention to count by twos, we in effect presuppose that he has an opportunity to mention other numbers, but that his intention makes him exclude these. To know that a man has an intention, we would have to have him faced with alternatives which are as available and attractive as any others, and have him reject them nevertheless. Those alternatives might be treated as selectable from some store, or as facing him in the shape of temptations, or objects, or lures, or occurrences.

When a man engages in an organic act, he goes through the moves which he had been trained to master. But he follows one on the other in a way that no one of them determines; at the same time, he vitalizes the activity and puts aside alternative courses or modifications which are then open to him, but which are not permitted by the intended objective. A man may walk to the store with the same gait as he does when he merely walks and arrives at the store. We can say that he intended to walk to the store only so far as we find a connection between the steps, and an exclusion of efforts and interests which could not otherwise be explained as simply. If he looks into a window on his way to the store, the intention to go to the store will then explain why he looked at this item rather than that, or why he stopped looking and suddenly began to walk again. All these occurrences could have causal explanations. One can be trained to make a smooth transition from one move to another, and to concentrate on what one is doing. But this does not yet go the length of accounting for the spontaneity which permeates the whole act, or for the ability to include factors which had not been considered in the training but which in fact make for a more successful completion of the act.

December 8

Every set of moves is governed by a future possibility. When we intend, we make that possibility more determinate than it had been. This determination is produced by our reading ourselves into the possibility; it is now our possibility, a possibility for us. And we can add further determinations through anticipation. No one of these determinations or any set of them ever gets the length of making the possibility wholly determinate. But the determinations which are imposed do have an effect. They delimit the moves that are open to us.

A more indeterminate possibility allows for more moves than one which is comparatively less indeterminate. It is not at once evident why this is so. After all, no matter what we intend, we can engage in irrelevant moves while getting to it. In what sense then do we make a selection of moves by increasing the determinateness of the possibility we confront and which we wish to realize?

It could be well argued that if we have a determinate possibility before us, we so far require whatever move will realize it. When we find ourselves engaged in irrelevant acts, we have made evident that we have allowed another possibility to function, for which that irrelevant act is relevant. The proper determination of a possibility will exclude such other possibilities, and therefore the moves which promote them. When we have a well-anticipated, focused possibility, we will engage in the moves which will realize it, and in no others. If we do not engage in such moves, say because we have not mastered them or because they are in fact impossible to us, the intended prospect is only the object of a hope or a wish.

On this view, there is an inescapable connection between the determinations which a possibility has natively or acquired, and the moves in which one will engage. The possibility is determined by an individual who is a source of moves; in the determination of the possibility before him through intent, that individual delimits himself by the possibility so as to require these moves and not those.

Possibilities could be long-ranged. What dictates that one will do this and not that now, that and not this next? Is this not due to the fact that the individual as he is now can do only one thing in a properly ordered situation if he is truly governed by the possibility he intends? At the present moment, facing just this possibility, he can do a number of things, but only one of these is what the end requires; he must now grip the bat and only then can he lift it. If he has as his intention the lifting or the swinging of the bat, he can do nothing more than grip it in this way or that. This does not preclude his adding details, or even other moves in the course of his transition from gripping to lifting.

We have here a case of preference, where the intended end has overwhelming value; less determinate ends in preference will lead to an interplay with what one inclines toward with what one has in view. Intention then is a way of making a preference operate primarily by virtue of the intended end, with the various moves that are open to us, all neutralized.

To reach what we intend it is necessary A] to make the end maximally determinate through our own focusing and anticipation, and B] to have all the moves, that are open to us now, have neutral or minimal value, thereby forcing to the fore that move which the end demands.

It is possible for a man to run to a base before he has even gripped a bat. The prospect of getting to first base could make him act in this way. What would prevent him? Nothing less than having himself be one who must now deal with the bat. He must, while thinking about going to first base, face the bat as that which he is to use. But he could use it wrongly; he could kick it or toss it away. It is such alternatives that the possibility will exclude if it is properly determinate. We have then also C] that there must be an acceptance of something here and now as that with which or at which one is to begin.

Two equally skilled men will achieve different results because though they will deal with C in the same way, they will fail either to determine the possibility to the same extent or will not take all moves to be equal in value, and thus will express a preference for one move that is more attractive, or easier, or more pleasant.

December 9

Three attitudes should sustain the threefold reference mentioned yesterday. To have the intended end at maximum determinateness (which is, of course, far short of the actual determination characteristic of actual entities in the present), it is necessary to be committed to it. The *commitment* is in effect an intensification of the intention, an acceptance of it as determinative of whatever moves we may be able to make. The second attitude is that of *detachment* toward the various moves, thereby enabling them to be on a footing with respect to the intended end. The third attitude is *resolution*, the acceptance of something in the present from the base of which we are going to make our first move.

These three attitudes must interplay. The commitment, the detachment, and the resolution, directed as they are at different entities though in rather oppositional ways, must be synthesized to yield a single, tensed act which is carried out from the present through the move or moves that the end requires.

An athlete must do at least five things: 1] he must master skills; 2] he must be committed to an end;   3] he must be detached from the various moves possible to him when he is about to engage in an act;   4] he must be resolute about starting in the present with such and such materials or muscles or at such and such a position; and   5] he must synthesize these so that the skills are exhibited in such a way that he does arrive at the end efficiently and well.

Skills make for a limitation in possible moves in one direction and an increase in another. Commitment makes for a tension which must be distinguished from mere nervousness, as merely keeping one focused on the end rather than worrying about the outcome. Detachment makes for a relaxation which is needed if one is not to be overanxious, or too finely tuned. Resolution in the present avoids the ambiguity or frustration of not being able to get started; it breaks through a possible indecisiveness, by making one identify himself with some present position or object. Synthesis allows one to perform the act as a unity and with some gracefulness, the more that it brings the various factors together without leaving them unsatisfied in any particular.

It has long been known that athletes must be at once tensed and relaxed. The swimmer shakes himself; the jumper steps about, the football player does calisthenics, etc. These are ways of getting relaxed. But at no time is this relaxation to interfere with the tension produced by the commitment. It was also well known that there must be skills mastered; that is what the training is primarily occupied with. But sufficient attention has not been paid to resolution and synthesis. The first is sometimes included under skills, for the runner is taught how to crouch, the diver how to approach and stand, the golfer how to place his hands, feet, and shoulders. These are skills that can be taught, but there is a difference between possessing a skill and being set to apply it. Resolution refers to the fact that the athlete is ready to apply a particular skill. This is the same thing as his being ready to engage in one particular move. We can therefore say of him that his committed end determines that he should engage in a particular move at the beginning, but that this move must be independently resolved upon. It is this preference for the initial move, together with the sanctioning of it by the end to which he is committed, that makes him begin the act in this way.

Since the very same move is endorsed by the end and by the resolution (it being one of a number which is faced by the end, but which the end selects by virtue of its compatability with the determinations of that end), the synthesis that is required in effect comes down to the carrying out of a move that has been doubly endorsed—by the end and then by the resolution. Since the move has been mastered as a skill, it would be more precise to say that there is a skilled move which is emphasized in one's resolution, and also among a number of neutral moves as that which is demanded by the intended end. The relaxation with respect to possible moves is a preliminary, just as the mastery of skills is. The act proceeds only when the end already determines a man (because he is part of that determination, as a factor in the making of the end more determinate than it otherwise would be) to engage in a move, which in the ideal case is what he has resolved to produce.

The end must be allowed to manifest its full power; that is why the relaxation is necessary. The resolution must be allowed to stay focused on a single move; that is why it must be directed to the present. A distinct commitment and a distinct resolution must be directed to the same move. The resolution is then supported by the intention's demand, and the intention has its selection backed by the resolution.

December 19

A well-turned act involves an interplay of a number of factors: 1] *Attention* is needed in order to focus on some delimited part of the future to make it into a relevant prospect with which one is to be occupied. 2] *Desire* is needed in order to intensify the relation we have to the prospect and thereby make the prospect more determinate. 3] *Intention* is needed in order to make the prospect have an effect on us in the present. 4] *Relaxation* is needed in order that we may be able to free ourselves of whatever inclinations and biases we may have toward this or that move, so as to enable the demands of the intention to be carried out. 5] *Resolution* is needed in order to make us take advantage of whatever facilities there be, so that an act in fact can be begun. 6] *Energy* is needed in order that the act be carried out by altering ourselves and what we encounter.

The intention may have over against it a rule or criterion in terms of which the legitimacy of the act can be evaluated, or it may contain the rule within itself as that which can be abstracted from it by freeing it from its stress on the prospect and its temporal reference. There should also be considerable training, so that the moves which begin with what the initial resolution demands can be carried out successively and well. And, of course, equipment and other conditions for the actual carrying out of the act must be presupposed.

Such a well-turned act is to be found in multiple areas—in athletics, in art appreciation, and in love. The most important aspects are the *commitment*, which results from a combination of desire and intention (presupposing attention), *relaxation*, which involves an inhibition of our inclinations, and *resolution*, which requires that we be properly placed so that an actual move, required by the commitment, can be carried out.

Commitment makes one tense, relaxation makes one open, and resolution enables one to act. Manuals for sexual performance, for the making of art, for training in a sport, concentrate mainly on the different moves which one must go through if the end is to be attained. But the end which calls out these moves is not that which an act, stretching over those moves, is aimed at. It is an end for being ready, or being well, or being efficient.

We concentrate on the mastery of moves with the implicit end for being ready, etc., only so far as we are ill. The various manuals are for individuals who are in a state similar to that of an injured person who must learn various moves in order to be able to walk. Those who are not injured in this way use a whole step as a move; the injured instead use various subdivisions of that step as the different moves that have to be mastered.

If one has an intent to love, or to appreciate a work of art, or to win a race, one cannot stop with the various moves which one might conceivably have learned to master in order to attain the end of functioning properly, but must go on to engage in the act of loving, appreciating, or running as governed by the intended end. More often overlooked is the need to relax with respect to what one is now to do, while remaining tensed toward the end. One can become overanxious and not be able to perform well enough to reach the end; relaxation is an aspect of the situation out of which a well-turned act is to be produced.

Relaxation is too often neglected, particularly in the West. In the East, with its emphasis on detachment, relaxation is more readily recognized as an important factor in every act. But there is then not enough attention paid to the commitment to an end. Too often too, there is not enough attention given there to the need to make a decision. As a consequence, in the East there is a tendency to do nothing. But we need not suppose that the only alternatives are a relaxation or a tension. Both are needed, and both must be supplemented by a resolution to take advantage of something now in order to engage in an act.

An act makes use of energy, and energy can be stored. This means that one might prepare for an act by trying to build up a larger reservoir of energy. The athlete has learned how to hold his breath longer, how to withstand fatigue, how to continue despite weariness. These can be learned by his going through exercises which do not resemble in their pattern any of the moves which he must make in order to carry out his act. Similarly, to appreciate and to make a work of art, it is necessary to have improved one's sensitivity and insight by going through a different set of moves. Something similar can be said with respect to sexual activity. The energy utilized might be built up by eating the proper foods, and achieving a good body tone. In all these cases, what is learned is a way of reaching the stage where one can have maximum energy used effectively in the production of some act, be it of running, appreciation, or love.

"All administrators are failures."

"All?"

"Yes, all."

"Presidents, generals, college presidents, foremen, deans, treasurers?"

"Yes, all of these."

"They surely are not failures in the sense in which those who tried for these posts and did not succeed in getting them are?"

"No, they are not failures in that sense."

"Nor are they failures in not doing most important work, and often doing it well."

"No, they are not failures in that sense."

"You have a peculiar sense of failure."

"I don't think so. I think a man is a failure if he perverts the aims of man, if he gives his life to doing things which are not what should occupy a man's full time."

"To run a country, to save a country, to make for the material prosperity of all is not man's work?"

"It is not. A man should be occupied with the final realities; these administrators, at best, are concerned with making it possible for others to live full human lives."

"Then they deserve credit for sacrificing themselves on behalf of others, or of mankind to which those others will contribute."

"Oh, I agree to that."

"But a man who does good to all or makes it possible for others to achieve a result they otherwise could not, cannot be said to be a failure."

"He of course does not fail to do good; but he does fail to be a full man himself. He sacrifices, if you like, the opportunity to be a full man in order to make it possible for others to be full men."

"Every martyr then is a failure?"

"No; the martyr yields his life on behalf of a higher good which he would have liked to attain without making that sacrifice. The administrator has no alternative; he just gives up his life so that good may be achieved. He does not envisage the possibility of having those goods achieved without his aid. The martyr reluctantly sacrifices his life; the administrator, if you like, does it willingly, and then without any assurance that this will result in others doing well."

"Would it be better if there were no administrators?"

"No. But that does not mean that those who accept this role are doing what it is best for a man to do. The most one can say is that they are not doing what a man should do, but are making it possible for others to do what they should. It is questionable, however, whether they do make this possible."

"Is it not good to direct society, to promote law and order, to see that work is done efficiently and well?"

"Yes."

"Then administrators are not only necessary but desirable."

"I never denied that; I maintained only that they were wasting *their* lives."

1967

January 6

A philosopher should be both generous and critical. But the generosity should precede the criticism. He who starts with a critical attitude will have too narrow a base in terms of which to consider all fields of knowledge and being. This is true of Hume, and in recent times of the positivists.

The generous philosopher runs the risk of accepting superstitions, errors, confusions, unjustified claims, and mere beliefs. But it is the function of criticism to get rid of these. One should not then, as Hume did, try to get to what seems to be the most elementary and inescapable items of knowledge and build in terms of these. Not only does he then not really know what is elementary and inescapable, but he does not provide for items which, though dubitable one by one, may not be dubitable as a class, and in any case may ground a domain to be dealt with, say, by statistics or probabilities.

Criticism should enable one to isolate the fundamental units and categories within each accepted domain. One may in fact treat Hume as doing just this: he accepted the world of ordinary knowledge (just as today Russell would accept the world of scientific knowledge) and then by analysis located what he took to be its ultimate inescapable elements. The acceptance of the domain and the analysis were done in private and did not appear in his work; otherwise it might have been easier for some of his followers to note the fact that his critical approach presupposed a generous acceptance of some domain.

Today phenomenology is a philosophy which is generous in spirit but is not critical enough. Analytic philosophy, on the other hand, is critical in spirit but not generous enough. This difference in emphasis shows that some contemporaries (John Wild, e.g.) who think these two philosophies are somewhat alike are not altogether correct. What should be offered is a critical phenomenology. This accepts all empirical data and then subjects them to careful criticism, making sure that the questions relating to necessity, privacy, transcendentals, religion, and the like are not begged or pushed aside.

The phenomena do not reveal an intention. How is it then that an intention ever becomes a topic for an empiricist even to dismiss? Does he accept common sense's reference to it in the first place, and then find that he cannot deal with it in terms of the narrow base he officially accepts? If so, it is evident that he starts off by being generous to common sense, but instead of analyzing this, turns his back on it to develop a philosophy which starts with a critical attitude. If he were a generous empiricist, he would have analyzed the meaning of "intention," and not denied it a role. This is what some of the more recent analysts apparently are doing, under the influence of Wittgenstein and Austin. But ought they not accept common sense's views on religion, the self, immortality, etc., in the same spirit? To deal only with the languages which relate to these is not yet to deal with what these intend.

We can know that there is an intention by seeing what would happen if we modified or rejected some end in view. If a man is walking, we do not know whether he is walking for a purpose or just ambling along. But if we hear him express an intent, or if we suspect one, we can characterize his objective as being too remote, too difficult to realize, etc., and see if his behavior changes. If it does, and if the change is pertinent to the suggested characterization of the end in view, we judge that the end is intended. Before that time, and surely after it, we use a reference to the intent to enable us to divide a series of occurrences into those which are appropriate and those which serve merely as occurrences slowing up the time for the accomplishment of the intended task.

The man who walks with intent and the man who ambles may both stop to look into the store window. But if we say to both that it is getting late, the former will stop looking, but the latter will not. If the former insists that he has an intent but wants to continue to look, we will have to say of him that he has confused an intent with a wish. An intent involves some control of acts here and now by the intended end.

January 7

Reading Kurt Goldstein's *The Organism* prompts the reflection that there are two basic types of disease. In one, there is a failure to attend properly to the ideal or to some other ultimate mode of Being; in the other, there is a failure to attend to the concrete and immediate. Goldstein's interest in the whole leads him to emphasize the first.

Without adhering to any of his observations or conclusions, I think it is possible to find that following out the implications of the first consideration will give some support for what he is contending. When an individual loses a grip on an appropriate end, he is involved in a world of detached particulars. He does not lose all hold of what lies outside that world; he replaces his former goals, intentions, or purposes by a vague overall objective having little interior determinateness. In order to recover an objective which is more determinate, it is necessary for him to reconstruct the particulars. His overall tendency would seem to be that of finding a specific end which is adequate to his capacity. When for some reason, such as brain injury, he loses a grip on some particular and the determinate end, he is forced to reorder the remaining particulars in such a way that there will be another determinate end to which he will then turn.

If we are not well prepared for an end which we seek to realize, we will have to expend more energy than otherwise. It would have been better if we did not try to reach that end, but instead focus on one which was appropriate to our preparation. If this is true, we do not try to reach that end, but instead focused on one which was appropriate to our preparation. If this is true, we do not try to outdo ourselves; we want to conserve the use of our energy. But great work involves the willingness to spend more energy. We can therefore say that if we start with the idea of excellence as defining what we are to do, all men are defective, but that some of them, the athletes, e.g., willingly expend extra energy in order to reach that end. The perfectly prepared athlete is one who can attain that end without this extra expenditure. But this is a consequence which follows only if excellence be an unchanging goal.

Every athlete, no matter how well prepared, must expend extra energy, for whatever he is prepared to do is never all that he wants to do. The goal that is before him is one which defines him as here and now unable to reach it without expending extra energy, and therefore as one who, in terms of that goal, must be said to be defective. This result, which is in consonance with what Goldstein maintains, is evidently paradoxical. This is due to the fact that he thinks of a need to expend energy beyond a normal or average as a sign of a failure, because of his supposition that there is a finite amount of energy available for the accomplishment of one's tasks. The fact of commitment, of will, seem to indicate that this is not a proper view.

That men do tend to find goals appropriate to their abilities would seem to be true on the whole; but it does not apply in all cases. It does not apply to those who are inspired by ends which are not usually pursued. It would be wrong to say that men who are thus inspired are ill in any sense. Consequently, it would be better to say that there are goals appropriate to the survival of the organisms, and that these must be modified to accord with what abilities and energies are available. We should then say that a man is defective only so far as he must spend more energy in order to accomplish what others can do with less, but that those who spend more energy in order to pursue goals which are beyond the reach of others, are instead superior because they are realizing superior goals.

We have then two uses of extra energy. In the one case, we try to come up to a norm, and in the other, we try to reach a more difficult goal. The first indicates that we are defective, the second indicates that we are dedicated. The first gives compulsive power to the end, the second gives it arousal power. The first defines the use of a certain amount of energy, and then remarks that the failure of some part of us demands that the rest must be quickened with the energy that would have been expended in the use of the failing part. The second instead faces us with an end which demands a certain amount of energy if it is to be attained, and in some cases elicits from the individual the energy needed.

A second type of disease is a consequence of the failure to attend to the concrete and immediate and instead to face a dislocated ideal or end. But such an end is the object of a fantasy or wish. The individual occupies himself with particulars without any reference to what is needed or wanted or desirable, and as a consequence, though something is done, no end is in fact realized. When athletes are trained by step-by-step methods, they tend to fall into this situation, and whatever victories or achievements they may envisage will be but dreams which they are not in fact preparing to realize.

Means and end must be in organic unity, the one consisting of particulars which are ordered by the end, the other consisting of an ideal, but somewhat determinate, goal which has an effect on the individual and thus on what he will now do with respect to the various particulars.

We have here another instance of the One and the Many, and the need to have both of these in interplay. The neglect of one of these does not mean the abolition of everything but the other, but rather the substitution of another not altogether appropriate or efficacious. If we reject some controlling One, we get an immanent One—and in the case of purposive beings, an additional transcendent but not pertinent One. If we ignore the Many or some part of it, we get another Many which will either have only a minimal order or will overwhelm the One, and at the same time have beyond it a Many which is appropriate to that One, though no account is in fact then being taken of that Many.

(I think the above is a good indication of a process of thinking which was not sufficiently worked out in advance, even in outline. As a consequence, it is not well ordered, very clear, or very illuminating. But I think it worthwhile to keep it here to show what way a mind might work when it has taken up some suggestions but has not spent time trying to reflect on what they mean before trying to write them out.)

January 8

Faced with a dichotomy of any kind, one can deal with it in a number of ways: *1] Parallelism* affirms that what happens on one side has its counterpart on the other; but it has no way of knowing that this is so, since it must stand on one side or the other, and has no provision for a perspective embracing both sides. *2] Epiphenomenalism* affirms that one side is a function of the other, without efficacy or reality of its own. But one can with equal justice have an epiphenomenalistic position assume the other side to be basic. A epiphenomenalist is therefore arbitrary or has two epiphenomenalisms, and thus repeats the dichotomy once more. *3] Attenuationism* treats one side as grounding the other, but allows the other to have some being. It seeks to express the two sides as limits of a single continuum, but since it starts with one side rather than the other, to the disadvantage of the side at which it arrives, it is subject to the same criticisms as the epiphenomenalistic view. (Whitehead used to say that the worst view he knew was neoplatonism; but his contention that the same categories apply to every entity, to God eminently as well as to the particulars of this world, is in principle the same view as that of the neoplatonists.) *4] Analogism* tries to bridge the gap by taking the terms used for one of the factors to have a different application for the other. But this has the defect, like the parallelistic view, of not really knowing what is on the other side, and like the epiphenomenalistic view, of having to choose one side as a proper starting point, when the other is also possible. *5] Progressivism* holds that the oppositional units come together in time or through the course of knowledge to constitute a single new whole where they are reconciled; but it is difficult to see how this whole arises, and when the process can come to an end. *6] Penumbration* holds that each side has the other as a penumbrum, but that this double state of affairs is what is initially given. We start somewhere in the middle and move to one extreme in order to explain the other extreme. The dichotomy here is the result of a separating out of what was initially together. This is the preferable view, I think.

January 9

If one were to deny the existence of teleology, and more particularly of purposes, intentions, or other determinations by what is not yet, one would have to suppose that different moves are the outcome of the reaction of parts of the body to what is confronted in the environment, and that any combination of such moves is the result of association, habit, etc., which necessitates that when one item is produced it triggers the next, and so on. Should one remove the bearer of the "not yet," say a lure or other inducement, one would presumably remove the stimulant and thus would be able to account for the fact that the series of moves comes to a close. But the denial has no way of accounting for novelties and creations in the course of the process of arriving at the end.

What is introduced afresh sometimes is relevant to the achievement of the end. From the standpoint of an achieved association of moves, all that is introduced is odd; but from the standpoint of one who accepts the teleological outlook, the end to be attained will define some of the moves as relevant and some as irrelevant, the latter being those which slow up the move to the end. For the rejectors of the teleological view, there is no end to be attained, but only an end at which one stops. They therefore will not be able to say of the novel anything more than that it does not appear to have any cause among stimulators of moves, or that it happens to be caused by some such stimulator without becoming part of the associated series of moves which terminates in some result.

January 11

A dictionary, by listing words in alphabetical order and treating them all as on a footing (with the exception of those that are rare or vulgar or slang), makes a number of assumptions. It supposes that words are detachable units; that they all have the same weight; that they all are to be defined in the same manner; and that they do not change in meaning in different contexts. It mitigates the dangers of these assumptions by quotations which show the words in sentences; by labeling some of them as technical; by quoting authoritative uses; and by listing different uses. But none of these devices goes the length of showing the emotional overtones, the ritualistic uses, or the exhortatory character of such words as "God," "love," or "noble."

A dictionary must approach all words from one angle, or turn out to have many different styles and approaches. But it is hard to know just what that angle is, and what right one has to take it. It is not a commonsensical one, for this does not embrace the technical terms (or if it does, it treats them in ways they should not be treated, since they have highly specialized uses in highly specialized contexts, unapproachable from the outside). Most dictionaries begin with a philological approach and a reference to classical authors' uses of the terms. But this does not suffice to let one know just what is meant by certain terms, even in the past.

There is surely a great difference between a definition of God and a treatise on Him, whether this be written by a theologian, an historian, a reporter of religious practices and expressions, or a philosopher. To trace back the term "God" to an Indo-European base which means "To call out or invoke," or to define it as a supernatural eternal being who rules the universe and perhaps created it, or who is attended to in worship with awe and reverence, is but to place "God" behind a closed door.

Not until one worships or until one in fact goes through the process of thinking about what transcends the here and now is one able to make a direct use of the term. "God" is supernatural and eternal, in a context of speculative understanding, religious practice, or theological systematization. We must first enter the context before we can know what the terms in the definition mean in the sense of having a distinctive grammar and use. And when we enter the context, we find that "God" takes on a wider and richer meaning than can be given by telling us that there is a context in which it occurs.

To read a dictionary properly, we must distinguish the context from the defined meaning, even though the dictionary makes no clear distinction between them, and then must go on to recognize that in the context the defined meaning will have a different value from what it has when stated as merely requiring that context.

The emphasis on the context would seem to go counter to all reference to things as they are in themselves, to simple denotations, to science, ontology, and other enterprises making realistic and objectivistic claims. But this consequence does not follow, since there are contexts in which something is faced as objective and real. To say that we are to understand what an electron is within the frame of a science is not to deny the reality of the electron, but only to maintain that the reality is to be known within the kind of conceptual scheme that science provides. It is to say that we do not get to some realities without first turning from the usual commonsense context to more abstract and formal ones, from the position of which one can recognize the entities which the terms are intended to denote.

January 17

It is often said by men that women are irrational. If by that they mean that women cannot think straight, that they are unable to do logic or mathematics, that they cannot follow an argument, or that they are unable to see flaws in arguments, the view is surely mistaken. What is being pointed to, I think, is the fact that very often women are signaling when they seem to be speaking or arguing. They want to proceed in an atmosphere of love or acceptance; when this does not seem to be present, they try to invoke it, or they complain about its absence. In response to a question or an argument, they will therefore not reply directly, but instead will say something which is intended to provide the atmosphere in which the question can be dealt with.

Should someone respond always to the signaling of the women, this would not satisfy them, for what they want is not an answer to the signaling, but a situation which would not require the signaling. Therefore if one were to attend to the signaling of the women in every case, he would produce a situation almost as unsatisfactory as if he did not respond at all. What is wanted by the women is a situation in which the signaling is usually not necessary, and an occasional remedying of the situation because of the signals. There should be some occasions when the signals are ignored, not only because they are not then that important (as they might be at some other time), but because there is a desire on the part of a woman for the man to retain his integrity and in a sense not yield to her.

Why is there this difference in the sexes? Is there not also some kind of signaling by men?

I think it is correct to say that both men and women live in distinct kinds of contexts, in part because of their biology, in part because of their upbringing, and in part because of the fact that the one is primarily visual and the other tactile in relation to the other. Whenever the context seems to be slipping away, or to be obscured, there is a tendency to recover it, either by a direct effort or through the aid of the other. The woman, because of the fact that the context for her is one of love or intimacy, needs the aid of the other, and therefore signals primarily. The man, because of the fact that his context is primarily a public one, responds to a loss of it by a retreat from the woman, by irritation, by a renewed insistence on the context where he works, thinks, is respected, etc. But this does not mean that she too may not retreat, be irritated, and make a renewed insistence, or that he too may not signal and look for help from her. Nor does it affect the fact that women have an interest in social affairs, and that men cherish a family life.

The interest in social affairs by women is predicated on the hope that the relation to the man has been settled, making the social affair an extension of what she achieves in the ideal case. The man's interest in the family, conversely, is predicated on the establishment of a satisfactory relation of himself to other men in the public world. But the family is not for him an extension of the other; it offers him a haven, a resting place. He therefore can be said to have two contexts, a public one which is primary, and a private one which has its basic tone determined in good part by the woman. She, on the other hand, has only one context which she tries expand endlessly.

A woman may have a career, and a man may have little interest in an interplay with other men. But the career of the woman is never as sufficient as it is for a man; she would like to have it if she could also be guaranteed the pervasive atmosphere of love, not in the career, but at home. He, on the other hand, even when not interested in an interplay with other men, has some concept of his status in the larger society as one who is to accomplish what a man should. This may not have anything to do with what others might approve or which they might know. Still he sees himself as a being in a world which is larger than his family.

January 26

The ethical and political man tries to introduce an obligated freedom into nature; the religious man tries to introduce a sustained faith; the artist and the historian try to introduce a purposed creativity. By a parity of reasoning, one should expect that the knower and the man of action would try to introduce into nature something which reflects both the reality of Actuality and the manner in which men function with respect to it. What could this be? Actuality is the Being which the particular actualities possess for a moment; the knower and the man of action, and particularly the athlete, could be thought to represent that Actuality. In a sense, all the other types of men represent their respective Beings or encapsulated forms of these. What is wanted is some understanding of the specific nature of the representation.

The knower and actor are carriers, instantiations of Actuality. They introduce into nature a sacrificial acceptance of Being, thereby making all actualities have a dignity they otherwise would not have. They all become recognized to be equal in worth, not in themselves as individuals, but as localizations of Actuality, and are thus far excellent. The excellence which the athlete is endeavoring to make manifest is an extreme form of what he can carry.

But does not the athlete 1] represent mankind, 2] show a defiance of nature, 3] strive for an excellence of man over against the opposition of nature, directly or indirectly in the form of other men or their presented obstacles? This seems to be the case. Does this mean that the athlete is a particularized form of the man of action, that the parity of reasoning we have followed does not apply, or that there is a way of reconciling the above considerations with the consequences which flow from making the athlete parallel the historic man, the religious man, and the political man?

The last question is badly put. The historic, religious, and political men do not face all of nature, but only certain segments of it, and so far as they do this, they qualify it over a limited area and then only so far as men are involved with it. In this respect they are not too different from the athlete. They too, like him, represent mankind, struggle with nature, and strive to exhibit excellence.

The athlete seems to differ from the artist and the ethical man (and their counterparts, the historic and the political man) in that he is occupied with exhibiting a human excellence, whereas they seem to be concerned with exhibiting an excellence that transcends them. To have the athlete parallel with them, he would have to try to exhibit the excellence of Actuality, i.e., the Being to possess which would make actualities perfected since they would then be eternal and self-contained.

The excellence of Actuality is mediated by the athlete in his dedication or self-sacrifice. He in effect is saying to all men "we *are!*"

January 27

One can profitably divide the demands imposed on the athlete into two classes. In the one would be those which refer to his capacities and skill—speed, control, stamina, power, durability, coordination; in the other would be those which refer to his spirit—determination, relaxation, decisiveness, teamwork, team-spirit, commitment, ambition, teachability, competitiveness, basic conceit, maturity, stability. How much of the first is needed? Is it possible to start with a man who has hardly anything of the first, but a great deal of the second? If one could, it would mean that a good trainer or coach could make anyone who was willing into a great player. The achievements of great coaches would seem to indicate that this is possible. On the other hand, it does seem to be the case that there are native requirements; a basketball player must be above a certain height, a pitcher must have a strong arm, a crewman must have strong legs. It is dubious whether coordination can be much improved by training. We find coaches with remarkably successful careers unable to do much when they take over poor teams.

We should expect a promising athlete to show a natural aptitude superior to other players. This aptitude may be in overall activities, or it may be in some sport which is other than that to which he is going to devote his athletic career. He must have a native strength, speed, and endurance greater than the usual. If he will back this with the personal stresses of the second group, he can hope to become a superb player.

We have then not only the problem of the maximization of resources through the use of a proper spirit, but the having of maximum resources. He who has maximum resources may not use them maximally; if he does not, he may not fare any better than one who has less than maximal resources but who uses them maximally.

The judgment of a young player cannot be determined by questioning him. Usually he is inarticulate; often he has other meanings in mind; and it is quite common to find that his background and experience lead him to give distinctive values to words and questions. One would do better to ask the questions of the managers, teachers, and even fellow players.

The various categories I have listed can be best utilized if they are used as pivots around which general questions are asked. Thus to find out if a player is really committed to playing in that sport, one might ask if he has other interests; or one might note what he does when he has an opportunity to show children how to play, or when he has a chance to study other players or games, or his own performances on tape, etc.

The player is usually conscious of his own desires; but if he plays on a team, he will recognize that in fact no one plays only for himself. The awareness of his role on a team by a team-player is an awareness of a conspicuous case of a player being a representative of his team. But the presence of spectators makes evident that in some sports it is also clear that he is playing as a representative of them too. Here again we have only a conspicuous case of what is common to all sports. In all sports, the player represents all men, even those who are not spectators and not interested in what he does. Does he not also represent more than this?

It is true, of course, that the player competes with nature, either directly or indirectly, and cannot so far be said to represent it. But he could be said to represent the Being of Actuality, which he then tries to exhibit as the Being which makes all men equal and which places them over against the rest of the space-time world. He would then be the counterpart of the basic inquirer who approaches all things from the perspective of the fundamental category of being and knowledge. That category has some taint of himself or of the mankind for whom he seeks to know and in terms of which he speaks; the very same category serves as the base in terms of which one acts.

An "authentic" act takes it start, not from a role in relation to other entities, or from the individual as unique, but from the base which is common to all men as distinct actualities. The action serves as a means by which a number of men are brought together as equally important, and as finalities over against nature. Where the religious man tries to bring about a more intimate relation among men, the man of action, and particularly the athlete, tries to control and conquer nature and thereby bring about a situation where men are ennobled as a totality of individuals over against nature. The ethicist and political man can be said to act on both men and things in order to harmonize them, and the artist and the historic man can be said to work on nature so that men may produce something which allows them to understand what that nature is.

This is not altogether clear, but it is nevertheless evident that it would not be altogether correct to say that the athlete is seeking excellence for himself or for man, any more than he is seeking to win or to achieve a personal result. What he seeks is to make the categorial nature, which is at his root, to be exhibited elsewhere. He represents mankind just so far as he tries to exhibit this categorial nature in the acts of himself or his team while he struggles with nature.

January 28

MY ALTER EGO: You defend a metaphysical pluralism in *Reality*, by holding that a single being is absolutely indeterminate, that this is identical with being nothing, and that nothing self-contradictorily is determinately the indeterminate that it is, needing something outside it to give it that determinateness. Why cannot the one being be internally determinate, i.e., have various distinctions or fissures in it?

I: Surely it might.

MAE: Well then, it would not be indeterminate in the sense you require.

I: There would have to be a distinction between the being and its fissures, would there not?

MAE: Yes.

I: Then the being would be indeterminate in itself and be over against the multiplicity of determinations.

MAE: But the determinations are not beings.

I: If they are not beings, in what sense can they be?

MAE: I think they are just the Being itself taken part by part, rather than in one swoop; the Being is articulated in a plurality of ways, and that is the end of the matter.

I: The parts would have to be distinguished one from the other, and all of them would have to be distinguished from the Being. The distinction would be a real distinction only if the parts were real and thus far over against the Being as such.

MAE: But then you are denying that they are only distinctions, internal articulations of the Being. You might as well speak of them as a plurality of actual substances over against the Being of Actuality.

I: Can you avoid doing something like that? Either the distinctions have being enough to stand over against the Being of which they are distinctions, thereby enabling the Being to be determinate as that which is over against and opposes the being of those distinctions, or they have no being, and then, strictly speaking, are not.

MAE: Such an argument should make you say that an apple cannot be red, for the red either is or is not something over against the apple. If over against the apple, it is apparently for you a being to be contrasted with the apple; if not over against the apple, it has no being at all. But I would say that the red inheres in the apple, and that it is distinguishable from the apple without being able to be over against or apart from the apple. It is, but is not a being which can contrast with the apple.

I: We can distinguish the red and the apple only because we abstract the red and sustain it in our judgment, or because we set the apple over against other substantial objects where the fact of its redness is irrelevant. By itself, in itself, there is only red-apple.

MAE: That is exactly what I am arguing for. By itself there is only x-y-z-being, where the x-y-z are like red, i.e., they are qualifications or specifications or distinctions which we can focus on, but which are not to be contrasted with the Being as it is by itself. Their presence means that the Being is not altogether indeterminate, just as the red means that the apple is not mere appleness, or even a singular apple without any color whatsoever.

I: If the red or the x-y-z has no being of its own, a contrasting of it with that which possesses it would be a falsification. To say that red is a color is already to take it out of the apple and place it alongside of green and yellow, etc., where it has its own rationale and interplays. No particularity by itself can oppose, and therefore be over against and provide determinations for a Being. Being forever is, but a particular only has a being; it shares in Being, and for only a contingent, finite time. What can be over against the Being must have some being of its own.

MAE: If each particular is not, I cannot see how the totality can be; and if there be a totality of particulars which is, I cannot see how we can avoid saying that the particulars are.

I: I think you are right. Each particular is, and the totality of particulars is, and both of these contrast with the Being which I call Actuality.

MAE: That still does not give you the plurality of Beings, for which you argue in your metaphysical pluralism.

I: That is right. So far as we have now gone, all that we can say is that, with the panentheists, we acknowledge a plurality of real particulars and a Being which is germane to them in their severalty and as a totality. I would argue for a genuine plurality of Beings, on the basis that the being of the particulars or their totality is not of itself strong enough to be other than the Being. Either the particulars are sustained by some second Being, which enables them to stand over against their own Being, or their own Being is held apart from those particulars so as to enable those particulars to have some independence of function. The first alternative would lead to the difficulty of having some alien mode of Being intrude in some other Being, and there hold that other Being's particulars over against it. But a Being, it would seem, has to do only with its own particulars; if it makes possible the independence of the particulars of some other Being, it must do so by sustaining that other Being as a reality which is held at an ontological distance from its own particulars.

Beings determine one another as Beings, enabling them to function in various ways with respect to their particulars. The holding of a Being away from its particulars is only one of the enablings made possible by some other Being; it is in fact the enabling which is made possible by the

Being I call God. The Being which is Actuality is held apart from its particulars by the action of God. God is that Being which allows Actuality to be over against its own particulars. By themselves, those particulars have not sufficient reality to maintain themselves against the incursion of their common Being.

To give adequate being to particulars so that they, without being identified with Being, can nevertheless be, it is necessary for some other Being, God, to hold the Being of those particulars, a Being I call Actuality, to be a Being for them. Apart from the action of God, they would not have being enough to be independent.

MAE: It looks to me as if God has only an ontological role. What about the God of religion? If God cannot get to the particulars which share in the Being of Actuality, they can't get to Him, and religion is impossible except as a kind of make-believe or a whistling in the dark.

I: The object of religion is God in a delimited form, God as encapsulated inside the Being which is Actuality, and who is therefore (something like a Spinozistic infinite mode or "particular") to be related to the God that is alongside the Being, Actuality.

MAE: Now you have the particulars which are germane to one mode of Being functioning inside another mode of Being, so that a given mode of Being would have two sets of particulars—or if one accepts your whole view, four sets of particulars, only one of which was its own, properly speaking.

I: I accept that conclusion. The particulars of a given mode of Being share in that Being, and thereby are; what is encapsulated has a being by virtue of a participation in a Being which is alongside of the encapsulating Being. A Being at one and the same time acts on other modes of Being and has "infinite" particulars functioning within the confines of those other modes of Being.

MAE: You have moved far from the consideration of a single Being having no determinations, and therefore a Being indistinguishable from Nothing.

I: I don't think so. Whatever determinations we acknowledge a Being to have, must have some being. But they do not have sufficient being of their own to avoid reduction to the undifferentiable characteristics of the Being. To give the particulars a being of their own, as distinct entities and as a totality, it is necessary to invoke a power which will allow or force their common Being to stand over against them, and thus allow them to function in independence of it—even though the being which they have is it, though in a limited form and for a limited time.

MAE: Aren't you saying that a Being by itself has no particulars over against it, but has them only as distinctions of itself?

I: Yes.

MAE: But then you in fact accept the position I first suggested.

I: I think not, and for two reasons. *1*] There are particulars, such as you and I, which do have being, and   *2*] it is not possible to have mere distinctions in a Being.

MAE: The two reasons together mean that particulars must be. But particulars are all contingent.

I: Each particular is contingent, but the entire realm of particulars is not contingent, being made to be by the action of other modes of Being on the Actuality.

MAE: You are saying that the question why there is something rather than nothing is answered by saying there always is some thing, but that no one thing is itself necessary?

I: Yes.

MAE: Yet that there always be some thing is a consequence of the action of some Being other than that Being which each of the things will for the moment possess?

I: Yes.

MAE: What a strangely complicated universe you picture. Not only are there four ultimate modes of Being, but each has its own set of particulars; each has one of its particulars, "an infinite," present in each of the other Beings; each Being is enabled to have a set of contingent particulars of its own, functioning independently of the Being; and each of the particulars has the Being in a limited form by virtue of the action of some other Being.

I: That's not altogether accurate. God, for example, doesn't need a God to enable Him to stand over against His own particulars. But He has other roles with respect to his own particulars which do need the help of the other modes of Being.

MAE: That's another complication; the point I am making is that yours is a highly complicated scheme.

I: Why suppose that the universe is simple, or simpler than I am saying it is? After all, I make only the distinctions I am compelled to make.

MAE: You just spin them out of your head.

I: You know better than that. I try my best to avoid making those distinctions. You don't object to the physicist multiplying entities so far as he must; I don't think I follow any other compulsion than the one that he does, though of course I am occupied with a different set of problems.

MAE: Scientists also seek simplicity. Mendeleff's table gave an order to a multiplicity of items.

I: True. That is why I think one must do philosophy systematically. A system provides the order which enables one to grasp the various ultimates in interrelationship. The problem is not that of recognizing more than one ultimate, but of understanding how the plurality is interrelated.

January 30

There is an analogue between the way in which actualities and Actuality are ontologically related and the relation which results when we take appropriate scientific attitudes toward complex actualities and the elements they contain. There is a similar analogue between the relation which actualities ontologically have to their elements, and the theoretically instituted relation which results when we try to think of Actuality and its actualities in abstraction from all other.realities.

Actualities and Actuality are, due to the action of other modes of Being on Actuality, independently acting realities. (There are eccentric particulars which, while acting independently of Actuality, nevertheless reflect its presence, and which function in consonance with it rather than in terms of an interplay with other actualities.) Actualities and their contained elements (and similarly, organically functioning unities and their subordinate reflex—and other—acts) are not altogether separate, with the consequence that the actualities will sometimes behave in accord with the way in which the elements do (gravitation, chemical reactions, etc.), and sometimes in the way the whole requires (the elements move when and as the intent requires).

When we try to deal with actualities and Actuality as though they alone were real, we have them intimately related one with the other somewhat in the way in which complex actualities are in fact related to their physical and chemical elements. When we try to understand one of the complex actualities in terms of its interaction with others, we find that we abstract from the confined elements, just as when we try to give a scientific account of the elements we abstract from the organic whole in which they are to be found.

Why is this? Evidently the kind of effect which other modes of Being have on Actuality is much more penetrating than the kind of effect which other actualities have on an actuality. The former allows both the Actuality and the actualities to function in independence of one another, the latter does not. Evidently there is an ultimacy to the reality of an actuality with its elements which is not characteristic of Actuality and its actualities, since in the former case there is some kind of unity which possesses both the actuality and the elements (thereby precluding us from speaking of the elements as "its [i.e., the actuality's] elements"). But we do not have such a unity in the other case. Actuality is prior (as are the actualities) to any unity of the two. But in the case of actualities and their confined elements, the primary fact is the unity of the two, with each having distinctive functions which may in some cases overwhelm the other.

When we speak of a self or a soul, we emphasize the unity of an actuality, such as man, as biased toward the actuality as a unitary whole; when we speak of a pattern or law of elements, we emphasize the unity of an actuality as biased toward the elements. A neutral way of speaking of the unity of an actuality with its elements (which of course are also actualities) is to refer to the inner side of a substance, the center of action, the being of actuality, and the like.

It would make for clarity, I think, if "actuality" were understood to refer to the entire being of an entity, as embracing a singular whole and a plurality of elements. The elements have a reality which the singular whole does not, though the singular whole does operate with such effectiveness that there are times when it governs and modifies the behavior of the elements. The singular whole, however, has no existence of its own; there is nothing like the whole as such. Yet I have sometimes confused the "actuality" with the whole. This is due to the fact that the whole, when it does operate, expresses more than the elements can, either severally or together, and to the fact that the elements have a reality apart from the whole, tempting one, in the light of the whole's effectiveness, to suppose that the whole also has a reality of its own. The actuality expresses itself as the whole under the limitations which the elements provide.

What is the correlate of Actuality? Is it an actuality in the above sense? If so, it would seem to be an actuality not altogether separable from the elements. Yet the elements can be seen to be part of a single domain of elements, and as such to constitute a domain of actualities all of which are oriented directly to Actuality, and not, as is the case with ordinary objects, oriented indirectly to Actuality via the actualities in which they are. We can either say that the elements never exist in separation from wholes (though the elements have their own laws) and that therefore there are no genuine actual elements, or that the elements do exist in separation from the wholes and that they are not directly oriented in Actuality, but occupy a domain of their own.

If we take the second alternative (to which I am inclined), when we ignore the wholes which are in fact inseparable from the elements in ordinary objects, we but recognize one single "whole" which is the domain of all actual elements. But should we then say that this latter all-embracing whole and the totality of elements are but phases of a single entity, a macroscopic actuality which is related to Actuality in the way in which ordinary actualities are related to Actuality? I think there is no reason why we should say so. Such a supposed macroscopic actuality has no role, does not interplay with other actualities, and does not seem to be able to affect the elements through the whole, or to have a whole which expresses it.

Consequently what we have is *1]* Actuality, *2]* a macroscopic whole, *3]* a totality of elements, *4]* complex actualities which *5]* express themselves as wholes, and *6]* contain, under restrictive conditions, a limited number of elements. When elements control the activity of an actuality, they in effect function as members of 2, particularly if it is the case that the wholes (5) in which they in fact are, are without efficacy, and thus do not affect the way the elements function. It is possible, however, to maintain that though the elements have a real function and can in fact determine the course of an actuality (and the location of the whole?), they never exist outside of limited wholes, and that as a consequence the idea of a macroscopic whole is at best only the idea of something merely conceived, a useful notion enabling one to do physics or chemistry without having to make any reference to biology or any other enterprise which takes account of other wholes or the actualities which these might express.

I do not know how to choose between these views; I incline toward the second as requiring the least number of assumptions, even though it makes the physicist and chemist deal with abstractions so far as they speak cosmically, and with concrete entities only so far as these thinkers recognize that their entities are subject to conditions and restrictions and sometimes modes of action which cannot be accounted for by any multiplication of the laws which govern the elements by themselves as forming a single totality.

Field theories of various sorts would make one incline to hold that elements form a domain of their own. But there is nothing incompatible between that view and the view that the elements are confined within different actualities. When the elements take a dominant role and make the wholes of actualities (and thus the actualities themselves) function in terms of those elements, the elements function in interrelationship with one another. When the elements function as part of fields or a final domain of their own, they are not yet elements taken in their concreteness. They are always part of actualities, but there are times when they are minimally restricted by those actualities. They are then to be understood to interplay with one another in fields. The largest of fields would be a macroscopic whole, were the elements in their full concreteness. We avoid the supposition that the fields are anything more than an interrelationship of the elements by taking the elements to be not ultimately concrete.

Wholes will always have their adventures in part determined by elements as having their own integrity; elements will have their adventures in part determined by wholes because, like the wholes, they are not ultimately concrete. Both wholes and elements are abstract to some degree, despite the fact that they have some efficacy with respect to one another. The only concretes are the actualities of which the wholes and the elements were aspects or parts or functions, and the Actuality to which the actualities are directly related.

Elements are not genuine actualities because they never get to the stage where they are able to function independently of anything else. Only if they could function independently of the actualities and Actuality could they be said to be genuine realities, but then they would have to be said to be distinct items within a genuinely distinct domain which was characterized by cosmic field laws and structures.

There are physicists who would insist on the ultimacy of their elements, and therefore would demand that one acknowledge a real cosmic domain for them. As a rule though, it is only certain philosophers of science, such as Sellars and Grünbaum who would be inclined to be so dogmatic. And if one is to be dogmatic with respect to the elements in this fashion, what stands in the way of a dogmatism of a similar kind with respect to the wholes? Such a dogmatism would say that the wholes are ultimately real as distinct units, but that they exist as such in a domain of their own and thereby achieve a relation to Actuality similar to that had by the actualities of which those wholes are sometimes a part. The result would be a phenomenological totality of "gestalten." If we reject the dialectic and the movement of Hegel, we would get some such view as this from him (though the English Hegelians, who also reject the dialectic and the movement, have instead accepted the view that only the totality is the real).

The being of an actuality, its inner core, is not an entity, but the very relating of the whole to other wholes, and of the restraining of elements so that they don't simply interplay with other elements. This in effect means that the inner core expresses itself in a double way with respect to the whole; it relates the whole to other wholes and to the elements as their restraining force. Because the whole has only a limited power, it is sometimes overcome by the elements. There must also be a distinctive act on the part of the core; without an acknowledgment of it, it is doubtful that we could account for the will, the concern (with its entailed self-identity), and perhaps even the mind.

This view raises many further questions. One of them, going back to an earlier part of the discussion, is that the existence of eccentric particulars shows that not all actualities need to be thought of as functioning in independence of Actuality; only the regularly behaving particular actualities should be so conceived. But if this be the case, ought we not also say that not all particles are under restraint, and that some of them are in direct relation with other particles which are in other wholes but there equally not restrained? This seems most reasonable.

January 31

There are two kinds of compulsions. One is linear, and is exemplified in logic. Here items are interlocked to constitute a necessary whole. The other is directive, and is exemplified in ethics. Here a demand is imposed on something else.

It is possible to have one of these compulsions without the other. We can imagine a logic which is self-enclosed—more sharply, a mathematics which has its items linked by necessity, but which has no bearing on what is here and now. And it is possible to have an ethics whose primary Good is without any interior articulation.

When we try to conform to logic, we take its internal necessity to be that which we would like to exhibit; we put ourselves in a position where the logic has both kinds of compulsions. When we think of the Good as in the mind of God or as supported by Him, we try to get the ethics to have both kinds of compulsions, but we do not actually get an internally determined compulsion for the Good. To do that, we would have to show that its denial would be self-contradictory, and this I think has never been shown.

If we start with an exemplified logic, we find that it contains no pure necessities. What we find instead is what Peirce calls "leading principles," i.e., contingent principles serving to connect antecedents with consequents. It could be argued that the linear necessity of logic is a product of the very abstraction which yields a logic apart from all exemplification. One can maintain that there is no actual abstraction and thus no actual linear necessity to logic, but that instead we envisage the case where, were the logic to be apart from the exemplification, it would have an internal necessity. We conceive it to be internally necessary when and as we conceive it to be apart from the exemplifications where alone it is to be found.

When we deal with the ethical, we can also maintain that the exemplified case is the basic one, and that the Good is to be conceived of as a lure only so far as we abstract it from the concrete case. We would then in effect deny that the Good in fact lured us, and that we were subject to its compulsions; what we would have would be the mere fact of feeling compelled without something having compelled us.

In both cases we would deny that there is any genuine directive compulsion, because there is no entity outside us which compels us. The necessity inherent in logic would be a necessity inherent in an abstraction, and the luring presence of the Good would be the presence of that which we had isolated and set before us. But we would then lose the validation of our inferences (since this requires an inherent necessity on the part of logic and a demand that we conform to it) and the presence of the Good (with its demand that we conform to it).

What the attempted elimination of a directive compulsion overlooks is that our conformity to logic (or the Good) presupposes a prior demand that we conform. It is that prior demand that is expressed in the directive compulsion. We are forced to acknowledge the inherent necessity of logic, because we are forced to admit the directive compulsion of logic.

When we come to mathematics, we find that it has an inherent necessity, but no directive necessity; we are not required to conform to mathematics except so far as we wish to engage in work requiring mathematical considerations. But we cannot say that we need not conform to logic except so far as we wish to engage in work requiring logical considerations, because logic offers a condition for the validity of any reasoning. We are compelled to be logical if we are to communicate, to be articulate, to be intelligible, and to understand. Mathematics instead offers a criterion only for reasoning of a particular kind.

It is common to speak of a third type of necessity, particularly with respect to God. He is not thought to be such that He has a plurality of components linearly linked. When we say that a cat is a cat, it seems as if we are saying nothing, or that we are offering a simple case of a linear necessity. But what we are in fact saying is that a cat can be nothing other than a cat. The so-called law of identity refers to the fact that there is no alternative to being what one is. But the necessity which is attributed to God is not the simple necessity that if He be, He is what He is. He is because there is no such alternative as "He is not." The alternative that is excluded is not "being a non-God," but not-Being as such. Identifying God with (a) Being, we then get a case of the law of identity.

I have previously argued that there is no Being which excludes not-Being; there are only Beings, each of which is eternal, and all of which are together necessary with a kind of linear necessity. Consequently, I reject the case of a something which cannot not be, reducing it either to an eternal reality which is part of a single singular necessary whole, or to an identity, which is then a limiting case of a linear whole.

A secret: Take the great philosophers' accounts of God, and free them from anthropomorphism, and you get a good statement of the nature of Actuality.

"A chicken is chicken." Analysts call this an analytic proposition. Youngsters might too, but they mean something different. For them, to be chicken is to be cowardly; this may or may not be a necessary truth. A logician would say the proposition means that an actual chicken is properly referred to by means of the word "chicken." A good number of apparently innocent sentences are ambiguous in this way, changing their meaning from approach to approach, from context to context. But it is hard to convince an analyst or logician that this is the case; they suppose that their own contexts or approaches are the only legitimate ones.

It is rude to say to a woman that she should bring home a fatted calf.

"In God we trust" treats God as an amulet. Had we more trust, we would have said "God we trust."

A faith that moves mountains is a faith with muscles; it would be better to have a faith that mountains move, for that would be a faith which could be sustained by awe.

An "exact" thinker would say that water does not run downhill because it does not run at all. This does not mean that we are justified in refusing to think carefully, but only that words alone should not be our guides.

"Let's have an end to beginnings" says the doer. And so he starts all over again at the beginnings with which mankind long ago came to an end.

"Fear makes cowards." And what made the fear? Was it not too much bravery?

February 1

A somewhat orthodox Christian theologian could use my discussions in metaphysics and theology by making some translations, denying some of my moves, and taking account of some neglected roles of God.

What I call "Actuality" he might call "God, the Being" or "God, the Substance" or "God beyond God." He could then refer to my Ideality as "God, the Son," to my Existence as "God, the Holy Ghost," and to my "God" as "God, the Father." The latter three could be thought of as confined within the orbit of the first. The three would be characterized somewhat the way in which they are in the *Modes of Being*.

To account for the fact that actualities face external possibilities, that they are subject to Existence, and that they are evaluated eternally, it is necessary to see the three "Gods" as held away from the actualities. This holding away is the result of the way in which God, the Being, possessed them. The three also have the function of enabling actualities to be free from Actuality, to be similar in nature to it, and to be spread over by it. These three roles are achieved by having "God, the Father," "God, the Son," and "God, the Holy Ghost," respectively, act on God, the Being. The three "persons" act on actualities; they also act on God, the Being. The action does not take place from Beings outside the God, the Being; it is the result of actions on God, the Being, by the Gods within this.

This interpretation denies that the "three persons" have any Being outside the Being which is God, though they do have a reality apart from it and from the actualities. There is no creation except in the sense that these "three persons" so affect God, the Being, that it enables the actualities to function in independence of it. Those actualities are like God, the Being, and are encompassed within it.

If we start with Actuality (which was just now identified with God, the Being) and acknowledge the other three Beings to have the power to act on it and on actualities, do we have any need to acknowledge any more than one ultimate Being? We cannot answer this question by saying that Actuality by itself would be without determinations, for the three persons provide this. Nor could we say that it cannot obtain a proper counterfoil, for the three persons together with all actualities could be said to be equal in power and counterthrust to the Being alone. We would no longer, of course, have the "three persons" merely in God; they would be just as much outside as in, and would act on Him as surely as He acts on them.

If we take the three persons to be Beings, we would have to acknowledge that each had its appropriate particulars, and that the Being in each case would be acted on by the others so as to enable the particulars to be in contrast with the Being. With the supposition that the three persons have no reality outside God, the Being, there is no need to suppose that there is more than one set of particulars—the actualities, among which we are.

This interpretation allows most of the *Modes* to stand, requiring mainly a discussion of the nature of Actuality, and an account of how the three persons act on that Actuality from within rather than as alongside. There would be no need for a discussion of how "four modes of Being" could be together, though the discussion of togetherness would be germane to any discussion of the One and the Many.

The crucial issue is whether there can be only one ultimate mode of Being (whether we call this "Actuality" or "God, the Being") provided that we recognize that in addition to actualities, there are also certain intermediaries which can be seen to be part of God, the Being (or Actuality) when they act on actualities, and to be over against that Being (or Actuality) when they act on it.

Can it be shown conclusively that there must be other Beings alongside of Actuality? Can it be shown conclusively that there cannot be or need not be, or even may not be, other Being alongside Actuality? For the moment I do not know how to reply to these questions. But if I cannot answer the first one, I surely have no warrant for supposing that there is more than one mode of Being, even if I cannot entirely preclude the possibility that there might be such.

It is to be noted, however, that if the three persons and the particularities together oppose God, the Being (or Actuality), they in effect constitute another Being with it, and that these two Beings must be united and separated by a comma and a period, i.e., be capable of merging to any degree and as well as being radically distinct.

What kind of being have the comma and the period? Should we say that they are constituted by God, the Being, and the rest? This would be to follow the lead of the *Modes* while restricting ourselves to two Beings. And the recognition that the three persons could be credited to God, and so far be over against the actualities, would allow one to make sense of Whitehead's various paradoxes to the effect that so far as God is one, the world is many, etc.

It is to be noted that if actualities are over against God, the Being, and the persons, they would seem to have an oppositional Being equal to them. But this does not seem possible. Despite the fact that the actualities face the persons as realities beyond them, those persons cannot be ascribed to the Being and cannot, so far, be over against the actualities. They must be over against the actualities only so far as they remain with those actualities over against God, the Being.

There is also the question as to the kind of power that the persons can exert. If they are not final Beings, are they able to affect the Being which is God to such an extent that He stands away from all particularities? Can we say that this power is much less than is needed in order to be alongside such a Being? But if so, what prevents the Being from absorbing those divine persons? Somehow one must show those persons to have enough power to stand away from the Being, and enough power to affect the Being basically, but not enough power, and thus not enough Being, to be able to oppose and be opposed by the Being. We could take this just to be a fact, or we could take it to be a consequence. If the former, we need not make any reference to other Beings; if the latter, we must. Therefore the issue hinges on the question as to whether or not the persons (which are encapsulated Beings) presuppose Beings beyond them, on a footing with Actuality, i.e., with God, the Being, on the hypothesis.

It is not necessary, of course, to be an orthodox Christian to make something like the foregoing interpretation of my views. Anyone can hold that there is one ultimate Being, with three subordinate powers, and an independently acting set of particulars, which are able to so act because of the way in which the powers act on Being. Avoiding the notion of persons, and sharpening the difference between God and the powers, the view can be assimilated to some of the discussions of the Hebrew theologians. (I don't know enough about the Arabic or Hindu views to know if there are parallel cases, though I would suspect there are.) The eternal ideas, the realm of nature, and God as occupied with human affairs, can be treated as powers which affect God, the Being, and are affected by Him, at the same time that they are finalities with which the particulars are occupied in various ways. Whatever difficulties, though, that the Christian theologian will have with the persons as somehow having power and yet standing over against the Being which is God, will appear in the Hebraic version.

February 5

When one asks "why" an act was done, a reason is expected to be given in reply. If that reason has the form of a cause, it can conceivably be of one of three kinds. It might be an intention, that which I had wanted to do; it might be a motive, that objective, conscious or unconscious, which makes me have to carry out that intent and which in fact moves me to act; or it might be some physical or social or psychological antecedent that caused my doing the act, voluntarily or involuntarily.

There are some who would think that no intention could ever be a cause, or at least could never be a sufficient cause of an act. What they would want, if they allowed a reference to an intention at all, would be a consideration of the motive or some physical or other cause as well. There are others who would think that no motive could ever be a cause, or at least could never be a sufficient cause of an act. They would want one to refer to some physical or other cause, and might perhaps allow one to bring in consideration of the intention. And there are those who would not accept a reference to anything physical as a cause for a human act; they would insist on bringing in some reference to an intention or motive as at least contributory factors making up the proper cause of the act.

What we have is a demand for a reason which is answered by a reference to a cause of a certain kind. To the question "why?" the answer then is "because of this cause."

February 6

The question "why?" directed at any action, may ask not after a cause, but after a justification. A justification offers not merely a reason, but a good reason, a warranting reason, a reason which would persuade another that one had not done something wrong.

If we ask after a justification, we do not accept a reference to an intent or to a motive as a proper answer. Our intents and motives may be described correctly, but they may not warrant the accepting of the act as a proper one. We want another to say, "It was a good act." Or if he cannot say this, we want him to say, "Well, it is not your fault."

Though one may not be responsible for having the intent or the motive that one has, one is responsible for acting in terms of them. The responsibility may do nothing more than show a defect of character or of personality, but it is sufficient to make us say that the bad act is to be attributed to us as beings who are guilty for having been the source of it.

To show that the act is a good act, we must show that it is required by some Being who is good, that it is an act which is intrinsically good, or that it promotes what is in fact good. Our justification can be that God demanded the act from us and God is good, or that this is the right act in that situation (a matter to be seen intuitively), or that it makes for happiness, or more goodness, or the establishment of some important value.

If we wish to escape responsibility for the act, we can answer the demand for justification by saying that it is in fact not our act at all. We do this when we refer to some cause of our act over which we have had no control, so that what we do is an outcome of that cause as operative in us.

The answer to the question "why?" is then either a cause (which might be an intention or a motive) or a justifying reason (which might be a cause, just so far as the justification is permitted to be not a defense of the act as good, but an excuse for oneself as not being responsible for the act). Incidentally, it is possible to conceive of God or some other finality as a kind of cause whose goodness makes the act not only necessary but desirable.

Even if we intend to do what is good, or have a motive which is directed at the production of the maximum amount of good, we do not justify our act by referring to our intent or motive. "Why did you do that kindness?" might be answered by "I intended to be of help" or "I am motivated by the concern to make him happy." Though these answers refer respectively to an intention and a motive, they do not justify the act unless and only so far as the act produces good, and they contain at least part of the reason why the act is good.

Does a good intent or motive offer at least part of the reason why an act is good? A good intent or motive can be followed by an act which is bad. But this does not yet mean that the goodness of the intent or motive does not contribute to the goodness of the act. If the intent or motive were bad and the act were good, we could still attribute it to a good man who acted well despite his explicit and implicit drives to do otherwise.

I think we should conclude that the goodness of the intent or motive does not contribute to the goodness of the act, or that if they do that fact is irrelevant. What we want to know is whether or not the act is good. Our justification for the act is to be found in the act itself, in the compelling good source of it which conveys its goodness to it because the act is inseparable from that source, or in the consequences of the act, consequences which we find to be good in themselves.

The justification evidently refers to a sustaining good cause of the act or to an intrinsic character of the act or its consequences. A reference to a good intent or motive will then but tell us that we are good men, not as sources which cling to and continue to define the act, but as possible occasions and perhaps even causes which remain exterior to the act and its goodness.

There is still another use of the question "why?" that is common in connection with action. One may ask not for a reason or a justification, but for an explanation. This we might do when we know that no justification is possible, since the act is bad, and when we know the cause. A man might hit another. He could have been aroused by something that he remembered, and this might have triggered off his act; to say this is not to justify the act, but to give a cause for it. If he wanted to explain the act, the cause might or might not suffice for this purpose. It would suffice if the cause were irresistible. If this were not the case, we would like to have some further condition stated, such as that he is a man who hits those who are smaller than himself, or who hits if he feels an impulse to hit, etc. The explanation thus accounts for the act by taking account of whatever causes there be and the conditions under which the causes operate. If we take the cause for granted, the explanation concentrates on the condition.

An intention or a motive can serve as an explanation. If they are not also causes, they will serve as the pervasive conditions with the acknowledged causes serving only as triggers or occasions.

February 7

When a man is unable to justify his acts, he tends to find a justification, i.e., an excuse, for himself. He may point to his intention, and try to excuse himself because he is a man of "good will." This is the alternative often accepted by administrators; some of them are shocked to find themselves criticized, since they thought that their self-justification was a justification for their acts.

Instead of referring to his intention, a self-justifying man might point to his motive. This may be conscious or unconscious. If conscious, he tries to excuse himself on the ground that he was interested in promoting a more valuable objective than that which is exemplified in the act. But he cannot justify a bad act by remarking on the fact that he has a noble aim. If the motive is unconscious, he may try to excuse himself by treating himself as subject to powers beyond his clear knowledge or control. He may blame his parents, his childhood experiences, his sudden impulses, etc. But all this goes to show only that he does not have the kind of control that other men have, or that his impulses, etc., exceed in force what is customary to other men. His excuse in effect is that he is not a man like others. But this in effect is a confession, not an excuse, though it may at times free him from criminal charges or may evoke pity on the part of others.

A similar excuse is attempted by those who refer to causes for what they do; they in effect say that they have been compelled to do what they do. But they either are caused as others are (and then they have to show why they deserve to be understood in ways others are not), or they are caused in new ways (and thus are either unable to resist in the way others can, or are subjected to unusual powers). The last alternative does give a genuine excuse, and in effect says that the act is not a human act, but one which happens to be mediated by a human. It is to this alternative we appeal when we are forced to act under the threat of death or injury by some superior power.

We can think of all these excuses as forms of explanation for the act occurring. If we do, then we should say that certain explanations are offered as excuses and that some of these excuses are self-justifications. A self-justification is an excuse, but when the excuse refers to uncontrollable forces, we have no attempt to justify, but only an attempt to account for the act, with ourselves serving as pathways or agencies having no affect on the act.

An explanation which refers to some general truth or pervasive condition—such as being a woman or a child, an official of the state, etc.—does not justify the act. Does it justify the actor? He who says it is his duty to obey his superior officer does not thereby justify the act in which he is engaged. He excuses himself either as one who could not avoid obeying, or as one who ought to obey because obedience here is a good. The self-justification or excuse in the second alternative tries to find something good in the actor at the same time that it is admitted that the act may not be good, and that this good in the actor does not justify the act. We have here something like the explanation which is offered by one who appeals to the demand of God; obeying this command, if at all voluntary, means that one is so far doing what one ought from the perspective of God, even though the act demanded may be bad as an act in this world. If one obeys involuntarily, one is in the position of a being who cannot control what determines him. Even if that which controls is good and means well, it is then a fact that the actor is but a mediator, and excuses himself as one who was made to do what he did. That the act is a bad one he may perhaps be unable to explain as having a cause in a good source, but this is irrelevant to the question as to whether or not he is responsible for it. His answer is that he is not responsible.

We excuse ourselves by absenting ourselves through an acknowledgment of causes and explanations which show that we were only intermediaries; that we had good intentions and motives is irrelevant. Because we are intermediaries, we can acknowledge causes and explanations which require something bad to occur. When we appeal to our intentions and our conscious motives, it is always to something good. When we appeal to our unconscious motives, we appeal to what uses us as intermediaries and thus to what may be itself a cause of bad acts.

A bad act must be attributed to ourselves or to something which uses us as intermediaries; either one or the other is accountable. The accountable being is to be characterized as bad because it is the source of the bad act. In neither case do we justify ourselves. We could justify ourselves only in the case where it is good for us to submit to, yield to, function on behalf of someone else who thereby requires us to do what is bad. Granted that one ought or must submit, and that as a consequence one must therefore act improperly, one in effect denies the right of oneself to act as a free agent. In effect then, one attributes the act to the source or the system requiring submission, and treats oneself as a mere intermediary so far as that particular act is concerned. But then one defines oneself as so far not a man. The fact that one is supposedly a good soldier, obeying his superior officer does not alter the fact that the act is being interpreted by oneself as issuing not from oneself, but from the system or the superior officer. The excuse is then that one is subject to controls at the time, even though they may have been voluntarily accepted at some other time. But if one is a puppet, one can be treated as a thing. Like one who is subject to uncontrollable impulses, one can then be confined and punished even though one might not be properly called responsible.

February 8

If an act is justified, we feel that we are justified. Such justification of ourselves is something like that which is achieved when we take ourselves to be the creatures of a good God. We accrete in both cases something of the goodness of something else—in the one case the goodness of the act, and in the other the goodness of the source of our act.

Sometimes we find ourselves with a situation where we are not sure whether or not the act is justified. Because the justification of an act has its repercussions on us, we seek, on behalf of ourselves, to find a justification for the act by attending to what would make it desirable, and screening out what would make it undesirable. I understand from Marcia Guttentag that this attempt at self-justification by a selective defense of the act is given considerable attention by students of "cognitive dissonance."

The attempt to bolster up one's act through selective considerations or "rationalizations" occurs only when the act is not taken to be self-evidently right, and there are no clear compelling causes or desirable consequences which make it right. The selective considerations add up to making the act a reasonable one, for what one initially finds is that the act seems to be right and is performed for that reason, but that one does not know that it is right. The reasonableness of the act is a consequence of the fact that we have found what makes the apparently right be truly right.

If we have reasons for an act, we do not yet show that the act is reasonable, for the reasons may be farfetched. But when we start off with the act being apparently right, we look for reasons which are persuasive: these make it be the right act for anyone. Instead of moving to some grounding reasons which suffice to make the act right, and this regardless of what anyone might think of the plausibility of those reasons, he who seeks to justify himself by showing that his act is justified, and then by means of selective data, builds up a set of acceptable reasons for the act. His selectivity involves a consideration of what is reasonable. His self-justification accordingly involves the achievement of reasons which are reasonable. This is a desirable outcome, but the price that is paid is the temptation to ignore countervailing evidence.

Selectivity operates within the frame of commonsensical or accepted beliefs; it finds a reason inside this frame, and is content to remain there, even if it be the case that the entire frame is questionable. A more stringent moralist would want to find an adequate reason, and then without going through a process of selection or without resting with the corpus of commonsensical or accepted beliefs.

Sometimes the selectivity is engaged in for the purpose of persuading others. Instead of serving as a means for justifying oneself for engaging in the act, the selectivity would be employed solely to make what might be self-evidently right appear to others as being right. Once again what is done is to make what appears to be right to be known to be right, but now it is something which appears and is known to another and not to oneself.

Where we try to make the apparent right be known to be in fact right, either for ourselves or for another, or both, we attend to the fact. We do not refer to our intention, motive, causes, or explanations, but solely to the reason which makes the act have an excellence in that situation. The effort testifies to the fact that what we want to do is what is in fact right, and that until we do see that it is so, we are restless and have some question about our own merit. A reason, reasonable or not, for an act shows that we are in fact good men. If the reason is reasonable, it shows that we are good men in a community, good men who are and can be known to be good men by others.

It is conceivable that we may not come up with a reason which is able to justify the act, but what we offer may be a reasonable explanation, a sensible base on which we can take a stand. We offer the reasonable explanation as a reason under the limitation that this is after all what a man is supposed to do, in the circumstances. We do not then claim that the act is right, but that it is the act that a reasonable man would engage in. If it is a wrong act, as it might well be in a dilemma or where the issue is not clear, or where we are in a crisis, what is being said is that no reasonable man would have done otherwise. In effect this is an excuse, similar to that offered by one who says he is subject to inexorable causes, except that here we do have a choice of acts. We are saying (on the assumption which all of us want to make, that the act is reasonable) that we could not have done otherwise. If the act is wrong and even one less preferable than another which was open to us, we excuse ourselves on the ground that we are reasonable men, men who act in consonance with the knowledge, spirit, and values of the community, or of mature mankind.

February 9

In *Nature and Man,* I treat the quality of a thing as something achieved from its outside; this outside is there said to be the product of a joint insistence by what is beyond the object and a resistance by the object. A subtraction of the insistence would apparently leave the resistance as a potential, defining its outside. This account does not say anything about the possibility of error, the knowing of "essences," or the way in which such observation of a quality could tell us about the thing itself.

What should also have been said is that we specify the generic result of a union of insistence and resistance (a point made earlier in *Reality,* where error is seen to be the result of a specification of a generic nature). It should also have been remarked that there is an expectative factor in our grasp of the quality, a point made long ago by C. I. Lewis. But this means that the expectation which was accredited to the concern we had, and which was to match the concern of the object, affects the quality. Also, since it was seen that the quality was a facet of a more comprehensive grasp, which included an adumbration of the inside, the quality should have been understood as exhibiting something of the insistence of the object, and not merely as being the juncture of a resistance with an intruding insistence. The quality should have been said to be such a juncture which is affected by an expressive insistence as well as by the concern. In this way, the quality would be recognized to exhibit features of the object as at once being something from the outside, something on the inside, and something from the inside. The "being on the inside" would, however, have to be understood as more than merely a center with maximum insistence, and thus as more than what the object would be if it were maximally close.

We are able to adumbrate the inside only because the inside does not remain static, but comes to expression in the shape of modifications of the outside, as this is modified by the intruding insistence of others. Our grasp of the "quality" or predictional aspect of the object is a grasp of the way in which the object's resistance qualifies an intruding insistence, at the same time that the result is affected by the insistence of the object and its concern. The predicate is then, despite its apparent simplicity, revelatory, in an obscure way, of the object as contrasted with itself as a mere "it." This conclusion reverses a rather common supposition that it is the "subject" which is the contentful, existing entity, with the qualities or predicates serving merely to characterize some phase or even accident of it. It also modifies the view that I have more or less held over the years, to the effect that the predicate was a correlative of the subject. It is that, but it is a correlative which contains something of the substantiality of the object as a being with an inside and which acts from the inside while it is being intruded on and resisting.

When we approach an entity from the outside and take it to be our outermost limit, we minimize the inwardness of the entity. It is only when we see the result to be attributable to the entity as its quality, that we are able to see it as revelatory of the object. The attribution of the quality to the object is evidently an opening up to the effectiveness on the quality of the insistence and the concern.

February 11

Holding tight to the idea that omniscience means knowing all that can be known, and not merely knowing anything whatsoever, we can say that God can predict every detail of a present occurrence before it takes place. He cannot know that round squares are red, because there are no round squares. He cannot know the present in its concreteness, because the present has an ongoing, a becoming, an experiential side which is only when it is taking place. All that God could conceivably know about such a present is the series of positions which something in the course of the becoming might occupy. He might predict what place will be occupied in successive moments of time, but what He cannot know is the becoming by which one moves from one of the places to the others. He does not get the unity from which the places could be derived by abstraction; He knows only the places as discrete particulars which are not interrelated in a dynamic organic way. He can know that they are to be so related, but the relating of them He must await and cannot know in advance.

Can we know an occurrence when it takes place? Yes, we can, because what we then know is not only the places we abstract, but the adumbratable dynamism of the whole in which those places are to be found. There is nothing to adumbrate in the future; our adumbrative act —and presumably God's—occurs only with respect to what is present. If God tried to look at the present in terms of what He knew of it in advance, He would find that his various places were occupied or swept along in fact. Could He not have predicted that they would have been swept along or been occupied? No, because there is nothing done to the places themselves when this occurs; the knowledge God has of them as mere places is correct; what is not known by Him is that they are interrelated, that there is a movement which goes from one to the other, making them into a single whole.

Why might God not know that there is a single whole in which the various positions of the moving objects are to be found? He could know of such a whole, but it would not be a whole which in fact contained the different positions. It is a whole which could be conceived to be only *with* positions. God can conceive of the whole *as* including them; He cannot conceive *the fact* of its including them. When He knows that the whole includes them, He does not in fact have the whole including them.

This view differs some from Aristotle's interpretation of the sea fight. Aristotle acknowledged only knowledge of the general. Consequently, he could see the sea fight only as that which in the future can be won or lost, and as that which is won in the present or which is lost in the present. But I think we can say that even if we know (and God presumably can know) that the sea fight will be won, we will still have only a general knowledge. To know now that the sea fight will be won is to have a knowledge which is more specific than the knowledge that the sea fight will be won or lost. But the knowledge in both cases is of the general. The particular sea fight that is won will be won in this particular way in a present.

We can add details upon details to the idea of the sea fight, but we will not yet come to the present. The present does not merely add details to the future; it gives it a body, an experienceable ongoing or becoming, a presence which makes it encounterable. Aristotle would not allow us to say that the sea fight can now be said to be won tomorrow, but there is no more difficulty in saying this than there is in saying that the sea fight will be fought tomorrow—which is what is meant in fact by saying that the sea fight will be won or lost tomorrow.

If an Aristotelian were to object to our saying that we can now know, or that God can now know, that the sea fight is won, we can object to him that he, on the same grounds, cannot know that the sea fight tomorrow is won or lost, i.e., fought. All possibilities are on the same footing; all fall short of the present. We do not get closer to the actual present by speaking of the sea fight as being won rather than of it being fought. Both expressions should, for analytic completeness, be written as expressions in which alternatives are hyphenated and not allowed to stand as separate entities. Both should be written as "x is y-or-(non-y)."

February 13

References to the past or to the future take their start from the present. They are references which need the present as a contrastive fact. The present is the domain of action, that which is experienced, that which cannot be known except so far as it is undergone or encountered, a process of making the indeterminate determinate. The future, in contrast, is indeterminate and inert, while the past is inert but determinate.

This view commits one to a radical empiricism in the sense that it demands that one acknowledge as distinctive and indispensable what can be known only by being experienced. But it is nonempirical as well, in that it takes the future seriously, refusing to suppose that its knowledge or being is a derivative from the experienced. It is nonempirical too, in that it acknowledges a real past which may never have been experienced by the one who recovers it historically. And, of course, it is nonempirical so far as it considers realities, such as God or the whole of space, which themselves need no reference from the base of a present—though, to be sure, whatever we know is known now and takes its start from something now. We know the future and the past as related to this present; but though we know God now, He is not known necessarily as related to the present from which we start. We can leave our start behind, transcend our present temporal position to concentrate on what is not in time at all.

The past and the future, though they are distinct from the present, and contrast with it, are also to be encountered in it, as was remarked in the book on history. We perhaps should go even further and say that the Being which is God (and the other three modes of Being as well), though nontemporal in nature (and known, not by moving from the base of the present to something to be understood in terms of that present, but by escaping from the present altogether), is to be understood as having some immanence in the present. The present moment is heavy with the past and the future; it has a sacramental nature, stands over against Actuality with an independent active reality, epitomizes Existence (and the space, time, dynamism which characterizes this), and embodies value.

The present is the locus of whatever there be. It is this without denying to other temporal modalities and to other beings the status of distinctive realities with distinctive functions, natures, and powers.

February 14

Different types of occurrences have different temporal spans. Those occurrences are present, but the acts which they exhibit differ in the extent of their spread. A war occurs in the present, but stretches over a longer span of time than does a battle.

There are three ways in which one might deal with the various times that different types of occurrences exhibit. The most common is the reductionistic; here we take some small unit, perhaps defined by the movement or discharge of some minute particle, and take all other presents to be nothing more than combinations of a number of such units. One would then be making an interpretation somewhat like that often heard in connection with the cinema, where it is said that what we confront is a sequence of stills which are replaced so rapidly that we have the illusion that we are seeing something move. Such a view is a variant on the Leibnizian idea that space and time, macroscopic objects, motion, and action are all illusions produced by our inability to make the fine discriminations necessary in order to discern what is in fact present.

The ultimate particles which are supposed to provide the units for this account of time are not directly known; whatever knowledge we have of them is either obtained a priori or involves some dissolution of what is initially encountered. (To suppose that what was so encountered is illusory is to suppose that what we experience is to be rejected in favor of what is not experienced but which may be reached through analysis, inference, and speculation.)

A second way of dealing with the plurality of times is to accept all of them as equally real. This is the alternative I have accepted. It involves one in the problem of reconciling all the different times, and faces one with the difficulty that there seems to be an all-embracing present which reaches from the beginning of civilization to its end, even though there is much yet to be done before we reach that end. The present of such a civilization would seem to be inseparable from an indeterminate, future factor. (By saying that the future is after but not later than the factors we would normally say are in the present, we do not of course escape the fact that the future factor is indeterminate in a way in which the factors that are before it are not.)

This second interpretation has the merit of doing justice to a world in which art, ethics, politics, religion, and science, in which walking, racing, games, plans, etc., can all be understood. It avoids the folly of reductionism with its rejection of what is experienced, and instead takes all types of experience with utmost seriousness.

A third alternative allows one to stay with experience, but avoids the generosity of the second with its acceptance of a great number of disparate presents. Here we accept a humanized present, one in which the individual refuses to diminish or expand the stretch required in order to experience common place occurrences. All other occurrences, smaller or larger, are then taken to be the result of abstractions and combinations of what is in fact experienced. We come close here to an existentialistic view.

This third view is not without its own difficulties. Not all of the commonsense occurrences are of the same magnitude. Does not gripping a bat constitute one occurrence, and taking a walk another? Does not gripping a bat constitute one occurrence, and taking a step another? And are these not of different magnitudes?

Nor does this alternative escape all the problems that beset the second. It does, however, allow us to eliminate some presents as being abstractions or products. It keeps us within a limited range of diverse presents, and allows us to avoid speaking of the present of the whole of civilization or even of a war. It also allows us to avoid speaking of the present of ultimate particles or their functioning, except as mathematically defined abstractions from the real basic time that we experience. In effect this means that those particles are denied ultimacy and perhaps even reality. This seems too high a price to pay, just for the sake of keeping in some consonance with commonsense experience.

We could conceivably divide experience into spans equal to a unit

act of attention, and then acknowledge that some kinds of attended occurrences have presents which are big with a past and future to a degree
others are not. What we would then have are vital presents of equal
length, all defined by a common, or minimal, or characteristically human
attention span, but some of which would have to have subsequent occurrences placed alongside of them as equally vital (though at a later time),
in order for their meaning to be properly expressed. A so-called larger
present would in fact then be a common present which was understood
to be in organic union with a present or presents of equal size that will
take place in the future. A so-called present walk or war would be a
stretch in which there were presents of the same magnitude as any commonplace occurrence, such as taking a step or aiming a rifle; but the
walk or war would be understood as having the meaning of subsequent
presents already implicit, or demanded, or inseparable from the actual
lived-in present, with its characteristic span of attention now.

Have we a right to favor a span of attention or even an experience
over what we can organize or can know through science and mathematics,
or speculation? The present must be understood to be ongoing, and not
to be knowable without experience or encounter. We must make reference to that present if there is to be verification, and a modal distinction
between what had been and what will be, and what is in fact occurring.
A reference to the subatomic seems to lead to the acknowledgment of
presents which are not encountered as ongoing; but this does not seem
to be a serious objection, for there is no reason why something may not
occur in a present which is too small for us to experience, but which we
can know in indirect ways. And it does seem to be the case that we do
live in a war or a battle, even though these may take days to occur. We
do seem to live in and through a symphony as a single whole.

Perhaps it would be enough if we distinguished two kinds of pasts
and two kinds of future. One kind would be made up of units or stretches
which were external to and irrelevant to what was happening in a fixed
length of a present; the other kind would be made up of units or stretches
which, though external to the present, were not irrelevant to it. In both
cases, the future would be later and the past would be earlier than the
present, but in the second case, what happened later or earlier would be
brought into organic union with what was in the present to constitute a
new domain. The extended present which embraced the past and future
would be a new product; it would be real but only because it had been
made to be so.

We could produce long-spanned presents after we have encountered a number of smaller presents and had joined them together. But when would we be joining them together, and in what sense would the result be real? Why should we favor a step or an aiming as occurring in a single, undivided, and unconstituted present, while supposing that a walk or a battle was made up of a plurality of such presents, but were united by us by virtue of our introduction of an idea of relevance or interest?

An occurrence is "organic" if a future prospect is operative in what occurs before it. It is present so far as encounterable content is ingredient in every portion. This last is possible if the future is affected by the encounterable content. An organic present occurrence has the indeterminate future operative in the encounterable, and at the same time has the encounterable effective in the future, making that future have a concreteness and determinateness which it does not have as a project or as that which is operative in the encounterable.

When and as we encounter concrete content, we also encounter fainter versions of it as affecting the future; when and as we face a future, we have the encountered concrete content affected in its meaning and direction. There is something to await when we are facing the encounterable content, but it is only a more intensified form of encounterable content as now resident in the future or as affecting that future. The battle is now making a difference to a succeeding battle; that previous battle makes that successor be a battle in which the previous battle is attenuated content, at the same time that the succeeding battle affects the direction of and meaning of the preceding battle. This latter operation of the succeeding battle on the preceding one does not occur except so far as the succeeding battle is not merely a battle but part of a war; it is a war as localized in the succeeding battle which operates on the present battle to make that present battle be part of the "organic" war, and it is the present battle as having an attenuated being in the war as localized in a succeeding battle which makes the present battle be part of the present of a war.

An actuality or an actual act has two kinds of relation to the future: it has the future as a prospect to be realized, and it has it as that which has been made relevant, by being infected with an attenuation of the actuality's substance or the substance of the actual act. The future in turn has two relations to them: it is a possibility before them, and it is a condition operating in them. There are analogous relations and roles that the present and the past have with respect to one another.

So far as the present actuality or act infects the future, we can be said to be in the present as a merely more intensive form of a common kind of content; so far as the future governs the present, we can be said to be organically connected with the future, since the direction and emphasis of the present is a function of that future.

Do we not, when we are in the intensive portion of the content, become aware of the fact that a less intensive portion is becoming more intensive and that what had been intensive is such no longer? Are we not, when we consider the future possibility, also aware of it as making a difference to what is actual now? The second question is obviously to be answered in the affirmative, for we know we are being guided just so far as we know that there is a future distinct from what we are in the actual present. But the first question makes one pause. It would seem that we should answer it in the affirmative, for we do seem to be aware that the battle or the walk or the war is not yet over, and that we are able to live through it.

February 15

An actuality is in the present. As a present entity, it contains within it something of the past. The way in which that past is present and the way it functions is discussed in my history book. But the actuality is also affected by the future possibility. The possibility limits the things which the actuality can do and become: if adopted by the actuality in intent or deliberate purpose, it controls and directs the activities of the actuality. I have been accustomed to speak as though inanimate things faced their appropriate possibilities as outside them in the future, and that only living beings, and particularly man, had those possibilities ingredient in them. But though it is true that the possibility which is relevant to an inanimate being does nothing to the being, and is of course not adopted by it, it does not follow that it is not ingredient in the being. To be relevant is to have a future prospect as part of one's being here and now, at the same time that that prospect remains outside as a possible terminus to be reached through a dynamic act taking time.

An actuality spreads its vital content into the future to make the future prospect have a qualitative tonality, continuous with but less intensive than that which the actuality itself has. This means that the present actuality must have had, when it was only possible, vital content which was continuous with the past. When a possibility is realized, evidently the vital content achieved from the past remains within it and functions as a factor determining the nature of the activity.

A possibility is a relevant, immanent presence in an actuality; it is also a realizable future, as well as an attenuated form of the present. An actuality is a distinctive, present being which has a past and a future outside it; it also has something of them operative on it, and locatable in it. (The locatable possibility must be distinguished from the possibility which had once confronted the actuality and is now realized as that actuality's form, or structure, or meaning.) A past actuality is a wholly determinate, fixed entity; it is ingredient in present actualities, and has what is future to it as a constituent. That future dictated the direction and type of act of which the actuality was capable.

The occurrences (which have their ground in actualities) are to be understood in terms of the actualities. They are to be interpreted as having all the components that the actualities have, but to have them only because of the fact that they are the actualities.

My life is being lived now; but it is a life which is now governed in part by what I had been and what it is now possible for me to be. It is a life which in its possibility affected what I had been and had done in the past, and which now in an attenuated form is the content of the possibility that still remains beyond and which I am to realize. My life as now lived throws its shadow across the future; it is now lived as it is, because what I had been and done throws a shadow across it. The shadow that is thrown across my life now becomes submerged in me to function as the encounterable past in me; the shadow, before such a submergence, makes the future that is to be realized already part of a single present of which the shadow-throwing actuality is the most intensive part.

The future as external to the present actuality does not have a future for itself. It is related to the actuality as a realizable possibility, as an ingredient control, and as a continuation of the present. A past entity does not have past items in it; it lacks substantiality. Instead, it is related to the actuality in the present as that which is external and excluding/excluded, as an ingredient, effective factor, and as that which had been directed by what is now present (so far as this is only possible and indeterminate).

1]   Past   Future

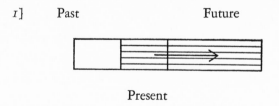

Present

The Present spreading into the future.

2]   Past   Future

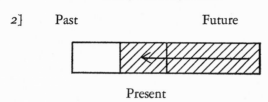

Present

The Future intruding into the Present and immanent there.

3]   Past   Future

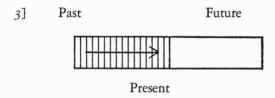

Present

The Past intruding into the Present.

4]   Past   Future

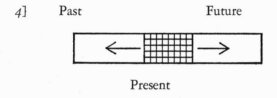

Present

The Present.

5]   Past   Future

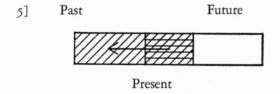

Present

The Present governing the Past. (The futurity [/ / / /] of the Present intrudes on the Past.)

A war can be said to have its entire span affected by the intrusion of the first battle, with all the subsequent battles merely sustaining the same intrusion, while taking over from their predecessors the intensity of being what is lived through or experienced sequentially. The first battle would mark out the span as being present, even though that battle gives way to other battles which are vital and in that sense present in place of it.

We have a sequence of vital presents occurring inside the single present of the war, where the sequence consists of maximal intensities, and the span of the war has a minimal but constant intensity. Each battle, moreover, is governed by the possible victory in the war. That possible victory, while it remains outside the present of the battle as its future, also intrudes into the battle as that which directs and alters it. As we continue with the war, the earlier battles are seen to be intrusive in whatever battle is being fought, at the same time that they remain outside it in fact as settled realities, and are infected by the present battle in the guise of a possibility which once governed them.

When we attend to the sequence of battles, we do not attend to the war; it is only when we attend to the constant minimal intensification that we attend to the war at the same time that we occupy a position where the intensity is maximal. Only when we take a position outside the war itself do we know that the position where the intensity is maximal changes; so far as we are in the war, we have a present which is constant and in which a change in the location of the intensity is to be known and measured by attending either to the battles or by seeing the distance which the war places between an event that occurs before it and an event that occurs after it. The magnitude of the span of the war is to be calculated in terms of units outside it, or in terms of the separation it provides for events earlier and later than itself. The last can be treated as involving a sequence of occupations along the span, or as the period required in order that the maximum intensity be present at every point.

A different answer was given in *Reality,* because it was there supposed that there were ultimate units of time; those units were taken to occur in gulps, such that there was no possible sequence to be found in them. But when we have such long spanned events as a war, which must be said to be as present as any supposed ultimate unit state or moment of time, we must take account of the fact that there are events encompassed in them which do occur as earlier and later, even while they are only before and after in the long spanned present.

In the long-spanned present, the before and after events do seem to have an intensity in an order of earlier and later. Must we not say that they have such an order of earlier and later only so far as we move from the common stable intensity of the long-spanned event to consider other kinds of intensities, and thus remove ourselves from the long-spanned event?

February 16

The future is a possibility to be realized. Through acts of attention, it comes into clearer focus. The future is also a controlling force in the present actuality. Through intention and purpose, it achieves greater and greater power. The future, finally, is the terminus of a present which is most intense in the actuality and least intense at the future. By an identification with one's acts and aims, the future becomes a more intensive part of the present.

Can attention, intention, purpose, and identification be together? If they could, the future would be external, ingredient, and present at once. But as external, the future is indeterminate, to be realized in the form of some subsequent reality; as ingredient, it is part of a more intensive whole where it offers some control; as present, it is intensive, ineffective, and continuous with the actuality.

So far as the future is present, it is neither external nor ingredient. The latter two can be together, for they express different ways in which the future is effective on the actuality. But as present, it is that which is defined by the actuality. The actuality to be sure, when it focuses on the future as a prospect to be realized, defines it as relevant to itself; but it is relevant as having a nature and a role which is distinct from that of the actuality, whereas as present, it is so far but an attenuated form of the actuality. It can be said to be external as a structure, ingredient as a power, and to be a content as present.

The intensive content of the present is that which makes the actuality existent, experienciable, and encounterable. But then why should not the future as present be so? If the actuality is individual, unique, undeducible, and unpredictable in its concreteness, the present content of the future should make that future also individual, etc. We would then seem to lose the distinction between the present and the future.

The future as present, by virtue of the incursion of the content of the actuality into the future in an attenuated form, must be determinate in the very way in which the actuality is, though it will be a determinateness that is fainter than that which is characteristic of the actuality. What is realized is not that determinate future; what is realized is the external future, and then through the activity of the actuality under control of the ingredient future. ("Ingredient" is here used in a sense different from that employed in connection with possibility in *Modes of Being*. In the *Modes*, the ingredient expresses merely the presence of the possibility as having been realized, whereas here it refers to the vital activity of the future in the present actuality.)

When and as the actuality is realizing the external future structure, it increases the vital content of the future that it has continuous with itself as part of one present. When the increase reaches the magnitude of the actuality, the entire present passes away. That passing away of the present is one with the realization of the future structure as the terminus of an act.

The act of realization is not the intensification of the content in the future. The intensification is a continuous process, making the determinate more and more evident, whereas the realization is a process which, though continuous, makes the indeterminate determinate. But once the process of intensification begins, it is indistinguishable from the process of realization, for both then involve a continuous increase in intensification of determinateness, ending with the realization of the future as a new actuality, a new act, or a new feature.

February 20

The future needs to be characterized in two and not in three ways, as was done in the previous discussions. Every actual entity brings into being a subdivision of the total future. In doing this it infects the subdivision with something of itself, to make that subdivision into a relevant possibility. The activity of the actuality continues the process of infecting the subdivision, and ends with making the possibility into an ingredient possibility in a new present actual occurrence. When the actuality has an ability to intend, it can initially make the possibility have a much greater intensity than a mere ontological infecting of the possibility can.

The possibility acts on the actual object as it engages in its acts. This it does in a minor way with inanimate things, and in a major way when the individual is able to have a purpose. Purpose is but a vital and intensely effective way in which the possibility is enabled to control what is done.

Intention (as well as the minor ways in which the present affects the future) dictates the sequence of occurrences which are to take place in order that the terminus of the intention be realized. If there be something which takes place that is not so demanded, it is to be treated as an obstacle delaying the achievement of that terminus. Without an intention (or the minor ways), one might act properly in each moment, but there would not necessarily be an appropriate order to what one had done.

Purpose (as well as the minor ways in which the future operates in the present) dictates what is now to be done. It does not tell us, though, just what place the present act has in a sequence of acts. However, if there were no purpose or any of the minor forms, one might well do nothing more than what is merely irrelevant to the achievement of the end, and therefore produce only a set of obstacles or hindrances in the achievement of some end.

Intent is needed in order to maximize the relevance of what one is doing; purpose is needed in order to maximize the effectiveness of what one is doing so as to realize the end. The less there is of intent, the less assurance there can be of an efficient, directed set of acts; the less there is of purpose, the less assurance there can be of action which will suffice to bring about the end. If there be only a minimal purposiveness, which is to say if there be only a minimal effect exerted by the future on the present, we can continue to have a clear way of discriminating between acts which are relevant and acts which are not relevant to bring about the end, but may produce only the latter. If there be only a minimal intentionality, which is to say if there be only a minimal effect exerted by the present on the future, we can continue to produce the kind of acts which are suited to bring about the end, but will not have them in a proper order, and therefore will fail to reach the appropriate end.

We can know what an intent is or that there is an intent by seeing whether an expressed statement of a change in intent, or an expressed statement that there is a change in a terminus which might have been intended, leads to a change in the order in which something is done. And we can know that there is a purpose and what its nature is by seeing if an expressed statement of a change in purpose, or an expressed statement that there is a change in a terminus which might have a purposive role, leads to a change in what is done. If a boy is walking, we can see if he intends to go to the store by seeing what he does when we tell him that the store is in the opposite direction; and we can see if he has a purpose to go to the store by seeing what he does when we tell him that the store is about to close its doors. In the one case, we make him see that what he took to be relevant moves are irrelevant, and in the other, that what he thought were sufficiently effective moves were not. We expect him in the one case to make a different set of moves, e.g., to change his direction, and in the other to make more effective moves, e.g., to walk faster, or to cut down such irrelevancies as looking into the windows of stores as he ambles along.

February 21

Intention, and the minor forms of affecting the future by the present, can be expressed as the operation of a present actuality on a domain of possibility in such a way as to yield a modal term. This can be expressed as: $(p)D = Xq$, where X is a modal operator.

Purpose, and the minor forms of affecting the present by the future, can be expressed as the operation of a modal term on a present actuality so as to produce an action. This can be expressed as: $(Xq)(p) = A$, where A stands for action.

One can purposively engage in an intention. But whether one does so or not, the purpose acts not on a mere actuality, but on an actuality which is making a difference to the domain of possibilities in such a way as to yield a modal term or possible q. The independence of intention and purpose, and of their minor forms, means only that the degree of one may not match the degree needed to make it in perfect consonance with the other.

By substitution, we can express the second formula as: $[(p)D]$ $(p) = A$. This is to say that an action takes place as the result of an operation of p by the product of the operation of p on a domain of possibility. When the intention is inadequate, the operation of p on D does not yield the operator on (p); that operator will be the result of a special effort. The "[]" are additions to the intent, marking the fact that a purpose has been introduced.

These considerations are pertinent to the examination of the meaning of "therefore" in an inference. This part of the inference has not been given much attention by me or anyone else. It is an action, and can be assimilated to the formula $(Xq)(p) = A$, or its equivalent $[(p)D]$ $(p) = A$. We should therefore be able to write an outline of an inference as:

$$\frac{p \qquad) \qquad q}{p}$$
$$[(p)D]\ (p)$$
$$q$$

or

equivalently as:

$$\frac{p \quad) \quad q}{p}$$
$$(Xq)(p)$$
$$q$$

"Therefore" is a special form of the action that takes place when a modal operator is imposed on an acknowledged starting point. The action which it exhibits has a terminus in the nonmodal form of the modal operator. Were there some other modal operator, there would be a "therefore," but it would not arrive at the q; we would then have an instance of a purpose without an appropriate intent. We would not arrive at the q either, if we had an intent without a purpose, i.e., if we had (Xq) but did not use it as an operator on (p). The prospective conclusion must operate on the accepted premiss if there is to be a terminus in the implied conclusion.

In the usual expression of inference, the "therefore" is a universal, identical in every context; but it is in fact a particular which starts from a distinctive beginning and moves in a distinctive direction with a power adequate to produce an actual conclusion.

The operation on the premiss is an operation on a proposition having a certain "truth" value. The operation allows the value or the proposition, or both, to remain unaltered, the limiting case being that of the value and the proposition being altered. From p with a "truth"-value (or as I once suggested we call it, a "property"-value) we can derive p with a value $\#$, r with a value $@$, p with a value $@$, or r with a value $\#$, where $@$ and $\#$ are different values. The operator (Xq) therefore must be capable of affecting the value, the proposition, or both the value and the proposition it operates on, to yield the result. In the above formulae where we have q expressed as the outcome, it must therefore stand for $@r$, $\#r$, $@p$, or $\#p$ as possible consequences to be drawn from the acknowledgment of $@p$.

February 22

The qualities which we know have both subjective and objective tonalities. The red we see is disturbing or soothing. What we confront is a juncture of ourselves reaching out, and of objects insisting on themselves. Sometimes the factor we introduce is dominant, and sometimes the factor that is introduced by the object is dominant. In the first case, we move toward feeling and particularly pain and pleasure, in the second, we move toward attribution and particularly predication. The subjective component is the element of specification (mentioned in *Reality*) which accounts for error; the objective component is, with respect to the specification, something general, though it achieves its own specification when it is part of the object.

The subjective and objective components are not adjectives of a subject and an object; they express the way in which the unitary being interplays with its component parts. Neither can therefore be reduced to a summation of the parts. Those who try to understand perception as though it were the action of brain cells or nerve impulses begin by reducing the objects to mere physical processes and then move on to suppose that the nerve impulses not only are simple summations of such processes, but that they can exist and function apart from the organic body. The various parts of the body—or if one wants, the very neutrons and other subatomic particles in the body—are unified by the wholeness of the body, and it is that fact which is expressed in an insistence affecting other beings and meeting their insistencies to produce a congealed relation which we can at times consciously acknowledge as a quality, oriented primarily toward the object and secondarily as a rule toward ourselves.

Why are there so many different expressions of the unity of whole and parts as color, shape, size, smell, etc? The above account requires the object to have a color and to contribute a generic form of the color to the joint product of the perceiver and itself. But there should also be similar contributions made regarding size, smell, taste, etc., which cannot be accredited to the presence of men or other perceiving beings. Those beings do add specifications, but they add it to what is real apart from themselves.

Perhaps the different features tell us different things? Can we not classify them as telling us either how, why, where, for how long, the whole is operating on its parts? Thus colors might tell us how; sizes might tell us where, shapes might tell us why, smells might tell us with what difficulty, and tastes might tell us for how long.

February 23

If one grants that there are four ultimate modes of Being, that the ontological argument must be grounded in an objective necessity, and that the necessities of which we know anything are logical, we might try seeing each of the Beings as the very being of some ultimate law. In "God and the World," I suggested that God was the being of the law of identity. It is not altogether easy to see how to characterize the other modes of Being. One can though, well argue that Existence is the being of the law of inference, since it is the domain of action, and inference is an act; that Ideality is general and this violates the law of contradiction, leaving it to be the embodiment of the law of excluded middle; and that Actuality is therefore the reality of the law of contradiction.

Concentrating for the moment on God, is the law of identity God as He is apart from all the other modes? If so, it cannot be the case that every actuality is to be analyzed as some compound of the law of identity. We would have to say that only the particulars associated with God are to be so analyzed. The ontological argument for God would involve an acknowledgment of the law of identity as having being only so far as it was endlessly multiplied, to yield God as at once one and many. But such a demonstration, if it were possible, would not show how God operated on other modes of Being, or how He could be encapsulated by the other modes of Being. We would have to argue at the very least that one of the applications of the law of identity was God in the delimited form He has within the other modes of Being. On such a view, actualities are to be understood to be multiplications, not of God in His purity, as a mere law of Identity, but of God as a combination of cases of such a law, which requires that it be multiplied in more limited ways and usually in the shape of actualities.

One could also maintain that God, as operating on the other modes of Being, subordinates the laws they exemplify, just as they in acting on God make the law of identity an instance of themselves. We could also make a place for God's role in enabling Actuality and actualities to be distinct in function. This would mean that God, in subordinating the law of contradiction *in concreto* (i.e., Actuality), would at the same time offer the actualities a limited form of the law of identity as that which they could be said to exhibit in a plurality of instances combined externally.

The first step to be taken would be to show that the proof of the reality of God is a proof of the reality of the law of identity as that which is instanced in a plurality of combinations of the law of identity. To be the law of identity, God would have to multiply it in the shape of a plurality of "divinities." We would have to show that the law could not be, except so far as it was also multiplied. These multiplications would be of a limited form; they would involve some instances of the law of identity combined externally. We might then go on to try to show that the law of identity, which was God the Being, would have to subordinate the other laws, and that in the act in which it did this, some one of the external combinations of instances of the law of identity would function as a being for the plurality of actualities, each of which would, from the perspective of that being, have to be treated as a plurality of identities.

The plurality of instances of the law of identity in God would have to have some meaning as external to the law of identity; or alternatively, God must face Himself as externally united with Himself. Or would it be a better supposition to maintain that God's identity consists in His being a Being in relation to a plurality oriented in Him? On this last view, the law of identity would have a singular term, God's Being, and another term which was internally plural, related as identical with one another. This in effect would amount to the claim that the plurality associated with a mode of Being was identical with it in meaning, or value, or range, so that the totality of items in a many would be coordinate with a one— or what is the same thing, that an immanent one of a plurality would be, with that plurality, equivalent with a transcendent one. The two ones in God would have the same meaning by virtue of Ideality (or the law of excluded middle), at the same time that the plurality was assured of being extended over by the transcendent One by means of Actuality, and was required by Existence to be a logical consequence of the Being.

The issue is somewhat confused in good part because I am trying to speak of what goes on inside other modes of Being where I have none but dialectical suppositions to guide me. Staying with God, all we could say for the ontological argument is that it will either try to deal with God as related to actualities or with God as related to the God who is related to actualities. The ontological argument in its traditional form would seem to be more pertinent to the latter than the former. Consequently what it should show is that the law of identity which has God as one term must have another term which is part of a plurality, or which becomes plural because it is the God for a plurality of actualities. The second of these alternatives would require that God could not be God unless in fact He was on one side the God of a plurality of actualities which required Him in some way to be internally plural, or that he in fact was on one side a pluralized member of a wider plurality, and as such a member was in relation to the plurality of actualities.

It would be neater if it could be shown that God, the Being, was self-identical only so far as He also was a unity for a plurality of entities, i.e., actualities, each of which was to be understood as some combination of identities. And this could perhaps be best done by trying to use the ontological argument to prove the identity of God with Himself-as-related-to-a-plurality-of-actualities. Later one might then go on to show that He was identical with Himself-as-related-to-a-plurality-of-possibilities and with existential locations, and that as a Being He subordinated the other modes of Being as so many different forms of logical necessity, just as they in turn subordinated Him as a law of identity subject to their laws.

If we go this far, perhaps we ought to say of the three-part argument for God (which I have maintained contains a teleological, a cosmological, and an ontological component) that the first part stops with God as the identities in actualities, the second with Him as related to those actualities, and the third with Him as a Being in Himself, and that after we have taken these three steps we can view it as the true ontological or fully articulated argument.

February 24

The "complete" argument for God starts with a teleological interpretation of identity as the necessity which God has. This identity is pluralized and refers to itself as single. But this single identity, which has a cosmological relation to the teleological form, instances the law of contradiction. To get it in its proper form, as an ultimate in its own right, one must move to the last phase and take the identity as a reality in itself. What is proved as a consequence of these three steps is not merely God as a reality in Himself, but God as immanent in the pluralized world, God as subordinate to Actuality, and God as in Himself.

The conclusion of such an inference would not be the "q" that was implied by the starting point, "p", but this "q" together with all the preceding steps. We should write it as: $q \& p \& \therefore$. What we conclude to is, in other words, not merely God in himself, but God in Himself, God as immanent, and God as relative to the Himself as immanent, arrived at by a process which begins with Himself as immanent.

When we think about this God—and *pari passu* when we entertain possibilities in wish and hope, or consider even idly the nature of anything that is not empirically confronted—we manifest the fact not in any particular act, but rather in the way in which we connect the various acts of inattention that we exhibit with respect to things to which we ordinarily attend. The meaning of my idle thought of the Queen of Sheba is given not by my unreflecting placing of my hand on the ashtray before me—for I might do this too if I had an idle thought about Alexander the Great—but in the way in which I relate such an unreflecting movement with others that I had made and will make.

An idle thought is an explanation for a number of particulars which are eccentric in the sense that they are not wanted, not attended to, etc. Everything we think of then, even if it be of that which is not on sea or land, has its public meaning, not contained in this or that object, but expressed as the rationale of what otherwise would be a set of unrelated and inexplicable occurrences. Without a reference to the idle thought, we could say only that my touching the ashtray is inadvertent or accidental. We would give up any attempt to account for the way in which this occurrence is followed by others that are also thought to be equally inadvertent.

This discussion (which is aroused by some talks I have been having with Robert Ehman) leads to the conclusion that every private act, or meaning, or experience, has its public form. This is not always to be found in a particular isolated act. It may be found in the way acts are related.

The reductionists, who would like to interpret all experience of qualities as movements in the brain, could improve their position if they were to take the experience of qualities to be explicable in their interrelationship by virtue of a reference to the brain movements, if they were to take the qualities to be the explications of the relationships of the brain movements, if they were to take the qualities to be congealed relations of the movements, or if they were to take the movements to be congealed relations of the qualities. If what they wished to do was to make the qualities disappear altogether, they would evidently lose whatever evidence they needed for the presence of the brain movements. All they can hope to do is to make the qualities account for movements or relations (between them) which otherwise would be inexplicable, or conversely, to have the movements account for qualities or relations (between them) which otherwise would be inexplicable.

We here come close to a Leibnizian position, for the quality or the movement (he would allow only the quality) can be viewed as a blurred union of a multiplicity of relations between movements or qualities, respectively. On the first alternative (which is of primary interest to a reductionist), a quality would be a blurred summary of a host of relations, and would disappear as soon as we had analyzed it into its constituent relations amongst the various brain movements. This would seem to lead us to say that the relations between the qualities are counterparts of the relations connecting one group of movements with another. Can such a position be maintained? Only if the aspects of the relations, which refer to the qualitative natures, were treated as adventitious and in the end unreal.

The reductionists should not try to correlate qualities with movements. They should correlate the relations amongst qualities with those amongst movements, and then treat the qualities themselves as summations of a totality of relations amongst certain movements of the brain. If they can do this, we should then also reverse the entire program and A] treat the relations amongst qualities as having a counterpart in relations amongst movements, and B] see the movements themselves as summations of a totality of relations amongst certain qualities. In the latter case, for example, we might speak (B) of a single movement in the brain reflecting the relations which a whole series of shades of red have to one another, at the same time that we take (A) the relation of that movement to other movements in the brain, to express the relation which the series of shades of red has to the series of shades of blue.

This approach enables us to have not only the eccentric particulars which reflect the quality of a mode of Being, but also the eccentric particulars which reflect the presence of qualities (or alternatively, the presence of brain movements), the one type of particular being movements, and the other being qualities. The existence of brain movements, for example, would be acknowledged in order to avoid treating qualities as eccentric particulars, particulars which had no proper rationale. The movements would tell us what the proper relation amongst those qualities should be understood as. Each movement would help us analyze the qualities into subordinate elements, and the relation of the movements to one another would be matched by the relation of the qualities to one another. As a consequence, the qualities would be seen to be no longer eccentric; their eccentricity would be shown to be the outcome of the fact that we had neglected their rationale in the form of brain movements. And the converse would be true of the movements themselves and their relations to one another from the perspective of qualities and their relations, thereby preventing the movements from being eccentric and inexplicable.

February 27

It is plausible to speak of sport as though it were a form of action. It could then be thought to be best understood as falling under the second part of *Reality*, as a kind of public treatment of Actuality. But it is perhaps more correct to see sport as one of four different forms of practical effort, each of which succeeds in getting to the being of a mode of Being in a public setting.

Sympathy can be taken to be the practical means by which one penetrates to the public side of Actuality; gainful work can have a similar role with respect to Ideality; sport would have a similar role with respect to Existence; sacrifice would have such a role with respect to God. In these various cases, what we face initially is a mode of Being as open both to a multiplicity of individuals and to a need to reach this Being through an action which penetrates beyond the public domain. These modes of practical penetration contrast respectively with speculative thought, mythology, intuition, and mysticism. But it must be confessed that they do not seem to have the reach or the richness characteristic of these latter. Is this because the latter start from more impoverished positions, or from positions which are more remote from the modes of Being than their publicly grounded counterparts?

February 28

One can achieve a purpose in two ways. One of the ways was discussed a little while back, and had to do with the conversion of an intended object into a purposed one. This method allows one to deal with a possibility as something confronted, but made to be effective in what is now happening.

A second way involves the utilization of a consequence or terminus of a set of acts. Here what is being used as a purpose is something concrete, something which in fact had been arrived at. This is a purpose which can be obtained as the outcome of an inference or in the course of training.

When we draw a conclusion of an inference, we replace the premiss. But, as the discussion of the three stages in a proof of God indicates, we can arrive at the conclusion—in this case, God as in Himself, as a mere Being—without altogether forgetting that we had acknowledged God to be immanent in things and to be a possible source of their existence, or power, or ultimate unity. But instead of presenting this result as was done the other day, it would be better to see the conclusion as something arrived at in the usual case and to be conjoined with itself as a possible purposive agent. It could be written as:

$$q.\ X(q)\,[(p)\ (\,.\!^{.}\!.\,)$$

where q is the conclusion, X is a modal term indicating "possible," (q) is an operator on (p), the original premiss, and on $(\,.\!^{.}\!.\,)$, the original process.

The conclusion of an argument gives us a detached q together with the possibility of using q as a purpose operating on the original premiss and course of inference. The detached q was arrived at by following the rule "p) q". The possibility of q functioning as a purpose allows us to dispense with the rule and the intention to arrive at the q. We of course had to start with the rule and the intention in order to get to the q as the outcome of an inference; but once we get to the q, we no longer need the rule and the intention.

The conclusion in the ordinary syllogism that Socrates is a mortal will have now to be understood as being part of a larger conjunction, of which the other component will be " 'Socrates is a mortal' having the role of a possible purpose." The purpose operating on "Socrates is a man" makes it into a premiss in the same way that the rule originally allowed it to be; operating on "All men are mortal," it makes this into an operation in which the "man" in the premiss is replaced by the "mortal."

A trainer knows what the last step of a training should be. But the student is taught one step after another; the last step is also learned the way the others are. The trainer guides the student in accord with a rule which the trainer has come to know, has habitually carried out, or acknowledges to be that which is to be habitually carried out. But he wants the student to master the steps; he therefore does not want to tell him about the rule or even to direct him to the proper end. He wants each stage of a process to be given full consideration and not to be thought of as merely a step toward the end. If it were so thought, it would be slighted, because the student would tend to crowd toward that end. But having learned the last step, the student must then be made to see that this can function as a purpose. The student in repeating the steps must now do so not merely as a sequence of detached acts, but as acts which are guided by a purpose. He learns first to pick up the bat, hold it, swing it, and hit the ball. Having hit the ball, he is now to see the picking up, the holding, and the swinging as governed by the hitting. This governance is not a governance by a merely possible hitting, but by an ingrediently possible hitting.

The difference between a merely possible hitting, a hitting which is arrived at by intent, and an ingrediently possibly hitting, a hitting which had taken place but which now functions as a purpose and thus is a possibility, is that the latter is affected by the entire context in which it occurs. The ingrediently possible hitting is an abstracted possibility, a possibility which depends on the achievement of an actual terminus. It is conjoined to the actual terminus only because it is abstracted from it. It would therefore be better to write the initial conclusion as:

$$q.Aq,$$

where Aq (abstraction from q) is equivalent to $X(q)(p)(\therefore)$.

An abstraction from q leaves us with the memory of the feel of q, of the fact that it had been experienced. It has an adumbratable experiential component even though it is only a possibility. To use it as a purpose is to allow the impact of the hit, the confrontation of God in Himself, the acknowledgment of a conclusion, to have some effect on the content which is being governed by a purpose.

March 3

There are a number of ways in which one can deal with a movement to some terminus in a rational way:

We can treat the movement as an act of substituting the terminus for the beginning. This is a procedure followed by some logicians in connection with inference. They start with a p, which is treated as an adventitious carrier or locus of some such property as "truth-value," and use substitution to replace the p by a q as demanded by some accepted rule. On this view, the character "truth" does not inhere in either the beginning or the end; the acknowledged beginning and end are just specific locations of that which was accepted to begin with, the domain of truth.

An alternative way of dealing with inference is more common. Here one starts with a premiss possessed of some such sessile character as truth. One then, under the warrant of an implication, converts that sessile character into a projective character, and through the act of inference, imposes it on q. The account should go further and show how the projected character is converted into a sessile character of q. That this is not done by logicians is due to a confusion between the "therefore-ing" and the result of it—a confusion which has characterized my thinking no less than others. One should distinguish between the process which carries the projected property "truth" and the act by which we accept that property and convert it into a sessile character of the detached q. We arrive at q while leaving p and the process of therefore-ing behind.

A third form of inference, which can serve as a model for learning theory, and the way in which intentions and purposes operate, starts with a q which is lacking some desirable feature, and has this operate on p in such a way as to make that p yield up the desirable feature to q. The q functions as a purpose affecting the p and the process of moving from p in such a way as to yield the q with the desirable feature. (The q is initially faced as an object of intent; the intent takes the rule as datum and converts it into a vector.)

I have argued in the past that we can derive an endless number of consequences from a premiss. Having a rule which directs us to one conclusion does not of itself guarantee that we will get to that conclusion. It is only because we guide the process by the intended result that we in fact arrive at the terminus as possessed of the desirable character.

If we take the third to be the proper form of inference, we will have to understand the previous two forms as inadequate, degenerate versions, or will have to see them to be in effect illustrating this third form—or both. I think we must say "both." No inference merely substitutes; the property of being true is integral to the proposition which is true—certainly when it is analytically true and when it is united with the facts by virtue of which it is true.

The property "truth," even if it were the case that it can be made to appear or disappear by an alternation in some exterior fact or in the way in which the proposition is related to fact, is in any case a property of the proposition p and not merely a domain or fixed nature which the proposition allows us to locate for a moment. And in the ordinary interpretation of inference, where we arrive at q along a route defined by a rule of implication, we have the problem of converting a sessile property into a projective in the beginning, and then converting a projected property into a sessile property at the end. How is this done? Why suppose it can be done? Why suppose it can be done without altering what has been projected? How can we follow the route of an implication without knowing the q is that at which it is to end? Implication as such is common to all inferences, but what is wanted is an implication which will lead us to get to a particular q. We would seem to need the guidance of the q in order to be able to follow the rule.

The third method of moving not only is applicable to inferences, training, and the carrying out of purposes; it allows one, as was seen the other day, to keep a hold on the previous steps so as to allow one to understand the terminus as that which makes the earlier stages have the nature they do. The sessile character of the p is worked on by the prospective q in such a way as to produce a sessile character in the q. There is no projecting and no alteration of the character of the p; there is only a production of a sessile character in the q, by means of the operation of the prospective q on the beginning.

There is still another way of moving which can be applied to inference. This is suggested in the discussion of God in the *Modes of Being*. Here the premiss offers testimony of some feature in the terminus. The premiss is here thought to be able to provide this testimony only because the terminus is that which makes that testimony present in the beginning. We take the fingerprint to offer testimony of the criminal by treating it as the beginning of a move to the finger, and from the finger to the owner of the finger. This kind of inference, though common in all human affairs, is not examined by logicians. They would be inclined to use the testimony as a premiss to which they would add a rule or law which will warrant the transfer of the property "truth" to the owner of the finger. But why and how did they come to have the owner of the finger, or a proposition about the owner of the finger to be the conclusion to which they wanted to ascribe the character "ground" or "true"?

The movement from testimony to the ground of it is in effect the movement from an adherent character which is not an essential part of the premiss, to a substantial reality which may or may not have the very feature which the testimony exhibits. If we apply this way of looking at the situation to the problem of inference, we will say, not that the testimony is a premiss which is to give us a conclusion along the route defined by an implication of the testimony, but instead that a sessile character which is adjectival to the premiss will be converted into a sessile character which is ingredient in, essential to the conclusion. But this operation will require a purposive use of the conclusion as that which we want to have understood as having the character essential to it.

A conclusion should be understood to operate, as in the third case, as a kind of purpose; but instead of working on the premiss so as to obtain for itself a similar sessile character, it is to be seen to operate on a sessile character which is not essential, so as to make it essential elsewhere. We can therefore take this fourth way of moving to be a special case of the third. It could in fact be said to start within or be a part of the third, for the third requires one to make the sessile character of the premiss or the premiss itself yield an external character which is to be gradually made essential to the q.

The third starts with a p in which the truth is ingredient or essential, and then works on it by means of the q to get the q to have a similar truth; but in this process, it has to get to the position where it has some feature or occurrence distinct from p and its truth, which can become the intrinsic or sessile feature of the q. No inference does anything to the premiss or its features; the premiss continues to retain whatever features it in fact has, so that even a change from a sessile to a projective feature is a change which does not deny to the initial p the continuance of its possession of the sessile feature.

In the ordinary inference we start with what is not testimony, since we start with *p* as having the sessile character of truth; but the operation of the *q* on this *p* with that character will yield a projective truth. That projective truth will then be worked on by the *q* until it becomes a sessile truth of the *q*. As such a sessile truth, it will, in the ordinary inference, characterize the conclusion but will not necessarily be ingredient in or essential to it. It is ingredient or essential only if we work on the projective truth, not merely to carry it to the conclusion, but to make the conclusion be. We get *q*, not as merely carrying the truth which was projected, but as having this as part of its very being, just so far as the projected truth is offering testimony, since testimony leads us from unessential features to substantial beings or to beings in which those features are in fact essential.

Most compendiously stated: The normative form for a rational process of moving from a beginning to an ending is to so operate with the ending on the beginning as to make a feature associated with the beginning have a more sessile role. The association may be one of ingredience, predication, or relationship to something outside, etc.; the more sessile role may involve the making of what originally was sessile into something which was more sessile because more deeply involved with the ending than it had been with the beginning.

March 4

Reflection on the third and fourth ways of rationally moving to a terminus, discussed yesterday, leads to the view that the normative form of an inference is one where we start with a sessile characterized beginning, operate on this by means of the desired possible terminus so as to produce a projective character which is then converted into a sessile character of the terminus. The account of the third method does not take into consideration the fact that the sessile character of the terminus is a more substantial version of the projective character, and that it may in fact be more substantial than the initial sessile character of the beginning. The fourth method does not take into account the fact that one starts with a sessile character which may be merely adjectival or may be integral to the beginning, and thus must be converted into something which is less substantial than the character of the terminus (which might conceivably be no more substantial than the character of the beginning). By speaking of the character as being more substantial, what is meant, of course, is that it may be affected by its carrier, penetrate it, be inseparable from the being of that character.

The normative form of inference allows us to understand training, learning, making, and inference. In training, we learn to do a number of distinct things representing stages in what will eventually be a single act. Each of these things is attended to by itself; it has a sessile character. But one must learn to do each with some readiness to do the next; the eyes must begin to turn, there must be a relaxing of the grip in order to move the bat in a manner other than that required for lifting it, etc. This learning to attend elsewhere is a producing of a projectile character. It is the beginning of a "therefore-ing," of the actual movement from the beginning. The act proceeds by intensifying this projectile character, to end with it as a sessile one. This means that as we turn from one act to another, and finally to the end, we concentrate on that end without further reference to an act beyond. The end terminates that act and is seen to terminate it by virtue of the sessile nature of the character. At the end there is a concentration, an explosion of energy, an involvement which has no fringe to it leading one to turn elsewhere, whereas in all the other steps there is always a fringe, and apart from the possible case where the beginning is characterized as being as substantial as that which is achieved at the end, there is always less concentration, less energy used, less explosive power exhibited at the beginning.

The entire process is, of course, guided by a rule, and that rule in the ideal case is made into the structure of an intent, with the beginning vectorially directed at the end as a possibility. By virtue of the fact that there is a substantializing of the projectile character through a transformation of it into a sessile character, every rational movement will have to be said to include a use of testimony, the passage from some acknowledged feature to that which could have been its source, but is always in any case a place where the feature is confined.

After an act has taken place, there is often a readiness to engage in another act. This is particularly true if one has in mind to engage in a long, drawn-out activity. Does this mean that we must end an act with a fringe to it, leading us to treat the character as projective? The earlier stages in the act involve an occupation with something here and now which is not separable from a vectorial reference beyond, which vectorial reference is filled out as the projective character. But the end of that act is an end for those earlier stages, and so far as the character which was initially projected is concerned, there is nothing further in the end, beyond the merely sessile character, which was produced by operating on the projected character. The fringe characteristic of the end, when the end is the terminus of an act within some larger movement, requires one to produce an entirely different projectile character from that with which one started—unless, of course, one is merely repeating the act another time. Or it may be the case that the larger movement's end serves only to determine what act is to follow on the given act, so that the fringe following the given act is to be filled out by the possible terminus of the next act as that which is to operate on the given act's terminus's character.

What seems to be true is that in the earlier stages of an act there are inseparable fringes which are the domain of the operation of the possible end, and that a subsequent act occurs within a fringe following on a given act, but which is usually operated on by a different possible end. That different possible end—and even in the case where the end is the same in kind as that which operated in the given act—does not operate, however, until it has been made into an object of purpose, whenever we have rational controlled movement. The given act ends with a purpose achieved, and if it is part of a larger movement, it must be made subject to a new purpose, whose end may, however, be the same in kind as that which had governed the given act.

Inference and other rational movements, though they may start with sessile and substantial characters, do not proceed to the end without first having gone to the stage where they are dealing with projectile characters, characters which are to be filled out in a process, and which at the beginning are no longer substantialized by the beginning. The movement to the end is the substantializing of this which is not substantialized at the beginning of the process of moving to the end.

Does the process end with the substantializing of the character? If it does, the q at the end is a limit of the process. But we hold the q apart from the premiss and process in the usual inference. We detach the conclusion, hold to it with its sessile character. This would seem to show that the process itself does not end with the character fully substantialized and sessile, and that we must engage in another act by virtue of which we tear the conclusion away from the process, and in that very act make the character entirely sessile and as substantial as it can be in that terminus. The transition, in other words, from the beginning with its sessile character to a projectile character, is to be matched at the end with a movement from a maximally substantialized projectile character to a simple sessile character of the terminus.

March 7

An ideal standard for behavior involves a reference to success— success in adjustment, in ease with oneself or others, in maintaining a job or a marriage, in fitting in with societal demands, in attaining a position of dominance, in achieving self-confidence, in doing what the majority or the dominant group may be doing, in having certain skills, in passing certain tests, in achieving certain goals. Those who cannot meet these standards have in root only two alternatives: they remain as they are, and then have supplementary aids provided which will enable them to get by, or they are helped to change their habits and patterns so that they can attain the level that others do.

The first of these alternatives can be carried out in one of two ways. The supplements to the defective situation may be arbitrary, or they may be quietings provided for by the majority. The arbitrary ways involve cheating, theft, violence, self-denial, protections, and the like. The quietings can come in the form of remedies, supplementary incomes, handicaps imposed on those who are already privileged, bonuses and aids to those who are not, threats, and sometimes promises.

The second alternative demands a retraining. It requires the underprivileged to start at some point below which they now are so that they can learn the skills and achieve the powers that others have. It is a method which may reveal that those who are being helped are in fact incompetent and cannot take advantage of the new opportunities being offered. But it must be tried, and only when it fails must one have resort to the other method, for the other confesses to failure and seeks ways in which the failure will not end with injury to the disadvantaged or to the society as a whole.

When it is shown that the Negro family is often one in which there is no father, and therefore no male with whom boys can identify themselves, a mistaken attempt to protect the Negro from being underevaluated leads some Negroes to defend the view that the boys identify themselves with their grandfathers, uncles, or even with the men who pass in and out of the house. In effect, this reply takes the first of the two alternatives, and then in the form of arbitrary remedies. Let it be the case that the boy does identify himself with his grandfather; it still remains a question whether such an identification is ideal, whether the absence of a father does not mean the absence of someone steady, responsible, of somewhat the age of the mother, able to play and be with the boy, etc. The quieting process of providing money for fathers who remain at home, or which provides clubs and games where the boys can come to know and respect adults is certainly more desirable than forcing the boy to make an identification with whatever male happens to be available.

To this last observation it will undoubtedly be replied that this is the kind of identification which is eminently suitable to a slum child. A similar reply is sometimes made to the observation that the slum child has an inadequate command of English, for it is then said that he fills up his vocabulary with terms of violence and slang which are adequate to his needs and well express his condition and ambitions and interests. But these are arbitrary supplements, and do not in fact bring the child to the position where it is able to be successful in the larger society; it still keeps the child in an inferior class, but allows it not to suffer too much, by giving it arbitrary supplements. We make an advance when quieting supplements are provided, for these at least allow the minority person to live in terms of which the majority approves, not because it keeps the minority down, but because it enables it to have a semblance of equality with the majority. But the proper answer would be one which enables the minority person to achieve the skills and exercise the powers that will enable him to achieve success by his own efforts, and thus not be one who has been propped up by the society or made to find some solution to his problem by arbitrary devices which do not change his condition, but only make it more tolerable or pleasant.

It could be argued that if minority people are to continue to fail to meet majority standards, they will have to find ways in which they do not depend on the majority for help. But this supposes that the minority is not a social responsibility for the majority. Social responsibility requires that the disadvantaged be helped by the advantaged. This help, if it is to make the individual successful not merely by easing the way but by virtue of his own achievements, should be provided in the form of aids that will enable him to improve his habits and rid himself of those which keep him disadvantaged because of an incapacity to do certain things needed for a successful life, no matter how this be defined.

In sport, we face something like these possibilities—arbitrary or quieting supplements. It is the object of training to provide for organic change, to make it possible for an individual to achieve the position where he can compete with others on a common basis. This illustration shows that the supplementing method accepts men as they are, and then tries to add extrinsic factors in order to make them function in public in what appears to be ways that do not reveal them to be disadvantaged. But they will be disadvantaged nevertheless in nature and effort, though not in effect. Training takes one away from such a situation; it tries to change a disadvantaged man into another kind of being, rather than, as is the case with the supplements, trying to change the situation in which he is by cutting down the factors that reveal the disadvantaged to be in fact not equal in skill, knowledge, intelligence, motivation, etc., with some of the advantaged.

One can suppose that those who are now disadvantaged are natively as able as the advantaged, and that the difference between the two lies only in the fact that the advantaged have been able to lay hold of supplements in a way denied to the disadvantaged. Some of the advantaged, to be sure, are not intrinsically superior to some of the disadvantaged; their advantage is the result of the fact that they have been, through birth, politics, accident, etc., able to make use of available arbitrary or quieting supplements. To the reply that the fact that they can lay hold of such supplements shows a superiority, it can be answered that this is a matter of historic accident or the result of an inheritance of an advantage once gained by forebears and which is not to be inherited. Among other things, this position forces into focus the question as to just what is meant by "natively as able." If it means that at the beginning all children are to be thought of as equally open to proper instruction, and that the same proportion of successes are to be found among children having different creeds, colors, and ancestry, it but points up the fact that we should see if we cannot provide young men and adults with the kind of education and training that would enable them to master the skills they intrinsically could have had, had they been educated properly when they were younger.

If what is meant by "natively as able" is that adults in disadvantaged groups have skills of their own, one must either maintain that those skills should be provided with outlets other than those now available, or that supplements should be provided to take up the slack which results from the fact that the skills are not socially viable to the same degree as are the skills of the advantaged. The first of these alternatives is inviting. It argues that the society should be changed in order that the skills possessed by the disadvantaged can result in social success. In effect though, this suggestion involves some kind of supplement, for it asks the majority to open up opportunities for the disadvantaged so that they can exhibit skills they now cannot, apparently in the hope that the result will be an organic change in the individuals or their offspring.

I think a democracy should recognize that the structure of its society is such that it does not take full advantage of skills possessed by the disadvantaged. The ideal standard to which the disadvantaged are often urged to reach, in effect emphasizes the skills that the majority has. A democratic society could have a wider range of activities than it does now. But granted this, it is also true that the disadvantaged lack some of the instrumentalities for success, and that these should be provided by introducing organic changes.

We should then have supplements, but these should be in the guise of opportunities which allow for the use of skills now not supported by the society or the majority. But such supplements, which merely allow for the use of the skills already possessed by the disadvantaged, should not preclude the effort to train the disadvantaged in skills which have proven to be successful in the society, not because they are the specific skills of a few, but because they carry out to the full the skills that all must have—such as the proper use of the language, the mastery of the technologies, the way to work with others, etc.

Behind this discussion loom some large questions: Do the disadvantaged, minorities, and the underprivileged have special skills, knowledge, power, or insights that will yield a maximum success for them and society if proper opportunities are provided for their use? Should the standards of the leading sectors be achieved by the underprivileged, etc., in the same way that the leaders once did, whether this be through organic change or by supplementation? Or, where it is the case that the leaders achieved their success through luck, historic advantage, or inheritance, can the others do anything more than violently demand the same degree of success, where the violence is but the sudden substitute for these adventitious advantages enjoyed by the leaders?

Every one of these alternatives has a role to play. Some of the success of the leaders is due to luck, some to superior opportunities, and some to training. But the most neglected and most interesting of the alternatives is the second, with its supposition that the disadvantaged have something distinctive to offer and that they need not a training which will make them like the others, but an opportunity, with its appropriate training, to enable them to use distinctive abilities. This does not preclude their being trained to do what the leaders did and to being given supplements to make up for advantages obtained through luck, etc.

March 8

A disadvantaged man may have the skills possessed by the advantaged, but by accident have not had the opportunity to exhibit them successfully. He might have only inadequate or improperly developed skills; or he might have a distinctive set of skills which have not had the opportunity to exhibit their viability in society. To remedy the first situation, one must deliberately recompense for what accident provided to the advantaged. To remedy the second, one must try to train the individual so that he obtains what the others have. To remedy the third, one must either provide for new opportunities or make some recompense for the denial of the opportunity to have the skills exhibited.

The American Indian is often said to have a temper and abilities which are not suited to a technological society. One might treat this fact under the first heading and say that it is the accident of history which prevents him from living a successful life today. We here understand the particular temper and abilities to be appropriate, not to our society, but to some society or other. If we take success in our technological society as the standard, we must move to the other alternatives. We must then say that the Indian does not have an adequate training in the skills necessary for success in our society; we will then try to have the Indian children go to schools where they will learn what the rest of society's children do. Or, should we find that they cannot learn, we will try to provide some recompense in the shape of protection, supplementary income, and the like, to enable them, despite their limitations, to reach a footing with the others. If we do not do this, we run the risk of having the Indian at some time try to achieve equality by violence.

The supposition that the Indian has distinctive skills and that these should be preserved in one sense is most consonant with the spirit of democracy, and in another goes directly against it. It is in consonance in that a democracy is supposed to encourage maximum diversity of individuals and attitudes and abilities; it is not in consonance in that a democracy works on the supposition that a common education will produce a random distribution of leaders, mediocrities, etc. We can reconcile these two opposing characterizations by viewing a democracy as a system which offers not a common education, but equal opportunities for diverse abilities to make themselves manifest with equal success. If these opportunities are not provided, there will be some special skills which will not be allowed to be exhibited, to the detriment of the society and the individuals who possess those skills. The individuals will then have to be recompensed or will achieve some of their necessities by violence. The recompense may be in the form of residual aid in the hospitals, charity, unemployment insurance, etc., or in the form of additions to income or the making of jobs. In either case, the recompense will be a kind of supplement, and will not do much more than allow the individual to fit in the society as it now is, without being internally altered for the better or being enabled to make a genuine contribution to the society.

The disadvantaged lack the training (to use the abilities that are natively theirs) or the opportunity (to use skills like those possessed by the advantaged, or to express their distinctive skills with the same success as the advantaged had to express their distinctive skills). The training or the opportunity must be provided, or some kind of compensation for the disadvantage will be provided, either reluctantly and inadequately, or deliberately and adequately. The very fact of being disadvantaged would mean that there is some training they do not get; if they constitute a single ethnic group, it would seem likely that they have been denied opportunities to carve out the world in a distinctive way that is of value to themselves, to others, and to society as a whole.

All the cases can be reduced to a denial of opportunity—opportunity to acquire common skills, to exhibit common skills, or to exhibit distinctive skills. There is a tendency on the part of those who defend the underprivileged to deny that there are distinctive skills, or to claim that whatever is distinctive is an advantage. They make the denial when they are emphasizing the fact that opportunities to develop and express common skills are needed; they suppose that the distinctive is always an advantage when they are emphasizing the virtues of the group.

What is needed is a clear understanding of what the acquirable common skills are, what must be provided if common skills are to be successfully exhibited, and what must be done if certain distinctive skills are to be allowed to be as successful as others have been in the past or by certain favored groups. Most civil rights and poverty programs concentrate on the second of these; most educational programs in the slums are directed at the first. They should not be allowed to obscure the significance of the third. The disadvantaged are aware of the third, and place an emphasis on those skills which make possible a readier upward mobility. And that is why European Jews attended to the law and medicine (for the good doctor or lawyer was employed by those in power), and the Negro occupies himself with sport and popular music as ways of passing beyond discrimination. But these offer openings only for a favored few. What is wanted is means for enabling the disadvantaged to make out as well as the rest, and thus to have about the same distribution of great successes and genuine failures as the others. If it were true that the Negro by and large has a special aptitude for sport or music, then that fact should be acknowledged in the form of opportunities to have money, dignity, self-confidence, and status to the same extent as now is the case with the whites.

March 10

In the usual inference, we end with the conclusion having the same quality as the premiss, and having it with the same intensity. If the quality is due to the presence of some outward fact (which makes the quality be the quality "true"), then the conclusion will be thought to inherit a projected form of this in such a way that it has that quality matching some outward fact. When we want to prove the reality of God, we want, however, to move from some unessential character of an actuality to an essential character of God. If the latter is of the same nature as the former, we want it to be ingredient in the latter in the way it is not in the former.

If we turn to the first examination of testimony in the *Modes of Being*, 4.15, we find that it attempts to use the otherness of an actuality as testimony for God, as the correlate other. But this approach not only demands that the actuality make itself into a representative of all else, but that the relation, despite its symmetry, have one import for actualities and another for God. This is possible if we take the actuality to be that which is other than the rest, so far as it is in the world with anything else. We can then say that the actuality changes its role from being directed toward or attached to other entities (besides God), to one where it subordinates the other entities to its individual being. When it makes this change, it continues to have otherness intrinsic to it, but it will have it intrinsic too to the contingent status of itself as a representative of all else.

What we have at the actuality end is an otherness which is intrinsic to the individual, but not to it as assuming the role of being a representative. It is, though, intrinsic to it as having assumed the role, for the role is subordinate to itself as an individual. It is the individual, as having assumed the role of a representative of all actualities and three modes, that is other than whatever is left. But that which is left does not have a role which it assumes. Consequently, the intrinsic otherness of what is left, which is the reciprocal of the intrinsic otherness of the individual, has a substantiality lacking to the actuality's otherness.

An actuality has an otherness which is intrinsic to it as an individual, as that which must be related to something else, and to it as a representative, through the assumption of a role by virtue of its being related to something else. The otherness is intrinsic in God in the way it is in the actuality, but it is more deeply imbedded than it is in the actuality acting as a representative (since though it is then intrinsic to the individual actuality, as such it is extrinsic to its role as a representative, except so far as that role has been adopted and subordinated to the individual). This means that God cannot be the absolute other except relative to the individual as a representative.

Testimony does not point to God in or by Himself, but only to

Him as related to the actuality. But if this is so, otherness does not tell us about an essential feature of God, and therefore not of God as He is by Himself. We would have to take another step and argue that nothing can possess the character of being an other unless it is something in itself, so that when we come to the cosmological and ontological phases of the argument, we would have to go beyond the testimony to the Being which not only sustains a character like that which is used as testimony, but which will allow us to free ourselves from a reference to that testimony.

The other two direct arguments of the *Modes* start with a different type of testimony. The position of 4.18 is that there is a mode of Being (Ideality) which is exterior to actualities, and that this exteriority depends for its presence on an exterior reality, God. God, it is testified, is an exterior reality which allows the mode of Being, Ideality, to be exterior to the actuality for which it offers a prescription. The position of 4.21 is that there is a mode of Being (Existence) which intrinsically is self-divisive, but which in fact is found to have a unity. This unity is in direct conflict with the self-divisiveness. In effect this says that the Existence has a feature, unity, which can be there only if its own essential nature, self-divisiveness, is prevented from having the upper hand. God is testified to as the Being who enables Existence to have a nature which is opposite to what it intrinsically has. That nature, unity, is thought to testify to God as a unity, so that what is being maintained is that the presence of a unitary Existence testifies to a unity which imposes a unity on what is anti-unitary.

The first kind of testimony speaks of an intrinsic character which is extrinsic to a role assumed; the second kind speaks of an extrinsic relation of a mode to an actuality which requires an exterior cause; the third kind speaks of an alien nature which overcomes what is native, just so far as that nature reflects the nature of a being to whom that alien nature is intrinsic. The second kind, however, succeeds in doing nothing more than showing that there is an exteriority, which itself might be God in a relational role. The third kind does not show that the unity which is imposed on Existence must be imposed by a unitary Being. When we take into account the fact that the reference to otherness in the end leads us to God as the bearer of the relation, and thus to God who does not have, as such a bearer, the nature of being an other, all three testimonies seem to be indirect in the sense defined in the *Modes*—as telling us about a source or power which is distinct in nature from the kind of nature accepted as testimony. The first kind of testimony does, along the lines of a usual inference, give us a God who has otherness as part of Himself in the way in which otherness is part of the individual, both as attached to something or other, and as subordinating all else within itself. But this is only to say that the God it arrives at is a cosmological God, a God in a cosmos, and not God in Himself—which is what is sought.

If we think of the athlete as one who moves through a series of steps to arrive at a point where he explodes with finality, we can make some use of the above analyses. The athlete can be said to be in a state of tension, trying to accomplish something, but he must get in the position where the effort is integral to him at that time in such a way as to require for balance a similar integral act. His concentration on an act here has its reciprocal in a concentration on a final act, but he can move to the final act only if he takes himself to be now at a nonfinal position. The effort to concentrate makes him similar to what he will be at the end, but he must at the same time assume the position of being one who is at a stage earlier than the last and proper one. His concentration must be accompanied by a dis-evaluation of the finality of that with which he is now occupied.

If we take the second form of testimony as our guide, what we have instead is the individual in a tensional relation to a prospective goal, which tensional relation is in fact maintained by the power of some more remote, indeed the final, goal.

If instead we take the third form of testimony as our guide, we have the individual as not yet fully organized, but subject to a unification by a prospective goal which can so operate only so far as there is a more remote, indeed the final, goal operating on it.

March 11

Following the clue of the account of otherness as providing testimony to the reality of God, one can approach the problem of learning in a way not previously discussed by me. The individual can be said to be polymorphously incomplete or tensed, and to master, and thereby identify himself with, a number of activities. This will leave him tensed with respect to the remainder, which in the ideal case will be the terminus of his efforts. The learner will, in short, not only attend to the stages which precede the final climactic one, but will include them within himself, so that as encompassing the final prospect, he is an incomplete and tensed being who has made the previous stages part of himself.

This approach can also be carried over to the mind-body problem.

The individual faces the heterogeneity of the world as encompassed within a rational whole. The nature of that rational whole he does not know, but he understands everything as somehow being encompassed within this, since it is presumably governed by a rationale. Experience, reflection, and teaching make him attend to laws, habits, probable courses, etc., of most of the things. The more he understands things in terms of such laws, rules, habits, etc., the more does he make them to be within his own rational life. What remains unexplained by these laws will either have to be viewed as irrational, inexplicable, surd, or will have to be thought to have a distinctive rationale of its own.

When we face an isolated aberrational case, we take it so far to be without a rationale. It is an accident, the outcome of luck, an instance of contingency. But when we have a series of activities which we cannot understand in terms of the laws, etc., we have used before, we are forced to credit it with its own rationale. And this is what we mean by the style of the individual. In the case of many animals, we are content to treat their sequence of activities as having only a bodily rationale as guided by an intelligence—which is to say by a capacity to grasp the import of some things for their welfare. We speak of an animal as having intelligence precisely because the animal behaves in terms of possibilities; intelligence is our term for the rationale which is occupied with the present in terms of the possible.

We speak of a man having a mind when he engages in a series of activities which cannot be reduced to mere intelligence. He does not merely treat the present perceived content as a sign of what is to be next, but relates possibilities to one another, governs his acts by the possibilities, and sees that what he faces as a possibility must have a different import (or in the limiting case, the identical import) for others that it has for himself. He shows that this is the case by making use of symbolic apparatus in language and by engaging in a series of acts which remain unintelligible unless understood to be produced under this type of guidance.

We know that a man has a mind when we know that what we have accepted as the rationale of all other things does not make his activities rational. We take his mind to be normal if it is an explanation of acts which are similar to those that other men engage in; we take it to be not normal, and therefore either better or worse than the minds of the rest, when his activities are aberrational and are to be explained by a reference to the individual's being occupied with odd possibilities in the way in which other men are occupied with their more conventional ones. Alternatively, we can explain his aberrant activities as being due to his occupation with the ordinary possibilities, but in a special way. The first of these methods emphasizes the imagination, the second the creativity or conditions to which one is subject.

We know what a man has in mind by seeing what he does next. We follow out the course of his action and modify our understanding of the nature of his mind accordingly. We did not come to know that he had a mind by making an analogy with our own, but by facing him as a locus of activities to be understood in a way in which the rationale we now impose on others cannot serve. A man can of course become routinized, and operate the way others do. We account for the things men do by referring to that which is common to all their minds, reserving a reference to the individual mind only so far as we seek to deal with a particular activity as occurring in a particular setting. All men will then be viewed as having similar minds with local notes. We move to the acknowledgment of their individual minds only when we see them making rational certain activities which others make rational in other ways.

We can know that others have minds, and can know what they have in mind. We cannot know the qualitative feel of their pains and pleasures, their thoughts and inferences. But we can act and expect in accord with them. This we do when we sympathize. We say to another that we know what he has in mind, or that we feel with him. These are precise expressions, revelatory of the fact that we do not repeat or penetrate to what he is on the inside, but are content to be in accord with him. If we keep abreast of his rhythms when he is in pain, we can be said to know his pain. And we can know that he has a pain because this accounts for his grimaces, his cries, his wincing, his retreats, etc. If he is making believe, we think we can sooner or later detect in his actions something which tells us that the rationale of what he does is to be found not in the set of grimaces, etc., which normally are explained as the forefront of a privately felt pain, but in a larger set which will deal with the former as an expression of a desire to deceive.

We see the entire world as being capable of a rational explanation, either as a single totality or as made up of smaller rational schemes, of which the minimal one is an individual man with a mind. This seeing is but the acceptance of the world as a datum for our own use of a mind.

It is because we want to understand, because we want to have an explanation of whatever we confront, that we accredit the world with a rationale. This accrediting is no deliberate act; it is part of the very act of acknowledging something before us. When we do this, we exercise our minds in a way that is not necessarily manifest in any act. So far no one but ourselves is aware that we have a mind. But others can be made aware of it by noting our expectations with respect to what we confront. We reveal our rationality first in our expectations which accompany our endowing the world with rationality; and then we reveal it in our particular acts which enable another to look at us as a source of acts which require ourselves alone to provide the rationale.

March 13

We intend by having a highly indeterminate future before us as that at which we wish to arrive. Every act we engage in before we arrive at that future is faced as something to be mastered. While mastering it, we continue to face the future as that which is yet to be mastered. From the very beginning, consequently, we are bifocal, having our attention directed at something to be done here and now at the same time that we look toward something to be done later, either as a mere end, as a desired climax, as that which completes, etc.

The more we fill out the means to the future we wish to arrive at, the more sharply does that future come into focus. The more we are men who have already managed to go through various stages, the more evident it becomes just what it is these stages are leading us toward. We get a more determinate idea of the future when we act purposively, but we get an even more determinate idea the more closely we approach it by going through the antecedent stages.

We face the future, finally, as that which is the finality for ourselves as having gone through the various stages. Before we arrive at that point, we are men who are aware that what we are to go through is for the sake of arriving at the finality. Teaching a person to master a complicated process should from the very beginning involve some effort to make him bifocal, so that he, while concentrating on an immediate task, is aware that there is a final task to be accomplished, and which he will see come into clearer focus when he completes his immediate task.

March 14

A prospective goal has three effects on the subordinate and antecedent things one is to do, and they have at the same time some effect on it. *1*] It defines them to be preliminary to it at the same time that they bring it into sharper and sharper focus in the course of being carried out. 2] It gives them a value or import at the same time that they define it to be a climax of what is done. 3] It makes a unity of their multiplicity at the same time that they bring it closer to realization.

Faced with some particular step in training, we must take it to be a means to an end dimly discerned, see that it has a value and meaning for that end, and that it finds a place in a totality of means by virtue of that end. Otherwise we cannot make it into a step in a single organic act, with that end intended or purposed.

When we use some such pattern as this to clarify the nature of testimony, particularly with respect to a proof of God (such as that offered in the *Modes*), we must recognize that the testimony is affected then and there by that to which it testifies. God should (in the *Modes*) have been seen to be the final terminus when and as an actuality makes itself a representative of the rest, and indeed to aid in the making of it such a representative; He should also have been seen to give the Ideal a meaning and value as that which is forever relevant to actualities. And He should have been seen to be that whose Being or nature or acts not only give unity to Existence, but that He is in the different beginnings of routes which lead to and are included in Him.

March 25

A game can be broken down into a number of factors. It involves 1] a challenge in the form of some obstacle or goal; 2] a standard of excellence or a statement of limits in terms of which the challenge is to be met; 3] a set of rules in accord with which participants are to act; 4] participants who are to meet the challenge; 5] an activity where the challenge is met by the participants in accord with the rules; 6] a record of the way in which the challenge is finally met.

1] The challenge in a game involving physical exercise may have reference to the need to master the body, to master equipment, to master the environment, or to face demands made by nature, animals, or men. The men may be copresent or may have existed in the past.

2] The standard of excellence or the stated limits mean that it is not enough to master what one confronts, but that it must be done with a certain striving to achieve excellence, or to accomplish the task within the set limits of time, or distance, or use of materials.

3] Without rules there would be mere play. The rules define the beginning and the end, the method by which one is to move from one to the other, the conditions which must be met if one is to participate, what would constitute infractions, and what must be done after such and such an act. The rules are exemplified in the game, and are there given details and interrelated, sometimes in novel ways.

4] It is possible for a man to enter a game and not be a participant. This happens at times with overheated spectators. And there are games in which the participants are subject to the penalty of having to sit out of the game for a period because they have fouled a certain number of times. A participant is defined by the rules and is the producer of a game. When it is animals that compete, or when machines are sent off on their own, it is still true there are men directly or indirectly involved. Those men can be said to be genuine participants, in somewhat the way in which an archer is a participant in the shooting of an arrow at the target. Both start the flight and then have to see what happens when the matter is out of their further control. In the case of greyhound racing or cock fighting, the direction of the contest is less under control than it is in the case of archery, but this seems to be only a matter of degree.

5] A game is played. Playing a game is a process by which one moves from the beginning to the end in accord with the defined rules. The playing is a single event, even though it may be played in a number of distinct sets, rounds, innings, periods, etc. It is a playing which stresses accuracy, speed, or endurance, or some combination of these.

6] If a game is part of a sport, some record of it is to be kept. The records we call "records," i.e., those which state the best results achieved up to that time under those circumstances, are merely the ones we use to define the standard which one ought minimally to meet in order to be a competitor of those who then or earlier had set us such a standard.

March 29

A contest occurs by meeting *challenges*, on the part of *prepared participants* who *act* in accordance with *rules*, to meet *standards*, so as to achieve *excellence*.

Challenges: Under this heading one ought to consider A] what have been the challenges in the past; B] how the challenges have changed; C] the nature of obstacles; D] challenges set by oneself; E] by fellow man; F] by fellow competitor; G] by the records of the past; H] by age; I] by sex; J] by race; K] by nation; L] by social background; M] by the estimate one has of oneself; N] by brute nature; O] by time; P] by space; Q] by causality; R] by the risk of pain; S] by the risk of injury; T] by the risk of death; U] by the joy of meeting the challenge; V] by the pain of losing; W] by the value of the winning; X] by the need to sacrifice; Y] by the need to deny oneself; z] by the need to separate oneself off from the world of contemporaries and irrelevant occurrences; a'] by how one is sustained by others; b'] by the achievement of health; or c'] by good body tone.

Is each sport defined by a different challenge? Are all challenges given or in part, at least, defined by the athlete? Are there challenges which sport could consider but does not now?

Preparation: This should deal with such matters as a] man's natural gifts; b] training by a step-by-step process; c] training by considering the whole transaction; d] training in a different kind of activity than the one the athlete is going to compete in; e] character building; f] strategy; g] tension; h] relaxation; i] aggression; j] the role of reflexes; k] specific problems raised by sex, l] age, m] race, or n] custom; o] the problem of diet; p] the nature of a warming up; q] spring training; r] recruitment of promising men to be trained; s] training rules and regulation; t] anxiety; u] fear of failure; v] the coach as model; w] practical judgment; or x] attitude toward future opponent. Are different preparations needed for different sports, apart from the concern with the particular muscles involved?

Participants: Under this heading one can consider the problem of a] the individual contestant; b] the team member; c] the problem of roles; d] the problem of loyalty; e] the difference between the athlete and the craftsman; f] between the athlete and the artist; g] between the athlete and the spectator; h] the change from the training to the participant stage; i] decisiveness; j] participating via machines; k] participating via animals; l] freedom; m] determinism; n] spontaneity; o] handicaps; p] amateur, q] professional; r] interference during play by managers, coaches, etc.; s] loneliness; or t] separation by sexes, ages, weights, experiences, training. Does one belong to something larger than the game?

Acting: The participant acts in an athletic contest by making use of his body with some skill and strength. The nature of his action can be considered under a number of heads: a] movement; b] unit acts; c] event of the game; d] rhythm of the game; e] unit game; f] crises; g] tactics; h] intention; i] purpose; j] against competitors; k] with teammates; l] gracefulness; m] its warlike nature; n] the effect of the context; o] the effect of the spectators; p] the effect of wrong decision; q] exhibitions; r] the letdown; s] effect of possible defeat; t] effect of actual defeat; u] role of possible victory; v] effect of actual victory; w] terrain; x] luck; y] identification with body; z] identification with team; A'] identification with equipment; B'] locus of the pleasure; C'] effect of hitting another; D'] emotions E'] purging; or F'] supporting others. Is there a difference between the acts of professionals and amateurs?

Rules: Under this heading we can consider A] general rules that apply to all sports; B] specific rules for a given sport; C] conditions in which the rules are to be applied; D] definition of a sport; E] habituation of rules; F] conscious acceptance of rules; G] comparison of rules; H] play; I] the number of games required; J] the modification of rules; K] rules for determining what is a record; L] rules for determining what is a victory; M] penalty.

Standards: Under this heading we should consider A] dedication; B] self-sacrifice; C] who sets the standards (owner, spectators, past, models); D] fair play; E] maturity; F] elimination contests; G] speed; H] accuracy; I] strength; J] endurance; K] the role of judges; L] different standards for professionals; M] standards for different ages; N] standards for different sports; O] drugs.

Excellence: A] Is this the true aim; B] should it be conscious; C] excellence with equipment; D] excellence in one's body; E] excellence in character; F] excellence in records; G] the feeling of defeat; H] the feeling of victory; I] anticlimactic character of the result; J] the role of competition; K] money awards; L] favorable conditions and handicaps; M] who gets the credit—trainer, participant, etc.; N] place of entertainment; O] different types of failure and different forms of cowardice, etc.; P] winning respect from opponents; Q] winning respect from spectators; R] overcoming despair and sentimentalism; S] change in the game because of equipment—vaulting poles, lighter bats, etc.; T] substitute for crime; U] religion; V] effect on future life; W] defeat as defeat of oneself; X] defeat as contributing to victory by man; Y] defeat as revealing man; Z] defeat as test of character; A'] defeat as indifferent; B'] defeat to be feared; C'] abstract opponent and concrete team; D'] is there satisfaction with result; E'] civilization and knowing others; F'] cost in training, etc.; G'] freedom from guilt, fear, self-doubt; H'] representative against machines.

April 1

Beware of the friendly philosopher. The true philosopher starts without any friends, and over the course of his life alienates the rest. This is not done deliberately; nor is it desired. It is inevitable, for he works at questioning the very categories in terms of which all live. This does not mean he is a sceptic or an iconoclast, for not only is his criticism laced with sympathy, but he may end his critical examination with an approval of what he set himself to examine objectively, coldly, and radically. But those who do not want even a suspicion of doubt to cross the field of their firm beliefs find him rightly to be an ever present danger.

Beware of the programmatic philosopher. The true philosopher does not outline a special method, or mode of thinking, or a set of categories that he is going to use. His is an exploration, and he is not sure just where he is coming out. But the programmatic philosopher refines a method and specifies a promise, all the while doing nothing effective to use the one or bring about the other.

Beware of the inconstant philosopher. The true philosopher changes his mind, sees the error of his previous views, and modifies his position under criticism. But the inconstant philosopher abandons a position under fire, and then assumes another. He reveals that his first position was not embraced after reflection on the issue from all sides, but was taken to be a consequence of the acceptance of some questionable assumption. Instead of merely abandoning that questionable assumption to take another which has the same defects, it would have been better for him if he had questioned the idea of starting with assumptions which were questionable. The inconstant philosopher is an honest man with an inadequate view of philosophy.

April 2

Granted that there is something that transcends the empirical world, one can approach it in a number of ways. One can make reference to it in the terms which one uses ordinarily, but now made absolute. This would seem to be the way in which the Whiteheadians deal with God, who is taken to be an actual occasion, like the things in the world, but nevertheless distinguished from them by his everlastingness, his completeness of memory, etc. The position is a variant of Leibniz's, whose God is a monad like the other monads, but one that is perfectly clear and capable of producing the others. But an extreme case of the particulars of this world is precisely what a transcendent is not; it is on an entirely different level of being and discourse.

One might deal with the transcendent as that which is outside the kind of language or concepts or method characteristic of the empirical world. Instead of trying to "know" it, one would try to give oneself to it, to immerse oneself in it, to identify oneself with it. This is the approach that the mystics take; it is also the position of Kierkegaard with his "subjectivity." The difficulty here is knowing that one is not in error, of making sure that one has given oneself to God rather than to the devil. Moreover, it is possible to give oneself to finite things. There should be no incompatibility between subjectivity and objectivity. Some mystics see this. Without abandoning the creeds and affirmations of particular religions, they seek to attain a special relationship with that God. But since they do have to leave the finite domain behind in order to become "subjective," they do not provide themselves with a proper guide.

One might insist on a distinctive kind of knowledge, having its own kind of claims, checks, methods, and the like. This is the route taken by the metaphysician. Without this, there will be an unbridgeable and perhaps unknowable gap between what is finite and the transcendent.

There is no incompatibility between this last view and one which insists that one can speak of the transcendents in finite terms functioning as eccentric particulars. Indeed, the intelligibility of the eccentric particulars in grammar or as things, depends on their being oriented in the transcendent reality. All the knowledge that is obtained in the previous alternative is now expressed in the last alternative, but in a distinctive context or grammar.

Anthony Quinton has remarked that those whom some thinkers would call philosophers, he would call sages; and those whom they called logicians, he would call philosophers. Is this only a verbal matter? I think not. At the very least it raises a number of questions.

Is it thought that the sages are a breed apart? Apparently so, for Quinton goes on to make a sharp distinction between those who are occupied with being precise and clear, and those who have vision. This would seem to indicate that, for him at least, the sages cannot also be philosophers. Would that mean that one could not have been or should not have been a philosopher (in Quinton's sense) before trying to be a sage? But there surely is no incompatibility between being precise and technical and analytic and having vision. Why not then reserve the name of philosopher for those who have both virtues?

If this last suggestion be followed, we can speak of logicians and sages as extremes which should be united. Neither type would have to be treated as superior to the other; only the two together would make the full philosopher. This answer preserves the "negative" aspect of Quinton's view, since it finds room for his "sages"; but it rejects his attempt to preempt the term philosopher for a certain set of specialists, and in that act preclude one from speaking of Plato, Schopenhauer, Neitzsche, and Hegel as philosophers. But in contrast with those who would oppose Quinton by contending that only those whom he terms "sages" are true philosophers, it emphasizes the fact that to have vision is also not enough. The vision must be articulated, worked out, communicated. But this is exactly what the systematic and great philosophers have done in the past.

Quinton's suggestion has the value of making one see that the eulogistic use of the term "philosopher" should lead to the recognition of a type of enterprise which embraces his two contrastive ones as extremes within a single whole.

April 3

Growing up involves in part a growing into a position in society. This is not easy, particularly for the young man. There is much to learn, far more than it seems he could possibly manage; he is shown only pieces of it, and is forced to manage in good part through trial and error. And the more surely he makes his way, the more surely he finds that life has become too easy. He has much energy to spend. Unable to spend it in the guise of one who conforms to the going ways, he either must express it idly in byplays, or violently in destructions and mischief. The answer to his answers has usually been to apply more and more discipline, but this in effect is but a device for making him conform, or at least not revolt from the given patterns. But he still has energy in reserve; if he is really prevented from making use of it, he is prevented from growing any further than the position in which he is now confined.

A better answer to his dilemma is provided in games and sport. These not only make ample provision for the use of whatever energy he may have, but they add the factor of discipline, and even demand at times prior training and preparation. The best solution is that of athletics, where one not only expends energy in controlled and disciplined ways, but strives for an excellence that goes beyond what mere exuberance or mischief could produce.

What makes a young man take excellence as a serious objective? He is just escaping from the romantic period. His diverse and unfocused energies and interests become polarized by any figure who stands out as the very epitomization of what a man can be. He models himself on someone whom he takes to be a model man, and it is with this in mind that he first turns to athletics as a world in which he is willing to live for a while.

This tempts a formula: in fear and terror one points primarily to Actuality as a final mode of Being; to have the situation under control one makes use of a representative of the Being, God, in the shape of some object of worship; to become the master of oneself one makes oneself into an instance of the Ideal; to express oneself with control, and thus to use the energy one has deliberately, one practices and creates. The first leads to knowledge, the second to religion, the third to athletics, and the fourth to art. The young man prefers the third because identification with a model is easier than the practiced control of one's creative energies. Having accomplished the identification, the control will be easier, but it will no longer be in the service of an art, but only in the service of the craft of mastering the means by which the identification can be carried out in fact.

April 5

When we detach ourselves from daily life in order to give ourselves to religion, mathematics, art, metaphysics, and the like, we put a bracket about the daily world. That bracket and the way in which it is put changes in accord with what we attach ourselves. One should therefore be able to say that there are public and empirical ways of determining what is privately entertained.

This overall relation to the empirical which we exhibit when we are attached elsewhere is a constant. It should therefore affect every encounter which we may have with empirical items due to their intrusion on us. The very act of bracketing the entire empirical world is one with the attempt to close off the influence of this or that particular empirical occurrence in that world. We do not attend to the particular occurrence, for on the hypothesis we are attending to something nonempirical instead. But we maintain our attitude toward this nonempirical so far as we have a characteristic way of thrusting away the entire empirical domain and its particular contents, when they force themselves upon us.

The religious man, for example, may exclude an intrusive noise by treating it as profane, secular, as that which is a temptation, whereas the mathematician may exclude it by treating it as irrelevant, vague, as that which is comparatively unintelligible. Remaining with these, what seems to be the case is that the one will see the noise as somehow offensive, whereas the other will see it as somehow perplexing. The more intrusive the item becomes for the one, the more he will reject, exclude, barricade it; the more intrusive it becomes for the other, the more he will be ready to question it, analyze it, bring it inside his initial frame. There will then be differentiatable activities on the part of both, revelatory of the fact that they have attached themselves to different kinds of realities which are nonempirical.

We will not be able to tell from an examination of the empirical just what particular items in the nonempirical realms are being attended to, except so far as we then go on to express ourselves in language, concepts, gestures, or activities, when they will reveal themselves to be eccentric particulars, particulars which do not behave as other particulars do, but which can be made intelligible by being oriented toward the nonempirical.

April 17

One can be said to obey a command if he does what is commanded, even though the doing be only a reaction to the sound heard. The dog does not understand what is being said, but it obeys if it has been habituated to behave in a certain way when it hears its master speak in a certain tone of voice.

Conforming to a rule, following a map, learning, following a recipe or instructions are not to be understood in the way an obedience to a command is to be understood. Sometimes an obedience to a command, though, has the pattern of a conformity to a rule. A rule interrelates various items to make a single structure or schema. To conform to this schema, it is not necessary to instance it, for one could conceivably act in such a way that the structure is not exemplified but is merely something held to or something claimed to be legitimate.

We conform to a rule by accepting various items and activities as possessing features designated in the rule. We use a map by acknowledging that such and such is a place which has the role of a beginning for a trip, and that such and such a set of moves by us is a traveling. The map tells us that such and such can be a terminating place and we, having accepted such and such as a beginning and such and such as a traveling, accept in the same way that such and such is the terminating place. When we subject this result to another test and find that it lacks a feature which we demand that a terminating place possess, we have the alternative of holding that the map is wrong, or that we were wrong to accept such and such as the beginning, or such and such as a traveling. We took, for example, the outskirts of the city to be a proper designation for the city, and we took driving to be a proper way of traveling. But we do not find that we are at a place which we can independently accept as that which the map says is the place at which we arrive. The map was for walking perhaps, or for planes, or we started at the wrong place, or we lost the way.

If we accept the map and the starting point, as well as the mode of traveling, the end must be accepted as being as appropriate as the beginning and the moves were. This is what it means to conform to the rule, to follow the map: it is impossible not to have such and such be acceptable, once we have this and that to be acceptable, unless the rule is not sound.

We are conforming to a sound rule when we accept such and such entities and moves as having certain predesignated features, and accept such and such entities, which terminate the moves, to have equally acceptable features. The entities, moves, and termini may not have such features; what they must have is the status of being accepted as having those features. If a recipe calls for one spice, we may substitute another; if it tells us to bake, we might broil, etc. The outcome may be a tasty, satisfactory meal, which is what the recipe promises and which we, in the way in which we accept one spice as satisfactory in place of that which the recipe requests, find satisfactory as a terminus. It may be a meal which from other perspectives is found to be spoiled, tasteless, etc. From those perspectives, we will be said to have failed to use the proper materials or to have not proceeded correctly—i.e., not followed the recipe. But that is only to say that what we accept as answering to the descriptions in the recipe may not be acceptable to others.

April 18

We conform to a rule when   1] having accepted certain items as meeting the conditions of the rule,   2] we go on to accept other items. The process of "going on" is proper just so far as it yields the other acceptable items. It makes no difference just how the process takes place; it is a process which conforms to the rule just so far as it ends with the other acceptable items.

If we have a rule of inference, and treat the process as a way of substituting the conclusion for the premiss, we acknowledge any number of acts as substitutions, providing they do give us that acceptable conclusion. We can cross out the premiss, write over the premiss, write below the premiss, etc. All these are equally satisfactory ways of substituting for the premiss if the end result is the acceptable conclusion.

We can now write *modus ponens* as:

1] $p \,) \, q$
2] $p \rightarrow p$
3] $\therefore$
4] $q \leftarrow q$

Line *1* gives us the rule. Line *2* gives us a proposition p, possessed of the sessile character truth. By placing it under the p of the rule (an act indicated by the arrow) we define it as acceptable as a beginning. We do not give it a transportable character; we merely say that though it has the sessile character "truth" it can function as the beginning of a warranted act and thus as though it had a transportable character. The third line is "therefore"; we make no prescription as to just what path it will take. All we ask is that it yield a q which we can thereupon take to meet the condition of an end (a fact indicated by the arrow which moves from the q, as arrived at by the process of "therefore," to the q as meeting the condition of the rule. More precisely:

1] $p \,) \, q$
2] p
3] $p \rightarrow p$
4] $\therefore$
5] q
6] $q \leftarrow q$

On this account there is no risk in inference. Nor is there any conversion of a sessile into a transportable character. All there is is the acceptance of some item as conforming to a rule (line *3*), an actual process (line *4*) which arrives at another item (line *5*) that is then taken to be acceptable in the very same sense and with the same justification (arbitrary, reasonable, habitual, conventional, etc.) as that which allowed us to produce line *3*.

This account seems to provide us with an encounter with the conclusion (line *5*) before we have it as that which is concluded to in accordance with the rule. Yet we seem often to infer and then look about for an encounter. But is this not to confuse two senses of encounter? The outcome of an inference is an encountered terminus which we then make conform to the rule; but what we want is to have the conclusion encountered in experience. This would require us to have an experiential process of moving to the conclusion in place of a mere mental process.

When we use a map or follow a recipe, we go through an experiential process; we experientially encounter the result. It is q of line 5 which, when obtained merely through a process of thought, that we do not find altogether satisfactory, even when it is made to yield line 6.

April 19

When it is said that we subsume the premiss under the rule, we in fact take two steps. One step involves the acknowledgment of the premiss as a true proposition; the other involves the acknowledgment of this true proposition as an acceptable beginning for the inference. When we come to the conclusion, either through the manipulation of diagrams, through a substitution, by an association of ideas, by using various proof structures, etc., we arrive at that which is offered as meeting the conditions of the rule for a proper terminus. The fact that we are not satisfied merely with an inference means that we want the conclusion not only to be acceptable according to the rule, but to be one which is true in the sense in which the initial proposition, which we used for a premiss, was.

The *modus ponens* is therefore to be written as:

$$
\begin{array}{lll}
1] & & \underline{p \quad) \quad q} \\
2] & p & \\
3] & p \to p & \\
4] & \quad p \to p & \\
5] & \qquad \therefore & \\
6] & & q \\
7] & & \underline{q \leftarrow q} \\
8] & & q \to q \\
9] & & q.
\end{array}
$$

The first line states the rule; the second gives us a proposition that is true on its own account; the third is the move from the true proposition to it as a premiss; the fourth is the move from the premiss to a beginning in accordance with the rule; the fifth is the inferential move; the sixth is the arrival at the conclusion; the seventh is the presentation of the conclusion as justified by the rule. After the inference is over, we can move from the conclusion arrived at to the conclusion as standing apart, and from that to the proposition as true by itself.

In the usual treatment of inference we ignore steps 2 and 3, and fail to see that step 4 is necessary if we are to have something on which we in fact can act. It would be more precise if we included a step which gives us the beginning by itself, and if we treated steps 2 and 3 as separated from the inference the way in which steps 8 and 9 are. If we follow this suggestion we get:

$$
\begin{array}{lll}
& 1] & p \ ) \ q \\
\hline
2] & p & \\
3] & p \to p & \\
4] & p \longrightarrow p & \\
& 5] & p \\
& 6] & \therefore \\
& 7] & q \\
& 8] & q \longleftarrow q \\
\hline
& 9] & q \to q \\
& 10] & q.
\end{array}
$$

Here the first line gives us the rule; lines 2, 3, and 4, give us a true proposition, a premiss, and a warranted beginning with that premiss; lines 5 to 8 give us the inference to a terminus, q, and a warranting of this as conforming to the condition of a terminus. This is the end of the inference. We can subsequently take the terminus and move to it as having an independently established truth (9), and finally take it as such an independent truth (10).

When we follow a road, the road has a role similar to that of a rule. But instead of being something privately undergone, the use of the road not only involves an acceptance of some position (2), the acknowledgment of this as a beginning of a trip (3), and the acceptance of it as a beginning of a trip on that road (4), but the use of it as a start (5) and the actual movement over the road (6), until we arrive at some other position (7) which we then attempt to justify as meeting the condition of an end of a trip on that road (8). That this arrival point can be the position at which we do something else is shown on lines 9 and 10.

The concern for lines 9 and 10 indicate that there is a conviction that what we arrive at has other roles than that of being arrived at; it is a position from which we can engage in other activities as well. An inference in conformity to a rule can tell us only that we do get a terminus which

meets the condition of the rule, but not that this terminus also is one
from which we can take a start in another direction if we wish.

April 20

Not every activity which starts with an acceptable beginning
and ends with an acceptable result is satisfactory. Otherwise there would
be nothing like a violation of rules, unfair play, and the like. The rule
defines a range of permitted activities, and it is only by staying within
that range that one can arrive at an end which can be offered as acceptable in the same sense as the beginning was taken to be.

A trip or a baking according to a recipe differ from a game in that
the latter is satisfied with producing a result which is acceptable as a
terminus that conforms to the rule. When we go on a trip or follow a
recipe, we want to have the terminus serve as the beginning of something
else—say a visit or an eating. When we treat the game as an instance of
a sport, the acceptable ending of a game is subject to a further test and
judgment, to see if it is to fit in with other endings. The commissions
which determine whether or not records have been made impose criteria
on an activity which conforms to the rules. They may at times eliminate
someone who has been victorious and followed the rules. Thus a com-
mission might wish to exclude a man of a particular creed or race, or
one who had previously performed as a professional in some other sport,
or one who was not of a proper social class. Even the Olympic Games
once had days for men of certain ethnic classes, who were not permitted
to compete with others.

Jim Thorpe was stripped of his honors and medals when it was discovered that he had played professional baseball as a youth; Kelly was
not allowed to compete in sculling because he was not an aristocrat. In
these cases we have men conforming to a rule by making an acceptable
beginning, engaging in activities which the rule defines as permissible,
and ending with what is an acceptable ending. But the entire enterprise
of achieving the ending, the very act of conforming to the rule is judged
adversely in these cases.

We could reduce a rejection of some result (even though it conforms
to the rule) by envisaging a larger rule, or an additional rule which is
violated. One could say that there is a tacit rule to the effect that the
competition, and thus the kind of beginning, activity, or ending, which is
permitted, requires that the contestants be of such and such a sex, age,
social class, color, etc. We could acknowledge such a rule for a particular

game, or we could acknowledge it only when the game is dealt with as an instance of a sport and thus as subject to criteria beyond those which are involved in a particular isolated game. If the rule be used in a particular game, we could still bring in another rule to determine how this game is to be treated in relation to other games. Consequently, we must say that there is always a rule of some kind which is added to the rule followed out in an isolated game and in terms of which the game and its results are to be evaluated in the context of the sport.

Mathematics is like an isolated game in that we are content to have the outcome be acceptable if arrived at in an approved manner and if its acceptance is like that accorded the beginning. We don't ask if the mathematical conclusion is legitimate apart from the rule-conforming process of attaining it. If we did ask such a question, we would have to refer to a platonic realm of eternal mathematical truths to which our result must conform, or to a world of scientific occurrences which our result is taken to refer to. But like the outcome of the game, the outcome of the mathematical thinking is an occurrence arrived at. It is not something concluded to in consonance with the rule until it has been taken to be an acceptable outcome, which is to say until it is identified as the kind of result which the rule permits to be terminal.

Usually we do not look to the rule to discover whether our activity is appropriate. The activity of getting to a result is guided by the result; we conform to the rule by intending the result and therefore enabling the result as a prospect to guide the way in which we make use of the beginning.

An intention can be said to make use of the conclusion as acceptable in order to guide the activity to the conclusion as a mere outcome. That outcome is acceptable precisely because it has all the way been under the control of the conclusion as acceptable. This means that there is no first arriving at a result and then seeing if it is acceptable as a conclusion for that rule, but only an arriving at a result which is necessarily acceptable because it is a result intended. One is still left with the question as to whether or not this result has an objective status apart from the act of arriving at it, so far as one is interested in something more than a particular game or a particular mathematical result, taken by themselves.

An intention makes it possible for the ending to be acceptable and the activity which arrives at it to be proper only because the intention is the rule given direction and made to operate through the agency of the prospective terminus. When we arrive at the terminus, we have gone through an activity and characterized the terminus as acceptable in terms of the given rule.

April 23

Fear is normally a warning of danger. It may lead one to a mistaken strategy, prompting one to retreat, abandon, sacrifice, or deny oneself, instead of advancing and struggling. The retreat, etc., may end with one in a worse state than would have been, had one struggled. The coward saves his skin for the moment, but he may win the abuse of others, the loss of self-respect, and perhaps even invite injury no less severe than that from which he had run away.

There is wisdom sometimes in running away; knowing what to fear, as Plato remarked, is part of the meaning of bravery. Fear as we speak of it ordinarily means fearing when one ought not to fear, or when one does not see altogether what the situation is and demands. It leads us to overestimate the threat and to under-evaluate what we ourselves can do.

There is fear of a physical nature, a fear that one might be physically injured. There is also a fear that one may fail intellectually. This is a strange fear for intellectuals to have, for the intellectual life is one which every honest man finds to be rewarding. If he does not succeed in winning the honors or respect of others, he may win the joy of discovery, or even the joy of seeing just where he had been wrong. At the very least, he presents himself as a model of what an intellectual is, of what it is like to be an honest man trying to discover something. He can act as a beacon for those who follow.

It is conceivable, of course, that a man might be misconstrued by all who live then and later; his honest struggle may be ignored or even interpreted as hypocrisy, self-exploitation, and the like. But his own life will have been lived properly, and so far as this is the case, he cannot possibly lose, no matter what others think. The outlook for most, however, is even more rewarding than that. Other men are usually perceptive enough to note one's basic virtues as well as one's vices.

The intellectual who fears to put pen to paper or to send off the results of his thinking denies himself the opportunity to see himself as others might, to subject his ideas to criticism by himself and others, and to possibly achieve the kind of success he would like to attain but now fears he will not have. The failure to adventure on the part of the intellectual but brings him to the stage which is of less value than that which he would have achieved had he engaged in the inquiry and failed to achieve the result he sought, for this, as was just observed, does allow him to live through the process of inquiry, and does allow him to discover what is not possible, and what it is he knows and does not know.

A somewhat related phenomenon is the hesitation on the part of some intellectuals to pursue a type of inquiry or to change a specialization so as to engage in activities which are more suitable to their talents, insights, and abilities. Too many continue to carry out the line of endeavor which they had been directed toward by their teachers or by the tradition of the profession, even though they are aware, often quite clearly, that they are not making progress or that the values and stresses of the chosen activity do not answer to what they are best able to master. They are afraid to cut themselves off for a time from the established or prevailing doctrines, forgetting that there is nothing like a fixed and established body of truths or methods, and that nothing can be achieved of significance without adventure and thus without the risk of failure.

May 1

A popular publican has recently said that on behalf of an ailing friend, he prayed in a Roman Catholic Cathedral, an Episcopalian church, and a Jewish synagogue. His remark raises a number of interesting issues.

He undoubtedly took his prayer to be a petition in which he asked for a favor from God. If this is true, he supposed that God "heard" petitions, and directly intervened in human affairs. But whether he petitioned or not, he evidently supposed that these various places of worship were appropriate places in which to present his prayer. He would be justified on the ground that they were all sacred places where men made the most direct or effective contact with God. (He said that he "touched all the bases," but this is evidently not correct, for there are many more than three religions.)

It could be urged that there is no need for a man to make more than one prayer. The efficacy of a prayer is surely not a function of the number of times it is offered, if it has any efficacy at all. One could even say that it makes no difference where the prayer is offered, for God is omnipresent, and can be reached at any place. But it is more correct to observe, I think, that it is never enough to be in a place of worship in order to be able to pray properly. If the place makes a difference, it makes it only for one who has become part of the religion itself. There can be nothing gained by a non-Jew praying in a synagogue; if his prayer is efficacious or appropriate, it is because the place or condition under which it is expressed is irrelevant. No one, merely by being in a place which is sacred by virtue of some religious occurrence or tradition, achieves sacrality by that fact. This is a conclusion analogous to that drawn by medievals regarding the eating of the Eucharist by a mouse; the mouse does not participate in the transmutation of the "substance," for this is a miracle occurring only for those who have faith.

These observations can be summarized in the alternatives: one can validly pray to God anywhere, or one can validly pray to God only when one is able to take advantage of the sacrality of some occasion or place. The alternatives are not exclusive. It is possible to hold that one can pray validly anywhere—for it is possible to maintain that every single place and occasion in the world is sacred—and yet suppose that one must take advantage of the sacrality of some particular occasion or place. The difference between the sacrality offered by some religious institution and that of an ordinary place is that the former does tie one up with a tradition and thus with some signal religious event where the sacral character is certified and intensified. In compensation, the sacrality of an ordinary place allows one to make reference to God as a cosmic being, whose efficacies and interests are not necessarily confined to those who follow some particular religious activity.

It is not clear whether our publican thought that he was addressing the same God from three different angles, or instead was addressing three different Gods. I suppose if pressed he would say the former was what he had in mind; but then it becomes a question whether it is necessary to approach God from more than one angle. In a sense, his actions were based on an implicit criticism of the different religions as leading us to only a dimension of God and not to God Himself; it was also implicitly supposed that some one religion might not be appropriate or satisfactory and that one had to take out insurance by taking advantage of all the opportunities. Were the analogy of a baseball player, who has to touch all the bases before he could get "home," pressed, one would have to ask if there were a special order in which one had to go to these different places of worship, and whether the prayer was efficacious only after one had gone through all three.

May 2

I have been scheduled to speak to the Yale Alumni Seminar next month on the question of a definition of the film. I had been under the impression that I would be part of a panel which would explore this question; it now turns out that I am to give an address on the matter. But as of the present, I am not very clear about the nature of the film as a work of art in contrast with other works.

One possibility is to see it as a combination of three ways of conquering the dimensions of Existence. The camera can be said to conquer space by bringing any position into prominence, making it represent all others. Juxtaposition in word or image can be said to conquer time, since it allows one to associate any moment with any other. Causality can be conquered by an imaginative replacement of a cause or an effect by any occurrence. The film can therefore be said to be a union of camera, juxtaposition, and replacement. This account combines a mechanical device with intellectual ones, but fails to do justice to the principle behind the mechanical device or to offer mechanical devices which utilize juxtaposition and replacement.

A more hopeful approach perhaps is to take account of long established ways men have employed to dislocate parts of space, time, and causality, and then seen how they might be recombined in order to illuminate the nature of space, time, and causality. Thus, a chronicle isolates occurrences according to date, and fails to link one item with another. A linkage could be provided, though, in a holiday or celebration. These would offer a new way of bringing together isolate times in a new aesthetically illuminating way. Similarly, an association of ideas can be taken to unite causal items which had been dislocated by our concepts, and which could be given an artistic form in fantasies, fables. Similarly, interest, status, power could be seen to be ways of isolating portions of space, which the camera might unite in any way it wishes, particularly with reference to the viewer. We can now take the film to be a combination of celebration, fantasy, and photography, and thus as ordering and relating space, time, and causality in themselves and in relation to one another according to the dictates of an artistic production.

The trouble with this last suggestion is that is does not take account of the fact that in the film the viewer is part of the entire situation. He does not contribute to its production, but he is taken to be a part of it. The suggestion also fails to make clear just how or why the film combines all these, and in what sense it is an art.

The problem is to get a definition of film which will show it to be a distinctive art, allow for the possibility of still other arts, relate it to previously known arts, and avoid taking it to be either the product of a number of arts, or to be the best or least significant of arts.

The previous alternative can perhaps be improved by dealing with time, space, and causality in somewhat diverse ways. The chronicle and the celebration can both be said to involve an isolation of certain moments, with the celebration there recovering its meaning in other moments. Interest and photography can be said to concentrate on the identification of places by virtue of some signal occurrence in them, and concentration and fantasy to involve the separation and then the juncture of events in a causal connection. On this view, film would be a union of celebration, photography, and fantasy.

"Celebration" seems too strong a term here. What is wanted is a reference to the fact that in the present we have opened to ourselves any moment of time. Since the time may be future, celebration will in some cases at least prove to be a misleading term. What the film does is to make any moment present, as the chronicle does, (since all items are on a level, despite their difference in date).

Apart from the film, a moment can be made present by having it enacted. "Enactment" does not involve a plot; it merely captures in the present an act which belongs in some other moment of time. An enactment, however, does not give us the occurrence as taking place in its own proper moment, which is what the film attempts to do. For an enactment to be present, yet as though it were at some other moment of time, it would be necessary to give it a setting whose purpose was to make the present observer take himself to be at some other time. We in short need an enactment in which the observer is transported to the appropriate moment, rather than one in which the occurrence is brought into the present. "Portrayal" would seem to be a more accurate term then than enactment, if one can free it from its usual association of involving a number of moments and incidents.

A portrayal can be said to be an artistic way in which chronicable items are presented. Keeping the other two terms fixed, we can now say that the film is a fantasied, photographic portrayal in which new affiliations and content are provided for causality, space, and time. The fantasy provides the connection, the photography the spatial presence, and the portrayal the temporal occurrence. The definition does not make evident, though, that the camera, and eventually the spectator, is present at the occurrence, even though the latter does not affect it or even help constitute it.

Though I had in mind the use of the still camera when I spoke of "photography," the term is misused in the above, for both the fantasy and the portrayal can be the object of photography, and the still camera can be used in the course of a film. What is wanted is a term which conveys the artistic transportation of a spectator into a part of space, in such a way that the spectator can be in it in the way in which he is in his present space. "Presentation" is a better term here than photography. As a consequence, we get film to be a fantasied, presentational portrayal.

May 3

Architecture bounds a space and enables us to enter into it. The film does a similar thing with a plurality of spaces. It can take any part of space and open it up for entry by the spectator.

The story portrays events and people regardless of time. The film offers a similar portrayal by visual means. It can take any moment of time with its content and allow us to be present in it.

The dance allows one to share in the dynamics of a production. The film extends the range of our sharing and the range of the cases where the dynamics can be exhibited. It can take any object or occurrence and link it dynamically with any other, and in such a way that we live through the movement from one to the other.

The film can then be characterized as the artistic opening up of spaces, times, and dynamics by visual means. It presents the one, portrays the second, and constructs the third.

The great problem for the film is to understand the logic by which one moves from one frame to another. We need not suppose that this question requires us to start with individual shots and build up a unity, any more than it requires us to suppose that it starts with a single unity which it breaks down into shots. Whether we take either of these alternatives, or combine them (which I think is what takes place, for what we unite in a single film are not shots, but sequences of shots which constitute a single filmic event), we must ask how we are to connect the different spaces, the different times, and the different dynamics, and then how the resulting space is to be combined with the resulting time and dynamics.

Architectural spaces are today related to one another in city planning, in landscaping, and in interior decorating. But the intent in these is not primarily to provide contrasts, tensions, and climaxes, nor to order them in an irreversible sequence. But the film emphasizes these. Japanese film makers seem to have this problem at the forefront, and they solve it better than other film makers do, to judge from a few of their films that I have seen in this country. The relations between the spaces is, I suppose, governed primarily by a given space as subject to contraction, expansion, and connection, as expressed in the close-up, the long shot, the fade-out, and fade-in.

Portrayals have usually been related by a plot. This dictated what portrayal should follow on what. The easiest way to relate portrayals visually is still through a plot, which leads one to first concentrate on this event and then on that. If we drop the plot, how can we make an artistic transition from one presentation to another? Experimental film makers face this as their main question; I do not know of any who has thrown light on the solution, either through his experiments or his comments. The talking accompaniment of the film allows one to use the techniques of story, but stories too can be developed without evident plot. One can follow the line of some other work as James Joyce did, but this makes the logic of one's activity presuppose the logic of some other. What is wanted is a logic for portrayals which are at once visual and vocal, and which despite the occurrence of simultaneous events (similar to the presence of a number of items under a given chronicled date) involves a juncture of occurrences at different times. Must not the logic be the very nature of time itself as allowing for contingencies, affiliations, contrasts, and oppositions?

A plot can be viewed as providing the logic of a dynamics, telling us what is cause and what is effect. But we need no plot in the dance, and need none in the film. Like the dance, the film can produce movements which relate acts in terms of their own structures. But here we are not content with the logic of the world's dynamics, as we are content with the logic of the world's time. Time is receptive to anything, but the dynamics of the world are more restricted. (Space seems to stand in between, for though it allows for strange neighbors who appear along different causal lines and who come to be at the same time in different places, it tolerates connections in the form of roads, communications, and an overall physical space which restricts what in fact can be understood to be at the different places.) The film need not treat one event as a cause; indeed it moves better if it treats every event as an expression of underlying dynamics which make one event be the condition for the presence of another. It is perhaps the intent of the film to reveal the nature of dynamics while taking advantage of its ability to enter into any space and time. This would make it a dynamic art primarily, and would in effect mean that it is a kind of dance which has a cosmic range, and is subject primarily to choreographic considerations in its determination of what frame or set of frames follow what.

May 4

The discussion of the last few days seems to apply to the film without regard to its being silent or not. But sound adds another dimension to the film, to make it something new.

Sound can be treated as a verbalization of what is seen. It then is the sound of the theatre, a sound exhibiting a plot. The sound can also be treated as a kind of musical accompaniment. It is then the sound of music with its own intrinsic rhythm. The first way of treating sound makes it too dependent on what is seen, whereas the second makes it too independent, even though as is the practice, the musical sound tries to catch the spirit of what is occurring.

The sound should be treated as a counterpoint, having its own rationale, as music does, and as having a reference to what is seen, as theatrical talk does. But the counterpoint moves in some independence of the visible; it may intersect it in various ways, lag behind it, anticipate it, and the like. One can hear a voice and see the body of another; the sound can stop or start at any part of a single visual event—and conversely, a visual occurrence can stop or start at any part of a single aural event.

We can retain yesterday's definition of film by adding to "portrayal," "aural and visual" where these are understood to be independent in principle, though capable of being used together, as they are in the theatre, or held to their own logic as they are in music and dance.

The film I have now characterized in terms of categories applicable to the other arts, but in such a way that it stands over against the nine arts I discussed in *The Nine Basic Arts*. It would seem odd if this were the only art that has this status. Would a "happening" be another instance? Could this be said to be primarily a performance which is united with composition and painting, because it encompasses an acted event which is paced in a distinctive, newly minted time and which is the very space that it occupies? If something like this can be said, then it seems as if we have a number of arts which emphasize one of the dimensions of Existence at the same time that they are united with the other two dimensions in a distinctive way. They would not be "compound" arts, but single, unitary arts in which the various dimensions of Existence are given a larger scope and a more independent role than they are in the nine basic arts (which also take account of the other dimensions to some degree, but always in a distinctively subordinated position).

May 5

In order to play, one must free oneself from the pragmatic concerns of every day. This is in effect what the *Gita* urges as one of the alternative ways of doing what one ought—to act, but to detach oneself from the fruits. In play though, we go on to impose a new set of categories on the items, or to produce creatively a new set of relations amongst them. When we move on to the game, we cling to a set of rules and restrict our creativity to what those rules permit. In both cases what we do is to attach ourselves to a local set of objects which with us is held over against the rest of the world. This which is held over against is taken to be other than that world. We have here a case where we achieve an "other than" situation without attaching ourselves to some other realm, as was suggested that we do in *The God We Seek*.

That to which we attach ourselves is related to what lies outside, by space, laws of nature, our own pragmatic concerns, and our associations in act and language. We are not then in and of ourselves, "other than." To achieve this result, we must ourselves relate ourselves to something. Only if the limited situation which we now hold over against the world were first faced as being over against ourselves can we be said to have found ourselves in ourselves. Otherwise, what we have over against the rest of the world is ourselves as in a situation.

A similar problem arises in relation to the athlete. He can be said to identify himself with his body, and then through that body with the situation in which he tries to become and exhibit himself as excellent as a body. But if he identifies himself with his body without first separating himself off from that body, he will never find himself as one who has a centrality over against that body. He, like one who plays or is in a game, when he identifies himself with his body, has attached himself to something in the world and thereby is enabled to stand over against the rest of it, but not in the way in which one does who attaches himself to some Being such as God.

The athlete, when he plays a game, attends to the rules, and those rules can be seen to be specifications of the possibilities which are distinguishable in the realm of Ideality. By clinging to those rules, he can be said to detach himself not only from the world outside, but even from the particular objects and occurrences in the game. He does attend to those objects and occurrences, but only as one who represents the rules. He is therefore like a religious man who returns to the affairs of the world as a representative of the God to which he had attached himself, when and as he detached himself from the world and retreated to a center from which he could be "other than" that world.

By attending to rules, an athlete is able to free himself from an attachment to every item in the world, including those which are involved in the game. Such a freeing from attachment allows the athlete to be other than the rest of the world. But to be "other than" the rest of the world is to be "other of" and "other for" what remains—in this case, the rules. When the athlete acts in terms of those rules, he once again becomes other of and for items in the world, and therefore one who is "other than" those rules.

Strictly speaking, if there be more than one mode of Being, an athlete cannot be "other than" the rules, any more than he can be "other than" God or Actuality or Existence, except so far as he is a representative of other modes of Being, or has detached himself from those modes of Being when and as he detaches himself from the items in the world. The last seems to be the easier way. When and as a man detaches himself from the world of things (actualities), he must, if he is to be one who is in himself, one who has found his center, detach himself from all modes of Being but one. To that one he must cling. He must make himself be an other of and for it.

The athlete should therefore see himself not only as separated off from the world of every day and the items which are involved in a game, but as separated off from Actuality, God, and Existence, if he is to be one who attaches himself only to rules or the realm of possibility which these epitomize or specialize. Yet if he separates himself off from Actuality, he will lose that condition which makes him the equal of all other actualities; if he separates himself off from God, he makes himself a purely secular being; and if he separates himself off from Existence, he cannot be part of a single space-time-dynamics. The alternative to this, that he represent Actuality, God, and Existence as he detaches himself from all the rest of actualities, and thereby faces the rules as other than them, seems to be a more difficult position to achieve, and is at least as implausible as the present suggestion.

If it be possible for the athlete to detach himself from everything else besides rules in order to be able to be in himself over against everything else but as involved with the rules, it is possible for one to do the same thing with respect to this or that object, institution, or occasion, just so long as respect is paid to some structure or other instantiation of possibility. But then when the individual returns to the world, he will face the world as that which is to be structured, which is to be meant, or as that which is to be seen from the perspective of the possibility to which the individual had attached himelf.

May 6

From the perspective of a Being, the particulars within its confines can be dealt with as only congealings, instantiations, or fragments of it; from the perspective of the particulars, the Being can be dealt with only as an abstraction, a generalization, or a distillate. What we need are two distinct vocabularies. But we must say something about the relation of the two, and this would seem to require a third vocabulary. To say for example, as I have said in the past, that contingent particulars possess Being and are not identical with it, raises the question as to just what it is that possesses Being. It must have some being, for nothing cannot possess. But if it already has some being, it cannot be true that it is to be understood as that which merely possesses Being.

I have dealt with this question many times under different guises. One way has been in connection with the mind-body problem, where it has been argued that the two are together in the shape of the emotions which have their own distinctive rationale; another has been in connection with history, where it has been argued that mankind in whole or part interplays with nature to constitute a new domain with its own rationale, methods, evidences, units, etc. I have also dealt with it in terms of a "theological space" which mediates God and the universe. It is, of course, another expression of the problem of the One and the Many, or Togetherness, discussed in the *Modes of Being*, though it is there argued that the final reality is a plurality of Beings for which there is no true unitary Being, but only a unity which has its reality constituted by the interplay of four Beings. The present problem is that of the relation of Being and particular beings, both of which are realities and even in a sense finalities, though the one is necessary and permanent and the other contingent and transitory.

Duns Scotus apparently was concerned with this problem. He solved it by conceiving of an indeterminate Being which was specified in the shape of God (or Being as a definite reality) on one side, and particulars on the other. The indeterminate Being was not derivative from either, and could not be characterized in terms provided by either. One has to deal with it in new terms. If God were the object of a set of transcendental terms, one would have to find a new set of such transcendentals to apply solely to the indeterminate Being. If, however, as I am inclined to hold, a Being (of which God is but one) and its particulars are ultimately real, the indeterminate Being would be a product of their interplay. This would not make it unreal any more than history or the emotions are unreal; it would merely account for its presence.

If consumption, enjoyment, existential involvement, and the like are the final ends of life, we are forced to say that men are occupied with the instruments for the production of these, and that women are in fact living the good life, just so far as the men make this provision for them. On the other hand, if we think of production, creative making, technological efforts, and work which has an economic value as primary, we must say that women are engaged in the means by which there will be a supply of workers qualified to do a good job.

The former of these is the position taken in modern societies of the west; the latter is that which had been assumed earlier and which is characteristic of those places where women are still in subjection, or which are not economically strong. But the former does sound paradoxical, since the men are persuaded, and have persuaded many women, that the work in which they are engaged is more important and provides them with a more satisfactory life than a woman has. Margaret Mead has argued that in every society, no matter what the men and women do, both the men and the women evaluate the roles and tasks of the men as being more important than that of the women. The present paradox would seem to stem from this fact.

May 8

Granted that women are consumers and men are producers in our society, it is to be noted that both seem to be discontent. The women particularly do not seem to relish the role of being merely consumers, even though this means that they are living with the fruits of the efforts made just to produce such fruits. This seems to point up the fact what is wanted is not merely the opportunity to enjoy what has been produced, but the opportunity to contribute to the production, and not merely the opportunity to work to produce what is final, but the opportunity to enjoy this. Both men and women need to enjoy and work, to be consumers and producers. If they have only one, they remain dissatisfied.

The satisfaction of work and the satisfaction of enjoyment or consumption need one another. If there be no satisfaction in consumption, the work becomes onerous; if there be no satisfaction in work, the consumption becomes deadly and inane. There must be a satisfaction both in striving and in achieving.

Winning a game cannot altogether satisfy; there must be something worthwhile achieved in the process of getting to the point where one wins. And the mere process of getting to the point where one wins also fails to satisfy; there must be something in the result achieved which satisfies.

It is possible to find satisfaction in an effort, even though one fails to achieve a goal. This points up the fact that what is sought is not victory as such, not consumption as such, but the opportunity to win or consume. Similarly, it is possible to find satisfaction in consumption even though one does not make a significant contribution through production. This truth is evidenced by the experience of spectators, collectors, and connoisseurs. They make evident that what is sought is not the having of a significant role in production, but an appreciation of what is significant in production.

The humble worker can find a significant place for himself in a vast enterprise by seeing his job to be, not significant—he knows it is not, and does not like to have the employer try to lie to him that it is significant—but one which has a place in a significant enterprise. He should be consulted about that larger significant enterprise, even though he engages in an activity which, though necessary, is not intrinsically important and does not have a large role to play in the totality.

May 10

Among the primary tasks of philosophy is that of distinguishing items which do not conform to the grammar of the main or accepted items of a situation. The tracing back of these items to their source leads one to consider another type of situation in which the items have their own distinctive grammar. The next and hardest step is to attend to the nature of the relation between the two types of situation. Some of these relations are constituted by the distinctive items; this is true of "theological space." It can also be said to be true of myth, where this is understood to be a vivid portrayal of the relation of God or the Ideal to the world.

There are some cases where it is questionable whether the relation is constituted by the items related. This is particularly true if such constituting requires the antecedent presence of the items as independent and so far unrelated in any sense but that of being members of an aggregate.

Are there any clear cases where the context, or whole, or relation (where this is taken to be something structural and concrete) precedes the items said to be related by it, so that those items, when considered apart from it, are abstractions, delimited versions of what they in fact are? It is of course the view of idealists, contextualists, sociologists, and pragmatists that the isolated individual is an abstraction, a mere delimitation of a situational term. But the reason why one hesitates to accept these views is precisely because they seem unable to account for the individual as functioning apart from, and even making possible, the situations in which they are found.

In connection with ultimate Beings, we ought to say I think, as is said in the *Modes*, that the Beings are prior to their relations in the sense that those Beings have a reality and a role not defined by those relations. They are always related to one another; but they also have a distinctive Being which they exhibit in so far as they are related to their own particulars. It is as related to their own particulars that they can be said to be subordinate to a larger context, but then only as Beings which stand over against one another as independent.

Each Being stands out as independent with respect to its own particulars. So far as it does this, it must be integrally related to the other Beings, and in this sense be subordinate to some larger context. This is not admitted in the *Modes*; that work denies that the Beings ever are subordinate to anything. But that to which they are all subordinate is indeterminate, their cosmological unity, and this can be said to be a product not of the Beings severally, but of those Beings just so far as they are severally independent of their own multiplicity of contained particulars.

The separation of a Being, either from other Beings or from its own multiplicity of particulars, makes it subordinate to a reality connecting it with its particulars or other Beings, respectively. One can with considerable warrant insist that the reality is prior to what it connects, and which in turn can be said to specify it and terminate it. But if we do say this, we must at once say that it is a reality connecting Beings, or a reality connecting a Being with its particulars, and that so far as it is one of these, it presupposes and is inseparable from the state where the Beings, or the Being with its particulars, are independent and final.

Accepting this conclusion forces one to say that the *Modes*, since it takes the Beings to be ultimate, and not subordinate to any reality, presupposes a state where each mode of Being is encompassed within an indeterminate Being that also encompasses its particulars. The *Modes of Being*, in short, presupposes that each Being is intimately connected with its particulars, and that each Being affects its particulars (and conversely). That is why we can find evidence of the Being by attending to some of the eccentric items in the realm of the particulars.

A philosophy of religion begins with an awareness of the interplay of God and men (or the world). The interplay makes God an other *of* the world and thus one who varies with it; it gives Him no reality of His own. To acknowledge that reality is to acknowledge Him as a God *for* the world, which is to say as a relative transcendent, a transcendent whose meaning is to be immanent or in interplay with the world. To acknowledge that He is absolutely transcendent, that He has a Being all His own, apart from any promise to be related to the world (which is what must be held by those who think of God as one who had Being before there had been a world and who never loses that Being even when He assumes the role of a creator) has always been difficult. It has led to such impasses as the acceptance of absurdity, of the unknowable, of negative theology, and of analogy.

But why, if there be no other Beings than God, might not God and the particulars be related in two ways, one intimately and the other as aggregates? After all, it is admitted that God is intimately related to other Beings and also aggregated with them; why can this not be true of God and the particulars? Is it not because God and the particulars, when treated as aggregates in a common class, yield God and a *domain* of particulars, which is to say, Existence, or in any case a Being which is as basic, and ultimate, and eternal as God?

The acknowledgment of the independence of a domain of particulars does not change the situation in principle; it merely leaves over the question as to whether or not there are other Beings besides God and the domain of particulars. That there are seems evident from the consideration of the nature of the Ideal and the nature of Actuality, the one the domain of possibilities, and the other the Being which they are oriented toward and participate in.

Whether we are dealing with two or four modes of Being, the particulars with which God is interplaying will, as over against Him, be part of a single domain having its own Being. But this claim would seem to mean that there must be eight ultimate Beings considered in the *Modes of Being*, since each set of particulars will have to have a being of its own, and as such stand over against its ultimate Being. If, on the other hand, one acknowledges only particulars and a totality of them, one will have the difficulty of showing how *all* the particulars can stand over against the totality of them.

Granted that a Being interplays with its particulars, and that it also stands over against them, the question that must be faced is how to express this fact. Up to now I have been speaking as though the indeterminate Being, which encompasses the Being and its particulars, were the result of a shift in perspective from the position where the Being is seen to be in independence of the other Beings. But what is not faced is the question whether there is in fact an indeterminate Being which the shift in perspective uncovers. An affirmative answer requires one to say that each Being and its particulars are independent realities and also embraced in some indeterminate Being. There would also be an indeterminate Being embracing all the Beings. One would then not only multiply the indeterminate Beings, and would be faced with the question of how it is possible to speak both of the indeterminate Being (with its encompassed entities) and of the particular entities as independent and aggregated. Would there not have to be a neutral position from which this double fact could be expressed? Also, it has previously been argued that God is needed in order to permit Actuality to stand over against its actualities, whereas now this opposition is understood to be a function of the fact that the Actuality is involved with other modes of Being, or with some other mode of Being which might not be God, and which does nothing to the Actuality except interplay with it.

I have now opened up a nest of alternatives, all of which seem implausible and undesirable—eight Beings, five indeterminate Beings, perspectivism, inability to find a neutral position, and non-independence of Beings from one another and of particulars from one another. I do not see my way clearly out of this situation.

One might begin by taking the interplay to be as well as to be seen from the position of the entities as independent; and conversely, the independence can be taken to be and to be seen from the position of their interplay. The attempt to take both perspectives at once must end with having both perspectives as separate at the same time, and so on and on. Here I am supposing that there is no being of the perspectives together and separate except, of course, in the thinker's mind, in contrast with the ontological togetherness and separateness with which I have up to now been concerned.

This alternative leads to the supposition that particulars face their Being not only as over against themselves, but as merged with other Beings, and that a Being not only faces other Beings as over against it, but as merged with their respective particulars.

Is the correlative of the Beings as together, the Beings as separate from one another; or is it the Beings as separate from their particulars? The correlative of the particulars as together with their respective Beings is particulars as separate from the Beings. If we take this as our lead, then the correlative of the Beings as together is the Beings as separate from their particulars.

Do we have the Beings (with the particulars with which they interplay) together with one another? Or are they together only as Beings? Are the particulars separate from their respective Beings only so far as the Beings are merged with one another? To the first I think we ought to answer that it is the Beings which are together, but that the reason for this is that they are interplaying with their respective particulars. To the second I think we ought to answer in a similar vein: the particulars are separate from their respective Beings, but the reason for this is that the Beings are merged with one another.

If merging means that there is an indeterminate Being in which the merged items are, we must say that it is because there is an indeterminate Being for each Being and its particulars that Beings can be separate from one another (and presumably the particulars can be distinct?). It is also the reason why the Beings can be separate from their particulars. But is not the converse also true? Is it not the case that because Beings are separate from one another, they can merge with their particulars, and because they are separate from their particulars, they can merge with one another? Because Beings are separate, there is an indeterminate Being for them and their particulars, and because Beings and their particulars are separate, there is an indeterminate Being for all of the Beings.

I am discontent with all these tentative conclusions.

May 11

A particular as involved with its Being is an independent reality over against other particulars. The various Beings are each involved with particulars when and as the Beings stand over against one another.

To say of something that it is independent, that it is a thing in itself, is to say that because it *is* involved with something else it *can be* involved with the very items with respect to which it is a thing in itself. Thus, it is only so far as an actuality is involved with Actuality that it can be taken to be a distinct actuality over against other actualities; it is only so far as an actuality is involved with other actualities that it can be taken to be a distinct reality over against Actuality.

Each particular and each Being is something in itself. Each particular is involved with other particulars and is involved with its Being; each Being is involved with its particulars and with other Beings.

To say something is in itself is to say A] that it is involved with particulars and with Being, and B] that so far as it is involved with one of these, it has the status of a thing-in-itself, over against the other. Every entity, particulars or Beings, is involved with particulars and Being or Beings. A reference to what it is in itself is but a reference to an involvement not now in focus. With equal justice we can say that every entity, particulars or Beings, stands apart from either particulars or Beings, but that as standing apart, it contains within itself the meaning and effect of either Beings or particulars.

A particular is sustained to be over against other particulars by the Being with which it is involved; a Being is genuinely a Being by itself only so far as it is a Being encompassing particulars.

We solidify an involvement in one direction in order to have an entity which can be over against entities in another direction. To speak of something in itself is but to solidify in an entity the Being, Beings, or the particulars which are involved with it.

When we say of a particular that it is over against its Being, we are saying nothing more than that it stands as a representative, that it is a congealed unity of all the other particulars as affecting it. When we say of a Being that it is over against other Beings, we are saying nothing more than that it is a Being which is oriented toward the particulars which it encompasses. When we say of a particular that it is involved with a Being, we hold it away from its companions; when we say of a Being that it is involved with particulars, we hold it away from its companions. When we say of a Being that it is involved with other Beings, we hold it away from its particulars; when we say of a particular that it is involved with other particulars, we hold it away from its Being. But in holding something away we solidify in it all the items with which it is involved in another direction.

This way of putting things takes involvement in a sense to be basic. It defines the thing by itself to be a solidification of involvement in one direction to yield what is independent in another direction. What is not yet clear is what the independence is, apart from solidification, representation, etc. Nor is it clear just where I am standing when I am characterizing the entity as involved in two directions.

An hypothesis which I have not explored would start with the idea of an indeterminate Being which spreads, not only over all the Beings, but over each Being with its particulars, and over all the particulars. This indeterminate Being could be faced as indeterminate relative to whatever determinations there could be produced by Beings or particulars. Taken apart from all the determinations, it would be an abstraction; taken as that which was determinate in some respect, it would be concrete, by virtue of that determination. It would not be exhausted in that or all the determinations. To see it as something real, one would have to take a start with it as determinate and then see it as spreading over all else as an indeterminate. What it spread over would make it determinate; each of the items would function in independence of the others. If we start with a set of distinct particulars, the indeterminate Being would spread over them as related to their Being, and over the Being as involved with other Beings.

This last statement, though, seems to cover a confusion. If particulars are independent of one another, they are then involved with their Being. But is that Being then involved with other Beings? Yes. When we have distinct particulars, the Beings are involved with one another and are not independent of one another.

When a Being is involved with its particulars, is it independent of other Beings or is it involved with them? Is it not true that it is independent of the other Beings only as involved with particulars, and that as involved with the other Beings, it is independent of the particulars? If so, should we not say that as made determinate by particulars, the indeterminate Being spreads to the Being-for-those-particulars, and that it can be said to spread to that Being only so far as we have it spread further to the other Beings? The indeterminate Being cannot, in short, be taken to spread uniformly; it spreads to the Being in the given case only so far as it is then and there made determinate by the Being. But then will it not be the case that the determinate Being will be over against the other Beings, and there will not be an indeterminate Being over all of them? (I am evidently wobbling back and forth among a number of incompatible ideas about independence, involvement, indeterminate and determinate, and affiliated ideas.)

Perhaps better: Indeterminate Beings have limits; one extends over particulars, another over Beings, and a third over a Being and its particulars. The limits in each case are determinate beings over against determinate beings of the same kind and of different kinds—Beings over against Beings, particulars over against particulars, and Beings over against particulars. There is no one single indeterminate Being, but three different types, and the reality of one precludes the presence of the others.

Determinate entities, both Beings and particulars, are prior to indeterminate Being. But this is only to say that indeterminate Being is prior to Beings in relation to their particulars. But we can also say that particulars and Being are independent of one another, which entails that the indeterminate Being for Beings (with those Beings) and the indeterminate Being for particulars (with those particulars) are both a function of the independence of the particulars and Being.

Can we speak of the independence of particulars and Being without somehow encompassing both? It would seem that we must have indeterminate Being prior to a Being in relation to its particulars, and that the indeterminate Being for Beings and the indeterminate Being for particulars are derivatives which come about only when we take our stand with the Being and the particulars as limiting entities specifying the indeterminate Being which spreads over both of them.

If this alternative could be maintained, we would have to say that the involvement of particulars one with the other is a consequence and not an aboriginal fact; a similar thing would have to be said regarding the ultimate modes of Being. But this is questionable.

Once again: There is an indeterminate Being which is specified as a Being and as a particular when it is set over against Beings and particulars. Conversely, when a Being or a particular is held over against other Beings or other particulars, respectively, they constitute an indeterminate Being. In the first of these expressions, indeterminate Being is prior, and in the second, it is derivative. But in both, the Being and the particular are determinate only in contrast with their respective Beings and particulars. Indeterminate Being is determinately over against Beings and particulars through the fact that its termini are a determinate Being and a particular.

From the standpoint of determinate Beings and particulars, indeterminate Being is a result of the fact that a Being and a particular are contrasted. From the standpoint of indeterminate Being, we have a determinate Being and a particular, only so far as indeterminate Being is, since it then must be over against all determinates. What is over against Beings, and what is over against particulars, is an indeterminate Being specified as a Being and as a particular, respectively. It is also true that a particular and a Being are independent of one another. One indeterminate Being is specified as particulars and another is specified as Beings.

Once again: every indeterminate Being, that which encompasses the Beings, that which encompasses the particulars, and that which encompasses a Being with its particulars, is a derivative from the entities which it encompasses, being constituted by the penumbra of the encompassed entities. But we can also envisage a prior indeterminate Being which spreads over the entire complex of Beings, particulars, and the combination of Beings and particulars. This indeterminate Being is prior, not in the sense that it existed before there were any other entities, but in the sense that it has a reality of its own, not constituted by the entities which it encompasses. It could in fact be said to be the determinate indeterminate Being that it is, only because it allows for the production of three distinct kinds of indeterminates by virtue of the constituting acts of various entities. But this supposition will lead us to suppose that there is a real indeterminate Being over against, not only the four modes of Being, but the particulars for those Beings. The solution to the problem is not yet at hand.

May 12

It seems to be true that particulars are always involved with particulars, and always have an independent status with respect to one another; that Beings are always involved with Beings, and always have an independent status with respect to one another; and that Beings are always involved with particulars, and always have an independent status with respect to one another. It also seems to be true that the indeterminate Being which encompasses all the Beings, all the particulars, and both in relation to one another, is an abstraction. Though it has no ontological status, it is through it that one achieves a neutral position. But the three subordinate indeterminate Beings which encompass Beings, particulars, and Beings in relation to their particulars, do seem to have some status.

Might not the togetherness of the particulars be nothing more than the Being for them? Could each kind of particular, or each distinct particular, offer a distinctive way in which the Beings are together? What then would be the togetherness of a Being with its particulars? Would that be constituted by the rest of the Beings and their particulars as over against one another? Or would it not be more correct to say that when and as the different particulars serve as biased ways of having the modes of Being together, and the different Beings serve as ways in which their own particulars are together, the overlapping of these two forms of having entities together produces the togetherness of a mode of Being with its own particulars?

We are left, on this hypothesis, with the question as to how a particular could be a form of togetherness for its own Being and other Beings, when it is confined inside its own Being. We would have to say that the particular is so related to its own Being that the Being adheres to the other modes of Being; the particular would be the togetherness of Beings via a given Being. Ought we not then say that a given Being is the togetherness, not only of its own particulars, but of these as related to the particulars in other Beings? Should not a set of particulars be the means by which a given mode of Being serves as a unity of all particulars, no matter what their Being? If we say yes to the first of these, we ought to say yes to the second—and it does seem plausible to say yes to the first.

We have then A] a particular is the togetherness in a biased way of all the modes of Being. As such it is an indefinite Being for those modes of Being. B] A Being is the togetherness in a biased way of all the particulars. As such, the Being is an indefinite Being for those particulars.

The indefinite Being in both cases is a distinct particular or a distinct mode of Being; it is only so far as it is distinct from other particulars or Beings, respectively, that it can be the togetherness of Beings or of particulars, respectively.

If we combine A and B, we have a Being as distinct, and the particulars as distinct. But we also have the Being functioning as an indeterminate Being for the particulars, and the particulars serving as an indeterminate for the Being as related to the other Beings. Their distinctness would be apparently identical with their togetherness in the sense that it is only as distinct that their correlatives are together.

We could consequently say of Being and particulars that A] all the Beings together are together with all the togethered particulars; B] all the Beings together are together with distinct particulars; C] all the particulars together are together with distinct Beings, and D] distinct particulars are distinct from distinct Beings. Indeterminate Being is to be found only in the first three cases, but in the first it is unaccounted for, while in the next two it is accounted for as being the meaning of distinct particulars or of distinct Beings in relation to their correlative Beings or particulars.

May 15

Particulars are each distinct; they are unit beings, and must be if they are to be together. A similar thing must be said about the ultimate modes of Being. And when and as the particulars are distinct from one another and the Beings are distinct from one another, the particulars and the Beings are together with one another. The togetherness of particulars with Beings is as primary a fact as that the particulars are distinct from one another and that the Beings are distinct from one another.

The child from the very start is linked to the Being which is Actuality and all the subordinate Beings within Actuality. But it is amorphous, and its togetherness does not involve much impingement by the Being. It is attached to the Being, but in such a way as not to be significantly structured and controlled by it. In the course of its growing up, it becomes more and more involved with other particulars, and as a consequence becomes more and more distinct and contrasted with the Being. As a consequence of its involvement, it becomes pragmatically alert, and therefore also subject to the categories that society and experience show are to be followed if there is to be a tolerable accommodation to the world about.

Because of some dislocation from one's present surrounds, perhaps due to a severe intrusion or injury, because of terror or fear, because of something wondrous seen or heard, one may turn away from the daily world and try to attend to what lies outside it. One then begins an adventure of recapturing the kind of connection the child had initially, but now with respect to a more specific form of a Being, and then in such a way as to make that Being part of one's structure. The life of the adult is one that is structured either by conventional and pragmatic categories or by the rules and principles which are devised and discovered in the course of the attempt to integrate the Being (with which one was loosely involved as a child) with oneself, in a more specific and controlling form.

This I think is the solution of the problem with which I had been occupied for the last week or so. It allows one to refer to all the particulars and all the Beings without having recourse to an indeterminate threefold abstract Being, for the togetherness of the particulars with the Beings is the position from which the particulars and the Beings are seen to be distinct entities.

May 23

Suggestions for the resolution of dualisms—mind-body, private-public, perception-science, Being-Beings, etc.:

1] Express each side as a set of reports or statements. View these as either items in a language or as distinct claims. Pair them with one another, perhaps on the basis of their coincidence in time. The pairing is itself something done in a language of a claimant. The two languages have different grammars and vocabularies, and the resolution consists in allowing us to use one or the other of these, since for each there is a counterpart. The one language does not take the place of the other; we merely attend to one as being adequate for our purposes, and know that whatever is claimed or said will have a counterpart in the other language. There is here nothing said about the origin of the languages, the justification of their claims, the validity of the correlation based on contemporaneity, etc.

2] The pairing or correlation can be said to have an ontological reference, and thus to tell us about what is neutral to the two reports. This gives us an ontological opening from the base of a linguistic approach. But we have no reason for supposing that the correlation has an ontological import alone, and that there is nothing answering to the claims of the different sides.

3] The different sides can be said to make diverse claims. The languages in each, therefore, must be interpreted as having meanings which tell us something about occurrences answering to the diverse expressions of those languages. There will be statements which refer to, say mental entities or events, and others which refer to physical entities or events—or the evidences for either of these. The correlation, though, could be thought of as a mere device by which we are able to keep these different claims abreast. There would be nothing answering to the correlation; it would serve only to allow us to go from one language or claim to the other, or to allow us to account for all that occurs by supplementing one claim with another. Though the correlation here has no claim to make, it nevertheless will be part of a language having only a syncategorematic function. The language could be said to be a "public" one, in the sense in which Wittgenstein has stressed. (This is also true of the languages mentioned in the other two alternatives.) It would be distinct from the languages which were correlated in that it had a grammar distinct from either, but it would not involve our going into some new domain which was nonlinguistic (or alternatively, noncognitive or nonempirical, etc.). We now have the two languages as basic, each making claims answering to distinctive facts; what would be reconciled would be the reports of the facts, leaving the facts themselves unbridged. But if the reports can be related, why not the facts which they report?

4]   The correlations as well as the items correlated can be viewed as having realities answering to them. The correlations, since they are functions of the correlated items, would have two roles—they would relate the reports, and they would refer to a reality of which the diverse reported realities would be aspects. This view is very close to that offered by me in connection with perception, where the "is" or copula serves to unite an abstracted subject and predicate to a reality which has the subject and predicate as aspects. It entails having three kinds of reports and not two, the third serving to refer us to what in fact unites or sustains the two, and having the additional role of connecting the reports of those two. One can justify this alternative only if one in fact can adumbrate the third reality and see the other two as aspects. This solution may be satisfactory in some cases, such as that of the relation of mind and body, but it is hard to see how it can be pertinent to Being and beings, or even to private and public. We have some grasp of an organic unity of which body and mind are aspects, but we have no grasp of anything which sustains Being and beings, or the private and the public. However, there is a real relation between Being and beings, and it is this real relation that can be referred to by the correlation. This brings us to the next alternative.

5] The two languages can be thought to make diverse claims which are correlated by a relation, itself making a claim, not to a reality which underlies the objects of the diverse claims, but to one which merely relates them. This relating reality can be a function of the related realities in the very same sense that the correlation can be a function of the correlated languages. This is an answer appropriate to Being and beings, provided that it be allowed that there is a sense in which Being and beings are related in another way, as merely together but separate. The private and public can be similarly treated by seeing the relation which in fact holds between them to be spatio-temporal, a locus of interplay which is what it is because of the penumbral interlocking and interaction of the private and public realities.

In all the above cases, we begin not with the realities, but with linguistic expressions taken either as mere items in languages or as carriers of meaning, and acknowledge the relation between them to be another item in a language or another carrier of meaning. All three languages or carriers would be part of one domain in one sense; they would all be faced by the individual as something which may or may not be referred to a reality beyond them. All of them would, as being faced by the individual, presuppose a solution to the private-public relation, since the languages would be public items looked at by a private being. We would have to presuppose the fifth answer in order to be able to entertain any of the other four.

May 25

Is the totality of actualities identical with Actuality? If so, it must be a Being, and have a nature and power of its own. But can a mere "totality of" have a nature and a power of its own?

But suppose we think of Actuality as a Being which makes the multiplicity of actualities be a totality? Apart from it, they would be a mere aggregate. This they could not really be, for to be an aggregate they must somehow be together. Their aggregativeness will have to be understood to be correlative to their being together, and this togetherness could be provided by Actuality.

Actuality as together with other modes of Being is correlative with itself as separate from them. The togetherness of itself with the other modes of Being does not demand that there be a Being which constitutes that togetherness. But there is no reason why the togetherness of actualities should not be constituted by a mode of Being. The togetherness of actualities will then be of a distinctive kind; it will be a togetherness which requires that there be a Being for them. Perhaps a similar thing must be said for the particularities pertinent to the other modes of Being: all of them have their togetherness constituted by their respective modes of Being. In all four cases, there would be a plurality of aggregated particulars and a togetherness which had a nature and power of its own which was the Being pertinent to those particulars.

What happens then to the supposed encapsulated forms of the modes of Being inside Actuality? Would we not have to say that the Ideal, for example, was striven for by actualities only so far as it was subordinated to the togetherness of the actualities? But the individual actualities are concerned with the Ideal and the other modes of Being. There seems to be no need to suppose that they are concerned with encapsulated forms of these, if the encapsulation has to be made by the togetherness of the actualities, for it is only when Actuality stands over against the actualities and when each mode of Being is seen to have its own particulars, that we seem to have a need to suppose that the other modes of Being in a truncated form, are encapsulated in Actuality.

The point perhaps becomes more plausible when we start from the perspective of Actuality and interpret this to be a reality which nevertheless bounds and makes the separate actualities be together. When and as it makes the actualities be together, it encloses limited forms of the other modes of Being. The togetherness of the actualities will then be separated from the actualities by these other included modes of Being.

But why suppose that there be an Actuality which has or is a Being, when it is enough to remark that the various actualities are together, and this togetherness has some nature, though not necessarily a Being or a power of its own? It is only so far as we must affirm that there is an Ideal (or Existence, or God) which is over against the actualities, that we are required to say that there must be a togetherness of those actualities as alone able to oppose and to be opposed by the Ideal (or Existence, or God). Must we not say that the togetherness of the actualities has a Being of its own, only so far as it is operated on by the other Beings?

But why should we say that there is an Ideal or other mode of Being in terms of which the togetherness of the actualities also is a Being? The only Ideal of which we know anything is one pointed at by particular actualities. They may all point to the same Ideal—indeed the very nature of a common future means that they must. But this is not the Ideal with its own particulars, but the Ideal as made relevant to the actualities. Only if we can argue from the latter to the former Ideal, from the Ideal as relevant to actualities, to the Ideal as having its own particulars, and then show that that Ideal must be related to the togetherness of the actualities as having a being of its own, will we be in a position to defend the view that the togetherness of actualities is a Being interplaying with the Being of the Ideal (and Existence, and God).

May 26

Let us suppose that Actuality is nothing more than the way in which actualities are together. We then have to choose amongst a number of positions:

1] The togetherness has no reality of its own. This would bring us back to something like the position of *Reality*. It was the awareness of the reality of Ideality as a kind of futured form of togetherness which forced me away from the position of that book. We could, though, maintain as a modified form of this alternative the view that there is a powerless kind of togetherness which is to take the place of Actuality, but that there are other more concrete and vital ones in the guise of Ideality, Existence, and God. These three would be concrete togethernesses of the actualities, and all of them together would be together in an innocuous unity or togetherness. This would bring one close to the way in which the *Modes of Being* is actually presented, with its absence of a concern for Actuality as a Being. But I have argued in this present work that there is a role that Actuality plays; it too is prescriptive, and it has a role to play with respect to the various other togethernesses. This puts it on a footing with them with respect to ultimacy and reality.

2] We can suppose that there are four forms of togethernesses for actualities. But in this way we would lower the status of three of them, since they would not have appropriate sets of particulars. We would have a togetherness of actualities, each taken as a final substance, and then the various togethernesses represented by Ideality, God, and Existence. But if they are to be on a footing with Actuality, they too should have their own particulars for which they are distinctive forms of togetherness. We should say then that Ideality, God, and Existence are ways in which the actualities are together, only so far as these togethernesses are understood to be specializations of some more remote types of togethernesses each with distinct items together. The actualities would be primarily together by virtue of the togetherness I before termed "Actuality," and secondarily together by virtue of the togethernesses provided by what I before called "encapsulated modes of Being."

When the actualities are contrasted with Actuality, or their primary togetherness, they are taken either individually or as together in the other ways. These other ways, are evidently subordinate to the togetherness characteristic of Actuality. The actualities are never together in the Actuality-manner as over against the other togethernesses which unite the actualities.

We have then three types of togetherness for the actualities. Whole united by these togethernesses, the actualities stand over against them. There is a primary form of togetherness, which itself is over against other primary forms of togetherness having their own particulars. These primary forms are related to the subordinate togethernesses (appropriate to actualities) as their transcendent grounds.

If this be correct, then Being in contrast with Beings is just a powerful, independently functioning, and substantial way of having a plurality unified. The distinctness of the unity from what it unifies means that the view cannot be reduced to a monism, while the concreteness of the unity prevents a reduction to a monadology.

The most appropriate way of contrasting actualities with Actuality is when the actualities are treated as individuals. Actuality on this view is the togetherness which is appropriate to actualities as such, apart from any other unification. Actuality is the togetherness of the actualities taken severally, as well as of them as together in other subordinate ways. Those subordinate ways give us the actualities together, not as beings but as values, contemporaries, and as standing away from the Actuality.

May 31

With a woman you must aim high if you are to reach low.

It is also true that you must aim low if you are to live high.

If all life is slightly ridiculous, then politics makes good sense.

In the end, the most one can show for a life is that one has become a man.

The pessimist: nothing makes a difference, not even indifference. The optimist: everything makes a difference, even indifference.

The follies of youth acquire no dignity with age.

A contented woman is paradise; but paradise is not possible in this life.

Men marry for sentimental, women for practical reasons.

If a child is father to a man, God help us. It would be better to have a man be father to a child.

Those who ask philosophers to conform to the criteria employed by scientists are like those who say to poets, "You'd be intelligible if only you would write prose."

How can you tell whether what a philosopher says is true or false? Take any occurrence, any fact, any thing, and see if it is not more intelligible in relation to everything else within the framework of that philosophic view. But what is it to be more intelligible? Is it not to see it as explaining the others? And what is it to explain? Is it not to see the source of its wonder, without losing its wondrousness? Here is a desk. To say it is an actuality is but to relate it to Actuality, Existence, etc., and to understand its contingency, its presence in a plurality, its spatio-temporal nature, in relation to Actuality, etc. To understand Actuality, we must signify it by aberrational entities, such as metaphysical terms, egos, totalities, the good, the true, the beautiful, etc.

June 1

Richard Rorty, in his splendid introduction to his anthology, *The Linguistic Turn*, once again challenges philosophers—more exactly metaphysicians—to show that what they say is correct. If they cannot, they are to be charged with writing "poetry" or nonsense. The challenge can be met in a number of ways:

1] Philosophy begins with anything wondrous and traces back from this to the source of the wonder. How do you know you have arrived at the source? If you find that on returning to the world where the original object appeared, everything is wondrous. The wonder does not disappear; it is not the function of philosophy to dissolve problems, but to answer them and show why they arise. Philosophy sees that everything is a problem if dislocated from ultimate reality.

2] Philosophy uses a metalanguage. This language allows one to give coherent and communicable sense to what in ordinary life is paradoxical, contradictory, obscure. How do we know that we have the correct language? If we find that we have made provision for whatever new paradoxes, i.e., for whatever new aberrational terms or occurrences that arise. Usually we find that the language we have been using is not adequate, and must therefore be changed. Philosophy is engaged in the constant enterprise of restructuring its language.

Following Ayer, Rorty also asks what counts for or against the position offered. If there is something wondrous or aberrational that is not accommodated, this counts against the position.

Does philosophy clarify, explain, substitute for, or refine common sense? It clarifies common sense in that it removes the aberrational from its domain. It explains common sense in showing how all of it, in a purged form, is wondrous, and how it accretes conventions, distortions, etc. It substitutes for common sense only so far as it uses a language relating to what is ultimate and distinct from the items in common sense. It refines common sense in allowing it to have a purged form separated off from accretions and aberrational items which do not fit its ordinary grammar.

June 8

Is it necessary that there be Being and particulars? A number of answers are antecedently possible.

1]   Neither Being nor particulars are necessary. There could conceivably have been nothing at all. The presence of either Being or particulars is inexplicable, absurd, brute.

One might try to get rid of this alternative in a number of ways. One might argue, as I did in *Reality*, that "nothing" is a self-contradictory idea, involving a reference to an indeterminate which is determinately what it is. But one who accepted the absurdity of anything would not be troubled by the absurdity of a nothing. It might, though, be effectively argued that the view that everything whatsoever is absurd involves ideas of rationality and intelligibility which need not be accepted, and that indeed the very intent of all inquiry is to understand that which is "given" and thus is in a sense brute.

The absurdity of what is or what is not, is but a condition for the achievement of an intelligibility. To say that there can be no way in which something is to be made intelligible is to be dogmatic, denying the value of an inquiry. It is presupposed that we must end where we began.

Still, it could be the case that all is absurd, and that inquiry in fact arrives at such a result. But will the inquiry be absurd? Will not the discovery of the irrationality of what is involve a recognition that there is something else, to wit reason, or mind, or inquiry, and must this not be made part of Being or particulars? We would then have to conclude that Being and particulars are absurd from the position of some part of them. Absurdity would then be a contrastive term and not an absolute one, and this fact itself could be viewed as an intelligible result, making evident only the substantiality, objectivity, and irreducibility of that with which the mind is occupied.

2] There might be only particulars, entities, actualities, the items acknowledged by atomists, physicists, commonsense men, Aristotelians, and radical pluralists. These different thinkers pick out different kinds of items to acknowledge, but all are agreed in affirming the reality of a plurality of finite entities which make up all that there is. Such views have the problem of accounting for the togetherness of the items, a togetherness which may be exhibited in their contemporaneity, their subjugation to some prospect, etc.

3] There might be only Being. This is the view of monists, who disagree amongst themselves as to whether or not this Being is God, Nature, the Absolute, spiritual or material, Nirvana, etc. All are met by pointing out that there are appearances and that there are philosophers who tell us that there is nothing but Being. Such an answer shows us that today, at least, there is more than Being. It does not tell us whether or not there ever could be Being in and of itself, without anything else. This alternative is in fact the position accepted by orthodox Christianity with its view that there had been a "time" when the universe had not been, and when God alone was, a Being in and of Himself requiring nothing else. This position must be examined again in connection with any attempt to show that there can be no Being without there also being particulars.

4] There might be Being and particulars, but these could be without having any reference or bearing on one another. This is the view of dualism. It comes up against the question of how there could be two entities without these being together so as to add up to two.

5] There might be particulars and a Being which was nothing more than the common nature of them all, without a reality of its own. As was suggested above in 3, though, we would be able to move away from this position by pointing to considerations in connection with particulars that required a reference to a Being as over against them. These considerations are A] something factual, B] something evidential, C] some "analytic" reasons.

A] We find the particulars, as subject to compulsions of various kinds, requiring a reference to a reality or realities which provide the source for these compulsions. But might these compulsions some time cease? Does not the Being have a nature which is not expressed or exhausted in these compulsions?

B] There are eccentric particulars which we cannot make intelligible except by seeing them to be the counterpart of a Being, in terms of which they cease to be eccentric. But must there always be such particulars?

C] Inside each particular there may be factors which belong elsewhere;

the particulars may be sacramental, future oriented, matters which an analysis would lay bare. But once again one may ask whether such factors are necessary.

A stronger analytic approach would try to show that the particulars cannot be the particulars they are, except so far as there is something else. They would be shown to possess an "existence" only because there is "Existence" as such—the Thomistic approach; or only because no one particular is ultimately substantial, but depends for its being on a substance —the Spinozistic approach. This is the "cosmological" argument freed from its misleading association with the term "cause," and kept free of a reference to past conditions, so as to concentrate on preconditions having an ontological status.

These three sets of answers all presuppose that there are particulars; they do not show that there had to be such, but only that if there be such, they ground arguments for the reality of a Being. The arguments need to be supplemented by a reciprocal set which starts with Being.

6]   There should be   A] factual,   B] evidential, and   C] analytic reasons for Being to have or be accompanied by particulars. If the case can be made out, we rid ourselves of course of the position accepted by orthodox Christianity that there could be a God who was without a "creation."

A]   The Being might be found subject to changes which had their source in the particulars. But such changes could stop at some time.

B]   The warrant for an acceptance of particulars might involve the acknowledgment of obscurities or nuances in the Being which could not be accounted for except as the result of intrusions into it by particulars. But such intrusions could conceivably stop at some time.

C]   The Being might be found to be, only so far as it had features which pointed beyond itself. God, it is sometimes said, overflows with love. But from this it does not follow that there is a terminus to this overflow, that the overflow ever gets to be separate from the source.

A stronger position would be one which showed that Being was such that it could not be, except so far as there were particulars. Being, for example, could be said to need for its very being the presence of particulars. Without them, it would be a mere general, not more than merely possible; the particulars would, by contrasting with it, give it determinations, allow it to be concrete. But why might not there be nothing more than the merely general? Must Being hold itself to itself to be Being; must this mean that it then must contrast itself with particulars? Must Being be incomplete and need to become complete by articulating itself over endless time with all possible particulars?

Throughout the history of thought, men have held in some form or other that there are Being and particulars. I for one have gone further to contend that there are Beings and particulars. But no one to my knowledge has shown that there must be both, but at best only that if there be one, there is reason to suppose that there is the other, and this usually only in one way, by starting with particulars.

June 9

The discussion yesterday tried to abstract from the question as to whether or not there was more than one Being. By doing this, it has perhaps precluded an answer to its problem, though the acknowledgment of more than one Being does not, of course, mean that the problem is solved.

A Being has a plurality (of particulars) just so far as it is part of a plurality (of Beings). A particular has a plurality (of Beings) just so far as it is part of a plurality (of particulars).

We do not know what kind of particulars there are, unless we know what kind of Being we are acknowledging. The formula regarding a plurality of Beings does not tell us about any one, and therefore cannot tell us about the nature of the particulars. If we know the nature of a Being, say that it is Actuality, we will know the nature of the particulars. But we will not know just which particulars there are. We could not know this, for if there were one set of particulars that we could know existed because demanded by Actuality, we would have a set of particulars which could not but be always.

From the base of Being, we cannot know why we have just this set of particulars at any given time; to answer that question, one would have to go back to antecedent causes. But why just that pattern of causation? Why just those antecedents? Why do just those laws prevail? The necessity that there be particulars in no way dictates the answers to these questions.

Starting with actualities, we do not know just what the relation of the different Beings may be to one another. All we know is that there must be a plurality of Beings of which Actuality is one. But the nature of the Actuality is in part determined by how it stands with respect to the other Beings. We cannot know just what the nature of Actuality is, either as determined apart from all the other Beings, or as related to them from the base of actualities. All we can know is that Actuality is the Being in which they participate; what more it is cannot be determined.

Do we now not approach the acceptance of an absurd, of a brute inexplicability? Why do we have the kind of universe of particulars that we do? Why do we have the kind of ultimate Beings that we do? These questions seem to require an approach from outside the particulars and the Beings, respectively. But if the only "outside" for these are Beings and particulars, respectively, we seem to have no way to escape an acceptance of inexplicables. To avoid such a result, one would have to be able to show that the very demand that there be Beings or particulars from the base of particulars and Beings, respectively, is a demand which requires that the Beings and the particulars be of a certain nature. But such a reply goes no further than to tell us what is needed in connection with Beings, for these Beings are concretionalized natures. Particulars, on the other hand, are distinct one from the other. They are more than natures concretionalized; they are natures individualized, pluralized, diversified. If we know that the Being with which we are dealing is Actuality, we know that its particulars are actualities; but we do not then know just what actualities there are. We will be able to find out what ones there are through experience, but that still does not tell us why the experience should turn up just those items and not some others.

Does the togetherness of Being and particulars require that there be one Being which is the locus of identity (God), another which is the locus of the law of excluded middle (Existence), a third which is the locus of the law of contradiction (Actuality) and a fourth which is the locus of the principle of inference (Ideality)? Why should this be so? But granted that the only things that must be Beings are logical principles concretionalized, what must their respective particulars be like?

Is the only answer possible to the question of why the particulars are what they are, one which embraces all the particulars of a certain kind— and this we do not have? Can we do anything more than extend our inquiry back and back, and also project it forward as much as possible, so as to have a larger set of particulars, and then try to show that if such a set could be completed along the same lines, such that there would be no particulars missing, the totality would be the correlative of the concretionalized law of contradiction, and would have to be fragmented amongst just those particulars? But this answer supposes that time has, or could have, a beginning or an ending, that there could even in principle be a completed totality of particulars.

We might be able to show that the laws of nature had to be what they are because this is required by the nature of Actuality. But unless we could then show that these laws had to be exemplified by particulars in a certain way, or by particulars of a certain nature in a certain order, we would still be left with the fact that there were particulars for which we could not account on the basis of Being or anything that it might demand.

June 12

The individual as a self-maintaining being, as one who is final by himself, is a togetherness of himself as an actuality and of Actuality as here and now. For him to be merely an actuality, he must release his hold on Actuality and involve himself with other actualities. As he stands final in and of himself, he is other than all the other actualities; they are his reciprocals. We can say they must be just this set of actualities for him to be able to be involved with them. This is the same thing as to say that what he is to become as an involved actuality is defined by whatever actualities there are, and these in turn are to be understood to be the negation of his actuality as part of a self-maintaining whole.

The recognition of the difference between an actuality which is a part of a private self-maintaining being and the actuality as involved with other actualities is one with the recognition that there are other actualities which together make up the articulate meaning of "non-I." There are many ways in which that meaning can be articulated, and this we find out through experience. But the totality of actualities other than myself is the totality which articulates the meaning "not-I."

One might analyze the "not-I" in two dimensions. One could refer to what was contemporary, and thus what was then and there also involved with self-maintenance; and one could refer to whatever actualities there had been, and thus what directly or indirectly made it the present thing it is—directly as its antecedents, indirectly as the antecedents of the other actualities.

Actuality becomes involved with other Beings when and as an actuality is involved with other actualities, but there is no past set of Beings to which one can refer. One might, though, refer to past states of the different Beings in the same way that one refers to past actualities.

Why are there any actualities? Because there are Beings involved with one another. Why are there any Beings? Because actualities are involved with one another. Why are the actualities what they are; why just this set? Because they are the counterweight to myself. But who am I? I am a self-maintaining private being. Why am I as I am? Because of what the actualities had been and what they now are. Might I not be? Of course; the reality of the actualities and Beings does not depend on my existence. But it is only because I know what I am, as self-maintaining or as an actuality involved with others, that I can say what Beings there must be and what actualities other than myself there must be—not in fact, but in principle—by pointing out that they make a set which articulates me, negated.

Why is myself negated, articulated in this way rather than that? I am articulatable in all possible ways; we cannot rule out the possibility that over the course of time all will be exhibited. But why in this order or that, why articulated now in this way? Perhaps this has to do with the way in which Actuality itself is articulated by the other Beings and the way these Beings are represented by encapsulated forms of themselves governing the activities of all actualities?

June 13

Is it more correct to say that the space with which the film is interested is architectural rather than painterly? Is it more correct to say that the dynamics with which it is interested is dancelike rather than musical? I have previously chosen the first of each set. But we can say that the space that is taken is filled, created, and concrete, and that the dynamics is essentially one which involves contrasts and harmonies. If we take this line, we can go on to define film as a dramatic movement of filled spaces associated imaginatively.

The dramatic movement is not the movement of a play; it does not require a plot; it does, though, have tension and resolution, and a thrusting toward a climax. It is a movement distinguishable from the temporality of the film, for it involves the association of different items as having a bearing on one another, whereas the temporality of the film is one essentially of rhythm, periods, beginning and endings. One could have the dramatic movement with a monotonous time, since the difference in the items might carry that movement—e.g., a shot could be followed by a fall and a death, and the whole nevertheless be the result of simple juxtaposition, rather than a kind of transformation from the beginning to the ending.

The time of a film is always the present, but the occurrences for that time might be past or future; in this sense the film can be said to be at home in any time. And the dramatic movement can take any items, no matter when they were supposed to occur, and relate them as "causes and effects." It is also at home in any space, and can juxtapose what is in those spaces, or more sharply, the spaces themselves in a dynamic way with an imaginative temporality. One could relate two spaces without dramatic movement, and one could relate them without much imagination in a temporal order.

Are there other arts which combine space, time, and causality in special ways? The present account goes from the third row in space (in the diagram in *Nine Basic Arts*) to the second in time, to the first in causality. That diagram means that the number of other ways is limited; is that all the arts there are or can be?

Of what is the film revelatory? Existence as such? Would an art which combined architectural space with dancing dynamics in a dramatic way also reveal Existence? How would its revelation differ from that of the film? What about an art which combined architectural space, compositional time, and musical dynamics? Or one which combined painterly space with poetic time and dancing dynamics?

Is it not more important to stress the fact that the film can treat of any space, any time, and any association? I think not, for we do want some kind of unity produced, and this is provided for in the formula offered.

June 15

Film: the art of juxtaposing photographed spaces and times, and integrating them with sounds.

The juxtaposing can be similar to that exhibited in music, in acting, or in dancing; the spaces can be architectural, sculptural, or painterly; the times can be compositional, dramatic, or poetic. The film has open to it any space, any time, and any sound, and any justaposition of them that enables it to be a work of art, as defined let us say, in *The World of Art*.

The film evidently gives us the nature of Existence more completely than any of the nine basic arts, since these emphasize either space, or time, or dynamics, and then concentrate on either bounding, occupying, or constituting the extension. In addition, through the introduction of sound, it takes these dimensions to be more complex than mere vision would allow.

No definition of an art is satisfactory if it precludes the possibility of other arts, any more than if it merely carries over the categories appropriate to some established art. Definitions of the film that I have seen all characterize it as a form of painting, or dance, or reportage, etc. None does justice to the film as a distinct art.

Other arts in the future might deal with other ways of juxtaposing photographed spaces, times, and sounds. They could also juxtapose photographed spaces and times with smells, tastes, touches, and kinesthetic sensations. They could juxtapose heard or touched spaces and times with sights, etc.

A touched space can be combined with a sight. The result should be different from that produced by combining a seen space with a touch. In the first case, the primary fact is a touch with explores and perhaps fills up a space; this filled-up, touched space would be integrated with something seen. This which is seen is, of course, spatialized, but the use to which it would be put would make an artistic whole with the touched [filled] space. If instead we start with a seen space, this will be filled up with items having definite spatial relations to one another to constitute a single spatial whole, which may be architectural, sculptural, or painterly in nature. That seen space would then be combined with touch. The touch will cover a spatial extension, but the combining of it would be in terms of what was needed by the seen space to make a new harmony.

Might we not speak here of a seen space combined with a touched space, and thereby reduce the above cases to one? I think not. The combination of a seen space with a touched space is different from a seen space with a touch, or a touched space with a sight. In the first, the geometry of the spaces is paramount; in the second, the touch is used to emphasize certain portions of the seen space; in the third, the sight is used to emphasize certain portions of the touched space. Even if in the first case we restricted ourselves to the area of touch or sight involved in the second and third cases respectively, we would in the first case be emphasizing the extensional relations of the touched or seen surface, whereas in the other cases we would be using the touch or the sight to force an emphasis, a contrast, etc.

More important: there are other ways of having seen spaces and times than through the use of the camera. They can be blueprinted, drawn, moved through, etc. There is not much point in showing what other ways than the film for taking account of the differences in various spaces, times, sounds, and affiliations of these, there could be, for the actual production of an art will give them an import and value no a priori outlining of them can. What is necessary is to show that there are other combinations possible than those which the film provides, that there are other ways of using touch, sight, etc., besides those which the film uses. And this I think is now evident.

June 20

Peter Kubelka has convinced me that part of my definition of the film is incorrect. He remarks that one need not photograph anything to have a film. One can paint or make marks on the film directly and then project it on the screen. Consequently, what ought to be said is that the film is a creative juxtaposition of screened spaces and times which may be integrated with sound. "Screened" here refers to filmed material which is projected on to a screen.

Some question arose as to whether or not there was a difference between a sequence of slides and a film. I think there is. A sequence of slides, no matter how rapid, is offered to us so that we can attend to each one. A film, no matter how slowly it is unreeled, is offered to us as that by means of which we can attend to a sequence of transitions or motions. A sequence of slides is a set of atoms; a film is an organic unit covering a number of frames.

I have found that it is not possible to see a film as a work of art without seeing it twice. The first time one is caught in the process of following the rhythm. One may be arrested by the photography or the plot, and may even see that it is a work of art. But the appreciation of that work of art requires some attention to the transitions from one space to another, one time to another, one type of juxtaposition to another. In this respect, of course, the film has an advantage over the dynamic arts, since these can be duplicated but never replayed exactly as they had been. The film is more like a spatial art, since it allows one to go over the old ground again and again, thereby making it possible for us to subtilize our judgments and to become aware of nuances we had originally neglected.

Despite its transitive nature, the film freezes time and dynamics in each frame, thereby enabling one to have them again and again. The phonograph record does something similar for music, and the script does something more remote but still somewhat analogous to this for the play. We seem not to have anything but the camera to give us a "frozen" dance.

June 28

The moral and intellectual level of politics can be judged by seeing what kind of men can be conspicuously successful there—Hitler, Stalin. Equally vulgar but not as vicious are Harding and Coolidge. It would be hard to find anyone to match them in other disciplines. Heidegger saluted Hitler; but he did not kill anyone. He was a disgrace to the intellectual life, but we think of what he did as a failure, a lapse, and not as a characteristic—but what Hitler or Stalin did, and what Harding and Coolidge did not do, expressed what they were completely, since they were occupied with nothing other than politics.

The only man who could do what should be done in a political situation is a dictator, for only he can avoid the mediocrity which is characteristic of committee judgments. But a dictator is a finite man and makes mistakes; he feeds on his authority and power, and loses his sense of proportion. The occasional success he can achieve is over-balanced by the blunders he inevitably makes. The best we can hope for is an individual who is checked but not suppressed by committees. This is, of course, what we have tried to do in America, but the division of powers has turned out to be a separation of powers, and not a check on their foolish use, except in special cases.

July 6

A number of thinkers have suggested that contrary-to-fact conditionals, particularly as used in science, can be treated as statements about a connection between the premiss and conclusion as related by some law and subject to certain initial conditions. This makes the contrary-to-fact conditional in a way dependent on the lawlike connection. But is it not the case that the contrary-to-fact conditional is an assertion alongside factual ones? Is it not true that a supposed factual assertion may in fact be a contrary-to-fact conditional?

Suppose it be the case that at such and such a temperature, such and such an expansion of a given metal takes place. Before we engage in the experiment, before we provide for the initial conditions which will hold in fact, we can state this lawlike truth. It is like a counterfactual, and yet there is nothing about which it speaks. But there is something it would speak of were it in fact to be operative as an actual connection between premiss and conclusion under operative conditions.

We can interpret a counterfactual statement as one which expresses the very truth expressed in a factual one, but as exhibited under conditions then not operative. The premiss of counterfactual of science must be related to some factual premiss in a specifiable way, and the conclusion should as a consequence be related to the factual conclusion in a similar way. When and as the premiss is altered, the conclusion should be altered. A set of counterfactuals explicates the meaning of the law which in the factual case yields only one instance.

Alternatively: a law can be stated with a set of variables. Any instance will involve the substitution of values for the variables. The counterfactual offers another substitution; all the counterfactuals together with the factual articulate and presumably exhaust the meaning of the variables employed in the most general formulation of the law.

July 7

Science deals with two types of entities, neither of which is identifiable with the objects of common sense. One type is the theoretical, that which is not within the scope of observation, and which is part of a system serving to explain the various laws science formulates in order to do justice to the second type of entity. The theoretical entities are constructed, sometimes because of observations, and sometimes as part of an effort to overcome contradictions and confusions and failures to encompass laws which characterized previous theories.

The second type of entity is dealt with in experimental laws. These laws are often said to be rooted in observations. And they are. But the observations are a mixture of two operations. There is the observation in a commonsense way of what is confronted, and there is the confronting through the corrective agency or instrumental device of microscopes, telescopes, precision rulers, and scales of entities within limited situations and under controlled conditions. One can, of course, say that what is seen in the second sense is nothing but a commonsense object, placed in a special context and approached from a special angle. But then the difference becomes evidently verbal, for what is ordinarily said to be a commonsense object is not merely one which is confronted without the use of any agency that leads to the acknowledgment of kinds of entities not otherwise confrontable, but one which is confronted in commonsensical contexts.

When we look at a photographic plate, we look as commonsense men. We also see the plate in a commonsensical context. Yet were we scientists, we might see on the plate various lines and marks which for us would be taken to be evidences of entities that might be confronted through other devices or that would be known only in a theory. We would see the lines and marks as commonsense entities, but we would treat them then as signs of something else. This consideration leads to a modification of the foregoing observation, and requires us to say that an entity which a scientist would accept may be symbolized by a common-sense one.

The commonsense man acknowledges signs and symbols, and uses commonsense objects to point to something else. Usually he uses them to point to other commonsense objects; but he can take this or that to sig-nify a God or Good Fortune or the force of Nature. He differs neverthe-less from the scientist, in that the latter uses the commonsense object or entity acceptable to commonsense opinion at that time, to signify either the first or second type of scientific entity—an object of a theory or some-thing in a limited and special context which dislocates the object from its commonsense roles and some of its meanings.

The science dealt with in the fourth chapter of *The World of Art* is theoretical science; the science dealt with by empiricists and pragmatists is the science of laws dealing with confrontable objects in limited and special contexts. A Galileo is inclined to neglect the second or to treat it as a mere instantiation of the first; a Dewey is inclined to reduce the first to the second. But sometimes we find that theoretically known entities are not and sometimes that they are instantiated by confrontable objects, or can be understood to express limiting conditions involving such objects. So far as they are not instantiated, we have a difficulty for the rationalistic account of science; so far as they are instantiated, we have a difficulty for the empirical account. They are not instantiated because laws are often explicable from many different theoretical standpoints and have a mean-ing and a validity apart from any of those standpoints; they are instanti-ated because theories sometimes provide grounds for deducing laws from other laws, thereby enabling us to confront entities we otherwise would not.

July 8

The view that theories and observations or observational laws are independent has been misconstrued by some philosophers of science as meaning that the two are unrelated in fact and are brought into such relation by correlating items in the one with the other. Putting aside the fact that such correlation requires one to take a stand which encompasses both sides and which cannot be defined merely in theoretical or observa-tional terms, there is the fact that no criteria are provided for determining what is to be correlated with what.

Theories seem to originate in two ways. One either tries to articulate some otherwise unintelligible or paradoxical phenomenon, or one tries to provide a relation between known laws or law-abiding phenomena. Both of these ways provide for theories which can be extended beyond the initial cases and which then might require some correlation with observational material, but only so far as this is consistent with the initial accepted correlation. This fact has been overlooked because the approach to theories has been made in terms of them as fully developed and expressed in variables requiring the use of models and a definite relating to matters of fact. But on the present account the variables are derived from constants, and there is initially a definite and justified relation with matters of fact. One avoids the supposition that the theories and laws are therefore not independent by showing that the theories are elaborated by themselves in their own terms, that other theories could be used to articulate or relate the observed, and that the items in the theories have objective counterparts in fact, constituting a world distinct from the observed.

To account for the fact that bodies fall at the same rate, and at the same time to avoid the paradoxes that Aristotle's account of falling bodies involved, Galileo treated bodies as aggregates of distinct atoms. The bodies were thus articulated as aggregates of atoms. There were no particular empirical counterparts for any of those atoms; all that the atomic theory did here was to explain how bodies which differed in size and weight were nevertheless equal as falling bodies, since their aggregational atoms all fell as distinct items, no one affecting, accelerating, or holding up the others. Starting with such a theory, one can go on to ask why it is that chemicals combine in such and such ways, why water boils, etc. These questions can be answered by adding to the initial theory the supposition that the atoms move in such and such ways. If one uses this theory to account for chemical combinations, one would of course have to identify the boiling of water as something which is also being articulated by the movement of the atoms. But this identification is only that of accepting a field or locus for an accepted mode of articulation. The number of atoms involved, and the type of movement in which they engage, will be determined in part by the predictable consequences which flow from the boiling and which can themselves be articulated in terms of a movement of a certain number of atoms.

The second mode of deriving theories involves a connection between observations of law-abiding entities or the laws themselves. Pythagoras discovered the empirical truth that the length of vibrating strings was in a clear functional relation to the sounds produced on a harp. The theory that there are waves set up by vibrating the strings is a consequence wrongly drawn from the theory that the sounds are related to the vibrating strings by waves in the atmosphere. We make a jump from one realm of discourse to another without warrant when we speak of the vibrating strings causing waves and these in turn causing sounds.

We can say that there are distinct sounds correlated with distinct lengths of vibrating strings, but it should be noted that the correlation here is well-articulated in the guise of a wave theory of atmospheric alterations, and that the termini of the correlation are not the sounds and lengths of string, but rather the beginning and terminal waves and what constitutes them. The sounds and vibrating strings are merely loci for those beginning and endings. The theory remains independent of the loci; its entities enjoy a reality of their own. What the theory does is to bring together clusters of the beginning and ending items by means of relations which have to do with those items in relation to one another and in disregard of the nature of the clustered wholes they constitute, or where they are located.

Taking a theory which may have originated in either of the above ways, one can draw consequences from it and see if those consequences articulate something else or relate other clusters. One must eventually free oneself from the initial application, turning the referential terms into variables so as to elaborate the theory in itself, without regard for the observational material. The formally developed theory is not applied to other cases; instead it allows for the guidance of extensions of the initial, more concrete, referential forms of the theory which articulated some observed matter of fact or related a number of such facts.

We work with a theory on two dimensions; on the one we continue to use it with respect to the observational domain, and on the other we elaborate it as a formal calculus. The latter is, of course, independent of the observational domain, but it is instanced in the referential form of the theory, the theory as an articulation or as relational with respect to observations. The latter is not instantiated by the observations or by those laws which, apart from the theoretical connections, characterize the observational data.

It is misleading to say with Nagel that "On the basis of the electromagnetic theory of light, a line in the spectrum of an element is associated with an electromagnetic wave whose length can be calculated, in accordance with the assumptions of the theory, from experimental data on the position of the spectral line." What is "associated" is a line in the spectrum with observations which had been articulated by the electromagnetic theory. The electromagnetic theory relates the observed line with the other observations. Accepting the view that the electromagnetic theory has objects answering to some of its distinctions, one can then speak of clusters of electromagnetic items being related in electromagnetic ways to other clusters of electromagnetic items. The nature of the clusters, i.e., the observed lines and the other observations which are articulated by the electromagnetic theory, are not topics for the theory, though the observed lines should be understood to be clusters in the same sense as are the other observed items which the theory serves to articulate.

Because the purely formal theory was treated as a system in itself, Nagel forgot to note its instantiation in a theory which articulated observable material or in a theory which served as a relation between observable materials. As a consequence, he overlooked the orientation of the instantiating theory (and derivatively of the purely formal theory) in one area of observation, and took the only problem to be the locating of the theory in some matter of fact which was completely independent of the theory. But the theory was completely independent of the matter of fact, only so far as it was also sundered from the initial items which it articulated or which it took as one term of its relational nature.

July 9

The clustered items which are connected by theoretically instituted connections have two roles. They are to be treated severally and therefore on a par with the items which the connections by themselves refer to (and as such will constitute a single world of theoretically acknowledged items), and they are to be treated as making a contribution to the nature and functioning of the clustering totality, which is made up of a unitary force, or meaning, or form, and the items.

What we come to acknowledge as evidence in a given commonsense or otherwise observable object for the existence of theoretically known entities is abstracted from something more complex—the commonsense or otherwise observable object. This is a function of the entities and has a nature of its own due to a unitary form. What the theoretically instituted connection does is to abstract from the commonsense or otherwise observable object those features which can be functionally related to other features. But it does not attend to the features; the features are merely loci for functionally connected units. That is to say the distinctive nature of the features, e.g., that they are lights, or sounds, or weights, etc., is being dealt with; what is connected is an increase or decrease in the intensity of light, magnitude of sound, or weight, etc. The items within the compass of the cluster make a difference to the intensity or magnitude of some feature, the feature itself being understood to be the product of the imposition of a unitary form, and thus to be explicable in terms not provided by the theoretically acknowledged items.

Marriage should be for better *and* for worse.

Israel now will be the Ireland for the American Jews, eliciting their loyalty unto the seventh generation.

Most men are rightly without self-confidence.

Truth crushed to earth will arise again, but crippled and bloodied.

Fear makes cowards of us all, but some do not need that goad.

Being half-educated does not preclude being wholly uninformed.

Two stupid, mutually supportive men are not necessarily more stupid than one; they are merely more confident that they are right.

All, work and no play makes jack.

The poor we will always have with us; that is because there always will be those with more money.

July 10

Theoretically formulated connections relate functionally dependent variations (i.e., variations which are functionally dependent one on the other) of observable phenomena. When we speak of the sun or of some distant star in terms of light rays, what we are in effect doing is foreshortening an account of the variations in the intensity of the light there, or of the way in which the light of the sun or star varies in relation to some other phenomenon.

The theoretically defined connections show the difference that theoretically defined entities make as they change in some way. The change is manifested not in its purity, but in the guise of observable features. The features themselves are expressions of the imposition of a unitary form, which clusters the theoretically defined entities, but the entities, when they vary, affect the observable whole and consequently the features.

The entities constitute a single domain. The differences in the features evidence the changes which the entities undergo as groups, though without any determination of those entities by the grouping. If we have a number of entities operating in a region, the region is not bounded off from other regions of entities. But by virtue of the constraining unity expressed in a feature, those entities will be clustered. The factuality of the cluster is expressed in the feature; the variations which the entities undergo as together making up a region of unclustered entities is expressed in the variations in the feature.

The features cluster the entities, and the entities determine variations in the features. The real object is not the entities nor the features, but the entities as together with the features. Where is that real object? Where is the astronomical sun? Where is the sun we perceive? What is their location with reference to the substantial sun that contains the one and exhibits the other?

The feature as separate from the items is distinct from itself as affected by their variations. The object is neither where a feature as separate is, nor where the entities by themselves are. The feature and the entities have domains of their own with their own geometries. The object is where the feature is effective, where the entities make a difference to the changes in the feature. This location is determined through action, where we can make a difference to the way in which the variations occur. It may also be known speculatively by purging the commonsensical object, along the lines suggested in *The World of Art.*

Not every feature whose variations are explicable in terms of the activities of a set of theoretically known entities is a unifying force; it may be a consequence of a unifying force and may vary while the unifying force does not. Nor is it the case that every feature will have its variations accounted for by the activities of a set of theoretically known entities. Some features will vary as a consequence of the action of something outside; others will be affected by variations in other features in the clustering object; still others will express the nature of the cluster as a whole, and this may remain fixed or constant. The relative brightness of an object may be the result of a change in the atmosphere; one's color may change with fever; transcendent characters such as beauty can remain fixed while the various features may vary in harmony.

Since a law can be stated as functionally relating observable features, we can treat a theory as a generalized version of a law, but one in which the new variables can be developed into a system apart from the law, and can have other laws as instances of some of the deductive consequences of itself.

We can reduce the version of theories as articulations of paradoxical phenomena to that of theories serving to relate variations in observable phenomena by taking the articulations to be ways of referring to observable features and relating these to other features. A body at rest can then be said to have atoms at rest which are theoretically related to the atoms at motion when the body is in motion. The motion of the body can be generalized and expressed in variables and the result given a theoretical formulation. This instance shows that the variables appropriate to an unanalyzed body are not appropriate to the atoms unless those variables are understood themselves to be articulatable into a plurality of subordinate variables. The issue then shifts to the way in which we are to look at the variables in a theory. Generalizing from observations or observational laws allows for variables which are themselves to be interpreted, not by instancing them in the cases from which they were generalized, but as encompassing or as being expressed in a plurality of subordinate variables.

July 11

A theoretically acknowledged *ground* is to be distinguished from a theoretically acknowledged set of *connections*. The former is what I have before termed "an articulation"; the latter is a theory proper.

All scientific formulations of a theoretical kind presuppose a ground. The nature of that ground is altered sometimes in the light of what the theoretical connections demand, but even then there is an antecedent presupposition that the ground is made of such and such entities which have been involved in such and such activities as testified by changes in observable phenomena.

Galileo's acceptance of an atomism was in effect the acknowledgment of that ground which defines modern science. The fact that his atoms have given way to electrons, protons, and the like, but shows the refinement to which our understanding of the ground has been subjected.

This approach allows one to reconcile the Democritean and the Aristotelian views. Aristotelians are opposed to an atomism, the Democriteans are opposed to the acceptance of any reality but the ultimate particles of physics. There is no necessary incompatibility between these views, provided one does not suppose that Democritus has given us an ontology, or that Aristotle's substances have no components having an independent reality.

The Aristotelian acknowledges a "matter" which his substantial form is to organize. Apart from that form, the matter is relatively indeterminate. But it is indeterminate only with respect to the organizing form. It need not itself be one unbroken extension; it could in fact be a plurality of ultimate particles which are organized by a substantial form. As involved with the substantial form, the particles are no longer individual separate entities; they are together as in a region, and function together to determine a difference in the observable features. The Aristotelian tends to make the particles, or the totality of them as making up a "material," to be entirely passive, but there is no intrinsic necessity for this. The Democritean is inclined to ignore or overlook the role of a substantial form; he takes the ultimate particles as constituting a domain of their own to be the only realities. But the fact that they occupy a domain of their own and act there on their own does not preclude their acting in concert in limited regions and there affecting the observable facts, at the same time that they are subject to a substantial form to constitute objects which can act in ways common sense knows.

Aristotle can be said to deal with the ultimate particles only so far as they constitute a single region and as such together determine the functional variations in observable phenomena. Democritus can be said to deal with those particles only so far as they are treated as distinct and interrelated one with the other, apart from any regional clustering.

The substantial form of Aristotle is not imposed on the particles as together; this is an analytic result. Whatever substantial forms there are also have a teleological role. As such they are possibilities as well, possibilities which are inseparable but yet distinct from the analytically discoverable forms of substances as here and now.

July 13

Is sound a feature? If so, what is it a feature of? We seem to perceive it in the way we perceive shape and color, which are adjectival to something substantial. Is it not that a sound is ingredient in a particular space? The substance is the spatialized sound; the percept is the sound as abstracted from a particular space.

When we refer to sound waves, we refer to the factors which explain the difference in time in the presence of sounds at different places. Those sounds are explained as abstracted from the places. All that is then being explained is the time at which the sound is present as a perceptual entity. The sound does not travel any more than light does; what we have are percepts at different times which can be accounted for by speaking of the activity of waves in another area and as involved in another kind of time.

July 17

A woman's reality is her appearance.
Truth crushed to earth is crushed.

Solitude: the one and the many.

The Marxist thinks that the right is always to the left.

Make an end to your beginning if you would not end where you did begin.

When the mind minds the body, the body minds the mind.

He was brave beyond belief: everyday he lived with himself.

Cowardice: Afraid to face the cause of fear.

Foolhardiness: Afraid to be afraid.

Courage: Fear controlled and ready to attack.

Fear: One surrounded by many.

Terror: Oneself in an unfamiliar guise.

August 5

Kenneth Schmitz (in a forthcoming review of *Philosophy of Process*, vol. 1), in the *Review of Metaphysics*, has raised two important questions. Are there not four ultimate languages appropriate to the different modes of Being? Are not some of the terms ascribed to one mode more appropriate to others, and therefore mislead or even misconstrue what is the case? The two questions are not unrelated.

We can answer the first question in at least two ways. We can argue for a single metaphysical but ambiguous language, or we can maintain that there are four irreducible, unmixable languages. Once again, these are compatible.

We have to begin with a metaphysical language which is ambiguous in two ways. It is ambiguous when viewed in terms of conventional grammar and vocabulary, since this is appropriate only to particular actualities severally and together. It is ambiguous too, in that it does not separate out the references to the different modes of Being. Once we arrive at the point where we distinguish the metaphysical language from that appropriate to particulars, we can go on to refine it so that its terms are applicable to the modes severally. In short, we have metaphysical language in the form of a language appropriate to the ultra-natural to begin with, and refine it later.

When we refine the language, we do not find that there are terms which have application solely to one of the modes. Instead we find that they are primarily appropriate there, and have a secondary usage in the others. This is to be expected, for each mode infects the others, and makes a difference to its nature and function. It is proper therefore to speak of "power" when referring to any of the four modes, but in only one of them does it have a primary use. It is possible to have a divergence of opinion as to just which one of the modes is most appropriately said to be or to have power in a primary sense. This divergence will give us only a difference in stress in the different views. I do not think this makes the kind of difference that has great implications for the soundness of a view.

Each of the modes of Being has a distinctive being and nature. Must it not have a set of terms appropriate to it in this guise, even apart from the kind of difference which the other modes of Being make to it? Even if we say that it is to be characterized by some such term as "power" used in a primary sense, we must use the term as constrasting with other primary terms, appropriate to the other modes of Being. If we are wrong to designate mode X as characterized by y when it is by itself, even though y has a primary role there and secondary roles elsewhere when the modes are seen to be in interplay, we will falsify X. But what does that falsification amount to? Does it not mean that we merely misname the mode? Yes; but this does not break the force of Schmitz's objection. The modes are not given singular designations by me; they are given clusters of terms, and his question points up the possibility that some of the terms in a cluster appropriate to one mode may belong to some other cluster.

An answer to this difficulty can be provided by finding a term which was more general and functioned as a variable for all the terms of a cluster. If one objected to the presence of some items in a cluster, one would then be objecting to some value of the variable. This would not be serious. What is needed now is a set of four terms which catches the spirit of the cluster, regardless of whether or not the items in it are correctly designated. And then one need not suppose that the generalized term which functions as a variable is in any way ambiguous. Instead one can suppose that it is a precise term having specifications only with respect to functions which are peculiar to it.

Given four primary terms referring to each of the modes of Being, we can proceed to specify functions for each, show how those primary terms have secondary uses inside the other modes, and show how the specific functions of each are qualified by virtue of the presence of other modes of Being in limited form.

At the present juncture of interest and knowledge, we seem to be able to speak of Ideality, Existence, and God more readily than of Actuality by virtue of the fact that they are encountered in encapsulated forms and as effective on actualities. They provide us with hints as to how they are to be designated in and of themselves. But it is Actuality which is the mode of Being that is ontologically pertinent to the particulars we confront.

The difference between Actuality and the other three modes of Being allows us to find values for the variables of the other three modes, with a consequent creation of a single variable or general term to designate the nature of those modes as standing outside Actuality. But we can make a direct reference to Actuality by means of a single variable or uniquely designating term. If we have a group of four unique terms, however, and follow the clue of the other three modes as to just which terms are appropriate to each of those modes in and of themselves, we will be in a position to designate Actuality by a process of elimination. But if we do not have such a group of four terms, we will have to forge a fourth to contrast with the other three when they are appropriate to the other three modes of Being taken severally and as unqualified by one another.

If we have only one term for each mode of Being, how can we have a grammar? How can we speak of it? How can we build up a system, since our terms will be mere names without content? The answer to these questions follows from the recognition that the modes of Being have multiple nuances in relation to their own particulars; if we want to deal with them in isolation from those particulars, we will find them to have multiple relations to, and therefore to be qualified by, the other modes of Being. Each mode of Being, we must consequently say, can be designated in a unique way, but that way will involve a reference either to its own particulars, or to other modes of Being (where the unique designation functions only as a primary emphasis).

So far as a mode of Being is taken in relation to its own particulars, and thus as being designatable by a distinct term which contrasts with the terms appropriate to other modes of Being, it will be conditioned by its particulars. It will be alongside them and will interplay with them in a common vocabulary. But it will need to be separated out in order to achieve a clarity and rationale of its own.

The unique designation appropriate to Actuality is repeated with variations in the realm of actualities. Some of those variations we have come to designate by such terms as "reality," "wondrous," "contingency." These terms relate to the actualities, but as having their orientation in Actuality; they require us to move away from those actualities to Actuality in order to locate their source and reason.

A consequence of the foregoing discussion is that we deal with actualities in terms appropriate to them as particulars, and also find ourselves using terms such as "wondrous" which require us to look beyond the particulars to Actuality. When we move to Actuality, "wondrous," "contingency," etc., should all converge into the unique term appropriate to Actuality as contrasted with the other modes of Being, but as related to its own particulars. Other terms such as "unity" or "beauty" will relate us first to the encapsulated modes of Being and then eventually to the modes of Being in themselves as related to their own particulars. If we do not move to the ultimate modes of Being from the base of these various terms, we will have them as an unintegrated heap of eccentric terms. If we try to forge a single language using these terms, it will be radically ambiguous unless the terms are given appropriate references to different modes of Being and the whole is systematized. We have one language appropriate to the modes only in the sense that when we move from one mode to another we change our language and emphasis.

To summarize: *1*] There is a single systematic language with different terms used in different parts. *2*] These terms are convergencies from terms appropriate to particular actualities. *3*] We make a direct convergence to Actuality, but only indirect ones to the other three modes, via their encapsulated forms. *4*] There are clusters of terms which specify the aboriginal terms appropriate to the modes by themselves but in relation to their own particulars; these clusters refer to the modes of Being as qualified by one another.

August 6

When we see or designate something as wondrous, we in effect are orienting it in Actuality. In order to deal with the entity as a mere actuality, we must dislocate it from the wondrousness. Wondrousness now becomes a free term. Allowed to remain alongside the actuality or the terms which are applicable to it as together with other actualities, it will be an eccentric particular. Given its own referent, it becomes a means for discoursing of Actuality.

Evidently we have a dislocation of actualities by virtue of the adherence of some such character as wondrousness (or unity, beauty, truth, facticity, being, etc.), an eccentricity of behavior on the part of that which made for the dislocation (when the dislocating agent is freed from the actuality), and a distinctive grammar (when the dislocating agent is allowed to have its own appropriate referent).

If one is immersed in a metaphysical exposition of the modes of Being, one will find obscurities in the object reflected in the account. There will be irrationalities, vaguenesses, gaps. If we distinguish between the

Being and the gaps or irrationalities—which we should, since Being is One and Self-consistent, whereas the gaps and irrationalities introduce breaks and divisions in it—we will, to begin with, have together Being as a unitary locus and Being as pluralized content. But if we refer these gaps and irrationalities to particulars as their source, we will be able to see Being as a unitary content.

In both cases we have a distortion introduced which we cancel by recognizing what produces it, and referring this to its source. This is clear in connection with the realm of contingent particulars; it is not so clear in connection with Being. It becomes clearer with respect to the latter when we see the entire Being as qualified and distorted by something. The focusing on the distortive aspect shows it to be a plurality. The attempt to deal with that plurality forces one to refer the items of it back to actualities as their source.

August 7

I do not think I have given sufficient concentrated attention to the question of the evidences in a Being of the existence of particulars. These seems to be of two kinds: those which involve the use of transcendentals, and those which involve the use of ordinary terms, categories, and processes of knowing.

When we detach some such terms as "wondrous," "being," "unity," "reality," from their carriers in ordinary discourse (thereby freeing particulars for their own proper designations and allowing us to refer the terms to Actuality), we find that we do not have the terms in their purity. They still bear the marks of having been carried by finite beings. It is possible, perhaps, to have them in their full purity, but only after we have attended to the fact that they are tainted by their carriers, even after we have separated them from those carriers and allowed them to refer to Actuality rather than be limited to certain actualities, or even to all actualities.

The second kind of evidence is provided by ordinary terms which, perhaps generalized and universalized, are taken to apply to Actuality. All attempts, such as Whitehead's and Hartshorne's, to take a Being to be a preeminent case of particulars make this move. But they end not with a sound grasp of Actuality or any other Being, but with a distortion of it.

Both kinds of references yield content which is vague, i.e., which cannot be made precise except by separating out contrasting terms. Instead of finding that "wondrous" or "eminently real" refer us unambiguously to a

Being, we find that they seem to have more than one meaning. We can get a single meaning by referring the pluralization of meanings to the plurality of particulars as intruding on the Being. They do this via our thinking, through the use of our categories and terms as limited and qualified by us finite beings. Freeing the Being from these ambiguities leaves us with terms such as "wondrous" as wholly distinctive of Actuality and untainted by any carrier in this finite realm. Freeing the Being from these ambiguities also leaves us with terms such as "eminently real" (which are but generalizations of designations of particulars) as not applicable to the Being, except so far as they can be non-relativized and made to be directly applicable to the Being.

A term such as "wondrous" seems to function as evidence both for actualities and for Actuality. It evidences the latter so far as it is seen to make actualities eccentric and to require separation from them before those actualities can conform to conventional grammars, observations, relations, etc. It evidences the former so far as in being applied to Actuality, it is found to be ambiguous and so far not altogether intelligible; the term is then seen to be a variable and not a proper name or singular term.

The designations of particular things, particularly when used in a preeminent sense, also evidence both actualities and Actuality. They evidence actualities so far as they are ambiguous when applied to Actuality; they evidence Actuality just so far as they serve as carriers for transcendental terms (which in turn infect them).

Two kinds of terms are evidently applied to Actuality—transcendentals and exaggerated forms of designations of particulars. They evidence actualities by virtue of their ambiguity, which becomes clarified when the terms are used distributively. Such use allows for a residuum transcendental which has a pure nature, untainted by being carried by a finite mind or man, but requires us to interpret the ambiguous, exaggerated form (which in its normal use designates particulars) as a variable for which the precise terms for the particulars are values.

Two kinds of terms also are applied to actualities. There are the transcendentals which are used to characterize the particulars but make them fall outside the province of usual grammar and use, and there are the usual terms which are affected by any transcendentals which they might carry. Both kinds of terms are eccentric in their behavior. If we free the latter from the role of carrier, they function in normal ways; if we refer the transcendentals to Actuality, they are ambiguous just so far as they are affected by the carriers we provide in the form of our finite minds, categories, and grammar.

In the case of Actuality, we have an appropriate term (a transcendental) which loses it ambiguity by being freed of the intrusion of its carrier, as well as an inappropriate term (an exaggerated form of a designation of a particular) which loses its ambiguity by being used as a variable for designations of actualities. In the case of actualities, we have appropriate terms (ordinary ones) which lose their eccentricity by being freed from the role of carriers, as well as inappropriate terms (transcendentals) which lose their eccentricity by being purged of all taint of their carriers, thereby becoming essentially proper names. In addition then to two terms which become appropriate when made unambiguous or noneccentric, we have two which turn into a variable or a proper name when made unambiguous or noneccentric. Or, once again: a term which, when made unambiguous, becomes a proper distinctive term for Actuality, will, when freed from a reference to a domain where it is eccentric, also become proper and distinctive. "Wondrous," for example, becomes a proper name when it is freed from ambiguity by being no longer affected by its carrier, and also when it is freed from eccentricity by being held away from the domain where its carrier functions. And a term which, when made unambiguous, becomes a variable for actualities, when made noneccentric by not being affected by a transcendental, will function in our ordinary empirical use and grammar.

There is a lack of symmetry here. We should expect to find the latter term to be a variable both when it is unambiguous and when it is noneccentric, just as the former term becomes a proper name of a Being both when it is unambiguous and when it is noneccentric. The lack is due to an improper analysis. Keeping in mind the fact that what becomes a variable is a special use of some term applicable to finite things (the "super-eminent," "the supreme actuality," etc.), we can properly say that this very term loses its eccentricity by being made into a variable.

What we have then are a proper name and a variable, both of which become ambiguous and eccentric by being used in domains that are not appropriate to them or when the terms are affected by items in another domain. The proper name of a Being is a transcendental which becomes ambiguous because it is intruded upon by its finite carrier, and which becomes eccentric by being used to refer to a domain of particulars. The variable is an empirical term which becomes ambiguous by being wrongly applied to Actuality, and becomes eccentric by being affected by the transcendental which it carries in multiple contexts. The proper name becomes ambiguous and the variable eccentric through the intrusion of something alien into them; the proper name becomes eccentric and the variable ambiguous by being made to refer to what are not appropriate objects for them. In summary:

Vagueness results when	a transcendental is affected by finitude	a variable is applied to Being
Eccentricity results when	a transcendental is applied to particulars	a variable is affected by Being

The variable provides us with evidence of the existence of particulars. We find that when it (in the guise of some generalized term applicable to particulars) is applied to Being it is an ambiguous term, one which seems to be univocal but which in fact shifts its meaning from case to case. (A variable has the same meaning in every case, the shift in meaning being given by the different values of it.) The proper name of Actuality also provides us with evidence of the existence of particulars. We find that when it is applied to Actuality, it too becomes ambiguous, forever tending to break up into a plurality of distinct designations.

The variable and the transcendental will provide evidence for Actuality only so far as they are eccentric, the one by being affected by Being, the other by being wrongly used to characterize particulars. This wrongness in use is a wrongness only so far as the full meaning of the term is involved. It is correct to say that this or that object is wondrous, but the truly wondrous, the wondrous in itself, is a Being, so that any attempt to speak of a particular as though it were wondrous in and of itself, or as though it exhausted the meaning of wondrousness, would involve a wrong application of the term.

There is nothing wrong in having terms that are vague or eccentric, or in having real things which are so. What is unsatisfactory is to have the vague so tensed that it verges on the self-contradictory, and the eccentric so peculiar that it contradicts the demands of what is otherwise acceptable. We dissolve both by turning them into unique designations or variables. The vague and eccentric transcendentals turn into unique designations of Actuality, and the vague and eccentric generalizations from particulars turn into variables. We get unique designations and variables, therefore, from both the domain of actualities and from the Actuality.

A variable differs from a vague and from a unique designation in that it has no object of its own. It merely offers room for various values. It is those values, one might say, in an ambiguous highly general form; but unlike the vague, it does not take the ambiguity to be objective. A unique designation differs from the eccentric and the variable in that it has a transcendental reference. It is connected with a reality and has a distinctive rationale in a distinctive grammar.

We see now that it is not correct to suppose that a transcendental is a "metalogical" term which has found an answering reference. The metalogical term is a variable, but a transcendental is a unique designator. Both variable and transcendental can be reached by trying to avoid eccentricity through a refusal to submit to the rules governing distinct particulars, but the one remains referential with respect to the world of particulars, and the other is turned toward Actuality. Nor is it correct to suppose that a variable gives us the least common denominator of a plurality of entities, so that it could be said to designate "Being" or realities of that type. A least common denominator is expressed by a transcendental. Both variable and transcendental can be reached by trying to avoid vagueness through a refusal to allow any determination of Actuality by actualities, but the variable remains oriented toward actualities and the transcendental refers to Actuality.

A variable tends to solidify itself into a term; it thereupon becomes either a vague designation of a Being, or an eccentric item whose grammar contradicts that of the particulars amongst which it is found. A transcendental tends to spread itself over the entire Being, and thereupon becomes a vague or an eccentric item whose grammar contradicts the particulars amongst which it is found.

The foregoing suffers from the fact that I have not made clear whether the intrusions are ontological or merely epistemological. That they are the latter is evident, but there seems to be ground for supposing them to be ontological as well. This, though, is no reason for slipping from one of these approaches into the other, unannounced, which I am afraid must have happened a number of times. For the moment it would be wise to stay with the epistemological interpretation, perhaps as expressed in languages, categories, or "terms."

Something like these observations must be extended to the other modes of Being alongside Actuality, or as encompassed by Actuality in a limited form. Evidently they apply to the latter, for actualities have no direct relation to other modes of Being. But the kind of difference actualities make to the encapsulated Beings, and conversely, should in some respects be different from that which they make with respect to Actuality. We will get eccentricity, but perhaps not to the same extent, in view of the fact that the encapsulated Beings are not final and therefore not basic enough to make a maximum difference. The vagueness, though, should be greater, in view of the fact that the actualities can be more intrusive and will have less remote and resistant Beings to operate on. We will then have maximum eccentricity of transcendental terms relating to Actuality and a maximum vagueness of empirical terms for actualities in connection with the encapsulated modes of Being.

If transcendental terms relating to Actuality have maximum eccentricity, we should be able to find them to be most recalcitrant to our ordinary usages. And if some empirical terms have maximum vagueness when referred to the encapsulated modes, we should be able to make them most readily yield evidence for the existence of actualities. The transcendental terms relating to Actuality are less vague than the empirical terms applied to the encapsulated modes, just as the empirical terms are less eccentric when they relate to actualities as subject to conditioning by the encapsulated modes. "Actuality" is maximally eccentric, more so than "Goodness," for example, and "most perfect" has maximal vagueness, more so than "most real," where the latter is thought to characterize Actuality.

August 9

There are three possible views to take on the difference in degree of eccentricity (with a correlative vagueness) or transcendentals. 1] It is possible to maintain that Actuality, because it is an ultimate mode of Being, is most eccentric, and that the others, because encapsulated delimited forms of Being, are less so. 2] It is also possible to maintain that Actuality, because it is more remote, is less, and that the others, because they are more involved with actualities, are more eccentric. 3] And it is possible to maintain that the state of being qualified and encapsulated is compensated by being more closely involved with actualities, so that all the modes, or the terms applicable to them, are equally eccentric. I opted for the first of these alternatives without examining the other two possibilities. (Reciprocal considerations will apply to actualities, or expressions of them, as they intrude on Actuality and the other modes of Being encompassed by Actuality.)

Is "Actuality" a more eccentric term than "Goodness," or "Divinity," or "Space"? It would seem to be so, because the others are already qualified in such a way as to be germane to actualities, whereas "Actuality" has a reference only to Actuality as it is of itself. But then shouldn't it be said that the intrusion of terms applicable to actualities should become more vague when treated as designations of Actuality, in view of the difference between the two kinds of reality, and that the intrusion of terms applicable to actuality on the encapsulated modes will be proportionately less vague? If so, I inverted a relation yesterday with respect to vagueness.

Is "actual occasion" more vague than "duty," "sacramental," "temporal," when the first is applied to Actuality and the others are applied to the modes of Being as encompassed by Actuality and relevant to actualities? It would seem so; the latter do say something about the nature of the encapsulated modes, whereas the first misconstrues Actuality and must be treated as a variable oriented toward the actualities.

"Actuality" is a transcendental which is eccentric to an extreme when treated as a particular term in ordinary discourse. "Actual occasion" (Whitehead's term for God as well as for a particular in this world) is vague to an extreme when treated as a designation of God. "Actuality" becomes a normal, uniquely referring term when made to refer to Actuality itself, freed from tincture by any carrier; "actual occasion" becomes a variable applicable to all actualities when the tension within it is seen to be the result of not distinguishing the variable from its values, and that value is then supposed to be a single name or designation of Actuality.

Does the capacity of actualities to intrude on Actuality, and conversely, affect the fact that the two are made to be distinct by the action of God? Does the intrusion mean that God is not sufficiently powerful to enable them to be really distinct? The acknowledgment that the impingement of the one on the other is epistemological will allow for a negative answer to these questions. God enables Actuality and actualities to be independent in their functioning, but this does not preclude some actualities, such as men with minds, intruding upon the Actuality (incorrectly) and using transcendental terms which correctly apply to it. Nor does it preclude the misuse of the transcendental terms by applying them to actualities. When the connection with Actuality is made by mind, correctly or incorrectly (and thus through the use of clear transcendentals or vague generalizations from Actuality, and sometimes with transcendentals which show the affect of their carriers), the separateness of the Actuality from the other basic modes of Being is allowed to stand out in clear focus.

We should expect misuses of ways of referring to the other modes of Being from the base of Actuality. There should be something analogous to vague or eccentric terms here, expressive of the fact that a mode of Being is being incorrectly dealt with through the agency of a transcendental which bears the marks of having been reached from the perspective of

Actuality even though it applies to another mode of Being. I am now close to the question which Schmitz raised. He in effect asked whether I did not mischaracterize some of the modes, not by using empirical terms for them, but by designating them with terms which pertain to other modes. If I did, I so far made transcendental terms eccentric. (They would not be vague, for transcendentals are vague only so far as they reflect the intrusion of finite carriers. We could get such vague terms, though, by using terms applicable to actualities to apply to the sources of the encapsulated modes.) We get an eccentric transcendental having a correct reference to some mode of Being other than Actuality by having the transcendental apply to actualities via the encapsulated form of that mode of Being.

Clearly, there are two kinds of vague transcendentals. There are those which are tinged by their carriers in the shape of particular actualities and which, when freed, become clear and distinct designations of Actuality, and there are those which are misapplied in the sense that they pertain to some mode of Being other than that to which they had, in their purity, been ascribed. And conversely, there are two kinds of eccentric empirical terms—those which are affected by the Actuality-referring transcendentals which they carry, and those which are affected by the transcendentals which are mediated by the encapsulated modes of Being.

August 10

Because of our memory, expectations, and the fact that we learn words through speech, we have in our vocabulary a number of terms for which we are not sure there are any answering entities. These terms are somewhat like those which Russell called "indefinite descriptions." They include such terms as "God," "Beauty," "the wondrous," "all space," and "redness."

When we try to find references for these, we find that the terms become either vague or eccentric. When we try to avoid the vagueness or the eccentricity, some of those terms are clarified as transcendentals, and others as variables.

An eccentric term can be said to violate the law of inference, in that its behavior does not follow the ordered structure of logic. A vague term can be said to violate the law of contradiction, since it permits of the juncture of terms which, when distinguished, are mutually contradictory. When the vague term is reduced to a transcendental, it becomes a kind of general term, violating the law of excluded middle; when the eccentric term is reduced to a variable, it becomes a kind of diversification which can be said to violate the law of identity.

An indefinite term expresses the fact that our minds relate us both to the transcendental and to the empirical, but in such a way that there is a pull of the one on the other. When we get the transcendental and the variable (or its values) in clear and independent focus, we have the two domains separated, and we are either then detached or attached to the empirical world in our language and attitudes.

Transcendental, variable, vague, and eccentric terms all have objects; it is the "indefinite" which is faced as that which is not known to have an object. We do not know whether or not it is just a word, or whether it has a reference.

When we make the vague give way to the transcendental and the variable, by freeing the first from its carrier and by referring the latter to particulars, and when we make the eccentric give way to the transcendental and the variable, by freeing the second from what it carried and by referring the first to a Being, we are left with a clearly designatable Being on the one side, the proper object of a pure transcendental, and with rationally developable particulars, the proper object of the values of the variable.

A transcendental is something like what Tillich called a "symbol" in that it is affected by the object to which it refers; it is a highly general, but nevertheless uniquely proper, name which achieves clarity the more integral it is to the Being which it symbolizes. When men take a secular use of the term "God" to be blasphemous, they are in effect saying that the secular use is also idolatrous in that it invests a secular thing with the kind of substance which adheres only to the term "God" or its cognates.

A transcendental would be a mere general were it not suffused with its object; a variable would be a mere concrete diversification were it not given stability by each of its values. We are forced to turn from the vague and the eccentric because we do not find objects which will allow us to overcome their inherent violation of some law of logic—in their case, the law of contradiction and the law of inference.

The Being at which the vague points does not have a plurality which will allow for the functioning of the law of contradiction. The eccentric violates the rules of the ordinary world, and therefore does not fit in that world. If we want to refer to a Being by the vague, we must give up the law of contradiction; if we want to refer to a plurality by the vague, we must turn away from the Being to a realm of particulars. If we want to remain empirical, we must give up the eccentricity of our empirical term by treating it as a variable, and if we want to keep the eccentricity but find for it a distinctive logic, we must turn toward Being for its referent.

We retain the fluidity of the vague while losing the vagueness by getting a variable; we retain the reference of the vague while losing the vagueness by getting a transcendental. We retain the empirical nature of the eccentric while losing the eccentricity by getting a variable; we retain the generality of the eccentric while losing the eccentricity by getting a transcendental. We do not know how to retain the fluidity of the vague and refer it to a Being, or how to retain a reference by the vague and keep it empirical. We cannot retain the empirical nature of the eccentric if we refer to a Being; we cannot retain the generality of the eccentric if we remain empirical.

A transcendental is not vague just because its object suffuses it; a variable is not eccentric just because its values order it, give it an empirical rationale. But a vague term which is not changed into a transcendental has no proper object and remains vague; an eccentric term which is not changed into a variable has no empirical content and remains eccentric.

August 11

A variable is a rule of diversification. Taken apart from all its values, it has no meaning with respect to other entities; it is completely fluid internally. In a sense it is doubly eccentric, apart from any disturbance from the transcendentals. Values not only give the variable stability from case to case, but enable it to have the meaning of being applicable to those values and not to others.

Confronted with an individual case which is impervious to previously known treatments, we usually find that it has two dimensions. One of these can be clarified as an internal designation of an organic unity (the limit here being a transcendental symbolizing a Being); the other can be clarified as a variable which is instantiated in a plurality of well-orderable cases (the limit here being a variable which encompasses the entire realm of particulars).

We may, of course, have indefinites which are to be directly reduced to transcendentals without residue, and others which turn into variables, but the usual cases are, I think, indefinites which compound both dimensions, and are dissolved by being made to yield transcendentals and variables.

"Variables" in the sense I am now using seem to be quite close to "metalinguistic" rules for linguistic expressions. The tendency of positivists has been to suppose that all indefinites will turn out to be such variables or nonsensical, in good part because they do not see that there can be an orientation toward Beings as well as toward particulars.

In logic, there can be a multiplicity of variables each of which refers to an indefinite pronoun and which can be distinguished by virtue of the reference of the pronouns to one another. "The *x* who was walking is the *x* who was smoking." But here the "*x*" is not a true variable, but an indefinite characterization of a particular. A true variable will refer to "any *x*"; it will be expressed therefore in some such expression as "Any *x* that walks is an *x* that smokes." Care must be taken though not to confound the intent here with what is conveyed by "For every *x*, if *x* walks then *x* smokes." The former is expressed through a capping of the *x* in the *Principia Mathematica*, whereas the latter involves the use of quantifiers.

What is the difference between "any" and "every"? The negation of "any" is "none," or "is not"; the negation of "every" is "some are not." We then have, "No *x* that walks is an *x* that smokes" and "For some *x*, if *x* walks, *x* does not smoke." I am not sure that these keep to common usage.

Quine takes "any" and "all" not to be equivalent (*Mathematical Logic,* p. 70), e.g., "Smith cannot outrun every man on the team," and "Smith cannot outrun any man on the team." But he takes the denial of "Smith can outrun any man on the team," not to be "Smith cannot outrun any man on the team." The denial of "Smith can outrun every (or any) man on the team," he takes to be "Smith cannot outrun *every* man on the team." "Smith cannot outrun *any* man on the team" is treated as saying that "for every or any man on the team, Smith is not able to outrun him."

In the negations we see that Smith, in not being able to outrun every, may nevertheless outrun someone, whereas in not being able to outrun any, there is no one he is able to outrun. In the negative cases, it is evident that "every" is collective and the "any" is distributive. "Any" here alone expresses a true variable.

"Smith can outrun every man on the team" I think is distinct (despite Quine) from "Smith can outrun any man on the team." In the former case, nothing less is claimed than that it covers every (possible) case of man, but in the latter, we say that you can pick out anyone you please and Smith can beat him. We can express the difference as a difference in quantifiers, (ϕx) Smith, and (Ex) Smith, i.e., "For every *x*, Smith can (or cannot) . . ." and "There is an *x* such that Smith can (or cannot). . . ."

"Any" can be taken to be the name of a variable for which we are assured that there is a value, whereas "every" could be used to refer to variables which are really names of collections or classes which may have no members. This interpretation is up against the fact that (Ex) Smith is usually treated as being satisfied completely if there is one case, whereas what is intended by "any" is a reference to all the single cases that there are. The proper way of writing "any" would therefore be "(Ex) Smith, and (Ey) Smith, and (Ez) Smith, etc.," i.e., "There is an x on the team and Smith can beat him; there is a y on the team and Smith can beat him, there is a z on the team and Smith can beat him, etc." This acknowledgment of a plurality is not true of "every," even though it need not be said that every always means that there are no instances of it.

Perhaps it would suffice if we defined "any" as "(x) implies (Ey), (Ez). . . ." "Every" we can then say is the variable without the values, and "any" is the variable with them, if we adhere to the modern view that every or all is purely general, and do not allow for the subordination of some (as would be the case in the usual square of opposition). Or, following a suggestion made by me a number of times, we can think of two squares of opposition, the one having no subordination of some, the other allowing it.

Have I got the negations exactly right? The negation of the above implication would give us a disjunction of universals implying a particular (Ex)-x. Is this all right? Perhaps the matter is of little importance; in any case a logician can patch it up, I suppose, without much trouble. What is important is the fact that a true variable is not necessarily quantified, but always implies a plurality of instances.

An organization, by holding itself over against the cases with which it is supposed to treat, tends to use transcendental terms of itself and leave over variables for the use of the cases. Those variables are defined by the transcendental use, in the sense that they are the terms which are to be referred to particular cases, when the transcendental is applied to the organism as a pervasive name, or as genuine symbol. We can say that it is the ability of the organizations to be able to sustain a symbol that permits one to have a variable for the actual cases. That variable is not possessed by the organization. Who possesses and uses it? It must be someone outside the organization who takes the variable to be that which is to be exhaustively expressed in a set of cases. He could conceivably make himself into an organization; in that case we would have to find another variable for the cases.

Following out this last suggestion, we have a transcendental use of a term leaving over a variable, which can conceivably be viewed as having two dimensions in a new organization, one of which is transcendental and the other of which is a new variable. On this view variables have values, but can nevertheless be caught up as indefinites in new organizations, thereby leading to the further division of the variables into transcendentals expressive of the new organizations, and new variables which refer to what lies outside the organizations.

Conversely, we can envisage a set of particulars and a transcendental which refers to an organization alien to them. That transcendental can be treated as indefinite with respect to some further organization. It will thereupon break up into a new transcendental referring to some further organization, and a new variable which extends over the details of the previous organization.

We come close to contemporary usage of terms if we speak of signs, symbols, and variables, the former being the indefinites, and the others being the signs when they are clear and have referents. When they are impure or misdirected and therefore unclear, they still remain signs, but will possess symbolic and variable properties not altogether appropriate to them, making them therefore be vague or eccentric.

August 12

When we find ourselves with an indefinite sign, i.e., one whose exact function we do not know, and of which we are not sure that it has an object, we try to use it as a symbol, or as a variable, or as both. A symbol is a general term. As a mere general, it violates the law of excluded middle. (Reified, it violates the law of contradiction, for then it is vague). The variable, on the other hand, is a mere rule of diversification. As a mere rule of diversification, it violates the law of identity. (Made into a value, it violates the law of inference.)

In order to avoid violating the law of contradiction, we must find an appropriate content for our general. This means we must find the object for which it can be a genuine symbol. Correlatively, in order to avoid violating the law of inference, we must find genuine values for our variable. This means we must find cases which allow our variable to be instantiated.

In a family, the mother is a symbol. And just so far as she is, the father functions as a variable. As such a variable, he has no other meaning than that of being able to be instantiated in multiple concrete cases outside the family. The richer the content which is accepted as value for the variable, the richer in meaning is the variable.

This illustration seems to indicate that the variable is a mere empty holding place which becomes eccentric if treated as though it were a term, and achieves meaning by virtue of the values we take to instantiate it. But when dealing with ontological issues, and using the variable as correlative to transcendentals, it seemed obvious that the variable ranges over all the actualities that there were. But this is consistent with the foregoing. A variable achieves new meaning as actualities change. The meaning of the variable is always given by whatever values it in fact is instantiated by.

We know that a variable is to be instantiated by all actualities. Can we say that a father, for example, is to be instantiated by all the possible places in the world and that so far as there are some which don't instantiate him as a variable, he is so far limited? But the mother symbolizes only this limited family. Why should this not mean that the range of the variable which the father covers has a limitation too? What would this limitation be? Does the intensification of the symbol, the amount or degree of adherence to its object, dictate what must be the range of the correlative variable? Is the symbol for a Being most intensive; is the variable which is its correlative therefore most extensive?

Do we have a problem of determining either the symbolic meaning of mother or the variable range of father in order to know the other's range or symbolic meaning, respectively? This seems to be a plausible hypothesis. Following it up, we can say that an organization is expressed by a symbol and is articulated in the structure of the organization. The more the symbol achieves concreteness, the more does the variable extend in range over particulars. There is no choice of the kind of particulars determined by either symbol or variable; all we have is the range.

Given such an indefinite term as "mental health," "education," or "government," we eventually arrive at a symbol which can have multiple degrees of intensification. As it increases in intensification, the range of a correlative variable increases in range. As a consequence, we move to the stage where we make "education," "government," etc., into symbolic terms of maximum concreteness, and leave over a variable. That variable is instantiated in actual occurrences within the territory or the reach of the power of the government. Even if the variable is obtained from the indefinite term which yielded what became the symbol for education or whatever, it is not to be understood to be anything other than what the instances dictate it to be. In a totalitarian situation, the variable would have alienated beings as instances; in a democratic situation, the variable would have as instances individuals who were educable as individuals, or who had recognizable rights, etc.

The discussion so far would seem to permit a variable to extend over the oddest cases. Why should not the correlative of the symbol of health or government or education or God be shoes, or subway cars, or elephants? How do we find the instances? Must not the symbol function as a kind of theory telling us what kind of entities would be suitable as values for the variable? If it did, this would mean that the variable was in some sense under the control of the symbol. Would this not deny its autonomy or equality with the symbol?

Suppose that there was a reciprocal determination by the variable and its values dictating the degree of intensification possible to the symbol? We would then have two cases of subordination. Suppose that these were to be treated as correlative? Would we not then be able to say that the symbol tells us something of the kind of entities that the variable can range over, and that the variable tells us something of the kind of content which is appropriate to the symbol?

In the case of the family, we can say that the instances defined by the symbol are what will support the family. In the case of health, we can say that the organization defines the variable exterior to it to have as instances what will promote the functioning of that organization. Ditto for government. Conversely, we can then say that the variable role of the father for the family defines what kind of symbol the mother can be, i.e., how well she can be identified with the family.

Better: the variable defines the content of the symbol to be that which serves to support the independent existence of the values of the variable.

Does it make sense to say that the symbol for a totalitarian government defines the kind of entities over which an otherwise unreferred variable might range? Must not the values for such a variable, since it is defined by the totalitarian system, be cases which support the system? But before it was suggested that the values were the alienated individuals, the very individuals who do not support the system. So far as the system symbolized is concerned, the variable must range over values which support the system; conversely, the symbol must be concretionalized by content which makes it possible for the values to continue to be. A variable for alienated beings, i.e., beings who are not merely outside but are opposed to the system, are to be independently determined; they will then be seen to dictate the content of a new symbol, for example, the symbol of a revolutionary movement.

An institution may divide itself into two parts, one of which is symbolically defined, and the other of which is constituted through a variable. This happens, for example, when the institution is engaged in the production of materials. We then have an internal bureaucracy or organization which is essentialy white collar over against the productive side which is blue collar, and which is to be judged in terms of the units it turns out—the values of the variable whose objects are defined by the bureaucracy. The two together can of course have a symbol and be faced with a variable which has to do with the market that is intended to support the entire twofold organization.

Does this mean that the internal organization of the white collar division of a shoe factory is different from one devoted to making automobiles, and that the two of them differ from one which, like a school, does not have products? (The educated children who might be termed their products are objects of a variable which is comparable to the variable for the entire organization of bureaucracy-shoe producing, and is not to be compared with the shoe-producing side.) Shoemaking and automobile making should differ, except so far as they are nothing more than instantiations of a single "money-making product."

Returning now to the initial problem, it follows that a variable covering the totality of actualities demands that there be a symbol of Actuality, which we may initially obtain from the same source where we got the variable, or which may be independently derived from some indefinite term. (Both the source and the indefinite term are vague designations of some Being.)

When and as we begin to refine our variable over all actualities, we begin to get rid of the vagueness which adheres to a general term which we then also possess, and for which we, too, precipitately provide content. We must have such a general term, for it enables us to know that our variable extends over actualities, just as having our variable extending over the actualities enables us to know that our reference to Actuality is through the agency of a symbol.

The symbol and the variable direct each other to appropriate content, and thereby make them function as genuine symbols and variables. The symbol without such aid is only a general, or has irrelevant content and is vague. The variable without such aid is only a method of diversification, or has become rigidified as a value and is eccentric. The avoidance of the vagueness or eccentricity for the one helps the avoidance of the eccentricity or vagueness, respectively, for the other. We come to have a grasp of Actuality through the use of a symbol because we are in fact dealing with all actualities via a variable.

August 13

It is the generality which can be abstracted from the symbol (and which the symbol concretized through its union with content) that tells us what kind of values there should be for the variable. It is the diversification of the variable (which is exhibited as distinct values) which tells us what kind of content there is needed for the symbol to be a symbol.

The generality was initially found to be eccentric through the attachment of content which is not altogether appropriate to it. The more eccentric the general, the more evidently it tells us what the content is that is appropriate to the variable. The vaguer the variable when it has been located in the non-empirical or organic, the more surely it tells us what the content is that is appropriate to the symbol. The content appropriate to the symbol makes the variable vague; the content appropriate to the variable makes the general eccentric.

We know that there are particulars for a Being because we find that our symbol has a generality abstractable from it which can be seen to function eccentrically. Said more ontologically, the nature of Being is such as to allow for a separation of part of itself in the form of a general or universal which behaves eccentrically. Conversely, we know that there is a Being for our particulars because we find that our variable can be treated as a mere diversification-principle which adheres to content that makes it have a vague meaning. Said more ontologically, the nature of a particular is such as to allow for a separation of a negation or principle of otherness which seems both to be and not to be, i.e., is objectively vague.

The eccentric general reveals to us what the content is over which the variable is to extend; the vague variable reveals to us what the content is with which the symbol is to be identified. The richer the symbol, the wider the range of the variable, and conversely.

An eccentric general tells us that there is content outside the Being, and that it is appropriate to a variable. A vague variable tells us that there is transcendental content, and that it is appropriate to a symbol. The variable loses its emptiness by acquiring content from the eccentric general, which can then become a symbol. The general term loses its eccentricity by acquiring content from the vague variable, which can then become a variable with empirical values. Ontologically said, negation or negativity acquires content from a universal involved in empirical contexts, and a universal acquires content from a negativity which has been involved with Being.

There is a looseness to Being which allows for a universal to behave eccentrically, and there is a looseness to the world of distinct particulars which allows for a principle of negativity to become vague. The looseness in Being is necessary in order that the Being have a nature, for the looseness enables the universal to become a symbol, and therefore to express the nature of the Being. The looseness in particulars is necessary if distinct particulars are to be united in a class, for the looseness enables the principle of negativity to become a variable for those particulars, so that those particulars, while distinct, are part of one world.

Why are there particulars? Asked from the perspective of a Being, the answer is that they enable Being to have a nature. That nature has a reality which is exhibited in a free universal that becomes eccentric through the acquisition of empirical content.

Why is there a Being? Asked from the perspective of particulars, the answer is that it enables the particulars to be distinct in a single world. The particulars are distinct in a world by virtue of a free principle of negativity that becomes vague through the acquisition of nonempirical content.

The only way for a universal to have reality is for it to be held away from that of which it is the nature, and thereby become involved in eccentricity; the only way for particulars to be distinct in a world is for them to be subject to a distinct principle of negativity which can acquire a content that makes it vague. For a Being to have a nature, the nature must be held apart from it, and this is done by that which makes it function eccentrically. For particulars to be distinct in a common world, the principle of negativity must be held apart from them, and this is done by that which makes it be vague.

The ontological situation cannot be remedied: there never is a mere Being whose nature is lost within it; there never is a mere world of particulars whose negativity is lost within it. But when we come to know, we make the nature be expressed in a symbol and the negativity in a variable, each with its appropriate content. The symbol is the nature oriented toward the Being, returned to it as much as we can make it be; the variable is the negativity oriented toward the particulars, returned to it as much as we can make it be.

There must be particulars to enable the Being to have a distinguishable nature; there must be a Being to enable the principle of negativity to have some reality. If a Being did not have a distinguishable nature, it would be indistinguishable from Nothing. If the principle of negativity did not have some reality, the particulars would be sheer others of one another without thereby constituting a single world of particulars. If the nature is given content to keep it distinct, it will behave eccentrically, revealing what the content for the negative should be. If the principle of negativity is given content to keep it a reality, it will become vague, revealing what the content for the nature should be.

The avoidance of eccentricity for the nature is one with making the negative function properly; the avoidance of vagueness for the principle of negativity is one with making the nature of Being function properly. When the negative functions properly, it is a variable; when the nature functions properly, it is a symbol.

Is there such a thing as an objective variable or an objective symbol? If there were the one, there would be a real principle of negativity which operates on particulars. If there were the other, there would be a nature which is inseparable from the Being, as a merely thinner version of it, but nevertheless distinguishable from it.

Once again: there must be actualities so that Actuality can have a distinguishable nature; we know that there are such actualities because we note the aberrant behavior of that nature. There must be Actuality so that actualities can be under the control of a negativity; we know that there is such a Being because we note the vagueness of the principle of negativity. The negativity exerts a greater compulsion than contemporaneity, affiliation, or futurity, because it is more ingredient in the context of the particulars. The nature of Actuality is less relativized than are the natures of the encapsulated modes of Being, because the actualities do not affect it as much as they do these others.

August 14

In creative work and in the growth of an organism, we have something like a symbol becoming more and more integrated with content. The fact is somewhat obscured because the content is being produced at the same time that there is an increase in intensification. In mechanical or analytic work, we have something like a variable for which we are obtaining more and more instances. This fact is somewhat obscured because the content that is provided is going to be dealt with by the same principle, so that the variable seems to have something like the nature of a symbol.

When we are engaged in analytic work, in stimulus response studies, in the mere collection of data, etc., we make use of a variable whose nature is exhausted in the cases covered. We are driven to attend to an organic account because we see the variable function as a term (for it adheres to content). But the variable as a term is radically vague; it is then at once that which has no content and is yet a definite kind of entity. In order to allow the variable to function only with respect to its instances, it is necessary to free it from the content which makes it vague. But this is one with making that content integral with a symbol or form of an organic whole. More sharply: when the behaviorist looks at the principle of behaviorism, he sees it to be at once that which is exhausted in the particular cases of behavior and that which is distinct from other principles. As both of these together, it is intolerable; to keep it in the first guise, the behaviorist must ascribe the content to an organic whole whose form is no longer vague but intensive. In this particular case, he must treat himself as one who as a single human being holds the doctrine outside the realm where it is used as a variable.

Conversely, those who work with organic notions, usually in the form of commonsense ideas, find that these sometimes function in aberrational ways. Some actions are found to be purposeless, and others, which seem in every particular like them, are known to be pursued purposively. We recognize creativity, planning, etc., in others, but the evidence we have is made up of disconnected items which make the plan encompass a plurality that does not appear to have a rationale. In order to avoid the aberration, it is necessary first to free the plan, or organic form, or symbol from the content which makes it aberrational. This is one with making that content be covered by a variable which is instanced in discrete items.

More sharply: if we have the idea of a plan or overall scheme, we find that it achieves support in a plurality of cases. But then it jumps over many cases which seem like the others. We can bring in those skipped cases by treating them as obstacles. But before we do this, we must see them and the others as all instancing the same variable, say that of being distinct items of action, or history, or behavior, or response, etc.

Where the behaviorist presupposes himself to be an organic unit, the organicist presupposes discrete data which he can clasify as all belonging to a single totality, and thus to exhaust some variable. The latter is given material to organize; the former starts with a whole which he can pulverize.

August 16

When a behaviorist or someone like that insists on dealing only with detached items, he necessarily presupposes the use of a variable which those items instance. That variable is distinct from other variables. So far as it is sustained by content, it is vague. It is then at once an instanced entity without meaning of its own and a definite variable over against other variables.

Without dissolving the state of the variable as instanced and yet as fixated with content of its own, we can ideally take it to be merely instanced, and then attribute the content to a symbol. However, as fixated, it is itself functioning as a symbol, though not as a clear one. The necessity that the pure variable have its content become part of a symbol is one with the necessity that the variable in its pure form be seen to be an instance of itself as part of a larger symbolic process. It is the variable as expressive of a single organic view which has itself functioning as that which is exhausted in values.

Conversely, when an organicist insists on dealing only with contexts or wholes, he necessarily presupposes items with which his organism is to deal. Those items are the objects of a variable. But the organic view itself is one view among many; it is an item which must instance a variable. Without dissolving the state of being a distinct item, we ideally take the organism to be a symbol and leave all instances (including that of the symbol itself) to be covered by a variable. This in effect says that a whole takes itself to be an instance of the variable it makes possible, just as a variable takes itself to be part of the whole which it makes possible. The one makes the variable, the other makes the whole possible, just so far as they detach themselves from the content with which they are initially associated.

A whole frees itself from improper content by allowing for a variable, which variable has the whole as an instance of something said, or done, or symbolized. A variable, on the other hand, frees itself from improper content by allowing for a symbol, which symbol has the variable as a part of itself or the symbolized. A whole refers to itself via a variable; a variable refers to itself via a whole.

Better: The occurrence of an organic view is a value of the variable which contrasts with that view. The meaning of a variable is a content for the organic symbol which contrasts with the variable. The recognition that the organic view is a meaning does not deny that it does occur; the recognition that the atomistic view is governed by an empty variable does not deny that the view has a meaning. The occurrence of the organic view is to be understood in terms which the organic view provides for the variable; the meaning of the variable is to be understood in terms which the variable provides for the organic view.

The organic view provides terms for the variable in that it specifies what the variable's values are to be; the variable provides terms for the organic view in that it specifies the kind of content that organic view is to symbolize. The organic view specifies the kind of values appropriate to the variable; the view frees itself from the values, since those values make it eccentric. The variable specifies the kind of content that the organic view needs; the variable frees itself from the content, since that content makes the variable vague.

August 17

The occurrence of an organic view is not eccentric; it is a good value for a variable of atomic entities. But the meaning of the organic view as affected by the occurring is eccentric. It loses its eccentricity by becoming the symbol of the organic content.

The state of being a variable is not vague. It is proper content for an organic view. But the functioning of the variable as affected by the content of the organic view is vague. The variable loses its vagueness by functioning as a mere principle of negativity.

The loss of the eccentricity in the first case, and of the vagueness in the second, is not achieved by slicing off the occurrence or the meaning, respectively. We merely take the meaning side of the organic view to function as a symbol, and the functioning part of the atomistic view to act as a real variable.

The organicist cannot get his view to stand over against the atomistic until he makes the occurrence of his view be a value of an atomistically functioning variable. The atomist cannot get his view to contrast with the organic until he makes the atomistic view be part of the content for an organic outlook. The organicist cannot be a pure organicist until he frees the occurrence of his view so that it can be the object of a variable; the atomist cannot be a pure atomist until he gets the meaning of that view to be content to be symbolized by an organic account.

I have been wobbling back and forth between holding that the state of being a variable or the meaning of a variable is content for a symbol or part of a symbol itself. I think the latter is more correct, for the content which makes the variable be vague is a meaning which adheres to that variable and which, as part of a symbol, adheres to the content of an organic reality. The last sentence of the above paragraph therefore must be changed so that it refers to the symbol and not to what it symbolizes. So far as the state of being a variable is part of the symbol, it is oriented toward the organic content, or more fundamentally toward Being.

The principle of negativity which operates on atomic entities is an intrinsic component of the symbol of Being. Conversely, the occurrence of the organic view is a part of the atomistic world, but it carries a meaning which transcends all the atoms and the variable that governs them. The principle of negativity is vague because it is operative in the symbol when it should not be; the meaning of the organic view is eccentric because it lives the life of its occurrence which is not in accord with what that meaning demands.

The meaning of a variable, how it differs from other variables, and the kind of values it can take, is part of the symbol of an organic view. The view of atomism, for example, is actually a variable whose meaning is part of the symbol of a Being. The occurrence of the organic view is one of the data of an atomic position. The principle of negativity thus, because it is part of a symbol of Being, is continuous with the Being; but it functions exhaustively in a plurality of atomic items. The occurrence of an organic view (or of a symbol of Being), because it is one of the data for an atomic approach, is subordinate to that approach. The principle of negativity as a meaning contrasts with itself as an operant; the symbol as an occurrence contrasts with itself as a meaning inseparable from content.

The language of metaphysics is evidently a language of symbols. The logic of symbols is indicated by prayer, psalms, and liturgy in religion; exhortations and criticisms in ethics; punishment and coercions in politics; in works of art; in historic influence. The problem of metaphysics is that one would like the writing to have something like the clarity and argumentative force of scientific discourse, even though its terms cling to their content the way in which a term such as "God" clings to God in religion. (At present the only widely accepted or at least tried method of dealing with symbols is through a dialectic, either Platonic or Hegelian in character.)

Collingwood and Cassirer offer historic and relativistic accounts of the use of symbols, but what one needs in metaphysics is a logic of symbols regardless of cultural change, though such change may have some affect on the vocabulary. It is not enough to say, as I have sometimes, that the logic of the symbols is to be discovered in a creative activity; this is true, but it does not tell us anything about the criteria and limits of the symbols thereby revealed. One guide could be the recognition of the kinds of entities which are acknowledged to exist and to be open to treatment by variables, i.e., class concepts and the like which are exhausted in their membership. It is the acknowledgment of these kinds which points up the content of the Being which is symbolized, and therefore tells us about those symbols, since these are but attenuations of that content.

There should also be a consideration of the way in which distinct items belong together, without forcing ourselves to consider only organic ways of having them together. They could conceivably be together in correlated and causative ways. These are not ways which conform to the models of the organic or the atomistic in the sense already discussed. If forced to decide between symbol and variable, one will have to opt for the former, and understand the symbol to be a sign which is inseparable from a context of some kind. This would be a tempting alternative were it not for the fact that the logic of empirical items seems to be not dialectical, but in consonance with a "linear" procedure.

Does not Kant teach us that a causal theory is a distinctive kind of "organic" view in which the category of causality is imbedded in content in the way I have been describing symbols? But his context is a mere flowing one, and the "logic" of his causal symbol seems to be a purely one-directional determination. His symbols adds something to the situation, whereas I have been considering only those cases where the symbol is an attenuated form of what is there in fact. With Hegel, one can say that there is a dialectic at work, not in the operation of a given symbol, but in the interrelation of the symbols (or categories in the Kantian sense).

Is the logic of symbols a dialectical relation of symbol to symbol? Yes. But the dialectic need not be Hegelian in character; it could be close to what I have been calling a mere principle of completion, used so as to see what something means when approached from the opposite side.

Granted all this, we want to know something of the way in which a symbol reveals. Granted that symbols are dialectically related, we still want to know about the symbolized. If we accept the present view that symbols are attenuated forms of the Being symbolized, and reject the Kantian interpretation of them as imposing an order on what is otherwise unordered, we still have the fact that there are many different kinds of symbols and symbolized, each of which deserves study apart from its relation to other symbols and symbolized. A scientist wants to study the relations which hold between entities; even if we grant that his domain is dominated by a symbol, we are still left with the problem of articulating that symbol, or of taking fractions of it in various empirical situations.

If causality or scientific inquiry is treated as though it required symbols, all we would have left for our variables would be the sheerest atoms. But things seem to hang together, and to be affiliated and disaffiliated in various ways. Granted that we have a context of causality to be dealt with via a symbol, we still are faced with the fact that we seek causal connections between particular items, and do this through a logic which is not appropriate to a symbol referring to an entire domain, nor to a variable applicable to a set of detached items.

We get a variation on the Kantian position by taking causality or some other basic category to be facing detached items and then assimilating them to itself. But instead of supposing that the category becomes more and more intensified in time, all we need suppose is that each assimilable item provides an occasion for a constant degree of intensification. We would then have A] an intensification which had degrees with respect to a static object; B] an intensification which had degrees over time; and C] an intensification which was constant with respect to items assimilated over time. The last would seem to provide the meaning of symbolization which is appropriate to "linear" inferences.

August 18

A symbol can function as a rule with respect to items covered by a variable. When it does this, the activity of assimilation is usually performed not by the rule but by a reality which embraces the rule and whatever items it can control. The symbol does not, of course, solely assimilate; it allows for a rejection as well. Growth and decay can be understood to be the outcome of the adoption and release (by the structure of an organism) of content which is governed by a variable, i.e., content which is made up of discrete items not affected by the structure.

If we treat the content as made up of discrete items to be ordered by a symbol, we return to something like a Kantian position with respect to the categories, with the difference that he seems to suppose the content to be continuous and indefinite, and does not envisage the case where the content might be released from the category at some later time, in the same or in a modified form of it as it was when first assimilated.

The symbol in adhering to content which is governed by a variable makes that content behave eccentrically, i.e., not as items which are merely together, to be dealt with statistically. Scientific theories of the linkage of these items with one another are tantamount to theories of cosmic symbols in which all those items are immediately imbedded. Theories which suppose that small groups of these items are enclosed in organisms to which those items are then subject to some degree may either start with the items as merely alongside one another, or as already ordered in some way in a cosmos.

The variable for a behaviorism takes discrete items of behavior as values. The behavioristic theory, however, makes use of a symbol employed by a man. That symbol relates the discrete items in stimulus-response patterns or in variants of these. This symbol is part of a larger symbol which relates to the man who uses the behavioristic theory.

In inference, we have a man making use of a rule with respect to items that were not governed by the rule, and which will yield us a separated conclusion also not governed by that rule. The rule is a symbol which is an attenuated form of the mind or being of the man, at the same time that it functions to provide a context for the items covered by a variable.

If it be permitted to commit the paradox of calling secular items "sacramentalized" because they are subject to the control of powers outside them and thereby become eccentric relative to their behavior as not subject to those powers, we can say that it is the function of a symbol to sacramentalize the items covered by a variable, as well as to adhere to a Being who may exercise the power to bring those items within the orbit of the symbol. It is not the symbol, but the items subject to it that are thereby made eccentric. But it is also true that the pull of the items on the symbol will make the symbol eccentric inside the context of the discrete items.

We have two kinds of eccentricity here; the eccentricity that is due to the fact that discrete items are brought into another domain where they are subject to new conditions; and the eccentricity that is due to the fact that the symbol which works on the discrete items is subject to the laws governing those discrete items. We should now expect to find two kinds of vagueness: the vagueness which results when a variable or its items qualify an intruded-upon symbol or a Being, and the vagueness which results when the variable or its items are qualified by a symbol or a Being on which the variable or values intrude. When and as variable or items become eccentric by being subject to a symbol or Being, they make that symbol or Being vague; when and as the symbol or Being makes the variable or items vague, the items make the symbol or Being be eccentric.

1] From the perspective of the symbol or Being, it is desirable to have the vagueness which comes from the qualification of the variable or its items by the symbol or the Being, for this vagueness affects only the variable or its items as in an alien domain. *2*] From the perspective of the variable or value, it is equally desirable to have the eccentricity which comes from the qualification of the symbol or the Being by the variable or the items, for this eccentricity affects only the symbol or the Being as in an alien domain. *3*] From the perspective of the variable or values, it is also desirable to have the vagueness which results when the symbol or Being is disturbed by the variable or its items, for then these make their presence felt. *4*] From the perspective of the symbol or Being, it is also desirable to have the eccentricity which results when the variable or its items are disturbed by the symbol or the Being, for then the variable or its items are sacramentalized. The vagueness and eccentricity should of course be eliminated if we want to have a pure symbol or variable; they are desirable only so far as they express an advantage exercised from one perspective.

When we use a rule of inference, we want the items to become eccentric because sacramentalized (*4*) as distinct beings, and (*1*) to be vague because the rule controls the items. We want the rule or the Being to be vague as a result of the control by the variable or its items (*3*) and to be eccentric (*2*) because it is part of a context appropriate to distinct values. When we use a rule of inference, we deny to the items the life they had before (*4*), and make them at once be identical and different in themselves (*1*). When we try to have a communicable language, we deny to the symbol or Being the transcendence they had (*3*) and make them behave in ways which violate their appropriate rationale (*2*).

An inferential rule is made to adopt items that thereby achieve a new career and lose the distinctness of being they had before, since they then are involved in the inferential context. The reciprocal is appropriate to communication, when we make the symbol, in particular, function in our ordinary communicative contexts and thereby become vague as at once meaning something not in that context and yet belonging to the context, and to become eccentric in that it is subject to the laws that govern non-symbolic entities.

A little while ago I took a symbol, or Being, or a rule, to be eccentric just so far as it appeared in an empirical context, and not because it no longer followed the rationale it had before. I took vagueness to be a consequence of a variable being a function and a meaning at once, and not because it was in a new context where it lost distinctness. Are the senses different? Perhaps not. By appearing in an empirical context, the rule, etc., is subject to a new rationale which is not appropriate to it as rule, etc. By being subjugated by a rule, the variable gets a meaning in addition to its function and thereby becomes vague.

I have not been consistent, I think, in the use of my terms. Should one say that the symbol becomes eccentric, or becomes vague, when involved in the empirical? Should one say that the variable or its values become eccentric or vague when involved with the transcendental? Or do both become both eccentric and vague?

August 19

From the perspective of a concrete pluralism, or from the perspective of a formal unity, the other is something which can be accommodated only at a sacrifice. The pluralism becomes eccentric by intruding on the unity and by being forced to function within the confines of the sacramentalizing unity; it also becomes vague, since the items are qualified by the intruded-upon unity and are thus distinct and yet united, secular and yet sacramentalized. The formal unity becomes eccentric by intruding and by being forced to function in a world of many entities; it also becomes vague, since it is qualified by the intruded-upon items, and because it is a meaning which is organic and yet is dispersed in those items.

We normally live with the formal unity and the concrete pluralism intertwined; we must engage in an act of abstraction in order to have them both in their purity. We can, of course, have the pluralism in a unity which itself will have a plural and concrete character with respect to some other formal unity, and conversely.

Formal unity and concrete plurality affect one another. The result is a double eccentricity and a double vagueness. The double vagueness is exhibited in the emotions; the double eccentricity constitutes a single rationale which characterizes action. The primary lived reality is an emotional possession of both formal unity and concrete plurality carried out in an intelligible practice.

Metaphysical speculation and empiricism (where this is taken to emphasize pluralism in the concrete) merely stress one side or the other of the emotional practical complex. And any organicism or functioning atomism but specializes the speculative or the empirical stresses.

The occurrence of the speculative view and its utilization of a plurality both make for eccentricity and vagueness; so do the encompassment and the meaningfulness of a plurality. The metaphysician tends to ignore the occurrence of his view and to look at the utilization only after it has occurred; the functioning pluralist (I say "functioning" to avoid a confounding with the speculative view of atomism) tends to ignore the encompassment and to take the meaningfulness to be exhibited in the plurality. The one concentrates on the use of a pure symbol and the other on the use of a pure variable. But in fact, the one finds his symbol turned toward the plurality and the other finds his variable turned toward the organic whole, with the consequence that they both become eccentric and vague.

"God" is a symbol, but it is also a word in the dictionary and has a common grammatical use; "shoe" or any other common term is a variable, but it is also a word which has a meaning differentiating it from other variables.

We can take our plurality to be men, facing the organic unity of a society or a state. The lived reality of them both is "emotional" and "practical." The emotional factor is expressed in private and civil rights and duties; the practical factor is expressed in adjustment and civilized living.

It is not yet clear whether the eccentricity of the formal unity (to concentrate on this) is due to the fact that it has an empirical side where it is one of a plurality, or to the fact that it makes use of something in the empirical world. The matter becomes acute when we speak of an organism, for here we have the organic unity antecedently involved in the world of pluralities, and also concerned with absorbing some others. And when we begin with the first use of a symbol on a plurality, we will have this symbol becoming eccentric because it works on a plurality outside it. So we have three cases—the unity as having an empirical pluralistic side, the unity as engaged in controlling or possessing something in the empirical, and the two cases together. The common case is the first, and expresses the emotional-practical situation; the second case is that of the use of a rule on content; the third case is that of a functioning organism which is already complex, as possessing elements.

The three cases can perhaps be reduced to one, by noting that the factual side of a formality is always with us, and that it is merely enriched or added to when there is a use of other empirical items. The case where we start with a pure symbol and make it operate on the empirical gets at the beginning of the process by which the symbol acquires its factuality. This would mean that we can envisage a pure symbol turned toward the empirical. In fact, however, we have already used the symbol by attending to it in this world, and thus initially have the case where the symbol has a factual side. The empirical use of a pure symbol is an idealized case, just as the having of the pure symbol or a transcendental use of it is.

August 20

A rule articulates a symbol for the purpose of dealing with a plurality of entities. A formal logic congeals variables into relative pronouns for the purpose of dealing with a single system. Correlative with the use of a pure variable which is exhausted in its values, there is the use of a pure symbol which is attached to a unity. The logic of the pure symbol in one form has been given by Hegel in his account of the development of the categories, for the categories are in fact symbols of the real, inseparable from the real to which they refer.

Is the only logic of symbols a dialectic one? No. There is surely a logic in a work of art; by following its rhythms, moving from tension to climax, etc., we come to make symbolic use of the work of art. The Hegelian tells us how to relate symbol to symbol, whereas in art we carry out a process which in effect is the achievement of a symbol that adheres to its referent. The Hegelian view can be assimilated to that of art by seeing the progression of the categories in Hegel to be a progressive achievement of an adequate symbol of the Absolute. Conversely, we can assimilate a work of art to the Hegelian view by taking each step of the work of art to involve the next step in something like a dialectical way.

Art seems to be more pertinent to the understanding of religious symbols than an abstract dialectic such as Hegel's. The trouble is that we cannot formalize it, or give rules in advance. Also, instead of looking at the object of the symbol, as was suggested by me in my presidential address to the American Philosophical Association, Eastern Division, in art we look at or work with the symbol or its parts. This limitation is also characteristic of the Hegelian dialectic. What is wanted is a logic of symbols which attends to the symbolized. We have something like this in mysticism, existentialism, and pragmatism, which in different ways concern themselves with distinctive logics pertinent to symbols, but which are developed in the concrete by attending to the subject matter.

Dewey states the principles for practical thinking, but applies them in each case so that they are integral to the subject matter. The principles are for him variables for the symbols that are in fact used. These variables are distinct from those which take particular entities as values. Or they can be treated as the latter when these are turned toward Being and not toward particulars. If we take the latter alternative, we can say that the same kind of formal considerations hold for a logic of symbols and a logic of signs or entities, but that the meaning of a logic of symbols is exhausted in a concrete embodiment of those symbols in their content. By the "same kind of formal considerations" I do not mean that the logical rules are the same in both cases, but only that both sets of rules can be stated formally. In the symbolic case, those rules are impotent, and the rules therefore are given a new role and meaning (i.e., they become eccentric and vague from the perspective of their formality), whereas when rules are used to deal with distinct entities they force the entities to become eccentric and vague (though the rules are perhaps modified to some extent, just as the being—as Cassirer would perhaps insist—is modified by the symbols of it).

We have evidently at least three important questions to settle regarding the logic of symbols. 1] Is there a formally expressed rationale of the internal character of the symbol? 2] Does one develop the logic of the symbol by attending to the symbolized; if so, how is this done? 3] Is there a logic interrelating the various symbols with one another? The first—to begin with a reasonable hypothesis—is answered by turning to rules and viewing them as directed toward unity. The second is answered in experience and perhaps in inductive logic. The third is answered by dialectic or by accepting the formal logic of ordinary variables, and rigidifying the variables to give us a similar logic, but one with meaningful terms.

If we know the answer to the first and third, do we need the second question? Can we say with respect to the first and third that we know we are developing them properly by noting whether the kind of aura we started with remains? Thus can we not say that if we still have awe as we divide or interconnect symbols of God, we are working in consonance with the subject matter?

A symbol is tied to its subject matter and as a consequence has its tonality affected by it. We know that we are following the logic of the symbol when we continue with that tonality or intensify it. This means that even in the understanding of a work of art we must, from the beginning, have a sense of an underlying reality and use its effect on the art as a guide that we are reading the work of art correctly. Any merely formal statement of the paths we are following in the interpretation are but dummies, though there is no reason why one should not state certain pivotal facts: indetermination, e.g., is to become determination, according to Dewey, or we must move dialectically, according to Hegel, or we must seek completion, as I have urged, etc.

The consideration of tonality applies to a plurality of symbols if they are directed toward the same subject matter. But suppose they are not? Must we not then look for a single subject matter which embraces the plurality of them, and see the symbols for the plurality to have a tonality expressive of the single subject matter? If, for example, we had a feeling of peace with one religious symbol, and one of enhancement with a second, must we not look for an underlying awesomeness of numinousness which these symbols are to possess in a limited form? The feeling of climax, etc., involved in the appreciation of a painting can be the foreground of a sense of beauty, and this can be a revelation of the space-time-dynamics of Existence.

We now have a criterion telling us when we are articulating and interrelating symbols correctly. But can we have guides or rules, or must we proceed by trial and error, noting when the tonality begins to fade or to intensify, etc.? We can have guides, based on a reflection of previous encounters, but the logic of symbols is essentially experimental.

Wonder for Actuality, Awe for God, Sublimity for Existence, and Admiration for Ideality could be said to be the tonalities that inform their symbols, and the subdivisions and the interconnections of these. These are criteria for the maintenance of the logic of the symbol; the guides will be dialectic, completeness, system, formal logic of variables, historic discussions, analysis, and indeed any device whatsoever that has in the past proved fruitful in clarifying and bringing one into closer harmony with the various modes of Being.

When we turn from a study of Beings to other unities, we should find something similar to the tonalities that symbols get from Beings. We are using the correct symbols with reference to man when we find that we become more intimate with him, that we can sense his moods or anticipate his responses, all of which are reflected in the tonalities that result from his being in harmony or in friendship or in love. Those tonalities are sympathy, openness, and joyousness.

What is the tonality that is appropriate to a symbol of an organization? Would it be the sense of being accepted, adjusted, being decent, or being free while bound? It seems to be all of these.

Civil Disobedience: Committing a wrong to right a wrong.
Freedom: Bound to choose.

No man's land: Women in conversation.
A lie is too restless to lie.
A cause can be because a being can cause.
War: self-destruction by a roundabout route.

We must distinguish between the individual who is in accord with a unity, and the symbol which that individual uses. When we say that decency, for example, offers a criterion of one's proper symbolization of an organization, we refer to the side of the individual that is public and organizational in role, and not to the individual who may himself be symbolized, and in any case uses and tests whatever symbols we employ with respect to organizations.

August 21

Many terms used in ordinary discourse have a symbolic import. "Father," "mother," "home," "my country," are normally used as symbols. It is true that they do not often increase in intensity. But it does seem true that the symbols convey to us something of the quality of their objects. What we then obtain is a feeling. This is to be distinguished from an emotion. The latter is a turbulent activity which can be removed through action; the former is a private state inseparable from an objective fact, without turbulence though capable of increase and decrease.

When a work of art is being made, we acquire a feeling of the nature of Existence at the same time that we purge our emotions through the action of making the work. Since a work of art is a symbol of Existence, when and as we purge ourselves of an emotion in the making of a work of art, we acquire a feeling answering to the majesty of Existence. The feeling is the subjectification of a quality characteristic of the object of the symbol.

If we were to suppose that all language is symbolic, or were to isolate that portion of it which is made up of such symbolic terms as "mother," etc., we could take language as a whole to be a symbol of mankind, and to be accompanied by a feeling of being right, or accepted, or allowed, or communicative.

The more we use a language, the more we feel at home with the users of it. This contention of course has limits; we do not necessarily increase our feeling with the persistent use of language. Many symbols become clichés and are used solely as signs. We can use language to abuse and hurt and alienate others who belong to our community. And, of course, God might terrify, and the word "God" can be used in perverse ways. In these cases we are using the symbol with respect to the values of a variable, as our emotional state indicates. This does not mean that the only feeling we can have when we use a symbol properly is a value-enhancing one. We can symbolize evil powers—as we seem to do when we refer to snakes, toads, or brute force.

When a work of art is produced, the emotions are purged; as a consequence, we often find ourselves with a kind of satisfaction. This satisfaction has often been taken to be the mere outcome of the purging, but if the above is right, it is a feeling which answers to the nature of Existence's sublimity or majesty. The excellence of the work of art is one with its adequate symbolization, and this is one with its proving to be a vehicle for the purging of emotions and the achievement of a deep feeling of satisfaction or completeness.

It is a question whether "beauty" should be viewed solely as a property of the art object by itself, or to reflect the art object's adequacy as a symbol. A fine work of art is, of course, a symbol integrated with Existence; it then and there has beauty. What is being asked now is whether this beauty is adherent in the work of art or in it as related to Existence. I am inclined to say the former, only because we often speak of the work of art by itself as being beautiful or not.

We should have as many basic feelings as there are types of Being— ultimate Beings, Beings which are encapsulated, and Beings as involved in different disciplines. On the basis of what I have already written, I should distinguish at least the feelings pertinent to the modes of Being; to Ideality, Existence, and God as encompassed in Actuality; and to the Beings which govern the worlds of action, ethics, art, politics, and religion —i.e., to the four modes of Being as involved in human activity and concern.

Analytic philosophy has the difficulty of not being able to distinguish sign from symbol, because it abstracts from feeling. Some have tried to shear off a factual or sign side, and set this in contrast with an emotional accompaniment, so that to say that something is good or desirable is but to say that it has such and such characters and we want you also to approve of it because of them—the "wanting to approve" apparently expressing the accompanying emotion. But this is to deny that the words themselves have a weight. Were the program carried out, poetry would be reduced to prose with an aura of emotion, and God would be a proper name which was used emotionally. But poetry is no kind of prose, and God is not a name, but a term of address, a symbol of an ultimate Being, or more usually of an encapsulated form of this.

If feeling accompanies a proper use of a pure symbol, he who feels must be separated from the symbol and its object, in contrast with the case where he is emotional, when he, as a pluralized body, interplays with himself as a unified mind, or when he, as one of many men, interplays with an organization or other unity. It is the function of religious rituals and of patriotic exercises to have feelings elicited which remain after the rituals and exercises are over.

Metaphysical discourse is symbolic and is accompanied by a feeling of wonder answering to the wondrousness of Actuality. There are other feelings, but these are either limited to encapsulated forms or are reached from the base of wonder or from the limited encapsulated forms. The feeling of wonder remains after the metaphysical work is done. Whatever emotions we have, because of our looking at things with undifferentiated minds and bodies, are partly purged in the course of the construction of the metaphysical system, to leave us as beings whose minds and bodies are distinct while we stand away from the symbols and their objects, as pure objective data.

It is reasonable, I think, to assume that men from the very first have a symbolic approach to all that lies outside them. This is accompanied by a feeling of being placed-in-a-world-which-is-ominous. All other symbols can be said to refine this original symbol, given initially in anything what-soever by which we refer to what is not ourselves. When we deal with variables or prose signs, we can be said to abstract from the symbolic situation. This is the position taken by existentialists.

An alternative view is that we are emotionally involved with Being to begin with, and it is in the course of the purging of our emotions through activity that we come to separate out, refine, and use symbols. The aborig-inal fact would be an emotional involvement of a finite being with Being or Beings and with other finites; action would lead to the purging of the accompanying emotion and the freeing of the individual to use symbols and variables in their purity and in relation to one another. When used in relation to one another, they would interplay as refined entities subject to some kind of control.

August 22

If there are feelings accompanying the use of pure symbols, par-ticularly of the modes of Being, ought there not be something correlative accompanying the use of pure variables? If we wonder when faced with the wondrous, and are in awe when faced with the awesome, what feel-

ings do we have when we are faced with Existence and Ideality, as objects
of pure symbols?

The answer to the first question might be that there is a sense of self
which accompanies the use of a variable. That sense of self becomes
sharper with a greater range and use of the variable.

The answer to the second question might be that we feel ennobled
when facing the Ideal, and that we feel that we ex-ist, i.e., spread out and
make a difference when we face Existence. The awe, ennoblement, and
ex-isting are felt most distinctly when we are dealing with the modes of
Being as caught inside Actuality; when we move to the Beings themselves, they get the tonality that accompanies mysticism (joyous unity?),
duty (happy responsibility?), and intuition (tragico-comic feeling?).

Men in carrying out roles function as symbols for organizations. They
then have a dimension of their own. Organizations, on their side, have a
rhythm and career of their own; they also provide various positions to be
filled. The roles are carried out through the agency of skills, and the
various positions are filled through the acceptance of individuals for
them. When the two mesh, we still continue to have the privacy of the individuals and the life of the organization. It is only when we hold on to
all four that we are in a position to solve the problem of the way men
should function in their organizations, and particularly the state. The
skilled man filling out a position, with self-respect and in such a way as to
allow the organization to continue and to prosper, is working out the nature of a civilization. There is here a constant need of adjustment of the
individual and the organization to one another, without loss to their
independence or integrity. The adjustment will involve exacerbations by
them of one another; these exacerbations will be minimized if the change
that takes place involves a simultaneous expansion of the individual in
his privacy and of the organization in its career.

In the current problem of the poor and the underprivileged and their
place in America, we find most men stressing either the need for new
positions in the society, or the need to have skills taught which will enable men to fulfill established or new roles, defined by society's positions.
There is some acknowledgment of the privacy of the individual, but little
regard for what this might be occupied with; and there is little acknowledgment in theory, though much in fact, of the need for the entire organization of society to continue to be in effective harmony and at peace. Men
need to have an awareness of the worth of themselves—which is not
identical with an awareness of the dignity of their ethnic background;
they must be taught skills, both old and new to make possible the fulfill-

ing of roles; and they must be met by an efficient and just order which provides positions, both old and new, which can be filled by all the members of the society. Today we need more stress on the first, without neglecting the others. It is not enough to have a job, even a good job, if one has no feeling of worth in himself or as a part of the organization.

To achieve the first, we must make evident what can be done privately; to achieve the second, we must make the organization be engaged in significant work and allow for significant functioning in it from any position. But all must at the same time be pointed toward civilized living, where the arts and sciences are produced and appreciated. Civilization is the product of the creative working out of the juncture of skilled men filling significant positions in organizations, while enjoying a privacy and facing a prospering order.

August 23

The private side of man, emphasized by Plato and Augustine and thinkers of the East, is occupied with the exercise of freedom in detachment from the empirical world. We have here the mind that speculates, has faith, acknowledges duties, and is unique. This private self is a condition for and a consequence of the individual as possessing skills. The Platonist emphasizes the conditioning dimension, and the empiricist the consequence dimension. The Aristotelian can be said to insist on them both, for according to him, virtues are habits achieved by actually engaging in activities.

Ideally the skills are matched by positions in society. As a rule though, there are skills for which society has no proper use, and there are positions for which many men are not qualified. There are periods and places where artists or actors or huntsmen, etc., have no significant role, and there are men who are not trained for any of the posts that the society can provide. Once again we have a consequence and a condition. The positions and the skills are both consequences in that the presence of positions prompts the teaching and learning of skills, and the having of skills has some effect on the organizations, prompting them to make some provision for those who have the skills. The fact that there are men who do not fit into the going establishment, either because they do not have the needed skills or because there are no positions open to their skills, shows that these conditions and consequences are not adequate to cover the entire situation.

We could say that if there are no positions open to men with certain skills, those men do not have the skills that are needed. But this is to use the going institution as the criterion of what is needed. We could with equal justice reverse this approach and speak of all cases of maladjustment as being the result of society not making positions open to everyone. But this would only emphasize the use of men as they are as the condition to which an organization should conform.

The positions made available by an organization are conditions and consequences of the organization itself. They are conditions in that they provide the articulation of the organization, enabling it to carry out its functions; they are consequences of it in that as the organization moves along its career, it requires certain parts of it to be filled out in various ways. The American Constitution seems to emphasize the positions as a condition, but a totalitarian state emphasizes the state as a condition.

The course of civilization involves the interlocking of skills with positions in an experimental, pragmatic effort to enable men to be and work together in harmony while the organization continues to function maximally. But this interlocking must not be separated entirely from the individual in his privacy or the organization as an ongoing reality. The private individual and the organization are themselves conditions and consequences of the interlocking of skills and positions, i.e., of the carrying out of roles. The private individual as condition for the assumption and carrying out of roles is today stressed by existentialists; the individual as consequence of the roles would seem to be the view stressed by Hegelians.

A civilized man would be one who carried out his role at the same time that he lived a private life and stood over against a distinctive organization.

In the past, I have sometimes spoken as though the organization was solely a means for the making of men. It is possible I exaggerated the fact that the individual is more important than the mere organization. On the present account, both individuals and organizations are means. The ideal result is to have both interlocked in roles, while each has its own being and distinctive career.

Thirteen different factors seem to be here involved: *1]* the individual in his privacy; *2]* the individual with his skills; *3]* the first as a condition or consequence; *4]* the second as a condition or consequence; *5]* the organization with its own rationale; *6]* the positions in the organization; *7]* the organization as condition or consequence; *8]* the positions as condition or consequence; *9]* roles; *10]* roles as conditions for privacies; *11]* roles as conditions for organizations; *12]* roles as consequences of privacies; *13]* roles as consequences of organizations. In the last four cases, the roles, though products of what has already affected and been affected by privacies and organization, themselves inter-act with those privacies and organizations.

Returning now to Actuality and actualities, we can distinguish: 1] the individual in his private feeling; 2] the individual as using signs; 3] the feeling as conditioning the use and choice of signs; 4] the signs as conditioning the feeling; 5] Actuality in itself; 6] divisions in Ac-tuality, perhaps those given by the encapsulated modes; 7] Being as a condition of the divisions; 8] the divisions as a condition of the Actu-ality, in the sense of limiting it; 9] symbols as junctures of signs and divisions; 10] symbols as affecting privacies; 11] symbols as affecting Actuality; 12] roles as affected by privacies; 13] roles as affected by Actuality.

August 28

There are three ways in which a symbol (and what it symbolizes) can become aberrant: 1] by its facticity; 2] through the intrusion of the variable or the values of the variable; 3] through the infection of an intruding variable or its values.

There are three ways in which a variable or its values can become vague: 1] by virtue of the meaning which pertains to them; 2] through the intrusion of the symbol or symbolized; 3] through the in-fection of the symbol or symbolized when they intrude on the variable or value.

The sign to begin with has the symbol and variable mutually infective though not necessarily to the same degree; the reconciliation of the two in a practical life involves their mutual infection with some approach to a similarity in degree.

August 31

The mind should be viewed as the orientating factor in man, and thus as that vector which relates him to Actuality and to the three modes of Being that are confined within it. No one begins with such a mind clearly separated from the body; he has the two intermixed to constitute a sign which has an emotional root and is to be explicated in practice. The orientating in the beginning is toward other actualities, but it is toward them only as going beyond them to Actuality.

Only after one has learned how to retreat from common sense is one able to use the mind as a distinct power. It then operates by making use of the content of Actuality or the other modes to control the use of variables. Most of our concepts are the result of the union of a grasp of some Being with some use of a variable having bearing on a limited number of actualities.

Consciousness and conscious functions of the mind are all the product of a release of its orientating aspect and a return of it to concrete situations. Only after this has taken place for a long time is one able to forge concepts of the Beings themselves, and make use of well-defined symbols to express what those concepts intend. Consciousness and thought will then be something like what Plato referred to by "reminiscence," for these operations express a return to an initial situation. There is a big difference, however, in the present view and Plato's, for he thought that thinking involved a return to a pure state of Being and thought, whereas I am now contending that it involves a return to a mixed mode where body and mind are intermingled. The pure state is desirable, but it is the outcome of an act of detachment from the mixed mode achieved after there had been a kind of blind symbolic contact made with Being.

September 5

If two or more men perceive something they may 1] perceive as individuals, 2] perceive as informant and respondent, or 3] perceive as a unity.

1] Epistemologists and psychologists incline to take individual perception to be the basic or only form. They seem justified in doing this, for it is always an individual who perceives, judges, knows. But one then tends to overlook the fact that there are categories shared by a number of men that may not be the categories which in fact govern their individual perceptions.

2] In *Nature and Man*, when dealing with the development of language and the development of mind, I emphasized the case where an individual takes note of something and another attends to his accompanying gesture and eventually perhaps to what the other attended to. This is an instance of our second form of perception. Here there is something common being noted, but the conditions for the noting of it which are set initially by one or a few individuals are accepted by the others. Those conditions may express something of the original individual's or individuals' biases and intentions. We take something like this position when we play a game such as tennis, and attempt to act in terms of conditions provided by the other player.

3] More common than either of the above two, and perhaps the normal case of which the others are specializations or perhaps even only idealizations, is where the individuals share a common vocabulary, categories, myths, beliefs, expectations, habits, and practical objectives. Here the objects are understood in terms which reflect the nature of the group and not of any individual in it.

When the individual knows something, he will undoubtedly subject it to conditions peculiar to himself; but the data on which he imposes these conditions will already be conditioned by the common outlook which he shares with others. He sees a common objective as that which is to be seen in individual ways; he knows what is common, usually before, and sometimes when, he knows as an individual. The common knowledge reflects a common inheritance, a common language, a common set of accepted principles of verification, and his position in a common situation. He need not have a grasp of these commonalities; it is enough for him to occupy some position with respect to the others, and there approach the whole from a particular angle. When a defensive football team awaits the snap of the ball by the offensive team, each member is concerned with a team-object, though each looks at it from a particular angle. We do not here have a plurality of angles which somehow intermesh; rather we have a single fact faced by a number from different positions.

September 6

An organization has a lived and a calendral time. The lived time may be that of a business corporation, a nine-thirty-to-five affair, or it may be a twenty-four-hour matter as it is in a family. The calendral time is a matter of recurring dates and pivotal occasions; in a state it makes reference to holidays and workdays, the times for financial statements, inventories, etc.

An organization also defines a set of positions. These are distinctive places in the organization having distinctive tasks and usually some connection with one another, so that something done in one requires something done in another. These positions might be divided into the essential and the conventional. The former relate to those without which the organization will not be of a certain kind—without rulers or sources of authority there is no state, for example. The conventional positions are partly a result of accident, and partly a result of a need or a desire to utilize whatever men or talents are available.

When men fill a position, they occupy limited places inside the organization. But the health of the organization depends in part on the ability of the men not only to utilize their abilities in the position, and thereby at the same time to express themselves and enable the organization to function, to be efficient, and to be steady and perhaps to grow, but also on their ability to realize common objectives and thereby enable the organization to achieve its ends.

The organization has an ideology pointing to a myth or to a personalized form of an ideal. That ideal can be made the objective of each of the men in the positions which the organization provides. But each man ideally will see the ideal as that which is to be realized by others in distinctive ways. Each will face the ideal as an objective which is to be diversely specialized.

Whenever a number of individuals function with respect to a common objective, something like an organization is presupposed. The common objective is a specialization of the organization's goal. Some individual or individuals can make the organization's goal an objective. This objective can be shared, but then the individuals do not occupy positions in the organization. So far as they have positions and look at objectives from these positions, they presuppose an antecedent commonality which specifies those positions in relation to one another and thereby dictates the nature of their common goal as something internally specified by the organization, and not serving as the goal for the organization.

If the goal for an organization is profits or peace or maintenance of power, it is usually desirable to have some individuals concerned with assuring these. But those individuals, as having distinctive positions in the organization, are actually occupied with one phase of the profits or peace; the other phases are dealt with by others in the organization. The phases, all said to be occupied with profits, or peace, or some such similar trans-organizational goal, in fact deal with specializations of the goal of the organization. The profit which a business might have as its goal is something to which the organization as a whole is directed. Whatever concern with profit is characteristic of this or that position is but a concern with a specialized form of profit which different positions realize in interlocked ways.

There is a difference, then, between the objective of an organization and the objective which is common to a number of interlocked positions. The one is rather constant, the other is constantly changing; the one is definitory of the nature of the organization, while the other is descriptive of its actual functioning. Each position specializes the entire objective. The specialization occurs not in the meaning of the objective, but in the way in which it is being realized. This distinctive way of realizing the objective, of course, can be itself accompanied by a specialized objective. But whether this occurs or not, from a given position we have the same objective that we find in another position, but which is approached for such and such realization in the light of the fact that it is to be approached for other realizations from other positions as well.

September 8

From the fact that a work of art is a symbol, three important consequences can be drawn. *1*] The internal constitution of the work of art, its tensions and climaxes, its nuances and contrasts, are distinctive ways in which this particular kind of symbol is produced. *2*] A symbol adheres to its object; the artwork consequently must be seen to be attached to the Existence which it symbolizes. *3*] The enjoyment of a work of art involves a sharing in the symbol and thereby participating in the reality it symbolizes. (The symbolic nature of a work of art is, of course, to be distinguished from its iconographic import or from any representation that it might provide or convey. The artist does not have to attend to the symbolic function; his concern is to make the work of art by making use of the medium and emotions in a creative act.)

One should expect to find distinctive symbols characteristic of the different ways of approaching the various modes of Being. Religious symbols, used both publicly and privately, bring one in contact with God in a way no other agencies can. The public symbol is expressed in the liturgy, and has the effect of affiliating men at the same time that it relates them to God; the private symbol is expressed in prayer, and has the effect of making a man open to the presence of God. In the latter case, the man identifies himself more fully with the symbol than the artist does, and as a consequence, attends not so much to the prayer as to the object of it.

The symbols of art are matched by the symbols of history, particularly as exhibited in historic narratives. These symbols are the product of the union of items which are connected by principles of relevance rather than (as is the case with art) by principles of organic completeness. To read an historic narrative properly is consequently to be brought into contact with what is portrayed. What is portrayed, to be sure, is in the past, but that past is also in a sense contained within the present and is there symbolically faced. The historic symbol, like the art symbol, but unlike the religious symbol, is somewhat opaque, forcing its user to attend to it primarily, rather than to what it in fact portrays, though it seems to be the case that a historic narrative is less opaque than an artistic work.

Ethics and politics also make use of symbols. By means of them, one is brought into relationship with the Ideal. The political symbol is primarily in the form of a myth, and is articulated or built up by having a plurality of positions interlocked. In every organization there is a set of interlocked positions which together constitute the myth that has as its object the objective of the organization. When individuals occupy those positions, they not only take on roles—which are the products of the interplay of their abilities or skills with the positions and opportunities made available—but accept and vivify the myths. In knowing the myths, they become attached to the objective of the organization though usually without any clear knowledge that this is the case. The myths may be built up from different positions; they are inevitably articulated by those positions. Nevertheless, they have a unity just as surely as a work of art has. It is the use of a common myth by individuals in diverse positions which enables them to be in consonance and to have a common direction toward the objective of the organization. (The ethical symbol seems to have a minimal content but to have a vital force, so that one who accepts it finds himself attached to the Ideal as that which obligates him.)

Since philosophy is occupied with ultimate reality, it must also make use of a symbol. An entire system can in fact be said to be a symbol of the mode of Actuality primarily, and incidentally of the other modes. This symbol is distinctive; it has within it a number of subordinate symbols reflecting the main distinctions of the ultimate Beings.

The subordinate symbols of philosophy have their own grammar. This is produced as the inquiry proceeds. They also have a logic of their own, just as the symbols of history have. But where the symbols of history are connected by a principle of relevance, those of philosophy are connected by reasons.

Because men have attended to reasons, they have been inclined to overlook the fact that the style of a philosophy is a part of it as well. Philosophy is not art; the style is not that important. But it has some importance; it expresses the way in which the various subordinate symbols are interrelated.

Do we distort a philosophy when we deal only with its arguments? What is the nature of the arguments as part of a symbol and thus as orienting us in a Being or Beings? Are arguments in and of themselves to be formulated solely by means of signs? These questions are not altogether independent. The first and third evidently are to be answered in the affirmative, and receive clarification in the answer to the second. Though each particular argument can be stated in a purely formal way and thus through the use of signs, the entire argument is to be taken as a symbol or a part of one, and is to be related to other arguments as supplementary, each contributing an element in a single outlook or emphasis. We here come close to what Peirce contended for against Descartes, when he objected to a linear development of a philosophy and opted instead for one which intertwined reasons to constitute a single rope.

The style of a philosophy does allow for a logical dissection of arguments. What it does not allow is a logical dissection of the relationship of the arguments one to the other; those arguments are related, not as mere conjuncts or as merely relevant to one another, or as contrasts and conditions, but as concordant and supportive thrusts toward a common factor, and eventually toward a common Being in which such a common factor is a part.

The logic of actualities proceeds by *modus ponens*. The logic of religion instead proceeds by affiliation; of history by relevance; of art by organic unity; of ethics by enrichment of value; of politics by enrichment of power; of philosophy by completion through reversal; and of action by completion by production. In the first of these, we move away from a beginning to a new terminus. In the others, we hold on to what we have achieved and try to make it function within a larger setting. In these others the logic, as it moves phenomenologically by accreting new items, also moves on in depth to give one a stronger grip on the symbolized reality, either through the provision of a stronger bond (as in ethics), or by enabling one to have a closer contact (as in religion), or in some combination of these, as in the other cases.

In the case of philosophy, we can make use of the principle of completion with respect to arguments as wholes, or with respect to conclusions drawn from such arguments in accordance with *modus ponens*. But why should *modus ponens* be usable at all in this connection? If *modus ponens* is appropriate to the plurality of actualities, is it not used improperly in connection with arguments relating to Actuality or any other mode of Being? But if we do not use it there, in what sense can we be said to use arguments at all? Is it not the case that a symbol can be constructed with the use of signs? Is it not the case that we can work inside a symbol in any number of ways without affecting the ultimate logic of the symbol in relation to other symbols? But then ought we not also say that if we use symbols for each of the modes of Being, we will need another symbol to tell us about their interrelationship? But is that interrelationship an object to be symbolized?

We are led to consider two ways in which an argument could be used —inside a symbol and with respect to the relation of the ultimate symbols to one another. If we speak of a principle of completion in both cases, we will have to distinguish them as "symbolic" and "non-symbolic," respectively.

Not everything is clear to me here. What seems relatively clear is: *1*] actualities as affected by limited forms of Ideality, Existence, and God, as illustrated by ethics, politics, art, history, and religion, are subject to conditionings by virtue of which they are interlocked to constitute symbols for those limited forms of ultimate Beings. *2*] The different modes of Being are governed by a logic of completion which does not involve the use of symbols, unless symbols can be used to align one with a set of relationships as well as to bring one into closer contact with Beings.

What is left over is: *3*] the kind of effect Actuality has on actualities and the expression of the result in a logic making use of symbols or items which together constitute a symbol. *4*] The kind of logic which is involved in the use of symbols each of which attaches us to Actuality.

September 9

A philosophic system is a symbol. The parts of it are interrelated by a logic of their own, just as a work of art has its parts related by a logic of their own, and a religious communion has its members related by a logic of their own. The interrelationship is in part due to the effectiveness of the Being which is symbolized. The affiliations of the members of a religious community, for example, give us the logic of the way in which the members of that community are related; but the affiliations are due to the operation of God on them. The connections of the elements of a work of art, similarly, while governed by the logic of a created organic unity, are affected by the Existence which the result is intended to convey. The artist—a point not made by me in the books on art—relates the various elements of the work of art, not as a man in isolation from the rest of the universe, but as subject to conditioning by Existence.

Not every element in a work of art answers to a distinction in Existence; nor does every element in history do so. Religious communities and individuals may have components which have nothing to do with the distinctions characteristic of God. A similar observation is to be made in connection with ethics and politics. It is also true of philosophy and action. However, this fact does not preclude the existence of distinctions in the grand symbol which answer to distinctions in the object of that symbol. Such distinctions are objects of symbols which are subordinate parts of the grand symbol.

We have then *1*] symbols of modes of Being given by an entire discipline—philosophy, ethics, religion, etc.; *2*] subordinate symbols which refer to distinctions in the modes of Being and which are related by distinctive logics; *3*] elements which must be united in order to produce the subordinate symbol or a grand symbol, but which themselves have no counterpart in the Beings or in distinctions within them.

The elements of a philosophic system are words and ideas. These may refer to actualities, and so far as they do, they are only signs. But we classify the actualities, bringing some together as complex and others as simple, some as men and others as subhuman. These distinctions do have distinctions in Actuality answering to them. Simple entities constitute a subordinate domain of their own, apart from their being clustered by the more complex actualities which are alone encounterable. Human beings, through the agency of their minds, are representative of Actuality and other modes of Being.

The treatment of actualities (in a philosophical system) as falling into various classes is therefore not to be understood to be empirical or scientific; the classification reflects distinctions in Actuality, somewhat in the way in which the various types of art reflect distinctions in Existence, and the way in which various types of religious activity—ritual, prayer, song, and help—reflect distinctions in God. (I have not previously given sufficient attention to the problem of classification; the only strong attempt I made was in connection with art, and this was done in relation to distinctions in Existence. But classifications of a similar nature with respect to Actuality, Ideality or God I have not attempted, in part because the distinctions in these have not been as evident as those in Existence.)

Actuality has distinctions answering to the major divisions amongst actualities. It also has distinctions which reflect the fact that it embraces delimited forms of the other modes of Being, that it is affected by the other modes of Being, and that it makes a difference to the other modes of Being. As a consequence, the symbol which is the philosophic system has a number of types of symbolic parts, as well as parts which have no symbolic role. The symbolic parts refer to the distinctions answering to the kinds of actualities, the delimited modes, and the modes which are alongside Actuality.

All these different parts of a symbol referring to Actuality are interrelated as so many distinct items which are equally real and which are completed by the rest. This interrelationship or logic is distinct from a grammar; the latter refers to the kind of rules required in order to produce sentences, whereas the former is concerned solely with the production of a symbol. This, though it may have a sentential form, is to be lived with or in, and not merely related to other sentences. (I am not sure how far one can carry out this distinction between grammar and logic, particularly if one refuses to suppose that all grammar is arbitrary in its rules.)

The symbol which refers to Actuality has relations to the symbols which refer to other modes of Being. It is related to them also by virtue of the principle of completion. The result here is not a symbol, unless a symbol can be employed to relate one to a relation of togetherness and not to a Being, in which case it is to be understood to be a super-symbol that is as distinct from the symbol of a mode of Being as are the sub-symbols out of which the symbol of a mode of Being is partly composed.

Sub-symbols and symbols are interrelated by a common logic, according to the present account. But this is perhaps an oversimplification. After all, there is considerable difference between a connection provided by a Being and a connection which has no reality of its own; it seems antecedently implausible to suppose that the two kinds of connection are similar in their functioning or rationale. The relation of the modes of Being to one another is evidently guided by a principle of completion, but the relation of the various parts of a mode of Being need not be so guided. There is no principle of completion leading us from space to time to causation, or from one possibility to another, or from one of God's powers to the others, and there need not be any such principle leading us from Actuality, as germane to complex actualities or to a functioning Ideal, etc., to simple actualities or to some other functioning mode within the compass of the Actuality.

It would seem then that there is a contingency governing not only the existence and behavior of particular actualities, but of the classifications to which these are subject, even though those classifications reflect distinctions in Actuality. Actuality has distinctions in it which cannot be accounted for by supposing that one of them is completed by all the rest. The distinctions are characteristic of the Actuality, but they cannot be accounted for, except by taking some account of the nature of actualities and of other modes of Being.

The view that the natures of actualities, as subject to a basic classification, are expressive of a distinction in Actuality, confirms the view I recently formulated to the effect that the variables which we use to refer to actualities have their range determined by symbols that prescribe the nature of the values for those variables.

Why should Existence have the three dimensions of space, time, and dynamics? Why should Ideality break up into the possibilities that it does? Why should God have just those powers of omniscience, omnipotence, and the like? Why should Actuality have distinctions matching complex and simple actualities, or the human and the subhuman?

Rules of perspective, relations of complementaries, and the like, all have to do with the grammar of a painting; the logic concerns the way in which the various colors and designs are interrelated to produce an adequate symbol of Existence. Similarly, the cross references of the various propositions in the *Modes of Being*, and the movement from conditioned factors to the conditions, are part of the grammar of the philosophic system; the logic of the system has to do with the relation of the modes of Being to one another, and the way they condition actualities to make them fall into various kinds. The primary kinds are those which require a reference to Actuality; the other kinds have to do with values, force, and affiliations. The latter require a reference to delimited forms of the other modes of Being.

The classification of the arts into spatial, temporal, and dynamic obviously answers to distinctions in Existence. But the manner in which these different dimensions are utilized by the different arts does not have such answering distinctions. They seem to reflect the different ways in which one can approach a given dimension of Existence, with apparently the same revelatory result. If this be taken as a clue, we should now go on to say that different kinds of actualities reflect differences in the way in which Actuality can be approached or represented. This will leave distinctions essential to Actuality, which express what the Actuality is, as interplaying with the other modes of Being in their ultimate or in delimited forms.

It would seem that we have certain essential distinctions in Actuality which relate to itself in relation to other modes of Being, and certain contingent distinctions which express the way in which those essential distinctions could be utilized by actualities. But then we are faced with the question as to whether the actualities are already divided into kinds and make this fact manifest in Actuality, or whether the kinds are a function of distinctions in Actuality, or of those distinctions together with some diversity in our approach to them. I think we must take something like the last tack and see the actualities to function in ways which become demarcated by virtue of the kind of distinctions which Actuality allows, and which contribute to the differentiation of the differing functioning actualities. Actualities differ in kind because they must approach Actuality in different ways so as to be actualities which are all equally real.

When we turn to organizations, we can make a related distinction between essential and contingent distinctions. Some positions are essential, making possible the reality and functioning of the organization itself; others are but anticipations of the way in which individuals, with different skills, will approach those basic distinctions, thereby constituting roles in the organization—or more strictly, constituting roles which unite skill and position, and thus make both individuals and organization function on behalf of a reality larger than either.

The family has positions for father, mother, and child. An individual who occupies the position of father gives himself and the position the function of constituting a role. The role of being a father is thus distinct from that of occupying the position of father. Many a man has the position without having the role, and there can be cases where men assume the role without having the position.

If both the role of father and mother are carried out properly, father and mother will pursue common objectives and thereby make it possible for the family as a whole to realize its appropriate goals—security, peace, persistence, and perpetuation. The common myth will work in them as a final cause; but it will be realized in different ways as the individuals act out their different roles.

The parents can look at their children from the vantage point of the myth (or familial ideology), and thereby see the very same object, but this will not preclude their dealing with the children in diverse ways. Something similar occurs when individuals make use of a common philosophy.

This conclusion encourages the thought that the different arts which stress space, the different arts which stress time, and the different arts which stress dynamics, offer equally satisfactory revelations of their respective dimension of Existence. A trio of them might yield a single complex symbol of such a dimension. If the former claim is justified, one can then go back to the kinds of actualities and treat them as so many different equal ways of referring or revealing a phase of Actuality. Difference in kind will then tell us no more than that there are different distances from Actuality which different types of actuality must traverse.

We can then distinguish five types of symbols: *1*] simple symbols of Actuality—Being, principle of equality; ground for actualities; principle of otherness; *2*] complex symbols of Actuality produced by combining signs or actualities as distinct items, but belonging together as members of a single kind, and conditioned by the Actuality; *3*] simple symbols of the other modes; e.g., God; *4*] complex symbols of the other modes; e.g., a religious community; *5*] symbols of the relationship of the various modes of Being to one another—principle of completion, togetherness; these are all complex, being made up of symbols of the modes in systematic connection.

1] The simple symbols of Actuality is what I had in mind when dealing with eccentric particulars in my presidential address to the APA, ED. I there attended to the fact that they had an aberrational grammar. They could be said not to have a logic except in the sense 5, where they are brought into relationship with other symbols of other modes.

2] The complex symbols are here somewhat like works of art. They are produced through the use of items which may have no symbolic function and thus may not answer to anything in Actuality. Each has a logic, in that it is achieved through a definite kind of operation on its parts. But it is questionable whether there is a logic connecting these complex symbols to one another; they could be said to be ways of referring to the Actuality from different distances. We do, of course, relate the different kinds of actualities to one another; we recognize their relationship in evolution, and we recognize the relationship of wholes of a macroscopic sort with physical elements (which constitute a domain of their own though clustered by the wholes). But this means only that the relationship of kinds to one another can be studied. When this is done, each kind is freed from its role as a symbol of Actuality. But it is not obvious that the totality of ultimate physical particles makes up a single symbol of the very same reality that is symbolized by the totality of wholes, though this I think is a consequence of the present supposition.

3] These symbols seem to have application both to the delimited versions of the modes of Being with which actualities are concerned, and with the modes of Being themselves as they stand away from such involvement and are interlocked with Actuality. (Strictly speaking we should have different ways of referring to these different symbols. Up to now I have been content with using adjectives to distinguish God, for example, as immanent from God as transcendent, or the God of religion from God the Being, but it would have been better to use distinct symbols for each.)

4] The complex symbols of the modes other than Actuality are the words, signs, acts, or beings of actualities. They are therefore similar in nature to the complex symbols that are used to deal with Actuality. This fact has been indicated by my referring to them as communities, works of art, and the like.

5] The logic of metaphysics is primarily concerned with the symbols which have to do with the systematic connection of the various modes, and thus with them as having a necessary reference to one another. The togetherness of the modes of Being, particularly as discussed in *Modes of Being*, is a distillation of the relation which connects the various modes. They need one another to complete themselves. They act on one another and are affected by one another. Their togetherness is not merely capable of degrees of intimacy but has a dynamics to it, expressive of the references of each to the rest.

September 10

1] Every organization has essential positions, without which it would not be that kind of organization

2] When positions are occupied by men, the men fill roles.

3] A role is a symbol, inseparable from a position.

4] The role as symbol is one of a number of equally valid and effective ways of referring to the organization as a distinctive reality.

5] The organization as a distinctive reality has its own objective, usually expressed in the form of an ideology or myth, and realized in the guise of particular objectives, the realization of which is begun here and now.

6] The men in their roles are occupied with the supplementary activity of realizing the particular objectives.

7] The men in their roles have a knowledge of the same particular objectives, though they approach them from different positions.

8] Ideally, the men in their roles have a knowledge of what is to be done in the other roles; the particular objectives which each faces is specialized by each and is understood to be specialized by the others.

9] The specializations of the objectives occur together with the presence and effective control of the objectives over the course of the specializations.

September 11

When we reverse the application of a symbol and apply it to actual entities via a variable, we make the entities fall into "natural" classes, i.e., to have natures. A symbol functions in such a case somewhat like an Aristotelian substantial form; it is a governing universal which makes otherwise uncharacterizable units have a meaning and a function. Without the use of the symbol, there would be no way of determining which entities are values for a variable. By operating on the actual entities via the variable, the variable is associated with items which the symbol takes to be appropriate to the variable.

There should be a converse operation which involves the application of the variable on the content appropriate to a symbol. The variable is a principle of diversification; by being applied on the content of a symbol, via the symbol, the content is differentiated. This enables the symbol to have an internal articulation, which may be sustained by means of subordinate symbols that are interconnected in accordance with the demands of the variable.

A symbol which operates on actual entities without the intermedita-
tion of a variable will itself act eccentrically, and will make the entities
act eccentrically as well. A variable which operates on the content of a
symbol, without the mediation of the symbol, will make that content
and itself both become vague. A symbol, though applied to actual entities, ceases to be eccentric when it is mediated by a variable; a variable
ceases to be vague when applied to symbolized content via a symbol. The
one becomes a "variabilizing" symbol, the other becomes a symbolizing
variable.

If we take "God" as our symbol, that symbol will make a variable
apply to sacramental objects. If we take God to be the content of our
symbol, we will make the symbol "God" apply to a differentiated content—God's different powers, for example. Sacramental objects behave
differently from other kinds, though to be sure they have a secular base
and as such conform to secular conditions. But purely secular objects,
no matter how familiar and regular their functioning, are also governed
by a variabilizing symbol, i.e., a symbol which applies to actual entities
as so many values for it.

Eccentricity is thus a relative matter, reflecting the fact that we
have accepted some variabilizing symbol without question. Vagueness,
too, is a relative matter, in that a symbolizing variable, i.e., a variable
which is applied via a symbol to the content of a symbol, acquires a
limited reference through the mediation of the symbol. We usually accept the mediation of a symbol without question, and look at all other
usages of a variable to symbolized content as somehow special.

A symbol applied directly to its appropriate content is neither eccentric nor vague, but then it lacks internal differentiation. Similarly, a
variable applied directly to actual entities is neither eccentric nor vague;
but then it lacks all warrant for applying to them rather than to something else.

We accept without question certain internal differentiations of our
symbols, and certain meanings for our variables. Theologians are accustomed to making the first of these moves, whereas analysts make the
second. A more persistent theologian than the usual would go on to use
his symbol to determine the range of his variables—variables which he
could discover by asking how it was possible for his symbol to have a
differentiated symbolized content. A more persistent analyst than the
usual, similarly, would go on to use his variable to make symbolizable
content internally differentiatable—content which he could learn about
by asking how it was possible for his variable to have a definite range.

Eccentricity is a contextual matter; it is possible to take some context as basic and regular and thereupon see other items to function eccentrically there; but vagueness seems to be an objective feature, expressive of the fact that something can be said to be both x and non-x. If there were justification in the symmetry which allows one to make correlative statements with respect to both symbols and variables, we would have to say that we cannot avoid having our discourse about particulars infected with vagueness. We confront a world of particulars only so far as we use a variable which is vague, just as we confront a Being only so far as we use a symbol which is eccentric because it deals with differentiatable content. ("Eccentricity" and "vagueness" are evidently not being used here to refer to the way in which items behave in an alienly defined context or to refer to the way in which a sign is given definite meaning by being applied to symbolized content without the intermediation of the symbol.)

There seems to have an intrinsic and a relative meaning for both eccentricity and vagueness. The intrinsic relates to the fact that any symbol or variable requires the mediation of the other; the relative refers to the fact that some mediation is accepted without question and all others are seen to involve distinctions otherwise unaccounted for, or to the fact that a symbol or a variable is applied directly on what is appropriate content only for the other. The latter could be termed "avoidable," the other "unavoidable" relative meanings for eccentricity and vagueness, where "unavoidable" entails presupposing some accepted base.

September 13

We men are bounded in many ways, and it is one of our needs to discover what those boundaries are and to see how far they can be stretched. Those boundaries relate to our minds, bodies, wills, to us as unitary human beings, and to us as actualities.

All of us are bounded by the past; what we are is in part what we have been, or what others had been. Our minds are governed by categories and beliefs which we have inherited; we reach into the past only so far as we can remember or can come to know through the aid of history. Our bodies are governed by habits which we have acquired in the past; they also are subject to diseases and developments that reflect the constitution which they have acquired via our parents. Our wills are also habituated; they are weaker or stronger depending on how we have used them in the past, and they are exercised today in the light of what they had accomplished before. As unitary beings, and thus also as governed by organic drives, we bear within us the experiences which we have undergone and also something inherited from our forebears. As actualities, we are part of a temporal series which extends far past the origin of the human race, and are part of a causal sequence which relates not to what we are as humans, but what we are as particulars in a contingent universe.

We all are bounded by the present, as minds, bodies, wills, as human beings, and as actualities. We are located in a limited space from which we make our perceptions and judgments, from which we act, from which we decide, from which we specify what is important and what is other than us. We could subdivide these, along the lines suggested in *The God We Seek*, into the focal and the peripheral, the mine and the not-mine, the private and the public, and the episodic and the constant. These distinctions could also be extended to apply to the past, for some items there are more focal than others, some are directly and others indirectly possessed, some are known only privately and others only in a public way, and some seem to be steady and others to occur only at certain moments or occasions. In the light of that fact, it would be better perhaps to make use of two kinds of divisions of boundaries—those that relate to the past, present, and future, where these permit of further divisions into the spatial and the causal, particularly with reference to the present, and those that relate to what I had termed "dimensions of experience." The latter relate to attitudes that can be taken toward the former, or to qualifications that can be imposed on the former.

We are also related to the future by mental intent and purpose, by bodily expectations and tensions, by willed determinations and commitments, by what is germane to us as individuals and human beings together, and by the relation all actualities have to future possibilities.

These various classifications deserve refinement. That refinement can be achieved in at least two ways. One can operate on them as part of an abstract form of classification, or one can take them as being germane to some particular enterprise. Ideally the two can mesh with one another after they have been somewhat independently developed. The above listing expresses more of an abstract refinement of what must have been a more primitive list of boundaries, more or less unconsciously accepted by me.

Sport can serve as one way of producing refinements rooted in what men in fact do. It involves an understanding of what a man is and what he, for the moment, in the guise of some representative or paradigmatic cases, has been able to do in pushing his boundaries to their present limits.

The sportsman is primarily concerned with his body as itself providing him with limits in the form of strength, endurance, grace, speed, synchronization, maturation, sex, and an adjustment to whatever environment he is in. But there is no sport without some judgment and decision, and thus without the use of the mind and the will. These, if more limited than they need be, will prevent a man, no matter how much he has extended himself as a body, from being as complete as he might be. A man with a superbly prepared body, but who has poor judgment and inadequate commitment, will not push himself or achieve what would otherwise have been attained. Nor can we treat these various dimensions altogether in isolation, even when we are willing to bring them together or to take them as supplements. The individual human being as a single entity and as a mere actuality must also be considered. As a single human being, he exercises a freedom to reach to, to push back, and to live in terms of his boundaries. As a mere actuality, he is subject to conditions provided by space, time, causality, and whatever ultimate realities there be, as well as by whatever actualities exist with him.

Suppose one were to look at all sports as involving a concern with boundaries? We would have to take some account of boundaries provided for life itself, by the fact of death, by language, knowledge, training, experience, and interest, even though some of these factors may have only a slight bearing on either the making or performance of athletes. Evidently we need a more systematic classification, and therefore more consideration of the abstract procedure before going into sports directly. This might best be achieved by concentrating on the problem of a body, since this is a primary consideration in connection with sports. We should see this body in its individuality, as the body of a certain type of man, as the body of a man, and as the body of an actuality. The body, in all of these guises, will have to be understood as that toward which we take diverse attitudes, and as that which is to be bounded as a mere physical entity, as a plurality of subordinate entities, as an organic entity, and as something to be used.

September 14

One may turn away from one's body, misconstrue or distort some of its features, accept it, make use of it, change it, extend it, or use it as an occasion for dealing with other things. It is a body of a definite age, sex, maturation; power, health, capacity; inheritance, habituation, responsiveness. It functions somewhat autonomously, or under supervision and acts in independence of or as interrelated with a mind. It can be treated by itself or in interconnection with other bodies.

If we turn away from the body, we are ready to acknowledge other realities, such as God or the Nirvana, or to pursue purely intellectual pursuits such as mathematics or metaphysics, or fantasy and mysticism. If we distort or misconstrue what the body is, the body will continue to function—as it does when we turn away from it—but in a minimal way. There are bodily functions that go on regardless of what we desire—though we may intensify or constrain, accelerate or vary them—such as the breathing, the heart beats, and the digestion. But when we misconstrue or distort these, or such other features as sex, age, maturation, and power, we place ourselves in positions and engage in tasks which we cannot or ought not to engage in, or which should have been replaced by others if the body is to be in health or to act efficiently.

The acceptance of the body may take the form of an identification with it, or an allowing of it to respond without control by mind or will or through any conscious effort. The allowing moves us to the position of self-indulgence, which can be expressed in extreme lassitude, or in the pursuit of pleasures or other objects of desire. The identification can be tacit in the sense of our acting authentically, without our trying to change the initial outlook or to modify the kind of efforts which we can make without thought. Or the identification can be explicit, accomplished by will or by training. In between these two means of identification is an identification which comes about through experience; here we at one and the same time allow the identification to occur tacitly, without control or supervision, and to be controlled so far as we take from what we experience only part of what we could have taken.

Only if there is a full acceptance of the body through identification can the body be at its best. It is not at its best when it is allowed to act without control, for the causes of its acting are of various kinds not all of which are desirable. The responses which are elicited may or may not be of benefit to the organism; the body may be overwhelmed by fear or terror, or lured by deceptive promises of security or pleasure.

We change the body when we identify ourselves with it, for we then being into play nonbodily factors that alter the way in which the body will function, and consequently what will happen to it and thus what it will be. We can also change the body by acting on it by making use of material about us. We can change it too by having it act. The tonality and the harmony of the body is altered when the body acts; the action of the body enables it to develop and grow as a rule, though it may at times weaken or over-constrain it.

We extend the body by having it forced to a test. We make ourselves engage in tasks which are greater than what we normally would have engaged in, or which are greater than one need to engage in in order to keep the body alive or in health. Sometimes we are forced to extend the body because we are placed in circumstances, economic or environmental, which demand that the body act in unusual ways. But even when we are in an ordinary state of affairs, we can extend the body by making it perform at its maximum in contests or in training.

We use the body when we engage in bodily acts—walking, running, digesting, blocking, attacking, and the like. We use it as an occasion for dealing with things when we treat it as a means. In the former case, we engage in a bodily activity without having any other end or objective in view; when we treat it as a means, we focus on something which is to be realized through the activity of the body. We may walk, for example, without having any place to go, or just for the sake of engaging in exercise; or we may walk in order to get to a certain place (a baseball game) or to engage in a certain activity e.g., racing against someone.

The age, sex, and perhaps even the maturation, power, health, and capacity of the body, can be taken to provide a challenge which one should try to meet. Though one is younger or older than most, one might try to see if one could do what they can; a female might want to see if she could do what men have done; and a male might want to see if he could deny his particular impulses or accepted ways of acting as a man in relation to women, at his job, in his society, etc. A man might try to recover the innocent movements of a child, even though he is mature, habituated, and traditionalized in a way the child is not. Even one's health could be taken to be a limitation, and an effort made to imitate the behavior of the sick, in order to understand them better, to elicit sympathy, to avoid work, and the like.

We are weighted down by the past in an inherited and in an habituated form. Our freedom depends on our ability to act freshly in the present despite what we carry over from the past. The past which we have must be utilized, controlled, altered, and sometimes suppressed.

Of course we are more than bodies; we are more than bodies and minds. At the very least, we are emotionally united bodies and minds which are also able to function in some independence of one another. We are also beings with wills. The bodies which we use or with which we identify ourselves are bodies which should be viewed as part of more complex beings. A complex being can be treated by itself, as an individual, or as part of a larger complex, as a unit in it. In the guise of a unit, it may stand and even function alone, but its presence and its acts will then be incipient or localized public acts.

The foregoing is not systematically presented; the various divisions should be justified.

September 18

Does every discipline have certain indispensable ideas, categories, meanings, principles? If it did not, we would be able to relate an earlier stage with a later—particularly if the distance is quite long and the discipline has undergone a number of revolutions—only as a part of a single continuum. Yet it is very difficult to determine what such basic, fixed ideas are.

Once men identified logic with the study of the syllogism; position was once thought to be an indispensable basic idea in physics; the number of elements or even what constitutes an element has undergone considerable change in chemistry. Is alchemy a part of chemistry? Is a chronicle, particularly an Egyptian chronicle, a part of history?

One way to answer these questions is, I suppose, to see what one could vary without losing the intent of an enterprise. This would mean that the intent was a constant. If so, how would it be discovered? If we tried to summarize what actual practitioners accepted, we might settle too soon for what had merely been taken for granted. Before the time of Cantor, one would have so defined mathematics that transfinite arithmetic, with its odd rules, would not be possible. And when we had only the natural numbers, a definition of number would have precluded the existence of imaginary numbers or irrationals. Why then were these accepted? Is it not because they were consistent with the intent of mathematics?

It is the intent of mathematics to find the necessity which links possibilities. Those possibilities may be outlined by various formulae. If one were to find formulae for which the previously known numbers would not suffice to yield a solution, the mathematician would be inclined to invent another kind of entity which would yield that solution. But surely this goes too far; it would mean that every problem could be solved.

Can we say that logic requires the use of such entities as "not," "or," "and," "any," and "some"? If we did we would have to say that the Peircean-Shefferian stroke function was only a device to reduce the number of symbols used, and that it in fact expressed some such combination as "either *not-p or not-q*." But might one, without making use of some such device, actually provide a logic which did not use all of the above notions? I think one could. What is essential is that we have ways of testing and ways of formulating valid arguments.

Once it was thought that the various rules of the syllogism told us how to formulate and test arguments, but now we have a wider range of arguments and different ways of determining which are valid or not. Suppose some one today denied that logic had to do with valid arguments? Might he not say it should merely list all the possible arguments? List all the fallacious arguments, at least according to type? Or consider only those valid arguments that interest mathematics or science? I think we would be correct in saying that he would then have extended the subject but retained a core. That core is legitimately called logic because of past practice. The extensions, though legitimate, make logic something which has other branches, to be designated through the use of adjectives. But this answer in effect says that logic does not have an essence, but only a core which can be designated in a permanent way.

Essentialism precludes additions, and in any case requires a priori or definitional beginnings, while relativism provides for no prescriptions to be imposed on arbitrary delimitations or extensions of the subject. What we can say is that a discipline has a definite nature which never changes, but which allows for supplements and for new ways in which the original items are divided and related. On the basis of this suggestion, we can begin by saying that history deals with relevant past items (thereby distinguishing it from a mere chronicle); theology with the God of religion; logic with valid argument; ethics with obligation and final ends; politics with state power; and art with created, revelatory objects.

What right has one to select these characterizations? It surely would not be enough to claim, if one could rightly so claim, that these characterizations alone do justice to all that has been dealt with under these rubrics. In any case, a premium is placed on what had been done. We would be inclined to say in the last century, were we to follow this lead, that psychology deals with the human mind. But today the tendency is for it to speak only of the behavior of living beings.

There are, I think, a number of problems here which must be distinguished. *1]* What are the ultimate elements, if any, in a given discipline? *2]* What are the basic or unchanging categories, if any, of a given discipline? *3]* What criteria are there for determining legitimate reductions or expansions of the acknowledged elements or categories? *4]* Supposing that one were to identify disciplines in terms of their import for clarifying or explaining basic modes of Being by themselves, in relation to one another, or some or all actualities, how is one to characterize other interpretations, particularly if they are accepted by most of those who take the discipline to be their major concern?

I think the only hopeful procedure would be to treat the disciplines in the light of their relation to different Beings, and then go on to show how the common practice in fact does conform to this idea, though perhaps under an unnecessary qualification or limitation.

September 19

What is a human body? The answer must be divided into a number of levels. 1] *Ontological*; 2] *Physical*; 3] *Chemical*; 4] *Biological*; 5] *Psychological*; 6] *Sociological*; 7] *Concordant*; and 8] *Subordinative*.

1] Ontologically, the body is a contingent, finite extended, complex entity, over against other actualities, and oriented toward Actuality. If we can turn from it, it can be only because we are possessed of nonbodily powers or natures, such as mind, will, spirit, occupied with transcendents and ultimate realities. We are occupied with these to some extent, and therefore always have the problem, if we desire to identify ourselves with our bodies, either of utilizing or ignoring the nonbodily dimensions and our interests in these.

2] There are some who would identify the ontological with the physical. This involves a double error. It supposes that the ontological is restricted to purely physical processes, and it supposes that the physical is restricted to the merely complex, or that the ultimate particles with which physics is concerned alone are real. As physical, the body is complex in the sense that it can be divided into smaller regions, and in the sense that within its confines there are subordinate entities having their own integrity, even though confined and to some extent controlled by the total body. As physical, the body is part of a larger spatial, temporal, and causal context. For those, like Leibniz, who take the spatial and perhaps even the temporal to be unreal, the ontological body is most evidently distinct from the physical, where this is understood to involve spatiality. Also, even though one were to assume that the ontological is necessarily spatial, one would have to distinguish this from the spatiality that is of interest to the physicists. The latter, as subject to relativity and quanta considerations, can be said to be an appearance or an abstraction from the ontological.

An attempt to identify oneself with the physical body is tantamount to an attempt to be part of a spatio-temporal, causal world as governed by physical laws and forces. One will then be characterized in terms of positions, masses, and changes. The features characteristic of the body as merely ontological will, of course, also be included, except so far as there is a refusal to consider any but the characters which are peculiar to a body as merely physical. On all the levels, though, the traits of a previous level are to be found; the new traits can be said to qualify the traits of the previous level without denying them an independent role on that previous level.

3] There are men who would reduce the chemical to the physical. But the reduction is of the same order as the reduction of any whole to a sum of parts. Chemical entities have valencies; they combine and oppose in characteristic ways. Because the body is chemical, there are disorders possible, and a way of referring to the body as healthily functioning, even though it does not act.

A physical understanding of the body, even if concentrated on the body by itself, will tell us about the effect that different parts may have on one another, and thus tell us about a harmony or conflict in the movements or effects of those parts. But the chemical unit is larger than any which the physicist will deal with, and it will interplay with other units in nonphysical terms to constitute still larger units. Water is a chemical which no study of hydrogen or oxygen or ways of merely having them together will tell us about; the water has genuine properties which are distinctive. The body's blood, spleen, oxygen, etc., are to be understood in nonphysical ways, though, to be sure, everyone of them has physical and ontological properties.

When a man tries to identify himself with his body as a chemical compound, or as a set or locus for a plurality of chemical compounds, he is primarily occupied with its functioning as a healthy organism. When he does this, he in effect is operating within the orbit of a biological view of the body. Were he to abstract from this biological view, he would have to content himself with seeing the body as an interactive system or systems. This minimum would suffice to make him attend to the fact that in identifying himself with his chemical body he was placing himself in a surrounding. To identify oneself with one's chemical body is to see oneself as capable of interacting with a chemical surrounding, without passing any judgment on the result as good or bad or even as desirable for the body.

4] The biological body is a unit which was born and will die; it has grown and decayed, and will continue to change and to decay. It must feed and may procreate. To identify oneself with one's biological body is to recognize oneself as a member of a part of the animal kingdom.

The biological body, we have come to learn, is one which has an inheritance dictating some of the features and abilities that can be exhibited. There are some who would speak of the biological body as though it were nothing more than the inherited factors, but this would make one overlook the fact that the biological body is a living body now working its way through present time.

When one identifies oneself with one's body, one may ignore individual, accidental, and sexual differentiations to deal with the body of a human. But these other features are just as surely a part of the biological as are such commonalities as life, growth, decay, nutrition, procreation, and death. A male is biologically different from a female; this man has a different biological body from that; the accumulated fat in this individual is not essential to him, but has a role to play in his biology. What now becomes clear is that a man can identify himself with only a phase of his biological body—say himself as male or as thin, or as unique, or as having such and such parents or genes. He could conceivably make a similar selection with respect to himself as chemical, physical, or ontological. Thus he might identify himself with himself as merely having functioning or malfunctioning kidneys; with himself as merely temporal; with himself as oriented toward Actuality. But these partial identifications require considerable sophistication; once we accept ourselves as chemical, physical, or ontological, we tend to overlook phases or distinctions within each of these. But in the biological case, we become aware quite soon of differences in age, sex, maturity, ancestry, and sickness.

5]   The psychological side of man has in the past been understood to concern man's mind, perception, judgment, will, and the like. But today there are many who call themselves psychologists who are concerned solely with behavior, primarily of men and secondarily (even where these become the main objects of experimentation) with other living or mammalian living beings. There need be no permanent division between these two sides; the individual as having a mind is also the individual who behaves in publicly ascertainable ways. But if we take the mind to be occupied with nonbodily objects then, unless we see these to make a difference then or later to the way the body functions, a consideration of the mind will not be pertinent to the question as to just what the body is. Yet it seems evident that the kind of thoughts we have do make a difference as to when, where, and how the body is going to function.

Putting aside the fact that the mind does play a role in determining how the body functions, a psychological approach to the body will deal with it in terms of what will provoke or inhibit its activities. Some of these provocations may be physical, chemical, or biological, but there are also some which have no pertinence to any of these—the learning of words, the mastering of special skills, the response to irritating sounds, sights, etc.

The psychological approach to the body should include psychoanalytic considerations. Without entering into the controversy as to just to what degree Freud was right or wrong, it seems to be a fact that we act in terms of the experiences we have had in the past, and that some of these operate on a level below consciousness. The body, psychologically viewed, is the locus of drives whose direction and insistence are determined in part by what the individual had previously undergone, even as long ago as infancy.

6] A sociological approach to the body sees it as not only part of a larger context, but as part of one which has distinctive humanized properties and effectiveness. Every human being is born in a family and lives in a society. There are other organizations besides these for most men. What they see and say, what they do and plan for, how they act even as physical entities, is governed in part by what the society endorses and rejects. Some sociologists are inclined to see every aspect of a man as instancing a social situation, so that even his chemical or ontological features are understood within the compass of sociology. But though men who fall out of windows are recorded as suicides, or murders, or accidental deaths, and though they may have their repercussions on insurance companies, hospitals, doctors, etc., it does seem to be evident that they fall at the rate that physicists determine. Social pressures may make ulcers likely, but the ulcers function and are cured through chemical means.

7] and 8] With the possible exception of one dimension of psychology, all of the foregoing relate to the way in which the body exists and acts, either by virtue of some intrinsic feature discoverable ontologically, physically, chemically, or biologically, or through some feature acquired through the impact of the psychological and sociological on the body. There are other impacts on the body, however, besides the psychological and the sociological—the speculative, the religious, the aesthetic. One can, of course, try to treat these as either psychological or sociological, but the same argument will force us to take the psychological and the sociological to be special cases of the chemical, etc. They have distinctive rationales and objects which can be pursued without regard for the functioning of the body. But each one of these can be brought to bear on the body. When this is not done, the body is coordinate with these; when it is done, the body is so far subordinate. The subordination does not mean, of course, that the body does not have powers of its own, or even that it does not go on about its own business when subject to these other influences; it means only that it is being treated as qualified by what is discerned in nonbodily ways.

There is a problem of the identification of oneself with one's body primarily because one has nonbodily concerns and must make an effort either to impose the outcome of those concerns on the body, or to ignore the concerns entirely and make oneself be merely a biological, etc., body. So far as there are plans and anything like deliberate control of what the body does, we have a kind of subordinating of the body, and this minimal degree of psychological influence is apparently the norm for most men.

All athletics can be thought of as an outgrowth of an initial tendency to impose control on the body in order that the body do what is wanted by the individual as a being who is more than a body, even when what is wanted is only something like food which is needed in order to enable the body to function. An animal that stalks its prey is not merely a body, but a body which is controlled, and then not merely to satisfy the body, but in order to satisfy it as a being which may have such nonbodily concerns as the feeding of its young.

I know that there are those who speak of the feeding of the young, and indeed of any activity, as a bodily one, entirely dictated by the various stimuli or conditions which happen to impinge on the organism. If one were to accept my position, one would have to take the organism to be more than a localized body; it has intentions and purposes, aims and objectives. If these be treated as leading to some kind of bodily satisfaction or involvement, it still will be true that the individual will be thought to be more than a body, where this is viewed as merely biological, chemical, etc.

At the very minimum, we must distinguish between the palpable body and the way it functions in response to what impinges on it, and the body as related to possibilities, remote objectives, and needed items, and therefore as subject to control by something which is not part of the body here and now, either as static or as functioning in accordance with the laws which interest the sciences.

If we accept the body with its essential features, we allow it to function without control. If we refuse to accept some feature or if we displace it, we subject the body to control. We then treat the body in somewhat the way we do when we deliberately impose some nonbodily condition on it; we inhibit, redirect, insist on the body to a degree that it would not otherwise manifest.

Unless our control is absolute, the body will continue to respond to conditioning from without. But unless we exercise no control whatsoever, the body will respond in terms of intentions and purposes, explicit or implicit, which reflect the fact that we have concerns which reach beyond the body.

If we start with the recognition of ends that interest us, we can look at the body as one of the agencies which we must use in order to attain those ends. Identification with the body, acceptance of some drive, rejection of certain tendencies or features, etc., will all now be interpretable as consequences of the attempt to utilize the body for some end. The training of the body, either in childhood or later on in connection with the mastery of skills or the achievement of athletic status, will all be conceived as preliminary means for readying the body in order to attain the desired objective.

An object can be viewed as something which is to be attained through the use of the body; it can also be viewed as something which functions as a boundary or barrier for the body. The two ideas can be collapsed into one. The body can be taken to be an agency which is to reach some prescribed end, having the form of a place, or a record, or a way of acting, and thus be an end to be attained only in the sense that we are required to pass beyond some point.

September 20

There are at least three ways in which one can accept a condition, whether this be in the form of a prescription, a boundary, a barrier, a task, or an end. One way is to sink oneself into the condition, to accept it as part of oneself. We do this initially as infants, and we do this to some extent when we enjoy ourselves, indulge ourselves, act mechanically or thoughtlessly, or carry out some skill. Precisely because we have minds which operate in some independence of our bodies, and because we do have to engage in something like an act of acceptance, some kind of control or influence is being exerted on the body. But for the most part, the course of the body dictates what it is that one will have in mind; the activities of the body at some later stage are in part governed by the memory of activities and successes characteristic of the being in the past.

To be entirely at the mercy of the body is to be a creature of every stimulus and of every impulse; it is to be lustful and indolent at different times. Almost every man is in such a condition at some period in his life. There seem to be some who are in it frequently. But the knowledge of danger and the promise of pleasure are nevertheless operative and show that the individual is more than the body as here and now responding as a mere biological, chemical, or physical entity. There will be times when the control is minimal or even absent—as, for example, when one is falling from a height—but in the ordinary course of life there is more control being exerted.

When instead of accepting the body, one accepts some instrument, some situation, or some task or end, a set of considerations, similar to those relevant to the body, is pertinent. We can sink ourselves into any of these, but we will normally do so in such a way as to modify them by virtue of what we were before we accepted them in this way. When we accept them, we in effect make the body function as an agency for their attainment or use. This amounts to our adopting the instrument, situation, task, or end as that to which the body is now to respond; there are controls exerted on it in addition to any which might have been exerted on it by itself. But we never lose ourselves entirely in these conditions; our intent or desire to use or accept the conditions keeps us distinct from, and allows us to control them.

There is the control we exert on what lies outside the body, and the control we exert on the body by virtue of what is beyond the body. So far as we can lose ourselves in these beyonds, just so far are we able to concentrate on having definite controls of the body. If there is a final end, there will of course be nothing further in terms of which that end can be controlled. But we can control that end in the sense that we can accept it in various ways and in various degrees, as was made evident in the discussion of freedom of preference and choice in *Man's Freedom*.

A second way in which one might accept the body or what lies beyond it, is a sharpened version of the first. It involves an acceptance of the body or what lies beyond it to some degree, while maintaining an interest in what it is that controls. We can sink ourselves in the body while attending to a task beyond it; we can lose ourselves in the task while remaining conscious of some further goal or of our intent to accomplish what the task requires. This is a method to which we often resort in the mastery of skills, in training for some further event, or in going through a complex activity. If we look at a task as part of a complex activity, we can take the first way; when it is occupied with a task, the second way, for the task is seen to be that aspect which allows the individual to avoid being wholly immersed in the body. Though no one is ever wholly immersed in the body, the first way does allow for a kind of internal or tacit governance of the body by ideas, objectives, intentions, and the like, whereas it is the point of the second way to stress a kind of external or explicit governance, accomplished by attending to something beyond the body when and as the body is being used and is governed internally and tacitly.

A third way allows for a tacit and internal governance of the body and of what lies beyond it; it allows, too, for a kind of control which is imposed from without by factors recognized to be distinct from the body, which is what is emphasized in the second way; in addition, it keeps itself focused on something without regard for the fact that it may not have a bodily import or may not affect the conditions, and may not exert control on the body or the conditions to which the body is subject. This third way is seen to be distinct from the other two when we take account of the fact that we sometimes attend to realities and ideals that have no bodily significance. We might, for example, dedicate ourselves to work on behalf of God; we will, while perhaps using the body and dealing with a situation in the first two ways, be focusing on a nonbodily reality. The body and the situation in which it is may then nevertheless be controlled, not for a better operation of the body or use of the situation (though this is not precluded and might even be said to be prescribed, according to certain views of the beneficent presence of God), but in order that the meaning of God be made more manifest. The body and the situation will then be made to function in ways which cannot be understood (even when there is benefit to the body and successful use of the situation) without recourse to the controlling reality or the control by our attitude toward such a supposed reality.

The first of these ways, the acceptance of the body, instruments, and conditions, not only characterizes the infant, but also the more mature, when these have learned how to move about successfully. The latter exhibit a control by habit and memory, by practical judgment and experience, which enables them to live in their bodies and in the world about without further thought or difficulty. This seems to be the stage which interested Dewey, with his theory that the individual does not think except to enable him to resolve situational difficulties which he usually deals with in a controlled, bodily way.

The second way is more characteristic of athletic contests. Here we have some goal—winning, breaking a record, doing the best one can, receiving a medal, getting applause, etc.—which we might accept in the first way, by submitting to them, but which continue to be distinct from the body and serve to control its activities. Sometimes there are athletes who are most at home in their bodies; their bodies function excellently, but the individuals do not have a clear goal in mind, or do not know how to use it in such a way as to make their bodies function as means for the attainment of that goal. If they do not have a clear goal in mind, they will not use their bodies in order to move in a single direction; if they do not know how to use the goals to control their bodies, they will lack determination or will.

The third way allows for an acceptance of a reality in somewhat the way in which the body or situation is accepted in the first or second ways. But what is then accepted has no direct pertinence to the body's needs or to effective living. It may have such pertinence, but this fact is to be known only by seeing how it conforms to the demands of that reality which lies outside the body's or the situation's contemporaries and the relevant future.

We know that some men function better than they otherwise would if they act on behalf of community, state, nation, or religion. Their loyalty may involve a complete immersion in the ideals or being of these entities or in realities beyond them; but it can also allow for the men retaining some independence from them, as the second way suggests, and can themselves be treated by the third so that the community, etc., are accepted only incidentally to a concern for something quite different.

The third way involves a control of the body or situation by virtue of an occupation with something not directly relevant to the body's needs or aims, or the nature of the situation. But, as was just suggested, this very method could be carried out with respect to an occupation with what is not bodily or situationally relevant. We could, for example, think about God in such a way as to enable us to control the idea of God; this in turn could be utilized to control the body or the conditions to which it is subject. The God thought about might be quite unlike the thought we have of Him, and this in turn might be quite unlike anything which the body or the conditions have as goals or relevant material.

Combinations of these three ways have already been hinted at. One can, for example, immerse oneself in the Being of God, as a mystic might. This immersion would conform to the first method of acceptance. One might hold on to this and yet be effective on the conditions in accord with the second way. And one could deal with those conditions, in accord with the third way, as not pertinent to the body, but nevertheless make the body so alter that the conditions are met. For example, a mystic might be absorbed in the Being of God, but in such a way that he makes the conditions he confronts into sacred objects. Those sacred objects in turn might be so concentrated on, that one will act to avoid certain moves and encourage others, as one does under the influence of taboos and ordinances.

September 23

There seem to be certain enterprises which are concerned with both the private and public sectors of an interest in some particular mode of Being or some limited form of these. Technology is concerned with both knowledge and action, acculturation with both art and history, celebration with both private and public religion. It would seem that therapy is equally concerned with ethics and politics, private values and public performances, and private performance and public achievement.

It is also true that therapy is involved with celebration, acculturation, and technology. This would seem to indicate that there is perhaps one basic private-public enterprise which can be stressed and broken up in a number of ways. If we emphasize technology, for example, the factor of acculturation will come out as adjustment, celebration will come out in the reasonable and conventional, and therapy will appear in the shape of a living up to contracts and other rules, with the attempt to demonstrate pride in workmanship, etc.

Is not sport an instance of therapy? If so, a classification of athletic events or topics will have to follow out something like the distinctions made in ethics and politics, and then recognize how technology, acculturation, and celebration enrich the result.

September 24

An alternative to yesterday's classification can be obtained by considering the practical ways by which one might function privately and publicly in order to achieve an experiential version of the basic disciplines. Education can be said to provide the way in which knowledge is achieved and publicly exhibited in the form of significant action. Similarly, sport can be said to provide the way in which a private ethical status is not only achieved, but publicly exhibited in organizational or public ways of existing. And then we would have work as the agency by which one creatively produces objects and makes them be significant in the course of the history of mankind. Finally, communication can be said (where it is understood to embrace the meaning of communion and community as well) to be the process by which the individual achieves a significance in himself by virtue of his relations to what is important, and expresses this in the manner in which he forms intimate junctures with others.

A study of education, such as I have already completed, should be followed by one on sport, which I am now in the process of working through. This should then be followed by one in economics and cognate subjects, and another by one on communications dealing with mass media.

This brief outline makes clear that the different practical ways of achieving the ends which are pursued theoretically in the basic disciplines impinge on one another, qualify one another, and complete one another. There is no education, for example, without the free, disciplined, bodily structuring produced by sport, work, and communication. Nor, to take another illustration, is there any genuine participation in sport which does not involve communication, work, and education. The emphasis in each case is on one of the dimensions, with the others playing a subordinate and qualified role.

A study of sport will follow something like the lead of *Man's Freedom* and *Our Public Life*, if the foregoing account is correct, and if these books really do justice to their respective tasks. This would mean that a discussion of sport would have to be considered under something like the headings: freedom, socialization, preference, choice, will, sacrifice, love, law, authority, power, etc.

This classification does not make provision for the difference between amateur and professional sports, between individual and team sports, between sports for men and women, between sports with and without instruments, etc. These can undoubtedly be accommodated, but the question remains as to whether or not there are other kinds of divisions which should be accommodated as well. But perhaps a beginning can be made by keeping clear just what is meant by the individual classified according to age, sex, maturity, and entering the public as an isolate, as skilled, or as part of a group.

This way of approaching the matter allows us to give consideration to the problem of conflict and death. But it does not make room for the view that sport is revelatory of reality—if it is—or of man, unless we see it as a kind of expression or evidencing of limits, as being somewhat self-reflexive and therefore clarifying the nature of those who participate in it.

If degrees of attachment to the Ideal be admitted, it might be possible to deal with the difference between play and game as involving a difference in degree of attachment. In a game, we accept and act in terms of a prescription; in play, we may follow rules and be guided by them, but do not allow ourselves to be prescribed to, and therefore are able to modify and break them without notice.

September 27

One way of looking at the problem of sports is to trace a progress from a mastery of oneself to a full participation in games. This progress has at least four stages. 1] There is the mastery of the body, through a union of knowledge with action. We have here calisthenics and therapy, training and self-discipline, all as a species of technology, though restricted to a utilization of the actual body and not involved in the production of instruments and agencies which promote activity in the public world. This stage has at least two parts: the becoming familiar with the body's parts and capacities, and the realization of the capacities through exercise.

2] Sometimes the mastery of the body is accompanied through the use of instruments of various sorts; this occurs in body-building and gymnastics. But there is a distinctive mode of mastery which consists in the individual becoming integrated with an instrument, so that they together become one functioning unit. We have a conspicuous case of this in polo; but hockey, tennis, baseball batting, rifle shooting, are also good cases. Here we have an instance of the attempt to unite oneself with what is outside oneself so as to constitute an excellent unit. The unit can be produced as a consequence of an effort to make oneself one with the instrument, or it can be produced in the course of an attempt to use the instrument, either in practice or in competition, in some wider situation. The former is the training in a skill, the other is the exhibition of one's accomplishments.

3] The competition or contesting of individuals in space, time and causal situations, as expressed in speed, endurance, and strength, may involve only the body or the body as attuned to some instrument. In either case, it involves the individual in relation to some boundary or obstacle which he must reach or overcome. The individual once again can engage in the effort to reach or overcome the boundary as a final act, or he can do this in the course of trying to achieve some other result, such as overwhelming another, making a record, getting an award, etc.

4] A final activity would be the becoming part of a community. Here we come to team play and team practice. The individual detaches himself from his own particular objectives to share in an objective of all, which he will carry out in his own way. The activity can be carried out by attending to each stage of the contest, or it can be governed by an awareness of the nature of the desired outcome, where this is distinct from the demands of the different stages. It in fact leads one outside the game as something participated in, to the game as shared by the spectators. The end which is outside the game in the same way that the situation is outside the body (when we are trying to achieve a mastery of a body while attending to the situation) is the game as sustained by and sustaining the spectator. The player does not attend to the spectator; he functions in the game as that which is made while he is trying to realize himself as a man.

In all four stages, we seem to have an effort which is an end in itself and which also functions as a means or a consequence in the realization of some further end. In the first stage, we have the effort to be at home in the body, in the second, at home with an agency, in the third, at home in a situation which is contested, and in the fourth, at home with others. When we arrive at the last stage, we have a community produced not only out of the players on a given team, but with the players of the other team, and with the spectators, to constitute a single totality in which all are adjusted to a rule-abiding set of activities.

The first stage can be treated, as was suggested, as a species of technology. It could equally be brought under the rubric of health. The second stage relates to skills. The skills could have been utilized for the promotion of work, but they become part of a consideration of sports just so far as they are developed in the course of an effort to perform well in some contest. The third stage, which I had previously designated as one having to do with work, has to do with the filling out of a situation, the actual playing of a game. This would be work, properly speaking, only so far as it was economically significant. It would otherwise be play, where this does not mean idle, spontaneous, unstructured activity, but merely that which is not economically important in that society, even when the men participating in it are paid, and those who watched it spent money to see it and to get to see it. The fourth stage involves a consideration of a factor which has not been focused on as a rule: the achievement of a union with the spectators to constitute for a moment a single totality having a semireligious tonality, where this is understood to involve an increase in intimacy.

Spectator misbehavior is, however, a conspicuous factor in many games. This is due to the fact that the individuals have identified themselves with only one side. Such identification is an extreme form of a loyalty to, or an acceptance of, one side of the contest. Such acceptance is similar to that which the player exhibits with respect to his own team.

There should be such acceptance, but only so far as this is a means to becoming part of a larger, more satisfactory situation. The participant or partisan who has no grasp of a larger situation which includes himself and the opposing team inevitably produces a larger situation characterized by antagonisms, chaos, conflicts, and even acts of destruction and violence, instead of one in which all are enriched by becoming more intimately and sympathetically united with one another.

In the first stage, the individual is making himself most alive as a body, and in that process forces himself to the limit of inviting death. In the second stage, the individual is making himself continuous with something outside himself, some instrument or animal or other agency with which he will constitute a single continuous whole; in that process, he moves to the limit of depersonalization. In the third stage, the individual is living through a contest, forcing himself to the limit in order to see what the limits of man are as defined by some outside condition or circumstance. He, in that activity, moves to the limit of becoming translucent, revelatory of man and the world in interrelation to one another. In the fourth stage, the individual is becoming part of a community where he at once communicates and forms a communion. In the course of that fourth stage, he risks losing his individuality. The entire athletic activity thus involves a risk of death, depersonalization, dehumanization, and loss of privacy. (I haven't these distinctions exactly right, with the possible exception of the first.) Failure results in these only in extreme instances. Before that time, we have injury, mechanism, humiliation, and inauthenticity.

September 28

To perfect the body as a means or as an end, we apply knowledge to actions. To perfect the way in which the body makes use of equipment and a terrain, we apply standards on public structures. To perfect the way in which one interacts with other men, we apply creativity to objective events. And to perfect the way in which a communion is achieved, we apply a private position to a public community.

The perfecting of the body raises problems in connection with maturation, sex, inheritance, knowledge, injury, health, and death. The perfecting of the use of equipment and terrain raises problems in connection with aptitude, mechanization of behavior, habits, training, practice, and skill. The perfecting of one's interacting with other men, particularly in contests, raises problems in connection with seeding, handicaps, victory, defeat, self-assessment, referees, the amateur, and the professional. The perfecting of the communion of men raises problems regarding rules, the mastery of particular roles, winning, losing, scores, and star players.

Records, drugs, competition, aggression, fun, ceremony, and even spectator participation, are matters that are pertinent to all the stages.

September 29

Identification has a number of basic forms. *1]* There is the acceptance of the body's activities, where it is allowed to function in response to stimuli without any, or at most a minimal, control. *2]* There is the acceptance of the body's ideal prospects, where one exercises control solely for the sake of enabling the body to function as it ought, i.e., at its best so as to promote the health and tone of that body. *3]* There is the adoption of the position of the body in the course of a concern with something beyond the body to be attained through the body's activities. *4]* When we come to the stage where man has moved from the position of being an unfocused individual to being a genuine member of a community, we have an attempt to forge an organic unity with equipment or a situation; here identification is the outcome of a process by which we try to make ourselves and something outside it constitute a single functioning unit. *5]* When we move to a contest, there is an identification with it in the sense that we are what we do; we make ourselves in the course of the contest; we accept the process of going through the contest as part of the activity of finding out and becoming something definite. *6]* Finally, in participating in a game, we identify ourselves with all the other participants; they represent us and we represent them.

We have, then, identifications in the sense of an acceptance of actions, an acceptance of ideal ends, an acceptance of the body incidentally in the course of an acceptance of some other end, unification, self-determination or self-making, and representation. One should perhaps add other identifications, resulting from the use of the equipment, and the treatment of a contest as one of the factors in the production of a state of representativeness. It might also be argued that one should also treat the representative stage which is involved in the participation of a game as a means that we can incidentally accept in the course of trying to achieve some such end as victory, approbation, health, etc. Equipment, contests, and games, in short, can all be incidentally accepted in the course of an attempt to realize some other end.

In all identifications, one runs the risk of not having gone far enough

or having gone too far. In connection with the body, we have awkward-
ness, illness, and lack of control; in connection with the equipment, we
have ineptitude, lack of skill, mechanization; in connection with the contest, we have injury and even death; in connection with the game, we
have fantasy or depersonalization (resulting from excessive identification) and maladjustment. There is, of course, maladjustment on every
level, so far as the identification is only partial, but the maladjustments
are distinct in nature, condition, and outcome.

One consequence of the foregoing is that we are willing to allow the
body at times to function without any but a minimum control, whereas in
all other cases, the identification requires us to exercise some control. We
control the equipment and the situation to some extent; we control the
course of the contest; and we control the way in which we will function
as a representative.

In all cases, identification seems to involve the modification of something by virtue of the acceptance of the acts, ideals, or being of something
else. The acceptance is a kind of submission, a refusal to impose a greater
control on what one confronts than is at least theoretically possible. So
far as there is control, there is subjugation, so that if there always is some
control, there will always be some subjugation no matter how extreme
the submission.

In connection with the first stage, we will have to face questions of
maturity, sex, and other organic handicaps or advantages. At the second
stage, there will be more of an emphasis on training, skills, and practice.
At the third stage, the emphasis will shift to judgment, spontaneity, and
flexibility. At the final stage, we have the problems of sacrifice, loyalty,
and cooperation. At both the third and fourth stages, we have to face the
question of the amateur and professional, drugs, referees, and penalties.

The last three stages all require some concern for rules dictating what
is allowed or is proper. The first stage also takes into account what is allowed or proper, not because this is a consequence of the acceptance of
rules, but because defined by external standards having a bearing on one's
position in society or as a man.

September 30

By attending to some remote goal, the more immediate goal is
often more readily achieved. There seem to be a number of reasons for
this. The remote goal allows one to attend to a variety of circumstances,
to relax toward various opportunities, and to take risks and thereby open

up the scope of one's creative realization of the immediate goal. It also leads one to restrict the kind of realization that will be allowed for the immediate goal. A goal by itself is always an abstraction; it is concrete only in a context. This context is provided for by the more remote goal which thereby allows one to see the immediate goal as requiring details and considerations which we would otherwise not provide. Finally, the remote goal sustains the immediate goal, particularly in an act of preference, enabling us to hold on to and realize that immediate goal even in unfavorable circumstances.

The remote goal thus provides a freedom, a limitation, and a persistence in the realization of the immediate goal. This does not mean that we always will benefit from having a remote goal. The remote goal may be beyond our grasp; it may be irrelevant to the realization of an immediate goal; it may lead us to take chances with the immediate goal which we would not have taken had we attended to that goal properly; and it may lead us to neglect details about the immediate goal because, instead of attending to it, we realize it incidentally in the course of our attending to and realizing the remote goal.

October 1

I have been struck recently by the number of men who have told me that they are primarily interested in sports as participants for the fun of the game, and that they were interested in sports as spectators primarily for relaxation. The two contentions are related. They point up a dimension of sports which is related to play in that it involves a contrast with work, involves one in something which has a value in itself, and which provides not revelation, or improvement, or the satisfaction of some deep drive, but simply pleasure of an uncomplicated sort.

If we approach sport from such a position, we find another explanation for the neglect of it by philosophers besides that of being an interest which concerns the vulgar, and therefore presumably is beneath the interest of respectable thought. Simple pleasures, such as those derived from eating, walking, breathing, free motion, and the like, all seem capable of being included under the heading of pleasure. Abstraction is made from the different enterprises as so many indifferent sources of the same qualitative result, leaving us with the quality of pleasure itself. That pleasure certainly has been dealt with by philosophers both as an occurrence and as an end which a man ought to realize.

Let it be granted that sport is primarily a source of pleasure for the spectator and for the participant. This need not preclude an examination of sport itself. It still becomes significant to ask why it is that one engages in sport rather than in something else in order to obtain that pleasure. Suppose one were answered that sport provides more pleasure, or that it provides it more readily, or that it provides it for more people? If this were all we could say, we would have to be content with making the empirical observation that sport rather than something else was a source of pleasure which we should cultivate. We would have no need to look into the problem of motivation, drives, etc., for these would all be explicable as means for making this desirable source available.

We are driven to inquire into the nature of sport, and the motivation of athletes, etc., because we see sport to answer to some need in man which reflects something of his nature. Sport is not merely a source of something desirable—in which case it might be replaced by something else or be abstracted from so that we can concentrate on that which it produces—but is itself desirable. Because in sport a man is enabled to identify himself with a community in a distinctive way and thereby become perfected, sport is a worthy topic for study. It is not merely a source, but an indispensable or unduplicable locus of certain values and offers occasions for achievements central to man.

The various enterprises which I have previously considered to be basic have all either had a revelatory function or have involved some utilization of a mode of Being. Education, though, has been treated by me as though it were a practical version of all the other enterprises. The treatment of sport seems to take us up a different path, since it is being approached, at least for the time being by me, as not revelatory, not involving some mode of Being, and not epitomizing a totality of enterprises. Perhaps, though, it can be treated as epitomizing a totality of activities to be approached in terms of categories provided for by different enterprises.

October 2

The history of the Jews, particularly in Poland, Germany, and the United States, offer suggestions for the solution of the American Negro problem:

The Polish-Jewish answer is to be part of a ghetto, living a life which is distinct from the rest of the population. This situation is initially imposed, but later it is chosen and desired. It precludes the people from having a full share in the country's culture, resources, opportunities, and history. Sooner or later it enables the more powerful force to find effective means for repression and perhaps annihilation.

The German-Jewish answer is to assimilate, to try to be a full part of the Germanic world while retaining some semblance of historic connection with one's inheritance. But such assimilation, as has been discovered, offers nothing more than a momentary mixture, to be dissolved with a new turn in the course of history.

The American-Jewish solution seems best. The Jews here retain their identity to a degree which is less than that achieved in Poland but more than that achieved in Germany. No blurring of lines is attempted; no delusion is allowed to the effect that one is an indistinguishable part of the whole. But there is nevertheless an insistence on having the full rights of a citizen, and for a full participation in all its activities. Were the Negroes to follow that lead, they would continue to have pride of race but would not try to form Negro blocs. In any case, they would never oppose having the whites help them. The American immigrant Jews did not disdain the help that the Christians and the wealthier classes provided in the shape of educational institutions, settlement houses, clinics, and the like, and they did this without losing their identity or weakening their conviction of their own merits and abilities.

We enter the world of play for no purpose, unless it be to enjoy ourselves. But once we enter it, we are ready to accept whatever rules are required in order that the play proceed. In connection with a game, instead, we have first an entry in order to allow ourselves to be contested, then a willingness to do this in consonance with rules, and finally an adoption of a play attitude or a work attitude with respect to what is done—i.e., an enjoyment of the participation or of a struggle to find our limits in the contest. In the case of play, we have no objective beyond it, though the play may promote a collateral enjoyment, whereas in the case of the game, there is a reference to a further end, achieved to be sure by playing the game, but having a merit of its own and having an import outside the game. This is not yet clear enough. What is evident is that there can be a play component in games, and that though games may be enjoyed, their objective is something else.

It is the fact that there is a further significant objective which justifies a philosophic interest in sport. (The same argument would seem to preclude an interest in play on the part of the philosopher. But this seems to be incorrect.) Sport brings one to the test, and thus to the discovery of what it is to be a man; it also has its cognitive and ethical dimensions, an exploratory grasp of the dimensions of Existence, and a production of a communion of the members of a community.

If play does nothing more than provide us with enjoyment, it would seem to be only a carrier or means not worth the philosopher's attention. It could be made to be a proper matter for philosophy if it be understood to provide not only pleasure, but a separated moment in time when one can spontaneously exhibit the potentialities which are man's.

October 3

There are at least three basic dimensions of behavior required of everyone. Without presupposing any idea of priority amongst them, they can be characterized as concerning the individual in himself, the individual in relation to others, and the individual as occupied with the good of others. There are, for example, exceptionally virile men and distinctively feminine women who live their lives mainly as expressions of their distinctive natures. Then there are those, not necessarily identical with the previous set, who are primarily occupied with others, say children, or the members of the opposite sex. And finally, there are those who put primary emphasis on love or friendship, or on a solicitude for others. We have here the motherly type of woman, who has this role even with respect to her husband, and the fatherly type of man who has this role even with respect to a sexual partner.

There are perhaps no humans who are without some trace of all dimensions. But a concentration on the first will make for a stress on a separation of the sexes, on an insistence on rights and duties, perhaps even conventionally defined, and on a self-centeredness, and perhaps even a selfishness of high degree. A concentration on the second makes one dependent on another; it involves constant interplay and, as a consequence, considerable self-discovery.

It is possible for a man to be unusually virile; but because of his insistence on male rights and privileges, his constant preening and self-regard, he may be unable to function well in the second role. Conversely, a man might function well in the second role but, because so involved with another, may be unable to maintain his own center of gravity sufficiently. He may be so occupied with the reactions of his partner, so concerned with functioning properly together with the partner as to make difficult the continuation of interests which reflect a basic masculinity— say an interest in sports, body-building, business success, etc. Finally, a man may be so deeply in love that he places his primary emphasis on solicitude, sympathy, admiration, submission, compliance, and the like. Such a person may also have no time, occasion, or interest in remaining a distinctively virile man, and could be so solicitous that he would not function as an adequate counterfoil to his partner.

We sometimes see interesting combinations of these dimensions. Taken in pairs, we have evidently three basic sets. A man who stresses the first two and is weak in the third is close to the norm of the successful male; one who stresses the first and third, but not the second, is represented best by the first when he turns middle age; the emphasis on the second two would be characteristic of the "family man" who has almost lost his independent life and outlook. These three types can be matched by similar ones embodied in women. The norm of a happy marriage in the upper classes would seem to approximate a man and a woman each of whom exemplifies the first type. When we have both of the third type, there is an involvement with one another that closes out the rest of the world. We have here an instance of a "grand passion" often ending in mutual destruction because of the lack of ballast in a primary selfishness. The second type, where both the man and woman neglect the role of being an interacting partner, to concentrate on being a distinctive, solicitous man and woman, is a result toward which most so-called happy marriages work. The ideal situation, though, would not be any of these, but evidently one where all three dimensions are exemplified by both.

The idea can be carried over into sport. There are those who function primarily as individuals, others who are exceptional in interaction, and others who are excellent teamplayers. It would be ideal to have all three, but we are fortunate if we can illustrate one of three types resulting from pairings of these three dimensions—individuals who function well by themselves and in interaction (relay racers, tennis partners), individuals who are also good team players (stars in football and baseball, particularly quarterbacks and pitchers), and interactive men who are good team players (men whose activities are guided by the situation in which they are, and with whom they are to make immediate contact, who never lose sight of the team needs (basketball players who repress their own tendency to star by making baskets and instead work with others in situations and as a team).

October 4

If we distinguish seven positions,   1] sexually distinctive;   2] sexually involved;   3] solicitous;   4] 1 and 2 together;   5] 1 and 3 together; 6] 2 and 3 together; 7] *1, 2,* and *3* together, we can evidently combine a male and a female in 7 × 7 or 49 ways. We could, for example, ask what would result from a male who, primarily oriented toward women (2), was involved with a woman who was primarily a female in outlook and who was also solicitous (5). If there were some tensions between them, one could then ask whether or not this was due to a lack of the other dimensions, or to an exaggeration of the present dimensions, both by themselves and with reference to the response of the other.

Generalizing this approach to make it embrace an individual by himself, an individual in reaction to another, and an individual as concerned with the welfare of another, the forty-nine cases would provide a schema for determining the kind of role an individual does and ought to play in a game. A generalized version of the example just used would involve a matching of an individual who was a good athlete with another who also was one, and in addition was concerned with maximizing the achievements and opportunities of another. This would give us a situation where a star, for example, was being fed by another player who might be equally good, but who was concerned with seeing that his partner was supported. We have something like this situation occasionally in basketball where a superb forward is constantly provided with opportunities by a teammate; we have a similar situation when a quarterback concentrates on some outstanding receiver.

October 10

Every enterprise in which we engage begins by our attending to a possible outcome. There are too many outcomes that could be dangerous and undesirable to make it possible to proceed in any other way. There is no difference between practical and theoretical activities in this regard. In intellectual affairs, we must be careful to distinguish the possible outcome from a possible conclusion; the latter has no reality except with reference to some premiss, and this occurs only after we have obtained a premiss by starting from a possible outcome.

Given a possible outcome (which we may entertain because it has been suggested by something, because the possibility interests us, or because we have it come to us as that which deserves to be realized, justified, or proven), we must move back to that which would justify it. This is sometimes taken to be a premiss. It is not. We must obtain our premiss from something which is not a premiss, for a premiss exists only so far as we have a pattern of inference and a possible conclusion. What we do is go back into our arsenal of facts, and focus on something which is relevant to the possible outcome, usually because it has elements which are seen to be elements of that outcome. This to which we turn may be a proposition or sentence, but we turn back to it as a mere fact. That fact is used as the beginning of an abductive inference which terminates in the having of a premiss, i.e., a proposition which has a character that can be transferred or transformed into a character of a conclusion, arrived at by conforming to the rule.

The move from a possible outcome to a factual beginning, and the move from a factual beginning to an acceptable premiss both can be said to have beginnings and endings, and to conform to rules. But if they be said to be inferences, and if the pattern of an inference is the acceptance of some end and the going back for a premiss for it, we will evidently have an infinite regress. What in fact we do is to go from a possibility to a fact, and from a fact to a premiss. These processes can be subject to criteria of excellence; they can be said to be valid or invalid, reliable or unreliable, but they are not inferences in the sense of presupposing an antecedent acceptance of another possible outcome and a movement back to some fact to start a process of deriving a conclusion.

Behind a possible outcome is some cause of our entertaining it; behind the fact to which we retreat for material for a premiss, is the outcome of a move from the possible outcome. What we must do is to transform the fact into a premiss by an abductive act. The structure of that abductive act can be formulated, and we can examine the move that accords with it, by making a proposition about the fact and arriving at a propositional substitute for the fact, but this will not give us our original abductive act. That act started with a fact and ended with a proposition to be used as a premiss.

The move from possible outcome to fact, and from fact to premiss, is duplicated in every act of practical life. But there, instead of converting fact into premiss, we convert it into a beginning which is to terminate in a relevant end, hopefully one which is like the outcome we initially entertained.

At first glance my book on education has nothing to say to those who are occupied with the problem of educating the underprivileged, or the backward, or those who have not been able to benefit from the usual form of instruction. But I think it contains in principle an answer for them. All education must start with a sympathetic instruction of children; those who are older but who are not in a position to benefit from instruction which ideally should be given to them must, without overlooking the difference in their ages and bodies, be treated in the same way that the younger children are ideally treated. We must find ways of telling them stories, and ways to awaken their sense of one another, and ways to make clear to them their rights and duties. This is perhaps best done by having them engage in games, plays, and similar activities, geared to their strength and aptitudes. On this, one can then build the knowledge that is needed. The mistake that is now often being made is to try to get this knowledge to them without making provision for the basis on which alone it can be achieved. The problem then is to find programs which are the analogue of those that successful or privileged children follow.

October 13

Without having a conclusion which we intend to reach, we would be faced with an endless number of possible outcomes. An inference presupposes an intending of a conclusion. But there is only a wish and not an intention if the possibility envisaged does not elicit certain acts which are relevant to the realization of the end intended.

A possible conclusion guides a number of moves: 1] we analyze it into components; 2] we move back into our arsenal of facts to find those components, if possible in the form of constituents of various propositions; 3] we synthesize some of these components, or their propositions, to constitute a single proposition which is to serve as premiss; 4] we take some of these components, or their propositions, to constitute a single rule which is to guide our inferential act.

The intended conclusion thus elicits the production of a premiss and a rule, but does this via a production of the components of the conclusion, the discovery of some of those components in what is now available, and the production of a premiss and a rule from the latter. Each one of these subordinate phases can itself, of course, be made the object of a deliberate effort, and thus be produced in what has something like this pattern; but then we will be engaged in doing something else than the preparing for the present inference. The elicitation by an intended conclusion, just like the finding of that intended conclusion, is an act which is not guided normally by a rule, but just occurs as a matter of fact, sometimes perhaps as the outcome of a trial and error effort to intend.

We only wish for a conclusion, if we do nothing as a consequence of facing it. We then deal with what is not relevant to bringing about that conclusion as a consequence of an inference.

We may have to be taught how to intend, say by being shown how to deal with only the possibilities that in fact do elicit what will contribute to the realization of what we intend. But then we will be taking advantage of some other intention, for example, the intention to learn how to intend. Without this intention we would not engage in directed acts. May we not, though, be conditioned so that we can intend? How can we when intention itself is a voluntary act?

An intent is not something completely enclosed in the mind, and which must be conformed to or somehow submitted to. An intention is an activity and elicits other activities, some of which may involve bodily confrontations and searchings. We must avoid the supposition that the acceptance of a possible conclusion takes one directly to a premiss or a rule. What is elicited is a consideration of components and propositions answering to facts, before one passes to the position where one has a premiss and a rule. Consequently, we must not speak as though an inference began with facts or propositions which are to give way to or are to be turned into premisses. The beginning of the inferential situation is with the intending, and this is a single act which involves the focusing on what is to serve as the source of the premiss and rule. There is no act of abduction to get us from the facts or true propositions to the premiss and rule, but only one continuous eliciting by the prospective conclusion.

It is to be noted that the source of the rule is similar to that of the premiss, the rule here being understood to be a leading, i.e., a contingently true principle, and not a logical or necessarily true one. Peirce, in his discussion of the logical principle as a component in every inference, makes the error of saying that the logical principle is not eliminable from its leading principle, whereas what his analysis in fact shows is that it is the leading principle and the premiss together which contain that logical principle. He says, for example, "Now, as L and P (supposing them to be true) contain all that is requisite to determine the probable or necessary truth of C, they contain L^1," only to follow this immediately by saying, "Thus L^1 must be contained in the leading principle."

October 14

Quine objects, on a number of grounds, to the supposition that there are analytic assertions. The most valid points out that the meaning of our terms can be imagined to have a different import in different worlds. To say, for example, that a cat is an animal, would be held to be doubtful in a world in which a robot was made to function as a cat now does, and even just made to look like a cat.

Quine tries to strengthen his position in two ways, neither of which I think can be maintained. One of the ways is to deny that a law of logic, such as the law of contradiction, is necessary, since it is possible to construct a system in which it is not used. But it is a mistake to suppose that a law is to be identified with the writing of it or the acknowledgment of it. If in avoiding the mention or use of the law we employ it, for example, by contrasting it with the use of it, we surely have not avoided it in fact. When, however, Quine speaks of such a law as presupposing a determinate world, he is on surer and more familiar ground, for he then affirms, with Peirce, that the law does not apply to the vague. Does this mean that the law is dependent on the contingent nature of the universe? If so, we can maintain the truth of the law by having it hold under the condition that it applies to whatever is determinate. This would not mean that we supposed that the world was determinate, but only that we held that the law was to be taken to hold only in a world in which every entity was determinate, or to that part of the world where the entities were determinate. The entire law could be made explicit in the form that for whatever entities are determinate, it is necessarily true that the law of contradiction is true. Would this make the law have something like the status of a proposition which said that in whatever world there were witches, they had supernatural powers? Yes; but does that not mean that both expressions are analytic, with the addition that the first also has its consequent in an analytic form?

Quine also contends that since there are many possible ways of translating an expression from one language to another, we cannot claim that there is a common core of propositional meaning that is shared both by an assertion and that into which it was translated. But there are good and there are bad translations. And the totality of legitimate translations can be said to carry out in sentential form a common propositional meaning. After all, translational rules are not sentences, but must be understood in propositional terms, i.e., as having a general meaning not exhausted in sentences.

October 19

When I look at a person, I see him in his face and his gestures. That is why I do not merely see a turned-down set of lips, but a frown. He is in the frown. But he is not exhaustively in it. He is also doing other things, and he is also perhaps intending, daydreaming, or having thoughts about God, or mathematics, or metaphysics, which may never come to any other expression. From the perspective of his gestures, etc., he is, as apart from them, only what he is in them, but more intense, and separated from the conditions of the world in which the expression is framed and by which it is conditioned. In himself, he is more than this. The gesture, like a sacred object, is a symbol which shares in the being of that to which it refers, but in so sharing it, leaves over the being by itself and whatever nature and career it might there have. We can know that nature and career, only by pushing beyond what the symbol can tell us to the presuppositions of this, to what the symbolized must be if it is to be that which can be symbolized and has a being apart from all symbolization.

It is possible, of course, for one to be deceived. One then intensifies the gesture of other expression incorrectly. This does not affect the fact that it is then correct to use the gesture, etc., as a symbol. The individual is in the gesture, but when we are in error, we intensify the gesture incorrectly, or—what is more usual—intensify it in terms which wrongly predict behavior of a certain sort.

Strictly speaking, we have at least two basic kinds of errors in the use of our symbols. 1] We intensify correctly, but misconstrue the empirical expressions that our intensified object will exhibit. We see that the individual is now sceptical, and we jump to the conclusion that perhaps he is antagonistic or of a bad disposition, etc., in the sense that he will manifest behavior sooner or later of an antagonistic or evil sort. 2] We intensify incorrectly, in the sense that we move from a friendly smile to a friendly person, when the smile may be a disguise for an antagonistic feeling or for the being of one who is in fact removed, detached, alien in relation to others, and in himself is defective as a person. The friendly smile might not be followed by friendly acts. Having intensified the expressed friendliness into a friendly attitude and then perhaps into a friendly person, we will more likely than not misconstrue the expressions which will thereupon be exhibited.

October 20

A rule of inference is a rule for a premiss and a conclusion. It must have a feature which enables it to be connected with the premiss. In the syllogism, the connection is the middle term. Aristotle takes the rule to be another premiss, but we can just as readily take the connection to be the rule which enables us to move from one premiss to the conclusion. When we do this, we make evident that there is something in the rule which relates it to the premiss.

The premiss is achieved by the intention. This focuses on a possible conclusion, moves under the influence of that possible conclusion to the constituents of it, from there to our funded knowledge to see if we can find warranted ways of accepting those constituents, and from there to a synthesis which can then serve as a premiss. The constituents and the various complexes in which they are may be propositions or propositional elements. But the kind of truth they then may have is quite different from the truth that is ascribed to the premiss. The premiss will get us to the conclusion via the rule no matter what we ascribe to the premiss. All that a valid inference requires is that *if* a premiss is true, the conclusion cannot be false. Or more accurately, *if* a premiss, and the rule when expressed propositionally, are true, then the conclusion cannot be false. But the premiss and the rule can in fact be false without affecting the validity of the argument, for every factor in the argument will be unchanged if it turns out that the world is such that what we call true is in fact false, or if the ground or occasion for a supposedly true premiss turns out to be something which is in fact false.

Does the intended conclusion not only yield a premiss, but the rule which we are to follow? It would seem so, for the premiss, as was just seen, could be said to be what I have been taking as the premiss as conjoined with what I have taken to be the rule. The movement from the intended conclusion ends with the premiss and the rule which is to operate on it. This does not, of course, mean that one could not begin by formulating a premiss or that one could not accept some rule or make up a rule. What it means is that so far as one has in mind some conclusion at which one would like to arrive validly, the ideal procedure is to have it elicit a premiss and a rule in interrelationship. We can say even that a conclusion is intended, only so far as it in fact so operates that we end with an acceptable premiss and rule.

A rule also has a terminus. What is the relation of this terminus to the intended conclusion, and to the actual conclusion? The terminus would seem to be a possible conclusion which is defined by the intended conclusion. The intended conclusion terminates in a rule, but the rule is one which is connected with the premiss and with a possible conclusion. That is why one can get to the actual conclusion as that which was originally faced as possible. The possible conclusion, however, need not be the intended conclusion. We might not in fact be able to arrive at the intended conclusion. If we could always arrive at the intended conclusion, there would be no theorems like Fermat's last theorem which we would like to prove but cannot.

There is no genuine reasoning unless we conform to a rule; i.e., unless we get to our conclusion in consonance with a rule. But what is it to conform to a rule? Wittgenstein rightly saw that we cannot think of the conformity to a rule as involving a rule, for this would lead us to an infinite regress. Consequently, he drew the conclusion that conformity to a rule was blind. But this conclusion was the only one available to him, only because he made a double supposition: rules are language items, and action had to do with items which had no natures. Knowing what a language said, we would not know what to do; all conformity to rules was, on his account, a result of convention, habituation, training, etc.

To say, "Open the door," is, to be sure, to reveal nothing of an actual opening or an actual door. Our behavior, Wittgenstein recognizes, when we hear the words, has a shape and a direction in no way conveyed or expressed in those words. But we try to conform to the *meaning* of a rule. This is not found by attending to the words. We read the words; we hear the words; we take account of directions, or of a map, by having them provoke thoughts in us. Those thoughts involve concepts and categories, and it is these which we take to be already exemplified in the particulars which involve a conformity to the rule. Our actions instantiate rules because the rules express universals or meanings, and our actions instantiate such universals or meanings apart from those rules. To say that we conform to a rule is but to say that the universal that we recognize when we attend to the rule is also recognized, and concretely embodied in the action which we perform.

Because our actions, when they conform to a rule, embody the meaning of that rule, we are able through an action to arrive at the conclusion which the rule terminates in. That conclusion is, of course, characterized by such designations as "truth" only so far as this has been warranted by the premiss and the rule. It does not follow that this warranted conclusion will in fact be true, because to be true in fact it must answer to something in the world. The inference has to do only with ascribing truth to the conclusion so far as the premiss is true. Or, more generally, we have a premiss which has some feature ascribed to it, truth or some other modality, or some such character as "interesting," "fruitful," etc., and ascribe it or a different character to the conclusion at which we arrive, in consonance with the rule.

Logical rules are analytically true. But as was remarked yesterday, they must, in their usual form, then be understood to apply to entities which are not general, vague, or in complete flux. This restriction might be taken to be sufficient to preclude the laws from being treated as really analytic, for the analytic is sometimes viewed as that which holds in all conceivable worlds, no matter what the guise, so that if they are restricted to those which are without vagueness, etc., they are thereby shown to be not analytic. But then we can express the laws in a disjunctive fashion so as to take care of the different kinds of conditions. We can say, for example, of the law of excluded middle that it says " 'x or non-x' or 'x-or-non-x,' " the one applying to the particular, the other to the general. Treated in this way, the law always holds but has a different form in different contexts. One could, I suppose, find some general form which would have these alternative expressions as instances, and that could be called *The* law of excluded middle.

Something similar could be done with respect to the law of contradiction. This holds only so far as items retain their distinctness. We could, therefore, express the law, so as to cover the cases where we have vagueness as well, by saying "so far as the items remain distinct, not 'x and non-x', otherwise 'x-and-non-x.' " This too could be brought under one heading to the effect that whatever is must be either distinct or vague, each to be characterized in its own way, the two of them being separated by virtue of a law of contradiction. The law of contradiction in its usual form would then be a law which had two special cases, one in which the law applied to discretes, and the other which required that the items lose their distinctiveness. So far as the items lose their distinctiveness, they do not, of course, violate the law of contradiction. The vague does not, in the instance of twilight, have a distinct light and a distinct dark combined, but instead loses their distinctness in the new result.

Flux fails to illustrate the law of identity in its usual form. But the flux is itself a flux. Here we have a case of the law of identity applying to something, but not to what it contained, or applying to both what contained and was contained. The law could be said to be the law of whatever context there was, and in some cases of what was contained inside the context, so far as this could be broken up into several parts. More generally, the law would apply to whatever was, and would fail to apply to what was not, i.e., to what was in flux, for this could never have a distinguishable being.

I have now dealt with the three laws and their possible exceptions in distinct ways. It appears, though, that all three of them could be dealt with in a similar manner. All apply to a context or totality always. They apply, though, to what these embrace only so far as what is embraced is distinct in a sense similar to that which characterizes the whole in which they might be abstractly distinguished.

Another way of putting the issue is to say: in the general, the law of excluded middle demands that terms not be separated from one another; in all other cases, they must be. In the vague, the law of contradiction demands that terms not be distinguished; in all other cases, they must be. In flux, the law of identity demands that no natures be specified; in all other cases, they must be. Put in these ways, the various laws hold in all cases, but they demand in their normal or usual use that the items be separate, distinct, or have natures; they tell us that their use in other contexts requires us to specify that the items are inseparable, indistinguishable, or without natures.

On this interpretation, the laws of thought do not break down, but they have one import in generals, the vague, and the flux, and another elsewhere. This interpretation has in common with the objections to the view that logic is tautologous, the recognition that logic does relate to a certain state of affairs; but unlike most of those who hold such a view, in the present alternative I go on to maintain that the state of affairs may be general or not, vague or not, in flux or not, requiring the laws to deal with separate terms or not.

October 21

Does it make sense to take a known object to be an intentional object, i.e., one which elicits the concepts or designations directed toward it? I think not, for the known object is the outcome of the use of the concepts or designations, and not the other way around. But the idea can be made plausible by modification. The object which is to be known is something pertinent to the powers of thought; it is something toward which the individual is directed, that to which he attends, or that which attracts, or lures, or stimulates him. We can conceive of the object to be known as making us attend to it as possessed of some universal feature. This attention need not be explicit or cognitive; it might be called "an intentional focusing." Such focusing is, of course, not conscious; it is an effect of the response which the object elicits. It is in terms of that focused object that we are able to say that our concepts are elicited. On this view, we have something like an intention being produced as a consequence of the operation of the object on ourselves, and this which is intended then operates to make us produce a concept that is directed at it. If it does not produce such a concept, it is of course not something intended.

Intention here is being spoken of in a way that is alien to ordinary usage. In ordinary discourse, an intention is a conscious act, whereas in the present case, it is a derivative from the act of responding to an object. Perhaps it would be better to call the responding an act of attending, and to consider attention as having a terminus in something which controls. Attention will then not be an act which realizes its object; it will merely record the object in the shape of a concept.

On this interpretation, an object elicits a response in us. One part of this is an act of attention, which terminates in an aspect of the object that elicits a concept. If it does not elicit such a concept, it is not an act of attention.

Attention is possible to animals. We do not, as a rule though, speak of animals as possessing concepts. We must either then abandon the term "attention," or signalize the fact that attention in the case of a man is different in kind from that characteristic of an animal. I think the latter alternative preferable. If we accept it, we must say that when a man attends, he produces a concept of that to which he attends, whereas when an animal attends, it merely keeps an object in focus without retaining any idea of it. Is this not a reason why animals can be accounted for in terms of habituation, stimulus-response, and the like, and that a man cannot? A man can continue to think about the object, draw implications with respect to it, modify and relate his thoughts about it, even when it is no longer present. Some animals pursue objects which are not present before them, but they do this apparently because they are now subject to causes which are in a chain leading to the object. The animals can attend to objects that are not present, but only in order to arrive at them, whereas a man can attend to them through the agency of his concepts which continue to function even when the object is no longer present, or even if it is not in existence.

October 26

In a complete flux, there is no identity. The law of identity can then be said not to apply to the realm of Existence. In a perfect unity of all, there is no law of contradiction. That law can be said not to apply to God. In the realm of the completely general, there is no law of excluded middle, as involving distinctive items. In Ideality, therefore, we have no place for it. Finally, the process of detachment necessary for inference does not apply where we cannot subdivide. In Actuality, therefore, there is no law of detachment, no inferential process.

We could make use of the logic of flux in the realm of actualities by having it apply to wholes for any accepted particulars. The logic of vagues could be found there by making it serve as the meaning of the sacred. The logic of the general can be found there as the meaning of universals. And the logic of non-detachment can be found there as the meaning of irreducible individuality. These "logics" are logics of finalities, and deserve to be exploited.

Theologians have a logic of vagueness, particularly in reference to the attributes of God. Brouwer could be said to have begun the logic of the general. Idealism stresses the logic of non-detachment, where one cannot deduce conclusions as standing away from the premisses, but where each item is accumulated in what comes after. Bergson has made evident the nature of the logic of flux. It seems odd to call these "logics," since this term is normally reserved for items which are not vague, general, non-detachable, and in total flux. But as these writers show, the different domains have something like a rationale and in this sense each has a "logic."

Identity, contradiction, excluded middle, and inference can be said to apply to ultimate Beings, but only so far as they are affected by actualities. Actualities provide definite units for God, persistence for Existence, distinct possibilities for Ideality, and different features for Actuality.

So far as actualities affect the modes of Being, those modes are subject to the laws that govern actualities; so far as the reverse affect is stressed, actualities are subject to the rationales of those Beings.

If now we turn to the actualities themselves, we can analyze them as substances in which four facets interpenetrate. Those facets are continuations of the modes of Beings. The facets can be abstracted and studied, but then they must be seen to be sustained by the modes of Being. The substances can be thought of as concrete togethernesses of all the modes of Being as interpenetrating one another in limited ways; they will then be something like a ",", as discussed in the *Modes of Being*, while the Beings together will be governed by a ".".

The modes of Being, other than Actuality, are mediated by encompassed forms in Actuality; but this does not affect the constitution of substances, though it does show that Actuality controls and limits the nature or functioning of the other facets of those substantial actualities. The substances, of course, are not derivative from the modes, for the comma is as basic as the period. But there will be many commas, each of which will be the locus of a distinct individual substance.

October 27

There are at least five basic logics. One of them is our established logic; it pertains to actualities, and relates premiss together with contingent rules to a conclusion, by logical laws having an explicit reference to the premiss and the conclusion as conforming to the three so-called laws of thought, and as being subject to a process of detachment which enables the conclusion to be held and asserted apart from the process of inference which arrives at it.

A second logic relates to the general, the domain where the law of excluded middle in its usual form, where items are disjoined, no longer prevails. This logic is pertinent to Ideality. It is a logic which relates generals to generals, and does so by taking some one or other general to be the condition which governs the achievement of the terminal general. It is this logic which is used by Plotinus in his derivation of lower levels, by Scotus in his movement down toward the individual, by Plato in the *Sophist* in his quest for a definition of the sophist, and by intuitionistic mathematicians. The latter make evident that the procedure by which one carries out the rule is through constructions. Without the intermediation of constructions, we will not move to the conditioned; the rule will tell us that the terminus is conditioned, but we will not know how to arrive at it. If this is correct, we must suppose that Plotinus, Plato, and others who employ this logic implicitly, at least, made use of a construction of the terminus. On this logic, one arrives at the terminus only by making something which, though conditioned by the premiss and in this sense subordinate to it, is lifted up to its level by the act of construction.

A third logic relates to flux and thus to the dynamic realm of extended Existence. Here there are no natures, and the law of identity, therefore, finds no application. We merely start in this logic at some arbitrary place, and come to an arbitrary end. It is the logic used by Heraclitus, the logic which governs Bergson's *élan vital*, and Whitehead's creativity. It is also the logic behind the action painting of a Jackson Pollock. It takes an act of decision or will to decide to come to an end of the process, and this act of the will is guided by pragmatic reasons. We find that it is more convenient, or conventional, or pleasant, to stop here rather than there. The terminus is without any special virtue; it is merely that at which we stop.

A fourth logic is obtained by attending to the vague. This logic is appropriate to God. It is the logic governing all movement from the exterior to the interior, of synthesis, and of abduction. To find out what a substance is like, we intensify its various features by making them affect one another, and eventually to constitute a unity where each interpenetrates the others. It is evidently, then, the logic which allows us to move from the four modes of Being to actualities; it is evidently, too, the logic behind the Incarnation with its attempt to show how the distinct natures of God and man can be one. We find this logic employed in Maimonides and Spinoza in their attempts to deal with the attributes of God, which are distinct apart from Him, but united and merged in Him, where they are concretionalized as well. The movement here is a movement of sympathy, union, appreciation, of attending to the increase in power and self-insistence on the part of the terminus.

A fifth logic relates to Actuality. Here we never let go of the premiss, but carry it forward into the conclusion. The logic here is one of non-detachment. It can be taken to be the logic of any context-governed view (and therefore the logic used by philosophic linguists); at its best it is the logic of Hegel, where the movement is guided by dialectic. Hegel's logic, of course, is also one where there is a conditioning by generals and an intensification into the vague. It is perhaps a logic even of flux, though I think the several points through which the dialectic must go preclude this last interpretation.

One might contend that here were three more logics appropriate to the plurality of particularities, which are pertinent to the Beings dealt with in the second, third, and fourth logics above. I have not thought this matter through sufficiently to be sure of myself here.

We are left with a number of problems. What relation do these logics have to one another? Must we not say that they are related in the way the modes of Being are, i.e., as diverse specifications of a radically ambiguous meaning, in this case "logic"? There would be no one logic subtending them all, but only a plurality of logics. Each of these logics could be approached from the perspective of the others and thus be subject to the conditions imposed by those others. Any attempt to look at them all, as I have done, will involve a beginning from the perspective of one, and detaching the meaning of the logic from its embodiment in a Being or in a realm of actualities, and then discovering that the logic is in fact embodied in some other domain.

Logics are really onto-logics. Each logic gives the structure of some domain, and when we envisage other logics, we in effect look at them as detached from the given domain. But when we want to work with a logic, we must embed it in its proper domain.

I am here in agreement with Quine in denying that the so-called logical laws are tautologous and apply to all possible worlds. But I disagree with him in that I take them to be onto-logic, i.e., to be inseparable from a certain kind of domain.

Ought there not to be a logic relating Actuality to its actualities? The encapsulated modes of Being to those very same actualities? Is this not the logic of conditioning, even though the actualities are not generals or particulars? All we can do in moving from Actuality is to arrive at the possibility of actualities; to get to the actualities themselves, there must be an actual construction, a making of the individuals. A similar situation prevails with respect to the encapsulated modes of Being, with the difference that the kind of construction required is radically distinct from that employed in the movement from Actuality, if the movement is to end with the same actualities.

What is the logic of the relation of the actualities to Actuality or to the encapsulated modes of Being? Is it not the logic of intensification, of a movement governed by a necessary law having to do with the vague? If so, actualities would be seen to lose their differences and to merge with one another as we approach Actuality. But we will not get the Actuality from the actualities; all we can do is to have Actuality as a possible outcome. To get the actual outcome, Actuality must enrich us as we approach it. Our movement is one of intensification provided by the very terminus we are trying to reach. This seems to be the movement that men in fact acknowledge in going from actualities to their God. It would seem to be the movement by which one goes from the actualities to the Beings of Existence and Ideality as well.

Our ordinary logic is not the logic for Plato's cave, for our ordinary logic relates to what is cut off from the modes of Being. The movement out of the cave is governed by the logic of the vague, and depends on the use of an intensification provided by the terminus to which we are moving, as Plato saw so well.

Each of the logics appropriate to the modes of Being has specifications in the world of actualities, just as the actualities and their logic can be given a role inside the modes of Being, or at least inside one mode and three encapsulated modes.

The logic of actualities proceeds through the use of signs; the logic of intensification, which ends in the vague, proceeds through the use of symbols; the logic of flux makes use of arbitrary marks; the logic of generals, and thus of conditions, proceeds through the use of cues which prompt one to attend to something conditioned; the logic of the indivisible (Actuality) or context proceeds through the use of evidence. It is to be noted that in connection with the vague, what would be the limit of union would be self-contradictory, were the items detached and yet conjoined somehow. Now they are blurred into one another; the logic proceeds from the less to the more vague.

I have previously argued that a philosophic system has its own method. Is this not to say that it has its own logic? I think so. But then there is a logic connecting the different logics. But a philosophic system is achieved in the realm of actualities, and thus involves a kind of abstraction in order to acquire neutrality. There is a logic which connects the various logics, but it is one which has to do with the logics as detached from their embodiment in distinctive realms.

A system of philosophy can be said to tell us of the common meaning of embodiment, of how the abstract logics are related in fact to their appropriate Beings. But those logics are embodied in different ways; a mark, e.g., is related to the flux in a different way than a symbol is related to an intensification of itself. A system of philosophy elaborates the meaning of the togetherness of the modes; this is an abstract logic. It would have to be a logic which was at once of the vague, the general, the dynamic, and the unitary or individual. But this does not seem possible, since it would involve the use of symbols, cues, marks, and evidences. There is something unresolved here.

It is also to be noted that the logic of actualities is an extensional logic, and the logic of the vague an intensional one. The logic of marks and the logic of cues, i.e., the logic appropriate to flux and that appropriate to generals are "practical" logics. The logic of evidences, with its accumulation and its retention of a context, is the logic of a game and thus of the reasonable. Here I approach fields I have not thought through.

Reverting now to the previous question—it is now 8 P.M., some hours later—if one follows the lead of the discussion in the *Modes of Being*, the logic of the philosophic system dealing with the four modes should be the logic of Actuality divorced from Actuality and thus made into an abstract logic, which is neutral by virtue of a divorce from Actuality. It nevertheless reflects the categories and logic of Actuality. That means that the logic of the entire work is one in which what is said in one place affects what is said in another; it is a context-scheme, and thus like an idealism. But unlike an idealism, which identifies its accumulative logic with the realm of possibilities (as it should, since that logic, like all the five logics, is an onto-logic), it is an idealism which is abstract. It becomes concrete only by being diversified by the different Beings.

If by perfection we mean the totality of the modes and whatever particularities there be, then this would be represented by an abstract logic. The ontological argument fails with respect to it, for it is an abstract perfection that never in fact exists.

The ontological argument in its usual form is one which takes perfection to be restricted to God, takes God to be perfect, and tacitly supposes that it uses a symbol of that perfection, the use of which inescapably leads to the being of the perfection. To say that the proof presupposes faith is to say that it uses a symbol whose intensification is guided by the apprehended substantial Being which is God. God's existence follows from His essence only in the sense that His essence is a symbol of which His existence is the intensification. In this case, we do not have a plurality becoming vague by becoming unified, except in the sense that the symbol as articulatable can be said to be a plurality, and God's existence as indissolubly one can be said to be the unified intensification of that plurality.

Religion makes use of symbols in the shape of sacred entities; those symbols participate in their object. They can therefore be said to be vague. But we have no right to suppose that ethics and politics make use of the cues characteristic of distinctions made for Ideality, that art and history make use of marks characteristic of distinctions made for Existence, or that knowledge and action make use of evidences characteristic of distinctions made for Actuality. This conclusion goes counter to the tendency of my observations made over a month ago about the different disciplines.

October 29

In religion, we make use of symbols, just as we do in trying to deal with the vague or any other movement from distinct items to those items interlocked in a more substantial and interior way. The symbols are an expression of man as a symbol, man as a sacred object. It is because the religious man starts with himself as a sacred object that he is able to function and express himself via symbols which are intensified in fact in God.

In art and history, we affect Existence with creativity and the human realm. In this way, we convert the marks that would be appropriate to a logic of the flux of Existence into the distinctive components of a work of art and the relevant items in a history. Analytic philosophers of history take it to be a domain of marks, but that means they forget the contribution that is made by the interplay of the human realm with Existence.

In ethics and politics, we affect the Ideal with the acceptance of ourselves as responsible beings. As a consequence of our converting the conditioned into the responsible, we make the condition assume the role of a prescription for us. In this and the previous (as well as in the next) case, the terms we use are more intensive (due to human involvement) than they are as items helping characterize the rationale of a mode of Being. In the religious case, we make ourselves into a symbol; in the other cases, we make marks, conditions, and evidences into significant components, prescriptions, and orientations.

In knowledge and action, we affect Actuality with our awareness of the aberrancy of their content. The knowledge and action, as was not always noted by me, is not any knowledge and any action, but knowledge and action which is revelatory of Actuality, and thus on a par with ethics and politics, art and history, private and public religion, which are respectively revelatory of the Ideal, Existence, and God. This knowledge and action takes account of items which are outside of the control of ordinary grammar and conventional behavior. They are occupied in fact with confrontable items that have been affected by Actuality to make them function in aberrational ways; those items are to be expressed by transcendental terms.

The recognition of knowledge and action as revelatory of Actuality is a consequence of the pursuit of the philosophic method of trying to see problems dealt with from multiple perspectives. It is because I saw that ethics and politics, for example, were revelatory of the Ideal, even though the Ideal in and of itself was subject to the logic of condition and conditioned, that I became aware of the role that man played in the production of the prescriptive function of ethics and politics, and saw the need to clarify what I had said about knowledge and action being related to Actuality in the way ethics and politics are related to the Ideal. Knowledge and action, if revelatory of Actuality, are to be distinguished from the knowledge and action which have to do with actualities, since such knowledge and action would not necessarily lead to any revelation of the nature of Actuality.

In all the revelatory activities, men first take material that is affected by some mode of Being and humanize it. The symbolic nature of sacred items is adopted by man so that he can share in the divine presence. The flux of Existence, which he arbitrarily has marked off, is qualified by his creativity and the human realm so as to enable him to discern the nature of Existence. The conditioning of the Ideal which is approached from the perspective of the conditioned is affected by his acceptance of the conditioned as his responsibility; he thereby is enabled to make evident the nature of the Ideal as an indivisible totality of conditions and conditioned. The context of Actuality, which is articulated in terms of evidences, is affected by man's approach through an acknowledgment of aberrational items; he is thereby enabled to use his experience as a revelation of the nature of the context to which those evidences in fact belong.

The previous discussion regarding Existence is restricted to a consideration of it as dynamic. But what of its spatial and temporal extensions? Is the logic of these like the logic of flux, when we take away all humanization by creation and the intrusion of the human realm? I think we can properly say that it is, for a space in and of itself has no positions or regions which can be separated off from any others, and a time in and of itself has no distinct moments. Both space and time in and of themselves achieve distinct components only through a humanization of them in art and history. Boundaries can be made in them through the use of arbitrary marks. So far we are justified in speaking of all of the dimensions of Existence as endless, and subject to arbitrary delimitation. It would make for clarity, therefore, if we spoke of endless extension in place of flux.

But is it not true that the objects in space demarcate it? Is it not true that there are genuine events and moments in time apart from our histories? I do not see how we can avoid saying this. But this does not affect the fact that in themselves space and time have no such demarcations, or the fact that only so far as we have art and history do we have what is revelatory of the dimensions of Existence as they are in Existence apart from all demarcations of objects and events.

October 31

If it be correct that man adds determinations to the various entities which the logics of the different modes of Being exhibit, we should say that the events of history are due to man's intrusion. Apart from him, Existence would not break up into periods, etc.

Man's intrusion might be thought to distort the nature of a mode of Being. But a logic is abstract, and structures what it encompasses. The additions that man makes enable him to reveal the nature of nuances in the modes of Being which the logic fails to reveal. Existence, for example, is no mere undifferentiated extension; the extension (or more accurately, the extensions) all have nuances which are accentuated by the beginnings and endings of history. That history is history as made with man's help; it is not to be identified with the written history which purports to tell us what the history is.

The nature of Existence is not expressed in a logic of marks; nor is the nature of God expressed in a logic of symbols; nor is the nature of the Ideal expressed in a logic of conditioning; nor, finally, is the nature of

Actuality expressed in a logic of evidences. All these logics need to be intensified before there is an adequate grasp of these modes of Being.

Some time earlier I had contended that the variables with which we deal with actualities need to be given meaning by symbols. But it now appears that symbols are appropriately used only in connection with God. What is wanted is either evidences or their intensification through human categorization, for the variables which deal with actualities are governed by Actuality and the meanings it has for us.

November 1

I have maintained a number of times that the world from the perspective of God can be treated as a multiplicity of identities. But if the discussion of the last week has validity, this should be but the prelude to a number of related claims. Existence is without the rationale of identity, and God can be thought to provide this for it. But we should also say, I think, that Ideality and Actuality also provide some kind of identity. Ideality provides for the identity of natures, and Actuality provides for the identity of substances. God's use of identity is with respect to the extensions of Existence.

So far as we acknowledge actualities, already the outcome of the production of identity by Actuality, and so far as we acknowledge natures, already the outcome of the production of identity by Ideality, the divinely produced identities will encompass both actualities and their natures. Something similar must be said with respect to the Ideal and Actuality. So far as Existence has been made the locus of identities through the presence of God, and the Ideal has yielded identities in the shape of natures in Existence, Actuality will not only turn existing actualities in to self-maintaining ones, but will provide a self-maintenance to the divine identities (allowing them to be in Existence though substance, and then as distinguishable) and will ground the identity-functioning natures which the Ideal provided. Similarly, the Ideal will treat both the actualities, which function according to the law of identity in Existence through the action of Actuality, and the divinely instituted existing identities as having natures, to be operative in Existence under the law of identity.

If the three modes of Being provide Existence with distinct types of entities which are able to be self-identical in Existence—though Existence itself precludes the presence of the law of identity—we should expect to find three modes of Being providing Ideality and its derivatives with prescriptions in place of its conditionings, three modes of Being providing

Actuality and its derivatives with distinctions enabling the use of inference, and three modes of Being providing God and His derivatives with separations which permit of the use of the law of contradiction in Him and derivatives.

The Ideal is not subject to the law of excluded middle so far as this involves items in a real disjunct, but it becomes so subject when operated on by Actuality, Existence, and God. These in different ways disjoin what the Ideal cannot, to yield prescriptions. Actuality is not subject to the operations of inference, for the items are kept in the context in an accumulative fashion; but it becomes so subject when operated on by Ideality, Existence, and God. In their different ways, they provide it with prescriptions. Finally, God is not subject to the law of contradiction, for He preserves all and is compelled to have them in a vague unity. In their different ways, Actuality, Ideality, and Existence operate on God to provide those items in Him with distinctness so that the law of contradiction operates there.

Each of the modes of Being has a logic of its own, where some law is defied or not given a role. Each of these modes of Being, nevertheless, finds some lodgement for the omitted law in two main ways: A] men intensify the appropriate items which the omitted law permits, thereby allowing one to discern distinctions in the mode that the items did not allow one to note, and B] the other modes of Being affect a given mode of Being so that it is made into a locus of the kind of items that would be subject to the omitted law. It is only the Beings in and of themselves, therefore, which can be said not to be subject to the different laws of logic; as dealt with by man and as qualified by the other modes they are so subject.

November 10

When we conform to a rule, we arrive at a terminus. What is wanted is the terminus as functioning apart from the rule, as that which can be used by itself without reference to the fact that it had been arrived at. This would seem to require, in the case of inference, another rule and process, relating to detachment.

The rule of inference and the process which follows this get to a terminus with an arrived-at truth value. To have the terminus possess its own truth value in the very same sense in which the proposition from which the premiss was derived had its own truth value, we must convert the arrived-at conclusion into a proposition which stands apart from the inferential process and the rule which governs this. Such a conversion can be called a "detachment." But a detachment is itself a process with a rule.

We are faced with the dilemma of having processes which are not constrained by a rule and therefore are in a sense arbitrary and uncheckable, or with rules which really govern and preclude novelty and the existence of anything outside their province.

I think we ought to say that the inferential process is a single activity which terminates in a conclusion that is detached from a process of arriving at a conclusion, but is not detached from a process of detaching a conclusion. There is one single complex rule which consists of the ordinary rule of inference, pRc, and a rule of detachment. The rule of detachment yields something which is separate from the process that gets to a conclusion with a truth value projected from the premiss.

A rule and act of detachment allow us to have a truth value which is possessed in a detached form. But it is a detached form which is derived from the projected form, and is therefore not the conclusion really separate. To get it really separate is the work of the content to which it is related in the same way as the initial proposition, from which the premiss was obtained, is related to its content.

The end of the act of inferring, which includes not only a movement of a projected truth value but a detachment of that truth value from the movement and thus a conversion of the truth value into a sessile one, is an end to which an external content can be given. The giving of the content is the isolating of the sessilly characterized conclusion from the process of detachment.

But is there no rule for the intrusion of content in the conclusion so as to make this in fact stand away even from the process of detachment? There is none, for we do not control the presence of the content; we discover this.

Is there then a risk in inference? There is a risk if we attend only to the ordinary rule of inference and the process it sanctions, for the rule and act of detachment go beyond this. But the ordinary rule of inference and the rule of detachment together show that the process of arriving at the detached conclusion is only an instantiation of the two rules together, and in that sense involve no risk. That the result may or may not be sustained by content outside it is something which cannot be known, of course, from the perspective of the rules and the instantiating process; but the presence of that content does not have to involve any risk of getting a result not sanctioned by the rules. However, the content may affect the nature of the conclusion, and in that sense the conclusion, which is one with content, may be different from the conclusion which we had arrived at through the complex inferential process. But the conclusion is not one with the content in any sense other than that in which the proposition, that we converted into a premiss, is different from that premiss, and then by virtue of the way in which the content affects that proposition.

We reason in order to achieve a result which is on a footing with the proposition which was true with a sessile truth, i.e., by virtue of its concordance with some reality or by virtue of the possession of some content. We use the rules of inference and the process (which I now take to include the rules and process of detachment) as part of a larger process which begins 1] with an intended conclusion, 2] moves under its guidance to a subdivision of this into parts, 3] to a discovery of these or some of these as sustained by fact, 4] to a proposition which affirms something of a content and is some synthesis of the found parts, 5] to a premiss and rule (which refers to a conclusion), 6] to a concluding and a detaching, 7] to end with a sessilly affected conclusion which is detached and which is to be sustained by a reality or content distinct from it.

It is not yet clear to me in what way the process of moving to the detached conclusion (6 and 7) is related to the process of arriving at the premiss and rule (1 to 5). I suppose the process continues to be governed by the intended conclusion and thus is a process which involves the union of premiss and rule in such a way as to give us an arrived-at, and then a detached, conclusion. Under the influence of an intention, (1) then, we move all the way to the detached conclusion (7), via an analysis of the intended conclusion (2), a discovery of what may be similar to the analytic parts of that intended conclusion (3), to a sessile truth-valued proposition (4), to a premiss and rule (5), to an arrived-at conclusion (6), and then to a detached conclusion, which awaits sustaining by content or a reality beyond (7).

The various logics which are appropriate to the various modes of Being leave out some essential function of this schema. Actuality fails to give us a detachment; God fails to give us a premiss; Ideality fails to give us a conclusion; and Existence fails to give us distinct items to deal with.

There is a risk in reasoning if one thinks of this as being governed only by the rule of inference as distinct from a rule of detachment. There is no risk if our process is one which conforms to both rules. But though there is no risk, we end with something which is not governed by the rules, just so far as what we end with is sustained by content or is related to a reality beyond it, which enables it to be free even from the detachment situation.

Inside the mere reasoning situation there is no risk; but that with which we finally end is outside the reasoning situation and, though it does not invalidate what we went through, yields a result which is transformed to any degree, and is so far novel and unpredictable. The unpredictable nature of the final outcome, however, is due to the fact that the legitimately arrived-at conclusion is allowed to be subject to the conditions of a world outside the reasoning and outside that conclusion.

November 11

Existentialism is a philosophy about women. That is why it does not interest anyone who knows anything about women. Feminine women particularly have no interest in it, and need not, since they live the philosophy in the concrete, with more substance and meaning than the philosophy provides.

Craftsmanship provides an objective form of psychedelic experience. It heightens experience by virtue of what is done to material rather than to the individual.

To provide structure for experience, we must turn away from experience; that is where structures are to be found and understood.

The arrow must be pulled back before it can move forward.

Ideally, a man provides the structure for a woman's existentialistic life.

November 23

1] Reasoning requires a conformity to rules.

2] The process of reasoning adds something to what the rule affirms, for a process is more than a structure. Either there is a risk in reasoning, or reasoning merely involves adding details to the general meaning which is expressed in the rule.

3] An inferential process takes us from a premiss to a conclusion for that premiss.

4] We reason in order to have a conclusion which we can hold apart from the inferential process.

5] We must arbitrarily and wilfully detach the conclusion, or we must detach it by following a rule of detachment.

6] A valid process of detachment must conform to a rule.

7] The process of detachment takes us from a conclusion arrived at inferentially to a conclusion which is detached.

8] Either we remain within the process which gives us a detached conclusion, referring back to its antecedent, or there is some way in which the conclusion can exist apart from any rule-abiding or arbitrary act of ours.

What we need and sometimes get is a confrontation by an object which sustains the detached conclusion, and therefore enables us to have it in a guise it does not have as merely arrived at by us. The novelty in reasoning is brought about by the addition that the confronted object provides.

The conclusion is usually altered by the object which sustains it. This is harmless for two reasons. A] The conclusion may be sustained in the same way as the proposition was sustained from which we obtained our premiss. We will then end with the kind of truth for our conclusion which we initially had for the premiss before it functioned as a premiss. Inference and detachment would then be intermediaries between a grounded beginning and a grounded ending. B] We can hold the sustained conclusion apart from the sustaining object just so far as that enables us to cancel out the difference which the object makes to the nature of the conclusion as something detached through an act of ours.

This result stands in opposition to a number of others. It opposes idealism, which is concerned only with a consonance with rules, i.e., with consistency. It opposes empiricism which is concerned only with processes and arbitrary terminal points. It opposes dualists, such as Wittgenstein, who think there is no bridge between a formal system or set of rules and the actual processes which we undergo (whereas I am holding that the process realizes the structure and becomes independent of it only at the end, when the outcome is sustained by a world outside both the structure and the process). It opposes correlationalists who offer an arbitrary correlation between the disparate domains of structure and process, without showing that there is a position from which this correlation can be offered. (So far as the process is itself consistent, they offer us a double idealism arbitrarily connected.)

Process is distinct from structure and cannot be deduced from it, but it also can conform to it by merely adding details to what the structure states. It is of course true that no one can know the nature of the process given the rules, but it does not follow that the converse is true. The process must be learned; what it is like must be taught in part by trial and error, but this does not mean that it cannot occur within the confines of a rule that is known by the teacher and perhaps even by the student. If the process were as alien to a rule as the Wittgensteinians think it is, we could not validate it by showing that it conformed to a rule, and therefore we would not be able to speak any longer of valid as contrasted with invalid reasoning.

Like every solution to a problem in logic, this has wide applications. Logic enables us to focus on a precise issue of a central nature, which is illustrated in a multiplicity of contexts. We can, for example, see the mind as a locus of structures (without denying that there are processes in it) and see the body as the carrying out of these structures. The body will end by placing what we have in mind in a world outside that body; the world will take from us what we have offered to the world in consonance with what we had in mind. The converse operation should occur as well; the body can be seen as a set of structures which the mental process will carry out and eventually offer to be sustained by other minds or objects. Thus the position I take with respect to something can be met in the mind by a process allowing me to conceive of a traversal of that distance from that position, and to acknowledge an object as at that distance to which I should bodily attend. Idealists forget the bodily role; materialists forget the mental role; dualists have only an arbitrary relation between them, since they take the two to be utterly alien one to the other.

We can deal with such matters as the relation of time to eternity, the world and God, perhaps even men and women, in similar ways. One of these can be viewed as giving the structure for the other. That structure is realized in a process that keeps to that structure, though acting in independence of it and as having a nature that is not deducible from it. The process will then be understood to end in something which must be taken from it by a world beyond.

If we take eternity to be the locus of a structure, time will be a process which comes to an end every moment by virtue of the fact that there are objects which sustain what it contains. If instead, we take eternity to be a process (as an Heraclitus might suppose, or a Schopenhauer or a Bergson), then time would be a structure which that process could be said to realize. The process would eventually terminate in one final content which was either arbitrarily terminated (as it seems to be in Hegel), or which precipitated its outcome (as it seems to do in Royce), or which was sustained by some Being (God, as in accounts of a Final Judgment).

Both women and men can be thought to provide both structures and processes for one another. What the one treats as structure the other realizes in a process which eventually ends with a conclusion that is sustained by a world beyond that process. The public world that the man brings home is realized (usually in the form of money) in the purchases of the woman; the structure of the family or household is realized by the man in his life outside, and is offered to a world which will carry it out in new ways. This is, of course, only one of many ways in which one can see the two to be related as structure and process.

Because the outcome of a process is sustained by something outside the process, it enables us to free ourselves from the process and incidentally to escape from any "playing of games." There can be no escape so long as we remain idealists and refuse to see that there are realities which can sustain what we arrive at through our intellectual or bodily processes. The outcome not only is given new content and thereby perhaps altered, but it is now placed in a context where the content is, and thereby gains new affiliations and connections. We can deduce an eclipse, but the eclipse that does occur is one which awakens admiration and superstitions, affects our vision and our light bills, etc. These occurrences could be deduced, but not from the eclipse as the outcome of an inference from the present position of the sun and moon and the laws of nature. They are deducible from a new premiss which is made up in part of the conclusion that there is an eclipse as modified by the actual occurrence.

Suppose one were to anticipate that the actual eclipse would have such and such consequences in the world? Could not one deduce this? One could, but from a different set of premisses than that which was used to deduce the fact of the eclipse. And this deduced factual eclipse, as involved in the world of men, etc., would itself have to be detached from the process of deduction and sustained by a world in which the eclipse was a part. That world would add more than details to the factual result; it would bring the occurrence of the eclipse not only in relation to what we deduced was in relation to it, but to the world in its history and spatiality.

Is it not conceivable that we might have a sufficient amount of information to enable us to deduce not an eclipse by itself, or a factual eclipse having such and such repercussions on men, but a factual eclipse as actually immersed in the world and thus as related to every part of it? Surely this is conceivable; we can imagine this to be the content of an omniscient mind. But then we must say, I think, that the very fact that this conclusion will be sustained by that world means that it will have relations to the future which are additional to what we could antecedently know. "Being sustained by the world in its totality" means that the conclusion will be caught in a worldly process relating it in the next moment to what could not be deduced as having just that relation to it. In short, we will have to say that the process of time will always take our conclusion and give it a career we cannot altogether anticipate, so that it will have relations to the future which we will have to confront in order to know.

November 24

Play can be taken to designate the entire spectrum of activities which are cut off from practical affairs, without thereby involving us in the affairs of ultimate modes of Being. That approach enables us to differentiate play from ethics, religion, science, history, etc. We will have at one end of the spectrum mere play, idle play, a play in which one merely fills up time. One can have rules for this play, as in solitaire, and even have a well-defined beginning and ending. But one's adherence to the rules of solitaire is dependent upon whim. This is true of all individual play. No matter how seriously one engages in play as an isolated individual, one does it merely to fill in time. It is therefore not to be identified with exercise, practice, self-teaching, and the like, which have express goals beyond the mere carrying out of the rules. At the other extreme of the spectrum is play in a game, where this continues to have some spontaneity, pleasure, and a losing of oneself in some role.

Is play revelatory of a world beyond in some way, the way art is? It could be said to be revelatory of the player's capacity to hold himself away from the workaday and other serious pursuits; of his ability to assume the role of a participant; and of his willingness to suspend violent termination and unapproved devices in order to attain a prescribed kind of result. But is it also revelatory of the world that lies outside the workaday world? Does it tell us something about Existence or some other modes of Being, particularly if no attempt is made to use it didactically? We move toward an answer by noting that in play one comes to see something of the meaning or nature of balls, water, sticks, strength, cooperation, and the like. But this is not yet to tell us anything about whatever finalities there be.

The absorption in play is like the absorption in art; we live within that world for a while. But where in art we use the work itself as a kind of icon for a reality beyond itself which it enables us to iconize, just so far as it is enjoyed by itself, in the case of play we have merely a withdrawal from the world which allows us to be open to what else there be. Play then is not revelatory in the way art is; it is revelatory in the sense in which faith is—the absorption in the content makes evident that there is something transcendent, without telling us the nature of that transcendent reality.

December 1

1]   If p is not possible, p could not be necessary.

2]   Therefore if p is necessary, p is possible. P is necessary entails that p is possible.

3]   A rule of inference is valid if, given truth it does not end in falsehood; this allows it to be valid if it ends in truth.

4] Therefore, if *p* is necessary, then it is implied by *p* as possible, and by *p* as not possible (or it is false, that *p* is possible).

5] By 2, if *p* is necessary, then *p* is possible, and by 4, if *p* is possible, then *p* is necessary. This means that *p* is necessary is equivalent to *p* is possible.

The escape from this paradox comes with the recognition that 2 is an inference in intensional logic, and 4 is an inference is extensional logic. 4 moreover presupposes that *p* is necessary, and should be written, "If *p* is necessary, then if *p* is possible, *p* is necessary." And 2, if it does use a genuine necessary truth, does not allow us to say that that truth is merely possible. The possibility of that truth is adjectival to it, i.e., is a conclusion in the realm of ideality which does not permit of the detaching of a conclusion.

Another paradox: There are other logics besides that which pertains to actualities. The logic for actualities requires distinct propositions which A] can be intended as conclusions, B] can serve as grounds for a premiss, C] can serve as premises, D] are formulated in rules which show connections between the propositions; it is a logic which E] arrives at conclusions, F] detaches conclusions, G] has those conclusions sustained by a world beyond. Some of these features are lacking in the other logics: God does not have a logic with premisses, Ideality has no conclusion, Existence has no rules, and Actuality does not have anything projected from premiss to conclusion. But we can formulate any rules whatsoever and use them in the logic for actualities, which seems to mean that the logics alternative to it can all be framed inside it.

The resolution of this paradox requires the recognition that the rules must be applied, and that any rule, such as that which did not allow for a transfer of some feature, though it is a rule which could be formulated in a logic for actualities, would not have a subject matter. To find that subject matter, one must either convert the actualities into different kinds of entities—generals, vagues, flux, or accumulation, or make the rules apply only to Ideality, God, Existence, and Actuality.

What is the difference between a logic for actualities, which makes use of odd rules and is applied then to modifications of actualities, and a logic which is appropriate to the modes of Being? More sharply, what is the difference between vagueness in experience and the vagueness of God, between the generals in experience and the generals in Ideality?

Is not what we find in experience A] located with other items not compatible with them, and B] somewhat impure, not entirely vague, general, in flux, or accumulative? This would mean that when we find some rules in use in connection with actualities, we look for something in experience to which they can apply, and eventually look to the ultimate Modes of Being for pure cases where they apply.

Does every rule have an application? I think we can say it does. A rule which told us to end every inference with a contradiction would be one which would not allow us to communicate. It is not because the logic of actualities is geared for communication that the above inference is to be said not to allow us to communicate, but rather that, among the rules which are not usable in a logic of actualities, are some which do not permit communication. There are other rules, such as those which relate to the various modes of Being, which permit communication but which are different from those which a logic of actualities uses.

Consequently, logics of intensions, modalities, induction, and abduction can all be said to have rules which could be treated as rules for a logic of actualities, but as having no application. It is only when we abstract from the concreteness of the actualities and their propositions, or when we turn to other realms that we can make use of these rules. Intensions concern Ideality, abduction concerns God, induction concerns Existence, and modalities concern Actuality. Intensions move from the less to the more general, abduction involves synthesis and unifications, induction has to do with a world of flux with nothing actually guaranteed to allow for a movement from one point to another, and modalities (but here I am not sure) allow for accumulations.

An induction, incidentally, concentrates on some limited part of the world and attempts to make an inference regarding the rest of it. That inference is futile unless the data of the premiss involves some connection amongst the items, warranting the statement that the connection will hold for other items. It offers an alternative to the Aristotelian view that there are natures in things which they can maintain; in contrast with that view, induction looks for evidence in the shape of high correlations and then concludes that there is a connection. In effect it denies only the view that we can have an insight into the nature of connections, and instead takes the position that this must be evidenced.

One can also say that an induction offers us a way of testing whether or not the evidence was reliable, for if we find that as a result of an inductive inference we conclude that all cases are the same as the cases we examined, and then find out we are wrong, we will challenge the idea that there really was a connection amongst the items which we used as evidence.

The connection amongst items may not be intrinsic to the items; it may be guaranteed only by nature, or habits, or practice. But in any case, the induction depends on our treating a connection as having a nature which will be manifest in other cases of those items.

December 6

We can deal with man in a number of ways. 1] We can view him as a *res extensa*, and thus divide him at any place and point, without regard to function or content. 2] We can see him as a host of physical particles. 3] We can treat him as a totality of chemical and biological units—oxygen, cells, blood, etc. 4] We can subdivide him into organs —legs, arms, liver, etc. 5] We can treat him as a single biological whole. 6] We can take him to be a perceptual being. 7] We can see him as an experiential being. 8] We can take him to be cognitive. 9] We can take him to be appreciative. And 10] we can take him to be speculative.

These can be viewed as occurring on different levels. But then we must note A] that on each level the affiliations are with other entities of the same level—and this even if they are not (except in the last three or four cases) human. B] The items on one level are affected by items on some other; what one perceives may dictate just where and how one's particles move; a feeling of stress has physical or chemical repercussions; an injury to the brain or even the kidney or arm has an affect on perception, the biological whole, etc.

We can now take one of two courses. We can say that the individual is nothing more than the outcome of the interplay of the different levels; or we can say that there is a unity which contains the various levels. The first supposition makes the individual into a function of the levels and their interplay, and must therefore change in nature and import from moment to moment, and even vanish when the different levels cease to interplay. The second supposition requires one to look at the individual from an entirely different approach; we will have to see the unity of all the levels as having a meaning and perhaps a reference which is not to be found on any of these levels. Thus it may be oriented toward the Ideal, as I suggested in *Nature and Man*, or it may be oriented toward four modes of Being, as I argued in *Modes of Being*.

The view that there is an orientation characteristic of an individual does not deny that there are levels, or that they interplay in the way the first suggestion allows. But it goes on to maintain that the unity has a distinctive nature and career, and that it enables us to say that the various levels belong to one being. The orientation makes it possible, too, to dislocate the items on the various levels from their affiliations, to make them all subservient, in restricted forms, to a common Being.

But we are still left with a question. Though it is true that the atoms in me have a distinctive way of behaving in me, and that as such they could be thought to respond, say, to a delimited version of the Ideal (concordantly with the response of other levels in me to other versions of that Ideal), I have not made provision for the fact that those atoms also function as part of a single totality of atoms. Must we not say that the orientating Being always plays a role to constitute the individual at his center, that it has more or less of an effect on the different levels, and that in an extreme case it may have no effect whatsoever—as say, when a man falls freely through space and thus behaves in terms of his atomic components? It could be said, of course, that the fall involves some bodily changes on an organic level. But this would be true, not because the falling atoms had an effect on the biological, but because the fall was taking place on a number of levels at the same time.

The different levels have their own times. That there should be occurrences on all the levels which take place at the "same time" means that there is a unity not a function of them. We should say, in contrast with what was said some time ago in these volumes, that the atoms are clustered together in an individual, not because of the nature of the individual as a whole, but because both the nature of the individual and the clustered atoms are subject to a common objective Being. This would not preclude the whole nature having some effect on the clustering, or the atoms having some effect on the nature; but it would allow for their partial determination by a common reality.

December 7

If there be a unity to the individual which is to be understood in terms of a reference to some Being, every dimension of the individual will have to be understood to be qualified by it. This will not preclude some one or more of the items in a dimension of the individual from acting in independence of the unity, by virtue of the fact that they are overwhelmed by the influence of other entities of the same kind. Those other entities will have a location outside the individual. Limiting ourselves to a plurality of atomic parts and an overall whole, it will be true at times that the atoms will function as a mere plurality of atomic parts—e.g., when falling—and it will be true at times that the whole will function as a mere overall nature—e.g., when intending to act.

A reference to the unity, as determinative of all dimensions, makes it desirable to distinguish two kinds of universals. There are those which characterize the individual or at least are attributed to it—size, shape, color, and perhaps even humanity. And there are the universals which express the meaning of a possibility toward which all the dimensions of the individual point, and which make it possible to speak of the unity of the individual as obligated or related to the future. Peirce's Scotistic realism evidently refers to the second, since it is a doctrine that universals control, and that they have a teleological import, though it seems that Peirce, and surely I, sometimes confounded this type of universal with the former.

The doctrine has some effect on our understanding of the different logics dealt with a while back. I argued that there was a distinctive logic for actualities, indeed that one which is commonly spoken of as an extensional logic. I also remarked that there was a logic which was dialectical, another which was occupied with generals, a third which dealt with marks, and a fourth which had to do with the vague, answering respectively to Actuality, Ideality, Existence, and God. Now each of these logics has some application in the realm of the empirical. In the world in which we live, there are entities or places which we can describe as dialectical, general, in flux, or as vague. Indeed one can argue that these are to be discovered in every actuality. There is a kind of genesis, a kind of generality, a kind of ongoingness, and a degree of vagueness which must be acknowledged if we are to do justice to the full being of an actuality.

The genesis of an actuality is a muted form of the dialectical development of Actuality. It is the latter as in interrelationship to the parts in the actuality. Both the genesis and the parts are subject to some final cause which modifies each so that they are somewhat consonant with one another. Genesis and the parts in an actuality are united in the idea of development, oriented toward Actuality. In a similar way, generals and the parts in an actuality are united in the idea of class, oriented toward pure possibility or Ideality. Similarly, an ongoing and the parts of an actuality are united in the idea of a practicality oriented toward Existence. Finally, vagueness and the parts of an actuality are united to make a member of a family by virtue of an orientation toward a common God, which is in fact referred to by the unitary being that possesses both the vagueness and the parts. (Of course, in the other cases there is also a reference to a Being by the unitary being as possessing the two dimensions dealt with.)

There would then be no pure logic of mere actualities contrasting with the modes of Being, each with its own pure logic. Instead we would have the actualities as unities in which a modified form of the logics of the different modes of Being was made concurrent with the other dimensions of the actuality. We could abstract from any one of the dimensions and get a pure logic, but the actual logic which governs the functioning of complex actualities in the world would require that we develop a new distinctive logic of genesis, classes, practice, and family. In these logics, the pure logic of, say dialectic, would be muted by virtue of the fact that it had to be copresent with the parts of an actuality. That muting would, of course, be the result of the operation of some mode of Being to which the total individual was related.

We would then have to say that a pure logic for actualities would have to deal with actualities as freed from all vagueness, generality, etc. This could be said to be true of the most elementary particles of nature, which would preclude them from being dealt with in the same ways in which complex actualities were dealt with, or it could be said to be true of any actualities dealt with in abstraction from all dimensions which reflect or mute anything about a mode of Being.

The fact that the vagueness in an actuality is but a muted form of the vagueness characteristic of God does not mean that the vagueness of the actuality is ever voided. Consequently, we need not expect to find the particles in the actuality to be entirely freed from any and all relation to that vagueness. The world of atomic particles is capable of functioning as mere particles, unaffected by vagueness, generality, etc., only as making up a single domain. But as making up such a single domain, they are governed by laws, etc., and these have the requisite generality, vagueness, etc. When we refer to a world and a logic of actualities, we make reference to particles which have a logic of their own, standing over against the logic appropriate to the generality, etc., of particular actualities. Those particles, though, will still have their extensional logic qualified by virtue of the reference of those particles to some reality which also affects the laws for those particles. Isolating the particles does not give us a set of entities free entirely from any limitation required by some other logic. As a consequence of the fact that the particles and the laws are referred to some Being beyond them both, when we abstract the particles from a particular actuality, we but provide those particles with a wider reaching vague, or general, etc., than that which was relevant to them when they were clustered in some more complex actuality.

The world of actualities, complex or simple, is a world of entities subject to the paradigmatic logic, but only as limited by the fact that there are four other logics in a muted form pertinent to other dimensions of those actualities. All the dimensions of the actualities are oriented toward four Beings, which make the actualities subject to a paradigmatic logic limited in four ways.

In a cosmological physics, where we try to deal with the ultimate particles by themselves, we would have to say that the appropriate logic for those particles is still genetic, classificatory, pragmatic, and affiliative, by virtue of the fact that the laws governing those particles are dialectical, general, in flux, and vague.

We would never have pure particles unqualifiedly subject to the paradigmatic logic. But we would presumably have the other logics in a pure form, for the various modes of Being seem to have an integrity or purity, untainted by actualities, which is not true of the actualities themselves. However, one might well argue that those modes of Being are and will always be intruded upon, and as a consequence will never be able to enjoy a pure logic, but only have such a logic muted by virtue of a need to cohere with the kind of qualifications which stem from actualities. On this issue I am not for the moment sure of my ground. Symmetry would dictate the latter conclusion, but an awareness of the nature of Being as contrastive with particulars, and the awareness that the vagueness, etc., peculiar to such particulars, is not identifiable with the vagueness characteristic of God, would lead one toward the former conclusion.

December 8

An actuality always has some degree of generality, vagueness, accumulativeness, and ongoingness. These features are delimited versions of the Ideal, God, Actuality, and Existence. As such, they offer muted ways in which the laws of excluded middle, contradiction, inference, and identity are violated. And they are interlocked with a logic in which those laws are all operative. The logic of actualities is a logic in which we can isolate delimited versions of other logics. These, in their pure and unlimited forms, are logics for the modes of Being and for actualities as over against generality, etc. The logic of actualities is not a mixture of the logic of generality, etc., with a logic of mere particulars; it is a distinctive logic in which we find all the four logics that are pertinent to the modes of Being, as well as that paradigmatic logic which relates to particulars.

What is the nature of an actuality as governed by this fivefold logic? What is the nature of the logic itself, as characteristic of the unitary actuality and as allowing for the abstraction of the five distinct logics? Is it not a vital, growing history, the kind of history which is sometimes called "philosophical history," where premiss, rule, process, conclusion are all produced? The five logics are all prescriptive, but the one logic in which they can be distinguished is but the boundary produced by vital history.

If we emphasize generality, or some other feature of actualities, and see this as united with the logic of particulars, we get a particular form of vital history. Generality and particularity give us a class with its distinctive logic; vagueness and particularity give us the act of self-completion, somewhat as portrayed in Whitehead's process of concrescence; accumulativeness and particularity give us a genetic logic; ongoingness and particularity give us a pragmatic logic. These various logics are the logics of a vital history, but ones which emphasize the ways in which classes are related to one another in a somewhat Marxian way; in which there is a genuine coming into being by entities; in which species originate in a somewhat Darwinian way; and in which the functions of items are stressed rather than their beings or presence.

These logics contain subordinate logics; a pragmatic logic, for example, contains the logic appropriate to Existence, though in a muted form, as well as a logic appropriate to mere particulars, though in a muted form. The pragmatic logic is a logic which dictates when one of these is to be dominant and when the other. And what is true of the pragmatic logic is true of the other logics just distinguished. Each determines when the muted form of particularity or some such characteristic as generality, vagueness, etc., is dominant, and thus when a law of logic will hold and when it will not.

Similarly, the one logic for actualities, the logic of their vital history, is a logic which dictates which one of the foregoing logics of pragmatism, classes, etc., is to be dominant and for how long. The one basic logic for actualities is a logic of vital history which is working itself out now and is exhibited in an unpredictable stress on a pragmatic or some other logic, itself dictating whether some muted logic is to be dominant.

The philosophical historian thinks he can isolate the logic of the vital process of history; the ordinary logician denies that there is any other logic but that governing particulars; the pragmatist thinks that the only logic is one within which one can find a muted form of the paradigmatic logic of particulars and a muted form of a logic appropriate to a flux. But the logic of vital history is being produced and cannot be abstracted, without turning it into a prescription, instead of a structure which is prescriptive only of what has already passed away. The ordinary logician may not have any object on which he can apply his logic and must, with Russell and the early Wittgenstein, create a world of atomic entities which are appropriate to that logic, instead of accepting the world as it is and then seeing what logic is appropriate to it. (The later Wittgenstein can be said to take the ordinary logic appropriate to mere particulars and to merge this with a logic of marks or conventions appropriate to a limited form of Existence so as to yield a pragmatic logic.) And a pragmatic logic, finally, is one which can be matched by a logic of classes, or a logic of genesis, or a logic of self-completion, whose claims to finality are as sound, and as unsound as its own.

We have four logics appropriate to the different modes of Being, and a fifth logic which is appropriate to actualities. The latter is constituted of a union of muted forms of the four logics with a muted form of a logic appropriate to mere particulars (the last is in fact the extensional symbolic logic exhibited in the *Principia Mathematica*). Those who would deny a need for the first four logics might say that we think there are modes of Being in somewhat the way in which Russell thought that there were logical atoms—just to have a counterpart for our logics. But if there be no such Beings, we would have no need for those logics, and could be content with saying that there is only one logic, the vital logic of history. From this we can abstract four logics of actualities, out of which in turn we can abstract a logic for mere particulars and a logic for mere empirically grounded generals, vagueness, flux, and accumulation. Or one could argue that there are logical atoms and also the modes of Being, and that the vital logic of history is but a blurred conjunction of them all.

It is my contention that there are four pure logics appropriate to the modes of Being, and that in addition, there is a logic of vital history in which actualities are qualified by the modes of Being, directly in the case of Actuality, and indirectly through encapsulated versions in the case of the other modes of Being. Epistemologically one could well argue that the modes of Being are tainted by actualities, but ontologically it does not seem as if this were true, since the Beings are possessed of a reality of their own. But do not the actualities possess a reality of their own? Yes, they do, but they are oriented toward and are conditioned by the modes of Being. Actualities make necessary distinctions in the modes of Being and activities there, but the Beings must first be for this to be possible, whereas actualities right from the start have a dimension of generality, etc. Actualities are always oriented toward Being, but the Beings are not oriented toward actualities.

No argument is satisfactory until it has the conclusion detached, and then has that detached consequence faced with content enabling the conclusion to be encountered. Anselm's ontological argument begins with an acknowledged encounter; the form of the argument is similar to that of Descartes, but Descartes has no real God to encounter, and thus has an argument which never gives us a conclusion we can use as a premiss or affirm apart from all argument. Anselm has such a conclusion, but he has it first, before he argues, whereas I come to it last in the *Modes of Being*, and then not in a religious guise, but as the object of a speculation. In *Philosophy in Process*, I have at times acknowledged various ways of confronting God as a transcendent Being, and thus as one who could be encountered as the sustainer of the conclusion of an argument to God.

Perhaps it would be better to speak of the various modes of Being as being affected by their appropriate particulars, and of Actuality, therefore, as being affected by actualities (as possessing generality, dynamism, and synthesizing unity), and to speak of the encapsulated forms of the other modes of Being as being affected by actualities (as possessing some genetic accumulative power and some other two traits, lacking only the one which they obtain from the encapsulated Being which they affect). In that case, we would have only one logic, a vital logic of history which would have a fivefold nature in actualities and a fivefold nature in the different encapsulated modes of Being and in Actuality. Each Being, encapsulated or not, would stress one of the five, i.e., primarily that which related to itself, but would stress this without ever having it entirely pure, since it would be affected by the presence of the other logics expressive of other facets of the Being and reflective of the effect of actualities on that Being. Conversely, actualities would always give more weight to the paradigmatic logic of particulars than to the four other muted forms of logic which express the nature of delimited versions of the modes of Being as characterizing those actualities. The vital history of the world of actualities, though it would have the same fivefold logic as the various Beings do, would be one which was primarily governed by the paradigmatic logic of particulars, and which at different times qualified this by some one or the other feature becoming dominant over the other features, but not over the particulars and their logic.

The difference in the stresses characteristic of the Beings and actualities precludes the supposition that they can be treated as versions of one another. But the fact that they are all subject to the same fivefold logic allows one to see them all as realities.

But what could a vital logic of history be like with respect to Actuality or the Beings which Actuality encapsulated? The Beings would remain, but they would undergo internal change in consonance with the course of the world of actualities. But do we not now make history a kind of sixth mode of Being exhibited in the four modes and in actualities? Not if we treat it as exhibited only in the Beings and actualities where its various components are stressed in different ways. There would be no single vital movement of history, but five basic stresses taking place concurrently. The fifth stress, characteristic of the actualities, will not make them severally or together be a mode of Being, for they will still be contingent items which adopt or accept the qualifications that Actuality and the encapsulated forms of the other modes of Being impose on them.

December 9

Some of the points made yesterday must be sharpened, and others must be abandoned:

1] The object of extensional logic—what I have called the paradigmatic logic, which makes use of all the laws, such as excluded middle, etc.—is the entire actuality.

2] That actuality may have subordinate parts, but each of these parts is itself a distinct object for the extensional logic.

3] Within the area of the entity for extensional logic, one is able to distinguish generals, vagueness, etc., so far as the entity contrasts with another entity for extensional logic. This entity in turn can be analyzed to reveal generals, etc.

4] The subatomic particles in an actuality are themselves to be understood to unite generals with extensional units, and to be united with generals, etc.

5] Though for logic there are just entities in contrast with the generals, etc., those entities are of different kinds by virtue of the fact that they have different analyses. One entity may make use of subatomic particles in interplay with generals, whereas another may have cells or organs in interplay with generals. Both the particles and the organs would be entities in an extensional logic, but would interplay with different generals and interplay with them in different ways.

6] Actualities are caught in a vital history so far as they are detached from Beings and are interlocked with one another.

7] As separated off from other actualities, an actuality functions as a mere extensional entity involved with the three encapsulated modes of Being. As such it accretes the characters of generality, vagueness, and synthesizing unity. In that guise, it can be seen as an extensional entity, but as interplaying with Actuality it will constitute with it a unity in a vital history.

8] There is a vital history, then, not only with respect to actualities, but with respect to each actuality so far as it is involved with Beings in an unqualified or qualified form.

9] Each mode of Being affects the others to constitute with them a vital history involving their constant adjustment to one another.

10] When a mode of Being is separated off from the others, it is subject to a pure logic having to do with accumulation, generality, flux, or vagueness. But since it then is interlocked with some particular, pertinent to it as that distinctive mode of Being, it will constitute with the particular a vital history. In the case of Actuality, there will be an interplay with some actuality to constitute a vital history where there is a stress on accumulation.

11] A vital history constituted by the intrusion of an actuality on Actuality has its counterpart in one which is constituted by the intrusion of Actuality on the actuality. There is, in other words, no one history which encompasses an actuality and Actuality. Instead, there are two vital histories. In one of these, an actuality, as separated from other actualities, has its generality, vagueness, and ongoingness interpenetrated by dialectic, and has them all under the dominance of the actuality in the role of an entity for an extensional logic. In the other of these, Actuality as separated from the other modes of Being, has its dialectic interlocked with generality, vagueness, and ongoingness as characteristic of an actuality which contrasts them with a dimension of itself in the role of an entity in an extensional logic.

12] When an actuality is in interrelationship with other actualities, it exhibits a vagueness, etc., which is intrinsic to it. That vagueness, etc., may have been accreted to it by virtue of the actuality's interplay with Beings, but it now possesses these features on its own, and in a form which reflects something of its own unity.

13] We have a history of Actuality with other modes of Being; a history of Actuality as affected by an actuality which has been qualified by the encapsulated modes; a history of an actuality as affected by Actuality and the encapsulated modes of Being; and a history of actualities, all of which have a fivefold nature, coming to expression always with the extensional side dominant and with a special emphasis on one or the other of the remaining four.

14] All of these histories have the same components to deal with; each functions in consonance with, but in independence of, the others.

But when we have two of them—one involving the interlocking of the actuality with some actuality, and one involving the interplay of actualities—we move constantly from one to the other, and never have one of them in an entirely pure form.

15] Actualities are never entirely freed from an involvement with Actuality; and they are never entirely freed from an involvement with one another. A similar observation is to be made with respect to Actuality. This means that the final, dynamic history is one in which what is primarily a genetic vital history for actualities is inseparable from a qualified dialectic appropriate to Actuality. At one moment an actuality will emphasize its own extensional reality, and at another moment it will, as separated off from the other actualities, be primarily genetic, due to the affect of Actuality on it. When it interplays with other actualities, it does, of course, have a genetic dimension (the outcome of an interplaying of its muted dialectic component with itself as an extensional entity), but that genetic dimension will be its own, whereas when it is primarily genetic in another moment, it will be so because it has been made to be so by the operation of a dialectic on it.

16] So far as the genetic side of an actuality is uppermost, we will not be able to distinguish any moments as constituted in different ways; yet one moment of the genesis will be due to Actuality's dialectic impinging on the separated actuality, and another moment of the genesis will be due to the fact that all the actualities are in interplay, each emphasizing the result of its own dialectic with its own extensional dimension.

December 29

If each of the modes of Being has its own logic, the problem of philosophic method becomes difficult. We must begin from the realm of actualities with its normal logic, and then use other logics in order to arrive at the various modes of Being. This means that there would have to be an act of detachment at the end of the use of that logic, enabling one to have a result which could be supported by the Being of the reality arrived at. Once it was so supported, the philosophic method would have to proceed according to the logic of that arrived-at reality.

Does that mean that we must begin with a dialectic? It would seem so. And then we must use that dialectic in order to get us to some other mode, say Ideality, which is subject to an intensional logic. We could proceed from the logic of Actuality to the logic of Existence directly, but if we go from Ideality to Existence, we must use an intensional logic to bring us to the position where we will use a logic of marks or arbitrary divisions. And by means of any of these logics, we can arrive at the logic appropriate to God, which is the logic of synthesis, and thus of the vague.

It would appear that a philosophic method is, therefore, one which goes only part of the way with dialectic, and the rest of the way with intensionalities, arbitrary divisions, and synthesis. But it first must make use of ordinary logic to arrive at the point where it can make use of a dialectic.

But are the encapsulated modes of Being to be dealt with by distinctive logics? Does not the use of symbols for the various modes of Being preclude the need to deal with a new kind of logic for each of them? What could be meant by a logic of mere marks, and what kind of knowledge could we get from it?

Since the encapsulated modes of Being are delimited versions of the various modes of Being (other than Actuality), it would seem that they are subject to the logics appropriate to their purer, freer forms. As encompassed by Actuality, though, they would be subject to some dialectical limitation, which would dictate the stopping of the various logics at points which those logics could not define.

The fact that the modes of Being are distinct realities contrasting with actualities requires that they be referred to, in the realm of actualities, by distinctive kinds of entities. Strictly speaking, there should be four distinct kind of symbols, and each kind of symbol will have to be dealt with, in relation to others of the same kind, by a distinctive logic.

Existence is a domain of flux, where the ordinary logic's capacity to allow us to transfer some feature of an antecedent to the consequence is no longer possible, since nothing remains constant in that realm. Whatever exists, to be sure, has beginnings and endings; there is relevance and causality. But all these seem to involve particulars as inextricably related to or qualified by Existence. Existence itself should have its own logic, but if this is a logic of mere arbitrary segmentations, there does not seem to be anything we can learn about Existence. But it is this very fact that we can deal with in a study of Existence; we can show why and how it does not allow for anything steady. Instead, then, of trying to make inferences in Existence, we can show how Existence functions so as to preclude inferences in it or in accord with it, in any significant sense.

If the above line be followed, ought we not then say that we need not employ dialectic in dealing with Actuality, intensional logic in dealing with Ideality, and synthesis or the logic of the vague in dealing with God, but should instead show how these various logics express what these realities are in themselves? If so, the initial supposition made to-day must be put aside. The method of philosophy would then be that of tracing evidences back to their sources, and examining the sources to see how they are in themselves, without requiring us to shift the kind of method we employ, except so far as we examine some particular item and find this to be subject to the logic of the reality in which the item occurs.

December 30

The evidences of the modes of Being are to be found in the realm of actualities. When we move from that realm to the modes of Being, we make use of the logic of actualities, but then require a detachment whose result is to be met by an encountered object, unless it be the case that the encounter took place (as Anselm thought) before the movement to the Being (of God) occurred. But if God is encountered before we actually infer to Him, and if Actuality is encountered after we have inferred to it, it would seem to be a reasonable supposition (in the light of the different natures and roles that the different modes of Being have) that the encounters with Ideality and Existence do not take place merely before or merely after we infer to them. In the case of Existence, it does seem as if we encounter it throughout the course of our inference to it, as constituting a forward thrust toward the conclusion of the inference, whereas in the case of Ideality, it seems that we encounter it throughout, but as a controlling condition, a "backward thrust," on what we do in order to arrive at it.

The movement to the modes of Being then is the same in all four cases in that it involves the use of the logic of actualities. But it is different in all four cases in that each involves a different kind of encounter with the object answering to the detached conclusion. Can this consequence be reconciled with the view that we refer to the various modes of Being by means of symbols, and that the world of actualities is to be dealt with by means of signs or variables and their values?

One way of attempting such a reconciliation is to see the inference from actualities to be made by means of signs, until we come to the detachment of the conclusion, which not only separates it from the inference, but converts it into a symbol requiring an encounter with a mode of Being. If that encounter took place before one had engaged in the inference, or had the form of a control over the inference, one would be exerting a pressure on the inferential process to arrive at a result which had the form of a symbol, whereas if that encounter took place after one had inferred, or merely over the course of the process of inference (which is to say if the inference was to Actuality or to Existence respectively), one would have to convert the detached conclusion into a symbol in order to make it adequate to what could be encountered, or one would have to await the conversion of the detached conclusion into a symbol by the Being when that Being was encountered.

In previous discussions, I said that a symbol participated in the Being which it symbolized. This would mean that the symbol was a symbol either of God or Ideality, so far as it involved an encountering with the symbolized result before we have a detached conclusion, and was a symbol of Actuality or Existence so far as it involved a detached conclusion which must be converted into a symbol before it can be a referent to a Being. In the one case, we prescribe that we must end a return from an encounter with a symbol, whereas in the other case, we find that that with which we end a sign activity must become a symbol before it can be sustained by an encounter.

When we arrive at a mode of Being, we can try to see what kind of activity it undergoes. It is this examination which requires the use of different logics appropriate to the different Beings. To know how God functions, we must move toward Him as a synthesizer, showing how the data which He confronts is, despite its apparent diversity and oppositionality of item with item, made into a single unity. Similarly, Ideality is seen to be a domain of universals or possibilities ordered in hierarchies, Existence is seen to be a domain of the self-divisive, to be stopped only at arbitrary points, and Actuality is seen to be a domain of the accumulative or dialectic. All of them, with the exception of Actuality, have been discussed in the *Modes of Being*; what was not dealt with there and what is not yet clear is what is meant by the dialectical functioning of Actuality.

Existence has no alien content with which it deals; its logic is an internal one. A similar observation must be made with respect to Ideality; the content with which it deals is contained within it, but it still has a being distinct from that content—which does not seem to be the case with Existence. God, in contrast, synthesizes items (His own particulars as well as those of other Beings as mediated by encapsulated versions of Himself) which are initially distinct from Him, whereas Actuality engages in a dialectic with respect to actualities and whatever might affect them.

Dialectic, in effect, is the production of a context in which we, given any item, can see how the very meaning of Actuality can be achieved by making the meaning of the item be continued into every other. Actuality is something like the absolute spirit of Hegel, which by itself dictates how the various items are to be related one to the other, and whose nature is exhausted by the totality of the items as related in an accumulative fashion. If we could speak of an end to the dialectic (which we cannot in view of the fact that there is time and therefore new items—or in Hegelian terms, new categories), that end would be identical with the very Being of Actuality, but would be internally articulate in the way in which that Being, as a mere Being, was not.

This approach supports the initial and not the last supposition made yesterday. We take account of the different logics when we take account of the manner with which the different modes of Being deal with a plurality of items. But this dealing is part of the very career of the modes of Being. Still, it is the case that there is a distinction between Actuality in itself and the items it accumulates; between God in Himself and that which he synthesizes; between Ideality in itself and the plurality of possibilities there hierarchically arranged; and perhaps even between Existence in itself and the totality of the parts into which it divides itself. Are there logics appropriate to these Beings as they are in themselves?

Since to be out of one context is to be involved in another, and since to be a Being by itself is either to be confronting items which are to be subjugated somehow or to be involved with other modes of Being without regard for any items to be subjugated, to speak of Beings in themselves is to speak of them either as interlocked with one another or as interplaying with particular items. In the one case, we will have a Being functioning as a synthesizer, as divisive, as hierarchically ordering, or as a dialectical unity with respect to the other modes of Being. In the other case, it will be a power at the beginning of an operation with respect to particulars; these are to be synthesized, made to oppose one another, ordered hierarchically, or dialectically accumulated.

In themselves the various logics apply to the various modes of Being, but only because in themselves they are incipiently related to something else—either other modes of Being or particular items. But this, in effect, means that both the initial and the later supposition of yesterday are accepted, for the distinctive logics would be logics for distinct types of particulars, and for their appropriate Beings as at the beginning of an effort to deal with those particulars or with one another.

The method of philosophy involves *1*] a logical move from actualities with a consideration of some kind of encounter, *2*] to a consideration of the various modes of Being as involved in distinctive ways with the actualities, directly or as mediated (with their own particulars or with delimited versions of themselves as well), and 3] to a consideration of the various modes of Being as involved with one another in terms of operations similar to those which they employ on their particulars (or on limited versions of themselves).

If we get to Actuality, we must see it as dialectical with respect to actualities and the encapsulated modes of Being. If we deal with it as apart from these actualities and the encapsulated Beings, we must see it as dialectical with respect to the other modes of Being. If we employ a dialectical logic on the Actuality with reference to the other modes of Being, we will not have a conclusion we can detach; but if we encounter one of these modes of Being, it will force a detachment of something in Actuality which will serve as a symbol for the encountered modes of Being.

Must we say that God is encountered in advance of an inference, not only from actualities, but from any of the other modes of Being? Or, in general, that whatever kind of encounter is provided by a Being for actualities is also provided by it for other modes of Being? This seems to be plausible, for the very nature of a mode of Being dictates how it operates with reference to anything else. God, we would then have to say, is intrusive on the other modes of Being, Ideality controls every movement toward it from the others, Existence permeates the relation it has to every other, and Actuality refers to and awaits the arrival of other modes of Being. Actuality must always be supplemented by an actual encounter with the others, if those others are to be reached; God has already encountered them in some form; Ideality directs them so that they are encountered; Existence enables each Being to be effective where the others are.

December 31

At least eight distinct kinds of excellence possible to men can be distinguished. 1] *Wisdom*, the result of the permeation of knowledge in and through the body. 2] *Styles*, the result of the utilization of knowledge on behalf of the body and its activities. 3] *Virtue*, the permeation of the ethical in the body politic. 4] *Being civilized*, political life under the control of ethical values. 5] *Monumentality*, the intrusion of the artistic dimension into the historic. 6] *Greatness*, the historic individual as qualified by an artistic sensitivity. 7] *Prophetic*, the permeation of the meaning of God in the community. 8] *Saintliness*, the acceptance of God by a man acting as the representative of men. All of the terms refer to the way in which men make a union of private and public ways of dealing with the several modes of Being. Some of the terms can undoubtedly be replaced by others which will prove more informative or traditionally better grounded.

Men can detach themselves from a reference to modes of Being, however, and become involved with one another and other actualities. When they do this, they turn away from wisdom, virtue, monumentality, and prophecy, to lose themselves in qualified forms of style, civilized action, greatness, and saintliness. They then make an insufficient acknowledgment of knowledge, ethical principles, art, and divinity. Such qualified forms can be termed *skill, adjustment, effectiveness*, and *leadership*. They are forms of excellence of men as together, with a minimal qualification or no qualification by any of the modes of Being.

A man can combine skill, adjustment, effectiveness, and leadership to constitute the single excellence of *maturity*. But the other forms of excellence cannot be combined, for it takes a lifetime to produce just one of them. Consequently, there are nine types of excellence open to a man.

The athlete is one who achieves maturity within the limited setting of a sport, and tries to move on to become excellent as a being with style, i.e., as one who in and through his body functions splendidly under the influence of good judgment and knowledge. He is not, of course, altogether cut off from the other types of excellence, any more than the other kinds of men are cut off entirely from the excellence that is possible to him. He cannot be as excellent as they can, nor can they be as excellent as he in their respective dimensions, for the excellence open to each requires full dedication to a particular type of life.

A better set of terms:

> wisdom, character, monumentality, leadership;
> mastery, justice, heroism, saintliness;
> skill, adjustment, effectiveness, affinity = maturity.

1968

If anything can happen after anything, induction is impossible; if we could deduce the consequence from what is present, induction would be unnecessary. On the first of these suppositions, the highest correlation between items is of no help whatsoever, for what is highly correlated now may not be highly correlated later. A high correlation of items offers not an index of what was to be in the future, but the prospect of finding out what the nature of something is. This conclusion comes somewhat close to Peirce's view; but instead of maintaining with him that induction is a self-corrective device which inescapably arrives at a final result—a supposition which denies novelty and variety, in contrast with Peirce's usual position—the present view holds that an induction is a means for directing us to a nature on the basis of some statistically significant result.

Given a high correlation between items, we do not yet know whether this is caused by some common power, whether or not it is an accidental result, or whether or not one of the items has the other as a function. All we can say is that we now have an indication where we might look for a nature having a relevant set of possibilities which are deducible according to the laws of nature, but which will be realized with some as yet unspecified novelty of detail. We might find that despite a high correlation we can discover no nature and no implicated possibility, and are so far dealing with what is only a chance occurrence. We will know that we have reached a nature when we can in fact deduce a consequence in accordance with natural laws, and then are able to verify our deduced consequence by encountering it as sustained by fact.

The nature and the laws which connect it with possibility are not to be found by examining the correlations which hold between items; the correlations, however, should stimulate speculative reconstructions which lead us to the nature and the laws. An appropriate inductive consequence is, "It is likely that there is a linkage between these highly correlated data, which linkage is grounded in a nature inseparable from possibility, one of whose instances is the high correlation." The likelihood here has no quantitative value; it is but a name for the desirability of a search for a nature which will have the high correlation as consequence. Any high correlation warrants us in making the search, but it in no way justifies the supposition that we will find what we seek. One can say it has a quantitative value as measuring the likelihood of finding the object of the search.

January 6

A bird should fly before it walks. The only question is, who is a bird?

Pioneer women attain a satisfaction others do not, because they are needed everywhere.

Even great clay figures have feet of clay.

Those who love best love most, and those who love most love best.

It is good to know that the Good is not as good as goods.

An athlete learns to accept his body, but only after this has been altered so that it is in consonance with what is needed in order that some prospect be realized. A woman also learns to accept her body, but in its basic forms. Both avoid an identification with the random, the aberrant, or even the impulsive. The woman, though, allows biological growth and ordinary care to do for her what the athlete achieves by training and practice. She can be said to have accepted her body passively.

Are there analogues of such passive/active ways of facing issues with respect to skill, adjustment, and affinities? Does experience provide a passive counterpart for skill, habit for adjustment, and a sense of identity for affinity? Something like these seems to be the case.

But would there not also be active and passive ways of making an individualized reference to a mode of Being as affecting a public dimension, so that we would have something matching to wisdom, character, greatness, and piety—say, adulthood, practical wisdom, self-acceptance, and a sense of being saved? It would seem so.

We should also expect to have an active and a passive case where a public activity toward a mode of Being is qualified by what one is in private. (I hesitate to add more terms; I sense that I am pushing toward answers only on the basis of a desire for symmetry. To be sure, I have found in the past that, when I try to carry out some general scheme, looking for instances and carving out terms so that the whole of it is filled out, I discover items that I did not know about.) The present scheme is not well thought through; there is something untidy about the division between individualized references to modes of Being affecting public guises, public activities directed toward modes of Being qualified by what one is in private, and public activity affected by the private; it looks neither complete nor grounded in principles which warrant its continued use and extension. It is at best a hint about some more satisfactory outline.

January 11

A fictional character has all the features with which its author has characterized it. In addition, it has all those features which are essential to its functioning as that kind of entity. If it is supposed to be a living being it must be supposed to have a heart, lungs, blood, and perhaps an Oedipus complex, even if the author does not mention them and they do not have a dramatic use, for they are presupposed in all the functioning of the character as a human being. What is not in these two categories is indeterminate. We cannot say if the character has hair or is bald, if the author has said nothing about these; we can, of course, maintain that the character is either bald-or-not-bald, but we cannot isolate one of these alternatives.

The features which the character has are all necessary to it; they are definitory of it. In this respect, they are like the features which are traditionally ascribed to God, for He is not taken to have any accidents, and to be eternally what He is. However, we need not suppose that He has no accidental characters; what we must affirm is that He has some characters which are essential. Those characters which were accidental would be somewhat like the indeterminate features of the fictional entity, just as those which were essential to Him would be like the rest of the features of the fictional entity. A fictional entity is like God in that it has necessary and indeterminate features, but the necessary features are there by fiat and are accompanied by indeterminate ones because it is a possibility, whereas God has necessary features analytically, and has indeterminate ones only so far as He is related to a contingent world.

The necessary features of a fictional entity are like the existence of God, in that they are required by the entity. If they were not, if they could be treated as though they were contingent, this would be tanta-mount to saying that the fictional entity was not at all. God necessarily exists or necessarily does not exist; there are certain features of the fictional entity which necessarily are or necessarily are not true of it—in the latter case, making the entity be other than it is, just as the necessary nonexistence of God would make Him be other than He is, if He necessarily exists.

God is like a fictional entity. His existence is parallel to the definitory features of a fiction. But unlike a fiction, God has His features apart from our designations or knowledge. We make a fictional entity be like God is, though with the limitations that we do not give it a necessary existence, but only certain necessary features, which define what it is.

If we say of a fictional entity that it exists, we say nothing additional to what we say by means of the other features, unless by "existence" we mean that it is nonfictional, that it exists in our world of actual entities, in which case what we say is false. If we say of God that He has such and such a nature, we say nothing more than that He exists, for the features are supposed to follow from Him as a Being who necessarily exists, unless we mean by the features those which He accrues by virtue of His interplay with the contingent world.

God's features follow from His Being; the features of a fiction are created by their author. God is so far perfectly determinate, and therefore can be said to have every property or its negation; the fiction has only some of these.

What is said of God must be said also of the other modes of Being. All finalities share with fictions aspects which differentiate them from contingent particulars; they also share with the particulars aspects that they do not share with the fictions. Finalities have the necessity of fictional features and the determinateness characteristic of the contingent particulars.

January 16

There are at least two ways to become the master of one's body. In one, the body is lived in, but in such a way that others yield to it; in the other, the body is used so as to overcome others. The first of these approaches is that of the glamorous woman; the second that of the athlete. Each has a perverse form. The prostitute and the brute take advantage of the weaknesses of others; the one has others yield because of their physical need, the other makes others yield because they are not strong enough to withstand. The perverse forms differ from the others in that they obtain their results not by a superiority achieved, but by an exploitation of a weakness in others.

There are two ways to master conditions. In one, that employed by the status seeker, some function is well performed so that others will assume a lower role; in the other, that employed by the powerful leader, conditions are mastered so that other men can be subjugated. Each has a perverse form, the one in the corrupter, the other in the criminal. They take advantage of the weakness of others, the one by assuming a higher status but not by merit, the other by achieving power through a cheating of others of their rightful possession of it, in the shape of property, rights, etc.

January 22

Philosophy does not invent another world than the world in which we partly live and which we partly presuppose. Its task is to clarify what we in a basic sense already know. This clarification is not achieved by an analysis of our language or what we confront; it involves speculation, dialectic, hypotheses, attempts to move away from what we confront to a higher ground from where we can see how things hang together.

It is, I think, correct to say with Wittgenstein that language sometimes idles. But instead of supposing, as his followers tend to do, that this means the language then says nothing, we should take it to point to the fact that there is perhaps another function which it performs. We make our language idle by bringing it into a context for which it is not designed. The language of sport is idle in a church, and the language of business is idle in a poetry reading. Just so, the language of metaphysics is idle in the world of common sense.

How can we tell the difference between expressions in the ordinary world which are confused or are produced by bad grammar, misconceptions, and the like? Must it not be by asking what the function of the language was: was it to clarify the workings of the practical world, was it to explain, to point to presuppositions, or to refer us to something outside the practical? When I say that I am *inclined* to accept what you say, I am using a term which is not, strictly speaking, appropriate to what has no horizontal, or vertical, or angle. We interpret "inclined" as a metaphor, because we see the purpose of the remark. When we say that God loves me, that there are possibilities, that substances are real, or (as Bradley might) that time is unreal, we refer to what the practical world presupposes. We try to indicate what happens there, what grade of ultimacy this or that may have. We take the metaphorical expression without much ado because we understand it in the light of an antecedently accepted purpose; we find difficulty with other expressions only so far as we try to deal with them from the perspective of an inappropriate purpose. We are caught up in wonder, perplexity; our attempt to resolve these by dealing with terms, or language, or assertion, in the context of practical or conventional affairs, fails to do justice to an initial insistence that what we are trying to say is not exhausted in any set of practical situations.

When a philosopher says "I do not know whether or not another man has a toothache," he does not intend to say that he does not use the signs other men do, or that he does not make the practical judgment to the effect that another has a toothache. Instead, he is pointing up the fact that the reasons for the claim are obscure, or that whatever reasons he can isolate are not well-grounded and that he knows no way of finding others. Philosophic perplexities do not reject facts; they merely point up the truth that they are wondrous, that they are perplexing, not for ordinary experience, but for an understanding seeking principles which apply elsewhere as well.

January 23

Wittgenstein often asked, "How would one teach the child the meaning of this word?" He supposed that the full meaning could be given to a child. When we teach a child how to use a word like God, or possibility, or Being, or reality, or substance, or Existence, however, we try only to help it avoid making obtrusive errors. We say, "Do not use the term 'God' except when you are in church, or when you feel kind, or when you think of someone who loves you always." The child will undoubtedly then think of God as a big man who owns the church or who is like its father, etc. To teach the proper use of the term, in the sense that it does apply to what is appropriate to it and which the child perhaps has glimpsed and which it in fact has referred to dimly in the use to which we have accustomed it, we must build explanation upon explanation. We must make an entirely new context by means of prayers, mercy, liturgy, references to history, holidays, and the like.

To teach a person the meaning of terms which have a metaphysical

import, we must first show him that the words are not to be used as
ordinary ones are, and then help him build up a context or language in
which the words will express the nature and role of something outside
ordinary experience. A similar observation can be made with respect to
private pain. The supposition that there must be authentic cases where
a certain behavior is a positive criterion for the existence of pain con-
fuses the initial satisfactory use of the term in ordinary discourse or in
the rough usage of children with the reference which can be made by
one who has passed beyond that point and thinks of the pain as a private
occurrence unaccompanied by any outward sign.

One can affirm that there is a pain in the absence of behavioral
criteria, and then go on to affirm that no behavioral criteria are necessary
and may never be present. We would not have come to the position of
acknowledging a pain, or a mind, or private feelings, or an ego, if there
had not been publicly acknowledged reasons for them and if we had
not learned some common language which uses certain public criteria
for the determination of whether or not such expressions are properly
used—initially. But we can, having learned this much, move on, and
follow the implications of what we have acknowledged. We can affirm
that the referent of the criteria transcend the criteria, and can be on its
own account. It can in fact be known in some other way, e.g., by building up another language around it, by another way of knowing, by seeing it together with other similar terms, by bringing some order out of
all the criteria, and by seeing how the criteria operate or showing why
they are necessary.

We use common terms, to begin with, to forge a distinctive language
of explanation. We do something similar in "our knowledge of other
minds." We do not merely infer these from behavior, nor make an
analogy with our own minds, as though we had a knowledge of these,
but instead build up a discourse which is explanatory of what we and
others do. We know that there are other minds just so far as we explain
and do not merely observe the behavior of others; we know those other
minds just to the degree that we have taken a position with respect to
what occurs, and allow that position to have content or meaning for
another.

We always start away from the facts, but we do not reflect on this
until we are led to. Someone makes us try to see how a number of facts
hold together or how they fail to hold together, and in that act we discover that he and we have minds.

We know that we have a mind just so far as we know that things fit together from one perspective; we know that others have minds when we see them fitting things together from their perspective, not because we make an analogy, but because ordering in a certain way means "mind." We could apply the term to another before we apply it to ourselves. The test or criterion that others have minds is given by the way in which items are organized from their perspective. The minds that we acknowledge are the explanation of the order, the ordering itself, the reality for which the criteria are criteria.

January 29

A theory of knowledge   1] presupposes real knowers in a real world,   2] presupposes itself as a theory about judgment and knowledge,   3] refers to judgments and knowledge that are possible and may be actual,   4] arrives at the point where it formulates the categories for an ontology, and   5] offers categories for embodiment by a real world.

An ontology   1] presupposes an epistemology as a theory about ontology,   2] presupposes itself as a theory about its users,   3] refers to ontological entities which dictate its grammar,   4] arrives at a point where it formulates the situation where knowing can occur, and   5] awaits the encounter of an actual knower who will carry out a knowing.

Can one replace "theory of knowledge" by "philosophy" and "ontology" by "religion"? A justification for this would be that philosophy is articulate and religion encounters. With reference to God, philosophy can arrive only at the point where God sustains a category of Him, but religion encounters Him in some way and arrives at the point where some theory about Him is possible.

Philosophy, particularly in its metaphysical dimension, deals with ontological realities in the same way that religion deals with God. The very use of metaphysical terms involves a confrontation with the referent of those terms. And religion, because it is practiced by men under limiting conditions, could be said to be imposing categorial limitations on God. He can be known for what He is only in a neutral ontology.

Linguistic analysts, idealists, phenomenologists, and subjectivists would insist that an ontology is only a theory which we formulate, and thus cannot be said to be talking of something in any other sense than that in which what was just called "epistemology" talks of something. Yet real men in a real world are being presupposed in order to make a theory more than an idle fancy.

We confront what we presuppose and that at which our theories terminate. An "ontology" is not just another "language game." It does not merely "speak" of substances, where an epistemology speaks of men judging or of judgments alone.

Does not all discourse involve an adumbrated? But is this not caught inside some other "language" which in turn entails another adumbrated? But if we have a circular system, this second adumbrated may be nothing other than that with which we began.

From this it follows that an ontology has at least two distinct kinds of encounters to consider: it must allow for the encounter of its categorially known epistemology, and it must allow for the encounter of its categorially known Being or Beings.

Should not the categorially known epistemology be recognized to be one of the categorially known modes of Being in some limited form? It would seem so. It should in fact be treated as an expression of actualities so far as they are representative of Actuality primarily, and of the other modes of Being secondarily. Consequently, what we should say is that an ontology makes reference to the various modes of Being, one of which under various restrictions allows for the formulation of an epistemology.

But, it will be objected, an ontology is only a theory, and therefore a kind of epistemology. Is this not only to say that we could take one of the modes of Being, and even a restricted form of it (as we have in the case an actuality representing modes of Being) and treat this as primary, with the other modes of Being functioning as presuppositions, sustainers, and termini of the study? I think so.

January 30

It is of interest to contrast two types of achievement. One is adventurous and the other is expansive. The adventurous begins at a distance from the goal and spends its energy in overcoming obstacles. It has exitement and drama, and ends in a climax of considerable intensity. It is the kind of achievement characteristic of a first or a young love, where there is a mutual discovery on the part of the lovers and an arrival at a moment of intimacy. The other starts where the former leaves off. It begins with an intimacy and expands this so that more and more is encompassed. It is the kind of achievement one would hope that the former will end in. The former can never be repeated for long. Not only do the obstacles become easier to overcome, making the climax less intense, but the climax has only a momentary existence and gives a result which has importance precisely because, and only so far as, it is novel.

Early romances fade, not because they were not genuine, but because they were not able to remain romances. If fortunate, the lovers will move to the stage where they can be expansive. The failure of many marriages is due, not to the fact that there was no love to begin with, but to the fact that the love was not transmuted into a love which is expansive rather than adventurous.

The distinction between the two types of achievement, here emphasized in connection with love, is rarely altogether sharp; there is always some expansiveness and always some adventure, but on the whole the distinction holds. The same pair of achievements can be found in business, sport, and intellectual inquiry. The first excitements of a field or enterprise must give way to an acceptance of the result as a beginning of an expansiveness, or we will have isolated achievements which will represent happy moments never to be built upon and never to be recovered.

January 31

Mathematics and logic are   1] precise,   2] applicable to the items before us, and   3] universal. "Water freezes" is not precise, though it does apply to items before us, and is a universal truth. A law about the behavior of neutrons is precise and universal, but not applicable to the items before us. "These men are brave" is not precise or universal, but is applicable to items before us.

Mathematics and logic tell us about our world of everyday things (2). They tell us that in any case where those laws do not hold, we do not have discrete and permanent items. Either we have something vanishing or coming into being or being distorted, or we have vagueness, generality, etc.

Physics offers constant laws for variable content, while logic and mathematics have a plurality of constant meanings for a plurality of constant contents. Metaphysics offers one constant meaning for a plurality of constant contents—or if one recognizes a plurality of ultimate realities, a plurality of constant meanings for a plurality of constant contents. Is metaphysics then a kind of logic or mathematics? No, for two reasons.   1] Where logics of vagueness, generality, etc., are alongside one another and a mathematics where $2 + 5 = 8$, for example, is alongside our usual arithmetic, in metaphysics meanings are linked, each requiring the other. Any one of these meanings could be taken to be prior to the others. It could be treated as a constant for all of them, with the other meanings as its content, without subtracting from its use as having its own distinctive content within its own orbit.

2] Ordinary logic and mathematics fail in this world, just so far as there are vaguenesses or so far as we, say, mix oil and water. But metaphysical assertions apply without exception to all the items in this world. They have a larger range of universality than logic and mathematics, just as these have a wider range than the laws of nature which, after all, apply only to physical things.

Laws of nature, ordinary logic, mathematics, and metaphysics do not brook exceptions within their field of universality. But the first three, because of the limitations of their field, make provision for alternative schemes. In metaphysics the alternatives have to do with realities outside the province of the other three in their standard forms, though within the province of the other three when these are taken to have distinctive meanings for distinctive kinds of content.

There is no reason why we could not find some linkage amongst the various logics, etc., somewhat in the way in which Poincaré translated the theorems of non-Euclidean geometry into those of the Euclidean. We could then say that there are four logics for the four modes of Being, and that these logics cannot be faulted. There is also a fifth logic which applies to actualities. This could be faulted by what is vague, general, etc., which are then subject to the other four logics.

We must not apply the metaphysical characterizations of the four modes of Being to the particulars of the world except so far as those particulars are affected by those modes. Consequently, we would have to say that if metaphysics and logic are identical with respect to the modes of Being, they separate with respect to particulars. Metaphysics considers the actualities, which are subject to the categories appropriate to the Beings other than Actuality, to be affected by those Beings, whereas a logic of discrete items considers the actualities, which fail to conform to its requirements, to be subject to another logic. Metaphysics, at the very least, gives a reason for the failures to which any one logic was subject in the field of actualities. A logic of discretes could offer reasons in the sense of saying that the actualities it failed to govern were vague, general, etc.; metaphysics tells why they are vague, general, etc.

Laws of nature, ordinary logic, mathematics, and metaphysics state necessary truths in the sense that they force us to explain why it is that there are exceptions to their principles. The reality of the exceptions is precisely what metaphysics tells us about, where the other enterprises are content merely to say that something must have happened which is unlike what happens in a world of fixed, discrete, etc., entities.

February 5

To the question, "What is the meaning of a *word*," Wittgenstein has, I think, given the correct answer. The meaning of a word is the use of that word in some language. That question should, though, not be confused with some others which sound at first as though they were equivalent.

The question, "What *meaning* does a word express," has the answer, "A rule of language in which the word is used." The meaning here transcends any particular use of the word; the word as used is an instance of the rule which allows for still further uses.

The question, "What meaning does a word *communicate* or is intended to communicate," has the answer, "That to which one attends when intending to speak to another."

Attention is an act referring to a possibility. The possibility to which we attend is a general which we convert into an object of intention just so far as we succeed in making it determine what we are to do. There might be some matter of fact, some plan, something imagined, which is to be treated as an intended object. This dictates to us a search for the beginning of a verbal expression and for the rule which this is to follow. If the intended object determines us to use a language, then we can say of that to which we attend that this is what we seek to communicate. We do not communicate the attended object, of course; we communicate our intention with respect to a word, which intention is to be accepted as that which prompts the other to attend to what we attend to.

We can know what it is to which another attends by seeing what he does when we offer him other alternatives to which he might respond. We know what it is which he intends when we see how he resists other possibilities which would lead to another course of action. The criterion for the presence of intention is the engagement in speech or writing with another and a reply of some kind in terms of the way in which he responds. Normally we take on trust the fact that another intends to communicate whenever he speaks to us.

Does the attended object prompt us to forge an intended object, or is the attended object converted into an intended object by being given new determinations and allowed to operate on us in certain ways? A causal theory preserves both the attended object and the intended object; it takes them to occupy different territories, the one perhaps being viewed as an abstraction from a confronted matter of fact, where the other is something merely conceived. But causality in the realm of mind is a difficult thing to show. And a theory of the conversion of attended objects into intended ones does not necessitate the denial of a continued status to the former. An attended object, no matter what its original home, can be made to function as an elicitation for a verbal activity and an acknowledged rule, and thereby function as an intended object for discourse. When this is done, the terminus of the discourse will be not some verbal outcome, but the discourse as inseparable from a semantical or denotative aspect.

Another on hearing me does not have the denotative reference that I have when I speak. But he hears me in this world we share. So far as this is true, he has an indefinite semantic reference. This he sharpens as he accepts the words as agencies of communication. Both of us, as it were, acknowledge that there is something to be encountered as we interchange our views.

When it is said that language expresses thought, what apparently is meant is that some of the intended objects are possibilities which were originally conceived by the speaker, and which may not have an experiential counterpart. Such possibilities are semantically connected with our language, but they in turn do not have a semantic connection with something real. Other possibilities we derive from matters of fact; they are located in those matters of fact, and therefore have a semantic connection with them. We immediately refer to those matters of fact when we intend to communicate what we have in mind.

Another on hearing me speak of something which he cannot locate inside his accepted semantical domain is forced to consider possibilities distinct from those which are abstracted from matters of fact. What possibilities does he consider? How does he know they are the possibilities that I, the speaker, had in mind? He may, of course, consider any possibilities whatsoever. But unless he considers those possibilities that the speaker has in mind, he will not know what the speaker intends. He must, therefore, go through a number of steps which determine not whether the speaker intends anything, but just what it is that he intends. The normal way of proceeding here is for the listener to communicate to the speaker some possibility; the listener in his reply will show the operation of some possibility functioning as an intended object, and will await the reply of the speaker to see if the listener had correctly identified the intended object. If the speaker replies that what is said by the listener is not satisfactory, then another intended object will usually be expressed by the listener, and so on. (It is being supposed, here, that an intended object uniquely dictates the expressions that are being used. This supposition is justified within the conventional situation of use and practice characteristic of both speaker and listener.)

Is there something a priori in this activity? There surely is something relatively a priori in the words that are used. The attended object, the intended object, the rule, and the method of experimentation and discovery characteristic of real discourse, are all relatively a priori with respect to what is said; they dictate its order and direction. Behind this relative a priori is an absolute a priori, expressive of the essential intention of a man, which is, I think, to complete himself, to perfect himself, to be able to deal with what is alien in such a way that its meaning, value, function, products, etc., are within his control.

February 6

1] That to which we attend may be converted by a desire into an intended object. Something seen can thus be transformed, by a desire to communicate, into something one intends to speak of in language. *2]* That which we intend is an operative cause or condition for the discovery of a beginning and a structure. *3]* So far as the structure is a function of the intended outcome and is inseparable from the premiss or beginning, it is a necessary whole or truth. It is contingent only so far as it is a mere pattern, separate from both antecedent and consequence, actual or intended. *4]* Logical rules are prescriptive in the sense that they demand that any beginning which we accept because of an intended conclusion must be transformed until it meets the requirements of the rule.

If we accept the fourth condition, could we not extend it to any rule whatsoever? Why not say that a rule in English is such that any word we want to use as a singular subject must have a singular verb? The rule of the language would then be prescriptive. We could; but our rule would have a narrow scope; it would relate only to English. In contrast, a standard logical rule applies to any entities whatsoever, just so far as they were distinct and retain their distinctiveness throughout the logical transaction.

Does this not imply that ordinary logic is a convention, but merely of larger scope than a language or a set of language rules, and that its only purpose is to allow for the communication of a larger variety of items to a larger variety of men? I think not. To make that point, we would have to show why it was that the logical rules had this privileged status, and why we could not instead take a rule of ordinary language to be that which defines the boundaries of communication. Or we could take some other rule, say one such as "Always replace *x* by a qualification of it," as that which could not be violated without making communication impossible. Logic (the ordinary sort, formulated in the *Principia* and its cognates) does have a larger scope than ordinary language, but this is because distinctness is a category whose failure of application demands the application of the alternative categories relating to vagueness, generality, flux, or dialectical accumulation (answering to the logics appropriate to God, Ideality, Existence, and Actuality).

What of mathematics? It seems to be the case that the formulae of mathematics summarize the results of discoveries, in which logical rules are used but not focused on. When we say that $7 + 8 = 15$, we express the nature of a beginning as connected with an ending, derivable logically. We can view $7 + 8$ as a premiss and the equality with 15 as a logical consequence of this (and conversely, of course, we could take 15 to be our beginning and show that the conclusion $= 7 + 8$ followed logically from this).

February 7

Leading principles may be conventional, but logical principles, which express the connection which leading principles and premisses have to the conclusion, are evidently not so. But we can take any logical principle and make it into the connection between a premiss and a conclusion, and then find another logical principle which relates the premiss and connection to the conclusion. Thus, if we have a logical principle relating to discrete particulars (the only kind Peirce considers when he makes the distinction between leading and logical principles), we can use this either as a connection for a premiss and a conclusion, or as the residuum which can be abstracted from any case where we have a premiss and a connection with some conclusion. A logical principle can, therefore, be derived from any inference where the principle functions also as a connection. It can also be found in any inference where the connection is provided by some other logical principle governing different kinds of entities.

If we have a logical principle appropriate to vague items, e.g., we can
1] use a contingent principle of connection which will take us from the

premiss to the conclusion appropriate to vague items, 2] use a logical principle pertaining to vagues (that they unite what would otherwise be disparate or conflicting) to take us from the premiss and connection (pertinent to vagues) to the conclusion, or 3] use a logical principle pertaining to vagues to take us from the premiss and connection (pertinent to other kinds of entities, e.g., generals, discretes, flux, or dialectically constituted wholes) to a conclusion which is vague because it absorbs the premiss and connection in the conclusion.

Peirce had too narrow a view of the nature of logical principles. He thought they were principles of one kind only. He knew there also was a logic of vagueness, and another of generals. I suppose, in the light of his discussion of thirdness, he would have allowed for a dialectical logic, and might, in the light of his insistence on chance, have allowed for a logic pertinent to flux. But he did not see that any premiss whatsoever could be connected by means of any of five types of logic to a conclusion, and that any premiss which had a connection of some kind with a conclusion could be said to be related, with that connection, to the conclusion by any one of five types of logical principle.

The acknowledgment of a plurality of logics and the fact that they could enter into one another's domain as connections, or could serve to be as necessary links between the others when these are made into connections (and thus yield a conclusion that is different from that which the logical principle with that premiss had produced), seems to bring us back to conventionalism and relativity. It also makes us modify Peirce's definition of a logical principle. He thought it added nothing to the situation; but if we are given a situation where we have a premiss and a logical principle together, we will not be able to introduce a logical principle of a different sort unless the conclusion (which is entailed by the premiss and the initial logical principle) is altered.

Peirce's definition is correct just so far as it applies only to logical principles pertinent to actualities. Given any premiss and any connection, whether this be a merely conventional one or a logical principle of any kind, the relation to the conclusion which the premiss and the connection yield is expressed by a logical principle that allows for a detached determinate conclusion. But if we think of a logical principle as that which necessarily relates a certain kind of entity in a premiss and a connection to another kind of entity in the conclusion, we can apply the logical principles pertinent to vagues, generals, flux, and dialectical wholes, and thereby get a different kind of conclusion. We will make the conclusion synthesize the premiss and connection, generalize them, turn them into marks, or accumulate them. The use of different logical principles makes a difference to the conclusion. But the principles will not, therefore, be shown to be contingent or conventional, but only to operate on different kinds of entities than those appropriate to the logical principles of which Peirce spoke.

We have here a situation something like that pertinent to truth and lie. It is sometimes thought that lies are but the negations of truths. But this overlooks the fact that truths are uttered in a context of acceptances, and that a lie not only says the opposite of a truth, but demands for its support an entire battery of other assertions or claims. To protect the lie, one must extend further and further into the domain of accepted truths and alter these, not because all truths are internally related, but because an assertion of a truth commits us to a context whose truths will not reject or conflict with other truths. A lie may reject, conflict with, or imply such rejection, or conflict with other truths not then envisaged, by virtue of its implications and consequences. A liar has no control over all the other assertions and claims which are accepted in the ordinary course of living or in some discipline, so that his lie eventually is confronted by something over which he has no control.

The ordinary logic of discretes is like truth, and the other logics are like lies, in that they cannot be carried on inside ordinary living without coming into conflict with what is ordinarily held. But just as a lie can become a fiction in a fictional world, so the other logics can become the rationales of absolute Beings.

We could also say, though, that a premiss together with an ordinary logical principle might yield a conclusion in which the premiss and the principle were accumulated. Then, following Peirce's definition of a logical principle, one could say that the initial premiss and principle yielded that conclusion, and that they together were related to the conclusion by a logical principle which has to do with vagueness. We seem here to have something analogous to the way in which the community's arsenal of truths is ruptured by the claims of miracles, political "big" lies, and the like.

None of the foregoing, or what I said yesterday, is altogether clear.

February 8

Suppose I conclude to something and find that this conclusion is arrived at by a process which does not conform to *modus ponens*? A Wittgensteinian would say that it conforms to whatever rule one might find in it. But this answer in effect means that one never makes any mistakes; whatever we do exemplifies or is the very being of the rules we acknowledge. Others would say that we evidently have made an error, a logical error in fact. But how can one violate a law of logic? The Wittgensteinian allows for no violations, but has no laws of logic which prescribe, while these others—usually traditional logicians—have laws of logic which are necessarily true, but which nevertheless can somehow be violated. A third alternative is better than either, I think: we never violate a law of logic, but we can get results which do not conform to the *modus ponens*. When we do, we in effect impose another law of logic on the result of a *modus ponens* to convert the conclusion into a conclusion in consonance with some other logic. We make no logical errors; our fallacies are the result of misinterpretation, of supposing that we are operating in this domain rather than that, or from taking some logical law as the law necessarily relating premiss and connection to the conclusion arrived at.

Given premiss, p, and rule, r, we arrive at conclusion c. Rule r may be a leading, i.e., a contingent principle, or it may be a logical law, i.e., a rule which applies to all conclusions which are determinate, accumulative, generals, in flux, or vague. I say "conclusions," for the various types of logic seem able to start with distinct terms and are characterized by the way these are used to produce conclusions of different types. When we use a logical law as a connection, r, we may or may not use it as well to constitute the relation of necessity connecting the premiss and the connection to the conclusion at which we in fact arrive. A logical law is one which provides the relation of necessity. It is used in an additional way when it is used as a connection or a rule; it then does not function as a logical law, though it still retains the structure that it had.

Logical laws are not conventions, for they are the laws which govern the connection between any p and r with whatever conclusion we do in fact arrive at. We do not reason in accordance with such laws; they are the product of a summation of p and r, a summation which may occur only after we have in fact begun with p and moved away from it in accordance with r. In saying that it is a product of a summation, it is not implied that the law is made by us, but only that it is operative only so far as we have both p and r.

We reason in accordance with connection, r, but the conclusion we arrive at is a conclusion rather than a terminus only because we, in moving in accord with r, still move within a situation in which p is the point of origin. A conclusion is a logical conclusion only so far as there is reference to the *p*, if only in the sense that it is expressed in the connection, *r*, as that with which *r* begins. And that logical conclusion is related to the *p* and the *r* in any one of five ways, answering to any one of five basic logics.

February 9

I have been wobbling back and forth these last days between the idea that logic offers the most general rules for entities, and the idea that it concerns itself with what necessitates a conclusion, given a premiss and a connection or rule. I think the latter idea is the more correct one, since it takes care of all the different varieties of logic, and also acknowledges each logic's inescapable necessity. Logic offers the most general rules only so far as it functions as a connection between premiss and conclusion; but this is a derivative use of the logical law.

February 12

The logic of the *Principia Mathematica* applies to the discrete, the quantifiable, the extensionally treated. The logic of accumulation applies to what grows and to what is usually taken as philosophical history. The logic of generals applies to the object of attention and to psychology. The logic of flux applies to the fact of persistence as studied in sociology, with its arbitrary beginnings and endings. The logic of the vague applies to creativity and perhaps to the domain of economics.

Do we need now to make reference to ultimate modes of Being? If we do, why should we not also make reference to an ultimate mode of Being having the rationale of actualities?

We are driven to acknowledge various logics as pertinent to various modes of Being when we find that the world of actualities (with which we begin) does not have these other worlds alongside it, and that these other worlds intrude on it as unitary powers. We would have no need to refer to the various modes of Being were the various logics to characterize the growth, etc., of actualities. We could then have five different logics applying to different parts of the spatio-temporal world. But we find, in addition, that these logics and their items intrude upon the world of actualities, and do so in a unitary way.

It is in the attempt to isolate the intruding powers that drives us to acknowledge the modes of Being as affecting the world of actualities. Should we find, while dealing with growth, persistence, etc., not only quantifiable, discrete items subject to the logic of the *PM,* but an intrusion on the growth, etc., by a unitary power having a rationale similar to that of actualities, we would have to acknowledge a mode of Being characterized by the logic we now take to have an exclusive reference to actualities. Do we find such intruding powers on the growth, persistence, etc., of actualities?

Can we take the growth, etc., to be localizations of the different modes of Being? I think there is no necessity for this unless we insist that the world can contain only actualities as subject to the laws applying to the discrete, etc., and subject to an extensional logic, so that the presence of any other kind of entity requiring another logic will be testimony to the fact that some other Being is intruding into the world of actualities. But growth, attention, etc., seem to be empirical phenomena on a footing with actualities, although it is the case that only actualities seem to be substantial and the others seem to be features of actualities (which conceivably can be understood as the outcome of the effect of modes of Being on actualities). If we understand growth, attention, persistence, creativity, as involving some "metaphysical" reference to Beings as intrusive on actualities, we deny to these, and to the disciplines which deal with them, a genuine empirical status.

Is a general or universal to be understood in the end as a precipitate or consequence of Ideality? Or is it not more correct to say that there can be generals which have an empirical being (such as the future as the terminus of a drive, or intent, or temporal structure), and that there are in addition prescriptions, which point to the operation of the Ideal on actualities? This latter suggestion, which seems better than the first, has a consequence the distinguishing of two kinds of accumulations, generals, flux, and vaguenesses. One kind is factual, real, something which occurs in the world of space-time and is to be understood in a language, or logic, or theory, or context which is alongside that of ordinary extensional logic as pertinent to discrete items (not all of which are substantial actualities). Another kind would be a unitary, intrusive set of items whose presence cannot be understood without the use of symbols which direct us to what is intrusive and has a being of its own.

This distinction between the two kinds of generals, etc., raises two questions. Are actualities only of one kind and generals, for example, of two? Does the Ideal intrude only on actualities to provide one of the kinds of generals, but not on vagues, for example, or even on those generals which do not owe their being to the intrusion of the Ideal? I think we must answer both negatively.

Beings intrude not only on actualities, but on other kinds of entities—generals, vagues, etc. One of the kinds of generals, vagues, etc., will be like actualities or other discrete items in that they will have their own rationales or logics. And there would be, as aspects of each one of these kinds of entities, features which could not be understood except by referring to exterior Beings.

We have then:

1] Actualities, dialectical wholes, generals, flux, and vagues. These occur in the space-time world, and are characterized by distinctive logics, alongside one another.

2] These very actualities, wholes, etc., are qualified by Actuality and its included delimited modes of Being, to give us features of the foregoing five kinds of entities.

The acceptance of both of these contentions leads to the conclusion that there is, for example, a generality characteristic of the discrete actualities (or better, the discrete entities which function according to *modus ponens*), and that there are also generals, wholes, flux, and vagues alongside the actualities. What we have then are five kinds of finite entities with distinctive kinds of careers, requiring distinctive logics. Each of the five kinds of entity has four kinds of features, to be understood to be the consequence of the intrusion of modes of Being in some form on those different kinds of entities.

February 13

A logical law expresses a necessary connection uniting a premiss and rule with a conclusion. On this view, the difference between the Aristotelian syllogistic, *Principia Mathematica,* *n*-valued logics, and "strict implication" is not a difference in logic, but only in the kind of premisses and rules that are permitted.

The only significant alternative we have had to the established logics, all of which relate to discrete entities having conclusions which are detachable, allow for a transfer of values, concern particulars, and are clear, are the intensional logics. These, though, have been developed by men who did not recognize that these logics end with generals, or accumulate the premiss and rules in the conclusion, etc., so that in the end the offered intensional logics turn out to be but variants of the old extensional logic.

The recognition that there are alternative logics is widespread to-

day, but somewhat blurred. Having discovered that the ordinary established logic with its respect for the various traditional laws of thought
does not hold in every case, there has been a tendency to suppose that
a logic is only a conventional language to be placed alongside any
other language. But it does not follow that if the ordinary logic does
not hold in every case, it is merely conventional in the sense in which
a language of butchers is conventional. The failure of one logic may
be (and, I think, is) due to the presence and operation of another
logic.

A logic can have a conclusion which   1] is detachable,   2] preserves the separateness of the items in the premiss and rule,   3] trans-
fers the property values, or some generalization from these, to the
conclusion,   4] preserves the distinctness of the items in the premiss
and rule,   5] denies any one of the above four,   6] denies any two of
the above four,   7] denies any three of the above four, or   8] denies
all of the above four. Since *1–4* allows for one case, *5* allows for four
cases, *6* allows for six cases, *7* allows for four cases, and 8 allows
for one case, we have sixteen cases in all. There are then sixteen different logics. Multi-values, languages relating to contingencies, logics
having to do with inductive and abductive rules, etc., all will fall under
one or the other of these sixteen.

Is any one of the sixteen more basic than the others? If so, which
of the sixteen is most basic? If not, is there something basic to them
all? Or are there a number which are basic depending on the point of
view we take?

The sixteen logics are possible only because there are sixteen possible conclusions which can be said to be necessitated, given premiss
and rule. One of those logics (case 8) has a conclusion which is accumulative, general, arbitrarily marked off, and vague; another (one
of those allowed by case 5) is accumulative, but particulate, with a
transferred property value, and clear. These and the fourteen other
kinds of conclusion might all answer to ultimate matters of fact
properly designatable as "actualities." All sixteen can be affected by
Actuality and the subordinate modes of Being to give us distinctive
types of features.

The ultimacy of Actuality demands that the feature which is accumulative be more basic than the others, in that the others occur
within its confines. But this fact does not tell us which, if any, type of
actuality is prior to the other fifteen.

The existence of various types of actualities seems to point up the fact that there is a plurality of types of entity, a plurality which is subject to ordinary logic. This result may be a consequence of the fact that we found our sixteen by the application of such a logic. (The application is itself apparently the result of the fact that each type of logical law has its own integrity.) If there be merit in this approach— and of that I am not altogether sure—we would have to say that actualities, in the sense in which I have previously understood the term as applying to substantial distinct entities, of which individuals, such as men, are outstanding examples, would be primary. This would allow for the reality and even finality of the other types of entity, but as occupying some less fundamental ontological position. A vague item, for example, would be an actuality perhaps only for perception, or for creativity, or for synthesis. It might represent a feature or function of a substantial actuality in the usual sense, or it might occupy a domain of its own, which in the end was derived from that of substantial actualities in interplay with one another. This might account for the fact that mankind has been so slow to recognize that there are actualities which are subject to a logic other than that appropriate to the substantial individuals we daily acknowledge in a somewhat unfocused and unreflecting way.

We have, then, as ontologically basic, a logic for substantial, individual actualities as subject to qualification, primarily by Actuality. This logic would exhibit the four properties of detachability, separateness, transfer, and distinctness; the features which resulted from the intrusion of Actuality would be accumulative, and may or may not have consequences which are separated and transferred, and which preserve the distinctness of the factors in the premiss and rule. These features would have subordinate to themselves other features which are the result of the intrusion of the subordinated modes of Being. As a consequence, we would use the ordinary logic to deal with actualities, and would use the logic of accumulation to deal with their primary features.

Are we justified in holding that generals, flux, and vagues are not ultimate in the very sense in which individual entities are? I think so, for the acknowledgment of any entities presupposes individuals which are particulate, possessed of an identity over time, and able to preserve their distinctiveness. It would be "existentially" absurd to try to deny the reality of individual, substantial actualities. This, though, does not go the length of showing that the other kinds of actualities are derivative from individual actualities. They could conceivably exist as independent realities. Consequently, what must be said is that individual actualities are existentially and ontologically real, and that the others may be ontologically real as well. This is sufficient, I think, to give priority to the ordinary logic so far as we are concerned with being accurate with respect to what is inescapably real in this space-time world, while leaving over the features of those actualities as subject to a logic of accumulation, which requires that what had been is somehow preserved in what follows. This logic of accumulation has primary place in each substantial individual actuality, but it can be extended to apply to any interplay of such actualities.

A logic of accumulation need not be cosmic in its application. It may apply only within the confines of an actuality or a number of them, and not carry over into another stage, as Hegel, Peirce, de Nouy, Teilhard de Chardin, and other historically, evolutionary, or progressively oriented thinkers hold. And, of course, it does not preclude the presence of features which are subject to the ordinary logic.

An individual being may have features which are not due to the intrusion of a mode of Being on it. Indeed, an individual being may have accumulative features which owe nothing to Actuality; the only accumulative features (or any other features for that matter) which involve a reference to a mode of Being are those which exhibit some subjugation to the demands of something having a cosmic power.

Why restrict the features to four imposed ones, and to five which owe nothing to the intrusion of modes of Being? Why might there not be a feature whose consequences were accumulative and yet which was not transferable (in that the truth value of the outcome was not determinable from the standpoint of the beginning)? After all, the different intrusions could intermingle, and any feature which was not due to the modes of Being could be a product of a number of tendencies or conditions in the object and in what environs it.

I think we must be content with saying that there are sixteen different kinds of actualities, of which the substantial individuals are the most inescapable, and that these have any one or more of thirty-two features, any one or more of sixteen of which may be the outcome of the intrusion of Actuality, or of the three modes of Being which Actuality subjugates individually or in combination. But Actuality will still be the dominant mode of Being, so that an accumulative imposed feature will be essential, though capable of being modified by the subjugated modes of Being. We could term that feature "essential" which followed the logic of the entity which it expresses, and that feature "basic" which reflected the logic of Actuality. Then, if we take actualities in their primary sense to be substantial individuals, their essential features would follow the ordinary logic, and their basic features those of Actuality. The individuals, like other kinds of actualities, would have other features as well, but these would not be essential, because they would not follow the logic of the individual actualities, and would not be basic because they showed the effect of the subjugated modes of Being. In addition, each of the kinds of actuality would have a distinctive kind of essential feature, while possessing the same kind of basic feature that characterizes individual actualities.

February 14

Forty years ago I published a paper on alternative logics. I there distinguished sixteen kinds. But that study did not deal with logics; it played variations on the definition of implication, and did not deal with the different kinds of necessity with which a conclusion might be connected with its premiss and rule.

The present distinction of the sixteen logics is the product of an attempt to formulate precisely the nature of the necessary connection characteristic of our ordinary logic. Every once in a while in the course of teaching, I try to formulate precisely some such basic notion, and thereby discover that I had been taking various matters for granted.

The attempt to make something precise forces one to distinguish, and also raises the question as to whether the focused item is the only case, and whether or not it is necessary. As a consequence, one looks at what is being excluded in the course of the process of making precise, and then tries to occupy the position of those excluded items, thereby discovering features which had not hitherto been noticed. In the present case, sixteen different types of logic are distinguished. Each one of these could have an instantiation in some distinct kind of finite entity. The sixteenth case, for example, which involves an accumulative, general, fluid, and vague outcome, requiring one to make arbitrary demarcations in a flux which absorbs what had been, and which defies the laws of excluded middle and contradiction as applicable to its components, seems to be expressed quite well in Bergson's *élan vital*, though he would undoubtedly object to the characterization "generality."

Not every one of these sixteen logics needs to be exemplified in the shape of final particulars. But no matter what exemplification they achieve, they are also manifested in the guise of distinct, essential features of the different kinds of final particulars. Those essential features give us the "natures" of those particulars. Each one of these features is a realized possibility, a can-be, which is now embodied and enriched by the present being of that in which it is, and which it can be said to express.

Whether or not there are in fact sixteen different kinds of finite entities in existence, there will be at least four imposed features, answering to the encapsulated modes of Being and to Actuality. Each makes a difference to whatever finite entities there be. Those encapsulated modes of Being and Actuality may infect one another in various combinations to yield any one or more of twelve features answering to the way in which the logics governing the imposing Beings combine. The logic pertaining to substantial, individual actualities does not, of course, combine with the others, for they are all defined in terms of a negation of one of its definitory dimensions.

We need not suppose that a logic which is, let us say, accumulative and vague in its conclusions, is the product of a combination of other logics. Instead, what should be said is that the influence of different Beings can be expressed singly or together with the others, thereby producing imposed features answering to any one or more of the sixteen possible kinds of features, each of which has a distinctive kind of necessary consequence.

We have, then, individual actualities which are existentially necessary by virtue of the fact that we are such actualities. Whatever happens is the result of the interaction of beings which are able to be and act as distinct entities, possibly together with any of fifteen other kinds of actual entity (which are as final and irreducible as the individual actualities). The individual actualities, and any of the others that there might be, have distinctive natures expressed in features which follow the very same logic that those entities do. Each of the existent actualities that there may be, in addition, may have any one or more of the fifteen other features that are possible, each following the course of a distinctive logic. What is an essential feature of one kind of actuality will, of course, be a nonessential feature of some other, and may in fact not be present in that other. There are as many essential features as there are distinct kinds of actuality, but it is a contingent fact that any one of these kinds has other types of nonimposed features as well.

In addition to the features which are not imposed on whatever kinds of actualities that there be, there are four types of imposed features revelatory of Beings. In addition, there are other possible kinds of imposed features that result from the way in which the different influences affect one another. It is conceivable that there might be no imposed features which reveal the Beings in their severalty. If that were the case, we could discover the four types of imposed features only by analyzing whatever imposed features we discover (which will be known by the way in which they subjugate or control or reorient the actualities in which they are), or by having an independent knowledge of the way in which the Beings affect actualities.

Because of the priority of Actuality to the other modes of Being in their bearing on actualities—due to the fact that those others are encompassed by Actuality, and the fact that all actualities, of whatever type, are oriented as equally real in Actuality—whatever actualities there be will always show a basic imposed feature reflecting the dominance of Actuality, and will exhibit features which tell us something of the other three modes of Being, severally or together.

We come again to the conclusion that there are individual actualities which bear the marks of having been imposed upon by Actuality and three encapsulated modes of Being. Those individual actualities, in addition, have essential features which express their natures and which follow a logic distinct from those characteristic of the imposed features. (Evidently something has gone wrong here—if there is no imposition of a feature answering to the logic of an individual actuality, there cannot be as many kinds of imposed features as there are nonimposed ones on individual actualities. There will be sixteen possible nonimposed features and only fifteen possible imposed ones on them. The other kinds of actuality will be able to have imposed features which are similar in nature and subject to the same logic as their natural, essential features. But like individual actualities, they will have no imposed features answering to the logic of actualities.)

When we are able to use ordinary logic, we know we are confronted with individual actualities. If we cannot use that logic, we either have 1] features of individual actualities which are not essential, 2] other kinds of actualities, 3] essential features of those other kinds of actuality, 4] features which have been imposed on actualities, whether these actualities be individuals or of other types.

February 15

An individual, substantial activity, of which living beings and the ultimate particles of physics are exemplars, have careers and relations to one another which conform to the ordinary logic with its *modus ponens*. In addition, they have natures which also function according to that logic. Those natures are ingredient possibilities which are achieved through the realization of possibilities confronted as future. This means that the natures of actualities result from the conversion of entities, subject to a logic of generals, into entities which are subject to a logic which (unlike the logic of generals) keeps the entities distinct.

In addition to a nature which is the product of the realization of a nonimposed possibility, though one which has its roots in Ideality, an actuality is subject to the imposition of an ideal possibility, which is focused on when the actuality becomes aware of its duties. Before that time, an ideal possibility controls an actuality in the shape of a delimiting object of concern.

An actuality is always oriented toward the future. The terminus of it in the future is two-fold: the actuality has an immediate objective in the form of a nonprescriptive possibility which it realizes as an ingredient possibility or nature in the next moment, and a more remote objective in the form of a prescriptive possibility which it is to realize together with all other actualities. The actuality may realize the latter possibility in a way that conflicts with its realization by other actualities, thereby leaving that prescriptive possibility so far unrealized.

An actuality is in constant interplay with its environment. That environment, as a limited portion of a larger cosmos, has the actuality as a delimited region. The distinction of the actuality from the cosmos, and in particular the environment, follows the logic of flux. That logic is one in which the process of interplay with the environment and the demarcation of the actuality from the cosmos is arbitrarily set. All actualities are there made contemporaneous by the power of Existence. This is manifested in each in an arbitrarily delimited, temporal, extended present. The extent of that present may be appropriate to the smallest particles, but it is an arbitrary delimitation for the larger ones.

An actuality also has a worth in affiliation with other actualities. As such it is sacral, and is to be understood as being subject to the intrusion of the divine in the shape of an encapsulated mode of Being. That imposition is manifest in the actuality in the guise of a feature which follows the logic of the vague. The feature has its import absorbed within a larger value constituted by the plurality of actualities. This larger value is the living being of the immanent God.

The three imposed features, answering to the prescription of the

Ideal, the compulsion of Existence, and the "persuasion" (to use White-head's expression) of God, are all within the confines of a fourth im-posed feature due to the intrusion of Actuality on the actualities. This feature follows the logic of accumulation, and expresses the equality of all the actualities as realities by virtue of their issuance from a com-mon past which they keep within them in some subjugated position (as was suggested in the book on history).

An actuality is primarily a finite entity which has issued out of the past. As so issuing, it has a future which it realizes by converting the generality of that future into a concrete, determinate feature. It there-fore requires a change from the logic of generals into one which uses the ordinary logic and its *modus ponens*. The actuality also has four imposed features, each of which follows out a logic that is distinct from the actuality's or from the nature which the actuality has by virtue of its realization of a future possibility.

An actuality is subject to the prescription of the Ideal and exhibits this in the guise of a feature which marks it as more or less fulfilled, realized, perfected together with others. It is also subject to the compul-sion of Existence and exhibits this in the form of a predicate of "ex-istence" contemporary with other similar predicates characteristic of other actualities. In addition, it is subject to the persuasion of God and exhibits this in the guise of its worth as affiliated with other actualities. These three features are all global in a double sense. They apply to all the actualities, and they characterize each as unities. They are not features to be found alongside the empirical ones. (The latter reflect what the actualities are as a consequence of an interaction with a lim-ited number of others.) The three features are subordinate to a fourth, which is also global in this double sense, and which makes the actuali-ties all equally real, as issuing from a past which they preserve in some sense within themselves.

An actuality must have the above five features, if what I have been arguing for in these last days has validity. In addition, it may have any number of empirical features, all subject to the *modus ponens*, any number of unitary features which have consequences that are to be de-rived by employing any one of the other logics or combinations of them, and any number of imposed features which express the conjoint influence of a number of modes of Being.

The necessary features of an actuality are all global. Its nature is expressed in a global feature that has no necessary bearing on any other feature. But it has four other features which are global in the additional sense of expressing what the actuality is in relation to other actualities. Those features follow logics which are distinct from that pertinent to the nature of the actuality. Whatever other features an actuality has can be determined only by an empirical study.

There may be other kinds of actualities than the individuals just now discussed. If there are, they will have natures of their own which will result from the conversion of possibilities into determinate aspects of those actualities. This would mean that the conversion of the future possibilities into determinate, ingredient possibilities would be accompanied by a modification of those possibilities, so that they will have a generality and boundaries, and be vague.

If an actuality conforms to a logic of generals, the features which express its nature also conform to that logic. As a consequence, the realization of the possibility will not result in the production of a determinate feature, but in one which is still general, though of a more specific form than the possibility it realizes.

Each type of actuality is subject to the impositions of the three encapsulated modes of Being and of Actuality itself. If the actualities conform to the ordinary logic, it will be because they have certain empirical features which, as instantiating and delimiting the ingredient possibility, are determinate. Ordinary logic, with its *modus ponens*, is a logic which deals with what is essential only in the case of the natures of individual actualities, as answering to the very being and careers of those actualities.

The foregoing presupposes that a realized possibility is an ingredient one expressing the nature of an actuality, a nature which conforms to the same logic as the actuality itself. If this supposition be dropped, we could say that any type of actuality may have features which are subject to *modus ponens*, by virtue of the way in which they realize the possibilities which represent their futures.

Common to all actualities, no matter what the type, are four global features which characterize each as a unity and as related to others. The actualities differ in their careers, in their natures, and in their empirical features, but all are subject to the prescriptions of the Ideal, the compulsions of Existence, the persuasions of God, and the demanding equalizations of Actuality.

Does not such a view compromise the integrity of actualities? It does not, for it merely tells us about the features which they all have, despite their difference in type. Each type of actuality is a finality having its own distinctive career, and each has a nature which it has forged itself in the course of realizing its relevant possibility. If we hold off the domain of actualities from the modes of Being, we will have to give up any common characterization of them all. We get a common perspective on them all only by approaching them from the position of some one or more modes of Being, though only in the one case of Actuality does the Being function in an absolute, unlimited guise.

The acknowledgment that there is a realization of possibility also enables us to speak of all the actualities in common terms. Other common terms relate to the pulsation of actualities, their achievement of worth, and to their equality in the present. Consequently, it would be more correct to say that we give up a common characterization of them all if we ignore the modes of Being to consider actualities only in terms of their careers or their empirical features. Once again: Each actuality, no matter what the type, has a nature which follows its type of logic; it also has four global features which characterize it as a unity and relate it cosmically to the others. In addition, each actuality's being involves a *1*] realization of a possibility, *2*] a bounding of itself off from the rest of Existence, *3*] an establishment of itself as a value to be evaluated eternally, and *4*] an establishment of itself as a present reality. These are the common denominations of actualities.

February 16

A nature cannot be taken to be identical with an Aristotelian form or essence, without raising the question of individuation. If the nature is the intelligible side of the actuality, what is not the nature will be unintelligible.

An actuality is not its nature; it has a nature. And that nature must be possible to it. Nor does the realization of a possibility in the guise of an ingredient possibility make the possibility fully determinate; a possibility always retains some generality, even when embodied. Since the result realized must be more than the possibility made ingredient or realized, this "more" would seem to be that which was not first possible, and in any case to be that which is not intelligible. We can avoid this result by recognizing that a nature is the entire actuality, but as separated from the actuality's insistence on itself in its environment. It is the actuality by itself, and as such is the actuality as fixed and intelligible. It is the realization of a possibility; it can be said to be an ingredient possibility with respect to the actuality as a dynamic entity. But it is not an ingredient possibility in the sense of being a feature alongside others, or as being sustained by a substance or matter.

When we isolate an actuality, we isolate it as a nature. That nature has implications which are in consonance with the career of the actuality, so far as this is necessitated and is not a mere function of a contingent interplay of the actuality with its neighbors. The concrete actuality is the actuality as in the context of Existence. It is this concrete actuality which realizes the possibility in the form of a nature, where it acquires details without ever becoming the actuality in its full concreteness.

What is in addition to the possibility is the dynamism of the actuality as directed at the other actualities. This is not something irrational; it is inseparable from the power of realizing the possibility. That power can be understood. Its particular magnitude and direction are possibilities which are realized when the possibility is realized. The magnitude and direction are not themselves realizations of distinct possibilities; they are consequences of the realization of possibilities. We can, of course, ask beforehand whether or not this or that realization will take place, i.e., whether it is possible. But we will then take the position of the possibility which is to be realized as a nature, and consider the possibilities which it grounds. There is no sheer possibility for this or that activity; there is a possibility which when realized involves such and such activity.

February 26

Some occurrences are used as evidence of others. We can avoid looking toward those others if we can deal with the original occurrences as bounded, self-enclosed. Though a religion requires a reference to a being beyond the ceremony, one could conceivably deal with the ceremony as itself the very meaning of God. Some such approach as this is taken by Wittgenstein when he deals with pain, for he seems to (and some of his disciples definitely do) take all the public manifestations, and the language which we conventionally use to express to others that we have a pain, to exhaust the meaning of pain itself. Similarly, when a pragmatist takes the scientific world to be but a way of reordering the macroscopic, he views the latter as self-enclosed, unable to lead us outside it to other kinds of entities. And when rationalistic or physicalistic thinkers reverse this process and speak of the ultimate realities as being those which physics will eventually discover, they read into those realities whatever information they may have, and thereby avoid the necessity of using those realities as evidence of some other type of reality.

If it were possible to view every kind of occurrence as self-enclosed, no one would serve as evidence for anything beyond. In compensation, we would not have to attend to anything else; we would know all that had to be known by studying how the component parts of the occurrence interplayed with one another and thereby produced whatever was real. (When we look at the entire scheme of things, of course, this is the only position we can take.)

Can every kind of occurrence be treated as self-enclosed? I think not. Growth, nourishment, acts of violence, compulsion, prescriptions, intrusions, all force us to look outside the confines of the occurrence to account for what does take place. What Peirce calls "secondness" is not something merely experienced as content; it is an alienating power, bringing one into contact, or forcing one to try to make contact with something outside the experience of the force.

Occurrences which drive us beyond them are taken to exhibit inside their confines something whose presence would violate a conservation law, were it not referred elsewhere for its cause and power. The feature as a mere phenomenon does, of course, have a residence in the occurrence; it is part of what Hume would call an impression. Yet as having residence there, it leads us elsewhere. Otherwise we could never tell the difference between a dead man and a murdered man. The latter is dead of course, but his death is one which makes sense only so far as it is related outside itself. The man, perhaps, had his hands tied and his throat cut. His heart, of course, stopped in the same way as the heart does of one who accidentally cut his own throat. The death of both cases occurs inside a bounded system; but in the latter case, we are unable to account for the hands that were bound, except by referring outside the man, and cannot account for the cutting of his throat as taking place after the hands were bound, except by making another reference beyond, which may or may not be to the being who tied the hands.

The existence of situations which are not conservative, in which an alienating factor is encountered, prevents a reductionism from being carried out. It denies the possibility of a Humean atomistic scheme, and also of the kind of view which Wittgenstein developed in the *Tractatus*. Descartes, and incidentally Hume, I think, when they tried to hold to their ultimate atoms, had to recognize that what they encountered were such atoms as intruded upon by alien elements. Their procedure was to refer those elements to another domain.

Confusion and habit, convention and error, all are knowable only because one has been able to identify a conservatively controlled situation and see that there were other items which were present with it that had to be located elsewhere. This need to refer elsewhere can be said to be only the reflection of the presence of Existence in some form. Because Existence is extensive and self-divisive, he who acknowledges anything existent is forced in that very act to move beyond it to something else.

It is true, of course, that a being exists in and of itself; it sits on its own bottom. But this observation is similar to the phenomenological remark that the compulsions, prescriptions, etc., are here and now with the being who suffers them.

We are driven outside by the nature of suffered content; this is relational. We cannot acknowledge it without being carried by it outside the place where we first encounter it. Confusion is the result of our trying to avoid the move to the outside.

But can we not remain in error indefinitely? May we not merely undergo the experience of being subjugated? If so, where is the need to refer beyond what is experienced? Must we not say that compulsion is discovered because we make an effort to assimilate it to what else we confront, and then find ourselves repulsed? Our first move is to bound what we face; the rejection of some item by the rest forces us to make a distinction and to locate elsewhere what is rejected.

These reflections are related to two forms of security which one might invoke when embarking on some adventure. One type of security involves the protection of the adventure itself by making sure it cannot be spoiled by a failure of some condition; the other type of security involves the protection of the adventurer himself in order to allow him a freedom to adventure. The latter is not sufficient, and must be supplemented by the former. The former could, though, conceivably be carried out without the latter. This is in fact the way in which calculating adventurers, say mountain climbers, in the main operate. They do incorporate some element of the latter, however. Training, a field base, rescue parties, etc., are provided for, at least in principle.

Men are more adventurous in spirit; women are more secure with reference to the world from which an adventure might start. Women, therefore, tend to insist on the latter type of security more than men do. Men, if well-organized, insist mainly on the former.

March 4

Since he who takes himself to be obligated not only insists on moving in a certain direction, but rejects and not merely ignores otherwise desirable or appealing alternatives, we could say that obligation is the persisting in a certain direction, combined with a rejection of others. The feeling of guilt for having violated an obligation can be ascribed to the lower state of energy one has when one has taken the alternative paths.

What of guilt sometimes ascribed even when not felt? If others ascribe the guilt, they presumably will act in opposition to the opposed guilty one. But suppose one ascribed guilt to oneself or abstractly defined guilt as the violation of an obligation? Must we not then say that someone would condemn the violator? Is this a prediction? I think not. It is a possibly contrary-to-fact conditional—were someone to know that I did so and so, and if he knew eternal principles of right and wrong, he would condemn me. But now we have lost our empirical grounding, for a contrary-to-fact conditional has no empirical, observable content.

We have a somewhat analogous situation when we speak, as most men do, of our theories determining what it is that we will select in fact. How could this idea be given an empirical meaning? Must we offer men various theories and then see how they select different things? But will this show that the theories make them do this?

It is in fact quite hard to understand how a theory or a set of categories, or a language, or some a priori set of ideas dictate what it is that one will notice. It seems to be true that what we have in mind makes us notice some things and not others. Only a biologist can tell what is being revealed in some biological experiment; the rest of us would not notice anything, or would perhaps notice what was not important. What we have here, I think, is a case where we acknowledge some antecedently determined boundary, and then see that what we confront fits into it.

Our categories and theories are ways of defining the nature of a possibility which is to be realized by what we accept as intelligible. It is not that we notice only what we have prepared ourselves to acknowledge; we in fact help constitute it. This view, of course, brings us close to a Kantianism where the ideas we have help constitute what is in fact known and perhaps even what can in fact be said to be. But we need not deny that things have their own boundaries and that what we notice or remark may be criticized for having failed to do justice to what the things are apart from us. Yet how could we know what those things were like? If all we know is bounded by and therefore constituted by us, must not every criticism of one set of categories be made in terms of another which just as arbitrarily constitutes another kind of world?

We could not hold the view that our ideas pick out certain items without our supposing that those items have some nature and being of their own. If we do not want to allow that things have a being and nature of their own, we must say instead that the ideas we have constitute the very nature and cognizable being of whatever there be. But we can   *1*] compare different categorial schemes and see what the difference is that they make to what is known;   *2*] follow the implications of what we know and see if it coheres with what we encounter at some subsequent time;   *3*] show that what we know when we assume one set of ideas clarifies and encompasses what we know when we assume another.

We do not suppose that the ideas of science are on a level with those of common sense; we know that the biologist sees what others do not, because he is a biologist. His ideas do not constitute the phenomena; they merely allow him to see what the rest of us do not. Some ideas pick out what seems to be real, in the sense that this accounts for what others discern, and more besides. These ideas select, in the sense that they focus on facets which others neglect and of which account must be taken if we are to explain this or that.

The question still remains as to how it is that any idea can have a selective role, and why it is that we see what we are prepared to see in some way by language, ideas, tradition, and the like. A first hypothesis might be that our ideas are like packages or boxes into which we want to make the data fit, and that we find that they fit more or less. This would mean that our ideas are not constitutive in a Kantian sense, but only serve as factual finders, to use an expression of Chauncey Wright's. We would start out with ideas that mark off certain data and when we found that those data did not act in consonance with those ideas, we would refine the ideas until they fitted the facts. The ideas would not select out the facts to be noted; they would order them, but not without allowing the facts to exhibit a recalcitrance to them.

March 5

Apart from all interpretation, expressed in concepts, language, gestures, tendencies to act, interests, etc., what we confront is a differentiated continuum, a kind of aesthetic panorama with nuances, emphases, lights and shadows, movements and rests which merge into one another. Our interpretations serve to demarcate and isolate some portion of this totality; the result involves a change in what is confronted, but this change may involve the recovery of the nature of that which was merged in the continuum.

This view opposes the Kantian in two ways. It rejects the view that there is nothing really discriminable in the given manifold (though it is not clear whether or not Kant himself held there was something discriminable there), and it rejects the view that what is produced by an interpretation is not checkable against and does not have to answer to the nature of things as they exist apart from the continuum—which is, after all, a continuum only for a human knower. We carve out parts of the continuum by means of our interpretations in the hope of thereby getting to the objects which the continuum merged.

How do we know that there are any such objects? Why not take the continuum to be the ultimate given, and take the result of the imposition of an interpretation to be the only thing that is knowable and real?

We find that our interpretations are not always satisfactory. The implications that can be drawn from our concepts or incipient activities are found to be not in accord with the alterations through which the continuum goes, or with the nature of the demarcated items that we subsequently obtain by the same means which we employed to get the original items.

March 10

A radical reductionist finally comes to a result which he can do nothing other than describe. All other thinkers find that A] there are some alienating factors which lead or point to something beyond, or B] that whatever one might attend to, at least categorically or in terms of a reason which has freed itself from a concern with contingent particulars, had an alienating factor.

A] Kant thought that there were alienating factors. He held that these were inescapable, but that there was no way of following them out to find what was at their terminus. Other thinkers, such as Schopenhauer, claimed that they had a special way of apprehending what was at the terminus of certain alienating factors.

The former acknowledges what he confesses he cannot really acknowledge; he points, but he does not know where, nor can he really explain why or show that there is something at which he points. The latter arbitrarily picks out some alienating factor; he is met by other thinkers who pick out some other. Where Schopenhauer intuits the Will, a mystic will intuit or lose himself in God, and a Platonist will find a dialectic to get himself to the Good.

B] Putting aside the question as to just what is a categorically known reality, the Hegelian view can be said to take every categorical item to involve a transcendent or alienating factor. The Hegelian then goes on to suppose that this factor ends in an item which can be reached by continuing the process by which the beginning had been apprehended —this though, of course, in the act of continuing the process is enriched, deepened, and modified. It is this latter emphasis that makes him a phenomenologist or idealist. But it is possible to be an idealist without making the supposition that every categorical feature has an alienating factor; and conversely, it is possible to suppose that there are many alienating factors without supposing that these are to be conquered by continuing the process by which we began.

The advantage of the Hegelian position is that the alienating factors are given a systematic grounding and that their termini are made part of the very process at which those factors begin. The disadvantage is that we seem to lose all reference to a world outside the circle of ideas or categories, a fact which becomes manifest today in the linguistic theories (which are verbalized forms of idealism) now current. Indeed, the very expression that language is a game, and thus self-enclosed, involves a denial that the language is referring to something outside, that it is spoken by someone and to someone. Once we recognize that what we know and what we say are known and said about what is not language, we can agree with the linguists, and not only admit but insist that we are using the words "know" and "say" in accord with common usage, and therefore legitimately criticize them for forgetting that language is used to communicate.

Is it possible to discover a way of generating or discovering whatever alienating factors there be, and learning just which agencies we must employ in order to apprehend what is at their terminus? By calling them "alienating factors," I have in a way anticipated an answer in part to these questions, for I have opened up the possibility that we can follow along the route of the factor and arrive at its terminus. In the process, we alter the way of apprehending, not necessarily in the Hegelian way by merely making explicit what we had been doing before, but by leaving our beginning behind in order to move on to deal with the terminus in a new way, as indicated by the alienating factor.

The alienating factor is itself an agency for knowing, but it is not necessarily one which ends in something infected by a relevance to us. The factor does not give us the object as it is in and of itself; we need to encounter the object, but it gives us something which contrasts with the beginning and sustains the alienating factor which made it possible.

A converse movement could be imagined, where the terminus of the alienating factor was itself discovered to be characterized by another alienating factor, which led us back to our beginning in its purity; i.e., in the very guise the beginning had when it was separated from the initial alienating factor. The beginning was apprehended in a distinctive way; it is a function of that way of apprehending it, in such a way as to subjectivize it. Only when the beginning was reached as the terminus of an alienating factor could we be said to know what it was as unaffected by us.

There are, on the basis of the last suggestion, two ways of apprehending. One of them gives us a content relative to ourselves; this is what we start with. We then recognize an alienating factor in it which brings us to a transcendent reality, and ultimately to a final mode of being. When we arrive there, we know what is the case, but we also see it as tainted by an alienating factor of a distinctive kind. The pursuit of that factor gets us back to the beginning, but no longer as affected by the knower.

This last suggestion could conceivably be reversed. We could maintain that what we apprehend of the beginning is what is true of it, and that it is the alienating factor which relativizes. But the alienating (what Hegel would call the negativing) factor is precisely that which not only moves on to new content, but which frees us from whatever limitation was characteristic of our start.

What the empiricist takes to be obviously true and objective, the "beginning," is in fact a subjectivized content which becomes true and objective only when we first move away from it by means of an alienating factor and then return to it via another alienating factor which begins where the previous alienating factor ended.

March 11

Inference, intuition, and dialectic are all alienating agencies, ending with something different from that with which they begin. I have previously argued that they never suffice to give us an object as it stands by itself, but only an object as having some relation to the beginning. Why is this? Is it not because these processes of inference, etc., are governed by rules, and that the rules refer the processes to termini which are related to beginnings?

If an alienating process is to terminate in an object, it must be self-alienating; when it comes to the terminus, it will free itself from the terminus, and free the terminus from itself. If this is not possible, there must be a resort to encounters or acts of detachment and the like, which allow the terminus of the alienating process to stand apart from that process.

A self-alienating process is something like that required in the cabalistic interpretation of divine creation, which takes God to withdraw Himself in order to allow creation to be. But whatever power of self-alienation the process of inference, etc., might have would seem to be a function of its terminus and not, as is the case with the divine creation, of its origin. The process seems to arrive at a terminus which an object or some other process alienates. Knowing, etc., thus arrives at a point where something alienates it. This which does the alienating of the alienating process could be known by attending to the new career which the terminus of the alienating process acquires.

We acknowledge an alienating process because there is something in what we confront which is accountable only so far as we turn away from the confronted. Our wonder and our perplexity are but the acceptance of the beginning of an alienating process. The process itself is revealed to be that which is alienated when it is seen that that at which it terminates functions in distinctive ways, independently of the alienating process.

We start with something independent of ourselves and move to what is distinct from this; but then we find that this which is distinct has a being of its own.

The alienating factor could be taken to terminate in that which assumes command of the content which the alienating factor developed from the beginning. Even the act of detachment, which is to follow on the act of inference, could be viewed as nothing more than the acknowledgement that the conclusion arrived at in inference is taken over and thereby achieves a new career in a world outside the inference. The alienating factor in these cases merely arrives at the place where some other order is in operation and which therefore makes use of the terminus at which the alienating factor arrives. But then can we know what this is which takes over? We can certainly know what happens when it takes over, for we can note the career of the conclusion. This is no longer caught within the process of our inferring. But we do not yet know the nature of that which takes over. Need this be anything other than a process, the very process which we see is governing the conclusion as freed from the alienating process of inference? Or there might be some new mode of apprehension which is appropriate to the process.

This new mode of apprehension, though, would seem to require a new alienating factor. We would then be in the same situation we were before.

March 12

If all alienating factors were like the inferential, we would end with items which could then be detached, and in that guise would be on a footing with the item with which we had made a beginning. The process of knowing the outcome would be in consonance with Hegel's approach, in that whatever method one employed in order to know what it was that one used to make a beginning would be employed to know what it was that was detached from the alienating factor at the end.

If there is to be knowledge of final realities, the alienating factor must be of a different sort from that characteristic of the ordinary process of inference. Even Hegel, since he thought that he was progressing closer and closer to the knowledge of the absolute, or alternatively to absolute knowledge, had to view his outcomes as apprehended in a somewhat different form from that characteristic of the apprehension of the items used for the beginning of the alienating process.

Kant and the positivists both recognize that there are alienating factors which terminate in items that, when held apart from those factors, could not be known in the way in which either the items used or the actual beginning of the alienating process was known. They conclude that the terminus is beyond our knowledge altogether, and that to speak of it is to speak nonsensically or dogmatically. But can we not intelligently recognize that the terminus of the alienating process is adopted by something which functions in a way not characteristic of the item which one used as the beginning?

The item that is used to allow us to begin the alienating process could be said to be known as it in fact is, either because we are capable of an immediate, true apprehension, or because when we use the item in the beginning of the process of alienation, we contrast it with itself as functioning as that beginning. The former is open to the criticisms of Hegel and Peirce regarding the immediate, the uncriticizable, and the unconceptualized. The second alternative allows us to say that the alienating factor alienates the item in such a way as to allow us to see the item over against itself as functioning as a beginning in the alienating process.

The item as offering us material for the beginning is itself known and qualified by a process of apprehension; by moving into the alienating process, we free the item from that mode of apprehension and see it as that which contrasts with itself as caught in the alienating process. When we arrive at the terminus of the alienating process, we have the reciprocal of the beginning of that process. When we allow that terminus to be sustained by something outside that alienating process, we provide a contrast for the terminus. When we try to know that which contrasts with the terminus, we bring it within the kind of context which characterized our initial apprehension of the item.

It is only when the detached item is contrasted with itself as the terminus of the alienating process that we know what the detached item in fact is like. In an inference, this would mean that we know the conclusion as a reality, not when we infer to it nor when it is independent of the process of inference in the sense of having no connection with it, but only so far as it is at once sustained by something outside the inferential process and contrasts with that which functions as the actual terminus of that process.

The actualities that we know are affected by our process of knowing. They achieve the status of being known as they are when we contrast them as confronted items with themselves as caught up in the world where they interplay with other items. Those actualities also achieve the status of being known as they are when we contrast them as confronted items with themselves as involved in the alienating process that terminates in an acknowledged finality. The latter is tainted by the process by which one arrives at it; but when we see it as sustained by something beyond it where it is subject to a new kind of rationale, we contrast it with itself as so subject to the rationale. The conditions of apprehension are not identical with the conditions by means of which we are able to know the terms of an alienating process. We can free ourselves from those conditions by using what was conditioned—a mode of Being, or more particularly, Actuality—as the beginning of a new alienating process which terminates in the acknowledgment of actualities. A mode of Being is known for what it is when we contrast it with itself as the beginning of an alienating process that ends with known actualities as able to be sustained by what is outside the alienating process which started from that Being.

The items that contrast with themselves as caught in an alienating process are themselves related to other items. When and as we apprehend them in the alienating process, we are able to see what they are as distinct items by themselves.

March 13

Whatever is confronted is in an alienating relation to oneself as that which stands apart, at a distance. When we know the confronted, we assimilate it to ourselves, leaving over the substantial being of the confronted. This in effect is to make the confronted divided into a content identified with ourselves and a being which stands away from this content. The confronted is then evidently itself subject to an alienating relation between itself as identified with ourselves and itself as able to be apart from such an identification.

When one apprehends the confronted in its guise of a reality which is alienated from its content as assimilated to oneself, does one then repeat the process by which one obtained content from the confronted? The Hegelian answer to this is in the affirmative. But I think it is more correct to say that one apprehends this in a new way. One does not get it as a naked object, but as that which is now the beginning for a new alienating relation. In accepting this beginning, one does not then alienate the content initially accepted (as I suggested earlier); the alienation of that content from the object as in an alienating relation to something further is already made when one accepts the content. But when one acknowledges the object as a beginning of a distinct, alienating relation, one looks back and sees the content to be that which is confronted initially.

We have A] the confronted, B] the assimilated content which we derive from that confronted, alien reality, C] the object which is alien to the content and which serves as the beginning of a new alienating relation terminating perhaps in some other object or some mode of Being. Once we have C, we can see B as that which can be confronted. C, though, once it is taken to be a beginning of a distinct alienating process, assumes something like the role that we had assumed when we confronted and assimilated, except that there need be no consciousness of something having been confronted. C ends with something which is assimilated as a terminus for it. The assimilation leaves over the being of this something. (In assimilation evidently the assimilated item retains its own integrity; it does not lose itself in the nature of the being which apprehends it.)

To apprehend the object which stands in an alienated relation to the terminus of a process that began with some object which had been alienated from content assimilated, we do not necessarily repeat the mode of cognition employed in order to confront, assimilate, or have an object serve as the beginning of an alienating process. But when we apprehend it, we inevitably assimilate it, and therefore leave over its being as that which is alien to what we assimilate. But now what is left over is part of another alienating process. If our apprehension of the object at the terminus of our alienating process is the same in kind as our apprehension of what we initially confronted, the object at the terminus belongs on the same ontological level with the confronted; they are part of the same world of being or knowledge. But we must apprehend the object at the terminus in a different way if that object is a Being.

The apprehension of a Being involves an assimilation of it to our understanding, but at the same time leaves it a reality which is related to other similar realities or to the kind of particulars we initially confronted. Which of these is the case? Does our understanding of a mode of Being lead to the alienation of that Being as that which is related to other Beings, or as that which is related to its own particulars? So far as I am a particular, and therefore have made the Being related to a particular, I must evidently leave over the Being as in an alienating relation to other Beings. But so far as I, in apprehending a Being, recognize it to be distinct from anything else I could know, my apprehension of it leaves it as that which could function with respect to me or other particulars in a new way.

This "so far" does not help. Which of these "so fars" operates at a given time? Must they not both be operative? My apprehension of a mode of Being is one with the freeing of that Being, to allow it to be in a relation with its particulars and with other modes of Being. It confronts them both. Should we concentrate on one of these, we but free it to function exclusively as a Being in the other guise. Before we have such a functioning, the Being itself could be in a process of emphasizing first one of these and then the other. It is first in a relation to its particulars and then in a relation to other modes of Being, or conversely, all apart from our apprehending. Our apprehension fixates one of the pulsations of the Being.

If a Being can be said to be in a dual relation, one prong of which refers it to its particulars and the other of which refers it to other modes of Being, must not each of the particulars also have a dual relation? I think so. Each particular is at once related to other particulars and to its mode of Being. Our apprehension of a particular assimilates it as content and detaches it, as a reality, from our apprehension. That reality is in a pulsational existence with respect both to the other particulars and to its own Being; we can therefore either proceed to infer to other particulars or to symbolize and thereby move to the Being.

The assimilation of content from the confronted leaves us with an object which is subject to two alienating relations. One of these takes us alongside other similar objects, the other takes us to a distinctly different type of being.

Is the content which I assimilate a neutral content, indifferent to the kind of relation I will pursue when I attend to the object left over? If it were neutral, what would lead me to go in one direction rather than the other? If it were not neutral, how could we face the object as that which could be said to be equally directed toward Being or toward other objects? The proper answer seems to follow from the recognition that our assimilation involves a bounding of the content either from similar content (to give us a distinguished particular) or from a ground in something more basic. The content, therefore, is not really neutral; by bounding it off from similar content, I set the object in an alienating relation to its Being; by bounding it off from a ground, I set it in an alienating relation to other similar contents.

March 19

Every item has three or four prongs which are alienating in the sense that they bring us to something which is distinct from that with which we begin. In knowledge, normally, we begin with some data which we confront and which we already understand in commonsensical ways. It is only after reflecting on error, confusion, and the conditions for knowledge that we take up the pursuit of epistemology and seek the grounds for what we know. Those grounds, as well as the commonsense object, have three or four prongs.

1] By an abstraction or through reflection, we are able to distinguish sense data, such as blue or square, as evidenced through sight, etc. These data have A] a prong in the form of an abstractive reference to such generals as color, shape, etc.; B] a prong in the form of a connection with other data on the same order with themselves, allowing us to connect various colors for example with one another; C] a prong which leads us to the adumbrative being of the entity which possesses the color or shape; and D] a reference to a Being in which the color or shape is oriented, though that Being is not characterized by the color or shape.

The one doubtful point here is whether there is a fourth prong such as described under D. It could be well argued that such a prong is possessed only by full-blown actualities. Yet so far as a color, etc., has an integrity of its own, it must either be oriented in our minds (which have abstracted it and allowed it so far to be distinct from that which it decorates), or it must be oriented in something which allows the color to have a being on a footing with more substantial actualities. The rationale of the color seems to go counter to the first of these alternatives, while its incapacity to act would seem to preclude the equating of the color's reality with that of an actuality's. I am not sure of myself here, but it does appear as though the second alternative were the more plausible, and that the reference to a fourth prong is but a consequence of my having worked out a fourfold scheme elsewhere.

2] We move to the adumbrated object by going through prong C. The adumbrated object is not the object as it is in itself, but the object as relatively transcendent to knowledge. It is related to a knower, but has a being apart from him (because it is in fact sustained by an actuality in its substantiality). The adumbrated object allows for generalizations and for an alienating act to the actuality, and perhaps also to Actuality.

3] We move to the object as it is by itself over against knowledge, by going through a prong which continues in the direction characteristic of C. But it is a different prong and has a different momentum, beginning and ending, and demands a different kind of cognition. When we are at the beginning of the prong in the adumbrated object, we taint it with ourselves maximally; when we arrive at the end, we taint it with ourselves minimally, and then only because the adumbrative object casts a shadow over the end of the prong. Not until we see the actuality as involved in relations to other actualities, to Actuality itself (these are like prongs B and D under *1*) do we have the actuality as freed from us and the adumbrative side of itself. The actuality seems also to have a prong like A under *1* in that it allows for a conceptualization, and thus a generalization of itself.

4] We can follow the prong from an actuality into other actualities (to give us an empirically knowable set of actualities, which are overlaid by commonsense conventions to give us the commonsense world) or to Actuality. If an actuality is recognized to have an ingredient possibility, to be existent, or to be sacred, we would evidently move from it, not to Actuality, but to the other three modes of Being as encapsulated in Actuality. Such a movement might be viewed as a special case of a movement to a generalization under *3*, along prong A, for when we isolate the feature, say of sacrality, we move away from the actuality which is sacred.

The movement to actualities or to Actuality is tainted by the actuality with which we begin. That actuality functions as a symbol for the

Actuality, but it is one which is as yet unconnected with other symbols. The connection with all the other symbols of Actuality is provided in the Being of Actuality. We will not have Actuality as freed from actualities until we refer the Actuality to its context, where it is interlinked with the other modes of Being along a prong similar to B under *1*.

Actuality has a prong leading to the other modes of Being; it also has a prong which allows us to move inside it in depth; and a third prong which allows us to move to the particular actualities under it. Once again we seem to have only three prongs and not four.

It is we who know actualities as substances, who know Actuality as their orienting reality, and who know Actuality as related to other Beings and to actualities. Do we not then taint the actualities with ourselves, and therefore arrive at the very position we were in when we confronted just the sense data, since we then have content which is not truly objective, but is tainted with ourselves, our categories, interests, language, and the like?

Is it enough to say that we make use of a symbol instead of a sign? I think not. A symbol will reach an object which is the symbol intensified. This operation works only for actualities in relation to Actuality. There must, in addition to signs and symbols, be *notions* which are appropriate to Beings by themselves (i.e., as related to one another and freed from their particulars, or as related to their particulars but freed from one another). These notions have the power of subjugating the knower to themselves, whereas the symbol allows us a freedom while it itself is swallowed up. Such a suggestion prompts the recognition of a *perceptum* which swallows up the object in the sense data.

We seem to have A] a *perceptum* which has become one with us, leaving only an adumbrative prong, a connective prong, and an abstractive prong, no one of which tells us what its terminus is: they merely point; B] a sign which has a conventionalized relation to its object or, if we are to follow it as it operates in nature, a prong which leads us to a reality distinct from it—the adumbrated object; C] a symbol which is a faint copy of the Being which absorbs it and other symbols, and D] a notion which is the rationale of a Being and which absorbs us in it, to allow us to become one with the relation which that Being has to others.

Though I have been mulling over these ideas these last few days, they are now at the stage which could rightly be called "sheer speculation," meaning by this that I have not only gone beyond the evidence, but that I do not see anything but the faintest outline of what seems to be necessary in order to allow us to know what is external to ourselves in this space-time world, and what is external to that space-time world as well.

March 29

The object of the mystic is to become one with God. It is not clear whether he wants to be one with the God of his religion or with God, the Being. When we speak of Jewish mystics, Christian mystics, Muslim mystics, we are evidently speaking of those who want to be one with the God of a particular religion. They seek to be in immediate relation with Him, as relatively transcendent, i.e., as not involved in a particular community or occasion, but as able to be involved in it and others as well.

No one achieves a relation of immediacy except mediately, i.e., as a result. And what is mediately made immediate, immediately mediates one to something else. In the case of the mystics, the mediation will be either A] toward Actuality, the Being, which encompasses God, B] toward other encapsulated Beings, C] toward the Being which is God, or D] toward actualities.

A] The relating of the relative transcendent God to Actuality seems to have been ignored in the literature except by those few who take God to be a product of some more cosmic process, a kind of precipitate. I suppose some such view could be extracted out of Schopenhauer, Bergson, Freud, and Jung. The mystics, or anyone else (say, by starting with some other encapsulated Being than God) who was related to Actuality in this way, would have to try to make Actuality itself be immediately apprehended, with the consequence that there will be an opening into a mediated reference to other modes of Being and to actualities.

B] The relating of the encapsulated God to an encapsulated Existence and Ideality would give us something like the fundamental relation which the demiurge is supposed to have in the *Timaeus*. Plato, of course, does not speak of these all being encompassed by Actuality, or having actualities over against them. Nor does he discuss just how we, in arriving at the Being of the demiurge, are inevitably related (as the demiurge is necessarily related) to Ideality and the existent receptacle. Nor does he tell us that all three, God, Ideality, and Existence, are limited forms of more ultimate Beings, though the term "demiurge" would seem to suggest that in that case at least, Plato had in mind some limited form of Deity.

c] So far as a mystic seeks to attend only to God, he has two stages to go through. He must make himself immediately one with the encapsulated God, and then try to make himself immediately one with the Being of God, which he, in becoming one with the encapsulated God, finds to be beyond himself, but related to himself by an alienating, i.e., a mediating, factor. Of course, should he arrive at the end of his quest and become one with the very Being of God, he will then find that he mediately faces other modes of Being and divine particularities. No mystic, then, can stop with being simply one with God. He does not, though, have to make a decision to move away from God. The more surely he is one with God, whether this God be limited, encompassed by the Being, Actuality, or by God, the Being, he finds himself over against other realities.

d] This has been partly anticipated. So far as the mystic identifies himself with an encapsulated God, he finds that he is at the beginning of an alienating relation to actualities. Should he, however, be united with God, the Being, he will not be related to actualities but to the particulars which are distinctly pertinent to that Being. He presumably will also be related to God, the reality, who is religiously relevant, i.e., to God as encapsulated in Actuality. (If God is also encapsulated in other modes of Being, which it would seem to be proper to infer, then when making himself one with God the Being, the mystic will find himself in alienating relations to God, as encapsulated in three Beings.)

It is not adequate to say, therefore, that when we become one with a reality, we are mediately related in two ways. The number of ways seems to be three at least—toward coordinates, toward some limited form of a Being, and toward particularities of a Being. The coordinates may be other particulars, other encapsulated forms of Being, or other Beings. The limited form of a Being may be one of four kinds (we evidently do not confront limited forms of Actuality when we confront the limited forms of other modes of Being, but we do refer to such limited forms of Actuality when we become one with Actuality). We refer to actualities when we become one with the encapsulated forms of three of the modes of Being or with Actuality; we refer to a Being when, starting with the encapsulated forms, we move not to their ultimate base but back to the actualities from which we started. (If we start with some modes of Being, other than Actuality, we refer back to some other kind of particularity.)

Most men think they are acquainted with actualities. The problem they think they have to solve, and that alone, is how to get from an immediate apprehension of these to them as realities apart from us. If I am right in the foregoing discussions, the immediacy with which these thinkers suppose they begin is something achieved. They had in fact begun with something in an alienating relation to them, and had gone through this relation in the act of knowing, to make the object (in some limited or abstract guise) be one with themselves. They thereby leave over the object in itself. That object in itself can be reached by going through an alienating relation, from the immediately-had content to the being itself—a relation which is perhaps best covered in sympathy and similar modes of experiencing.

The object in itself, when made immediately one with oneself, but places one in alienating relations with other actualities—i.e., with encapsulated modes of Being, and with Actuality, all of which can become immediately possessed, to leave over other alienating relations. Whatever is immediately apprehended can, from the position of something else immediately apprehended, be acknowledged mediately; whatever is mediated can be made immediate.

In this account, the movement from what we immediately grasp in perception is dealt with as though it allowed only one mediation to the real object. But if the above dissection has merit, there should be two other mediate relations which this immediately grasped perceptual content should have—to coordinate perceptual contents, making for an aesthetic experience, and to something analogous to the encapsulated modes of Being. What would these be? Would they be ourselves as having ideas, being involved in inquiry, and making a claim to truth? But do we not then turn inward? Ought we not turn outward toward nonhuman realities, as we do when we start with actualities, the encapsulated modes of Being, or any mode of Being? It seems so.

Our first step allows us to consider facets of ourselves which are something like counterparts of the encapsulated modes of Being. The next stage seems to be that these counterparts point us toward ourselves as the counterpart of Actuality, though we are just actualities.

There is no need for the first step of knowing to be on all fours with the other steps. But if it is not, an explanation should be produced showing why it is different. This I have not been able to find. It seems in fact more plausible to say that when we make perceptual content immediate, we not only are in alienating relations to other similar content, but that we refer, not only to actualities, but to aspects of them which are the counterparts of encapsulated Beings. We will then have alienating relations to other content, i.e., to the forms or meanings of actualities, to their dynamism or extensionality, and to their worth or dignity, at the same time that we have an alienating relation to actualities as the locus or orientation for those meanings, extension, and dignity.

But now we seem to have a reference to actualities from the content we have immediately, as well as a reference to them via meanings, extension, and dignity. If so, why do we not go directly to the actualities, without first trying to make the meanings, etc., immediate? Why, similarly, do we not go directly to Actuality from actualities, without going through the encapsulated forms of other modes of Being?

The answer to these questions is that we can and often do. We stop with encapsulated modes of Being only when we are occupied with questions of religion, the source of prescriptions, or with a controlling environment. But we could go directly to Actuality from the actualities without considering these. Similarly, we stop with something like worth, extensions, or meaning when we are occupied with values, scientifically interesting dimensions, or with judgments and inferences with respect to the empirical. But we could go directly to actualities in sympathy, etc., from a beginning with perceptual content possessed in its immediacy.

March 30

Epistemologically we begin (i.e., have immediately) three mediated (i.e., alienated) contents. We are *coordinated* with other actualities, are *correlated* with perceptual content, and are *conditioned* by a privacy. We can proceed to make any one of these mediated contents into immediacies by moving along the alienating relation. Normally, we attend to the content with which we are correlate, and by becoming one with it in perception, find that we have over against us a coordinated perceptual content and a correlative actuality, and are conditioned by a limited form of the Ideal, Existence, and God. When we move to a substance or actual entity, we once again find that we have a three-pronged relation beyond it—we are coordinate with other substances, are correlated with Actuality, and are conditioned by limited forms of the Ideal, Existence, and God. When we move to any one of these limited forms, we find ourselves coordinate with the other two, correlated with Actualities, and conditioned by Actuality. When we move to Actuality, we find it coordinated with other modes of Being, conditioned by the limited forms it encompasses, and correlate to actualities. When we move to the actualities, we arrive at the beginning of the epistemological movement. The epistemology ends with our movement to the substance.

An actuality is correlate to the perceiver, to limited forms of Being, and to Actuality; the limited forms of Being are correlate to actualities, to Actuality, and to themselves as unencompassed by Actuality. Actuality is correlate to actuality, to the limited forms of Being which it encompasses, and to itself as encompassed in the other modes of Being.

If we had not wanted to know actualities, we could have moved, not to the perceptual content, but in time or space to the other actualities or to our privacy, the one in order to extend the range of our knowledge, and the other to learn something about ourselves. Both movements involve the making of these mediated items into immediacies which themselves are in three mediating relations. Thus, if we move back into ourselves, we find that we are coordinate with other privacies, that we are correlate with actualities, and that we are conditioned by what we perceive. If instead we had moved from what we confront to other actualities, we would at that time find that we were coordinate to still other actualities and the original actuality from which we started, and that the actualities were all conditioned by limited modes of Being, and were correlate with Actuality.

April 4

I have argued that an inferred result needs to be backed by an encounter. Because we have not encountered an immortal soul, I have hesitated to affirm that the soul is immortal, despite the fact that it makes sense to say that it is so when consideration is taken of the reality of a persistent, responsible being, and the fact that the soul (or more properly, to avoid theological implications, the self) has an existence now overlaid by the existence of the living body. But this view holds only with respect to consequences, outcomes, that which is conditioned. It does not seem to hold with respect to conditions, presuppositions. We need not encounter the self, or mind, or privacy, for these are presupposed by what we do encounter. We arrive at them by tracing back to its source some compulsive component in the encountered.

Is a mode of Being a consequence or something presupposed? The argument that God must not only be reached through inference, but encountered, supports the view that God is a consequence. But as a Being, he is surely presupposed by anything which owes its being to Him. We must say, I think, that He and the other modes of Being are all presupposed by factors in experience, and that all of them are reached by an inference that needs supplementation by an encounter. We arrive at them as presupposed through a presuppositional inference. That at which we arrive through a presuppositional inference is the very reality which is encountered as the supplement of the inference to a consequence.

The movement to Actuality from the base of actualities is primarily a movement to a presupposition, to that which is the Being in which all the actualities in some sense partake, in such a way as to really be by themselves. It is not immediately evident that we also reach the Actuality as a consequence that must be supplemented by an encounter with it.

The movement to God is primarily a movement to a consequence requiring supplementation by the Being of God or some delimited form of this. It is not immediately evident that we also reach God (in contrast with what was said just before) as a consequence. If this is correct, then we would have to say that the movement to God, the other, in the *Modes of Being*, does not need to be supplemented by an encounter (as I say it must), because it is an inference to a presupposition and not to a consequence.

The inference to Ideality seems to be primarily an inference to a consequence, though we seem also to encounter its necessitating us, and to arrive at that encountering side of it through an inference by presupposition.

The inference to Existence seems to be primarily to a presupposition. We seem also to have it as a consequence in its cosmic guise, and therefore as that which must be encountered, and which in fact is encountered in the form which we come to know in our presupposition.

What is needed now is A] a clear distinction between inference to consequence and inference to presupposition; B] a precise characterization of both types of inference; C] a recognition of just what items are reached by only one of these types of inference; D] a recognition of just what items are reached by both; E] an understanding of how the outcomes of both types supplement one another.

Kant distinguished these two modes of inference in his *Critique*, calling one metaphysical and the other transcendental; Peirce distinguished them as deductive and abductive; rationalists distinguished them as the analytic and the synthetic. None of them faced all the above issues.

April 5

Inferences can be distinguished according to their differences in leading principles inside a particular type of logic, or according to the demands made by different logics. The problem of presupposition and consequence raised yesterday requires a consideration of the differences in possible logics. We move to the modes of Being by ordinary logic when we attend, as was done in *Modes of Being*, to otherness, universals, the unity of Existence, and look for what these evidence. When we arrive at the terminus of the inference, we must back the result up with an encounter. But when we move back to presuppositions by following up the clue provided by some kind of compulsion—existentially brute, ethically obligatory, divinely affiliating, and actually equalizing—we make use of a different set of logics. These result in the "production" of the encounterable material as well as a reaching of it; (i.e., a becoming one with that at which we arrive). For example, to accumulate the premiss in the conclusion, as is done by following the dialectical logic appropriate to Actuality, is in effect to change the conclusion into one which has material that can be encountered—or more sharply, that is encountered when and as it is arrived at.

We can arrive at a particular mode of Being by following our ordinary logic, as well as by following a logic singularly appropriate to it, and which is in effect a logic making use of symbols rather than signs. When we move back to minds, selves, and the like, we follow one of the logics appropriate to a mode of Being, but as applied to a restricted territory. We get back to a mind as a presupposition by the same logic by which we get back to the Ideal as a presupposition. The self is reached by the logic appropriate to Actuality. What finite occurrence is reached by the logic appropriate to getting to God or to Existence as presuppositions? Is it man as a locus of natural rights, and man as a center?

April 6

Do we, in moving to presuppositions, necessarily make use of the same logic that we use when we understand the nature of the presupposed? We should say that we do, if it be the case that the beginning of our inference involves a fragment of that at which we arrive.

In connection with the movement to Ideality, we start with actualities as obligated, or as having ingredient possibilities, or something like that. But if this is so, then we should say that the movement to God does not begin with actualities in the state of being other, but rather with them as sacral objects, or with their otherness understood to be sacral in nature. If we start with a secular otherness, we will get to God as a mere Being which is distinct from all else. If we start with a sacral feature, we get to a God of religion, and if we start with a sacral otherness, we get to a Being which has made a difference to the actualities.

It would seem to be true that we must start with the actuality as sacral, for otherwise we would not know that it is God to whom we could refer. If it be said, as I have in a number of places, that actualities have an inwardness and that the other that they need must have an inwardness too, and that this can be provided only by God, we overlook the fact that the other modes of Being might have inwardnesses too, though of a different sort than God could have.

If an actuality must be sacral in some sense in order to be the beginning of a movement to God as presupposed, then every mode of Being would have to be presupposed in the actualities with which we begin in order to be reached as presuppositional Beings for those actualities. We should say, I think, that the actuality is sacral and so far allows us to reach the encapsulated God as a presupposition, but that the actuality is also an other, and that this forces one to move beyond the encapsulated form to God, the Being. Similarly, we should say with respect to Ideality and Existence that our initial move is to them as encapsulated by virtue of some facets in the actualities which are like them, and that we move to them as Beings only because the facets are inseparable from another feature which requires for its presence the operation of Beings and not their encapsulated forms. Since the Beings do not operate directly on actualities, they can be said to be presupposed by actualities only so far as those actualities take on the role of representing everything else. It will, for example, be an actuality as representing all actualities and Actuality, God, and Existence which presupposes Ideality, the Being.

In connection with Actuality, the movement to the presupposed goes directly from the actualities. The actualities will each be. But they will not be identical with the Being which they are; they will *have* the being, and refer to Actuality as their presuppositional Being.

An actuality allows for four movements to presuppositions; in three cases, it exhibits some factor such as sacrality, intelligibility, or extensionality, which leads first to encapsulated modes of Being, and then (when the actuality takes on the role of a representative) to the modes of Beings themselves. In the fourth case, that of Actuality, an actuality represents all else, and in that guise has Actuality as the presupposition of it, as the Being in which the actuality partakes.

An actuality on this account will have four representative roles; it will represent as a being, as intelligible, as extended, and as sacral, and will thereby have the four modes of Being as presuppositions. In the case of Actuality, the actuality represents as a being directly; in the case of the other modes of Being, the actuality will first be characterized by the encapsulated modes of Being (which it also can be said to presuppose) before it is able to function as a representative of the modes of Being themselves.

If we started with different facets of actualities in order to get to the encapsulated Beings as presuppositions, and then to the unencapsulated forms of those Beings as presuppositions, it would be correct to say that we proceed by using the actualities or facets of them, or our own designations of them in distinct ways. We use either four kinds of symbols, or four distinct types of referents of that for which only one would properly be a "symbol." (Possible designations for the others could be icons or categories for the Ideal, creations for Existence, and sacrals for God.) Each of the four would follow a distinctive logic, the very kind of logic appropriate to exploring the Being in which the logic terminates, since the logic will begin with a fragment, i.e., a less intensive facet of the Being. The use of them will contrast with the use of signs and propositions. These begin an inference to the modes of Being, making use of the ordinary logic with its *modus ponens*, discrete truth values, and separated conclusions, and must be backed by an encounter.

Following this clue, we can move to mind as a presupposition only by A] using something like a symbol, and B] starting with something intelligible, or abstract, or an instance of the Good.

April 11

The mind can be said to be the general to which all other generals or universals are to be referred. The reference involves the use of a logic which moves from the less to the more general, and thus does not make the ordinary use of the law of excluded middle. In a similar way, we can be said to use the logic of dialectic to get to the self. Similarly, we can be said to use the logic of marks to get from any part of us in space and time to ourselves as centers. These centers are merely at some arbitrary place within the spatio-temporal-dynamic extendedness which we exhibit. Finally, we move to the individual as a locus of value, or worth, or dignity by making use of the logic of the vague, and thereby bringing together into a single unity what would ordinarily be said to be opposed according to the law of contradiction.

There are three movements from aspects of the objects before us. They go A] to ourselves, B] to encapsulated modes of Being, and C] to the Beings themselves. These movements follow distinctive logics, depending on the kind of entities at which we arrive, A, B, or C. Exploration of each of the entities at which we arrive will follow the very logic which was employed to arrive there. Consequently, to know just how mind functions, we would have to have recourse to a logic in which factors are not set over against one another by the law of excluded middle, but are conjoined as disjuncts to constitute a range or universal which is to be specified in the guise of one or the other of a set of excluding items. The mind will have the structure of something like "*A*-or-non-*A*."

It is desirable to work out the nature of these different logics. But it would be an error to try to imitate the practice of logicians in the Aristotelian-symbolic logic tradition and make up a set of distinct postulates from which theorems are to be derived by using the *modus ponens*. One would then be taking as model some other logic than the one that is to be studied.

Can the logics be indicated in any way but in use? If so, we could not generalize them, use them again and again as rules or principles which have a meaning, or as structures apart from this or that specific use.

If it be true, as was just held, that a given logic might terminate in an aspect of an individual, in an encapsulated mode of Being or in a Being as such, it would seem that the logic has a generality which allows it to be understood apart from a particular use. It would have a range of application (which would, of course, also be true of the traditional logic); also, it could be examined apart from this or that use. We should, therefore, taking account of the range of the application, be able to state the nature of its logic. The statement may not require the use of postulates, or other devices used in connection with the traditional logic. What will it require? Will there be many different leading principles which could be used in each?

April 12

A possible method for expressing the nature of the various logics would be to take the assertions of the *Principia Mathematica* and operate on the conclusions in such a way as to obtain the conclusions required by the other logics. Thus, if we start with some such assertion as $P.).P \lor Q$ (which expresses the entailment or necessary truth that is pertinent to actualities), we can subject this to the principle of accumulation, and convert the $P \lor Q$ into $P(P \lor Q)$. This is equivalent with $P \lor PQ$, and this in turn is equivalent with P. In effect, this would make the use of a logic of accumulation yield a conclusion identical with the premiss. Since $P.).P \lor Q$ can be treated as the paradigm of all the assertions made in the *Principia Mathematica* (for every assertion in that logic can be said to be some variant of a repetition of the premiss as disjoined from something else), instead of having an alternative logic, we would end with having a subdivision of the logic of the *Principia Mathematica.*

Instead of trying to obtain new logical rules by some kind of operation on the assertions of the *Principia Mathematica,* one might try instead to make a difference to the operation of *modus ponens.* Given *P.).P v Q,* the *modus ponens* proceeds by first asserting the *P,* and then by virtue of the assertion of the logical law and the *P,* asserting the conclusion *P v Q.* A logic of accumulation would require that the *P* which we initially assert be accumulated in the *P v Q.* But it does not say that this accumulation is a mere addition; it is a dialectical move in which the *P* is merged with something else, but in which we continue to hold on to the *P* even while we are affirming the *P v Q,* somewhat as we do when we remember as we perceive, retain while we are hearing, refer back as we expect. But is this not to say that the logic of accumulation is but a logic which stops at a conclusion as something arrived at, rather than with it as detached from the process of inference? I think not. The conclusion is detached, but it is detached in the guise it has as that which is arrived at. The *modus ponens* would operate here in a distinctive way. Our conclusion would be *P v Q,* but treated as that which had been concluded to from *P* (and presumably from *P.).P v Q* functioning as a rule).

If we are to have a logic of accumulation, we must affirm that there are laws for it. Our paradigm would be *P ⊃ . [(P v Q) ⊃.P.(P ⊃ . P v Q.)]* That is, the statement of the paradigm of the *Principia Mathematica* would be modified so that the conclusion it allows would imply the initial antecedent, *P,* and the whole of which it is a part. We would connect the the conclusion of the ordinary logical assertion by *⊃,* which would express a relation that the conclusion had to the premiss and the whole, a relation which would not permit one to separate off that premiss and whole from that conclusion when using the *modus ponens.*

According to the foregoing, we keep the *modus ponens* in its ordinary use, but modify the assertion of the *Principia Mathematica*—which was the idea I ventured at the beginning of today's discussion—by having the conclusion, to which we will conclude and which we will assert apart from its premiss, as a conclusion which implies or is inseparable from that premiss (and the whole or rule) at the very same time that it is held apart from the premiss and the rule. The *modus ponens* would operate to give us a conclusion which is distinct from the premiss and rule, but one which nevertheless was, as distinct, inseparable from some form of that premiss and rule.

If we take this last as a proper approach, we will have to take the logic of the Ideal to be one in which the ordinary conclusion of $P v Q$ from P would be modified to become P-v-Q, where "-" represents a connection which does not permit of the separation of the disjoined items. Similarly, the logic of the vague appropriate to God would be one in which the conclusion of $P v Q$ would be modified to become $P.Q.$ And the logic of Existence, which is a logic of marks, would merely have as a conclusion some Q having no necessary bearing on the $P.$ All of these conclusions would be derivable by using the *modus ponens.*

To this a defender of the *Principia Mathematica* would undoubtedly reply that our supposedly new logics are nothing but sets of contingent rules, having no necessity in them, which we subject to the ordinary use of a *modus ponens* to get what would obviously not be necessary conclusions. To assert $P) Q,$ according to a logic of Existence, is to assert what is not necessarily true; to then go on to assert P and thereupon conclude to Q by *modus ponens* would be correct, but would also merely illustrate how we properly derive a conclusion when we make use of rules which are not necessarily true.

The reply to this objection is that the laws of a logic have a reference to a particular type of domain, and that the logic of Existence, for example, seems to consist of deniable rules only because we either suppose that those rules are rules for some other domain, such as a world of actualities, or because they are held apart from all application. But then the question arises as to just how the domains function in the operation of the laws. Do they introduce modifications in the forms which are indefinite as held apart from these domains?

April 15

If alternative logics are treated as though they made use of what the *Principia Mathematica* would treat as a non-necessary truth or rule (or as Peirce termed it, a leading principle), it would seem that they make use of the *modus ponens,* and that their detached conclusions are the necessary outcome of the use of a non-necessary rule and premiss. Consequently, we would have just another instance of the use of ordinary logic.

It is also possible to treat ordinary logic as one which operated on the result of an alternative logic; ordinary logic could be conceived as merely imposing on the outcome of an alternative logic another condition, so as to yield the kind of conclusion which the ordinary logic requires. Given a continuum, for example, where we arbitrarily mark off some point as premiss and give the same truth value to some arbitrary point as conclusion, we can then go on and make this conclusion yield a conclusion which receives a truth value from the arbitrarily designated conclusion in the continuum.

Still another approach would distinguish between the conclusion which is part of an inferential whole and the conclusion which stood apart from this, the latter alone being the conclusion we want in the ordinary logic. We could say that the conclusion of an inference is one which accumulates the rule and the premiss so as to become the conclusion for them; that as something intended, it is more general than the premiss and the rule; that as that which is merely arrived at, it can be maintained indefinitely in a continuous time; and that as a distinct conclusion, it is the outcome of the merging of the rule with the premiss, with each justifying the other. On this view, alternative logics all remain within inferential wholes, where the ordinary logic moves beyond such a whole to a detached conclusion. This conclusion it obtains by first getting to a conclusion presupposed within an inferential whole that the other logics help define.

Granted that Hegel's is a logic of accumulation and not of the vague (so that the basic fact about it is not that the antecedents are somehow merged in the synthetic outcome, but that the synthetic outcome has the antecedents within it as subordinate meanings which perhaps can be discovered through analysis), we would do it less than justice if we said that the synthetic outcome is one obtainable by ordinary logic (through the introduction of a ruling principle which says that if we have a and not-a, we get b, and then proceed to affirm a and not-a and in accordance with the rule obtain b, or even b as implying that there had been an a and a non-a). We would do it less than justice, too, if we took that logic to express an inferential whole as though it never actually moved away from a beginning, to come out with a conclusion distinct from and actually existing apart from the antecedent.

We can formulate the various logics formally as making the following distinct types of assertion:

> Ordinary logic of discretes: $P .) . P v Q$
> Accumulative logic of Actuality: $P.).P) Q$
> Idealistic logic of the General: $P v Q.).P$-v-Q
> Existentialistic logic of the Continuum: $P .).Q$
> Divine logic of the Vague: $P,Q.).P.Q$

We can say of each of them that they express necessary truths, just so far as a reference is made to the kinds of entities that are being dealt with. The attempt to deal with any of the last four as a variant of the first involves a change in domain and a change in the kind of entity. *P .).Q* of the existentialistic logic looks like a contingent proposition in ordinary logic, but it is in fact a distinct kind of proposition; it becomes a proposition in ordinary logic only when the *P* and *Q* are altered in nature from being arbitrary points to being units of meaning, and when the connection between them is changed from that appropriate to discretes to that appropriate to a continuum. Our formulation of the alternative logics must avoid using some such constant as ") " for this seems to make them all use the same kind of connection between premiss and conclusion. Consequently we should express the four logics somewhat in the following way:

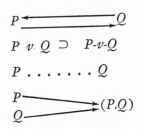

$$P \longleftrightarrow Q$$
$$P \; v. \; Q \; \supset \; P\text{-}v\text{-}Q$$
$$P \ldots \ldots Q$$
$$\begin{matrix} P \\ Q \end{matrix} \longrightarrow (P.Q)$$

April 16

Normally we write out formulae using distinct symbols for distinct ideas, and consequently presuppose a world governed by ordinary logic. When men try to express different logics, they therefore run the risk of writing them in accordance with the suppositions pertinent to a different logic. I think now of Heyting's formulations of intensional logic; those formulations conform to the requirements of the very logic to which Heyting wanted to offer an alternative.

Nevertheless, we want formulations of logical rules. One way of obtaining these is to make use of brackets of various kinds. We might write the five logics as follows:

1] Extensional: *(P)*   *(. > .)*   *(Q)*

Here each item is separated from the rest.

2] *Dialectical*: $(P \overset{\longleftarrow}{\underset{\longrightarrow}{\hspace{1cm}}} Q)$

Here there is a forward and a backward reference.

3] *Idealistic*: $[P \ v \ Q \supset (P\text{-}v\text{-}Q)]$

Here there is a single whole as terminus.

4] *Dynamic*: $[(P) \ldots \ldots (Q)]$

Here the connection goes from one isolate term to the other.

5] *Convergent*: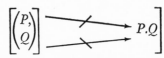

Here the connection goes from isolated beginning to a completing terminus.

I suppose these various formulations require modification and refinement, but what is now clear is that they are different in structure, and in what they allow to be separate. I suppose distinct kinds of brackets would have to be devised for each of them, with corresponding different signs for negation and other logical constants.

These different logics could be viewed, too, as being involved in their different concrete domains in different degrees. The first, the ordinary logic, though characterized in the same way as its domain, is exterior to that domain. The second, the dialectical, since it holds on to the initial term, is completely absorbed in its domain. The third allows for the conclusion to have a distinct nature apart from the beginning, which is nevertheless inseparable from the connection to the conclusion. The fourth has only the connection between beginning and end completely involved in the domain. The fifth reverses the third and has the conclusion not entirely separable from the connection (which leaves the beginning behind).

Alternatively, one could view the logics as being involved in their different concrete domains in the same degree, but to be involved in one another's domains in different degrees. To state a logic in formulae like those pertaining to another—say, expressing the logic appropriate to dialectic in the symbolism of an extensional logic—would be to use the symbols of a logic external to its domain to express a logic which is more intimately a part of its domain. The expression in an extensional logic could be seen to be one which changes its meaning and requires a distinctive kind of domain, when it is treated as an alternative logic.

April 17

Strictly speaking, an extensional logic does not arrive at conclusions; it merely acknowledges one of the externally related items which its formulae allows. The ideal method for it, therefore, is the truth tables. (When one refers to a conclusion, one should take account of both the premiss and the rule as that with reference to which the outcome is a conclusion.) Because we arrive at a conclusion through an inferential process, an extensional logic must have an act of detachment which will allow the conclusion to stand apart from the process. But we do not have an act of detachment in connection with the other logics.

Dialectic, by holding on to the antecedent, though in a subordinate role, gives us an outcome which is distinct. Idealistic logic also retains its antecedent, though in an altered form, leaving the initial state and the process outside the situation where we possess the altered form. Dynamic logic can do nothing other than acknowledge something which is detached from the premiss, since the outcome is an arbitrary mark distinct from that premiss. And in a convergent logic, the process is together with the outcome, leaving the antecedent behind.

Using the symbolism of the *Principia Mathematica*, we can express a convergent logic—a logic which seems to be singularly appropriate to vagues, history, God, and emergents—as:

$$P.Q \supset (PQ)$$

where the $P.Q$ represents conjoined items which retain their separateness, and the bracket about them as simply conjoined in the consequent denies that they can be separated. The proposition looks like a necessary truth; but its meaning in an extensional logic can be denied. We can have a consequent which will allow for the separation of conjoined items. The assertion in fact has the form:

$$P.Q \supset R$$

where R is understood to involve items similar to those with which we initially began but which are now inseparable. To acknowledge P and Q

inside R is to make an abstraction from the latter, even when we characterize R as an inseparable union of P and Q, for the R does not allow for the distinguishing of these items, even to allow us to say that they are merged.

$P.Q$) R is a contingent truth as held apart from any domain where it is constitutive of the structure of that domain. To make it subject to a *modus ponens* will not convert the logic we are using into an extensional one, except so far as the *modus ponens* is then seen to have need for a supplementary act of detachment. It will have a need for the supplementary act so long as it is treated as a contingent truth. Taken to be integral to its domain, to have its beginning with a symbol and to end with the symbolized, the *modus ponens* will yield a detached conclusion by itself.

The outcomes of these various logics are arrived at by a *modus ponens*. They are separated from their beginnings. Can their outcomes be called conclusions?

The outcome of a *modus ponens*, used in connection with a dialectical logic, is a conclusion, referring as it does back to the premiss; it is nevertheless detached from that premiss as it stands by itself, for it is a conclusion that we get to from the premiss only so far as that conclusion maintains a hold on the premiss, as an antecedent for the conclusion. The outcome of a *modus ponens*, used in connection with an idealistic logic, also possesses the premisses from which one began; it therefore is a conclusion which is detached. The outcome of a convergent logic's use of *modus ponens* is one where there is a separation from the beginning, but a maintenance of a hold on the process of getting to the outcome; consequently, it too can be termed a conclusion which is detached. But in connection with a dynamic logic, since there seems to be no connection between beginning and outcome, there is no *modus ponens* that is needed; or if one likes, the very connection between beginning and ending is nothing but the "therefore" of a *modus ponens*, so that we arrive at something which is a conclusion of a "thereforeing" and still is detached from the beginning from which the thereforeing took its start.

Today's discussion treats the *modus ponens* as pertinent to all the logics, and recognizes that in all of them it provides us with a conclusion, and therefore with an outcome which has reference to the beginning and the rule one uses. In connection with the nonextensional logics, the rule is formulatable in the symbolism of the *Principia Mathematica*. When the rule is used, we move from the beginning to the outcome by a "therefore." That "therefore" can be understood to be identical in all the cases. It allows us to arrive at different kinds of outcome, four of which have an internal reference backwards toward or into the premiss. It can also be understood to express a distinctive type of act in each logic. Thus, we can say that we go from $P.Q$ to (PQ) in an emergent logic by asserting $P.Q$, and also $P.Q$) (PQ), thereby getting (PQ); or we can say that we go from $P.Q$ to (PQ) directly under the aegis of the rule $P.Q$) (PQ) without having to assert the premiss in a *modus ponens*. The first of these ways gives us a conclusion which still refers back to our beginning, and thus does not give us the (PQ) as a detached result. The second approach seems to be more correct. Consequently, we should say that in connection with the logic of convergence, we have a rule which seems to be a contingent truth in the logic of the *Principia Mathematica*, and that we move in consonance with it once we isolate the premiss. Our movement is from $P.Q$ to (PQ) without an assertion of the rule $P.Q$) (PQ).

An extensional logic gets to a conclusion by asserting the rule and the premiss as antecedents in a *modus ponens,* and then subjects the result to an act of detachment. The other logics get to a conclusion by moving from an accepted position under the guidance of an accepted rule, and arriving at a conclusion that in fact is held apart from the premiss and the rule, because the rule is not asserted, and the premiss functions as a beginning of a process. But now it is evident that we do not have different kinds of "therefores," but a different set of uses for a "therefore." In an extensional logic, we use it after the assertion of a rule and a premiss, but in the other logics, we use it to detach a conclusion, i.e., an outcome having some reference to a premiss, under the aegis of a rule.

According to this account, all the logics are concrete logics. But we are able to work with an extensional logic without paying attention to actual entities. Is not something similar possible in connection with the other logics? Is this question related to the fact that in connection with extensional logic we have an act of arriving at a conclusion, to be followed by an act of detachment, whereas in the other logics the detachment is part of the act of moving to the conclusion? Must we not write the rules of the nonextensional logics in the form of extensional, logical, necessary truths, and then arrive at the conclusions of those nonextensional logics by distinctive "therefores" which not only detach the conclusion, but convert it into a guise it does not have as merely formal?

It seems reasonable to say that the answer to the first question is affirmative; so is the answer to the second. The answer to the third is negative; there is no reason why we cannot formulate any kind of result or operation. Why not say that we have the rule, for example, $P.Q$) (PQ) which is to be used in *modus ponens* by converting it into $P.Q$) PQ when it is used as together with $P.Q$, but subject to a distinctive movement so that the outcome is a detached conclusion (PQ)? But why should not the conversion also be expressed formally? Is it not the case that in the foregoing we do express the conversion formally? After all, we do write $P.Q$) (PQ) as the rule, but make use of it in such a way that it functions as an antecedent in a converted form, and is then connected, with the premiss, with a conclusion which has the guise of the consequent of the given rule.

On this last supposition, the various nonextensional logics all have rules which have the form of contingent truths in an extensional logic. When we infer, we can make use of those rules as antecedents. In that act we convert the rule into a necessary truth in an extensional logic, but thereupon subject this truth and the premiss to a process which terminates in the consequent of a nonextensional logic. A rule of a nonextensional logic will then tell us how the process must proceed from the necessary truths of an extensional logic. We can also use the logical law of an extensional logic as a guide for a process, and then convert the law into an antecedent which has the form required by a nonextensional logic. This, together with a premiss, allows us to arrive, through a distinctive use of a "therefore," at the detached conclusion needed by an extensional logic. When we follow this latter procedure, we evidently undo in the process what was done in order to convert the extensional rule into an antecedent for the process of inferring.

If we start with a guiding rule for a nonextensional logic and see the beginning of our inference to be produced by a conversion of this rule into an antecedent having the form expressive of a law in an extensional logic, we can then view the *modus ponens* as undoing what we did to get that antecedent, so that the outcome is what the nonextensional logic requires. For all five logics, we can then say that they begin with the formulation of rules of distinctive kinds, but that they change the nature of those rules when they use them as antecedents which, together with premisses, function as the beginning of an inferential process. They all have distinctive ways of "thereforeing" which result in the conversion of the consequent of the rule (when this is made an antecedent) into a detached conclusion of the kind required by the logic. This approach in effect makes the procedure of a logic subject to conditions characteristic of another logic—it, for example, starts with an extensional logical rule and then after converting this into some non-extensional antecedent proceeds according to a nonextensional "therefore" so as to arrive at the conclusion needed by an extensional logic. This shows how an extensional logic can be dealt with in a manner analogous to that used in connection with the other logics.

What was just outlined was a way of using one logic in the body of another, and this I think is important to see. What is still wanted is an understanding of how to use a logic without reference to any other.

Will it not be sufficient to recognize a rule to be a guide, and then take its antecedent to be the beginning of a distinctive process ending necessarily with the consequent of that rule? Such an approach seems to do justice to the nonextensional logics. Applied to an extensional logic, which states rules that are necessarily true (the assertions, for example, of the *Principia Mathematica*), we will then affirm the antecedent of the rule and use the *modus ponens* as a mode of "thereforeing" which gets to the conclusion of the stated rule. We would then get back to the position that rules are never antecedents, but always remain as guides. The *modus ponens* would then be stated as:

$$P \;.). \; P \; v \; Q$$
$$P$$
$$\therefore$$
$$P \; v \; Q$$

where the $\therefore$ would be understood to refer to just that kind of movement which goes from the given antecedent to the given consequence. This would be a detached conclusion by virtue of the fact that it was arrived at under the aegis of the rule and yet was made to stand apart from the premiss. Its "conclusion" aspect would be found by having it under the rule. While its "detached" aspect would be found by separating it from the P by means of the distinctive $\therefore$.

But isn't $P \;.). P \; v \; Q$ necessarily true? Not as a rule of inference; it is necessarily true as the rule for a distinctive "therefore." But this is the same kind of observation we can make in the other logics whose formulations would be contingent truths in the logic which takes $P \;.) \; P \; v \; Q$ to be a necessary truth.

But isn't $P \;.). P \; v \; Q$ necessarily true apart from a use in inference? Is not its denial self-contradictory? Yes, of course, for the self-contradictory here means that the terms remain distinct and opposed but are yet conjoined. In a world where no distinction of opposed terms was possible, the contradictory of $P \supset Q$ would not be self-contradictory, but a merging of P and $-Q$.

Would the contradictory or denial of a rule for a merging logic, $P.Q \supset (PQ)$ —to use the symbolism of the *Principia Mathematica* again —be $P.Q \supset P \lor Q$? Or would it be $P.Q. -(PQ)$? Can we state the contradictory properly, if we use this symbolism? Is "contradictory" the right word to use here?

What is evidently needed is a way of stating the necessity in each of the logics. Obviously, a logic of merging, which does not make use of the law of contradiction, cannot be understood by treating a denial of it as though it contradicted it. But what should it do?

April 19

The denial of an expression using a symbol might be the use of a sign. Such a denial involves a movement outside the logic which is appropriate to the symbol. Or one can formulate a denial of the assertion making use of the symbol; this will be the contradictory of the assertion. Such a contradiction, at least in the case of the logic of merging, will have to be forged by taking advantage of another logic. As making use of signs, it necessarily takes us out of the logic which is being denied. But we can nevertheless formulate the denial for the logic by recognizing that this denial will have a relation to the logic which is distinct from the kind of relation that the denials in other logics have to the assertions of those logics.

The denial of an extensional, necessary truth is $P (\overline{PQ})$; of an accumulative, $P(-PQ)$; of the idealistic, $(P \lor Q) (\overline{PQ})$; of the dynamic, $P (\overline{PQ})$; and of the merging, $(P.Q) (\overline{P} \lor \overline{Q})$. The extensional logic, no less than the others, formulates its contradictory in terms alien to itself, for though the contradictory is usually written as though the conjunction of the antecedent with the denial of the consequent was like any other conjunction, it is in fact one in which terms that are *necessarily* separate are merged together. We state the terms as separate, but what we intend to say is that they would be self-contradictory if we could make a union of them. The conjunction would be a necessary falsehood; the necessity of that falsehood is not conveyed by a mere conjunction. The very fact that we put the terms together without a dot in the denial of the extensional logical truth points up the fact that we must go outside that logic to express its contradictory; if we put dots in, we will not get a contradiction.

But why should all the denials be expressed by mergings? On the one hand, this looks as though the denial of the truth of some necessary assertion in a merging logic is expressed in that logic, and on the other hand, it seems to favor a merging logic for the expression of the contradictory of the assertions of any other logic. The justification of the second of these observations justifies the first.

Perhaps the denial of a necessary truth must be expressed as a merging? But then one would expect the other forms of expression would be most appropriate to the other logics. Will an extensional logic tell us what is implied by what we assert, an accumulative logic tell us the conditions of an inference, an idealistic logic tell us what we intend, a dynamic logic tell us the nature of the process of inference, and the merging logic tell us the nature of the denials? Each of the logics will then be applied on the results of the others, for different purposes.

April 22

There are five types of denial. In addition to that characteristic of extensional logic, we have a denial in accumulative logic in the form of a reversal: the denial of $P .). Q)P$ is $Q)P .). Q.$ In the idealistic logic, the denial is determination, the assertion of P by itself. In the dynamic logic, the denial is replacement, the demarcating of $-P$ instead of P. And in the merging logic, the denial is dispersal, the affirmation of $P v Q$ in place of the initial or final conjunction.

If there be any warrant for these negations, we will not have a negative sign, such as that employed in the extensional logic, except in the dynamic logic. We can think, though, of determination to be a kind of negation (following Spinoza), and the dispersal of the merging logic as the rewriting of the negation of a conjunction. This would leave only the accumulative logic without a negation, unless we think of reversal as the result of a negation of the connection going from P to Q, and from there back to P.

Do we have enough now to make a logic? Yes, if all we had to do was to make up truth tables. But truth tables are appropriate only to an extensional logic. Though it is possible to see all the assertions of the *Principia Mathematica,* or at least all the nonquantified ones, as variants on $P .). P v Q$, it is a fact that they are at least distinguishable as offering instances of various laws—e.g., distributive, associative, etc.—of use in mathematics. But such distinctions would seem to be irrelevant to the logic, and tell us only about the behavior of various variables viewed as somehow not part of a necessary logical whole.

If we take an extensional logic to have an endless number of theorems derivable from P .). $P v Q$ by making substitutions of various sorts in the Q, we should look for a similar formula in the other logics and get a host of theorems in each by a somewhat similar substitution. Can this be done?

April 26

A radical descriptivism would try to give an account of whatever was confronted. It would, however, be faced with the need to abstract from the multiplicity of details which any particular object possesses, and would surely have to neglect some of the many objects which are in fact confronted. It is a program that can never be carried out.

That a radical descriptivism is not practically possible still leaves the question as to whether or not it is theoretically possible. I think it is not, because it too would want to distinguish between the veridical and the illusory, the real and the unreal, the fictional and the factual, the permanent and the episodic, the good and the bad, and the true and the false, and would want to keep the distinctions fixed and clear. Having made the distinctions, one could then go on to describe what was inside each category, and in this sense seem to have a descriptivistic philosophy. But the move away from such a philosophy would have been begun in the making of a categorical distinction between the accepted and the rejected items, between what was imposed and what was given, etc.

A phenomenology tries to be descriptive, but only after it has bracketed off some of the pragmatic factors which were in fact encountered. It is a descriptivism within limits. The bracketing also takes place in an empiricism, but without notice, for an empiricism proceeds by discarding the world of every day to concentrate instead on some abstract aspects or analytic elements in that world or its objects. Its distinction between the given or experienced and the derived, or between the given or experienced and the fictional, is a basic categorical division.

One can object to the view that the content of a category is constant, but this would not mean that the category was not a basic one indicating a domain which was bounded off from others. One can object that the categories offered by thinkers in the past have been found to be relative to their languages, customs, history, interests, etc., but this would not deny the fact that such categories were offered in the attempt to mark basic divisions amongst the items in the world.

Philosophy is the quest for ultimate categories, and begins with the acknowledgment of certain categories as presumably ultimate. It does not deal with the latter in a purely abstract way, as mere categories, but always as having some bearing on subject matter. The development of the philosophy is a criticism of the initial suppositions in the attempt to determine just which categories are basic. That very quest is built upon the acknowledgment that there is a division in the world which is more than a division of degree; i.e., that there are items which belong under one category, and other items which belong under others. Those categories are 1] fixed, 2] universal, 3] intelligible, and are to be found presupposed by everyone, including those who deny that they exist.

A philosophy may be mistaken in insisting on this or that category as a true category; it is not mistaken in holding that some categories are ultimate, marking fundamental, basic distinctions in the nature of things. Even one who thought that all categories are man-made, reflecting man's interests, makes a difference between those categories and what they categorize, between man's conceptual apparatus and the given data on which these are used, so that he has as basic two categories, one of which is a set of changing concepts and the other of which is that of a given.

One way of determining which set of categories is the proper set is by trying to abjure their use and thereby discovering that they are employed. Another way is by accepting some items in experience and then discovering that they refer one to others which are by nature "other" or "alien" to them. It is possible that items in one category may differ only in degree from those of another. But it does not follow that all the items in one of the categories then differ only in degree from the other. It may be true that some entities which are not alive differ only in degree from some of those which are alive, but this would not entail that all the living differ from all the nonliving only in degree. Would this not mean that item X which differed from item Y in degree would be different in kind from item Z, even though it had been classified with it? If a nonliving entity is different only in degree from a living one, then would not the living entity have to be different in kind from other living beings which differed in kind from the nonliving? I think not. As differing in kind, it would be distinct, but as differing in degree, it would be indistinct and therefore not sharply distinguished from some of the items in the other category. But some of the items in each of the categories would be distinct and would, therefore, contrast with distinct items in the other category.

The basic problem is to know how to move from a given item to other items as occupying distinct categories. As was suggested, this question is answered by discovering in the item facets or factors which can be made intelligible only by referring them, for their source and meaning, to items in another category, permanently marked off from the first.

Russell made a distinction between knowledge by acquaintance and knowledge by description. His use of "description" is almost the opposite of that used above, for it means for him an indirect knowledge, a knowledge of something obtained from another through that other's account of what he had experienced. I use the term to express what is encountered.

Is not Russell's distinction between what is immediately or directly encountered and what is not, subordinate to the distinction between the real and the unreal, the illusory and the factual, the true and the false, etc.? Does it not occur inside each of these categories? Yes. But does not this mean that they are also to be subordinated to his distinction? If we have the classes True-Direct, True-Indirect, False-Direct, False-Indirect, it would seem to be just as true to say that the Direct-Indirect dichotomy is basic as the True-False one is.

Russell's division is as basic as the other, but it is epistemic and not ontologic in import. Not unless epistemology is subordinate to ontology and never conversely (which I do not think is the case), would his distinction be always subordinate to the other.

An idealist has only one entity to describe—the totality or absolute. For him there is no distinction between the essential and the derivative, nonessential, or accidental; all features are essential. We get a difference between the essential and the accidental only if we hold to something like a doctrine of external relations; a theory of internal relations makes all features essential, interlocked items descriptive of the whole. But since the idealist does isolate items, even if only as abstractions, and deals with them in external relations to other equally abstract items, he must, at least with respect to these, recognize a difference between the essential and the accidental.

It would be accidental to an abstract relation or feature that it should be considered by me now. When we bring in this consideration, we would just so far make the abstract relation or feature concrete; the features that the abstract relation or feature then accretes would be essential to it as so involved with me.

In a Humean world, every item has only essential features; each is what it is, with whatever characters it may have. His is a world of multiple absolutes, each to be described in essential (there are in fact no other) terms. His is a world where everything is only a sign of another; the idealist has only symbols.

A symbol involves an encounter then and there with the object of the symbol, but in a limited form; the symbol is but the most attenuated aspect of its own referent; to have the symbol is already to be in some possession of the object of the symbol. To get a better grasp of the object of the symbol, to have that object more fully than it is in the guise of the symbol as initially encountered, one must move on. This moving on is achieved under the pressure of the object of the symbol itself, a fact which is signalized in religion by the contention that one achieves a faith in God only so far as one has been made the subject of God's grace.

To get to a mode of Being from actualities (or from some other mode of Being) one makes use of symbols. The actualities (or the modes of Being) are seen to possess a nonessential feature, a feature which is not intrinsic to them as by themselves, and to owe it to the action of a mode of Being. The "accidental" will then be a symbol of what is an ultimate reality. This contention reverses the usual interpretation, which takes accidents to tell us of nothing beyond themselves, or only of that which is adventitious. But even Aristotle sees his "accidents" as testifying to the existence of matter or the action of other entities. Though he speaks as though the accidents told him nothing, he in effect takes them to be symbols of matter or of other entities.

To know what is accidental of an actuality is to know more than would be known if one concentrated on the essential in it—provided that the accidental was a symbol of an ultimate mode of Being. The accidental would then be more important and revelatory not in its specifity, as having this or that guise, but in its categorial aspect, in its being as accidental. The occurrence of the accidental, not the nature of the accidental, in short, is revelatory of a reality which is ultimate.

April 27
(Roslyn, New York)

There are two kinds of accidents, those that testify to the presence of a mode of Being, and those that testify to the presence of other actualities. Those that testify to the former are features which refer one to something that has to do not only with the actuality with which one begins, or with some actuality which has been isolated, but with a plurality of actualities and finally with all the actualities. They are in fact permanent features of all the actualities. Being is one of these; a common future or Good is another; contemporaneity is a third; and affiliation is a fourth. The acknowledgment of these features presupposes that we know more than one actuality, for they characterize the way in which actualities are together.

In the *Modes of Being*, an attempt was made to go directly from one actuality to God; that approach is alternative to the one here being considered, and if carried out with respect to all the modes of Being, would require us to find a way of going to them all from features in a single actuality. The consideration of what is discussed in the *Modes of Being* is complicated by the fact, however, that it was there supposed A] that we were trying to go from one mode of Being to another, and B] that an actuality could function as a mode of Being or as a representative of one.

Holding aside for the moment the question whether or not one can get to a mode of Being from a single actuality, it is true that we can get to other actualities or rather to the fact of their being and power from a consideration of a single actuality. The so-called secondary qualities are transient features of an actuality. Though they do symbolize the nature of that actuality, they also reflect the presence of other actualities as providing the condition or causes for the presence of those qualities. The qualities could be treated as ultimate beings, as Hume does, but then we could not account for change, coming to be, action, all of which require something which remains to act.

If we could demonstrate that there are 1] accidents which characterize single actualities, and that these all refer us to other actualities, not in their specificity, but as beings having the power to produce those accidents in the given actuality, as well as 2] other accidents that pertained to all actualities, but were permanent rather than adventitious, we would be able to demonstrate that there were five types of Being, four of which were ultimates and affected all the actualities, and a fifth which was another actuality which was part of a domain of actualities.

It does not seem possible to derive anything which prescribes to a plurality of actualities, from any one or any number of them. But if we grant there are accidents which originate with the modes of Being, we will have to show just what dimension of those accidents is contributed by the actualities and what by the Beings. We will also have to show that the accidents which were said to be the result of the operation of actualities on one another were not in fact produced by the Beings.

Having being, contemporaneity, futurity, and affiliation are pyramidical relations. They not only stretch between actualities, but they refer back to Beings. The meaning, say of contemporaneity, is that actualities are together in time and that this togetherness is intrusive. Unlike a secondary quality, it not only tells us that there is a power outside it, but tells us the nature of that power. A secondary quality is not a symbol of its cause, exterior to the place where that quality is located. But a feature referring to a Being is such a symbol.

Is it conceivable that a Being might impose on actualities not only relational features, but others which have a bearing on each of the actualities and are modified in nature by those actualities? After all, having being has not yet been shown by me to be a relational character, as contemporaneity, affiliation, and perhaps even futurity are. Unless we can show that having being is relational, we cannot define the accidents which lead to Beings to be relational, involving a plurality of actualities. And unless we can show that what is not relational must be referred to other actualities' actions or presence, we have not carried through the distinction between the two kinds of accidents.

One way of dealing with having Being as a relational notion is to see it as a One for a Many. Given a single actuality, we would not be called upon to make a reference to Actuality, as Being; but the single actuality could not be understood without reference to other actualities (by virtue of the argument that a single entity becomes indistinguishable from nothing, since it will then lack determinations, which are in part determined from without, thereby raising the question as to whether determinateness does not offer a category for all accidents which demand a reference to other actualities). But those actualities could not be considered to be equally real, equal actualities, except by virtue of a reference to a common ground of Being.

If this be granted, we are left with the question as to whether or not secondary qualities might be the outcome of the operation of modes of Being (directly or indirectly), but as modified by each of the actualities, and then without reference to the presence of any other actualities. Were this possible, there would be accidents which were modified and others which were not modified by actualities. The former would have a singular import, whereas the latter would reflect the constant and omnipresent nature of the Beings from which both types of accident originated.

We find that we can correlate and even produce singular accidents by altering the position or role of other actualities. This is an empirical answer to our question. And though it be true that an accident points to a reality capable of giving the accident some being, only those accidents which are permanent and universal require a reference to a reality which is permanent and ultimate. This is a kind of negative but dialectical answer to our question. What is still to be shown is that it is not possible for a Being to be the source of the accidents that are characteristic of actualities in their severalty. Is it not enough to remark that those accidents differ from case to case, thereby pointing up differentiating causes, for the causes might be the same, and the several actualities might qualify the product in different ways to give us different accidents.

Might it not be sufficient to observe that a number of actualities, though distinct, share the same kind of accidents, that a number of them, for example, are yellow, but that others lack this character? No, for we could then say that they fall into different classes and as such specify the action of a Being common to them and some other entities, all contrasting with still others. We would have to show that the accidents were individuated, and yet were common to a number. But they would have to be shown to be individuated by something other than the actualities in which they were resident. Since they were individuated and present in only some actualities, we could not attribute the individuation to Beings, but only to actualities.

How can it be shown that secondary characters are unique to each case, but that this uniqueness is not due to the unique entity in which it is resident? This might be done by showing that the essence of the entity precludes its making a unique difference to what is imposed on it, or by showing that the accident is divisible into a symbolic dimension and a referential one, and that the referential is precisely that which is not part of the actuality, and that it nevertheless is unique. What is to be shown is that the yellow of this flower tells us about the being and nature of the flower. Because the yellow is transient, it owes its presence to something else as well; as transient, it has a distinctness or uniqueness which requires a reference to only some of a number of actualities.

The time of the occurrence of the accident could perhaps mark off the accident as distinctive, and lead us to refer to something which brought it about. But that time would, after all, be a time which was characteristic of other accidents as well. What is needed is a feature of an accident which emphasizes the fact that it is imposed, and which precludes it from being imposed by a Being or an encapsulated form of one.

Why not have recourse to what I dismissed as an empirical reason? We could then say that all accidents require us to make reference to other actualities, but that some of the accidents lead to the others as correlatives, subject with the given actuality to common conditions, and that other accidents lead to other actualities as sources. Or better, that we are led to other actualities as sources, and then find that they are also correlatives. Or that when we acknowledge other actualities for whatever reason, we find that they function both as correlatives subject to permanent conditions and as sources. Or that they are found to be subject to symmetrical relations pointing us to Beings and to asymmetrical relations pointing us to them as sources (even though they may themselves be subject to converse asymmetrical relations which, together with the first,

have the appearance of being symmetrical). Some of the symmetrical relations would be irreducible, leading to Beings, and others would be
reducible to asymmetricals leading us to sources in actualities.

An alternative way of making the last point is to see the symmetrical
relation as a symbol of a Being and an asymmetrical relation as a symbol
of one of the terms. Those accidents which refer us to Being are symbols
of the Being, whereas those accidents which refer us to another actuality
are symbolic of the original actuality. When we see something as an
accident, we can therefore ask if it is symbolic of an actuality; if it is not,
it is symbolic of a Being, and conversely, if it is not symbolic of a Being,
it is symbolic of an actuality. Or even more completely, one kind of accident is a symbol of the entity in which it is resident and of the being of
other actualities, and another kind is a symbol of the nature of a Being
and of the beingness (as presents) of actualities. We get signs when we
misuse these symbols, or when we wish to refer to the natures of other actual entities or to the actualities that are present.

April 28

The being of a quality is due to another actuality, but the nature
of that quality is the result of the nature of the entity which possesses
the quality operating on the quality.

The being of a symmetrical relation is due to two actualities. Its
nature is the result of the operation of the nature of a Being on the symmetrical relation. This makes the quality into a symbol of the being of
another actuality and of the nature of the actuality in which it resides.
And it makes the symmetrical relation into a symbol of the nature of
some ultimate mode of Being, at the same time that it is a symbol of the
being of the related actualities. (The symmetrical relations to which reference is here being made are permanent, cosmic ones, such as contemporaneity.)

Just so far as a mind can be taken as a representative or epitomization
of the Ideal, as the soul of God, as centering the body, and as a self, we
should be able to see ourselves and other actualities in symmetrical relations whose beings depends on us and on those other actualities. The
nature of those entities in turn depends on ourselves in the guise of self,
soul, mind, or centering body. This would mean that if we understood
the relation which we have to other actualities, we could use that relation as a symbol of ourselves in the guise of self, etc. Such a view means
that we would have two roles, one in which we were one term related to

another, and the other in which we functioned as the transcendent ground of the nature of the relation, enabling one to use that relation therefore as a symbol of our own nature.

If we shear off from a quality what is owing to another actuality, we should be left only with a mere symbol, which owes whatever being it has to the fact that it is a symbol inseparable from the being of that which it symbolizes. The self, etc., which we took to be the ground of the nature of a relation we have with other entities, could now be said to be that which is also symbolized by the qualities we exhibit. Conversely, the self, etc., on this present account would be the ground for the nature of the quality we exhibit and for the nature of some symmetrical relation we sustain with respect to some other actuality. In the one guise the self, etc., is a representative of some Being, whereas in the other guise, it is merely a reality which has its outermost boundary in a quality whose presence is determined by the action of another actuality. The other actuality gives the actuality a boundary in the shape of a quality whose nature is an expression of the bounded actuality.

April 29

If we try to restrict ourselves to what we experience, and try to report what we find, we soon see that we must A] select some of the items which we face, for some of them are too dim, too remote, or too trivial for us to be able to deal with them carefully; B] select some of the aspects that the selected items have, for they seem endless, and a number of them seem to fall within the same obvious categories, such as taste or visibility, etc. We have no warrant for believing that that which we ignore has no value. It may or may not require a different kind of understanding from that which we accord to what we selected. And we must eventually return to what we had ignored, to see whether it can be accommodated within the frame that we find appropriate to what we selected.

An alternative approach would be that of starting with anything taken at random, and thus regardless of whether or not it be dim, remote, or trivial, and then randomly selecting some features of it. The random selection could be repeated any number of times as a way of checking what we had already determined on the basis of our examination of what we had previously selected.

It is not possible to avoid all selection, for at the very least we must use a vocabulary, and this will require us to attend to what we know; we also have pragmatic needs, old associations, interests, and strong confrontations, all of which force to the fore some items and require the neglect of others, at least for a time. Whatever it be that we select, we can take it to be final, as that which is to be accepted in the guise in which it is then found—but we will then presuppose that our selecting has no effect on what we selected. If our selecting had such an effect, we would have to separate off this effect from the item to see just what it was that we confronted. This affecting may be human or individual, i.e., characteristic of every individual or peculiar with such and such a weight for some individuals. If the latter, we can perhaps catch or compensate for it by varying the approach or checking our result against that which is reported by others; if the former, we would have to know something about the object as apart from men, or something about the way in which men deal with objects, so that they inevitably modify what those objects in fact are.

That with which I stop may be taken by me to be a final entity, existing then and there without further support, and this even if it be only a color or a shape. But we could have picked out objects which are involved in various pragmatic roles. Can we, in either case, by looking at the confronted item, know something about others, at least *that* they are, or that they are perhaps the conditions or the causes of what we now face? If we knew that confronted items were accidents either of actualities or of something else, we would know that there were other beings. If the accident is a quality of an item, it tells us that another being had power enough to give the accident a being, thereby making that accident a symbol of the other being; if the accident is a feature which refers to another item (such as being affiliated with, contemporary with, equally real as, or co-intelligible), it will be a part of a single symbol, the relation. The relation in turn will be a symbol of some Being that qualifies the relation.

April 30

When we begin, where we must begin, with everything whatsoever that we accept without question, we find ourselves in a dilemma. To accept everything is to find that we are involved with some items and not with others, and as a consequence are about to jettison the latter for the former. To remain within the commonsense world is thus to remain either with everything that we in fact face and deal with, or it is to insist on what we have been accustomed to insist upon. The former will be possible only so far as we avoid the latter. The acceptance of everything is thus a result achieved by an act of *detachment*. This is but a special case of a *fixating*. We must, to accept the world as merely confronted, abandon it as in fact faced.

The cult of experience, of mere phenomenological description, of sense data, and the like, are all possible only because a preliminary step has been taken to abandon what one has in fact emphasized. The pragmatist would insist on this observation, but remark that he at least has held on to what is practical or experienceable, the very items which he in fact insists upon as a commonsense man, and that he, the pragmatist, unlike all others, is therefore true to the beginning and the life of men; but he then forgets that the ordinary man is involved also with trivialities and follies, and that the acknowledgment of the practical is therefore the result of a selection and a fixating on some items.

We can fixate on A] the practical, B] the arresting, C] the qualitative, D] the humanly significant, E] the entire panorama, F] the structural, G] ourselves, H] the perplexing, I] the excellent.

A] The practical, as was just indicated, has us in its grip. We begin our reflections there; our vocabulary is geared to it; we are caught up in it; it polarizes our world, giving us a significant foreground and background. It presupposes that we retain a knowledge of what had been, and have some grasp of what might be. It is essentially a summational knowledge, making use of what has been learned from others, or from our own encounters. It is devoid of adequate controls, and is oriented toward our middle-level activities. We gain more control, become more practical, when we understand how to manipulate machines. We go behind these when we know what the principles are in terms of which machines can be made and controlled. The most pragmatic of men is thus one who refuses to be caught inside the daily practical world.

B] The arresting stops us. We cannot avoid attending to it. The practical is arresting in this sense, too, but the arresting need not be practical. We can be arrested by the unusual, by what blocks the practical, what seems to be irrelevant to it. Men are not always geared toward action; they have moments of leisure and idleness, and can be torn away from their practical concerns by something startling or shocking. Even one who, like Dewey, would want to hold that we think only when we are prevented from acting—a view traceable to Peirce and eventually to Bain—recognizes that men reflect, though Dewey thinks it is only to make it possible for them to proceed better in the practical world. Yet, for the time being, he who reflects has turned away from the practical to follow out or to understand the arresting.

The arresting is in part a function of the individual who stops; depending on what is familiar to him, how alert and perceptive he is, and what it is that he is involved in, he will find different things to be arresting. Some men will find certain items arresting where others will see nothing; and presumably some men will find everything whatsoever to be arresting.

c]   A long philosophic tradition focuses on the qualitative. This could be thought to be the arresting, or it could be thought to be that which is most evidently or easily fixated, or that which is omnipresent. The qualitative is normally thought to be made up of a plurality of items. This plurality has two forms; there is the plurality of different sensible modi, and the plurality of items within a different modus. There is sight and sound, and there is yellow and brown. He who would remain with the qualitative must, at least in the beginning, make a choice as to whether to concentrate on this or that mode of sensible perception, or to avoid raising the question of how we come to have the datum, and then must concentrate on this or that item. He who does this will have carried out the process of fixating one step further. And then it becomes a question whether he can remain with even one datum for long, not only because this is in the process of changing or even passing away, but because it has an endless number of nuances.

d]   The arresting, the practical, and the qualitative, particularly that which we unreflectingly focus on, are all humanly significant. Our interests, our language, our attitudes enable us to fixate these. The qualitative locates things for us, and affects us in various degrees; the practical catches us up in its career; the arresting stops us and forces us to attend to it.

More generally, we are tempted to fixate on whatever is of human interest, what makes a difference to ourselves here and now, or what promises to do so quite soon. Still, it is the case that astronomy is an early discipline and that it is produced by men who have freed themselves from an interest in what is significant to men. To be sure, it began with a consideration by sailors and farmers of what was important to their welfare. But it was then seen to be understandable only so far as one attended to the astronomical bodies and movements in their own terms. And there is the fact that even the most primitive of men has his myths, his stories, his idle pleasures and sports. When existentialists concentrate on what is humanly significant, they select out of the totality of the humanly significant only those items which they think *should be* significant; they deliberately cancel out what a man in fact takes to be significant if they think it is "inauthentic."

e]   The differences in content which the previous approaches produce prompts the consideration of the entire panorama which we in fact confront at every moment. To see this panorama we must, of course, detach ourselves from the arresting, etc. Only then do we allow every item to be part of a single aesthetic continuum, of one total experience, and can try to say what this encompasses. The saying will of course divide the panorama, for our language is not only broken up into words, but involves emphases and selections. The panorama also is constantly shifting, and any attempt to add to it or to describe it is up against the fact that it must either abstract an aspect of the panorama, hold it in mind, or abstractly define it—all of which involves a loss of a simple confrontation with the panorama. We will still not be able to avoid the arresting, etc., except by deliberately cancelling it out whenever it intrudes. We will therefore have to fixate the panorama in contrast with anything that might try to divide it. In any case, we will have moved away from the simple confrontation of the content of experience.

F]   There is a constancy to the changing panorama; there is stability to the practical; there is something common to the various items in a qualitative mode, and to the various arresting items and what is humanly significant. Men note the boundaries of things, the way they are related one with the other; they summarize experience in terms of rules and plans; they make guesses, inferences, predictions, and promises in the light of what is discerned of the structures in what is confronted, whether this be the commonsense world, the practical, the arresting, the qualitative, the humanly significant, or the entire panorama.

Science is grounded in the awareness that these different approaches are all inadequate and imprecise. It attends initially to the structures found in some one or all of these, and tries to see how it might order them. It soon finds that it cannot be content with the items as they appear —which is what an Aristotelian science would like to do—and must cut beneath or suppose that there are other kinds of items which could be interrelated in such a way as to make for precision in the acknowledgment of facts and accuracy in the formulation of predictions. If it is content only with making more careful observations and connecting the results in stable ways, it is an empirical discipline; but if it formulates theories as to just what the ultimate items are, and relates these by laws which are not similar to or perhaps reconcilable with those which characterize the practical, the arresting, etc., it is a theoretical science. In either case, we do not rest with what we initially accepted.

G]   All the foregoing concentrates on the data that we confront, even when this is supposed to be something internal to ourselves or constituted by us. No one of them turns inward to look at us, who are producers in part or whole of the data, or at least must be acknowledged to enable the data to be present. Even if we take our minds to be but searchlights or passive receptacles allowing the data to be unaffected in activity and perhaps even in nature by us, it is a fact that we do acknowledge the items, speak a language, have our own internal feelings and assessments.

One might well argue, with Wittgenstein, that without a public language we cannot communicate and perhaps make intelligible just what we are undergoing, but it still will remain true that we have an internality without which the external makes no sense or has no reality. We are at the center of the world we confront, and sometimes become aware of ourselves as having this role. To know what is in fact real, it is desirable to know just what we contribute to the data that we suppose was objective, to be merely noted.

Do we have a set of categories, drives, attitudes, approaches, languages, etc., which alter or hide the nature of what is before us? And does each individual add to this his own personal experience and interests, to make what he confronts into something no one else can know? We must turn to ourselves to get the answer.

A shift from the data we confront to ourselves as confronting them not only presupposes some one or more of the fixatings discussed above, including the scientific, but involves an isolation of one type of entity as contrasting with all others. Its acknowledgment, therefore, introduces a categorial distinction which divides off the private individual from the public world. But this is only one of many categorial distinctions that are possible. Some of these have already been taken for granted—the practical and the impractical or idle, the arresting and the uninteresting, the qualitative and the quantitative, the humanly significant and the humanly insignificant, the whole panorama and its parts, and the structural and the content. The question then arises as to whether or not there are other distinctions to be made, what the basis for making them may be, and whether or not they but illustrate a way of working inside those previously distinguished, particularly the humanly significant and humanly insignificant, or the whole and its parts.

H] None of these questions arise for the ordinary man. He goes about his business, making various distinctions in terms of various conditionings, his own interests, the demands made on him, the places he finds himself, his language and the like, all without reflection or criticism. But, like everyone else, he is sometimes perplexed by what he finds, by gaps in his knowledge, by apparent irrelevancies and unclarities, and is forced to separate what he is sure of, at least at that moment, from what he is not in order to free himself from the perplexity. He could, of course, remain in the perplexed state and attend to the content, himself, or both of them, but then of course he would have opted for a part of the panorama. Perplexities usually, though, are stimuli to reflection, action, detachment, and the like. They therefore become the occasion for a detachment from what is faced, thereby enabling one to attend to something else, which may offer a substitute or an explanation for the perplexing.

Those who can be said to have a philosophic temperament will find everything to have a perplexing aspect. The very fact that something occurs, the fact that objects have this or that trait, that they come to be and pass away, that they change, that they have such and such neighbors, that they allow for understanding, that they are distinct from oneself— indeed from any facet or aspect—may prove perplexing to a sufficiently sensitive, critical, or imaginative man, thereby putting into question every and any item he may find.

In contrast with religion, which glories in the existence of the paradoxical, the philosophical temperament seeks to dissolve the paradoxical, or to find its source and then perhaps to return to the world where the original perplexing item was found. The philosopher then discovers everything to be perplexing in the sense of being an object of a justified wonder and delight. The mastery of the perplexing, either by making it vanish or by recovering its ground and thereby seeing how and why everything might be properly viewed as wondrous, drives him from the perplexing to something else. If he sees all the previous approaches to be ways of emphasizing this or that perplexing fact, he can see them as providing an occasion for moving to their explanations or conditions.

1] All the previous distinctions could also be seen to be instances of what in some sense is excellent, superior, basic, whether this be viewed as objective or humanly defined. The very fact that something is fixated would argue for its being treated as excellent, if only for the purpose of being considered by us. Even something evil, ugly, undesirable, would be excellent in this respect if it were treated as something to be fixated. But we would soon have to distinguish between those items which, in addition to being excellent for fixating, were excellent in themselves or in reference to other entities which could have been or which might also be fixated. The distinction between the excellent for fixating and the excellent in some other sense introduces a categorial distinction between excellent for some purpose and excellent apart from this, or excellences for different purposes, which may or may not leave over some items which were not excellent in any sense except that of being open to a fixating.

Every one of the foregoing ways of dealing with the data has been emphasized in the past and seems to be worth emphasizing today. But whether some or all of these be emphasized, sooner or later one must return to the question of how they relate to the commonsense world with which we began. We could argue that that world has been replaced, but we would then have left over the unsolved problem as to how it ever was confronted; we could argue that it is a function of some combination of the items on which we fixated, but though some philosophers have claimed to do this, they have failed to show that the commonsense world in all its variety and complexity is such a product. We could argue that the commonsense world alone is real and what we have fixated are but facets of it, but since these supposed facets divide the commonsensical world in ways which it does not natively exhibit, the facets would seem to have a reality which is more than that of being simple derivatives or functions of the commonsense world.

The distinctions we have made are distinctions which have their roots in the commonsense world. They in no way show that that world is unreal or replaceable. Everyone of them seems to be capable of having a being of its own apart from the items which the commonsense world accepts; yet each of them seems to demand a carrier in us or in the world. One who, like Hume, wants to deal with the qualitative as though it alone were, not only replaces the commonsense world with which he, like everyone else, begins, but cannot account for laws, science, practice, or a future in which his distinctions will hold.

The simplest procedure would be to locate the fixated items in the world with which we began. But this will force us at once to ask how they are connected, and whether the fixated will provide us with a clue as to just what it is to which it is to be connected. The discovery that it is a clue to the being of that in which it is not made to inhere, and a clue to the nature of that in which it inheres or which is the source of it, is the beginning of the adventure of discovering what else there is besides that on which we have fixated and whatever we take to carry this.

In every case except that of the whole panorama, we can suppose that what we have fixated on is carried by the whole, and therefore offers a selection from this. We can take what we have fixated to be irrelevant to what carries it—the Aristotelian view of accidents—or as offering a symbol for the nature of its carrier, or for the being of what caused it (or, in the case of a relation, for the nature of a final Being or a derivative from this and for the being of the terms that sustain the relation).

More carefully said: that on which we focus may have the following relations to the gross macroscopic world of every day with which we began: the focused may   *1*] be alongside the gross;   *2*] have the gross as a product;   *3*] be an effect of the gross;   *4*] accompany the gross;   *5*] be sustained by the gross;   *6*] sustain the gross;   *7*] operate on the gross;   *8*] be operated on by the gross;   *9*] testify to the gross;   *10*] be testified to by the gross.

1]   To place something alongside that from which it was isolated, in order to examine it more carefully, is in effect to treat it as the foreground of a panorama.   *2*] The initial material could be treated as a function of the operation of the items focused on, whether these be in only one category or many.   *3*] That on which we focus can itself be thought to be a function of that with which we started. The last two cases are faced with the problem of knowing whether the product is everything excepting what we focus on, or everything including what we focus on.   *4*] This case is to be distinguished from the first; to be alongside is merely to be allowed to have an external relation, but to accompany is to be somehow related in such a way that the two are abreast.   *5*] The Aristotelian position takes what it calls accidents—for which qualities would be a good modern instance (though he includes quantity, position, place, etc.)—and takes them to be sustained at least by the objects with which we had originally to do, when these are purged of irrelevancies. This position evidently is one of two—in one we attribute the focused to the original objects, and in the other we attribue it to those objects only as altered somehow so as to be nothing but objects in and of themselves.   *6*] The focused may also be thought to sustain the objects. I know of no one who has held this position, but Whitehead in his view that events sustain objects, would be a good guide.   *7*] The pragmatists sometimes suggest that the focused is an operation to be employed on the substantial realities which presumably are left over when we attend to the manipulatable in experience.   *8*] What is left behind, particularly objects, could be thought to be expressed in the guise of the focused, and in that sense to be a way of operating on it, determining its career and nature.   *9*] The view I have urged just the other day takes what we focused on, particularly in the guise of a quality, to testify to the nature of that in which it is said to be resident and to the being of that which is supposed to be its cause.   *10*] It is the intent of a submicroscopic science to take its realities to testify to the presence of what we experience in the gross; carrying out this idea into the larger frame with which we are now dealing, we can say that the residuum of the gross world with which we began offers a testimony to the presence and reality of that on which we have focused. We do not need that testimony, of course, since we have the focused content; but the knowledge that the gross world does testify to this shows that there is an essential, referential nature to that which we left behind when we focused on the arresting, the qualitative, or whatever.'

These ten cases need careful study. The problem of the return to the world after we have departed from it has never been treated with sufficient care even by those who, like Buddha, think it imperative to return. They know what their message is, and where they should return; but they do not seem to care to tell us what they think is the relation of the message to the world. I suppose they take it for granted that the message overwhelms the world, transforms the world, makes it become an instance of the message. Translated into the present content, this would mean that where the world is returned to (in the shape of the residue after a focusing), that to which we return is transformed so as to become an instance of that on which we focused, or from which we derived the focused content.

May 1

Having concentrated on something in the world in which we live, we are faced with the problem of returning with what we had isolated. Perhaps it is not possible to return? Then we ourselves, as men who isolated what we did, serve to relate that on which we concentrate and the residue. Our problem then turns out to be that of relating the isolated, via ourselves or directly, to the residuum in the world with which we began.

Whatever be the relation that we take to hold between the isolated content and the residuum of the world with which we began, we must justify our decision to affirm this by producing some evidence. Without evidence, our assertion that the two domains are coordinate, that one is dependent on the other, or that one is more real, etc., will be arbitrary. If in the end we can find no evidence, we will be left with the brutal fact that we are treating the domains in a certain way, and are thereby merely expressing what we are, or desire, or intend.

1] To affirm that items are alongside one another is but to say that they are equally real. This means that they are oriented in ourselves or in something else which defines them, despite a difference in nature, to be of equal value. If attention be paid not merely to the domains, but to the various items in them, and the same question be asked as to how they could be alongside one another, we will be driven to consider more special relations.

The relations in one domain could conceivably be identical in kind with those characteristic of the other. If we suppose that they are necessarily different, we will be faced with the question as to whether or not they are therefore different in reality. Strictly speaking, though we have only the question of relating the isolated and the residuum, if we look inside either domain, we but continue the process of attending to some factor and holding the rest aside, thereby raising the subsequent question as to how we are to reunite them. If the reunion is to be achieved by bringing items alongside one another, it will require a reference to what makes them equally real.

The evidence justifying our saying that the isolated and the residuum are alongside one another is given by the kind of being that they have. We must see them as having their distinctive beings and assertiveness subjugated to a single Being which coordinates them, giving them an equal status, freedom, and career.

2]   The isolated and the residuum could be thought to accompany one another. They would then keep apace. This means that they are contemporaries. We will then have to see both of them as having a reality in themselves, even a temporal career by themselves, and yet as subject to a temporal movement not within their control.

If the temporality of the residuum and the isolated content be given by ourselves (as beings who hold them "at the same time"), we will have to ask ourselves how it is possible for them to have times of their own. In the end, on the hypothesis, we will have to deny private times to them; this should force us to give up the hypothesis that we give them their temporality. We are driven to affirm that the residuum and the isolated are objective, that their contemporaneity is not provided by us, and that each has its own time, and as such is subordinated to a common temporal movement.

3]   One of the domains might be a function, a product, to be accounted for by reference to the other. This will require the product to have a being which is referential to the past, i.e., to a being which it now possesses, but only so far as it is related to that which produced it. We can determine whether this is so or not by seeing if the modification in the possession will have a corresponding modification in the production; or we can see if they are in a temporal order, since production does take time. The latter alone offers us the needed evidence. We are able to take the arresting, the pragmatic, the qualitative, the structural, etc., to be a cause or an effect only so far as we see that its being is due to the residuum and that it comes after that residuum. Consequently, we must see the residuum as being at a preceding time. The evidence would consist in showing that though the isolated had a being of its own, it could have this only so far as it was temporally subsequent to the residuum.

4] A somewhat related idea is that of dependence. But here, instead of a temporal sequence, we have a coexistence. The isolated content will be properly treated as dependent on the residuum, or conversely, the residuum will be treated as dependent on the content, if its being is derivative but occurs at the same time. This derivation is ontological, yielding a result which is not entirely separable from its origin. The result should therefore reveal something of that origin. In effect the result should be a symbol of that origin, telling us something of its nature or being. It tells us of the nature if it is or so far as it is an exfoliation of that on which it depends; it tells us of the being if or so far as it allows the nature of the dependent to be dictated by something else.

5] The isolated content or the residuum can be taken to be a structure operating on the other, a way of ordering it, making it intelligible. It will then be something which is to structure the other, and as such will be a rule or intelligible principle, serving to clarify and interrelate that on which it operates. A pragmatist takes the formal to be such an operator; a scientist might take the residuum as an operator on the isolated submicroscopic content, enabling one to move to where the latter can be found.

6] Either the isolated content or the residuum can serve as a testimony to the other. This means that it will have an affiliation for the other, at the same time that it tells us about the nature of that which it is affiliated. The affiliation can be seen from the adherence of the so-called accidents to the substance, or by the way in which one object is more intimately involved with another in the other's domain than it is with its own companions.

To affirm that the isolated and the residuum are alongside each other, we must have evidence that they are equal in being; to affirm that they accompany each other, we must have evidence that they are contemporaries; to affirm that they are in a relation of being operated on to that which operates on, we must have evidence that the operator provides a structure for the former which is then a representative of the intelligible or ideal; to affirm that they are in a relation of testifier to testified, we must show that they are affiliated; to show that they are in a relation of product to producer, we must show that the former is a symbol of the being of the latter; to show that they are in a relation of dependence, we must show that the dependent item is a symbol of the nature of that on which it is dependent. It is possible for something to be a symbol of the being of one item and of the nature of another; this is the role played by accidents. These are at once products and dependents, being products of external objects and dependent on the objects in which they are normally said to be resident.

If we fail to find anything in common, or any kind of connection between the isolated and the residuum, we must, as was indicated above, see them as related by ourselves. Then we will have to deal with them as merely alongside one another, equally real because contained in us; or as accompaniments which, despite their individual rhythms, are subject to one common human time; or as in a relation of operator to content, with ourselves providing a kind of schema for a category and its content; or as offering affiliations enabling the one to adhere to the other. Or they will be in a relation of cause and effect, or condition and conditioned, and this will mean that we will provide the connection between them, serving to transmit the being of the cause to the effect, or the nature of the condition to the conditioned.

We are faced, evidently, with the same problems whether or not we make ourselves into the relationship between the isolated and the residuum, or take this relationship to occur outside us. When we take the latter position, we see our act of isolating to be essentially epistemic, and the return but a way of recovering the real world; the former is ontologic in the sense that it supposes that isolation separates a content from another but within the area of our individual being.

The acknowledgment of coordinate beings, contemporaries, operators, and affiliations, all involve the acceptance of symbols of ultimate Beings. The acknowledgment of causes and effects, and conditioned and condition are acknowledgments of Beings, without giving us an understanding of their natures, or of their natures without an understanding of Being. It all comes down to the recognition that the isolated and the residuum are symbols of some common relation which itself perhaps is a symbol of something else, or that they possess in themselves something of what they symbolize.

Our words are signs because they are either alongside or accompaniments of what occurs. This means that we, or an objective reality, function as a power which makes them equal in being to or contemporaries with one another. Treated as equal, we get a purely correlational view of the use of signs; treated as contemporaries, we get a behavioristic view, where action governs the way in which they are together.

If a word is to be a symbol, it must be shown to be operated on, dependent, caused, or affiliated. When taken to be a contemporary with, or equal in being to, its object, it is treated as a symbol of an encompassing being, since it refers us to a relation, for which it is a term. Consequently, even the most arbitrary sign will function as a symbol in some respect. It will be a sign only when it is used to refer us merely to a nature, even though that nature is ingredient in what is alongside, accompanies, is a cause, or an operator. If a word refers to that on which it is dependent or to that with which it is affiliated, it will properly be a symbol, even though it be arbitrarily instituted, as the word "God" is.

When we look at the isolated and the residuum, we may see one of them as the symbol for the other. It will be a symbol of the being of a coordination, of a contemporaneity, of a structuralization of one part of it by another part of it, and of a power of affiliation, as well as of the being of a cause. It will be a symbol of the nature of that on which it is dependent. (The dependency may itself be an instance of an affiliation, in which case the symbol will be of the being of the relation of affiliation, and of the nature of that with which it is affiliated.) The relations of coordination, contemporaneity, structuralization, and affiliation may in turn be taken as symbols. They then symbolize the nature of an ultimate Being directly, or in the form of a delimited version of it inside the Being of Actuality.

Is it also true that we have a symbolization of the relation which we might institute between the content we isolate and the content which we leave behind? Can we say of our isolated content, or of what is left behind, that it symbolizes a human relation of coordination, contemporaneity, structure, or affiliation, or that it symbolizes a relation of causation or dependence which allows it to symbolize the being of the cause or the nature of that on which it depends?

Causation and dependence seem to be relations which not only are symbolized by the effect and the conditioned, but allow one to symbolize the being of the cause and the nature of the condition as well. Why is this? Is it not because in these cases we have an asymmetrical relation, whereas in the others we have a symmetrical one? Even if the causes and the conditions are reciprocal, we have asymmetry, since there will be different causes and conditions in both cases, whereas in the symbolization of the being of the relations of coordination, etc., there is a symmetry of the relation with respect to the terms, as being equally necessary and on a footing.

But it was just said that affiliation was symmetrical and yet that we could symbolize the nature of that with which something was affiliated.

This, though, follows from the fact that affiliation, though it involves a symmetrical relation between entities, as somehow belonging together, does permit one of them to be subordinated to the other. In the case of structuralization, we not only have a coordination of what is structured, but a subordination to the structure. In the case of affiliation, we have a relation which is biased in one direction; in the case of structure, we have a bias toward a structure. In the one we have a symmetrical relation ending in a bias, in the other we have a bias toward one of the domains functioning as a symmetrical relation. Coordination (of beings) and contemporaneity seem to be both symmetrical without bias. We can of course have symmetrical affiliations, as we sometimes have with men and with chemicals; and in a Kantian schema, we could have structure and content in a strict symmetrical relation. This means, I think, that the asymmetrical cases are specializations of the normal symmetrical ones.

Can there be specializations of coordination and contemporaneity which will exhibit some kind of bias? Would the adoption of a point of reference serve, in the one case, as a standard of what it means to be real, and in the other as a standard of what it means to be present? Apparently. If so, we can say that the isolated or the residuum is a symbol of the being of a relation which in turn is a symbol of the nature of some Being, but that in special cases we will have A] a standard of reality, B] a point of orientation, c] a subordination of content, and D] a dependency of an affiliated. The case of causation is perhaps an instance of the bias which makes content subordinate to structure.

If dependency is a case of the bias of affiliation, and causation of the bias in favor of structure, ought there not be cases of the bias of standards and the bias of orientation which have a similar empirical import as dependency and causation have? It would seem so. A bias of standards is provided by man, whether he be part of the isolate or the residuum. If he is the relation between isolate and residuum, then the bias will show itself in terms of that in which he is interested. But unlike the existentialists, we should then say, not that things become real or have value or meaning only as related to man, but that the reality they in fact have is a reality equal to that of man's. Man's *reality* is the measure of the *reality* all things, showing them, by virtue of the relation of coordination, to be of equal reality. We are now left with the relation of contemporaneity, and the bias toward what is accepted as the present, or the point of orientation. With but a slight bow to physical relativity theory, we can say that any domain (or any item in one) can be taken to be present and all others treated as contemporary with respect to it.

We have then four basic symmetrical relations which are symbolized in their being by the terms, and which in turn symbolize the nature of ultimate Beings, and four biased forms of these which yield the cases where we have a symbolization of a standard of reality, of an orientating present, of causality, and of dependence, in which one term symbolizes the other as a measure, a locus, a being, or a nature. (The measure is a being and a nature as united together, and thus represents a Being, whereas the locus is being and nature as alternative, and thus allows us to take the present to be contemporary natures or contemporary beings.)

It is now possible to refine what is said in 4.06 of the *Modes of Being* with reference to testimony by a mode of Being with respect to God and other modes of Being. The supposed testimony is a feature which is either alongside, accompanies, structures, or is affiliated with, the mode of Being with which we start. One must not take for granted, as 4.06 does in *Modes of Being*, that we have testimony in the form of an affiliated feature, one that is predicable of the mode of Being, though owing its presence to the action of God. Depending on the status of the feature, we are forced to acknowledge distinctive types of relationship between the given Being and some other, and to acknowledge at the terminus of that relationship a Being appropriate to just that kind of relationship. Thus, if our Being is Actuality and it has a feature which is a structure of or for it, we are able to infer to the being of that structure, and via the bias which that structure has toward the other term, to infer to the Being of Ideality. The feature is a symbol of both the relation and the Being.

The argument of the *Modes of Being*, translated into the above account, is that an actuality has a feature which is a symbol of the relation between itself and the being in which it is resident, a symbol of the relation which it terminates, and a symbol of the other terminus, which defines the nature of the asymmetrical relation that the given feature terminates.

These considerations sharpen a difficulty. If God is the source of affiliations, we seem driven to say that an accident adheres in a substance by virtue of the action of God. The result is awkward, even if we depersonalize the idea of God and acknowledge only a delimited form of God as the source of the affiliation. The affiliation, after all, is only epistemic; the accident is a resultant of the actuality in which it inheres, as acted on by other actualities. Only when we detach the accident and ask about its bearing on an actuality does the question of affiliation arise. If we start with the actuality, the relation to the accident is one of conditioning, and we then have the accident in the position of a content for a structure. If we stand neutrally between the approaches of affiliation and structurali-zation, we get ordination and contemporaneity to which both the actual-ity and the accident are subject, the one though biased toward the unity of them as real, and the other allowing for a bias toward either as the locus of the present.

Since affiliation (and the others) is a symmetrical relation in its normative form, to speak of its being present when we start with accident is to seem to contradict oneself. But an affiliation of accident and actual-ity is a two-way affair, though it does not exist except so far as we have already detached the accident and asked after the way it fits with the ac-tuality.

In all cases, we start with distinct entities, but the symmetrical rela-tions that connect them mean that we take as our point of origin a unity, either one or the other entity, a rule or structure, or something dependent. The fact that we also have degenerate cases, where we have asymmetrical relations, should not be confused with the existence of a point of origin, which allows for symmetrical relations. In degenerate cases, we make the unity a standard, and take one of the items to be an orienting point, one of them to be a structure, and one of them to be an accident. (Though it is traditional to take qualities, etc., to be the accidents, it is possible to see the substance as an accident of the qualities, that which inheres in them, somewhat as the soul is thought to be sustained by the passing phases in Buddhism.)

A point of origin is merely a beginning. A standard involves a digni-fying of something, sometimes making it or taking it to be of superior worth or reality because of its explanatory value. A structure is no more important than the content which it orders. But a cause is explanatory of its effect, and a causal law is explanatory of the fact that its items are temporally related in an asymmetrical order.

May 2

I have been more than usually confused in connection with the discussion of structuralization and causation yesterday. It may be the case that the isolated or the residuum functions as a structure for the other as content. But this is only a special case of a situation in which the isolated and the residuum are related to one another by a structure, which can have the biased form of an asymmetrically formulated law of nature or causal law. The important point is that the relationship between the isolated and the residuum is a structure, a form, with both of them as the terms.

Should one of these terms be a structure for the other, it would have something like the role of a formal summary of the other, to which it would be formally related. In any case, the residuum and the isolated would both be symbols of the structure which links them, and this in turn would be a symbol for an Ideal Being in a limited form.

In all our cases, a man can take it upon himself to utilize the relation as a symbol, thereby intensifying the relation on the one hand and moving to its referent on the other. Affiliation can be assumed to be that which is to be intensified and spread by religion; contemporaneity can be seen to involve a force which is to be grasped by art and interplayed with in history; structure can be treated as an instance of a prescription which is to be taken as the object of obligation or the guide for legislation; coordination can be recognized to involve a relation whose insistent terminus controls the other three and has a direct effect on the residuum and the isolated as parts of the same universe of reality.

A man intensifies the relation of coordination by equating himself with others in action, or by privately assuming the position of the terminus of coordination, Actuality, as the perspective proper to knowledge. He intensifies the structural relation by embedding it in others through law-abiding activities, or by privately making himself the bearer of the terminus, Ideality. He intensifies contemporaneity by participating with others as members of a social group in an interplay with nature, or by creatively grasping the nature of a binding force in art. And he intensifies his affiliations by sharing in a liturgy or by privately reaching to the objective of a symbol.

On this approach, the emphasis on man is what leads one, via structuralization, to ask about evolution or other possible ways in which he might be related to preceding but different kinds of beings. The advisability of exhibiting the structure, and then as enriching the terms, will lead to a consideration of ethics. The acknowledgment of Actuality assures one that the realities acknowledged by science will be accorded the same reality as that attributed to man. (The existentialists and the reductionists agree in holding that men and things differ in reality, the one thinking that man has a reality to be denied to other entities, and the other thinking that ultimate particles have such primary reality.) The acknowledgement of affiliation allows one to distinguish between accident and essence, or the adventitious and the permanent. Finally, contemporaneity extensionally spreading over disparate items will—depending on what we take as our starting point—allow us to have presents of different magnitudes.

May 3

When we return with what had been isolated, we can humanize it, by taking ourselves to be the focal point. We thereupon become representatives of Actuality, offering a measure of what is real; representatives of Ideality, assuming the responsibility for the exhibition of structure; representatives of Existence, assuming the guise of masters of the brutal; or representatives of God, assuming the position of an affiliator or judge.

It is to be noted that we can function as such representatives only so far as the residuum and the isolated are part of the encountered world. We have testimony in that world for ultimate realities only by virtue of the kind of relation the items have to one another, and not because of the nature of the items. The nature of the items (properties or accidents in Aristotle's sense) tell us about the nature of that which is affecting the place or nature of the residuum or the isolated. When we come to the modes of Being, the testimony to the reality and presence of others is given not by the relation—though the relation must be there—as connecting what is essential to the Being and what is merely coordinate, accompanying, co-structured with, or affiliated with the Being, but is given by the feature related in one of these ways to the Being.

A factor related to an empirical item tells us about the nature of another such item; the relation of the factor to something else tells us about a reality beyond the factor and that something else. A factor related to a mode of Being tells us about the nature of another mode of Being, but it does so only because it is a factor, i.e., something not of the essence of the initial mode of Being, but related to it. The relation which the factor has to the mode of Being has been assumed by me in 4.06 of the *Modes of Being* to be one of ascription, affiliation, or predication, which is to say as though it were a relation which instantiates the nature of God. But that emphasis is due, I suggested recently, to the fact that we look at the Being and the factor from the perspective of the factor. Had we looked at it from the perspective of the Being, we would have seen the two to be in a relation of source and expression, thereby instancing the Ideal; had we taken them as coordinate, we would have taken them to be realities oriented toward Actuality; and had we taken them to be accompanying, we would have seen them to be governed by Existence and thereby made contemporary or coexistent.

When we come back, in a humanizing fashion, we have a biased form of the relation. Only when we take still another step, that of neutralization, where we see the residuum and the isolated to be governed by relations apart from our imposition, do we have the objectively real.

We begin, then, with acceptance, move on to isolation, then to examination, then to a humanistic return, and finally to an objective situation. From the humanistic, we move to a Being only so far as we are representatives, assuming the role of such a Being with respect to the residuum and the isolated. From the neutral position, we move to a Being once we recognize an element of compulsion in what is also essentially universal. What offers testimony is both universal and necessary. (Kant suggested that the universal or the necessary could be taken as evidence for the presence of the other, but this does not appear to be correct. There are universal occurrences—properties—which are not necessary, and there are necessities which concern limited situations or areas, such as the necessity exhibited in a law of nature pertaining to ultimate particles.)

When a man is a representative of Actuality, he can see other entities to be real by virtue of their common orientation in Actuality, and to be real in the very same sense he is; representing Ideality, he sees himself to embody and to insist on some structural ought to be; representing Existence, he sees himself to be existent and to be occupied with subjugating it as outside himself, either by creatively making something or by interplaying with it; representing God, he sees himself to be a locus of judgment and to be capable of judging, classifying, or in the more general case, of affiliating item with item. This, and the preceding stages, are usually prereflective. The neutralizing stage is also prereflective to some degree, but it is carried out only when one becomes aware that one is not at the only place where the relation can be said to begin. We must recognize that other entities could provide the standard for reality, could condition us, could define the present, or could provide a measure of affiliation or true judgment. Once we make this acknowledgment, we have achieved objectivity. The preceding stages can all, of course, be made the object of a reflective act, but we begin and go through them without knowing, to end with what is mainly humanistic, but is spotted here and there with what is objective, not in the sense that it is external or independent of us, but as offering a proper point for beginning or grounding the relations of coordination, etc.

May 4
(Roslyn)

When a man functions as a representative of a Being, he at once embodies a relation and imposes this on others. He therefore does epistemically what the Being does ontologically. To accept the result of his imposition as objective is to permit him to be in a relation to the residuum and isolated together, similar to that which they have to one another.

His functionings as a representative or as a unit in a relation to the residuum and content are properly to be understood within larger contexts. There are in fact four basic stages, and each one of these has five parts. The four stages are experience, isolation, examination, and return. Inside each there are the stages of acceptance, compulsion, use of standards, humanization, and neutrality. Experience begins with acceptance and ends with compulsion; isolation ends with standards; examination ends with humanization; return ends with acceptance of the content other than the individual as having a value of its own, deserving to be treated in its own terms, so that in effect it is a move to neutralization.

That which we accept on our return is treated initially from the perspective of affiliation, proceeds to structures, then to coordination, to end with contemporaneity. Or is it more correct to say that we start with coordination, move to structure and contemporaneity, and end with affiliation? Also, there should be four distinctions of this sort made when we humanize. In fact we should say something similar with reference to the other stages of acceptance, compulsion, and standards. That is, it is not enough to remark that experience, for example, begins with acceptance; the acceptance itself will be an acceptance which presupposes that we are in a condition of affiliation, structuralization, coordination, or contemporaneity with respect to the experienced content. But now we seem to be on the road to an infinite regress.

May 5
(Roslyn)

There are four stages: experience, isolation, examination, and return. Each of these stages has four phases: acceptance, compulsion, evaluation, and unification. Each of the stages begins with a different one of these, and ends with that with which the next begins. Experience begins with evaluation and ends with compulsion; isolation begins with compulsion and ends with acceptance; examination begins with acceptance and ends with unification; return begins with unification and ends with evaluation. (I am not confident of the sequence, nor of just how a given stage begins and ends.) At the end, when we return, we go through the four stages to end with a phase where different types of relation are distinguished.

Whether or not the last stage of a return, with its neutralization and

distinction of the four kinds of relation, illustrates the phase of acceptance or evaluation is perhaps unimportant. The important consideration
is that the last stage gives us a set of entities which permit the symbolization of ultimate realities.

At the first stage are not all the phases and the various kinds of relations merged? Is not the progress to the last stage a progress of a distinction of phases and of a distinction of relations at the same time? Why is
it that we initially begin with a stage where there is a lack of distinction
in phase and in the relations which in fact connect entities? Is it not that
we cannot distinguish the phases or the relations until we have in fact
been forced away from a merging, then forced ourselves to examine, and
then been forced to return to the residuum from which we have separated ourselves? The stage of immediacy of ourselves and anything else
is also the phase where nothing is distinguished in either.

Are we not forced away, made to examine, and made to return, by
virtue of some operation of the finalities? Is it not true that we are in immediacy only so far as we are subject to some other power? If so, this
fact is to be discovered only at the end, when we have succeeded in distinguishing different ultimate Beings.

Immediacy has all affiliated items, but without appreciation for what
they are; compelled to move away from this immediacy, we find that the
isolated is coordinate with a residuum and has coordinate items in it;
forced to examine the isolated, because of the knots and eddies in it, we
discover that the various parts accompany one another in various ways;
forced to return to the residuum because of the incompleteness of the isolated and the intrusion of the residuum, we discover that they are linked
by a structure oriented in ourselves. The insistence on the rights of other
entities by themselves, or by us on reflecting on their presence, makes us
attend to their appropriate affiliations, and therefore to the various kinds
of objective relations which connect isolates with residuum, and the items
in each with one another. (This too is not altogether right. It is the result
of my mixing, without sufficient check, systematic considerations with
some grasp of the different stages. In the back of my mind is the thought
that whatever occurs is governed by the operation of the finalities at
which we finally arrive—a position which is characteristic of both Plato
and Hegel.)

On this account, knowledge begins with a blurred form of what is
real. Were we to begin with the real, we would eventually have to find a
ground for knowledge. Knowledge would offer a special form of the relation which entities have to one another, and the ontological situation

would be characterizable as a blurred form, or rather an incomplete form of the ontological situation. I am now repeating something of the argument of *Reality*.

Does it make sense, and is there any justification for the statement, that the development of an ontology is governed by the movement to the position where knowledge will be achieved? Such a view means that reality governs the progress of knowledge, and that truth or true knowledge guides the structure of an ontology and perhaps its historic understanding. The real world would seem then to produce or contain a being, man, who is in a state where he moves to the position of knowing that reality. The reality that he knows is a reality which made it possible for him to know it. Is reality incomplete unless and until it contains a part of itself which knows the whole? Is reality then in a process of self-awareness? Conversely, is knowledge a process of objectification or externalization, the making of what is blurred or formal have a reality, and therefore to be transformed into objective, distinct realities?

To answer these questions in the affirmative is to take reality to be engaged in a process of coming to know itself via man, and for knowledge to be engaged in a process of localizing itself in a real world. My present concern is with the former. Why should reality be incomplete and be pressing toward self-awareness to be achieved through the necessary or even accidental presence of a man? These questions are rightly directed against a Hegel. I need not be bothered by them. All that the present discussion seems to require is that we affirm, once we have man, that the process of his knowing moves toward reality, and does this because he is subject to a control or guidance by that reality. The explanation of this fact might lie in the peculiar nature of man, who is at once a reality and not only knows but becomes perfected through knowing.

Is man a being whose progress in knowledge is pulled by his being, which in turn is affected by the total reality of which his being is a part? The energy for knowledge should have its source in man's being, even though this energy is utilized in the knowledge process in accord with the demands of knowledge. Is it perhaps his distinctive being which is behind the compulsion to hold away something out of the totality of experience? Some of the content does pull him along and force him to isolate it from the rest, but does this not occur only because he already is a distinctive being who stands away from some of the content, even while he is epistemically merged with it as an experiencing being? He is a distinctive being who can be forced to have a special relation to some of the items with which he was involved in his experiencing.

Man can be said to be involved in a constant effort to achieve an equilibrium between himself as an experiencing or thinking being and himself as a particular actuality. The first develops under the pressure of the second; the second grows to make it possible for him to be a knowing being, only because there is some discrepancy between himself as a being and the truth of that being. What is this discrepancy? It was suggested before that this discrepancy is between what he is and his self-awareness. A being needs to possess the truth of itself, in order fully to be. This result, taken cosmically, is Hegelian; keyed to the individual, it comes closer to Socrates and Kierkegaard.

May 6

There seem to be two senses of "ought." There is the "ought" which obligates, and which, if not realized, marks someone as guilty. This "ought" is realized somewhere, somehow; otherwise a real possibility would be precluded from realization and would just so far not be a possibility to be realized. "Ought" also stands for an ideal state of affairs; its non-realization marks something as defective. This defectiveness need not be made good. The defective being will be under tension, and will be in disequilibrium so long as it does not reach the ideal, but it may never do this. The ideal, as that which might conceivably not be realized, will be only a logical possibility, a conceivable state of affairs that may provoke the action which promotes its realization, but which is accepted and pursued, without obligating.

A guilty man is defective, but a defective being need not be guilty. A guilty man faces an ideal as that which obligates, but other entities face an ideal as definitory of their own perfectibility. Hegel supposes that the two kinds of ideal are one, and that in fact whatever ideally ought to be in fact is.

The various stages through which we go from immersion to return are prompted by and terminate in Beings. The Beings can be said to produce the movement of their own acknowledgment. Being then is a voyage toward self-awareness. This is mediated by man, but that man is only a contingent product of the restlessness of Being. Being is restless just so far as it is not self-aware, and when fortunate, arrives at the production of man who is able by his process of knowing to grasp Being as fourfold.

There is a similar movement in the objectification of knowledge. The restlessness of any item of knowledge is due to the fact that a man is not yet properly part of the total reality. His attempt to become part of that reality, by defining himself in contradistinction to the rest and then finding how he is to be related to it so as to do justice to himself and it, begins with his possession of some item of knowledge. He may remain with this forever, but if he persists in his reflection, he discovers that its completion in the end must mean the transforming of what is known into the form of what in fact occurs. The tension toward being a form for what is real makes a man make himself more and more an integral part of the real.

This second move seems less plausible than the first.

May 9

I have been trying to see if there is not an ontological force behind epistemological movements, and a cognitive drive behind ontological processes. So far there have been only blind stabs in the dark. Here is another try:

Actualities are each seeking self-completion. The achievement would place them in a position of dominance with respect to the rest. The ideal result would be one in which an actuality that was self-complete was not dominant over the others. This could be accomplished by an actuality making itself the representative of all of them by assuming on their behalf the meaning which would complete them. This is accomplished by a knowing of ultimate Beings in the shape of conditions that govern the actualities and their connections one with the other.

Beings affect the world of actualities in different degrees. They are universal, but not uniform, in their effectiveness. They would become uniform if there were some actuality to operate on their behalf, to take upon itself the role of dealing with the particulars in their particularity, but in the light of the meaning of the Beings. This is achieved when a man detaches himself from the humanistic return to experience and allows himself to be one who returns the examined material to make it subject to a relation known to symbolize the Beings.

There are then two movements, and both make use of man and his knowing. The first is a movement in the world of actualities. It fortuitously comes to its ideal end when a man adopts the position of a knower who represents the ultimate conditions binding on all. The second is a movement of Beings. This fortuitously comes to its ideal end when a man sees what he knows to be the very structure controlling whatever is, including himself.

The first movement is an ontological one, with knowledge as an instrumental agency. From the perspective of the world of actualities, the second movement is an epistemological one, since the Beings involved are considered only so far as they come within the purview of a cognizing man. But we could reverse this interpretation also, and see the first movement as epistemological, making use of the activity of actualities to get to the epistemological result of a representative cognition, and see the second movement as ontological, making use of man's cognition to get to the position where the Beings are taken as uniformly conditioning all actualities, despite their different resistances.

Both ultimate realities and actualities are Beings. Each deals with the other from its own perspective, as instancing it in some way. It recovers something of the objectivity and independence of the other when it deals with it as an autonomous epistemological domain, for then, while still in some sense an instance of the reality or actuality, it has a rationale and intelligibility, and therefore a career of its own. Should we take one of these, the ultimate realities or actualities, to be our initial base, the other will be seen to have an epistemological role. It can be freed from this role only by taking it seriously, giving it full weight as an independent domain. It will then appear to be ontological in character, requiring the other kind of reality to function in an epistemological way.

Actualities need completion, but are best served when this is achieved without dominance. Beings need uniformity, but this is most properly achieved when it does not affect the independence of the actualities from the Beings or from one another. Men, by representing actualities, are completed, but do not dominate; men, by representing Beings, see all actualities including themselves to be under the aegis of uniform conditions, i.e., of Beings in the guise of relationships where each actuality is allowed to be itself.

May 10

Once again: Actualities are subject to conditions, of which the laws of nature are only some. A world of actualities would be at its best if each of the actualities actually possessed the conditions which control it and others. So far only some men have achieved this state, and then by adopting, through knowledge, the conditions which govern them and other realities. The knowledge of conditions is one of the achievements of actualities. If every actuality could have that knowledge, the world of actuality would be made up of entities which intellectually mastered the very conditions that master them.

On the other hand, Beings deal with actualities as instances of themselves, but find that those actualities are not entirely amenable to this role. They are instances which do not function as instances, having their own careers. Beings would be most effective if every actuality were to make itself an instance of those Beings. This would require them to function as representatives of those Beings.

The drive in actualities is to master what conditions all of them; the success of Beings is to be found in the adoption of representative actualities. The actualities use man and knowledge as a device by which the conditions can, despite their universality, be made ingredient in an actuality; the Beings are ennobled by man allowing himself to be a full instance of the Beings. The acknowledgment that there are relations governing the residuum and the isolated, and that man is one of the terms in such a relation who nevertheless knows it, means that he is a knower who encompasses what relates him as a term, and is a reality who functions as an actuality, but in such a way as to be in consonance with the demands of the relation.

If we start with actualities as beings, we can see man as a knower who is a full reality by virtue of containing in his knowledge what conditions him, and thereby indirectly all other actualities. If we start with Actuality or with some subordinate Being, we can see man as an actuality who allows the Being to be fulfilled. This is done by his functioning as an actuality who represents the Being. The knowing in the one case carries out the need to control what conditions, and the knowing in the other case carries out the need to function in accord with universal principles or conditions.

If we think of Beings as primarily meaningful, i.e., as through and through intelligible, we will see man to make the being of himself as an actuality be nothing more than a carrier of the meaning; if we think of Beings as primarily realities, we will see man make his own reality represent it. If we think of actualities as primarily conditioned realities, we will see man as a reality who makes those laws into his substance, subordinating them within himself as an actuality which is more than a meaning.

May 18

What does an entity gain by having qualities? What do the qualities gain by being in the entity?

These questions suppose that we have the entity and the quality apart from one another, if not in fact, at least in thought, and that we try to see what happens when they are brought together. From the perspective of the quality, two things occur: the quality is coordinated with the entity, and it is swallowed up into it. The first of these allows the quality to benefit from the copresent power of the entity, to be that which can crowd out a place for itself in space and time; the second of these allows the quality to benefit from the activity of the entity, to be in the places and involved in the situations which the entity is in.

From the standpoint of the entity, the quality is in a relation of intelligible consonance with it and in the relation of accompanying it. In the first of these ways, the entity gains a position in the realm of experience and observation from the quality, and in the second becomes, with the quality, subject to some power that keeps them abreast and thereby allows the entity to benefit from the way in which the quality is related to neighboring qualities. Though we have here a connection of accompanying which is symmetrical, it is operative and knowable, apparently, only from the perspective of the entity itself.

There are analogous relations and benefits to be found in the union of majority and minority, white and black, and similar cases. In these, the separated items achieve power and effectiveness from what is left behind, and that which is left behind achieves orientation and rational, experiential meaning from the separated. From being integrated with the white majority, a black minority can be said to gain the power of the latter just through being coordinate with it, and this while retaining its own identity; at the same time, it gains effectiveness by allowing itself to be carried by that majority. The majority, on the other hand, can benefit by seeing itself and the minority to be subject to a rule of law, and also to a brute force which has both of them in its dynamic grip.

May 20

The treatment of qualities in relation to a residual object, as benefiting the quality by having it acquire power and effectiveness by being coordinate with and merging with the residuum, expresses a situation relative to an observer. The converse, the benefiting of the residuum by the quality also expresses a result relative to an observer. Here we should say that the residuum benefits from the rational evidence which the quality provides regarding the nature of the residuum, and from the brute presence and identification which it allows an observer to acknowledge.

If we desire to deal only with a neutral situation, we cannot avoid a symmetrical reference to the residuum and the quality. We would then have to say that they are related as coordinately real and oriented in Actuality, as terms in some basic rational whole, as accompaniments of one another in a dynamic world, and as synthesized in a new totality.

From the perspective of the observer, we can say that a quality provides the residuum (which could conceivably be a scientific object) with evidential material, from which an observer could rationally move to an understanding of that object, and that the quality also defines a present and a boundary in terms of which we can locate the residuum. When we view the matter neutrally, we can give preferential status to neither the residuum nor the quality. The two of them together must be understood to be termini whose natures and careers are to be understood in terms of relations which instance ultimate realities. They are equally real and final as coordinate; they are evidences of one another in a rational scheme as instancing an Ideal; they are coordinate in an extensive, dynamic realm only so far as they are subject to a cosmic force; and they merge one into the other to constitute a new synthetic unity only so far as this is itself but an instance of God.

To the question, What is God like? the proper answer is that He is not like that, i.e., He is not to be compared with some familiar object.

The untrustworthy do not trust; they know how unreliable a man can be.

Familiarity breeds contempt in the contemptible.

It was Freud's superego that invented the id.

There's no right to *civil* disobedience, but there is a right to question what the state does, by one who stands apart from the state. To question laws by remaining within the scope of law, even while expressing a willingness to accept the law's penalties, is to do civil wrong. The violation of a law, if it is not to be a legal maneuver, must be a consequence of the pursuit of another good, in terms of which the entire idea of the state is put into jeopardy.

We violate a law either inside a law-abiding state or outside it; as the former, we merely carry out the practice of lawyers, for it is their task to challenge the statutes, to test the laws, to determine the boundaries of what is permitted and forbidden. He who robs a bank challenges in his act what his lawyer will challenge in argument. He who civilly disobeys does outside the court what the lawyer does in the court, except that the former appeals to his conscience and presumably is acting on behalf of the good of others. But then he is hard to distinguish from a Robin Hood. The right opposition to the law is achieved by ignoring the law and following out some other norm, not by remaining within the orbit of the law and questioning this or that provision because it does not accord with one's belief or conscience, or even with some ideal or position achieved from another perspective.

When a man assumes another perspective and finds that one consequence is an act which goes counter to an established law, he should be seen not to challenge that law, any more than that law is seen to challenge him. Two systems are now in conflict, and are to be adjudicated not by either one, but by some third which will appeal to history or revelation or divine commands or eternal truths to determine just which one (and to what degree) is right.

A good deal of discussion, particularly on social questions, fails to have meaningful confrontations, in part because *conditions* are confused with *causes*. A condition encompasses an entire field, making it have a distinctive tone; a cause is one of the operative factors inside the field. The Civil War has any number of causes, from the growth of industrialism in the North, the cotton gin, the desire for independence on the part of the southern states, and so on. But the pervading condition was that of slavery. Though Lincoln's Emancipation Proclamation came late and as a special measure, and though he would have retained slavery if he could have saved the union, it is nevertheless true that the atmosphere of the country was radically qualified by the fact of slavery.

I suppose it is something like conditions that Page Smith had in mind when he said that the historians present at major engagements usually assess it correctly. Those historians obviously miss many of the causes; some of the causes are hidden in as yet unpublished documents. But what the historians need not miss is the pervading temper, the characteristic and distinctive conditions that prevail at the time.

How are those conditions discovered? Is it these conditions which the advocates of "Verstehen" have in mind, and therefore which are impervious to the criticisms directed at the formulation of causes?

The conditions are discovered, I think, by noting the way in which the various parts of the field hang together, how they relate to one another, how they cluster, how they separate, how they function, and how they contrast with similar parts in other fields. The discovery does require a Verstehen, but this does not leave the rest of the historic investigation to a pursuit of causes, if these be understood to be causes in the sense in which physicists use the term. Causes in history are different from physical causes. They differ in nature, power, rhythm, time, etc. (as I have tried to make out in the book on history).

June 2

If an entity is nothing apart from a relation or context, we seem to have nothing that is there to be related, or in the context. But if it is something apart from a context, how could we know it, since cognition itself involves a relating, a contexting of the item?

The only escape from this difficulty that I can envisage is to recognize that it is the entity as embedded in one context, and thus as in relations to other entities, which is the entity that is to be related in another context and by another relation. When the entity is related in the new way, it becomes detached from the context in which it had been. It offers itself to be newly related only so far as it is in fact related in another way, but it is in fact related in another way only so far as it is separated from that old context. The old context and the new must be different in type. It is not as father of my children that I am able to sit at the typewriter, but it is as father of my children that I am able to be oriented in Actuality, or to be occupied with an ideal good.

All relations in one kind of context are internal, but an entity as involved in these internal relations is now "externally" related to, i.e., separated from, detached from, entities in a different kind of context. To have it actually related to these entities is to have it internally related to them, and this requires that it be separated from the entities with which it was previously internally related.

We have here another demonstration of the need to take account both of an empirical world of particulars and of a transcendent reality. It is only because the particulars can be internally related to the transcendent reality that they can be said to have a being apart from the relational role they have in the empirical world. We have here, therefore, also a demonstration of the need to recognize the reality of an empirical world. We should not allow this to be dealt with as a mere appearance or as a neoplatonic adjective to an ultimate reality. It is only because particulars can be related to one another that they can be said to be internally related to a transcendent reality, and thus be entities which (by virtue of their interconnection with the other particulars) are able to have a reality distinct from the transcendent with which they are internally related. And we have here a demonstration, too, of the need to recognize more than one transcendent, for it is only so far as a transcendent can be internally related to other transcendents that it can be said to be externally related to a particular, and thus be something real apart from that particular.

Were I, as father of my children, internally related to my typewriter, say by a relation of sitting before it, I would be nothing more than the convergent unit for the relations uniting me with my children and with my typewriter. But I have a reality apart from these. Instead of this reality being a mysterious I-know-not-what, it is an intelligible relational state of being internally connected with a transcendent reality.

It is I, as an actuality, who has a being that is related to typewriter and children, but as so related I no longer have a being. I have a being—where this is understood to require a relating to a final Being—only so far as I am not internally related to typewriter and children. But now I but open up another paradox, for what I seem to be saying is that I have a being only so far as I have nothing to do with any other particular, and that I am related to other particulars only so far as I do not have a being. But this difficulty is only verbal. The being which I have is spent in serving as a term in the relations to other particulars; in that sense I have a being when I am related to them. But I am merely a being only so far as I am internally related to Being, i.e., to a final reality, Actuality. The reality I have as a particular, I spend serving as a term in an internal relation to Actuality; in that sense I am a particular in relation to an ultimate mode of Being.

As in one kind of relation, I am not in the other, but this does not mean that I shift my position from moment to moment, but only that the search for the entity which can enter into a certain kind of relation but gives us a side of it as in another kind of relation. A particular (and a transcendent, of course, as well) is at once in two kinds of relation. As that which has a role in one kind of relation, it is able to have a different role in another kind of relation.

June 3

Yesterday's discussions have a bearing, I think, on some of the issues connected with minorities, and particularly on those relating to the militant blacks today. It has been remarked that a number of the leaders of the militant blacks speak in one way to fellow blacks and in another to the whites. To the former they are belligerent, incendiary, exhortatory in tone; to the latter they are mild, conciliatory, reasonable, and friendly.

It is easy to speak of them as hypocrites, but it is perhaps more accurate to see hypocrites to be specializing and distorting—which is not true of some of these leaders—a proper shift in attitude which should characterize men as they move out of one context into a radically different one.

The black leader is one among the blacks. He is a leader because he stands away from the rest, and enters into some kind of representative role in relation to the whites. (The rest of the blacks can have only an indirect relation to the whites, a relation which may be distortive.) When speaking to the blacks, he is part of a context with them; he treats himself and them as parts of a minority which is to confront the whites. The whites they are to confront are mediated by the leader. He is in relation to the rest of the blacks as one who is able to be related to them. He is able to be related to them because he is in fact in a relation to the whites. Conversely, he is in relation to the whites as one who is able to be so related, and he was able to be so related because he is in fact in a relation to the rest of the blacks. The being he has in himself, as in relation to the other blacks, is the being of himself as one who could be related to the whites; the being he has in himself, as in relation to the whites, is the being of himself as one who could be related to the blacks.

The being of the entity in a given context represents itself as related in another context. To represent itself as related in another context is but to have as its local essence the nature that it has by virtue of the relation to other entities in that other context. The black who represents other blacks to the whites not only is actually in a context with those other blacks, but functions as a unit who expresses what the black nature is like.

It is desirable for the members of a minority group to recognize that they belong together. In this way they do not deceive themselves into believing that they belong to some other group, or that they do not share in the advantages and disabilities of being part of that minority. But they ought not to treat themselves as though they were only this, for they then treat themselves as though they were only terms in a relation, beings in a context, without individuality and reality of their own. They will then inevitably distort the kind of relation they ideally should have with the majority. Instead, they should epitomize the entire context (in which they as minority members are a part). They should have in their being the very nature which they accrete by virtue of their place in the context. They should see themselves as concretionalizations of the very natures they have as terms in the context of being a member of a minority. But this requires that they in fact then function as members of a different context—in the situation now being examined, as members of a context in which they are together with the members of the majority.

The minority and majority function in this analysis somewhat as particulars and beings did in yesterday's discussion. But today I have said much more clearly that the being which an entity has by itself is nothing other than the nature which it accretes by virtue of its place in a context in which every item is internally related to every other, and that this being is had only so far as the entity is in fact part of another context—and conversely, that the entity is part of another context only so far as its being consists in its possession, as a unit, of the very nature which it owes to the presence of other entities.

In each context, each entity has a nature which is to be understood to be a function of the presence of the other entities. But every one of these entities can offer a presence to the rest and be affected by the rest only so far as it is. But this which it is, is not different from itself as related, except that it is made into material to be relationally determined in a different context. The thing-in-itself is then the thing in relation, but freed from the other items in that relation. It is the thing as possessed only of relational characters which are substantialized there by virtue of a reference to the other entities which dictate the nature of the characters.

An entity evidently then has a relational character in two guises. It has it as in an internal relation, and it has it in an external relation. The former requires the entity to be in an external relation to something else (when the entity has a different relational character), and the latter requires it to refer to the entities with which it in fact is in internal relation. The entity as *having* relational character X is the entity as identical with a relational character Y, but freed from other entities (of a different kind) in fact, and therefore merely referring to them as termini for its meaning, Y. The entity, as relational character X, is the entity as in an internal relation to others of the same kind.

An entity is its relational character; there is nothing more to it in that context. Yet the entity is not the relational character which has a place in a certain context. These apparently opposite statements are reconciled by recognizing that in a context there are nothing but terms, each of which is only as internally related to all the other terms, and no one of which has any being of its own, and therefore no nature of its own distinct from what it is as a relationally determined term. And by recognizing, in addition, that the being which it offers to be internally determined is some other relational position in some other context. A term as in one context has no reality of its own. It has a reality, and thus is more than a mere term, only so far as it refers to the rest of the context, and is therefore involved with others which are the termini of a reference rather than coordinate terms. It is as referring to the rest of the context that the term is a being, and it is as such a being that it is now able to be part of another context. As part of that other context, it becomes a different term, with itself in the guise of the initial term functioning as the being or material for this new term.

It is a black who is related to blacks, but it is a black *man* who is able to be related to whites; it is a black who is related to whites, but it is a *spokesman* for blacks who is able to be related to the rest of the blacks.

A simpler way of saying all this would be to state that the terms in one context are the material for the terms in another. The material is qualified by the presence of the other items in the other context, to produce a new term. We have then at least two associated terms, each serving as the material for the other, and each constituted of that material as affected by other items in a context other than that from which the material was obtained. But the reality of the individual must not be overlooked. The term as material is the term in only a referential relation to the items with which it had been in fact related as mere term. A term must, in short, be understood to be detachable from the very items and context which made it be the term that it is.

A term then evidently has two roles—a referential and an actual relational one to whatever items constitute a particular context with it. It is a self-transcendent entity which has a referential involvement with other entities only so far as it has an actual involvement with them, and conversely.

Why not stop at the last statement? Why go on and say that as having a referential involvement with other entities, it is material for an actual involvement with another set of items? Is it not because *1*] it cannot have an actual involvement unless it provides material for this; and *2*] some account of how it could have a referential involvement must be provided, requiring us to take account of a different actual involvement?

To *1* it might be replied that it is as having a referential involvement that it is material for an actual involvement, and to *2*, that a referential involvement is but an analytic result. But to this it can be answered that a referential involvement which served as material for an actual involvement would be nothing more than a potential term, which already possessed in potentiality all that it was to have in fact, and that an analytic result would still not tell us how something could ever enter into a relation.

An idealist would persist in the argument and say that we have nothing but an actual involvement in one context, and that any consideration of a referential involvement was the result of an act of abstraction and the conversion of what is real into what is at least relatively unreal. But how and by whom such an abstraction can be produced is inexplicable on this view.

This position can be connected with Berkeley's. He took the real to consist of qualities which had no being outside of the relation of perception. In order to account for the reality of the qualities apart from human observation, he treated those qualities as being in a relation to God. The relation to God was different from the relation to man, and the qualities consequently were different (though he does not make a point about this), depending on whether they were passively related to men or were actively expressed by God. We need not, however, restrict ourselves to qualities, the relation of perception, or the Being of God. As a consequence, we can say that it is I, a father, who is real, and I, a reality, who is a father. If we now go on to distinguish different kinds of qualities, say the usual primary from the usual secondary, we can also say that it is I, 5′6″, who is white, and I, white, who is 5′6″. The "I" in these cases has only a verbal value, expressing the fact that the appositive expression, 5′6″ or "white," is substantival, a material for the white or the 5′6″ respectively. The latter are secondary and primary qualities, involving a relation to something else.

June 4

Each feature, whether it be a secondary or a primary quality, or something else, is faced as that to which one has private access, and as that to which others have access as well. But what we know is also known as an object, i.e., as that which has being apart from its relation to an observer, or knower, or a group of them. We know an object, which is to say we know that to which we and others have access, as material for a feature which is related to another kind of reality, in another kind of context.

But is not knowledge of an object a way of relating it to us, so that it becomes part of a context with us? Does this not reduce the object to a particular kind of feature which contrasts with the features to which we had access, only as a primary quality differs from a secondary? The answer is in the negative, once we understand the question as asking if the object is in the same kind of relation to us as the perceived qualities are. The features which are the object are symbols of that to which those features are related, and we in apprehending those symbols make ourselves part of the symbols. For us to know an object is for us to function symbolically, to be attenuated versions of the object, which itself is an attenuated version of the reality with which it is related.

This conclusion seems to make the object a function of that to which it is related, and neglects the fact that there is material on which the reality will work so as to constitute the object. Just as a magnitude—in contrast with a size which is a primary quality having a meaning only in relation to some other size—is a secondary quality functioning as material for the size, and just as a "feel"—in contrast with the secondary quality such as white which has a meaning only in contrast with some other secondary quality—is a primary quality functioning as material for the quality, so a particular as constituted by the context of particulars is the material for the feature which is the object as related to an ultimate reality. Similarly, the object as constituted by the relation that connects it and an ultimate reality is material for the qualities which are produced by virtue of the presence of other items in the context of particulars. The object is an attenuated version of an ultimate being, but the attenuation is to be accounted for. And that accounting is provided by taking into consideration the fact that the object has the role of symbol only because it is distinct from that which it symbolizes, and it is able to be so distinct because its material is provided by the context of particulars.

Our own qualities symbolize us, but the qualities we perceive do not, except in the sense of evidencing our presence and power to do something to the material we confront. The objects we know symbolize ultimate realities, and enable us to be such symbols too by virtue of our transcendence of the perceived qualities. We can say, if we like, that our relation to the symbols makes those symbols into relational items similar in nature to the perceived qualities to which we have private access or to which we and others can have access. But we will then overlook the fact that the qualities are related to us as used and user, known and knower, whereas the symbols, i.e., the objects, are related to us as the less to the more attenuated, the limit to the center.

I have now tried to deal with the question of perception and knowledge without invoking a substratum, a surd, an I-know-not-what, a thing-in-itself beyond all understanding. But have I succeeded? Have I not brought in the idea of a "material"; have I not spoken of a context which is distinct from any of the items in it, or which perhaps does not allow for any items to be in it except as arbitrarily demarcated positions in it? The material, however, is not something surd; it is the perceived or known as that which is qualified by new kinds of entities. The positions in the context all have the guise of material, i.e., are features which are not constituted by that context.

June 6

The philosopher feels two goads: "Get back to the beginning"; "Get to the end." The tension that results is expressed in a system.

The Platonist tends to emphasize the beginning; the Aristotelian tends to emphasize the end. We bridge the two in a dynamic system which, unlike Hegel's, is not itself the end, but which makes the beginning relevant to the end.

There is something forbidding about absolute purity. Is that perhaps why one must approach God through a religious institution?

June 17

Let us name some horses:

        Bastard: out of Wedlock
        Bankrupt: out of Business
        Ankle Hemline: out of Fashion
        Interruption: out of Order
        Metaphysics: out of In
        Alienated: out of It
        Types: out of Sorts
        Injury: out of Spite
        Out: of Damned Spot
        Outer: out of Out

June 18

What is real? An easy and not a bad answer is that it is whatever is not a fiction, not an illusion, not a word, or not a contradiction. But does this mean that what I believe, imagine, remember, are real? Does it mean that there is no reality to the fiction, illusion, or word? Does it deny the reality of what may not be subject to the law of contradiction —the vague? Does it allow reality to past entities, or to future possible ones? No one of these questions has a clear answer in the above negative formulation of what is real.

A fiction is something; it is real, but the fictive entity portrayed in the fiction is not real. The fictive entity is constituted by a mind; so is what I believe, imagine, my illusions, and my words. The real is that which is not constituted by me. This would seem to imply that the solipsist confronts what is not real. It also would seem to imply that a Fichtean non-ego is not real. What does it have to say to a Kantianism, particularly one which was so expressed as to make the categories be expressions of an individual mind? It would say to it, I think, that since there are data, and since the categories, when imposed on the data, are transformed (in the sense at least of being united with the data to constitute a new entity), the new entity is real, even though we contribute a vital component to that entity.

But suppose one were to pursue such reasoning in connection with fictions. Are not fictions also in part only constituted by us; do they not work over data in the form of ideas, contents, memories, etc., which are then subjected to a conditioning by us to produce a new entity? They are, but the data here are mental in nature. Consequently what is to be said is that a real entity, even if partly produced through the act of our minds, is one which has a dimension that is not constituted by our minds.

Is a nightmare entirely constituted by our minds? Is the remembered? Is the predicted? Is the possible? Are all these real? I think we must say of all of these that just so far as they have a component which is not of our making, they are real. We do the remembering, but our remembering may be inaccurate precisely because it obscures or distorts the nature of the component which is not constituted by us. To be sure, we remember only what is in our minds, but what is in our minds is not, as remembered, constituted by us now. We may remember some fiction which we had once conceived; when it was conceived, the fiction was not real. But it is now a fact that we once had a fiction in mind; when we remember that fiction, the fiction is a datum for our act of remembering, and is so far not constituted by us now.

We make predictions, but the predictions are the outcome of an inference subject to rules or laws which are not constituted by us, and therefore yield outcomes which are so far not constituted by us. And if there are real possibilities, as I think there are, then when we envisage these, we but face that which has a reality apart from us, though, of course, not known except so far as we attend to them.

To speak as though what made something real was a content on which we imposed categories is to generalize from some limited cases. In most cases in fact, what we have are objects, substances, events, which we eventually acknowledge by our minds, without in any way constituting them by means of our minds.

June 19

Perception involves a judgment, and therefore is able to be veridical or not. The judgment articulates what is confronted, breaking it up into a location, a nature, and an adumbrated being. Since these are derived from the confronted, and since they are objectively there in an intensified form in which their distinctness is overcome, evidently the elements of a perception are symbols of what is perceived. And the entire judgment—since it purports to give us the object, though as first divided before it is unified (where the object is instead unitary before it is divided by us in perception)—is a symbol of the unitary object.

Symbols, then, are not merely for referring to Beings of which they are attenuated forms; they are capable of being used in connection with what we encounter in daily life. The words we use to express a judgment about these (and its components) are of course only signs, having none but a conventional association with the perceptual judgment or its object.

A philosophic system makes use of symbols, each of which is an attenuation of a mode of Being or some derivative from this. An entire philosophic system unites a multiplicity of symbols to constitute a single articulation of what is ultimately real. It therefore corresponds to a perceptual judgment. Both the system as a unit and the component symbols in it are attenuations of that to which they refer, the unit answering to the unitary Being or Beings that transcend the empirical, and the component symbols answering to distinctions which we have made in the Being or Beings.

There is a difference, however, between the kinds of symbols we use in perception and the kind we use in metaphysics. In our use of the former, since we are practical men, we are guided by our interests, subject of course to limits imposed by the confronted. In our use of the latter, though, we are involved with what is not practical; our distinctions will either be arbitrary or they will be determined by the object of our symbols. If we have no insight into or "intuition" of Being (as Maritain calls it), the distinctions must be arbitrary.

What is an "intuition of Being"? According to Maritain, it involves some special faculty, obscured normally in the course of our daily living. I think he is right, but the view does seem as if it were created ad hoc in order to get one to the place one would like to arrive. But if we allow that we do have some grasp of transcending Beings as having a bearing on what is going on here and now, we can attain the intuition by the intellectual effort of trying to see what such Beings would be in themselves, as detached from their involvement with what is going on here and now. Such an effort will involve the use of a distinctive way of knowing, but it will not be a way which is either unfamiliar or very difficult to pursue. All of us in our daily commerce constantly separate objects from their relation to us, and thus come to know them as they are apart from us. The separation from the relation to us is most readily achieved by seeing that what we are related to is carried by the rest of the object—or if one likes, by its "matter," by experience, by a context in which we too are. When we refer to the ultimate modes of Being, there is, however, no matter or experience to which we can refer the relational meaning of the Beings, and thereby find what the Beings are in themselves. But there is a context: each Being is related to other Beings. It is the acknowledgment that there are other Beings which are related to the given one that allows us to free the given one from its involvement with us and to allow us to have an intuition of it as apart from us.

June 20

When we subtract from a feature that aspect of it which is due to the presence of some entity other than that in which the feature inheres, we seem to be left with nothing other than the entity, with a nuance which has no being or nature apart from the entity. On such a view, we have only the entity as a single unit, and certain nuances stressed and isolated through the action or presence of other entities.

This way of looking at entities has the advantage of freeing us from the Aristotelian substance-accident distinction, and of not requiring us to make reference to a power which is to unite the entity and its features. But it has the disadvantage of treating the entity as though it were isolated; everything about it that was due to its relations with others would be really impertinent to it. This in effect denies that it is a part of a context with others just as surely as it is outside that context. Though an entity has features which it owes to others, at least in part, those features, even as determined by those others, are *its* features, and tell us about it. Such a conclusion drives us to acknowledge something besides the features and the entity. What could this be?

If we view the entity, as contrasting with its features, as a One contrasting with some elements in a Many, we can look for another One which has the role of a unity for that One and Many. Such a unifying One is something like what Thomists call an act of Being. There is an act of Being which unites entity and features. The union can be of many grades, all occurring at the same time, from a merging to a mere concurrence. This act of Being is to be understood to refer to the Being of a final Actuality. It is an act of Being which is possessed by the resultant union, and is not identical with it. The entity is contingent, because though it is, it is by virtue of a possession of its being; finalities, instead, are Beings, and are therefore not contingent.

An entity can be said to face in two directions—toward an act of Being and toward publicly determined features. As facing the former, it possesses being, and as facing the latter, it has a public import.

A feature, as determined by both the entity and other entities, faces in three ways. It faces the act of Being, the entity in which it inheres, and the entities which partly determine its nature.

We will be supposing that the entity and the features are not real or have no reality apart from the act of Being, if we treat them as having a status apart from or prior to the act of Being. We should say that the act of Being at once makes them be, distinguishes them, and relates them. But now we seem on the verge of making the entity and the features be neoplatonic emanations from the act of Being, itself unexplained. We must, moreover, account for the being of the entity as it is related to a finality, and for its being as related to other entities. In the former guise, it is a participating being, but in the latter, it is a distinctive, limited being.

The entity is a being, though it participates in a higher one only so far as the entity is in relation to other entities. As related to a higher Being, it contrasts with its features; as related to other entities, it expresses itself as features which are reciprocally determined by the other entities, each of which possesses the being that has been participated in.

Perhaps better: An entity is at once finite and contingent. It is finite just so far as it is a being, but then it is related to a final Being. It is contingent because its being is something had in the sense that it overflows it in the form of expressions and impositions on others, enabling it to be in a context with other entities. There is no act of being apart from the entity; there is only the entity, but now in the guise of a finite being related to a finality, and now in the guise of a contingent being related to other entities. It is as related to the others that it has features, and these features have being by virtue of the overflow of the being from the entity.

June 21

An actuality is just a term in a number of contexts:

1] One context is extensional, making the actuality contemporary with others.

2] A second context is structural, making the actuality appropriate to others.

3] A third context is that of unity, where the actuality is compatible with others.

4] A fourth context is that of finality where the actuality is made to be equally real with others.

5] Each context gives the actuality a being but only as a term related to similar terms.

6] Because an actuality is in a number of contexts, the nature of it as term is richer than that which it has in any given context. It appears to be substantial for a given context by virtue of its place in other contexts.

7] Because an actuality is constituted by its context, it will appear to be substantial with respect to any smaller context where it achieves features by virtue of its interplay with the items there.

8] If it is detached from one context, an actuality will be occupied with another context; it will refer to that other context, interplay with it, as a contrasting reality.

9] A context, as a contrasting reality, may be faced as that which is pertinent to actualities; or it may be faced as that which has an integrity of its own, as that which an actuality makes an effort to accept for itself and others, with itself perhaps functioning as a representative for those others.

10] There is then no act of Being, as was suggested yesterday, but actualities in the role of complex terms, components of which are the terms in particular contexts, and actualities in the role of isolated entities each occupied with the context as having an integrity of its own.

11] A context is a being relating and terminating in beings in the shape of terms. But the terms are not produced by the context or contexts, as is evident from the fact that they can face the contexts as realities over against themselves.

12] As involved with other actualities, each actuality is substantial with respect to the context which encompasses all actualities. This is the reciprocal of 7. An actuality is thus substantial in one sense when it is viewed from the perspective of a context, and thereby delimited and related to but a few items; it is substantial in another sense when it is viewed from the perspective of its relations to particular items, and recognized therefore to lose something when merely related in some basic context, which has no regard for it and whatever other actualities there might be.

13] When separated from other actualities, an actuality can retain the substantiality it had with respect to them only by contrasting with the context, and thus by treating that context as a reality which it needs.

14] When involved with a context, an actuality constitutes another context with it then and there. This latter context, unlike the others, is constituted by substantial realities, and does not, like them, terminate in mere terms.

15] To be involved with a context is to take it to be a being over against a being, i.e., over against that which is involved with it.

16] The substantial reality of an actuality with reference to other actualities is the actuality as detached from the context with which it could be involved.

17] An actuality is inevitably caught in a set of basic contexts (*1–4*), each of which is a being that gives the actuality the being of a term. An actuality, too, is detached from contexts, possessed of a being of its own. As such it interplays with A] other actualities or B] contexts, to constitute specific contexts which are constituted by the interplaying entities then and there, the one (A) under the aegis of a context or contexts, the other (B) not.

18] An actuality has being because it is subject to primary contexts. It has being because it contrasts with the being of primary contexts. And it has being because it is affected by and affects other actualities. The first form of being is the reciprocal of the third.

These observations are set down mainly as pivotal notions in terms of which the problem is to be solved. They do not bring us to the end of the problem, for it is not altogether clear in what sense actualities are, what their unity is like, how Beings can be at once contexts and objects with which actualities are involved or with which they contrast.

The being which an actuality has through the immanental presence of a Being, in the guise of a context for it and other actualities, is continuous with that immanental Being. This reveals the actuality to be contingent. To be itself in itself, it must possess the very Being which determines it; but this means it must contrast with that Being. It does this by existing only as an actuality with other actualities and then separating itself from them in the guise of their representative. The immanental Being gave the actuality the being of a term, but this was substantialized through an actual interplay with other actualities. In detaching from those other actualities while epitomizing them, the actuality has reality sufficient to enable it to deal with the immanental Being as something it seeks, thereby treating it as a Being relatively transcendent to that actuality.

As constituted by other immanental Beings, an actuality is able to stand away from a given one. But it acts on that given one, not as constituted by other immanental Beings, but as the unity of all the terms that all the immanental Beings provide. The question that remains is what is the source of that unity, what is its nature, how is it to be understood. Is it not the actuality as interplaying with other actualities? On this view, "being the father of my daughter and son" (or similar relational features) would be the unity which is able to act on some Being. But this surely cannot be correct, for the state of being a father is dependent on something which can have that state, and this would seem to be the unity of which we are in search.

There seems to be a conflict between an approach in terms of a detachment from one kind of entity with an involvement with something else, and an approach in terms of an achievement of being from some common, more basic reality, where entities can be detached only if they are something outside all contexts.

Do not these troubles issue from an attempt to deal with Beings initially as though they were only contexts? How could they be contexts if there were nothing for which they were contexts? Must we not, therefore, start with Beings as correlative with finite entities, each distinct and oriented or involved with the Beings, and then see that they achieve a relation to one another only because the Beings become immanental in the guise of a context for them? We would start, on this supposition, with finite entities contrasting with and involved with Beings, and with an involvement of the entities in one another, at the same time that there is an immanental presence of the Beings. The finite entities would then, right from the beginning, be involved with Beings over against them and with other finite entities, but as subject to a context provided by those Beings. The unity of the finite entities would be twofold, in relation to the Beings and in relation to one another; as in one of these relations, they would not be in the other. The immanental role of the Beings could be taken to give a meaning for the separated Beings to act upon and thereby make the finite entities be.

We would have the finite entities doubly constituted, on the one side by Beings with which they were involved, and on the other side by contexts in which they were caught. The Beings by themselves would have the entities as terminal points, but these would be different in kind from the terminal points in the contexts.

We would then have two kinds of termini for Beings; in the one case, we would have distinct, unrelated finites which were limiting notions of those Beings; in the other, we would have interconnected finites functioning as limits of a context. Each type of limit would affect the other, to constitute a distinct actuality interacting with other actualities. This actuality could act on the Beings or on other finites. Such a view (which comes quite close to a Thomistic view that essences are limited forms that impose some limitation on existence and thereby constitute real finite entities) gives each of the limits a power with respect to the other, enabling them both to become detached from their conditions so as to constitute a new entity.

We could envisage Being as a kind of pyramid or triangle, with the base angles acting as the product of a meeting of precipitation and a radiation, each enabling the other to stand apart from its conditioning Being and thereby, with it, to constitute a unitary actuality at once related to the precipitating apex, and to the radiating contextual base. Such an approach, of course, takes its start with Beings and not with actualities. It must not be thought to provide anything more than an analytic account of the nature of actualities, a fact which makes it possible for us to reverse the procedure and see Beings also as the joint product of two conditions, one determined by the way in which actualities act on one another, and the other resulting from an actuality's effort to continue to be.

It would be an error, though, to take either one or both of these approaches, if this meant that there was first one kind of reality and then another, or as if they were not irreducible except for analysis. And yet we need not suppose that either has a unity all alone, since we can say of each that in one guise it offers the content for itself as able to function in the other guise.

Because it is determined in a context, an actuality is able to be related to a Being. As that which had been determined through a relation to a Being, it is able to enter into a context. Because it is related to a particular actuality, a Being is able to function as a context. As a context, the Being is possessed of a power to act on actualities.

The actuality or the Being, when constituted in one direction, serves as the carrier of what it is as constituted from another direction. In both directions it is a unity, but the unity is biased toward the side which is then being constituted.

June 22

On and off last evening, during the night, and on my hour walk this morning, I have been thinking of clarifications and alterations in yesterday's discussions, particularly those concerning the issues raised toward the end.

A final reality, either in its absolute form apart from all particulars (what I have termed Actuality) or in a limited guise where it is relative to particulars (what I have called encapsulated modes of Being), can be said to overflow and to stretch out, to exhaust itself in points of energy, and to terminate at various positions. The juncture of the two is a unitary actuality. The points of energy detach the positions, and the positions detach the points of energy.

Reciprocally, actualities symbolize different finalities in different ways. They might converge, be merely alongside one another (even at their most intense), be submerged, or merely point to a finality (answering to the encapsulated forms of Ideality, Existence, and God, or to Actuality). At the same time, those actualities, by virtue of the way in which they refer to one another along vectorial lines (as I suggested originally in *Reality*), constitute finalities in a relational or contextual role.

On this view, we account not only for the being of actualities, but for the being of the ultimate modes of Being, and this without supposing that either is in fact derived from the elements which are analyzed out of them.

In what respect and by virtue of what are actualities contingent? From the perspective of Beings, it would seem that they would be necessitated termini. If we say that they are contingent through the fact that they provide a unity beyond that which the Beings contribute, we will be faced with the fact that the Beings must also be said to provide a unity beyond that which the actualities contribute. Must we not say that the contingency of actualities lies in the fact that though the actualities are necessitated by Beings as points of energy and as positions, when the one becomes subject to the other, we have contingency?

It is not the unity of the actuality, but the fact that as a position it is a unity, i.e., has energy, and as a point of energy has a position, that makes it be contingent. It *is* a being in itself, but *has* a being in the sense that its energy and the position are part of Beings, and so far are only possessed by it and are not part of its being. Position and energy are part of the being of actualities, but only so far as position detaches the energy, and energy detaches the position from their source.

A number of questions remain. 1] Why is an actuality contingent? If we say that the energy and the positions are pulled by their sources away from the actuality so that there can be a constant reintegration of the two, we seem to give what were before termed analytic components a reality of their own. We would also have to determine what could reintegrate them. But we can say that the coincidence of energy and position, permitting of a unity, is a contingent matter. The unity of an actuality involves a dislocation of the energy and points, to make the energy and points (in the guise they have as outside it) be not coincident with one another, except for undetermined periods.

2] A question also arises with respect to Beings. Why should they not be contingent in the same way in which actualities are? Is it not because they are intensifications of the actualities and thus cannot be subject to limitations which the actualities exhibit? The unity of a Being preserves the very factors, without distortion, that actualities provide.

Actualities make a unity in such a way as to define the two expressions of Beings (position and energy) to be without necessary coincidence. So far as we see the actualities from the perspective of the Beings, we will see them as not unified, but as dissolved into distinctive units of energy and distinctive positions. The Beings themselves, however, have a unity which define the contributions of actualities to them to be necessarily coincidental. So far as we see the Beings from the perspective of the actualities, we will see them as necessarily unified.

What I hope is only another way of saying the same thing, the unity of an actuality occurs outside the reach of the Beings, in the sense that it makes the energy and positions unified in a way that is not necessarily identical with the way in which they are unified in the Beings. But the unity of a Being occurs where the contributions of the actualities come together. These contributions are already outside the actualities. A number of actualities symbolize an intensified version of themselves; the actualities coincide in fact in the Being. The Being is more than their coincidence, but only by intensifying their result. A number of actualities overlap to constitute a Being in the guise of a context; the vectors of actualities coincide in fact. The context is more than their coincidence, but is so only in the sense of subjugating them.

An actuality seems unable to intensify the terminal energy and positions of a Being; it allows these to penetrate one another but only by distorting them. A Being, on the other hand, does not subject its analytic factors to another transformation.

But surely a Being alters the distinct contributions made by distinct actualities? Yes, but only in the sense of giving them new weights, and not in the sense of making them coincide in new ways. Their coincidence is intensified and then evaluated from the perspective of the intensification, whereas the actualities take coincidental elements and alter them as they interlock.

Both the Beings and actualities have unities of their own, the one being understood to be an intensification of the factors into which it can be analyzed and which are due to actualities, the other being understood to be an interpenetration of the factors into which it can be analyzed and which are due to Beings. (The interpenetration changes the way in which the factors are in fact coincident in the Being.)

It is in their interpenetration that energy and position are at once separated off from their sources, and constitute the distinctive unity of an actuality, a unity which changes their natures. It is in their intensification that symbolization and vectoriality are at once separated off from their sources to constitute the distinctive unity of a Being which intensifies their natures. The intensification always has the same result no matter what the symbol or the vectors. A symbol and a vector could be viewed as intensifying one another to contrast with the energy—power is perhaps a better term—and position which primarily carry one another. An actuality is never properly centered; it is either a unity turned toward the source of power or toward other positions; but a Being is always properly centered, being analyzable into a convergence of symbols or into reciprocal vectors.

When an actuality is detached primarily in position, it does not face the Being as a context. Instead, it faces other entities, i.e., other actualities or the Being, as the source of power. When the actuality is detached primarily as a power, it occupies one position alongside others, and thus is in a context. It is there related to other positions. It helps constitute the context by the way in which these positions are vectorally related.

The unity of an actuality, to put the matter in still another way, is the power or the position as encompassing the other. This unity contrasts with the power and the position as analytic factors, or as factors which are connected with their sources in final Beings. The unity of a Being is the juncture of actualities but intensified, and thus as though each factor enabled the other to penetrate beyond the point where its source (actualities) could take it.

When we abstract the position or the power, we do not destroy them as constituting a unitary actuality. But we do then view that unitary actuality as providing a *tertium quid* for them. Having nothing but a position and a power as effete abstractions, we look for something which will bind them together. This is only the position and power as already interpenetrative, and therefore as constituting a unity. That unity may function with respect to the abstractions as a mere juncture, as a power controlling their functioning, as a structure making them intelligible, or as that into which they are to merge. Correlations emphasize the first, symptoms the second, Aristotelian substantial forms or purposes the third, and the object of judgment the fourth.

If the foregoing can be maintained, some corrections must be made in some of the contentions made at previous times. It will not be altogether correct to say that finalities are Beings and actualities only have a being. Both are, and are equally ultimate. The contingency of actualities is not due to the fact that they have being, but to the fact that the constituents of their being have a reality of their own as part of finalities, and that they are then together in a nonpenetrative way, whereas an actuality has them interpenetratively with a consequent distortion of what they are as part of or as continuous with their sources.

The nature of the encapsulated Beings, Ideality, Existence, and God, as involved with actualities, will have to be understood to be inseparable from themselves as having Beings apart from those actualities, and to offer a context in which they are related one to the other. Actuality, too, will have to be understood in a twofold way; it will be an ultimate Being by itself apart from actualities, and it will offer a context for them, making them equally real, i.e., each as real as the others.

Actuality is a precondition, not only for the reality of actualities, but for the reality of the subordinate modes of Being. But then it would seem to follow that the other modes of Being, as ultimate, will not be real except so far as they are subject to Actuality, unless this be understood, as it was by me some time ago, as meaning that Actuality enables them to be real when standing in contrast with their own particulars. Without the action of Actuality on them, the other modes of Being as alongside Actuality will be merged with their particulars.

Ought not there to be a consequence to the effect that each ultimate mode of Being is constituted by the other modes of Being (and not merely by its particulars) in somewhat the way in which actualities are constituted by the various Beings in their twofold guise, except that perhaps we need not make reference to a twofold guise here, but only to the fact that there are three distinct modes of Being which offer factors which are analyzable out of the unity of each?

Once again I return to discussions of the various modes of Being. Perhaps at this time I should make a strong effort not to deal with them, since they are by now presumably running the risk of becoming fixed ideas, all the more so perhaps because I do not feel that they are. They serve, I think, only as means to allow me to focus on some very difficult and neglected questions. But it could be objected that so much of these discussions offer only alternative ways of dealing with some fundamental problem and show no advance over what was done before. Usually they leave the reader with no knowledge of where I stand. But that is because I am exploring. And I do think that the ideas offered are often illuminating and suggestive. Also, I find that when I try to concentrate on actualities, I inevitably am driven to look to Beings in order to account for what would otherwise remain inexplicable.

Unless Actuality is to be a Being superior to all the others, the reality that it bestows on what is within its confines cannot be superior to the intelligibility that Ideality bestows on its particulars, or the worth that God bestows on His particulars, or the extension that Existence bestows on its particulars.

June 23

Yesterday's discussion brings me closer to the solution of a problem that has been troubling me for some twenty years. Given the origin of a human from the combination of sperm and egg, how account for the unity and the personality of the individual, and yet avoid the Thomist view that men (but not animals) have God-given souls, or the materialistic view that there either is no personality or that it is a mere function of the bodily parts? I would now say that both sperm and egg are unitary beings and that they interpenetrate as such unitary beings to yield a new entity. That new entity does not deny to the sperm and egg their distinctive beings, but it does take them as together to be different in nature and function from what they were when apart. When integrated in the unity which they constitute together, they continue to have distinctive beings and properties. The sperm and egg thus have three roles: *1*] apart from each other; *2*] as united with one another; *3*] as distinct from the union which they constitute by virtue of their interpenetration.

Chemicals are to be understood to combine in a way similar to that in which sperm and egg do. But the sperm and egg constitute a power which reaches out to encompass whatever the body of sperm and egg adds to itself. The sperm and egg, as mere bodies, are but one side of themselves, the other being given in their power. The power and the bodies (extended positions) are owned by the unity they together constitute. The power and the body are encompassed by the unity which functions in some independence of them, and which in fact seeks to realize its own objective through the use of that body and power.

The sperm and egg come together to constitute a new unity, not merely as bodies but as powers as well. It is the union of the bodies and the union of the powers which interpenetrate to give a single unity. In chemicals, the resultant unity has no independent functioning; in animals, it is occupied with other objects as increasing the range of the power, as making for the maintenance of the body, or as allowing the unity to encompass a limited region of bodies with which it is affiliated. But in the case of man, the unity has more independent powers, of which one major expression is that of the mind. The mind can itself be empowered as a will or a purpose, and it is in this guise that it is seen properly to be the correlate of a body.

The new self of the new individual is not the egg's privacy somehow maintained; nor is it a juncture of that privacy with the privacy of the sperm. In the first case, we fail to provide for the contribution of the male, and in the second case, we violate the ineluctable privacy of both sperm and egg. Yet it is true that some animals have been produced through the stimulation of the egg without the sperm. This stimulation must be thought to separate the body from the power in such a way as to require a new unification which will be as basic as that which is produced by the meeting of sperm and egg, and therefore of their bodies and powers.

June 24

An actual entity can itself, in whole or on any dimension, be treated either as a power or a position with respect to other entities, whether these be actualities or abstractions from these. The account of the juncture of sperm and egg must therefore be understood not to involve bodies apart from powers, but unitary beings. One of them will function as a power and the other as a position, the two of them actually being not mere bodies, but unitary entities in which the bodies are now of primary interest.

When we turn from the union of sperm and cell to the complex organic beings, we find that these include within their confines—more evidently than is the case of the sperm and cell, though these too must be recognized to encompass smaller actualities within their confines—other actualities. Those other smaller actualities are unities which are as real as the larger actualities. But the larger ones act as powers with respect to the others as positions, and conversely as positions with respect to the others as powers. In all of them, power and position are interpenetrative. So far as a larger being functions as a power, we take account of those features of it like decision, will, macroscopic activity, purpose, growth, etc. These are interlocked with the mere magnitude, mass, etc., provided by the contained items. So far as a larger being functions as a position, we take account of those features of it which place it (with the contained elements as units) in gravitational and electrical fields.

A body can be contrasted with some quality that it has. The body then is inseparable from a larger unity of which it is a factor; it is the larger unity which, via the body functioning as a position or a power, is then united with the quality when we predicate or when we reflect on what the quality does for the body, and conversely. The quality is normally thought to be a quality of the body alone, but we can see in the case of a blush or a flush that it may in fact be ingredient in the body in such a way as to tell us not merely about the body, but about the entire being as more than a body, i.e., as also having another dimension of either power or position and as a consequence, a unity of its own.

We normally view the body as a kind of power, and thus treat the entire unity which is emphasized in the guise of the body as a kind of power, when we contrast the body with a quality. The quality tells us the position of the body in a world of perceptual objects. But the reverse is also possible: we can see the quality as a power and the body as a position when we see quality as an anticipation of where and how we might act, and the body as merely the base or material on which we will then act.

The interpenetration of the power and the position are best understood perhaps along the lines of a Thomistic or Kantian interpretation. The Thomist takes every actuality to be the product of the imposition of existence on an essence, thereby bringing the latter into actualization; the Kantian takes every actuality to be the product of a meaning or concept in an experiential setting, thereby making the concept function in new ways—or as I have previously put it, to have implications it did not have before. But both the Thomist and the Kantian ignore the reverse process. Both take the unity to be biased toward existence or experience, and do not see that it could just as properly be understood the other way too, and that the combination of these two biases will yield us a unity which itself has to be related in some biased way to other entities.

From the standpoint of power, we can say the meaning of position is that it gives the power a geometry, forcing it to operate on this rather than that, here rather than there, etc. From the standpoint of the position, we can take the meaning of power to be the adding of implications to the position, telling us what is to follow as a consequence of that position, though there is no deducing this from the position by itself.

Because terms like "essence and existence," "concept and experience," "potency and act," all are biased in one direction, toward existence, experience, or act, we cannot use these terms without misleading. But "power" and "position" do not seem to be good substitutes, the one because it begins to entrench on uses in physics, and the other because it keeps us to a spatio-temporal context. We should find terms which are more plausible and more general conjugates. "Limits and terms," "units and *relata*," "units and nuclei" are some alternatives. The last might be the best if nuclei are understood to be inseparable from vectors with different senses which overlap one another. What is most important is the recognition that either one can be taken to be a potency for the other as act, or an empty meaning to which the other is to give vitality or human significance.

Not unless we are sure just what the two sides of a Being contribute can we be sure what kind of unity is characteristic of actualities. Or, not unless we know just where the unbiased unity of an actuality is can we be sure just what the sources of the units and nuclei are, or just what the units and nuclei are as apart from their juncture. The recognition that Actuality dictates that all actualities are to be equally real forces one to take an organic (or any other complex) being and recognize a unity in it which is distinct from that which is exhibited by the being as a whole or in its aggregated parts. Instead of thereby dissolving the actuality into these two, what we have instead is a recognition that it is as such a unity that the actuality is able to be oriented toward Actuality and other (but limited forms of) Being. In this orientation, the unity can be taken to be the being of the actuality, having nothing to do with the encompassing and the encompassed actualities. The encompassing and encompassed as united make a third kind of actuality which is as real as the other two, when these two are taken apart from their involvement with one another.

We have been accustomed to recognizing the reality of the encompassed entities as apart from the encompassing ones. But what would the encompassing entities be like apart from the encompassed? What is the nature of an organic being, such as a man or an animal, when viewed apart from the actual cells or smaller entities within its confines? Must we not see this as purposive, as directed toward some other entities, in ways not possible to encompassed entities? The fact that in theory or fact we might have the latter without the former, but never the former without the latter, merely points up the fact that the latter can be broken down into units and nuclei, whereas the former cannot, but must instead function as either a unit or nucleus for the encompassed entities which then have the role of being nuclei or units respectively.

We cannot accord the encompassing actuality the same kind of reality that we grant the encompassed to have, except so far as we see the former as but a unit or nucleal (and the latter as but a nucleal or unit) dimension of the total being which results from the juncture of the two kinds of actuality. When we speak of the encompassed as nevertheless having a reality of its own, we must take this to be but an index of the fact that encompassed items can function as unities outside the confines of the encompassing entity, though they then will have properties distinct from those which they now have.

If there is truth in the foregoing, there are no preferential factors, and there are none that are unintelligible. Many problems will be left over. And it will be hard to determine often just what factors are involved. It is hard to know, for example, whether mind, purpose, concern, etc., are to be attributed to the factor in an actuality which unites with the encompassed entities, or are to be attributed to the unity of these as expressed in some limited way or through one of these factors. To attribute them to the factors is to simplify the problem, but it is also to deny them the role of being expressive of the actuality as a whole. I think it is more correct to see them to be expressive of the actuality as a whole. The organic nature of a man is identifiable, I think, with the substantial form of the Aristotelians. But this still leaves us with the question as to just what the properties of that form may be. If I understand them, the Aristotelians are inclined to take the substantial form of man to be his soul, and this to be expressed as mind, concern, etc. But then what is the resultant substance?

The substantial form need be credited with nothing more than the power to confine parts, to offer a unit or nucleus for these parts together, and to prove an avenue for the expression of the unity. All that the Aristotelians say is expressed by the substantial form can be said to be expressed through it, by the unity it helps constitute.

June 27

I am not altogether satisfied with "unit" and "position," but I am not able to say exactly why. "Generality" and "singularity" are better terms, I think.

Each of these can be separated out of an actuality in one of three ways. It can be *prescinded, abstracted,* or *dislocated.*

1]   It is prescinded when it is held apart in the very guise it has as interlocked with the other. It is then in fact the actuality formalized (if it be a generality) or isolated (if it be a singularity). When we speak of the nature of something or of it as an entity or object, we prescind.

2]   It is abstracted when it is dealt with in the guise it had before it had been affected by the other. Such abstractions give us the Platonic form or Aristotelian form for the generality, and gives us the mere feeling (as Whitehead called it) or the mere hecceity (as Peirce after Scotus called it) for the singularity.

3]   It is dislocated when, as abstracted, it is related to other abstractions with which it in fact constitutes the one dimension of some Being. When we think of generalities in a hierarchy of complexity or excellence, or when we relate positions in space or time, we dislocate the generalities or the singularities from their place inside an actuality and assign them a different place inside a context.

We return from prescinding by merely replacing the unity which we have formalized or isolated so that the consequences which follow from the singularity or the generality in fact will be forthcoming. Before we come back, we can contrast one prescinded unity with a correlative unity. A nature is to be contrasted with an entity; both of them are the unitary actuality, but deprived of a capacity in one direction or another.

We return from abstraction by finding the correlative abstraction and recognizing that they interpenetrate one another when they in fact are part of an actuality. A form contrasts with an hecceity, and each is to be seen to be affected by the other in the actuality.

We return from a dislocating by subjecting a generality or a singularity to the operation of the other in such a way as to detach it from the other members of its context. A generality as part of a hierarchy or a position in space has a nature which it loses when it is subject to the disconnections provided by the other.

I came to consider these three types of separation in the course of an effort to get clear the nature of a quality in relation to the object where it is normally located or to which it is attributed. A quality is an accident in the sense that it does not follow from the nature of a generality; it is a part of a singularity. As something perceived and held apart from an actuality, it is part of a singularity in a context of singularities. It is to be related to the other items in the context and to a generality as that which will dislocate it and thereby make it part of an actuality.

When I asked what a quality contributes to a substance or the substance to the quality, I was evidently attending to a part of a dislocated singularity, but ignoring the fact that this singularity was then related

to other singularities. Also, I was contrasting the singularity with something concrete rather than with a generality which would have the double
function of separating the singularity from its companions, and of affecting the nature of the result, to produce a new unity of the singularity
with the generality.

A quality such as green or square or warm is a part of a singularity
in relation to other singularities. If we attend to any one of these, we
tacitly make use of a generality to separate it off, and then focus on a
distinguishable but not separable part of that separated singularity. The
generality as capable of separating off the singularity from other singularities is identical with the abstracted generality (thus presupposing
the separation and operation of the singularity!), but without there being
any unity for the generality and the singularity. The abstracted generality
(or singularity) is correlate with an abstracted singularity (or generality). They do not make a unity, but they presuppose one which contrasts
with them.

The prescinded generality and singularity are unities of generality
and singularity, with one of the factors denied the power to subject the
other to new conditions. The abstracted generality and singularity are
a pair of abstractions incapable of subjecting one another to new conditions. They are sustained by themselves as subjecting one another to
new conditions, though we may neglect one or the other as performing
this role so as to have its correlate in a prescinded position. The dislocated
generality and singularity are a pair of contextualized entities which can
be focused on only so far as they make a pair. We have then, in reverse
order, a paired generality and singularity, a connected generality and
singularity, and a pair of unities of generality and singularity.

The pairing of dislocated items is achieved by forces not particularly
pertinent to these items; if they are encompassed, merged, etc., it is without regard for what they are. The juncture of abstracted items is exteriorly produced, but by a unitary power that possesses them. The union
of prescinded items involves the recovery of a unity which each one of
them has delimited.

When we refer any quality to an actuality said to possess it, what
we do is either to pair it with a generality in articulation, to join it with
a correlative abstraction in a judgment of perception, or to allow it to be
captured by the unity of itself and a generality. Even if treated as lesser
and to be merged with its paired generality, in the first case we have a
unity of intent; in the second, a sustaining unity; and in the third, a unity
which subjects it to new and additional implications. Ordinary predication of a quality, as telling us something about an object, is the third;

it tells us what will be contributed to the rest, and what the rest contributes to it. But in this third case, it must be remembered, the locus of the quality is not a substantial object, but a formalized unity. It is an accident with respect to that formalized unity A] because it cannot be deduced from it;   B] because it is a differentiated part which has no reality of its own;   C] because it is what it is because of other items in a context with it, having nothing to do with the nature of the formalized unity with which it is to be united; and   D] because it operates in the concrete, as united with the formalized unity, in a way that cannot be determined by considering it or the formalized unity, by themselves.

A quality is, then, not simply a predicate of a subject; it is a predicate together with a subject in the first case, a predicate united with a subject in an adumbrated unity in the second case, and an abstracted subject completed by another abstracted subject in a unity beyond either, in the third case. In the first case, we presuppose an alien source of matching; in the second, we acknowledge a unity in which it and its mate are embedded; and in the third, we acknowledge a vitalized form of itself as the unity from which its own isolated unity was prescinded. "Red" is joined with "car" in the first case; in the second, "red" is joined with "car" as embedded in "red-car"; in the third, "red (car)" is united with "(red) car" to yield "red-car." The "red-car" in the second case is merely pointed at and sustains the "red" and the "car"; in the third case, it is a being with a unity of its own with distinctive implications. Though for practical purposes the different reds and different cars are indistinguishable, and though there is undoubtedly a nucleus common to them all, they are different generalities and singularities with distinctive natures, locations, and functions.

June 28

The unity for a pair is used, the unity adumbrated is acknowledged, and the unity of an actuality is yielded to.

These unities are relevant to different kinds of entities. When it is said, for example, that a red car is one that has been painted red, and could have been painted some other color without affecting it as a car, the red is dislocated. As prescinded, it is a red which is shaped by the car, and which is punctuated by windows, wheels, etc. As abstracted, the red which had been prescinded is bracketed off from the car to appear merely as a surface or mere phenomenon.

In the usual talk about predicating a color of an object, one tends to speak of a dislocated color, when what is needed is a prescinded one. In the usual talk about the contingency of the color, one tends to take the object as relatively fixed, but then reference should be made to the abstracted color, for this alone is correlative with that object (itself something abstracted). And in the usual talk about color as an accident, one holds the color away from the object in which it has been found, and therefore deals with the dislocated color.

In all cases, the color is symmetrically related to the generality, though we may miss this fact because of our acceptance of the generality as the factor which we wish to unite with a singularity, or the color part of it.

July 3

Quite a while ago, I suggested that there was some justification in thinking of sport as a form of art. I viewed it as an improvised dramatic event which revealed something of the nature of man. But I am not now confident that this judgment can withstand much criticism. There is first the fact that one can take art to be occupied with the production of beauty, whereas an athletic contest is itself the object, with a possible objective of achieving success in the shape of winning, the production of excellence in the players, and an aesthetic satisfaction in the spectators. And then there is the fact that though art is encapsulated, separated off from daily life, just as sport is, the work of art is removed to a second degree, whereas sport is removed only to a first degree, where degree entails a reference to the kind of activities and effects which are relevant to the activities of daily life. The players in a dramatic event or the dancers in a dance assume a role; the energy they expend, the strains they undergo, are all subordinate to what is being presented; but the players in a game spend themselves in the game; they involve themselves in its production in the sense that they give themselves as unitary beings to its existence.

To this it can be answered that an artist gives himself entirely to his role, and lives out the role only by expending himself in the process. That answer I think is good. But then one ought to go on to remark that the artist gives himself to the world of art, to the fact that there is a reality which is to be conveyed through the carrying out of the role or through the giving of himself, somewhat as the religious man gives himself to the world of religion, and while occupying a position there endeavors to make contact with some further reality. The athlete, in contrast, does not seek to convey anything; he does not give himself to the world of sport, but to the carrying out of a position in which he makes it possible for the game to be produced. He is like an actor who merely carries out the role of a father without any awareness of the intent of the entire play, or the fact that being a father not only is a role in relation to other roles (for this the good athlete also knows), but expresses from one angle the entire meaning of the play. An athlete who was an artist would be one who batted the ball, not merely as a baseball player inter-locked with others, but as one who was guided and controlled by the (perhaps unconscious) desire to exhibit the nature of man by making the interlocked roles carry the transcendental quality of beauty or grace. Grace is a factor in a good athletic performance, and an exhibition of the nature of man is one of the consequences; but in art we have beauty as the main objective, and an exhibition of the nature of reality (and in special cases, the nature of man) to be the controlling goal.

Were a dancer to throw a basketball, he would not tense his legs, arch his back, relate himself to the rest of the court or the other dancers, or even throw in a way in which a basketball player did. His throw would be controlled, not by the need to get the ball in the basket, but by the need to express something through the act of putting the ball in the basket. In the one case, we have an objective to be skillfully achieved; in the other case, we have an expression to be completed in beauty by means of the objective which also concerns the other, but which will not be achieved with the same skill that the other shows.

July 18

Perception requires a form of analysis, indeed a conceptual analy-sis. Let us take a familiar illustration, "this book is red." This is written by the *Principia Mathematica* as ϕa. Here the "a" represents the "this book" and the "ϕ" stands for "red." The "red" is thought to be ascribed to the "this book." Despite the fact that both Whitehead and Russell have strongly objected to what they called the subject-predicate view of judgment, they here exemplify it more conspicuously than it is to be found anywhere. For them, the ϕ is to be ascribed to the a. But if it is ascribed to an a which does not possess the character ϕ, the attribution will be self-contradictory, since it will ascribe to a a character which it is in fact without; a would in this case be an a which lacks ϕ and yet has a ϕ ascribed to it. But if a already has a ϕ character, the ascription of ϕ to it will yield a tautology.

Both ϕ and a are abstractions; they are correlative derivatives from an accepted apprehended content. We should rewrite the initial expres-sion, "ϕa," as "(ϕ) (a)" to bring out their correlativity. Since the a here is an abstraction, it is not identifiable with the subject of the discourse—

what Dewey called the subject matter in contrast with the grammatical subject—instead, it is a kind of variable like ϕ.

Russell was convinced that a was the object of a proper name, and that such a proper name named an existent which presumably was a spatio-temporal entity. But it was soon evident that all of our familiar names had connotative elements and could not be used merely to designate a mere a. To this difficulty, two answers were open; one was given by Susan Stebbing who maintained that proper names were achieved only at the end of analysis, and that they designated ultimate simples; the other answer was given by Quine who maintained that every proper name could be interpreted as a kind of ϕ; Socrates, for example, is an "x who socratizes." The first of these answers leads to a Leibnizian world of simples, the second leads to an idealism where we have only generals (with a referent to an x which could conceivably be the entire totality of things, or could be broken up into what Bradley called "finite centers," mere localizations which were beyond conceptualization but were needed to give the abstract universals some footing in a world beyond themselves).

When one asks where the abstractions are, and follows this with the awareness that we isolate the ϕ and the a while we continue to keep in focus an apprehended content, we see the desirability of treating both of these factors as the very apprehended initial content, but as biased from different sides. On this view, we should write our initial formula as "(ϕ_a) (a_ϕ)." Each is here the initial given frame, biased toward one of the factors. When we consider ϕ or a by itself, we either make a further abstraction—which should, I think, merely provide us with something like "ϕ_{ϕ_a}" and "a_{a_ϕ}"—or we recognize that we are merely ignoring the submerged or recessive other component of it. We could imagine a ϕ or an a; we use words which do have this kind of detachedness, allowing us to speak of a ϕ without any reference to an a or conversely, but so far as perception is concerned, we do not have the one without the other, either alongside or as a submerged factor. The initial whole is now in disequilibrium with one factor dominant.

"ϕ_a" and "a_ϕ" are the factors which we must unite in a perceptual judgment claiming to be true, and which as a matter of fact are united by us only so far as we continue to hold on them as together, undivided from one another in an adumbrated content which we then and there confront. Those factors are not themselves perceived; they are conceptual products, products achieved by our concentrating either on the indicated or contemplated sides of the single, undivided, apprehended content. This apprehended content, with which we begin and which we conceptually analyze into biased versions of itself, is not identical with the adumbrated; the latter is what is left of the former when we contrast it with conceptualized, analytic components. It is the initial content having a position in contrast with what we have analyzed out in order to form a judgment; it is the locus of those factors as apart from us, whereas the initial content is faced as without those factors, for we have not yet distinguished them in it or held them apart from it.

The real object, an actuality or substance, approached from an epistemological point of view, is the adumbrated as united with the factors we have isolated to make our judgment. We, in making our judgment, provide a point of equilibrium for the two biased factors; we stand between them, offering them a unity in which they can stand as extremes, balancing one another. But they are also oriented in the adumbrated, thereby becoming factors of a perceptual object. It is as together with that in which they are oriented that they constitute a unitary being. They achieve the status of such a unitary being (I am speaking, of course, from the vantage point of the epistemological process, for apart from this there already is a unitary actuality) by being oriented in a larger world. That orientation is expressed by "it is the case that."

The entire set, united factors plus the adumbrated in which they are oriented, is itself oriented in a larger world, and just so far constitutes a single unity. As in that larger world, the unity has consequences which do not follow from any knowledge of the factors or of the adumbrated or their unity. The unity, from an epistemological point of view, is that which is achieved only because the orientation in the world (which can be said to be a world of experience, after Kant, or a world of nature, after Spinoza) is for the factors as together with the adumbrated. We can also get to that unitary being as in the world through sympathy and love. Or we can acknowledge the reality of ourselves, and see that this involves the contrasting of ourselves, the insistence and resistance of ourselves with reference to what is as basic as ourselves. That contrasting, to be sure, may not be possible without our invoking or recognizing the exercise of power on the part of a reality capable of endowing other entities, which differ from us in accessibility, value, and perhaps even mode of existence, with a dignity equal to ours.

July 19

Since f or ϕ is conventionally taken to be a predicate to be ascribed to a subject, a, it is likely to be misleading to use such marks even when they are seriously qualified. It is tempting to refer to the isolated items as f_a and a_f, but the former looks as though it were not really different from $f(a)$, and the latter does seem to give us a mere a with a referent or subordinate mark. Perhaps it would be better to speak of a name and a characteristic, and express them as NC. Then the framework would be NC, and the isolated elements would be N_c and C_n. But we must remain aware that N is no singular term; it is as abstract and as repeatable as C.

The union of the isolated elements is provided by us in a judgment. It is also provided by the adumbrated. When we approach ontology from the perspective of epistemology, and ask about the real object as apart from us, we refer the entire perceptual situation, of structured items and the adumbrated in which they are oriented, to a world beyond them. The referring of all of them to that world is the acknowledgment of them as together, as constituting a unity. The referring can be verbally expressed in some such form as "it is the case that."

When we orient the total perceptual content in a world beyond ourselves, we in effect provide ourselves with an object which contrasts with us, though it does so, of course, not in its own terms, but as sustained by the larger context. We get to acknowledge it as an entity on its own only so far as we see ourselves and it as subject to powers which equalize our reality, subject them to a common future, make them contemporary, and affiliate them.

We and other objects are not merely in relation to one another, and as such subject to powers which have a transcendent origin. We are related to the beings which have a transcendent reality. How are we related to these? I think I have in the past taken it for granted that we are related to these either by virtue of a power which they exert on us (a view specialized in the doctrine that no one can reach God without God's grace), by virtue of a power which we impose (which is, after all, what is needed if our symbols are to be pursued to their referents, which are intensifications of them), or by both of us together (if we take full account of the fact that each has its own reality and its own power of detachment from what is alongside it).

If there be any parity between a being as related to those alongside and to it as related to a transcendent (or conversely to a particular from the position of a transcendent), we should say that the relation between a particular and a transcendent is due either to a power which the totality of particulars imposes, or to a power which other transcendents impose. But there is no such parity. Firstly, particulars are related to other particulars by means of a transcendent, and the transcendents are related to other transcendents by means of penumbra from each. Secondly, a particular, to relate another particular to a transcendent, would have to somehow act, not on the other particular, but on the situation which that other makes with a transcendent. Thirdly, there would be another, and apparently unnecessary, action by other transcendents connecting some given transcendent to a particular; but why it should take on this role, and then only when the particular detaches itself, is not evident. Fourthly, when a particular detaches itself and thereby provokes the action of other particulars to relate it to the transcendent (on the hypothesis), the transcendent is presumably detached as well, and when the transcendent detaches itself and thereby provokes the action of other transcendents to relate it to the particular (on the hypohesis), the particular is presumably detached as well. Why the double action takes place is not evident, and in any case requires us to affirm that the relation between transcendent and particular depends on the exercise of the power exerted by both transcendents and particulars. It would be simpler to affirm that particulars and transcendents have penumbra, and that these overlap to constitute a single situation which is sustained by the joint presence of both, regardless of other transcendents and particulars.

But then why can we not say that the various particulars are related to one another by virtue of their overlapping penumbra (which is the position stated in *Reality*) without invoking any transcendent? The reason is that they are all *compelled* to be equal, to have a common future, to be contemporary, and to be affiliated. We will have to invoke an exterior force to provide for the relation of particular to transcendent only when we find that they are compelled to be in a relation to one another, only if they have a relation which cannot be explained except by looking outside the confines of both of them, severally and together. This conclusion gives support to the view that particular and transcendent are related to one another only so far as they represent the other particulars and transcendents, respectively.

July 20

It is common to speak of a theory determining what it is that we will know or select. But one can with equal justice speak of selected content as serving to mediate theory, or more particularly, of theoretically known entities related to singular intensities by means of selected encountered content. We can speak of the theoretically known as being dictated by what we have perceived, and can also speak of the perceived as being mediated, by the theoretically known, to an experienceable world. The point is that the theoretically known stands between the perceived and the experienceable world and that the perceived stands between the theoretically known and a singular intensity.

The two mediations can each be pursued independently, since we can start either with the perceptual or the theoretical. But we can also have them together, in which case we have a union of the theoretical and perceptual (an encountered intelligible), mediated both perceptually and conceptually to a singular intensity embedded in an experienceable world.

July 21

Proceeding as if we had a mere perceptual situation or a mere theoretically defined object to begin with involves some distortion of the facts. From the very start, we have the perceptual situation guided by a theoretical control—more specifically, a principle of selection—and a theoretically defined object focalized by an apprehended perceptual content—i.e., by one in which the various factors have not been isolated and related.

The initial fact is a juncture of a theoretically defined object—which is not diffuse hierarchically as was suggested yesterday, but is a variable with possibly diverse instantiations—and perceptual elements. These are unified severally and together by virtue of a unitary meaning for the perceptual elements and a sensed insistency for the theoretical factor. The unitary meaning and insistency together orient the initial, theoretically understood, perceptual situation in a singular part of a total, experienceable world. Together the meaning and insistency express the fact "that" what they together exhibit is so objectively.

We are inclined to suppose that our reference to the external world —and analogously, that our reference to any residuum after we have made an abstraction from it—involves a predication, precisely because we have left the residuum behind. But we do not leave it behind in the sense of shearing off something from a base. Rather, we have it as an unfocused item which we must correlate with what we focus on. The true residuum is the juncture of what we abstract and what we leave behind; it has the two of them undivided. We, in trying to bring them together, recover in some way that true residuum as something which has a being in a larger world.

July 25

I do not think I have been as clear as I should be on the question as to just what happens when a possibility is realized. It is not correct to say that details are added to the indeterminate possibility, for every detail is itself a general. Nor is it enough to say that the indeterminate possibility becomes determinate, for not only must account be taken of the actuality itself, which is more than any feature or set of features, but it is not evident just what being determinate means. I think what should be said is that the realization of a possibility is performed by an actuality which is itself determinate in the sense that there are consequences and truths about it which could not be deduced from a complete knowledge of its features. The possibility, in being realized, becomes part of the actuality, and as such shares in the overall fact that there are truths and consequences true of the result that are not true of the possibility, no matter how many details or specifications it might have.

The existentialists see that there is more to an actuality than a set of features; but then, because they accept a rationalistic view of knowledge, they take the "more" to be something absurd, beyond intellection. Leibnizians tend to suppose that the being of an entity is exhausted in its features. They cannot therefore tell us the difference between a possible world that has been chosen and that very world before it has been chosen. What I am now maintaining (and which I have maintained more or less coherently in the past) is that the realization of a possibility is the involving of it in situations and adventures which cannot be deduced from its nature. We can understand what the actuality is by seeing that its new features and consequences are features and consequences which are accreted by it, by virtue of the fact that it is in a context and has powers which it is known to have only in experience. (This view is not too far from Kant's account of the difference between the imagined and the existent hundred dollars, for what he says of the latter is that it has every feature of the former but that, in addition, it is involved in experience.)

We are still left with the problem about the acquired features which the actuality has. Were these not possible before they appeared as features of the actuality? If so, how could we use them to explain the difference between realized possibilities and those possibilities before they were realized? Must we not say instead that the accreted features are only possibilities of possibilities and thus have no status as possibilities until there has been a realization of other possibilities? We must say this, but that will still leave us with the question of the nature of the possibilities once the other possibilities were realized. Must we not go on to say that the possibilities of possibilities are actualized when and as the possibilities are, but are the result of the action or presence of other actualities or of the exercise of power? I think so. This seems to imply that there are possibilities (the possibilities that depend on the realization of the possibilities which an actuality realizes, or even which a number of actualities realize together), which are constituted when and as they are realized; they have no antecedent status as possibilities. Being a possibility is an analytic fact about them as products of the realization of other possibilities.

On this view, an actuality would realize a possibility by subordinating it to itself, thereby subjecting it to conditions and endowing it with features and consequences which do not flow from its nature. In that act of subordination, it at the same time involves the realized possibility in relation to other actualities. Those relations are then and there actualized when and as they are constituted as possibilities. There is nothing actual which was not possible, but some actualizations are not preceded by possibilities, but constitute those possibilities when and as those actualizations occur.

A reference to "actualizations" here is likely to be misleading, since it does seem to suppose that there is something which is to be actualized. It would be better to speak of some occurrences or features which come to be only when and as their possibilities do. Those could conceivably be brought into being inside the realm of Ideality, but only so far as they are then and there exhibited in fact in an actuality which has some empirically determined features and consequences, some of which have repercussions on the possibilities.

It is necessary also to recognize that in the realm of the Ideal, no possibilities are marked out with distinctive boundaries. An actuality inevitably focuses on the Ideal in such a way as to bring into relief an inseparable part of the Ideal. Realization involves the provision of boundaries and thereby the separation of that which has been focused on. This separation makes determinate only the status of the possibility; it does not make the possibility itself determinate, for determinateness is the result of a subordination within actuality, itself determinate.

It now sounds as though a realization involved a transportation of a part of the Ideal into the realm of actualities. But realization of a possibility cannot involve a loss to the Ideal; it can mean only a sharing in the Ideal, in somewhat the way in which a sacramental object shares in God. There is a possession of the Ideal in a limited form by the actuality in such a way as not to compromise the activity of the actuality or its possessing the nature that it has. But to this it must be answered that an actuality can be recognized to have a career apart from its sacramental status, whereas no actuality is without features, which have been realized. This is true, but it serves only to point up the fact that the different ultimate Beings have different kinds of roles with respect to actualities.

An actuality occupies a part of Existence and shares in the Being of God as a whole; it is oriented in Actuality as a whole without sharing in its Being, and it duplicates in a subordinate form the specified but inseparable possibility which it focuses on in Ideality. This last observation brings us back to something like the observation made in *Nature and Man* to the effect that the self renews itself at every moment, by realizing its own possibility again and again.

July 26

An actuality is a self-maintaining being. This self-maintenance is achieved by separating out a position and specifying a meaning. Such a contention presupposes that there are a number of positions and a generality of meaning. The actuality can recover the position and the specific meaning that it now has; if it gives up the former, it moves; if it gives up the latter, it changes.

Were there no self-maintenance, we would have neither rest nor persistence, movement nor change. If there were only self-maintenance in the sense of resting on its own bottom, it would be private and eternal. Self-maintenance involves the separation off of a position from a continuum of positions and a specification of a general meaning. The continuum of positions and the general meaning are factors in a final Being. But as now terminating in an actuality, they are the materials enabling it to be a contingent being.

The act of self-maintenance is the act of possessing a segment of the positionality and the generality, which the actuality confronts because of its encompassment within Actuality. In that act of possession, the actuality expresses itself as a public particular in relation to other particulars. The expression is one with the unification of the self-maintaining being (with its separate position and specific meaning), with positionality and general meaning. It is when and as these are united that the actuality is expressed as a public particular.

The contingent actuality, possession by self-maintenance, and expression as a particular in a context of particulars, are all the same in content. They are also identical with the substance in a field, a selected object of apprehension, and the elements of perception. If one likes, one can speak of Actuality as analyzing out of the self-maintaining actuality mere positionality and a generic meaning, and take these to be reintegrated by the actuality in an act of self-maintenance. The self-maintenance unites with the positionality and the generic meaning when and as the actuality expresses itself as a particular, contrasting with other particulars in a public context.

It is not necessary to suppose that the positionality and the generic meaning are in any way derivative from the Being of Actuality. We can treat an actuality as itself separating into these factors and reuniting them by separating out a position and specifying the generality. There will, of course, be a context for actualities which has its roots in an ultimate Actuality, and there will also be a kind of meaning which is derived from the Actuality; neither of these is to be identified with the context and meaning which a distinct actuality faces and makes use of in its act of self-maintenance.

July 27

So far as positionality and generic meaning are external to the actuality, and thus are material which it is to intensify and unite, the actuality's unity and its self-maintenance are also separate from it. Each has as much right as the others to be considered to be the essential part of the actuality; each makes its contribution to the final result.

If one takes positionality and generic meaning to be the beginning of an activity which ends with an absolute unity, we get something like Whitehead's account of an actual entity. This starts with a grasp of conditions external to the position now occupied and moves to the position where these are united absolutely, at which point the entity ceases to be a present entity, to become part of the data to be used by a subsequent entity. But there is no absolute separation of the conditions from one another; an actuality never faces mere positionality and mere generic meaning outside itself as a self-maintaining being and then tries to solidify these into a single unity. It is a unity which is maintaining itself; it has a hold on the positionality and the generic meaning. Instead of breaking up the former into completely isolated or bounded positions, and instead of specifying the latter in the shape of a limited meaning then and there enjoyed, it occupies a position at the same time that it fends off the rest of the positions, and specifies a meaning by negating other meanings. Its boundary as a position and its specific meaning are separated from the other positions and meanings, not by having an unbreakable border, but by being held to in an act which thrusts outward to oppose other positions and meanings.

It is tempting to suppose that the positionality, generic meaning, self-maintenance, and unity are all expressions of the modes of Being—Existence, Ideality, Actuality, and God, respectively. They can all, to be sure, be taken to be instantiations of these Beings, when one starts from the perspective of these Beings. But they are more than such instantiations. Firstly, the modes of Being affect the actualities as together, and not severally; secondly, the modes of Being are immanent in the world of actualities as powers, or influences, and not as contents.

The positionality of an actuality is its position freed from the meaning; the generic meaning is the specific meaning of the actuality freed from its positionality; the mere unity of the actuality is the unity as possessing and operating on positionality and meaning; the act of self-maintenance of the actuality is the dynamic being of the actuality, viewed in abstraction from what does the maintaining and what is the material for this.

An actuality is not a completely self-enclosed entity, but one which is constantly moving from an internal diversification into positionality, etc., to a unity of all these, with neither the diversification nor the final unity ever being achieved. The actuality is related to other actualities through its expressions. These occur when and as the unification of the positionality and generic meaning are maximized—an occurrence which takes place only when and as positionality and generic meaning are faced once again as data for the achieved unification of them. The expressions of the different actualities are in a context which is quickened by the brute compulsion of Existence, the prescriptions of the Ideal, the persuasive affiliations of God, and the definitory equalizations imposed by Actuality.

Positionality and generality are unified when and as they are distinguished and faced as data. The more firm the unity, the more evident and insistent the positionality and generality as content to be unified. When we speak of the unity of the actuality as that which acts to maintain itself by intensifications of the positionality and generality, distinguishing a position in the one and specifying a meaning in the other, it is necessary to keep in mind that it is distinct from the unity of the actuality as that which refers to a positionality and a generality as still waiting to be unified. The unity of an actuality, in other words, is to be thought of as concentrated in a unitary actor, and to be dispersed from that actor to the content on which it acts. The interpenetration of the positionality and generality involves a facing of them as distinct and as needing to be united.

An actuality seems to recoil from its position and meaning, to make itself a nucleal unity facing positionality and generality, which it then tries to recapture, only to find that in the recapturing it in fact makes itself nucleal again, facing positionality and generality again. The actuality as a single complex unity has this nucleal unity of specified positions and meaning facing positionality and generality.

If we were to get in between the beginning and ending of some act of self-maintenance, we would find that neither the nucleal unity nor the positionality and generality are in sharp focus. But we would then have arrived at the position where we have the unity of the entire actuality in sharp focus. There is a bias toward the nucleal unity and the positionality and generality, or a bias toward their copresence in the unitary actuality. The rhythm of the actuality is not from positionality and generality to nucleal unity (as in Whitehead), but from a nucleal unity, with its correlative positionality and generality, to a complex unity in which these correlatives are not sharply distinguished.

What persists? What is identical through time? Is it the nucleal unity, or the complex unity of a not sharply differentiated nucleal unity with its correlative positionality and generality? Evidently the complex unity which can be said to go from the stage of a mere structural connection between nucleal unity and its correlative positionality and generality to the stage of a dominant power from which the nucleal unity and its correlatives can be abstracted as mere terminal points.

An actuality pulsates as an effective-ineffective complex unity. When most ineffective, the nucleal unity and its correlatives stand out in focus as requiring unification; when most effective, the actuality has a position and a specific meaning and a nucleal unity as facets of it. The nucleal unity in both cases, of course, is to be understood as involving an interpenetration of generality and positionality.

To speak of unity as effective and ineffective is to view it as spread out over the nucleal unity and the correlative positionality and generality. If, instead, we take up the position of the nucleal unity, we can see the encompassing unity as not only relating the nucleal to its correlatives, but as relating the result to the public particularity of the actuality. The encompassing unity encloses the nucleal unity and its correlatives at the same time that it makes them the topic of an expression in the form of a public particular.

The approach via ontology, just given, is the reciprocal of an approach via epistemology which begins with perceptual elements united with a selected object of apprehension so as to be oriented in a field having an intensity at a focal point. The field, with its intensity, is identical in content with the nucleal unity and its correlatives; the perceptual elements are identical in content with the public particular. The nucleal unity and its correlatives ontologically analyze the perceptual orienting field; the perceptual elements judgmentally analyze the public particular. It is also true that the nucleal unity and its correlatives analyze the encompassing unity of the actuality, and that the perceptual elements analyze the selected object of apprehension. But the latter analyses occur within their own domains, whereas the former involve analyses into elements of another domain. In the case of the latter analyses, we find out the components of something; in the former, we find out what the counterparts of something given is, but in a divided form. We analyze the selected object of apprehension as well as the public particular into perceptual elements; we analyze the encompassing unity of an actuality as well as the perceptual orienting field into a nucleal unity and its correlatives.

We can think of a mode of Being as expressing itself in a necessary meaning and in a characteristic compulsion. It could be said to distinguish these in the very effort to allow them to be pure, and that it then must have them together. Either it will engage in a pulsation which will reunite them when and as it keeps them apart, somewhat the way in which an actuality does with its factors, or it will look to the actualities themselves to be so many diverse ways in which the union could occur, by giving the generic, necessary meaning the widest range of specifications and by allowing the compulsion to possess that which it in fact compels.

If we take this line, must we not also take something like the reverse as well, and see the Beings as somehow synthesizing the positionality and the general meaning of an actuality? I think not, unless we at once add that the positionality is intensified until it becomes a source of compulsions, and the general meaning becomes finalized as a necessity.

The unification of the nucleus and its correlative positionality and generality is the work of the unity of the actuality. This evidently is something like Aristotle's substantial form. In uniting the factors, it at the same time expresses itself as an outside, and thus as that which is in a public context with other entities.

A similar description is pertinent to the epistemological situation. The unification of the perceptual elements (indicated, contemplated, and adumbrated) with the fixated object of apprehension is the product of our claim that this is true. It involves an orientating of the resultant unity in a field with a maximum intensity at a certain spot.

The nucleus and the correlative positionality and generality are the same in content, but differ in function. So do the perceptual elements and the fixated object of apprehension. The unity of the first (the actuality or substance—and not "object" as I have been inclined to call it recently) involves a duplication of content with diverse functions. The unity of the second (properly called an "object" and not a "substance" as I have been calling it recently) involves a similar duplication.

The unification in both cases is a pulling in of the diverse—the positionality and the generality in the one case, and the perceptual elements in the other—toward the nucleus and fixated object of apprehension, respectively. This act of pulling in is inseparable from a precipitation of the result in a context—in the one case, a public domain of outsides, and in the other, a field of objects.

Substances, as in public together, are identical in content with themselves as separate, but differ in function. Similarly, the objects in the field are identical with themselves as unified actualities, but differ in function. The differences are like that of occupying a position and having the position relative to another position—to use an illustration appropriate to substances. (An illustration appropriate to objects is like the difference between the fact that something is so and so, and the *claim* that it is true that something is so and so.)

July 28
(Ann Arbor, Michigan)

The substantial unity of a being in itself is its substantial form. This expands and contracts. It has a nucleus and generality as terms, and unites them with the nucleus (when it is given an outside as part of a context). In the case of perception, the claim that something is true comes after we have the perceptual elements and a fixated object of apprehension. That claim could be said to start with the elements and the apprehended as terms, and to end with them as united, and in that act grasped in an intensive field. (An earlier suggestion that the nucleus, when it possesses its correlative, also faces this as external, should be discarded as in conflict with the idea of the rhythm of the substantial form.)

We are left with the problems of A] the identity of the substance, B] the way the substantial form stands in relation to the atomic or physical parts of the object, and C] whether there are analogous problems to A and B in epistemology. A] In the case of man, the identity can be contained in the nucleus as a self. But in addition, like everything else, it has its identity in the substantial form which remains individual and constant, no matter how specific it makes the meaning. B] The substantial form should be thought of as governing the ultimate parts. These parts are not parts of the nucleus, for the nucleus can be identified with a self. They are parts within the area of the nucleus and the correlatives, both when united and when distinguished. They do not affect that union. A particle must itself have its own substantial form, with a correlative nucleus and generality. c] In the case of perception, we have a timeless truth in the claim we make, and have physical carriers of the claim in the guise of actions, attitudes, particles, etc., in the claiming being.

We can arrive at the modes of Being via the compulsions they exert on a plurality of actualities, from the position of some one mode of Being, and from an aspect of an actuality. We then use a distinctive logic—accumulative, intensional, existential, or divine—and find these also exhibited in the concrete at the terminus.

The movement from aspects of particulars to the modes of Being differs from case to case. We proceed to God from a different position and in a different way from the way we do, say with respect to the Ideal. The *Modes of Being* says we can proceed in any way we wish. But it does not make clear that the movements are really different in the kind of *modus ponens* they could be said to exhibit. The movement which is divine-like absorbs the symbol; the existential movement departs from the symbol; the movement which is Ideal-like generalizes from the symbol, and the movement which is like that of Actuality accumulates the symbol. If we use one of these logics to mediate between the other logics, we will get not to the object of a symbol, but to an aspect of that object.

To go from a particular piece of space and time to the whole of it via the logic of flux is merely to start at an arbitrary point and move out endlessly, stopping at an arbitrary point in an endless field.

Is the sacramental side of an object really vague? Do we move to God by absorbing it?

July 29
(Ann Arbor)

If we allow rules to be contingently true, we get five logics, or better, five types of inference, by changing the *modus ponens*. If we insist that there is only one *modus ponens*, we will instead have five different types of necessary truth, each embodied in a different kind of content. What is necessarily true in one of the logics will be contingently true in the other. We change the *modus ponens* when we are concerned with the movement to the ultimate Beings, but we change the necessary truths when we are concerned with knowing the structure of a Being. Also, when we deal with the vague, the general, the flux, and the being in the empirical world, we acknowledge different kinds of necessity and different kinds of *modus ponens*. (Symbolization, in short, has a distinctive *modus ponens* depending on what kind of symbolization it is, contingency to necessity, specific to general, part to whole, or diversity to unity.)

Ordinarily, we suppose that we have only the necessity characteristic of the realm of determinate objects, where we drop the premiss, keep to the same level of discourse, transfer a truth value, and relate elements in a purely extensional way.

An alternative approach to yesterday: we can begin the movement to finalities from a mere happening together of actualities; from the fact that they answer to one another's needs; from the brute compulsions to which they are subject; or from the unity of the field of their diverse presences. Each finality has its own set of particulars, which are arrived at by the converse of the movement by which we can get to the finalities. But only in the case of actualities do we in fact move from particulars to the appropriate mode of Being; in the other cases we start with actualities, too, and therefore with what is not a particular for any other mode of Being than Actuality. An actuality's substantial form, though, might be considered as being in the same relation to the parts of a complex actuality as Actuality is to an actuality—or better, perhaps, in the same relation as the unity of an actuality is to the parts of the actuality.

July 30
(Ann Arbor)

An actuality falls at a rate dictated by the fall of the several parts in it, as Galileo made evident. But it falls as a single being. The weight of an actuality is enclosed in the region of the substantial form. The mere weight is an abstraction from this, but in the case of an aggregate, it is a direct description. Perhaps this is one of the differences between a living and a dead body. The former weighs what the latter does if the latter is a moment later; but where the latter has weight as its immediate predicate, the former has it mediated or sustained in a qualitative whole.

August 5
(Ann Arbor)

From the perspective of a Being, the particulars which are germane to it multiply its efficacy and allow for an aggregational activity. Each Being, though, has a distinctive relation to its own particulars, and as a consequence is multiplied, allowing for aggregation in a different way than the others do. Actuality is multiplied in individuals who act at their best with deliberation and freedom. Ideality is multiplied in stresses which are aggregated only when distinguished by actualities. Existence is multiplied in regions which are aggregated only so far as they are occupied by actualities. God is multiplied in "persons" or attributes which are aggregated only so far as they are effective with respect to actualities.

Put this way, it seems as if aggregation is peculiar to actualities, thereby treating the particulars for other modes of Being as somehow being multiplied only through the aid of actualities. But this denies the integrity of a mode of Being and the particulars which it governs. We can save the above distinctions by taking the reference to modes of Being, other than Actuality, to point only to encapsulated modes of Being. We will then have to look for distinctive reasons in each of these modes of Being for their having characteristic particulars when those Beings are freed from encapsulation.

Staying with Actuality and the three encapsulated modes of Being, what we do have is the reverse of the process by which we reached the Beings through symbolization. What is the logic of this movement? In religion, we have a doctrine of Grace, which might serve as our guide. How does it function?

After we have determined this, we still have to determine the way in which God is related to His attributes or "persons." Do we not have a logic of modalities, of compulsions and demands to use in connection with the way in which the Beings are related to actualities, and a logic of exfoliation or delimitation governing the way in which the Beings arrive at (or we, from the position of the Beings, can arrive at) the particulars which are distinctively pertinent to them?

If we take the idea of Grace seriously, we should say that the act of moving to particulars is an act of empowering or ennobling what is confronted.

Grace turns a secular into a sacramental object; the Ideal turns an actuality via ideal demands into a representative of others; Existence subjects them to a power. Equally, though, we can say that Beings, in coming down to actualities, lower their own power somehow, thereby balancing the increase achieved in symbolization. It is to be noted that symbolization is due to us, whereas the descent (as now described) is entirely the work of the Beings. A problem still remains.

August 6
(Ann Arbor)

If we begin with Actuality, as a final Being, we can ask   A] are there any evidences of the existence of actualities;   B] what transformation must the Being undergo if it is to provide a premiss for the movement to actualities;   C] what is the nature of the process by which we go from the premiss to the conclusion;   D] what does the realm of particulars look like from the perspective of Actuality;   E] what is the relation between the premiss and the conclusion;   F] what guide do we now have for understanding the relation of other modes of Being to their particulars;   G] what guide do we have for understanding the relation of the encapsulated modes of Being to actualities;   H] what guide do we have for understanding the relation that Actuality, in an encapsulated from, has to the particulars appropriate to other modes of Being?

A]   The evidence for a Being was found in an "accident"; that accident had some kind of compulsiveness for a plurality of the actualities. The answer to the first question is the reciprocal of what has been characterized as compulsiveness of some kind, imposed on a plurality of actualities. Do we find a diversity in the single Actuality which we cannot account for except by looking outside it for the source? Actuality seems to be diversified in a way that is alien to its nature. It is subject to contingency in the sense that the diversification alters in content in ways which could not possibly be understood from the perspective of the Actuality. Do we have evidence that this is so?

B]   The movement from the fact that actualities are compelled, to the compulsion itself, is a movement from factuality to symbols. A different movement is needed to move from the presence of the diversity in Actuality to the diversification itself. This seems to be a movement from factuality to a variable.

C]   The premiss which compelled actualities provide is Being in its most attenuated form, as contingently exhibited; it is Being which exists only in the guise of a plurality of contingencies referring to one another. The reciprocal of this would be the distinctiveness of actualities as contingent beings. The former is a symbol of what is unitary and intensive; the latter is a variable which is subject to more and more sharp divisions. In the one case, we go from premiss to conclusion by intensification, and in the other by sharpening divisions, breaking up the variable into values.

The process of symbolization, we saw earlier, was subject to some modified forms of *modus ponens*. What is the process which moves from a variable itself to that variable dissected into values? It is related to a submergence in experience, a giving of oneself to what is present. It is like the process of making a perceptual judgment. If we think of the variable as incipiently divided, the process is one of analysis.

D] From the perspective of Actuality, actualities are only finite centers, mere points of Being. They are itself multiplied and interrelated, but necessary, or at least as having a necessary nature which is carried by unknown substances. Actualities cannot be grasped from the perspective of Actuality except by altering the Actuality or the evidences that it exhibits, so that we already have something of the nature of actualities under limitation.

E] The relation of premiss to conclusion in the case of Actuality and actualities is a relation of entities similar in kind: we either have attenuated versions of Actuality in the form of symbols, or we have undivided variables which are to be analyzed out into specific actualities.

F] If actualities can be analyzed out of variables derived from Actuality, there might be said to be different kinds of analyses. These make it possible to obtain values from the variables that are obtained from other modes of Being.

G] The encapsulated modes of Being are all relativized with reference to actualities, and thus already exhibit something like the character of variables. These variables are to be dissected into actualities and not into what is pertinent to these modes of Being when no longer encapsulated in Actuality.

H] Inside other modes of Being, Actuality has an encapsulated status where it is relative to the distinctive particulars of those modes of Being. If we can speak of it as sustaining a variable, it will be a variable which is dissectable into those particulars and not into actualities.

I think I have now clarified the issue somewhat, without, however, coming to a clear conclusion regarding the logic or the process which allows one, who has acknowledged a mode of Being, to acknowledge a relevant set of particulars.

The suggested analysis must not be taken to be the reciprocal of a merging, except in the case of God and His particulars. In the other cases, it must be conceived of as the reciprocal of accumulation, hierarchy, or part-whole. In the first of these only, "accumulation," is there a retention of the items with which one begins, so that here alone we have a dissection into what before had been utilized. In the second hierarchy, we have a movement downward, a movement of specificity which never gets to an individual. In the third, part-whole, we have a movement from whole to part where the part is arbitrarily demarcated.

If we are to arrive at determinate actualities from premisses which are not dissimilar to them, we must evidently be working in the realm of determinate logic. Though we can say that we there have a movement of dissection, specification, selection, and articulation, which start with evidences found in Actuality, and in limited forms of Ideality, Existence, and God (and which yield actualities only so far as these limited forms of Being are inseparable from a reference to actualities), we must have concluded to their determinateness before we can move to the determinate actualities.

Alternatively, we have a movement from different compulsions by symbolization to different kinds of sources of compulsion, and from different kinds of diversification in a unity to a diversity of separates by means of compulsions of different kinds. The diversification in a unity can be thought of as the unity as a perfected symbol. We would then have compulsion and a movement by symbolization to the unitary source of the compulsion, and perfect symbols with a movement by compulsion to a diversity of separates.

August 7
(Ann Arbor)

Have I in the last few days been looking for ways in which I can move from quality to quantity, from generality to specificity, from whole to part, and from unity to diversity—or more specifically from "being fat" to weighing over 200 lbs., from being a man to being a German, from space or time to here or now, and from the Trinity to the particular persons acknowledged in Roman Catholicism? The quality, generality, etc., must already be variables and thus already be of a different order from the Being which sustains them. All of them involve a use of the *modus ponens* in its ordinary form. The conclusion will involve an encounter if the premiss is really distinct in kind from the conclusion, unless we can somehow exhibit the difference in the process of inference, by modifying the *modus ponens*.

Our premiss must be a quality for a quantity, a generality for a specificity, a whole for a part, and a unity for a diversity. The inference will move to the being of the quantity, etc., by itself. The fat is a fat for some quantity—it is a variable without a precise lower bound. Do all movements from quality involve a quantity without upper, lower, or both bounds? Do all movements from generality involve an unspecifiable number of specifications? Do all movements from whole to part involve an indeterminateness with respect to the magnitude of the part? Do all movements from unity to diversity involve an unspecified order of procession?

Or do we begin with variables as having an indeterminate range of values, the indeterminacy being expressed in the quality, the indeterminate, separated specifics being expressed in the general, the indeterminate magnitudes being expressed by the whole, and the indeterminate sets of relations being expressed by the unity? Do we identify the quality, etc., with some determinate item as a beginning, and proceed to identify it throughout its range? If so, we would begin with a quality which is quantified as such and such, but as requiring further specifications through the aid of the acknowledged quantity, etc.

Or do we begin with the quality as quantified in one form, and then make use of that method of transformation throughout? For example, do we begin with fat already specified as 200 lbs., and then proceed to a further quantification of the fat by a related way of producing determinations? The specification of the fat as being no less than 200 lbs. involves a reference to other weights as well, thereby showing that the specification is partial. The quality as quantified in this one way is the premiss for another qualification of the quantification in other ways.

A quality becomes an operator producing determinate quantities in a determinate order. The quality, apparently, becomes interpreted as the rule for moving from one determinate quantity to another, a rule which is actualized by starting with an accepted quantity.

The quality, to begin with, has nothing to do but provide evidence for the quantity, since it is a rule for quantities. The *modus ponens* for the quantities exhibits this rule.

We can begin to move to quantity when we change the quality in itself into a specific quantity and a rule for the production of quantities. Similarly, the general is made specific and serves as a rule for the production of other specifics. Similarly, the whole is delimited, and serves as a rule for the production of other regions. And, finally, the unity is diversified and serves as a rule for connecting diverse elements to one another.

The quantity, etc., function as a beginning of a *modus ponens* by virtue of the fact that they specify the quality. The quality in the domain of quantity begins a definite way of getting the next quantity. The quality, as it were, says that quantities are arranged in a numerical order of succession beginning with this quantity *x*. The acceptance of such and such a quantity as the beginning is one with the acceptance of such and such a procedure for getting the next quantity.

If the last observation is valid, we can continue and say that the general becomes translated into specific meanings with an accepted way of getting them separated from one another, that the whole is translated into a region which bounds another region, and that the unity is translated into a plurality which is then given a certain order. In effect, what is being said is that these are diverse ways of speaking of something like a rule as it functions in an actual inference by which something is in fact produced. Let us call this "utilization." Utilization is then the converse of the operation of symbolization which starts with entities already taken to be creatures or items in some other domain, and proceeds to a more intensive version of them. In utilization, we start instead with quality, etc., understood to be already quantified and proceeding, in accordance with the rule-guide of the quality, to yield other quantities.

The foregoing leads us to say that Actuality is recognized to be subject to determinations which cannot be accounted for by reference to it. The attempt to account for the determinations involves the translation of Actuality into an actuality, together with a use rule for the acknowledgment of other actualities in accord with the determinations suffered by the Actuality.

In an ordinary inference, we acknowledge *p* to be a premiss only so far as we accept the rule to be expressed as *modus ponens*. The acknowledgment of the premiss is one with the use of the premiss in an actual inference. The rule can be said to be a stimulus for the acceptance of *p* as the beginning of the inference and of the *modus ponens* as the mode of proceeding to this rather than that ending. The movement of a *p* from outside to the position of a premiss is what the conversion of the rule into a utilized operative involves. At the end of the operation we must let go of the final term so that it can be an item which is related to the terminus of the rule as the initial term was related to the beginning of the rule.

We have, in the case of the modes of Being, a movement to the diversifications which those Beings are seen to suffer. From this we move to an acceptance of some beginning, and follow that move with an act which is under the guidance of the diversification, in the sense that it proceeds by *modus ponens* to go to an item which the rule warrants. But there is no need to look to the rule or to conform to it; the rule is already operative in the process of getting the next item.

This discussion allows one to say that a theory has been utilized when it not only is translated into some accepted datum, but when it leads to the production or acceptance of data of such and such a kind expressed in the theory. A theory about electrons accepts such and such to be evidence of the electrons, and such and such to be the proper way to proceed to determine some new state or new set of electrons. The acceptance of the electrons or of the proper way to proceed is not an act of subsumption of the electrons, or of the procedure under the rule; it is the rule itself, the theory itself utilized by our taking our start at such and such a datum and proceeding to such and such an end. What makes this datum be accepted? Must not the theory have a plurality of divisions within it which require it to be expressed as a theory of electrons, and must not the acceptance of this and that as electrons be due to the fact that they accord with the joints of the theory? We note a number of data and the way in which they are distinct from one another; the theory by allowing an acceptance of the data as in accord with its joints at the same time tells us to proceed according to *modus ponens*.

Instead of saying with respect to the movement from Beings to actualities or other particulars that one has an initial datum, the present discussion indicates that we proceed by acknowledging a number of data. In accepting these as the data for the theory, we thereby define the nature of the interval between them which is to be traversed by *modus ponens*. We make the Being as determinate as possible in the guise of a plurality of determinate particulars, and proceed to connect these and to provide for still other particulars on the basis of the way in which the particulars are related in the Being as so determinate. We might not want fat to be expressed by any number of pounds, no matter how large, but only by a certain class of such numbers; the acknowledgment of the limits of the application, or even that there is more than one number appropriate to the fat is essential to the use of the term as a variable which is utilized in dealing with values.

Should we not now distinguish different ways in which a Being might be identified with data, and the way the data and the Being are to be connected in fact? In the ordinary use of *modus ponens,* the rule serves to give a formal account of what we are in fact doing. But in the case of the various Beings, we can say that the copresence of the actualities is contingent, that the separation of the specific meanings is not complete, that the magnitudes of the parts is yet to be given, and that the relations of the diverse to one another is what is still to be provided. There would then be five utilizations of the *modus ponens*—the normal, characteristic of actualities, and four others which express different functions serving primarily to dictate what kind of relation a number of items have to one another.

In the laborious and circuitous fashion that these preceding comments reveal, I have arrived at the view that there are four types of symbolization by which we move in accord with different forms of *modus ponens* to Beings, and five types of utilization by which we use a rule to allow us to order data. There is a fifth form of *modus ponens* which is used with one of the types of utilization—this is the normal employment of a rule with respect to propositions about actualities or with respect to the actualities themselves.

Utilization, even in the case of actualities or their propositions, involves the acknowledgment of at least two data, usually those which represent a beginning and an ending. In the case of actualities, or their propositions, we want to transfer something from the beginning to the ending. In the movement *to* Beings instead, we want merely to intensify our symbols in one of our four ways. In the movement *from* Beings, though, we want to characterize the kind of connections the beginning and the ending or other data have to one another.

Utilization, as the remarks about theory indicate, has wide application in science. It can be extended to all practical problems, where we start with some program or ideal state and try to give it application. We then determine whether we are looking for ways to allow the different data to be independent (contingently connected), to be separated by virtue of their natures, to occupy regions, or to have an order of procession or merit.

August 8
(Ann Arbor)

It is tempting to forge a theory by making a number of observations, and then trying to see what formal system exhibits the structure of the set of observations. But not only does the Galilean refutation of the Aristotelian observed rates of falling bodies show that this is a method with insufficient explanatory power, but the observations are themselves selected, and are therefore not as innocent as they at first appear to be. If we have a formal scheme which seems to be effective in some areas, we should try to see if we cannot analyze the observation in such a way as to yield components which can be predicted to conform to the structure of that formal scheme. Should we not be able to make such a prediction, or should the scheme not be able to provide a basis for deducing other laws than those which seem to govern the observed phenomena, as qualified by gross interferences, or for deducing laws which seem to apply to the analytic products of those observations (and thus should our scheme fail to predict further phenomena or analytic items similar to the initial products, or those having a clear relationship to them as effects, combinations, etc.), we must try to modify the initial scheme or find some other.

In the case of ultimate Beings, we are presumably able to examine what is in fact ultimate, whereas in the case of theories, we have only our own constructions to consider, or (if we attend to necessary totalities of mathematics or logic) only limited schemes which may not be appropriate to the phenomena in which we are interested. But in the case of theories, no less than in the case of Beings, we want to understand the world of actualities as exhibiting necessities, not in themselves, but in their interconnection. When we derive a separation of beings, or specific meanings (still under the aegis of a common meaning, though), or regions, or different types of relation holding in the diverse parts, we exhibit the power of the Beings as variables or rules which are inescapably exhibited. Actualities, for example, are necessarily contingent because Actuality is manifested as a variable which is to be exhibited in a plurality of actualities. These are sundered from one another through the utilization of the rule which Actuality exhibits.

We would like to find theories which have the same role that the variable form of Actuality has with respect to the realm of actualities. If there were nothing but the ultimate particles of physics, we could say that the proper physical theory was but the variable form of Actuality; but there are other actualities besides these particles. Our theories in science are theories about a limited number of phenomena for which we would like to provide variables which will yield necessary connections between the acknowledged particularizations.

Had we no evidences of compulsions, we would not know what a good symbol would be. Similarly, if we had no grasp of the diversifications to which Beings are subject, we would have no clue as to how to choose amongst possible theories. But to this it could be objected that it took centuries of genius to discover such basic laws as those governing the fall of bodies in a vacuum. Why were these not suggested by some acquaintance with Actuality? Firstly, those laws apply only after Existence had been broken up into regions; and secondly, they require one to re-interpret gross phenomena as aggregates of ultimate particles to which the laws apply, thereby leaving to a side the actualities so far as they are more than aggregated. Similarly, men have made use of many different symbols, totems, evidences, as beginnings of processes of intensifications reaching to Beings; but the ones we take to be satisfactory presuppose that we have already moved out of the realm of ordinary activities. The satisfactory symbols require us to interpret them as inseparable from what they symbolize.

Our theories can be considered to be approximations to the statement of the diversification to which Actuality is subject, as applicable to ac-tualities. Those actualities are also conditioned by relations to limited forms of the other modes of Being. Our symbols can be considered to be approximations to the statement of the source of compulsions which have been suffered by actualities.

Our symbols move in four directions, whereas our theories move in only one, since they have to do only with Actuality and its relevant actualities. But this merely points up the fact that in addition to the delimited symbols which lead to relativized and limited forms of the modes of Being, there are intensifiable beginnings outside the realm of actualities which lead to those other modes of Being in their finality.

Matching our theories are symbols of Actuality; matching our begin-nings with appropriate particulars for other modes of Being are utiliza-tions of diversifications in those modes. These utilizations could be called "characterizations." Our theories are characterizations of Actuality so far as we can achieve these by taking account of only some actualities in certain kinds of relations to one another, (but still subject to the influence of limited forms of other Beings). Our intensifiable beginnings, of which symbols for Actuality offer but one type, lead to different Beings. Our accepted symbols are beginnings for a move to Actuality so far as we can free those symbols from modifications by other Beings.

Ideally, we could have a single theory for all actualities, and this not by the usual procedure of reducing the complex ones to aggregates of ultimate particles. And we could, ideally, have a single, splendid type of symbol which would take us in the most direct way to Actuality. I have in fact been speaking as though we had such a symbol in the acknowledg-ment of the fact that all actualities are equally beings. If this is so, why do we not have a perfect theory for all actualities? Could we not be said to have such a theory if all we expect to be able to get from a movement from the diversification of Actuality is the acknowledgment of the independence of actualities and the determination of the necessary division which allows them to be contingently together? A more specific theory concerns more specific relations, such as those which govern the sequence of the relations they will bear to one another over time. Similarly, a more vital symbol concerns more intensive compulsions, such as those which are acknowledged to be present in men who have subordinated other actualities to themselves in the guise of tools, and who therefore themselves function as symbols which represent those others immediately, and other actualities by extension. Such an intensive symbol does not get us to the full Being of Actuality, but only to it as diversified by man and his concerns. Whereas in the one case of the theory, we come to learn something about some selection of actualities, in the other case of the symbol, we come to learn something about some selected aspect of Actuality.

The perfect theory is cosmological, and ends perhaps only with necessary distinctions, permitting the actualities to be contingent. The perfect symbol is ontological, and ends perhaps only with that aspect of Actuality which is seen to be necessary. The whole Actuality would be seen to be necessary (with a contingent diversification), had we the right symbol, just as the totality of actualities would be seen to be broken up into parts related necessarily, had we the right theory. But we must be content with dealing only with an aspect of Actuality as at once necessary and having a contingent diversification. (Hartshorne rightly speaks of the ontological argument as ending only in an aspect of God. He then goes on to affirm that God also has "accidents" which cannot be deduced from that aspect. he does not show that the accidents must be, but his view and the present are otherwise very close.)

Can we move from the aspect which we arrive at with a proper use of a limited symbol to the Actuality as such? Can we move from the actualities that are covered by the best of our theories to all actualities as occupants of the same universe? Since the symbol and the theory are appropriate to their respective limited termini, such a movement does not seem possible. Instead one must try to find other symbols of a more penetrative kind, and other theories which are more inclusive. How?

The best symbol is indifferent to the nature of the carriers for it; the best theory is indifferent to the nature of Actuality. The one begins with the meaning of Being as unified, and seeks to find the unitary Being which is or has that meaning; the other begins with diversification, and seeks to find the actualities which exhibit this amongst them. The one remains a meant, unified Being, even though rooted in a plurality; the other remains a diversified view, even though rooted in the single Being of Actuality. There is only a single Being as unified for the one, and only a single diversification for the other. Just as we today cannot grasp the one diversification, but express subordinate forms of it in our different theories applicable to different groups of actualities, so we cannot grasp the full meaning of a Being unified, and must be content with a grasp of part of that meaning as caught in different symbols.

I have been pressing the symmetry of symbol and theory here, and trying to characterize one in the light of what I think I discern is true of the other. I know that theories are limited in range in fact, and I am, therefore, supposing that the symbols we have are also limited, not, of course, in their range, but in their capacity to give us the Actuality in its fullness, even when we move to Actuality by an intensification of the symbol. The symbols we have of Actuality, in short, are being viewed as capable of giving us only an aspect of it, no matter how intensified they become. They bring us only to the essence of Actuality, not to its Being as dynamic. But we could in principle get to the Being, just as in principle we could have a theory for all actualities.

The "accidents" of Actuality—what Hartshorne calls "accidents" of God—are the different diversifications of it due to the effect of actualities on it, just as the necessary separations of actualities are due to the utilization of different theories on different groups of actualities.

A successful comprehensive theory will shift in its offering of connections as the data differ in kind; a successful perfect symbol will end with different necessities as it comes to rest with different aspects of the Actuality. Each must be content in the end, not with a single, mono-valued answer, but with a multi-faceted answer which changes connections with changes in empirical data, or changes types of necessity with changes in aspects of Actuality. What is wrong with the best of our symbols today is that we cannot make them attend to different aspects and different types of necessity in Actuality; what is wrong with the best of our theories is that we cannot make them change their types of connection with a change in types of actuality.

Turning now to an actuality and its subordinate parts, we are led to say that a proper understanding of the unity of the actuality requires us to acknowledge that its subordinate parts are related necessarily in different ways just so far as they are different kinds of parts—organs, chemicals, physical, etc. And we are led to say that a proper understanding of the plurality of the parts requires us to acknowledge that the actuality has different necessities in it, depending on what aspect of its unity we happen to arrive at. Symbols do not guarantee just what aspect we will reach; and what is true of symbols is true of any reference of subordinate entities to the actuality in which they are. Theories do not guarantee just what kinds of contingency will be acknowledged; and what is true of theories is true of the unity of an actuality as that which governs parts. One must be told what aspect we have arrived at, what kind of contingency is being necessitated.

It is not hard to distinguish in such a being as a man the different types of parts which must have different kinds of relations to one another. The heart is related to the liver in a way that is different from the way one blood cell is related to another, or to the urine. But it is not so easy to distinguish different types or aspects of unity in him, such that approaches from some part will end with one or the other of those aspects and never with all of them as united, and that the aspects will be found to be characterized from these contingent approaches by different types of necessity. But it is perhaps this difficulty which has stood in the way of our understanding the nature of complex actualities.

I, for one, surely (and I think others as well) have not noted that the unity pertinent to organs is not necessarily identical with the unity pertinent to molecules. Once we say that they are different, it is not a great matter to go on to say that if we start with either molecules or organs, we can arrive at one or the other of these unities, or (better) at aspects of the unity of the actuality. Each will give us a different aspect of the unity, just as different parts of the diversification will give us different data and relations when properly utilized.

By a rather circuitous route, I have now arrived at the position of saying that Actuality (and the unity of actuality) is multi-faceted; that we arrive at different facets, different "essences" of it, from different starting points or symbols (or from different kinds of parts of the actuality); that there are groups of actualities whose members have different natures from those of other groups; and that we arrive at those groups and the relations the members of them have to one another from different parts of the diversification in the Actuality, or (what I trust is an equivalent expression) from it as exercising different kinds of roles with respect to its encompassed particulars. Yet if we had a perfect way of taking the actuality as a single unity, we would not be able to get to all of the parts it encompasses in a single move; we would arrive at one or the other set of such parts, but in such a way that we could, with a shift in emphasis, get to the other parts. And if we had started somewhere among any kind of parts to get to the unity, we would not get to the unity of the actuality but only to facets of it, but in such a way that we could move on to other facets by shifting the approach from the given starting point.

We are now left with the need to clarify the "unity" of an actuality in such a way as to make evident that it has many different aspects, each unified. It is diversified internally. And it can be approached from many different types of parts at the same time that it permits of a movement to one set of parts while allowing for a movement to other sets of parts with a shift from one part of the unity to another—which is possible so far as the unity and its aspects are diversified in the sense of being articulatable.

The physicist does not move to the unity of an encompassing actuality. He is not interested in his particles as clustered, but only as forming a single domain. The anatomist who is concerned only with the difference between the musculature of the arm and the leg has a similar attitude. Who then is interested in the clustered particles and other parts? The mystic or monist does not move to actualities because he is interested, not in the diversifications of his final reality, but only in it as a Being. Who then treats it as a ground for a utilization of actualities? Who is concerned with the unity of an actuality as utilized so as to allow us to deal with the encompassed parts? Is it anyone other than the philosopher in all these cases? The theorist who restricts himself to what is in common-sense objects is in effect one who is dealing with parts of a general theory; or conversely, he is occupied with clusters, and is so far not a scientist engaged in measuring or predicting, but rather a philosopher occupied with the different task of understanding complex actualities. He is dealing with limited theories that are sources of clusters.

August 9
(Ann Arbor)

It is important to distinguish between a movement from a theory to its components and a movement from a theory to data; and it is important to distinguish between a movement from data to a summary statement of them and a movement from evidences to a theory. In all four cases, beginning and ending are similar in kind. In the first and third cases, where we move from theory to components and from data to summary, we take the beginning to dictate the kind of consequence we will reach; in the other two cases, we transform items so that they conform to the conditions required by the outcome. The actual movements through which we go in fact begin with the first and go on to the second, or begin with the third and then go on to the fourth.

To go from　*1*] a theory to its components is but to analyze the theory; to go from　*2*] a theory to data is to utilize the theory so that data are identified and the connections amongst them revealed. To go from　*3*] data to a summary is but to bundle together the data; to go from　*4*] evidences to a theory is to use symbols with increasing intensifications. The first move is like that of saying that fat means no less than 280 lbs., and the second is like that of saying that if someone is fat, he is no less than 280 lbs., and can be up to 350 lbs.—after which he is grotesque. This second formulation is not altogether satisfactory because it is put in an hypothetical form and thus might conceivably not have an instance. Better perhaps is: since this man is 280 lbs., he remains fat if he does not go below this or over 350. The third move is like saying that 280 lbs. can be taken as a unit and then can be termed "fat." The fourth move is like saying that since this man never gets below 280 lbs., he is fat, or the 280 lbs. that he has are shaped in such and such a way, and therefore we can see him as fat. In the third move, we merely have a totality of units or pounds; in the fourth movement, we have the pounds contoured or structured, and move from this to the quality of the contour or structure.

These distinctions are important, though not yet precisely enough formulated. One reason for the imprecision is my failure to make clear what the unity of an actuality is—a question parallel to one which asks what the being of a part is. There is a unity which is the referent of the parts, and there is a unity which includes both the former unity and the parts. There is also the unity which refers to parts, and there is the unity which includes this unity and its parts.

Is there a difference between the unity which is a referent of and the unity which refers to the parts? Is it the difference between the unity which we arrive at from evidences, and the unity which can be used? If so, there should be two more unities—one which is a summary of the parts, and the other of which is analyzable into parts. And then there must be, in addition, the unity of all these unities, including the unity which encompasses all the unities and all the parts in all their roles. And any one of these could be said to have aspects or facets.

The plethora of unities now distinguished can be brought into some order by recognizing the unitary organic entity as allowing for divisions into different kinds of unities and different correlative parts. Within the organic unitary being we can distinguish,　A] the unity which is a meaning dissectable into referents to parts;　B] a unity which is a meaning that can be utilized and is in fact utilized in the functioning of the parts;

c] a unity which is merely the summary of the fact that the parts make a totality; D] a unity which is the unity of the evidences that the parts together provide; E] distinct unities for each of the above four, which keep together the original unity and the parts. When we deal with such a question as the fall of a complex body, which in ideal conditions falls at a rate dictated by the individual falls of the ultimate particles, we tend to speak of c, but in fact we should be speaking of the complex individual in which c is but one facet. In the complex individual, the unity and the parts have four roles—the unity is a dissectable meaning and the parts are the dissecta, the unity is a meaning utilized by the parts, the unity is a summary of the parts together, and the unity governs the common features of the parts as together. The organic being seems to be both of the last two together, with the first two serving only as ways of dealing with unity and parts as referents to something of the same kind, but in the guise of divisions or unifications of that with which we begin.

Is the organic unity a union of the utilizable meaning and the parts utilized, together with the governing unity and the clustered parts? The first would tell us why the body falls at the same rate every other body falls, no matter how large, since the fall is dictated by the same utilized data—the ultimate particles. The second would tell us why the being falls as a single body and not merely as an aggregate. The unity of these two tells us that a single body falls at the rate which is dictated by the fall of an aggregate of ultimate particles, or conversely, that the ultimate particles fall together in a single body. If we attend only to the clustered items, we will know the unity of the being only as that which has them together; if we attend only to the utilized unity, we will know the particles only as pertinent to that being, and not as interchangeable with any other particles and thus as subject to a universal law for particles.

The being, as having a utilizable unity, has its parts function in unusual ways by virtue of the functioning of that unity with respect to other unities. As having clustered parts, the being has its unity functioning in the way the parts dictate. The fall of bodies idealized emphasizes the parts (and even goes so far as to forget their clustering), while the commonsensical role of the being emphasizes the unity (and even goes so far as to forget the independent role of the parts). We have mere unity and mere parts only so far as they constitute the unity of the organism.

A being treated as the unity of mere unity and mere parts is misconstrued. The being should always be seen to be the unity of the clustered (and thus unified) parts, with the utilized (and thus diversified) unity. To speak of the organic unity we must, therefore, either see it as the equilibrium of these last two, or refuse to speak of it except as a distinctive type of unity primarily functioning now as one and now as many.

Are these observations limited to organic entities? Only so far as the unity which is dissectable into clustered parts and a utilizable unity is recognized to have a distinctive role, with powers and consequences which are not functions of the factors into which it could be dissected. If the utilizable unity and the unity of the cluster be termed "meanings," it is easy to see that unsuspectingly we have come to a conclusion similar to that arrived at in dealing with perception—we start with an aboriginal unitary item and divide it into two biased forms of itself, one bias stressing the meaning and the other the discrete parts, each with something of the other in a subordinate role. To get to the meaning by itself or to the parts as unrelated to the meaning, we would have to concern ourselves with a meaning for all the particles whatsoever, or what comes to the same thing, for all the particles as forming one world.

The realm of physical particles is inseparable from a submerged meaning, which is one of two biased forms of the unitary nature of the cosmos as a single whole. (In epistemological terms, we would express this as a single system in which theory and content required one another.) A law for the particles is a unity for all of them; the activity of the totality of the particles is governed by the nature of the whole of which they are a part.

When we speak of the nature of the whole by itself, we suppress acknowledgment of the subordinated particles. When we speak of the particles by themselves, we suppress acknowledgment of the submerged cosmic unity. The whole is always connected with submerged particles; the particles are always connected with a submerged whole. To have particles and whole equally prominent is to acknowledge the unity of a cosmos from which these can be derived as biased versions.

The present reflections bring us to the point of seeing that suppressed meanings or particles are to be arrived at from the vantage point of the dominant factor by utilization or symbolization, respectively. No matter what we have abstracted, we are left with the fact that we are connected with something else. That something else is to be arrived at by recognizing the dominant factor to be subject to a modification before it provides a ground for a movement to the other factor.

To get from the particles to the meaning which is suppressed, but inseparable from it, we must first recognize that the particles are together. To get from the meaning to the suppressed but inseparable particles, we must first recognize that the meaning is articulate. If we try to understand the suppressed item, and do not, as is usually the case, try to understand the item as occupying a dominant role, or as part of a totality in which it does not have a biased position, we will have to engage in an act of symbolization which does not progress by intensification, or in an act of utilization which does not progress by dividing the particles sharply one from the other.

A successful symbolic act does not move from clustered particulars to the diversified meaning (for this is relative to the distinguished particulars). Since what is wanted is the meaning by itself, it moves to the meaning or unity which is analytically obtainable from the organic whole. This is done by placing the bias on mere meaning and suppressed particulars instead of on a diversified meaning which is relevant to suppressed utilized particulars. Similarly, a successful utilization moves from a diversified meaning to distinct particulars as biased forms of the original whole and thus as inseparable from a suppressed meaning.

We have then two sets of biases: there is the bias of the diversified meaning correlative to a bias of a clustered set of particulars, and there is the bias of a mere meaning correlative to a bias of mere particulars. A bias always has itself as a suppressed or recessive item in a correlative biased item. A complex actuality is to be analyzed into mere biased meanings and particulars in inorganic cases. Only in organic cases do we find a meaning governing the parts and the parts utilizing the meaning. Perhaps a similar distinction should be made in perception, between judgments which report on the substantial form of an object and those which do not. The latter yield biased items which are like mere meanings and mere particulars, whereas the former yield utilizable meanings and clustered particulars with their respective suppressed factors.

Substantial forms are not usually thought to be balanced by clustered particulars, and one might perhaps consider cases where we have one of these without the other. But these appear to be degenerate cases. The bias toward a substantial form leaves over a bias for clustered particulars; the movement from the substantial form is to what can utilize it; and the movement from clustered particulars is to the mere meaning.

The combination of utilization and symbolization gives us a unitary substantial form and divided particulars, each of which absorbs something of the domain from which we begin. The organic being must be said to have a unitary substantial form which, though standing by itself, is what it is because it has been and is the intensification of the clustered particulars. It also has particulars, each of which is divided from the others through the operation of utilizations of the substantial form.

We have a dominant set of clustered particulars with a recessive substantial form over against biased clustered particulars which are dominated by the substantial form. The dominant clustered particulars move by symbolization to the substantial form of the original organic being, and the utilization moves to the divided particulars of that being. (Symbolization and utilization are, of course, not the appropriate terms to use when we are speaking of the mere internal structure of the being, but I keep the terms, for the moment, to provide continuity with the previous discussion.)

August 10
(Ann Arbor)

I think I have not kept sufficiently steady the fact that we arrive at the terminus of a symbolization by a process of accumulation. The failure is due to the fact that the terminus is the entity at its richest and yet known to be that which has some relation to the starting point. When one thinks of the terminus as something in itself, one overlooks the accumulative character of it. As in itself, it is to be thought of as containing the meaning of the beginning. The beginning is derivable from it by attenuation. When then we start with actualities as contingent beings (or with clustered particles), we move to Actuality (and to the substantial form) as a Being (or as that which is one distinct component in the actuality). We move not to the correlative biased form of the contingent compelled actualities (or the clustered particulars), but to the biased form which is correlative with mere actualities, as distinct individuals (or to the biased form which is correlative with mere particulars). But do we then not move from the factors derived from an organism to those which are involved in what is a mere whole or aggregate? No, because the Being and the substantial form, as was just remarked, are accumulative factors, so that the arrival at both of them is an arrival at that which is possessive of the meaning of the contingency (or the clustering).

What I think may be but another way of saying this is that the organic whole does not have a mere form or meaning and particulars, but has these as possessing the very meaning of a clustering or the very being of the contingency of the particulars, respectively. When we go from the biased clustering or the biased substantial form, we move to the substantial form as a mere being, but one which contains the meaning of clustering. We do not go to the mere particulars, but to those particulars as divided in consonance with a general meaning or substantial form. The movements of symbolization and utilization go from the clustering to the unitary meaning, and from the diversified meaning to the distinguishing of the entities. The abstracting of the factors, which is the same as the obtaining of biased forms of the original unity, involves an emphasis on the clustering and the diversification of meaning at the same time that it abstracts the meaning and the particulars from the whole in which they are.

In the case of perception, we ought to say that we do not merely have biased forms of the original object of awareness, but that in those forms the dominant factors are seen to be involved with the unitary aspect of the plurality and the plural side of the unity. This is due to the fact that the original whole is given a role in the abstracted biased factors. This fact is overlooked when we speak of the whole as made up of a mere unity, or substantial form, and the particulars. It is these as organically together; the abstraction of the factors takes account of the organic unity by having those factors not as mere unities and pluralities, but as diversified unities and unified pluralities, each capable not only of having the other suppressed while it is dominant, but each allowing for the achievement of the other as dominant through an emphasis by symbolization or utilization. The symbolization and the utilization begin from a side of the dominant factor and get to the suppressed as having both unity and diversity.

Better: in isolating the factor of form or content, we not only make one of them dominant, but suppress the side of it which is similar in kind to the correlative item. When we want to refer to the dominant, we must bring the suppressed side to the fore and then move to the dominant by symbolization or utilization. In the case of the contemplated and indicated, this means that a mere contemplated is merely a dominant with a suppressed side which is specifically experienceable, and that the indicated is merely a dominant with a suppressed side which is unitary. When we utilize the contemplated, we divide the indicated and relate the parts of it, but only after we have brought to the fore the side of the contemplated which is experienceable. And we symbolize only after we have brought to the fore the unity of the indicated.

We could use the unity of the indicated to symbolize the unity of the contemplated, just as we could use the diversification of the contemplated to give the indicateds. Instead, when we synthesize, we merely try to recover the original unity by allowing the contemplated to function as a dominant for the indicated (in the guise of a penumbra) and conversely, without paying attention to the suppressed side of the dominant in either case. The expression ϕa used in the *Principia Mathematica* tells us about the utilization of the ϕ, as making distinctions possible in the a; it tells us nothing about synthesis or about symbolization.

Are we now led to say that we can so utilize the contemplated as to arrive at a necessary division amongst indicateds or that we can use the indicated as a symbol so as to get the intensified contemplated, if only we bring out the diversification in the contemplated and the unity of the indicated? Yes. A contemplated seen to be diversified is a usable rule for dividing the indicated; an indicated seen to be united is a symbol for a contemplated which is intensive.

And we should say that clustered particulars, when we emphasize the cluster, function as a symbol for the unity of a being; and that diversified meaning will give us a set of divided particulars, when the diversity is utilized. We should say that a theory, or a law, or a rule, or a measurement, will be utilized when we bring out the diversification of them, the fact that they are variables, and with this diversification move to the at present recessive content (or, more exactly, move to the content as dominant with its own unity and the meaning recessive). The movement ends with an embodied, necessary order amongst the particulars. Both symbolism and utilization, in brief, start with the recessive side of a dominant factor of a biased whole and move to the acknowledgment of the other factor as dominant.

The relation of a substantial form to its parts goes, via the diversification of the form, to the separation of the parts by utilization, and conversely. The two together, the symbol and the utilization, dissect the organic unity of the being. The organic unity is related to powers beyond it as a representative of other beings.

When we have a problem of the relation of theory to content or practice, we do not have anything more in the relation between them than the combination of utilization and symbolization; there is no unity which has a role of its own. But there is a utilization, not of the theory as such, but of its diversified side, and there is no symbolization of the parts or content as such, but only of the unitary side. In the case of measurement, for example, we can say that we but utilize the diversified nature of formal rules or that we symbolize the formal scheme by means of the unity of the domain which we are measuring. We have a similar situation in connection with Actuality and actualities. But we must avoid supposing that the actualities we know are abstractions from a larger totality which includes the Being of Actuality. There are divided actualities, and there is Actuality which is diversified as a structure; we explicate the unity of the one and the source of the other by reference to the Actuality and actualities, respectively.

It is the unity of the compulsions in the different cases that evidences a Being; it is the diversification in the Being which evidences the plurality, i.e., that they are separated one from the other as distinct entities. The

compulsion exhibits the necessity imposed by the unity; the division of
the particulars exhibits the necessity imposed by the diversification; the
diversification exhibits the contingency of the particulars, and the intensity of the Being exhibits the contingency of the beginning made to
get to it, i.e., that this or that particular is a representative starting point.
The compulsion in the realm of particulars gives the evidence, and the
unity of it tells what it is the evidence of; the contingency of the diversification tells that there is some exterior cause operative on the Being and
the diversification in the Being tells what this is—a contingent set of particulars. Utilization gets to particulars as contingent entities necessarily
divided. Symbolization gets to the unity as a necessary being which has a
contingently accumulative intensity.

August 12
(Ann Arbor)

We should distinguish A] evidence *that*, B] evidence *what*,
C] a method for utilizing evidence, D] a terminus of the utilization of
the evidence, and E] the togetherness of the termini of the utilization
of evidence.

A] The evidence *that* is the presence of accidents, i.e., features which are
not explicable by the items in which they are. We have evidence that
there are Beings, or at least the Being of Actuality, when we see the actualities under a compulsive necessity to be together. We have evidence that
there are contained actualities or particles when we attend to the diversification in a Being or in a being.

B] Evidence *what* tells us the nature or kind of entity at which we are
to arrive. Evidence what, for a Being or an actuality from the vantage
point of contained particles, is given by the unity of the compulsion to
which the evidence is subject. The evidence what, for actualities from the
perspective of Actuality, or for particles from the perspective of the substantial form, is the contingency of the diversification, the fact that it has
one of a number of possible roles.

C] Evidence is used through a symbolization which employs the evidence *what* in actualities or particles to arrive at a terminus by a process
of accumulation. Evidence is also used through utilization, which uses the
evidence what in Actuality or in a substantial form to arrive at a terminus
by a process that makes necessary cleavages in the terminating data.

D] The terminus of a symbolization is an accumulative, necessary intensity; the terminus of a utilization is a necessarily ordered set of particulars.

E] An accumulative, necessary intensity is together with a necessarily ordered set of particulars in a unity which may have a power and nature of its own. Any attempt to deal with either the intensity or the particulars by themselves will involve a use of that unity in a biased form. One will then get the intensity as a substantial form having a repressed component of particulars and a repressed side of diversification. Or one will get the particulars as having a repressed side of being united and a repressed component of a single substantial form.

Since the set made up of Actuality and actualities is not more than the two of them together in a single context, and has no power or being or unity of its own, an acknowledgment of the operation of symbolization or utilization is but the acknowledgment of a movement from a biased form of the Actuality and actualities as together. The recovery of the unity is the seeing of the Actuality as an accumulative intensity which is necessarily one, and the seeing of the actualities as a necessarily divided set of contingencies. But before we see them as together, we have them as data or as evidences—which is the normal way of facing them, though without an awareness that they are evidencing or serving as data. We take them in the normal way to be final entities. But they are in fact dominant factors in biased unities by means of which we arrive at the correlative biased dominants. We use a repressed side in the dominant with which we begin the movement to the correlative biased dominant. To see them as evidences, we must attend not to the form or the particulars, as though they were isolated, but as affected by their repressed sides, i.e., by the contingency of a diversification which is repressed, and by the necessity of a division amongst contingencies, which is also repressed.

This "normal" way of dealing with the components is characteristic of the Thomists. They have God on one side, perfect and self-enclosed, and actualities on the other, dealt with as mere contingencies to be analogically related to the other. But the God that is self-enclosed is part of a larger whole, as is the set of contingencies. (They see the latter, not the former, of these as "parts" of a larger whole.) Any inference they make to God, even one which is carried out by faith, starts with evidence of God's power and unity, evidence which is found in the realm of particulars. If they looked more sharply on their God (either in the guise of a finality to which we have given the name "Actuality" or as connected with actualities), they would have discerned a contingent diversification in Him which evidences the presence of actualities.

God, as self-enclosed, is a unity which has a contingency of accumulations constituting His intensity. Actualities as making up a realm of their own are so many contingencies related necessarily in some way—

inferential, separative, etc. When we want to account for the contingency in the one and the necessity in the other, we take these to be termini of inferences which are due to the action of the other. But by itself, each has the contingency and the necessity as part of its "self-enclosed" reality, though of course as an "accident."

August 13
(Ann Arbor)

The unity of the organic being can be expressed as a combination of a compelled clustering, accumulatively moving toward an intensive unity, and a contingent diversification being exhibited in a necessitated separation of particulars. The termini of these movements is not included in this expression of the unity. But those termini can be taken as final limits or as encompassing a whole range of intensities and particulars. If we concentrate on the outcome of the symbolization and utilization, the organic unity is very rich; if we concentrate instead on the beginning of these processes and credit all else to the termini, the unity is very thin, consisting only of the compelled clustered entities in the role of symbols, and of the contingent diversification in the role of an operating rule of division. The unity does not have these components in a distinguished form; they are discoverable only by seeing what is recessive in a dominant factor and by what agency one can move via the recessive to the other factor as dominant.

Do we have here a clue to the mind-body problem? Can we say that the relation of the mind to the body is a component of a more fundamental unity, and consists in a control of the body by means of a contingent diversification, i.e., by means of one possible principle for articulating the body, and that this has a reciprocal in the form of a compelled unification of the body which symbolized a final, formal unity? This is at any rate a view which is compatible with that suggested in *Nature and Man*, where it was seen that the mind was a more developed form of a control over the body. Still, we must not overlook the fact that the mind has a function of its own. It is to be seen as the terminus of an accumulative act of symbolization by the body—the bodily parts formally united—just as the body is to be seen as the terminus of a necessitated division of the bodily parts. It is the accumulative product which is the mind with a role of its own, just as it is the required way in which the plurality of the parts of the body is constituted that determines the way in which the body functions as a body.

The mind is the operative principle dictating how data are necessarily related—the law, as it were, of their connection. The body by itself is constantly converging at the richest possible unity of its parts. These expressions are the result of focusing on factors in an aboriginal unity. If we want to treat the mind as working apart from the body, we attend to it as a dominant, so that it is only an accumulative intensity. If we want to treat the body as apart from the mind, we attend to it as a dominant, but only as a plurality.

The transition from life to death is but the recognition of the fact that the body as part of a living being has a correlative dominant in the mind, and that both of them, mind and body, are part of an organic unity. In death, when we have a mere body, we find the form of an aggregate taking the place of the mind, and the aggregational nature the place of the organic unity.

In connection with Actuality and its actualities, we have real entities which are intensive and pluralized (but which nevertheless have an accumulation and a necessary division that can be explained by reference to one another). We also have, respectively, a contingent diversification and a compelled clustering in each. These evidence one another.

The quantification of a quality discussed some time back can now be expressed as the problem of utilizing the contingently produced intensification of the quality so as to produce discrete units from data. There has to be an acceptance of some data so that the separation amongst them can be established by means of the quality. The reciprocal move to quality depends on the acknowledgment of the quantity as a unified and compelled totality of parts, which functions as a symbol for the quality. The evidence that there is a plurality for the quality to control is given by the contingent diversification found in the quality. This contingent diversification is nothing other than the generality of the quality, its capacity to function as a variable.

The acknowledgment of the unitary actuality, when approached from the perspective of a unification of biased factors—a contingent accumulation of final intensity and a necessary division amongst contingent particulars, the one mediated by a contingent diversification utilized, and the other by a compelled cluster symbolizing—involves a reference beyond it, analogous to that accomplished by orientation and expression when judging, or when starting with analytic factors of an actuality as a being. The reference in the case of an organic being is to the future to which it is obligated. This referring can be viewed indifferently as a form of expression or as a form of orientation.

In the case of Ideality, Existence, and God, their relation to their own pluralities, and conversely, involves a different mode of symbolization and ends in a different type of division amongst the items in the plurality than is true of Actuality and actualities. The persons of the Trinity in orthodox Christianity, e.g., are members of a plurality in a relation of procession governed by God, the substance, who must be understood to have an accumulative intensity expressive of His preservative powers. The three persons must be understood to symbolize the divine substance by virtue of their common Being which at once compels and unites them.

God as relative to actualities lacks finality. The actualities are compelled and unified by God, not as beings, but as sacramental objects. This means that the actualities are not to be viewed as though they were part of a plurality necessarily divided through the utilization of a diversification found in God, but as already compulsively clustered by God, and thus as part of a domain of sacramental objects. God is to be seen here not as a final Being, or with an accumulative intensity, but as a Being having the power to provide for a clustering of actualities. To be sure, an acknowledgment of the symbolic power of a sacrament will lead us to God as accumulatively intensive, but it will be an accumulative intensity only relative to the power of that symbolization. Apart from the symbolization, the God relative to actualities will be a unitary diversification, i.e., a variable with a single meaning and function. (Analogous observations are to be made regarding the Ideal and its distinctive kind of parts, and regarding Existence and its distinctive kind of parts, and regarding both of these as relative to actualities.)

God and the actualities, as involved with one another, constitute a single whole which, though it is not organic in nature, nevertheless has a nature and a role. The role is, I suppose, expressed in the idea of the Holy Ghost of Roman Catholicism as being efficacious in this world.

These reflections, directed toward speculatively acknowledged entities, should provide a needed guide in the solution of more specialized problems, such as the use of a rule and the following out of a command.

Doing something is so different from understanding something or from the formal structure exhibited in a command or rule that it is tempting to suppose with the Wittgensteinians that we can get along solely with the doing. But it is the rule and the command which tell us how to punctuate the doing. While we have only the doing—and this is what we have when we see another or hear him speak—we do not note the utilization of the rule or the obeying of the command. But were there no such utilization or obeying, the acts of the individual would be arbitrarily bundled together, and would therefore, not lead to the acknowledgment of any principle of diversification in the rule or command. Each act would be separated from the others in contingent ways, thereby precluding the acknowledgment of any law or predictable outcome.

Some modern psychologists, with their attempt to stay only with what they think is verifiable and thus in their eyes "scientific," welcome such a consequence. They are content to say that there is a law only so far as the public data fall into statistical groups which do not conform to a random distribution formula. They infer from their groups that there is some kind of connection amongst the data, and thus in effect move to a summary statement of what they have discovered. But this in no way allows them to predict anything about data not yet described, or discovered, or used.

If there be an actual clustering of data, we have evidence for the exercise of some power beyond them, and we then presuppose that the data are there and somehow connected with one another in a way that a principle justifies—a principle which is an articulate version of the power. If all blue-eyed females are near-sighted, or if, say 40 percent of them are, in contrast with 5 percent of the females who have eyes of a different color, we have evidence of a power beyond them; the nature of that power can be known only so far as we know how to symbolize by means of that particular 40 percent. The beginning of a method for making such symbolization is given in Peirce's theory of abduction—though I think I have shown that this is but the ordinary logic with a new *modus ponens*, or new necessary truths with the old *modus ponens*. The power dictates the grouping of those females with blue eyes. If we now ask how those particular females are related one to the other and want an explanation for that relation, we will have to find connected with the power a principle of diversification, which is to say a variable which will, when we accept this or that female as appropriate to our investigation, allow us to move on in a systematic way to other females. In the particular case, we will begin by accepting this or that female as blue eyed, and will then take them all to be necessarily individual, i.e., to be separated from one another by Existence. Were they not necessarily individual, we would have no warrant that our sample was restricted to females in the same world. But now I am once again beginning to lose my bearings.

If we see someone writing down 2, 4, 6, 8, . . . we can ask the empiricist what he means when he says that the person should continue "in the same way," and why he thinks the activity begins now with these numbers and does not include those written down last week or those which will be written down next year. To answer these questions, one would have to take account of a rule and of a diversification which were being used to cover just those items as now making a unity. Conversely, we can say to a formalist, who would contend that the person was counting by twos that he should tell us what is meant by "twos" and "counting." These meanings are not exhibited in the formal statement. Nor can he tell us how his rule can be used again and again. He cannot answer these questions unless he takes account of the fact that the counting is involved with data,—i.e., it is a rule to be used and that there is a plurality of numbers which allow the rule to be used in a diversified manner, which is to say, as a variable ranging over values.

August 14

A radical empiricist would undoubtedly reply to the criticism that he could not say what is meant by "counting in the same way," by saying that all we mean is that we in fact have the items in a sequence and that we predict with such and such probability that the next numbers will be in the same sequence. He would claim no necessity for the fact that the odd numbers are skipped; he would hold that they are skipped by virtue of an established process, called habit, which has a probability of being exhibited again. He would not look outside the actual sequence for an explanation of the sequence; there is, for him, no necessity in it to be explained, and no assurance, therefore, that the same sequence will take place. If you ask him if the man is counting by twos, he will say that he has up to now mentioned the even numbers.

The empiricist would not claim that there is a counting, or a counting by twos, or a rule which necessitates that the next numbers be even. In short, he would take the occurrences for what they are then found to be. But he could not decide that the numbers begin with 2 and end with 14, let us say, unless he knows that 2 is the first number and 14 the last to be considered; but this requires him to know that what was said to him a moment ago, e.g., that it is raining, is not relevant to the counting by twos. He cannot know what is relevant without some rule or principle which dictates that such and such items form a cluster, i.e., a necessitated unity of contingent items.

Similarly, a formalist can answer the question as to how he knows his rule is a rule to be used by saying that the meaning of "rule" is that it be used. A rule implies its use, and this implication does not demand of us that we pay attention to any data. But an implied use is not an actual use. The formalist says that does not matter; what is wanted is that we acknowledge a rule that is involved with our data; we do not provide data for a rule or ask if the rule is in fact to be employed. But the formalist cannot account for the diversified use of his rule. The rule is employed on different data. It operates to interrelate the data, and this fact, or even the possibility of it, the formalist cannot know without taking account of the presence of the data as to be dominated by the rule.

Kant's schematism faced the question that the categories might not have an application. His answer was that time and space allowed his categories to be used with respect to the manifold given in experience. When Kant turned to the transcendental deduction of the categories, he saw that the manifold could not have an intrinsic necessity, nor be the manifold for a single experience except so far as it was governed by the categories. He therefore was able to avoid the criticisms just now levelled against the formalists and the empiricists.

Hegel could be said to be the most radical of empiricists in the sense that he took the actual state of affairs to be necessarily clustered in and of itself, with a self-defining beginning and a self-defining end, thereby precluding the need to refer to any rule or abstract category telling us about the procedure or about what could count as appropriate data. Equally, one could say that he was a radical formalist in that he had rules whose being consisted in being used (categories), and that this use involved a necessary diversification. So far as he stressed the former, he was a phenomenologist, and so far as he stressed the latter, he was an idealist. Following his lead, a formalist could insist that the meaning of any rule was given in its use as a variable, and an empiricist could insist that the nature of the data is such that it had a self-defined beginning and ending, and built-in ways of being related. But it is a fact that rules have a unity by themselves and some of them are not used; and it is a fact that data are scattered and irrelevant to one another, and that some beginnings and endings are arbitrary. But to this one might reply that all concrete rules are variables, and that only abstract or formal and empty ones are not (and are thus not genuine rules), and that all ultimate data were clustered and well-bounded, and only abstracted data were not. The one, though, would neglect the sheer plurality of the data, and the other would neglect the sheer unity of the rule. And it would be hard to see how either could account for the "abstract" rules and sheer data. Further, one could reverse their positions and maintain that the supposed rules and data were fictions, that what the formalist and empiricist called "abstractions" were in fact the only rules and data with which we were familiar, and that with respect to these a reference to the other factor was necessary to account for and clustering.

Rules dictate spacing, clustering, and boundaries; data dictate diversification, i.e., variability, and applicability of the rules. If we try to give up one of these, we must, in Hegelian fashion, read the other into what is left, to give us a concrete dialectic of rules or a self-defining whole of data. Any rules or data which lacked these features would be treated as abstractions, distortions, or falsifications. This is the procedure which reductionists are required to follow. A materialist, for example, must so understand the material world that there is an intrinsic necessity to the ways in which the data are related and to the fact that they are all the data that there is or can be; and a mathematically minded philosopher, say a Pythagorean, must so understand his mathematics that it is spread out over the world necessarily because of its nature. A Leibniz takes the heroic step of denying the variability of his rules and their usability, and in principle supposes that the rules are the data without variability or application, except by arbitrary fiat. A positivistically inclined empiricist could, with equal justice, say that we arbitrarily bound data and space them.

Suppose we ask these reductionist why they did what they did? I suppose they would fall back on convention, custom, habit, and the like. But would not this in effect be invoking rules and data of a different sort from that with which they were originally content? Would they not have to say that any account they gave of the arbitrariness would itself be arbitrary? Their reductionism would, in effect, but begin an infinite series of arbitrary judgments, all having as their beginning a set of rules which were exemplified in diverse ways, and data which were unified. But then would it not have been better to have been bolder and to have said that the data just happen to be clustered and self-bounded, and that the rules just happen to be exhibited as a set of items all having the same nature or general meaning?

The most radical rationalist and the most radical empiricist would not claim to have made arbitrary selections, but would instead claim that the data just happen to form this collection and to have this boundary, and that the rules just happen to have this use and range, and that is the end of the matter. There would still be the fact that the one would emphasize the data and the other the rules, but one could argue that the difference between them was only verbal, since whatever the one said or predicted, so could the other. There would be only the single fact of a plurality of items exhausting a domain and being related one to the other in such and such a way. In effect that answer would come back to something like that to which I have already concluded: there is a fundamental unity within which we can distinguish rules and data, each needing the other. The only difference—and perhaps it is not even a difference—would lie in my contention that the rules and the data had a nature and a function of their own, making the rule dominate the data, and making the spaced and bounded data have a different import from what they had as a mere collection.

He who remained with the supposedly concrete fact of the ruled-data would have no explanation of the whole which he was acknowledging. He would have to be content to describe just how in fact its elements were related to one another. But on the present view, the ruled-data would be explained. We would make provision for the understanding of the nature of rules and the occurrence of data without compromising the fact that they do occur as parts of some more inclusive situation, which need not—as the alternative view supposes—be more concrete or real than the parts. In effect, the difference would amount to the recognition by me that the supposed abstractions have a reality and a power of their own. This would be denied by the other views. But such a denial means that there cannot be an understanding of individual items, of aggregates, of ideal rules not employed or perhaps even employable, or of controlling forces which are operative on the data. And when we turn to the relationship of one of these acknowledged unities to others, we will be faced again with the problem of the way in which they are related to one another, and of their roles as aggregates; or we will be faced with the problem of the laws which govern the occurrence of future events, or of the way in which groups of entities function as units.

The reductionist view fails not only to do justice to the evident, independent, real functioning of rules and data, but to the fact that a unity of rules with data is related to other unities of rules and data by means of rules. The reductionist seems to work only at the point where we have arrived; he fails to do justice to the independent functioning of the constituents of the items he acknowledges, or to the way in which the items he acknowledges function with respect to one another, or are confined to certain types of activity.

August 15
(Ann Arbor)

There is a strong tendency today to deal with God as though he were wholly immanent in the world. The world must then be understood to be a sacramental one, and no true role will be assignable to purely secular objects any more than there would be one assigned to a God apart from the world. There is some point to such a position if it be taken to define what is meant by a religious situation, but there seems to be no warrant for taking it to express the nature of things. Like other reductionists, the immanentist will not be able to account for the fact that the things in the world have a unity which is produced only so far as we take those things, not in their severalty, but as together subject to a compulsion. He will be unable to show that what occurs is subject to a God, since the God will be just what He is then and there exhibiting Himself to be. For the immanentist, there is no God, as it were, in reserve, no God who judges, no recalcitrant items, no sinners, and in the end, no salvation.

A similar set of problems confronts one who tries to treat the mind as a dimension or aspect of the body. Usually those who take this approach today try to identify the mind with the brain, overlooking the organic nature of the individual and the fact that he is involved in a larger world. A better approach would be one which took the mind to be an abstractable aspect of a single, organic being involved in a larger world. But this view, which would have the benefit of dealing with a living body and an actual occurrence and not with an isolated being or an aspect of it, has the difficulty of not being able to explain what it means to be conscious, how the mind can guide the body, or how the body can have its multiple efforts and activities and parts unified in a self-identical meaning. In any case, a body which had the mind as an aspect or function would be a body related to the world beyond in a way that other bodies were not.

One might, though, try to deal with consciousness as a development from an original sensitivity or mood, brought into some focus by pain and pleasure, and given its conceptualizing power by a capacity to face articulated grounds for the pain and pleasure. Whatever the details of this development may be, it does seem as if it could be achieved by a body in relation to other bodies, provided that we take bodies to be not merely mechanical combinations of particles, but unitary organisms. The body would then be thought of as interlocked with others, and as having a disequilibrium with respect to the future; isolation of the disequilibrium would be an isolation of the dimensions of mind, itself but a dimension of the entire being. The mind would express the unitary functioning of the organism with respect to what lies outside it; the body would be controlled by what the mind discerned; the mind itself in turn would be understood to be the principle which allowed for a plurality of roles without loss of identity, and which could be viewed as the accumulative product of a convergence of the various roles and parts of the body.

I do not see clearly in what sense the mind could be treated as an accumulatively arrived-at unity, or in what sense it governs all the divisions and diversity of roles of the body. The latter point could perhaps be made if one took the mind to be the locus of forms, not all of which were consciously faced. Indeed, if one took this approach, one could perhaps make sense of the fact that the mind was an accumulatively arrived-at unity, for the different degrees of intensity characteristic of the accumulation would express different grades of mind. We would, in the final accounting, have to recognize the independent functioning of the mind, the fact that it had some being of its own, since it does seem to function in independence of the body when it is involved in the consideration of mathematics, logic, metaphysics, theology, and ethical ideals. But this independence might be conceived of as an achievement to be understood only after we had treated the individual as a single organic being, within which we could distinguish a mental dimension and a correlative set of bodily parts and functions.

There is a way of understanding Aristotle's *De Anima* which allows one to suppose that he took the mind and body to make a single unity. But this is a position which presupposes his doctrine of a separate Active Reason. On the view I have been elaborating the last week or so, an Active Reason would have a correlative Matter, which was as final, and had roles and a nature which was just as basic and as effective, as the other. The Active Reason would be accumulatively intensive and have a diversifiable meaning; the Matter would be divided necessarily and form a single whole; the features of each would involve an explicit or tacit reference to the other.

August 16
(Ann Arbor)

Whether one supposes that the form (or meaning, or substantial form, or structure, or essence) has a meaning and role and perhaps a being of its own or not, and reciprocally that the material elements function and exist apart from such a form, it is always the case that there is a unitary meaning and power to the entity in which these are found. One does not, therefore, escape from the acknowledgment of a "metaphysical" unity to an entity, no matter what one decides about the role and status of the components which can be found within it. All one can do is to decide whether this unitary nature is at the limit of thinness or has some thickness beyond this. It has minimum thickness only so far as maximum power is given to the processes of symbolization and utilization and/or to their termini; it has maximum thickness when the processes and the termini are diminished in power, and the termini perhaps denied the capacity to have a reality and a power of their own.

Those who avoid a Platonism or a physicalism compensate by having an intensive inwardness. Those who avoid an intensive inwardness (which functions with a genuine thrust outward toward other entities and toward the future) inevitably have to grant some reality to the formal and to the physical, where the latter is understood to refer to the ultimate particles or the plurality of ultimate entities confined within the being with the intensive inwardness. A metaphysics which insists on the primacy of Beings and actualities does not have an intensively rich reality which encompasses both; it takes this to be a product or function of the Beings and actualities. But those who insist on a close conjunction of actualities with one or more Beings in their full reality, or in some delimited guise, are forced to give more weight to their juncture. And thus we have those who put so little stress on God or man that in compensation they have nothing to acknowledge as real but the Church. These are matched by men who put obligation before the prescriptive Ideal and the men to which they are prescribed, or who put the process of history before the individuals involved and the nature with which they interplay or the political whole which they forge from this nature.

The situation is not altered when we engage in a reductionism and attribute to the physical whatever we can derive from the formal, and then deny the role or presence of the formal, for what we do then is to transform the physical into a set of unitary beings within which we can discern the merely physical and the merely formal, or structural. Reductionism, in effect, gives us physical entities with an inwardness (and thus as allowing for termini in the guise of mere physical entities and mere structures or forms) and an outward thrust that is as "metaphysical" as the Platonism they tried to eliminate. Reductionism (here presented in its usual form of trying to avoid Platonism) thus does nothing more than shift the locus of the inwardness and outward thrust as having a reality and force which is equal to that of the discarded Platonism and physicalism as interacting.

A behaviorist is a disguised believer in inward workings of the beings he studies. He does not see this because he has his eye on the behavior which seems to be a public phenomenon. But his account of this behavior does lead him to speak of habits, dispositions, reward mechanisms and the like. If, to avoid this consequence, he tries to confine himself to a mere description or to a collection of different behavioral acts, he will have no warrant for attributing these to anyone. He cannot speak of their being produced or emitted, but only of their having an accepted origin at those beings. He might watch what is done to the beings and report perhaps what the beings then do, but he cannot speak of cause and effect, or of conditioning and the like, for these involve a reference to an entity as having an inwardness where the input is somehow connected with the output.

But why may not the organism be treated as a mere knotting device, and the output connected with the input without the organism being thought to condition or cause it? But we will then have to admit that a knotting device has a characteristic structure and power, and has these integrated so as to make for an actual knotting. To this a reductionist might reply: "I intend to refer only to the ultimate physical particles and combinations of physical laws." But combinations of the laws involves some kind of unification, and the submission of the particles to the combinations involves an interplay of the kind I have been exploring.

A reductionist might now go on: "Computers offer a model of what I mean. They are the result of complications of ordinary laws governing physical particles or of some easily understood combination of them. Such computers have no ideal form, and do not have an inwardness, or an outward thrust." But the ideal form is in the mind of the designer and in the programming; it is imposed on the machine. We call it a "computing machine" precisely because it is relevant to such programming. Man and the machine make a single organic whole. It is comparatively easy to see that a man in this situation is like a form, in that he is accumulatively intensive in his meaning and operates as a variable with respect to the functioning of the machine. But it is not evident that the machine has necessarily divided contingent parts (though perhaps this is a fact exhibited in the design of the machine and the programming), and that it symbolizes the man.

It is now evident that I was precipitate in saying that man is accumulatively intensive in his meaning relative to the machine. All we have a warrant for saying is that he is a variable with respect to the machine, and that the machine has necessarily divided parts. But this would seem to mean that man and the machine together have a rich inwardness. Such a result would require us to give a kind of richness to the unity of man and machine which is greater than that of the man, at least in contrast with the machine. The unity has something like the richness of an historic event, but like this, its power is given it by the factors which constitute it. If we are to avoid this result, we would have to say that the interaction of man and machine as expressed in the design and the programming is but a continuation of man himself, and thus is an expression of his inwardness.

The outcome of the present discussion is that we must acknowledge an aboriginal inwardness as well as inwardnesses which are derivate expressions of the former. One of the expressions can be carried further into the body of the machine to give it a semblance of autonomy and humanity while still allowing it to remain a mere machine.

August 17
(Ann Arbor)

Yesterday's consequence could be avoided by taking man to be the substantial form for a machine. The inwardness of the juncture of the two would then be at the extreme level of thinness, and would not be a derivative from the inwardness of man. He would be understood, in relation to the machine, to be accumulatively intensive in himself. He would also be the terminus of a symbolic use of the machine, converging on that which is unified and to be a variable in the use of the machine. Reciprocally, the machine would be seen to be a plurality of parts having its own functioning, and at the same time to be the locus of the utilization of man as the being who has the meaning of a principle or rule for the machine.

By taking this position, one allows for the machine to be a mere machine, at the same time that one sees how it could be made to function as a symbol (by being treated as a unified compelled entity) and to be part of a larger complex, of which man is the other part. At the same time, one could see man functioning as a variable (account being taken of the fact that he is concerned with a contingent set of data in the guise of the machine) exhibited in the diverse workings of the machine.

The reductionist on this account would be one who allowed the machine to be as "intelligent" as possible and yet saw that this was, as unified, the outcome of the application of an intelligence exercised by man; he would allow that there was an inwardness in the whole make up of man and machine, but would deny it any substantiality of its own. Man, he would say, would be accumulatively intensive by himself and also as the terminus of the machine taken as a symbol; the machine would be pluralized in itself and also as the terminus of the utilization of man as a principle of intelligibility. The contingency of man's variable nature would be evidenced by his actions, and the necessity of the parts of the machine would be evidenced by the fact that it was being used. Man would be understood to be not a mere conglomeration of parts, but a single, functioning whole which has an imposed unity and a symbolic role, once it is seen to have an imposed unity. The way the machine functions would have a necessity to it, too, which was to be accounted for as the outcome of the utilization of whatever rule man imposes on it.

The utilization and symbolism involved in connection with man and machine is, of course, the act of a man. When and as an individual functions as a form for a machine, he also acts in this double way. Were the relationship internal to an organic being, it would, of course, be analytically expressed as an ontological version of utilization and symbolization—perhaps as governance and dependence, or orientation. In the former case, apart from the human activity, we either have the potentiality for such activity given in an actual compelled unity of the machine and an actual imposed contingency in the accumulation of the intensity, or we have a mere aggregate of the man and the machine, the first functioning by itself as a mere accumulative intensity and the other as a set of parts distinguished in some rational manner. Neither would refer to or depend on the other, or show any evidence for the other. We get such evidence only when we have a compelled unity imposed on the machine, or have a contingent accumulation terminating in the accumulative intensity of a man.

Though we may be able to satisfy ourselves that the divisions of particulars are either non-necessary or that the necessity is integral to the domain of particulars, and though we may also satisfy ourselves that the intensity of a meaning is not contingent in its accumulative nature or that the contingency is characteristic of its accumulative nature by itself, we are always faced with the fact that there is a unity imposed on the particulars and a variable use or import to the meaning. The imposed unity and the variable use are evidences of the effect on the particulars and meaning by the meaning and particulars, respectively.

August 19
(Ann Arbor)

A stone rolls down the hill. I have in the past taken the stone and the hill to be wholes. Like aggregates, they were supposed to act as a consequence of the activity of their parts, but like individuals, were supposed to have a functioning nature of their own. But this answer has difficulties. The stone rolls, and the rolling is as distinctive as the stone. There is a causality on the level of stones. There are avalanches and caverns. If we did not allow any causality to wholes, we would also have to deny causality in politics and history.

A possible answer stems from existentialism. It maintains that a stone and its causality were genuine objective occurrences, but only as constituted by man. Apart from man, there would be no such thing as a stone rolling and hurting an animal, or denting in a tree, or blocking a stream. But then what is there apart from man? And is it not true that stones can block streams and did so even before there were men, and apart from anything they might think or believe?

Reductionists, who usually are opposed to existentialists, are here somewhat in agreement with them, so far as they think that the stone and its causality are artifacts. They differ from the existentialists in supposing that there is a real objective occurrence of physical particles. My account of wholes is somewhat allied to this view, though of course, unlike it, it grants some reality to the stone.

We do more justice to the rolling stone if we take it to have a nature which can trap energy within its confines. The stone will still lack the power to initiate action, but it will be active in the sense that the trapped energy will be expended in accord with the nature of the stone. The stone will roll as a single whole in which the energy that is available is made to conform to the demands of the nature of the stone.

In the case of an individual, the substantial form governs the use of the energy; it dictates how the parts are to be clustered and the entire being is to behave. But in the case of a whole, the nature that it has does not determine how the parts are to be clustered, but only how the unity of their energy is to be spent. The whole, of course, lacks the inwardness of the individual, without compromising the degree of reality, intensity, or divisiveness which is characteristic of the termini of its internal referential activities.

The nature of a whole dictates to the parts in the sense of determining something about their divisiveness; but it does not control those parts. The parts are united to constitute a single cluster; this union is not compelled by the nature, but is only encompassed by it, and then in such a way as to offer a type of utilization which is not united with symbolization to constitute a distinctive functioning or substantial inwardness. An individual has termini of maximum intensity and particularity at the same time that it has a maximum inwardness capable of expression, and a directed or deliberate causality, at least in the case of men. A whole, instead, has termini which may be as rich as that of the individual, but which are not capable of utilization or symbolization to the same extent, with the consequence that the whole does not have an inwardness of its own, and does not compel a unity of the particulars or make the intensive nature of the whole contingent of the presence of just such and such particulars.

An individual's nature is accumulative in and of itself; in addition, there is a symbolic reference to it which is identical with the beginning of this accumulation. We can say that the individual's nature begins at the unity of the particulars, or we can view it as beginning at some more intensive portion of the accumulation which began with the particulars. In the case of the whole, there is no such continuity. The nature of the whole begins at a remove from the unity of the parts; the parts do not just happen to be clustered, but they also are not compelled to be so in the sense in which the parts of an individual are. The nature of the whole bounds them, but does not control them. But this is enough to allow them to symbolize the nature of the whole. Reciprocally, the contingent variable usability of the nature of a whole is not the product of the functioning of the parts on the nature of the whole in the way in which the variable nature of the substantial form is a function of the parts of the individual. The nature of the whole is given internal nuances without being given the power to express itself with respect to a plurality of distinct data. But this is enough to allow the whole to be utilized as the nature which the parts together exemplify.

The minor symbolization and utilization characteristic of a whole combine only in the sense of providing a conjoint trap for whatever energy is received by the whole from other wholes, and which it will expend according to the rhythms of the whole and the demands of the situation.

Like the individual, the whole has an intensive nature which has an accumulative character, but unlike the individual, the nature is more sharply divided from the compelled unity of the particulars which could symbolize it. Like the individual, the whole has a plurality of related parts, but the relation of these parts as distinct entities is more sharply divided from the variable nature which they utilize. The unities of the particulars in the two cases are compelled in different ways; so is the variability of the natures. In the case of the whole, the unity of the particulars is at the limits or boundaries only, but in the case of the individual, it governs the relations amongst those particulars. In the case of the whole, the variability of the nature is not fully articulated, whereas in the case of the individual, it has a definite lawlike nature, dictating what must be the case with such and such particulars, if such and such are accepted as data.

Wholes, then, are not individuals or aggregates. But like individuals, they do have a characteristic use of energy which can be expressed causally. Like aggregates, they do not have parts whose symbolizing compelled unity can be viewed as part of the nature, and do not have a nature whose contingent variability can be viewed as in control of the parts.

This account of wholes allows for their being and functioning apart from men, and as distinctively different from that of aggregates or individuals, with a causality of their own. That causality has a time span and laws which are different from those which apply to the aggregated parts or to the clustered parts of an individual. Aggregated parts function as members of a single cosmos of similar entities; the clustered parts of an individual are controlled by it to some extent. The parts of a whole, like the parts of an individual, because not aggregational, have behaviors which are different from those which a physics could determine, since they are subject to the causal activity of the energy utilized by the juncture of the distinctive symbolization and utilization which is characteristic of a whole.

Is a family a whole? Can we say of it, A] it has a nature of its own; B] this nature is accumulatively intensive; C] the nature is symbolized by a distinct set of particulars; D] the nature has a variability to it, E] the particulars have a unity, F] the nature is utilized by the particulars to provide some determination of the relations amongst them; G] the nature does not control the parts; H] the parts do not produce a perfect variable in the nature, I] the family has a causality which is neither controlled by the nature nor dictated merely by the parts? I think so; that is why the family can be studied dynamically in sociology and in anthropology, and why we need not succumb to a nominalism (which reduces the family to its members) or to a "group mind" (which turns the family into a superindividual).

The cosmos, understood to be the domain of the juncture of all the actualities with Actuality and the subordinated limited forms of the other modes of Being, is like a family or any other whole. It can, therefore, be seen to have a causality without our thereby supposing that it is another final Being or another actuality. It is a being which is as real as these, but which nevertheless has these as constituents. In religious terms, this means that the domain constituted of God's grace and man's concern with God has a being and a causality of its own, but only so far as and because it involves the mutual partial use of God and man to constitute a unity capable of trapping energy stemming from similar kinds of combination of God and man, to give the history of a religion. It also means that man's religious activities are not as fully symbolic of God's nature as His own parts are (which are continuous with His nature and introduce contingency into Him), and that God's grace is not as controlling over man as it is over the parts of Himself, which He in fact not only unifies, but necessarily relates one with the other.

The relation of man to God, as an object of religion, is that of termini in a whole. This is also true of the relation of the parts of God to God. The difference is that God in religion is not a finality, and that the causality is confined inside this cosmology. God and his parts constitute a distinctive cosmology from ours, in which the nature of the whole attains maximum possible reality, without ever achieving the status of a Being or an inwardness characteristic of an individual.

From this it would seem to follow that sacramental objects are not as symbolic as I have been taking them to be. They lack the symbolic power of the parts of a true individual, where the parts are controlled and unified, and divided and necessitated, and where the nature is both made into a contingent variable and is continuous with the parts and thus is accumulatively intensive. A similar conclusion will have to be drawn with respect to actualities in relation to Actuality; they are related in a whole which has a vigor and a kind of unity that is greater than any of the finite wholes of actualities that might exist, but is not as inward and as usable as is the unity of an individual.

Is it true that the cosmological whole is more closely bound together than such wholes as stones and water? Our uncertain knowledge of Actuality, our absence of data on the behavior of the cosmos, the independent being of actualities, and the apparent lack of influence by Actuality, all point to the conclusion that the cosmos is a rather thin whole. This requires us to change the remarks made above about the nature of actualities and Actuality, the various other Beings and their parts, and man and God, etc. On the other hand, it is also a fact that we find the actualities compelled in various ways, and thus to be necessarily united by virtue of a power stemming from various Beings which are symbolized by the unity of the actualities and affected by the actualities in their severalty, and in turn utilize the power and are affected by the nature of Actuality. These last observations, though, do not go the length of showing that the actualities are more effectively united or are more intimately symbolic than the parts of actualities are, or that Actuality is made more definitely into a variable, or that it is more completely utilized than actualities are. I think it wiser to say that the cosmos is less well integrated than an actual individual is.

Wholes affect one another. Does this mean that there is an energy which they transmit to one another? Apparently so, for otherwise there would be no genuine causality between them. But wholes are produced through an interconnection of form and particulars, in contrast with individuals which have an inwardness that is as basic as these termini. Also the behavior of the whole depends on the functioning of the parts. But so does the individual's. Must we not say that in both cases we have a contribution from the termini, or alternatively, that the utilization and symbolization are sources of the energy of the unit, and that, in addition, there is a synthesizing of this energy in both cases? In wholes, the synthesis yields a mixture, which has a power of its own, whereas in individuals, it has a unitary nature and drive. In the whole, the dominant fact is the reality of the termini. The unity which expresses their interplay is enabled to function as a unit only because its boundaries are determined by those termini. But the unity of the individual has a meaning and a thrust of its own, enabling it to subjugate others and not merely to interact with them.

August 20
(Ann Arbor)

The form and the particulars of a whole interplay to constitute a single area which has the power to synthesize the energies issuing from those termini. The synthesized energy is the characteristic causal power of that whole. The area has no capacity to affect the form or the particulars, and has no other function but to make the synthesized power be single in nature. This characteristic of a whole is to be found in the individual as well—that is why a whole is to be found in every individual, and why it can be achieved in death, at least before the corpse becomes a mere aggregate of items spatially close together.

An individual has, in addition to the feature which it shares with a whole, the power of an inwardness. This not only affects the nature of the energy produced by its termini, but affects the termini as well. And these termini act on it as a unit, in addition to contributing to the energy which that inwardness utilizes. Termini and inwardness thus interact on one another. At the same time, there is an area of energy which functions as a unity, but which is to be understood as the product of the activity of the termini.

The interplay of inwardness with the termini involves not an interchange of energy, but a control and qualification of them. The inwardness achieves a direction from the substantial form, and a location from the parts. The substantial form receives the status of an active power, and the particulars receive the status of items used by the inwardness. The inwardness is not a product of the termini (as the area of the whole is). It has a reality of its own, and exists as long as the individual does.

A whole can be said to be self-identical over a period of time, by virtue of the constancy of the area within which the termini are united as powers. An individual is self-identical, in addition, by virtue of the power of the inwardness to maintain itself as an effective agent with respect to the termini, even while the termini dictate the direction and the location in which it will find expression. The inwardness of an individual defines it to be a basic reality; the area of a whole defines it to be a reality whose existence depends on the functioning of its termini as correlatives. The termini of a whole have a basic reality, and in fact can be individuals, as is the case in families, societies, and similar groupings. But though the particulars of an individual could be individuals (as they apparently are in the case of the final physical particles confined inside organic beings such as men), and though those individuals could be qualified by an inwardness, they are precluded from functioning as independent entities. The organic being is not less basic than the particles, for it has an inwardness of its own; the particles are no less basic than the organic being, for they have their own inwardnesses. But the particles are precluded from acting as full individuals; their inwardness is prevented, while they are parts of the organic being, from giving them direction or from making them effective, except under the qualifications provided by the substantial form and the inwardness of the organic being.

The individual, I said some time ago, was the outcome of an interplay of positionality and essence, where "outcome" is to be thought of not as a causal product or as something which comes about after a time, but as that which is to be analyzed out into the factors of positionality and essence. These factors can be said to be constitutive of the inwardness and of the whole, being made up of an inwardness (with termini at a substantial form) and the ultimate particles and their compounds.

Positionality and essence tell us about the nature of a unity, whereas substantial form and particles tell us about the factors which determine how it will function as a unity—e.g., as a mere whole or as an individual as well. The ultimate particles, of course, do not have distinct parts as the organic individual does, but they do have positionalities and essences. Still, an ultimate particle does function as a unity, and if it has an inwardness, it must also have an area which, on the foregoing account, must presuppose the operation of two termini.

Should we say that ultimate particles are not true individuals? We seem to have no warrant for supposing that they have an inwardness of their own, and we do not seem to be able to hold that they have parts. An answer: inwardness can be aboriginal, and an individual need not have a whole as an abstractable element. An inwardness affects and is affected by termini, and allows for the abstraction of the area of the whole only in the case of compound individuals. In the case of final particles (which need not be simple in Leibniz's sense, where there are no divisions of any kind, and no extensionality within which it fits or which it exemplifies), we have an inwardness that can be understood in terms of positionality and essence. This inwardness is causally effective, but it has neither form nor particulars to affect or be affected by. A compound individual benefits from the fact that it encompasses real particulars and that these have correlative to them a real intensity which has a being of its own, not in the sense that it exists by itself, but in the sense that while acting and existing only in relation to the inwardness and the correlative particulars, it has a power, a career, and a use of its own.

August 21
(Ann Arbor)

Like ultimate particles, finalities are without subordinate parts or anything analogous to a substantial form. Their inwardness is aboriginal, just as any individual's is, but unlike an individual's, theirs is neither affected by nor affects any termini. Like every actuality, ultimate or not, their inwardness is to be understood to be analyzable into two components, analogous to the positionality and essence in terms of which particular actualities can be understood.

Actuality is without position, and there is no Being from which its essence could be thought to be an extension. But Actuality could be analyzed into one component which stems from the other modes of Being, and another which stems from the actualities. The former is threefold in its origin, though single in its import as an analytic factor. It can be termed "indeterminacy," which is the common character of Ideality, Existence, and God, as ultimate modes of Being in contrast with Actuality. This indeterminacy is correlative with "unification." I am not satisfied with these terms. But this need not obscure the fact that they represent not actual constituents out of which the Acuality is produced, but analytic factors whose combination gives us Actuality in the same way that positionality and essence give us a particular actuality. And what is said of Actuality should have counterparts in the other modes of Being. Each should be understood to be the union of a meaning, which is divided into the conditions that the other three modes of Being impose on it, and a condition which is imposed by the "accidents" or particulars of that mode of Being.

It is tempting now to think of the particles and the Actuality as more basic (since they are simple) than the actualities which are between them, and to make no reference to any other realities as parts of either. The particles and the Actuality make some reference to one another; together, through utilization and symbolization, they constitute wholes having a causal power, though no individuality or effective inwardness. But compound individuals are not only as basic as any of the elements which might be found within them or the Actuality in which they are and toward which they are oriented, but there is no warrant for the belief that there was once a time when there were only the simple particles and that the clustering of them (and the existence of compound individuals within which the clustering does occur) is derivative from a subsequent occurrence.

The factors into which we analyze Actuality are on a footing in it. When we try to concentrate on one or the other side of Actuality—as related to other Beings or to actualities, we emphasize one of the factors without abandoning the other.

Actuality is evidently analyzable into the contributions made by the other modes of Being, for it is one of them, needing and needed by them. But though Actualities are oriented in Actuality and are confined within its compass, and cannot be thought to be without it any more than it can be understood without them, it is certainly not evident that they can be treated as analytic components of it. References to their compelled unity or to the kind of divisions that exist amongst them, and which could be explained as resulting from the utilization of a principle exhibited in Actuality, do bear on this question of the analytic nature of Actuality.

A better set of terms for the factors is "inwardness" and "finality." Each makes the other determinate. Together they constitute the unitary Being of Actuality. In each mode of Being, the meaning of finality is different, by virtue of the fact that it is in turn analyzable into three constituents which are other than those appropriate to the meaning pertinent to another mode of Being. Just what the particulars of each of the other modes of Being might contribute to the Being is not easily seen, in good part because there is no sure knowledge of just what those particulars are as real entities. But for the moment we can say that they too contribute an inwardness to their appropriate Being, but that this inwardness is different in meaning from that characteristic of particular actualities.

August 27

Paul Fitzgerald argues (from a number of different bases) against what he calls the "Halfway Theory" of the future. This theory is rather close to that which both Hartshorne and I have defended independently over the years. Fitzgerald (in his *Review of Metaphysics* article) wrongly takes the theory to suppose that the future is "real only to the extent that it is causally determined by the present or the past." The theory, instead, takes the future to have a reality of its own apart from causal conditioning. But Fitzgerald is right to remark that it supposes that the future is indeterminate.

Fitzgerald asks the theory to explain how it would deal with an entity which exists now, but "whose existence at the specified future time is causally contingent." He asks if the expression fails to refer, but is supposed to refer, since the existence at the future date is now causally undetermined. I, though, deny that the expression refers to something, because there is no possibility of a possibility. An existent individual now is possibly existent in the future, but that possible existent does not now have some contingent feature or possibility; it has only essential features.

Fitzgerald thinks he has an additional problem when he refers to the causal determination that he will be a father five years from now, but that the sex and structure of his child are as yet undetermined. Yet in this case, too, we have only the possibility of being a father or of there being a child. The possible child is of course male or female; this "male or female" is a necessary feature of the possible child. The child itself, though, is not now male and not now female. When and as it exists, it is one or the other. Before the child exists in fact, it is only a possibility, and the features of it, even its being male or its being female, are possibilities of that possibility. Such possibilities do not have any reality.

The fact that a possibility depends for its being on the reality of something else does not mean that its realization occurs later than that something else. When and as the child exists, it realizes the possibility of being male or of being female, though these possibilities were never distinct possibilities in the future. The realization of the possibility of the child is one with the separation out either of the possibility "male" or "female" from the single possibility "male-or-female," and the realization of that separated possibility.

Fitzgerald asks if a "future event is causally determined, or nearly so, if an irreducible statistical law can be used to predict its occurrence with a 90 percent probability." Since we are here presumably talking of an individual case, the answer must be in the negative. Even if the prediction had a 99.999999 percent probability, it will not yield the individual case.

He thinks the theory has difficulty in being reconciled with relativity views, but this objection is the result of a confounding of philosophical and physical questions.

He thinks that statements about occurrences could be timelessly true, and that "it involves a linguistic mistake to speak of their changing their truth values status." He overlooks an alternative: those statements are indeterminate and the addition of a date to them is but the addition of a number. An indeterminate statement does not become true. It is replaced by a true determinate statement.

He supposes that the theory makes an unjustified distinction between causal laws and justified predictions regarding the future. But surely there is a difference between laws as having a dynamic import and those which are implicative. So far as causal laws are viewed dynamically, they are indistinguishable from productions of future contingencies; so far as they are viewed as structures which can be expressed formally, they are indistinguishable from inferential rules. Predictions presumably relate to the former, and so far are not now true or false of individual cases. So far as we can say that causal laws will hold in the future, and that these are are very laws we now have, we but reaffirm the nature of time, or the order of things and the like, and thus merely affirm something about the necessary structure of the world.

We can speak of "predicting" that the causal laws will hold in the future, but we then use predicting in a sense which is different from that used when we say that because of such and such a causal law holding or operating, such and such a result will come about. Alternatively, we can say that the causal laws that hold now will hold in the future as encompassing the relation amongst possibilities, and that any particular instantiation of those laws cannot be ascertained until that future becomes present. In advance of the conversion of the future possibility into a present actuality, we can only deduce what it is that the structures allow. The only possible prediction we can make now is identical with the only possible deductions we can make now, given such and such a present and such and such laws. All other so-called predictions are educated guesses.

He asks why one does not withhold truth, not only from particular predictions, but from putative law statements, until all possible countercases have been made or shown to be impossible. We should withhold it from both, and for the same reasons.

He says that the Halfway Theorist holds that there is no objection in principle to a lawlike statement's being true now, and thus to its being a genuine law, even if some of its instances are as yet future. This seems to be a weak objection; the truth of a law does not depend on the presence of all its instances. Why then, he goes on to ask, does this theorist "object in principle to granting truth or falsity to certain other statements about the future, such as universal nonlawlike statements which have no past or present counter-cases but whose future falsification is a causally contingent matter?" Precisely because these statements are functions of their instances. Suppose then that we do have counter-cases occurring which show that the law does not hold? Either we must say that the law has stopped holding or that we were mistaken in thinking it was a law.

He thinks that "future particulars are included in the universe of discourse over which its variables range." This is not true, for there are no future particulars. He goes on to say that "if the law does not include real future particulars in its universe of discourse then it has no bearing on the future, and whether true or not, cannot be invoked to show that certain future particulars are causally necessitated by what has happened." But here he explicitly supposes that it makes sense to talk of future particulars, which is precisely what the theory denies. We must deny that "the reality of the future particulars is presupposed by the truth of the future-bearing law."

He thinks that to be a future *B* means that *B* will occur. But this is true only of a possible *B*; it is one thing to say that *B* will occur and another to say that the *B* which is future is the *B* that in fact occurs, for what in fact occurs is that future *B* transformed into a present actuality.

Most of Fitzgerald's difficulties seem to come down to the consideration that we can now say of the future certain things that are true—that such and such possibilities will be realized, or that such and such laws will prevail. But these are but ways of saying that the possibilities are real possibilities, and that the laws are structures of the world in which we are, and thus can be said to hold of the future as well as of the present. But what is the difference then, between a law as holding now and that law as holding of the future? As law, they are one and the same, differing only in that there are instances for the one and not for the other. Though a law is said to hold regardless of the occurrence of instances, any instance in which it does hold does give to the law the status of being a law holding or effective or operative in the present. As so operative, it differs from itself as in the future as an actuality differs from a possibility. The difference does not lie in the structure of the law, but only in the way in which it is related to an actuality. In the one case, it is vivified by an actuality, and in the other, it is referred to by an actuality. As vivified or instantiated by an actuality, it is present and actualized, and as referred to, it is merely a possibility.

INDEX OF NAMES

INDEX OF SUBJECTS

Artists: 706; Existence and, 487; free play, 131; gamesman and, 138; love and, 89

Assertion: analytic, 526; from lies, 587

Assimilation: Jews and, 520; symbol as rule, 466; terminus and, 613

Association, scientific theory, 432

Astonishing, the, 65

Astronomy, 651

Atheism, 67–68

Athletes: 308–10; accepts body, 572; artist and, 706; attitudes, 294; body and, 157–58, 397; body control, 506–7, 509–10; body mastery, 574; challenge, 152; craftsmen, 129; dedication, 202–4; defeat and, 231, 267; dislocated ideal, 302; energy, 301; excellence, 569; forms of testimony, 370; identification, 218; interest in, 259–60; knower and, 307–8; retreat from world, 261; settings, 200; specifications, 206; training of, 204–5; woman and, 157

Atomism, 14, 463–64, 465, 469, 470

Atoms, 431, 554, 556

Attachment: play and, 397, 512

Attention: action, 295; bifocal, 373; communication, 584; foci, 265; future, 343; games, 193–94; intention and, 582–84; response and, 533

Attenuationism, 303

Attitudes: behavior and, 521

Authority, 155

Autobiographical, 13, 69–70, 92, 114, 125–26, 143, 145–46, 158–59, 183, 221, 235–36, 391, 595

Awe, 321

"Backward thrust," 565

Bad act, 325–29

Base prospect, 283

Base united realities, 219

Baseball, 193–98, 270, 274–77, 279–80, 290, 292–93, 391, 707

Basic conceits, 225–31

Basketball, 522, 523, 707

Batters (baseball), 193–95, 197–98

Battle: Aristotle's sea fight, 333–34; plurality of times, 186–92; present and, 165–66; sports, 129; times, 338, 342

Beauty, 475, 707

Beginning: beginning-ending, 284; "end to beginnings," 321; wave theory, 432

Behavior: aberrations, 176–77; basic dimensions, 521–22; eccentric, 211; human body, 504; intention and, 174, 300; pain, 577

Behaviorism, 40, 467, 756

Being[s]: accidents, 644–45; actualities and, 52–56, 114, 615, 673–74, 696–97; Actuality, 27–28; aggregational activity, 723; apprehension of, 614; behaviorism and, 756–57; coherent pattern, 143–44; conceiving and encountering, 12; contexts, 690–93; contrast with Beings, 416; data and, 729; demiurge, 618; dialogue on pluralism, 310–14; differing pluralities, 251; dualisms, 412–13; entities and, 689; evidence for, 24; exposition of, 441–42; feeling and, 475; final realities, 42–43; finites and, 693; God, 574; instantiations, 29; intrusion of, 180; intuition of, 687–88; knowledge of, 25; life and death, 210; linear necessity, 321; mere Being, 459; minimal metaphysics, 10; negation and, 460, 464; only Being, 419; on the inside, 332; particulars and, 398–99, 402–11, 418–23; plurality of, 100; plurality of times, 185; prior to relations, 401–2; projects and retrojects, 188; qua Being, 13; relations to actualities, 51; relativization of, 18; relevant to actualities, 121–22; sacral actuality, 598; self-awareness, 671; singularity, 124; speculation and, 109; symbols and, 467–68, 647, 660; symmetry, 663; theories and, 731; Trinity, 323; two sides of, 701; ultimate, 11–12; unity and, 695

Belief and doubt, 323

Betrayal[s]: aberrations, 176–77; character, 169–71; intention, 174; speaking and evaluation, 241

Bias: meanings and particulars, 740–41; of standards, 662–64

Biased factors, 741–42

Biography, 24

Biology, 78–79, 81, 210, 213, 503–4, 605

Bird, 572

Birth, 282

Blacks: militant, 679–80, 682

Blame, 327

Blasphemy, 450

Bodily roles, 498–99

Body: acceptance of, 203; as challenge, 151–52, 244; athletic excellence, 569; birth and death, 282; concern with, 497; contexts, 182; identification with, 205, 516–17; interests in, 257–58; levels of, 502–10; man as totality, 78–79; mastery of, 513, 515, 574–75; mind and, 39–40, 156–58, 180, 746, 754–55; my body, 262–64; outward potentiality, 145; perfecting, 515; process and structure, 548; relaxation,